Mika Hein

Wimp

THE ARMCHAIR
BOOK OF BASEBALL II

THE ARMCHAIR LIBRARY

THE ARMCHAIR QUARTERBACK
THE ARMCHAIR AVIATOR
THE ARMCHAIR MOUNTAINEER
THE ARMCHAIR BOOK OF BASEBALL
THE ARMCHAIR ANGLER
THE ARMCHAIR BOOK OF BASEBALL II

THE ARMCHAIR LIBRARY

THE ARMCHAIR
BOOK OF BASEBALL II

Edited by John Thorn
Illustrations by Bernie Fuchs

Foreword by A. Bartlett Giamatti

CHARLES SCRIBNER'S SONS
New York

To Susan

Library of Congress Cataloging-in-Publication Data

The armchair book of baseball II.

(The Armchair library)
1. Baseball. 2. Baseball stories. I. Thorn,
John, 1947–   . II. Title: Armchair book of
baseball 2. III. Title: Armchair book of baseball
two.
GV867.A753 1987   796.357   86-27883
ISBN 0-684-18772-8

Composition by PennSet, Inc., Bloomsburg, Pennsylvania
Manufactured by Fairfield Graphics, Fairfield, Pennsylvania
First Edition

Parts of the foreword by A. Bartlett Giamatti have been
adapted from the speech entitled "Baseball and the American Character," which he delivered to the Massachusetts
Historical Society on October 17, 1985.

CONTENTS

Foreword by A. Bartlett Giamatti   ix

Introduction   xiii

CHARLES C. ALEXANDER: "Don't Come Home a Failure"   1
The crucible that made Ty Cobb.

DAVE ANDERSON: Sandwiches at an Execution   14
Friendly fire: how Steinbrenner canned Howser.

ROGER ANGELL: The Interior Stadium   17
Baseball's best writer's best writing.

MARTY APPEL: Noting the Milestones   26
Celebrating Ron Blomberg, Paul Pettit, and other titans.

RUSSELL BAKER: Idylls of the Kid   33
Joe D. hits seventy with a java jolt.

BOB CARROLL: Nate Colbert's Unknown RBI Record   36
Unknown even to Colbert—a neat bit of sleuthing.

BILL COLSON: The Over-the-Hill League   42
They knew there would be no mañana.

BILL CONLIN: The Ten-Minute Collapse   46
A compact dirge for the phutile Phils.

SAM CRANE: The Men Who Invented Shortstop   49
An old-time player recalls Dickey Pearce and George Wright.

ROBERT W. CREAMER: Do Not Go Gentle: Talking, Talking,
Talking   55
Stengelese: a guide for the perplexed.

CANDY CUMMINGS: How I Pitched the First Curve   70
The title says it all.

JIM DEVLIN: "I Am Honest, Harry"   73
A crooked player's poignant plea, 1878.

E. L. DOCTOROW: Family   75
Who fools whom—a Faustian riff from Ragtime.

LEO DUROCHER with ED LINN: The Santo Explosion   80
"The worst argument I ever saw in a clubhouse."

RAY FITZGERALD: Tony C, as in Courage, Comebacks, Coronary   93
What might have been for Tony Conigliaro.

G. H. FLEMING: The Merkle Blunder   96
A Rashomon-like view of the infamous "bonehead play."

PETER GOLENBOCK: Roger Maris   105
A mystery wrapped in an enigma—the reluctant home-run king.

ERIC ROLFE GREENBERG: Hero   122
Worshipping Matty, from perhaps the best of all baseball novels.

ZANE GREY: Old Well-Well   136
Not a shoot-'em-up: Grey once played pro ball!

STEPHEN S. HALL: Baseball's Dirty Tricks   143
Corked bats and scuffed balls . . . are they worth the effort?

MARK HARRIS: Henry Wiggen Goes Up   147

JOHN B. HOLWAY: Hilton Smith Remembers   165
Satchel Paige's other—and better?—half.

DONALD HONIG: Max Lanier Remembers   177
The 1940s in St. Louis and south of the border.

ROLFE HUMPHRIES: Night Game   186
"That each of us was a player for a moment"; a poem.

BILL JAMES: A History of Platooning   188
When and how did it start?

PAT JORDAN: A False Spring   198
Prospect to suspect; from the splendid autobiography of a pitcher.

NEAL KARLEN: Bad-Nose Bees   212
Ex-dopers, head cases, and rebels—the San Jose Bees of 1986.

GARRISON KEILLOR: Old Hard Hands   226
When a boy needs a friend; from Lake Wobegon Days.

JOHN LARDNER: Remember the Black Sox?   231
Chick, Swede, Shoeless Joe, and the rest—a 1938 view.

FRED LIEB: "Hits Are My Bread and Butter"   244
The lot of the official scorer is not a happy one.

SPARKY LYLE with PETER GOLENBOCK: The Bronx Zoo   251
Billy and George and Reggie and Lou: feeding time.

JERRY MALLOY: Out at Home   262
How baseball drew the color line in 1887.

TIM McCARVER: How a Catcher Calls a Game   286
Mind over batter.

WILLIE MORRIS: The Phantom   295
Until he discovered The Old Scotchman's trick, he was just a phan.

NEW YORK *WORLD*: Armless, Legless Baseball Pitchers   309
That was the headline of this bizarre story, 1898.

GRANTLAND RICE: That Man from Mudville   312
The further adventures of Casey.

MORDECAI RICHLER: Up from the Minors in Montreal   320
What kind of name is Expos, *anyway?*

LAWRENCE S. RITTER: Edd Roush Remembers   329
*"The 1919 White Sox were good—but the 1919 Cincinnati Reds
were* better.*"*

ANDY ROONEY: Real Men Don't Wear Knickers   337
Would a baseball player reply, "Quiche my ash"?

R. D. ROSEN: Strike Three, You're Dead   339
A major-league murder mystery.

PHILIP ROTH: Center Field   346
Alex, the Seabees, and the Duke; from Portnoy's Complaint.

DAMON RUNYON: The Soul of Wit   350
A backhand paean to the box score.

WILLIAM SHAKESPEARE (& friends): Bard at the Bat   353
The play's the thing . . .

ROBERT SMITH: Of Kings and Commoners   357
A portrait gallery of bygone demigods.

JOHN PHILIP SOUSA: Balls and Batons Forever   375
The "March King" (and pitcher!) extols the Great American Game.

JULES TYGIEL: "The Only Thing I Wanted to Do
Was Hit the Major Leagues"   378
Going from the Negro Leagues to the minor leagues, 1948–55.

BOB UECKER: Catcher in the Wry   396
The .200 hitter's last hurrah.

BILL VEECK with ED LINN: An Epitaph for Harry Grabiner   400
Harrowing.

ROBERT WHITING: You've Gotta Have "Wa"   404
In Japan, the nail that sticks up shall be hammered down.

WALT WHITMAN: On Baseball, 1858   417
America's poet on America's game—little-known reportage.

GEORGE F. WILL: Don't Beep in My Outfield   419
From cheating to Chiti.

TED WILLIAMS: Jousting with the Knights of the Keyboard   422
How to handle the press—a tip from Jim Thorpe.

THOMAS WOLFE: The Sound of the Ball,
the Smell of Old Dry Wood   428
Baseball and the weather of our lives—a letter.

Permissions   431

Foreword

Baseball grew with the country, its origins and first examples Ante-Bellum, its growth and first golden age coterminous with Reconstruction and the period through the First World War. Baseball grew in the surge toward fraternalism, fraternal societies, sodalities, associations, and aggregations that followed the fratricide of the Civil War. Baseball also showed who had won the war and where the country was building, which was in the industrial cities of the North. It was and is a conservative game, remembering its origins or even making up origins (as in the myth that Abner Doubleday invented the game in 1839 in Cooperstown, New York). In a fashion typically American, baseball carried a lore at variance with its behavior; it promoted its self-image as a green game while it became a business. That gap in baseball between first promise and eventual execution is with us to this day, as it is with us in so many other ways.

Genteel in its American origins, proletarian in its development, egalitarian in its demands and appeal, effortless in its adaptation to nature, raucous, hard-nosed, and glamorous as a profession, expanding with the country like fingers unfolding from a fist, image of a lost past, evergreen reminder of America's best promises, baseball fitted and still fits America. It fits so well because it embodies the interplay of individual and group that we so love and because it conserves our longing for the rule of law while licensing our resentment of lawgivers.

In *Democracy In America*, Alexis de Tocqueville implicitly characterizes the American capacity to invest any principle with the character of religious belief when he shrewdly says, "The Americans have combated by free institutions the tendency of equality to keep men asunder and they have subdued it." He leads us to an understanding of our American moral hunger for egalitarian collectivity, which impels us as individuals to aggregate and then to invest the aggregation with numinous meaning, over and over again, as if for the first time every time. This American capacity for religious awe, especially when applied to our social and political institutions, at first enchants and then appalls those from other cultures. They find it difficult to comprehend how so many different institutions can be laden with significance akin to religious value merely in order to expunge class and other distinctions and to promote and protect egalitarian diversity.

If such a characterization may be at least suggested by a sympathetic French observer in the 1830s, what can we learn of ourselves from an observer who did not visit and leave, but who left and visited? In 1877, Henry James published *The American*. The hero is Christopher Newman and we meet him in the Louvre. The year is 1868. The confrontation between the new American man and the Old World, urban and aesthetic in its values, is initially less striking than the contraries embodied in Newman himself. "His eye," says James, ". . . was full of contradictory suggestions: and though it was by no means the glowing orb of romance you could find it in almost anything you looked for. Frigid yet friendly, frank yet cautious, shrewd yet credulous, positive yet sceptical, confident yet shy, extremely intelligent and extremely good-humoured, there was something vaguely defiant in its concessions and something profoundly reassuring in its reserves."

In this eye, this Ego Americanus, there are contraries more complex and tensions more clear than in the generalizing characteristics of Tocqueville. But our French visitor wrote in the 1830s, when institutional coherence promised to subdue the centripetal force of equality. James writes in the 1870s. By then the promise of a more perfect Union had been broken by a savage Civil War. Now America would, once again, be compelled to compose or recompose herself in the aftermath of division and upheaval; once again, free institutions, baseball now among them, would have to play the role of subduing the tendency equals have to be asunder. Now there was no escaping the gap between America's promises and her execution of them. Post–Civil War America was complex in darker and subtler ways than Tocqueville could have foreseen. The matter of race would now forever claim the American conscience, if not its consciousness. That compound whose mix forms the American character—of moral energy and pragmatic efficiency, optimism and guile, admiration for the maverick and love of the underdog, and respect for law—would be forever flecked with race-anxiety.

Law—defined as a complex of formal rules, agreed-upon boundaries, authoritative arbiters, custom, and a set of symmetrical opportunities and demands—is enshrined in baseball. Indeed, the layout of the field shows baseball's essential passion for and reliance on precise proportions and clearly defined limits, all the better to give shape to energy and provide an arena for equality and expression. The pitcher's mound is comprised of a pitcher's rubber, 24 inches by 6 inches, elevated in the middle of an 18-foot circle; the rubber is 60 feet 6 inches from home plate; the four base paths are 90 feet long; the distance from first base to third, and home plate to second base, is 127 feet 3⅜ inches; the pitcher's rubber is the center of a circle, described by the arc of the grass behind the infield from foul line to foul line, whose radius is 95 feet; from home plate to backstop, and swinging in an arc, is 60 feet. On this square tipped like a diamond containing circles and contained in circles, built on multiples of three, nine players play nine innings, with three outs to a side, each out possibly composed of three strikes. Four balls, four bases break (or is it underscore?) the game's reliance on "threes" to distribute an odd equality, all the numerology and symmetry tending to configure a game unbounded by that which bounds most sports, and adjudicates in many, Time.

The game comes from an America where the availability of sun defined the time for work or play—nothing else. Virtually all our other sports reflect the time clock, either in their formal structure or their definition of a winner. Baseball views time as daylight and daylight as an endlessly renewable natural resource; it may put a premium on speed, of throw or foot, but it is unhurried. Daytime, like the water and forests, like the land itself, was assumed to be ever available. When it was not, the work of playing ceased. Until, that is, the lights in stadiums brought day to night and let the day worker watch (or engage in) play in the false sun of the arc light.

The point is, symmetrical surfaces, deep arithmetical patterns, and a vast, stable body of rules ensure competitive balance in the game and show forth a country devoted to the ideals of equality of treatment and opportunity; a country whose deepest dream is of a divinely proportioned and peopled (the "threes" come from somewhere) green garden enclosure; above all, a country whose basic assertion is that law, in all its mutually agreed-upon manifestations, will govern—not nature inexorable, for all she is respected, and not humankind's whims, for all that the game belongs to the people. Baseball's essential rules for place and for play were established, by my reckoning, with almost no exceptions of consequence, by 1895. By today, the diamond and the rules for play have the character of Platonic ideas, of preexistent immutabilities that encourage activity, contain energy, and like any set of transcendent ideals, do not change. The image of the place for play, varied in reality, now often domed or carpeted, lit up at night, but unchanged in our mind's eye, is a shared image across America. In the lore of a society whose mobility has always been one of its distinguishing features, the baseball field is an image of home.

What is baseball, and indeed so much of the American experience, about but looking for home? *Nostos*, the desire to return home, gives us a nation of immigrants always migrating in search of home; gives us the American desire to start over in the great green garden, Eden or Canaan, of the New World; gives us the concept of a settled home base and, thus, the distance to frontiers;

gives us a belief in individual assertion that finds its fulfillment in aggregation, a grouping with the like-minded and similarly driven; gives us our sentimental awe of old ways; gives us the game where the runner runs counterclockwise for home plate.

The hunger for home makes the green geometry of the baseball field more than simply a metaphor for the American experience and character. The baseball field and the game that sanctifies boundaries, rules, and law, and appreciates cunning, theft, and guile; that exalts energy, opportunism, and execution, while paying lip service to management, strategy, and long-range planning, is finally closer to an embodiment of American life than to the mere sporting image of it.

In this splendid volume, the reader will find diverse perspectives, from different eras of our game's, and country's, history. Ample material out of which to construct one's own view of the role baseball plays in the life of a person or of a people. Ample material to assemble a vision of the ongoing pleasure of the game as it renews itself with every pitch, every game, every season. Baseball is best played in the sun, on grass; but it can also, like literature, be played in the head. And there it lasts longest, and never loses its abiding innocence. There, the gap between promise and performance disappears.

A. BARTLETT GIAMATTI
President of the National League
of Professional Baseball Clubs

Introduction

As good as baseball is at its very considerable best—say, games six and seven of the 1986 World Series—for me it is even better in the recollection. To know something of the game's past rounds out the perception of its present, connecting the two in ways that are often trivial, occasionally profound, always satisfying. The 1986 World Series opened with a 1–0 shutout of the New York Mets by Boston Red Sox left-hander Bruce Hurst. A reading of tea leaves, or chicken entrails, or whatever it is oracles read these days, would have revealed the following: the last time a Red Sox team won a World Series was 1918, when another Red Sox left-hander won the opener with a 1–0 shutout. Whose shutout was it? Ruth's—an anagram of Hurst. Oracles not being what they used to be (to the determinedly nostalgic, what is?), the 1986 Red Sox did not win the Series in six games as their 1918 forebears did. But they were only one strike away. . . .

Baseball is a backward-looking game, in which every action on the field resonates against plays imprinted—in the mind's eye and in the record books— long ago. Baseball's undertow of history is powerful, drawing fans and players to the statistics, to old-timers' games, and to Cooperstown, summer after summer. What other sport has so rich and vibrant a past, so copious an accounting, so honored an alumni? Only cricket may be mentioned in the same breath.

"Only connect," advised E. M. Forster in *A Passage to India.* His prescription pertained not to the national sport of England and India but to humankind, increasingly solitary in its progress through this century. In America, where culture, class, ideology, and religion fail to unite us, baseball is the tie that binds, connecting fathers with sons across the inarticulate void of generations, connecting the immigrant with America, connecting the man with the vitality of his boyhood and the boy with the prospect of his manhood.

Baseball's hold, as strong as an embrace, as casual as a pat on the back, binds this book as it binds our people. From Walt Whitman's report of a rugged game played before the Civil War to Neal Karlen's look at the drug-ravaged careers of the 1986 San Jose Bees, from the paean to the box score by Damon Runyon to the rigorous statistical analysis by Bill James, this collection of writings celebrates the game that is more than a game.

The kind response to the first *Armchair Book of Baseball*—which I introduced by complaining that "I could more easily have gathered a book three times this size"—has permitted the publication of a second, every bit the equal of its dad. The general principles of selection are the same two that prevailed first time around: to bring together the best writing that, when collected, would present a panoramic view of the game; and to select only one piece by any one writer, thus denying the temptation to reprint *The Glory of Their Times* in its entirety. (I have violated the second guideline, sort of, by including one bit by Peter Golenbock flying solo and another in which he ghosted for Sparky Lyle, and by including two wraith-writer jobs by Ed Linn.) I have also sought to avoid frequently anthologized pieces, so you will not have the pleasure of reading again a portion of Ring Lardner's *You Know Me Al* or James Thurber's harbinger of Eddie Gaedel, "You Could Look It Up." Oh, well . . . perhaps in *The Armchair Book of Baseball III*.

I wish to thank artist Bernie Fuchs; editors Marta Goldstein and Elizabeth Rapoport of Scribners; designer Alan Benjamin; and, as usual, friend and collaborator David Reuther. For bibliographic help, Tom Heitz, John Blomquist, and Bill Deane of the National Baseball Hall of Fame; for general aid and bonhomie, the Society for American Baseball Research; for leads to specific pieces, Jim Carothers, Ralph Graber, and Bill Felber. And for nothing specific but everything that counts, Susan, Jed, and Isaac.

JOHN THORN
Saugerties, New York

How did Ty Cobb get to be that way? Paranoid, obsessive, bigoted, sensitive, cruel, he was as complicated a bundle as ever stepped onto a ball field. The shaping of this compelling personality began in the cotton country of northeastern Georgia. Charles C. Alexander's fine 1984 biography opens in that region called The Narrows, where William Herschel Cobb, a twenty-year-old schoolteacher, married twelve-year-old Amanda Chitwood. Tyrus was born in 1886, and the itinerant family eventually settled in the small town of Royston. There his father became, successively, the mayor, newspaper editor, and state senator. The Cobbs were accomplished, respected, and proud—until August 1905, when a shotgun blast stained the family honor and strained young Ty's faith in humanity.

CHARLES C. ALEXANDER

"Don't Come Home a Failure"

Convinced that education was the key to both social progress and personal advancement, W. H. Cobb kept after his children to get as much as they could from the schooling available at Royston and then look forward to college. He had particularly high hopes for Tyrus, obviously an intelligent boy who might very well become a lawyer or a physician. Yet while he did capably in arithmetic and grammar and even won a couple of prizes in school oratory contests, the boy would not apply himself the way he should, seemed distracted by too many things outside school.

Tyrus Cobb also gave signs of being stubborn, high-strung, and quick-tempered. In the fifth grade he beat up a fat boy for missing a word in the class spelling bee and thereby giving victory to the girls' team. Not that young Cobb was normally so scrupulous in his own spelling. It was just that the kid had flubbed the boys' chance to win because he hadn't worked hard enough. Joe Cunningham, who lived next door to Tyrus and was his best boyhood friend, sensed that there was something in him that made him different from the other town boys. "You saw it the moment you set eyes on him," Cunningham said many years later. "He just seemed to think quicker and run faster. He was always driving and pushing, even in grade school."

Besides spelling bees, that drive and push found expression in footraces, rock throwing, tree climbing, and various other demonstrations of boyish physical prowess. Once young Cobb insisted on walking a tightrope stretched across

1

the street in the center of town. Clearly, he was something of a showoff, but he was also a born competitor, obsessed with winning. "I . . . saw no point in losing if I could win" was the simple way, as an old man, he expressed what he had felt even as a boy.

Eventually it was baseball that became the main outlet for the boy's competitive energies. As was true in small towns throughout the country, the principal manifestation of Royston's collective existence took place at local baseball games. From the 1890s up to the 1920s baseball was far and away the most popular form of athletic competiton in America, and going to baseball games was one of the leading forms of entertainment and recreation. On Saturday afternoons all summer, a big percentage of the white townspeople and even some local blacks (carefully kept off to one side) turned out to see the local aggregation compete against some nearby community's team. They called it town or semipro baseball, because sometimes the team members split a few dollars contributed by their followers. Although such baseball was the source of most of the talent that eventually made it into the major leagues, the older boys and younger men who played for the town teams knew how remote the possibility was that any of them would ever be "discovered" by a professional scout. Mostly they played for the fun of it.

Royston went in for baseball in a bigger way than most places its size. Besides the Royston Reds in their flaming flannels, there was also an organized team for younger boys called the Rompers. A right-handed thrower and left-handed batter, Tyrus played for the Rompers until he was about fourteen. One Saturday the Reds found themselves without a shortstop for a game with Commerce. Pressed into service, the frail-looking boy handled eight chances without an error and, by holding his hands apart so he could get better leverage on the big bat he had to swing, managed to slap three hits through and over the infield.

Soon after that Bob McCreary, who managed and caught for the Reds, clerked in the local bank, and was the son of one of the town's physicians, talked Tyrus's father into letting the boy go with the team to Elberton, some 20 miles south on a spur of the Southern Railroad, in the heart of the peach country. As a brother in the Masonic Order, McCreary promised Professor Cobb that he would look out for Tyrus, make sure he behaved himself. At Elberton, Tyrus again got three hits, the last one driving in the winning run. Later on that summer, playing center field, he saved a win over Harmony Grove with a diving catch. For that the Royston people showered the field with coins, and Tyrus picked up $10 or $11, the first money he ever made playing baseball. And he experienced what it was like to be cheered by a crowd. "Once an athlete feels the peculiar thrill that goes with victory and public praise," he said sixty years later in reminiscing about those early exploits, "he's bewitched. He can never get away from it."

By that time Tyrus had already angered his father by trying to trade some of the professor's books for a new baseball glove he had seen at the local dry-goods store. After the Harmony Grove game, though, he no longer had to make do with the old ragged glove he had sewn together himself. He also ordered pamphlets on "how to sprint" and practiced making quick starts for the next base. Baseball had become the focus of his life, and in the summer he played anywhere and as much as he could when he was not having to sit in Baptist Sunday school, work the fields on his father's farm, or listlessly tend to chores around the house in town.

He even played in North Carolina during warm-weather visits to his relatives there. Although the Cobb children evidently saw little of their Chitwood kin, they made regular trips by train up to see their Cobb grandparents. Tyrus grew very close to his "Granddad Johnny," a feisty, imaginative little man who captivated him with tales of bear hunting in the mountains and also taught him the finer points of 'coon and 'possum hunting. His grandmother healed his cuts, scrapes, and bites and kept his digestive track cleaned out with an array of mountain remedies, and his Aunt Norah often drove him in her buggy into Murphy or Andrews so he could find some boys to get up a ball game. Tyrus seems to have had his happiest boyhood times with the North Carolina Cobbs, going there not only in summertime but sometimes during the mid-winter school recess, as well.

He was there early in January 1902 when he received a letter from his father. In later years he would carry that letter on his person and eventually have it printed. Writing under the letterhead of the Franklin County Board of Education and signing himself "Yours affectionately, W. H. Cobb," his father commented on the 2 inches of snow that had just fallen at Royston. He was glad that Tyrus was up in "that picturesque and romantic country" where there was "solitude enough to give nature a chance to be heard in the soul." To see "God's handiwork among those everlasting hills," to hear "the grand oratorios of the winds" and "the rush of her living leaping waters"—all that was a vital part of the education he wanted his son to have. To be truly educated was not just to "master the printed page"; it was also "to catch the message of star, rock, flower, bird, painting and symphony," to have "eyes that really see" and "ears that really hear and an imagination that can construct the perfect from fragment." "Be good and dutiful," he went on, "conquer your anger and wild passions. . . ." Be guided by "the better angel of your nature," not "the demon that lurks in all human blood and [is] ready and anxious and restless to arise and to reign."

"My overwhelming need was to prove myself as a man," wrote Tyrus Cobb many years later about his feelings in his adolescence. Clearly, proving himself meant winning and keeping the approval of the imposing man he called not "Pa" or "Papa" but "Father." For all his rhapsodizings about the education of the soul through contact with nature, W. H. Cobb expected his ball-playing son to master lots of printed pages. Yet the boy simply could not share the ambitions his father had for him. Tyrus was supposed to go to college and eventually enter law or medicine. He might even attend the U.S. Military Academy and embark on a career as an army officer. But he had to settle down and apply himself, even though the boy was convinced that he "could never match my celebrated father for brains." It was not easy being Professor Cobb's son. Too much was expected of him at school and in the town. Both his scholarship and his conduct were supposed to be exemplary—and neither was. "I felt guilty," he remembered, "that some great, vaulting ambition hadn't seized me beyond handling hard hoppers and line drives."

Tyrus dutifully went with his father to Carnesville, the county seat, so he could meet Col. W. R. Little, one of the area's foremost lawyers, and browse in the colonel's law library. But he found the reading to be "dry as hell" and decided right then that the law was not for him. Maybe medicine. He began accompanying Dr. Moss on his travels around the southern part of the county. On one occasion he assisted Moss in removing a bullet from a young black whom a white boy had shot in the stomach. Tyrus administered the chloroform and, at Moss's direction, felt around inside the youth to see if he could find the bullet. When he found nothing, Moss declared that the slug must have missed the intestine and sewed the patient up. Somehow he survived. Tyrus, his hand covered with gore, had discovered that the sight of blood and exposed tissue hardly bothered him at all. Conceivably he could become a surgeon. But try as he might, he simply could not work up much enthusiasm for a life in medicine.

About that time Tyrus had occasion to see plenty of his own blood when he accidentally shot himself in the left shoulder with his .22 rifle. After he got the bleeding stopped, W. H. Cobb jumped on a train with his son and took him the 75 miles into Atlanta to see a battery of physicians presumed to be more knowledgeable than the country doctors at home. Although they lacked X-ray equipment, the Atlanta doctors were able to determine that the bullet had apparently bounced off Tyrus's clavicle without breaking any bone and then lodged somewhere in the vicinity. Unable to locate the bullet, they sewed up the boy's shoulder and wished him well. The wound healed nicely, and the small slug remained inside Tyrus Cobb's shoulder for the rest of his life.

Being shot seems to have interfered not at all with young Cobb's ripening baseball career. Armed with his own bats, made, with help from Joe Cunningham, of prime ash in the same toolshed where Joe's father built coffins for local deceased citizens, Tyrus became the star player on the Royston Reds. Having grown to about 5 feet 10 inches and 150 wiry-muscled pounds by the time he was sixteen or seventeen, he played both infield and outfield, ran the bases with abandon, and hit whistling line drives. In March 1902 a trip into Atlanta and out to Piedmont Park, where the American League Cleveland Broncos were doing their spring training, heightened his baseball passions. Befriended by Bill Bradley, Cleveland's hard-hitting third baseman, Tyrus took pictures of the players with his little box camera and generally reveled in his first encounter with real professional ballplayers, and big leaguers at that.

Back home, as he later put it, "my father held me down, withholding acceptance of me as the man I yearned to be." School no longer held much interest for the youth, and inasmuch as Professor Cobb thought baseball a waste of time, Tyrus could find no way to please this man who awed, intimidated, and frustrated him but whom he nonetheless loved deeply. No doubt W. H. Cobb also loved his son, but he seems to have been the kind of person who carefully guarded his emotions and, even with his own wife and children, found it hard to show affection. Sparse with his praise, he was quick and sharp with his criticism. It seemed to Tyrus that try as he might, "I couldn't reach him."

In the spring of 1903 the youth finally did reach his father, for maybe the only time in his life. He threw himself into putting in the cotton crop, plowing and seeding from dawn to nightfall, sweating alongside the black hired hand. As the tender plants began to grow, he discovered a new warmth and intimacy with his father, who started talking with him about their crop, about work mules, about the competition American cotton producers were increasingly meeting from foreign-grown cotton, about whether they should sell or wait for prices to rise. Tyrus was so enthused by it all that he got a job with a local cotton factory and learned how the cotton was ginned, baled, graded, and moved to market. Everything he learned he discussed with his father, who was pleased that at least his son showed a good head for business. Tyrus Cobb would later think back on 1903 as "a great year in my life," the time when "Professor Cobb 'bought' me as his son. . . ."

Yet despite the new closeness with his son, W. H. Cobb had not changed his mind about the folly of baseball. Tyrus felt guilty about taking a few dollars for playing for a team over in South Carolina, because if word got around that he'd played for money, he would be ineligible for college athletics—if he went to college. For Tyrus that was still an open question. Early in 1904, however, he took a step that was bound to decide the issue once and for all. Despite the surge of love he had for his father, "I still felt that I was being held in some sort of bondage. So I decided I would become a ballplayer and get away."

A local athlete named Van Bagwell had had a tryout in 1903 with Nashville in the Southern League but had not made the team. That winter he told young Cobb that he believed Tyrus had the talent to make it in professional ball. That helped the boy get up his courage secretly to write letters to each of the teams in the South Atlantic ("Sally") League, which had just been formed over the winter as a Class C circuit with franchises in six cities in Georgia, South Carolina, and Florida. He included a little information about himself and asked for a tryout. One reply came back, from Con Strouthers, manager and part owner of the Augusta Tourists, saying that Cobb could come to spring training if he wished but that he would have to pay his own expenses. A couple of days later a contract arrived specifying a salary of $50 a month—if Tyrus made the team.

Dazzled as he was by the contract and the prospect of a professional career, Tyrus dreaded having to tell his father that he was leaving and that he needed money for traveling and living expenses until he got his first check. First he revealed his plans to his mother. Amanda Cobb—a kindly enough mother, it seems, but not a major factor in the boy's life—told him to go ahead if he had to and kept the matter to herself. Tyrus waited to confront his father until the night before he had to report at Augusta. Professor Cobb, whose hopes for the boy had swelled over the past year, responded with a stern lecture that went on for hours. Tyrus, he argued, was at a critical point in his life; what he did now might determine his whole future. He stood a good chance to end up "a mere muscle worker." Baseball was filled with no-accounts who drank and gambled and ran after lewd women. The boy could not argue, only keep saying, "I just have to go."

At last the man gave up, opened his rolltop desk, and sat down to write out six checks for $15 each, which he gave his son with the admonition for him to "get it out of your system." Early the next morning Tyrus Cobb, age seventeen, stepped aboard a Southern Railroad car for the journey south to Augusta. Although the trip was only about 85 miles by rail, it took nearly all day, because Tyrus had to change trains at Elberton and again just across the Savannah River at Calhoun Falls, South Carolina. It was late afternoon by the time he got into Augusta on the Charleston and Western North Carolina.

Augusta, Georgia, in 1904 was a thriving little city of something more than

40,000 inhabitants. Proud of its wide downtown streets, its new trolley line, and its attractive neighborhoods, Augusta was an important nexus of the cotton trade and increasingly noted for textile and iron and steel manufacture. Besides Atlanta, it was the biggest place Cobb had ever been.

The next day Cobb donned his red Royston uniform and took the field at neat little Warren Park, home of the new Tourists. He amazed and amused manager Strouthers and the other players by cutting in front of fielders for ground balls and flies to the outfield, making wild dashes from base to base, and generally going against the accepted procedures of the workouts and intrasquad games. He stood around hoping somebody would let him up to the plate for a few swings, but rarely did the other men, nearly all older than he was and most of them with professional experience, give him a chance to hit. When the Augusta team played the Detroit Tigers of the American League, also training at Augusta, Cobb watched from the bench. Nor did he get into any of the other exhibition games.

When the season started, all the Augusta infield positions were occupied by veterans. Strouthers's first baseman was being stubborn about signing his contract, so the manager had to shift his center fielder to first. Inasmuch as there were only fourteen or fifteen men still with the team, Strouthers had no choice but to put the young recruit from Royston in center field on opening day, April 26, 1904, at Warren Park against Columbia. Hitting in seventh place in the lineup, Cobb responded with a single and double in four times up against a pitcher named George Engel and scored two runs. Engel helped himself out with a home run, and Columbia won the game 8–7.

It was an impressive debut, or so Cobb thought. As it turned out, it was a moment of glory and nothing more. After he went hitless the next day, Strouthers called him into his office and told him that his first baseman had just signed, his center field could go back to his position, and he could no longer use Cobb. What the boy had dreaded but had not let himself believe could happen had happened. Now he faced the prospect of going back home to his disapproving father and acknowledging that he had been right, that baseball wasn't really a practicable career, only something he'd had to get out of his system.

Confused and depressed, Cobb wandered back to the little hotel where he had a room. There Thad Hayes, a pitcher from Alabama who had also just got his release, told him about a semipro team over at Anniston, Alabama, being managed by Hayes's friend. That team needed a pitcher and maybe an outfielder, as well; Cobb should come along with him to Anniston.

Released outright by Augusta, the boy was thus a free agent who could play wherever he wished. Still, he felt compelled to talk over the matter with his father. At the local telephone office he was astonished and overjoyed when W. H. Cobb told him to take the job at Anniston. But whatever happened, "Don't come home a failure." "In giving me his blessing, his sanction of my quest for success in my hour of defeat, my father put more determination in me than he ever knew. I had the shivers when I hung up." So Cobb described his feelings when he recalled that moment more than a half a century later.

Cobb and Hayes used most of the little money they had left in getting to their new team. Anniston, a smoky mill town in northeastern Alabama, was a member of a loosely organized outfit called the Tennessee-Alabama League. The league was not officially recognized by professional baseball's ruling National Commission and thus was not part of what was called Organized Baseball. Yet even as an "outlaw league," it was considerably above the level of competition Cobb had known with the Royston Reds.

Playing two or three times a week in towns around northern Alabama and southern Tennessee, Cobb soon was the league's leading batter, according to the rough statistics the various teams kept. Although he may not have been greatly affected by Baptist Sunday school back in Royston, he did intend to live rigorously by one Biblical injunction: put not thy light under a bushel. Playing for Anniston was fun, and at $65 a month plus free room and board, he was doing a lot better financially than if he had managed to stay with Augusta. Sooner or later, though, he had to get back into Organized Baseball.

Grantland Rice, the sports editor of the Atlanta *Journal*, began receiving regular communications from Alabama attesting to the sensational exploits of the young outfielder Cobb. Written in a variety of cursive styles and signed with names like "Jones," "Brown," and "Smith," the letters and postcards continued to come until Rice finally wrote in his column that "over in Alabama there's a young fellow named Cobb who seems to be showing an unusual amount of talent." Not until many years later, when Cobb told him about it, did Rice learn that it was really Cobb who had sent all those notices touting his ballplaying talents. Nor did Cobb himself learn until after his father's death that W. H. Cobb had clipped Rice's column and carried it around to show his friends in Royston and Atlanta.

After about three months with Anniston, Cobb received a telegram from the Augusta club inviting him to rejoin the team. By that time the Tennessee-Alabama League was about ready to collapse, anyway. In Augusta, Con Strouthers had sold his interest in the club and resigned as manager, giving way to catcher Andy Roth. Cobb first made sure that Strouthers, for whom he had vowed never to play again, was really gone, then hustled back to the Tourists. He reappeared in the lineup on August 9, again against Columbia. His return to the Sally League proved less than triumphal. Playing all the outfield positions at one time or another, Cobb appeared in thirty-five games during the remainder of the season and finished with an uninspiring .237 batting average, thirty-third among some fifty to fifty-five regular players in a league that had only one .300 hitter.

Back in Royston for the off-season, Cobb could bask in the adulation of his friends. His father remained unimpressed even when Cobb banked the $200 he had saved and showed no signs of having lost his virtue during the summer away from home. Again it was necessary for him to work hard at the Cobb farm, this time sowing the winter wheat crop, before his father warmed up and was again willing to offer praise for something he had done.

Otherwise, Cobb tramped the woods, sometimes hunting but mostly just staying outdoors as much as he could, and wondered about his future. It was just possible that he might not be good enough to go very far in baseball. He gave some thought to enrolling at the University of Georgia to start the long years of study that would lead to his becoming a surgeon. That would please his father. Over the winter, though, he got an inquiry from Andy Roth about whether he planned to play for Augusta again in 1905. The eighteen-year-old veteran of less than a third of a season in Organized Baseball wrote back saying that he had to have $90 a month. Remarkably, Roth and President John B. Carter agreed to Cobb's terms, and the youth prepared to give baseball another try.

Cobb had grown another inch and put on a few more pounds since the previous spring, and he was faster than ever. More determined, too. In 1905 the Detroit Tigers again trained at Augusta, having agreed with the Augusta owners to return in exchange for first claim on whatever players Detroit liked on the local team. When Bill Armour, the new manager of the Tigers, showed up at Warren Park for the first time, second baseman Herman "Germany" Schaefer greeted him with an account of the wild antics of a kid on the Augusta team named Cobb. According to Schaefer, Cobb wanted to steal a base on every pitch, tried to take two bases on singles, even tried to go from first to third base on bunts. "He's the craziest ballplayer I ever saw," said Schaefer.

Yet the Tigers soon began to take the kid seriously. In the two exhibition games Augusta played with Detroit, Cobb rapped a single off Bill Donovan, one of the Tigers' aces, another off Jesse Stovall, and a single and triple off Eddie Cicotte, a Detroit semipro star the Tigers had signed and subsequently decided to leave with Augusta.

Cobb started the season as the leadoff hitter and regular left fielder for Augusta. His hitting was mediocre in the early going, and his erratic base running and outfield play dismayed his manager. He also got on Roth's nerves by complaining that the team lacked discipline, that it was, in the baseball parlance of the day, a "joy club." Cobb himself soon "fell into the spirit of things. I was fast losing my ambition to go higher in the game." At one point Roth wanted to sell his troublesome young outfielder to Charleston for a token $25, but the owners thought otherwise, and Cobb stayed.

By mid-July the Tourists had lost fifteen of their last twenty games and were drifting in fourth place in the six-team league. Not that they lacked talent. Besides Cobb, the Augusta roster included three other future major leaguers: Cicotte, who pitched two no-hit games that year; Nap Rucker from Crabapple, Georgia, who roomed with Cobb on the road and pitched a no-hitter of his own; and infield Clyde Engle. But it was not a good ball club. Roth finally turned over the team to outfielder and team captain George Leidy, although Roth stayed on as first-string catcher.

Soon after Liedy took over, Cobb, in a game at Savannah with his team leading 2–0, took his position in the outfield eating a bag of popcorn or peanuts. (Accounts vary.) As he munched away, a fly ball soared in his direction. Trying to hold on to his snack at the same time that he pursued the ball, Cobb missed making the catch, and a run scored. Although Augusta went on to win the game, Manager Leidy was not amused by Cobb's gaffe. What followed that night was a scene that might well have been lifted from one of the period's books of boys' fiction, wherein a well-meaning but irresponsible lad is straightened out by the wise counsel of an older man—father, minister, employer, or whatever. In this case it was George Leidy.

A journeyman minor leaguer whose main ambition now was to have a few successful years as manager, Leidy asked Cobb to ride with him on the trolley line out to a local amusement park. As they rode and later as they strolled around the park, Leidy talked quietly but earnestly, telling Cobb that he had to stop fooling around, that he had a lot of ability and a great future in baseball if he worked hard to make the most of his talents. He went on to describe life in the big leagues—traveling in comfortable Pullman cars, staying in fine hotels in big cities, eating good food, wearing expensive clothes, gaining fame and success. On other nights, as well—while they ate together, took in vaudeville shows, or just sat on hotel porches—Leidy continued to boost Cobb's confidence and determination. Completely won over, Cobb promised henceforth to become the best ballplayer he could possible be.

In the mornings at the ballpark Leidy worked with Cobb, teaching him the intricacies of the hit-and-run, the delayed steal, hitting to the opposite field, and above all, the art of bunting. Hour after hour Leidy threw to him and Cobb bunted at an old sweater placed to either side of home plate. He worked on sacrifice bunts, on drag bunts, on faking bunts and slapping the ball past third basemen. And in the games in the afternoons, Leidy let Cobb do what he wanted at bat and on the base paths, confident that with what he had learned, the kid would usually do the right thing.

Within a short time Cobb had become the outstanding player in the Sally League. His team continued to flounder, but at the end of July the baseball tabloid *Sporting Life* could report that "Cyrus Cobb" was the first in the league that season to make 100 base hits. The club's owners raised his salary to $125 a month. Meanwhile, scouts from Detroit and other big-league teams, as well as Indianapolis of the American Association, turned up regularly at Augusta's games. Henry "Heinie" Youngman from the Tigers sat on the bench with Cobb one day and questioned him about his background. The Macon first baseman told him he had heard Cobb was about to go up. Now it seemed only a matter of time until Cobb could notify his father that he had made it into the big time and was on his way to the kind of rewards and recognition his father had envisioned for him in more traditional endeavors. For a few days during a home stand he happily hosted his seventeen-year-old brother, Paul, a good semipro ballplayer himself, who had come to watch Cobb in action.

Early on the morning of August 9, 1905—"the blackest of days," he later termed it—Cobb received a telegram in Augusta from Royston. His father had been killed in some kind of shooting accident. Cobb agonized through the slow, zigzag train trip back to Royston. Tired, bewildered, desolated, he arrived to hear a story of unbelievable horror. His mother, they told him, had shot his father.

What he probably was not told—at least not to his face—was that for some time it had been common gossip in Royston that Professor Cobb's pretty wife had taken a lover. The gossip must eventually have got around to W. H. Cobb. On Tuesday evening, August 8, he had told his wife he was going out to the farm for a couple of days, hitched his horse to his buggy, and left the house. Paul and Florence were staying with friends. Later that night Amanda Cobb went upstairs to the room over the front porch she shared with her husband, locked the windows (even though the temperature had been in the nineties that day and it was still warm and humid), and went to bed. A little later W. H. Cobb was seen alone on foot in town. Shortly after midnight Amanda Cobb was awakened by a noise on the porch roof. A figure she could not make out was struggling to raise one of the windows to her bedroom. Grabbing the loaded double-barreled shotgun that always stood in a corner of the room, she pointed it toward the window and fired once. After what witnesses later described as a considerable interval, she fired again. Approaching the shattered window, she peered into the darkness to find her husband lying in a widening pool of blood.

At the Cunningham house next door, Joe Cunningham heard the blasts and ran over to see what had happened. There he found, as he described it to his daughter many years later, "the worst thing I ever saw." Although Professor Cobb was still breathing, he had a gaping hole in his abdomen, and one of the shotgun blasts had literally blown his brains out. The young man ran to get Dr. H. F. McCreary, who pronounced W. H. Cobb dead at 1:30 A.M. He found a revolver in Cobb's coat pocket.

The next day a coroner's jury heard Amanda Cobb give her account of the shooting and others testify about what they had heard and seen. By the end of the day the coroner's jury had ordered Amanda Cobb's arrest on a charge of voluntary manslaughter. W. H. Cobb's funeral was held on August 11 at the Cobb house, where people crowded in and overflowed the front yard and into the street. He was buried at the local cemetery in a coffin built by Joe Cunningham's father, with the professor's Masonic brothers officiating at the gravesite. The day after that the county sheriff arrested Amanda Cobb, and the local justice of the peace set her bond at $7,000. She was quickly able to post the 10 percent of the bond necessary to keep herself from having to spend any time in jail. By the end of the month a grand jury sitting at Carnesville had returned an indictment against her. Her trial was to take place that fall.

Tyrus Cobb left no account of what he felt and did in Royston during that dreadful time. He did spend four days after the funeral with his mother, brother, and sister. That he was able to get himself together in fairly short order and resume his baseball duties suggests a great deal about the young man's will, concentration, and above all, his continuing drive to confirm his father's trust. Now, though, it was also a matter of upholding the family's reputation at a time when scandal and suspicion hung over it. The best way to do that was to achieve such success as a ballplayer that people would have to respect the Cobb name and especially his father's memory.

Cobb rejoined his team on Wednesday, August 16, at Augusta, where the previous week the local newspaper had tactfully reported his father's death. Against the Charleston Sea Gulls he made two hits in the first game of a doubleheader but went hitless in the second game. By that time George Leidy was out as manager of the Tourists, and Andy Roth was in again. Whoever managed Augusta no longer much concerned Cobb, though, because three days after he got back, he received formal notification from Charles D. Carr, now club president, that he had been sold to the Detroit Tigers and was to report to that team by the end of the month.

By August the second-division Tigers were plagued by an accumulation of disabling injuries and down to three outfields, one of whom, the veteran Duff Cooley, was hobbling on one good leg. Club Secretary Frank J. Navin and Manager Bill Armour had to pick up somebody to help the team finish out the season, and the club's finances would not permit the purchase of a player from the upper minor leagues. So Augusta, at the bottom of the minors and where Detroit already had an option to buy whichever player it wanted, was the logical place to turn. Good reports had reached Detroit on infielder Clyde Engle, who could also help out in the outfield. But Bill Byron, a native Detroiter umpiring in the Sally League (en route to a notable career in the National League), told Heinie Youngman that Cobb had greater promise. In Detroit, Bill Donovan, whom Cobb had impressed in spring training, told Armour basically the same thing. So for $700—the price agreed to in the spring for the player Detroit chose, plus $200 thrown in because he was being taken before the season was over—Cobb, still four months short of his nineteenth birthday, became a big leaguer. "I only thought," he later said, "Father won't know it."

Cobb played his last game for Augusta on August 25 before a fine Friday crowd of about 1,400, against league-leading Macon. His solid hitting and dashing style on the bases and afield had captivated the local "bugs," as baseball fans were called in those days; and when he came to bat in the bottom of the first inning, a group of them met him at home plate with a bouquet of flowers and a gold watch. He stammered his thanks, shook hands all around, waved to the crowd, finally got into the batter's box, and struck out. Subsequently, he singled twice, stole a base, and threw out a runner as the Tourists took another defeat, 5–0. Cobb's final-game performance gave him more than forty stolen bases (third in the league) and, with the Sally League season ending in a few days, ensured him the batting championship at .326. Taking chances in the field, however, had been costly. His thirteen errors gave him the lowest fielding average among outfielders appearing in more than a hundred games.

As would often be the case in his baseball career, Cobb both won the admiration of the paying customers and left a sour taste in the mouths of the club management. Just before he left Augusta, he groused to local sportswriters that he should have got part of his purchase price and that in fact he'd been ill treated all season, being kept at the bottom of the salary scale on the team. Whether or not his complaints were justified, one could well understand his ill temper. Although his big-league adventure awaited him in Detroit, he still had to go by Royston on his way north and, however briefly, again be a part of the mess at home.

Cobb was on his way to Detroit in earnest by Saturday night, the twenty-sixth, traveling at the Augusta club's expense. The trip of some 700 miles should have taken about thirty hours, but Cobb missed his connections in Atlanta and Cincinnati. Exhausted and bedraggled, he finally arrived about 10:30 P.M. on Tuesday after being en route from Augusta for something like four days. Carrying his Augusta uniform roll, a small grip, his little Spalding fielder's glove, and three bats in a cloth bag, he alighted from the train at the Michigan Central terminal in Detroit and looked around at "what for me was an unknown land." Nobody was there to meet him. Hiring a horse-drawn cab, he had the driver take him to a cheap hotel that turned out to contain a burlesque house, as well, near the Tiger ballpark. There he paid $10 in advance for a week's worth of room and board.

Meanwhile, notices about his purchase had appeared on the sports pages of the Detroit papers, giving sketchy facts about his background and indicating that his arrival was imminent. On August 27 the Detroit *Free Press* printed a photograph of Cobb in street clothes. It showed a thin-faced young man with a slightly hooked nose, somewhat jugged ears, small but intense blue-gray eyes, and a full head of finely textured, reddish-blond hair parted in the middle. Three days later Joe S. Jackson, chief baseball writer for the *Free Press*, remarked that all those on the Detroit team who had observed Cobb in the spring had been impressed by his speed and that Bill Byron thought he was one of the fastest men leaving the batter's box he'd ever seen. Noting that Cobb had led the Sally League in hitting, Jackson added, "He won't pile up anything like that in this league. . . . If he gets away with a .275 mark, he will be satisfying everybody." That same day Tyrus Raymond Cobb played in his first game in the major leagues. There would be 3,032 more.

After winning 103 games in 1980, his first (and only, it was to transpire) season as skipper of the Yankees, Dick Howser was eased out of the job in a highly uneasy news conference. Dave Anderson reported the "execution" with restraint and craft: "I've always been a believer in letting people hang themselves with their own words," he later wrote. Howser went on to manage the Kansas City Royals to the World Championship, and George Steinbrenner went on to further executions—at this writing George has since fired seven more Yankee managers.

DAVE ANDERSON

Sandwiches at an Execution

Near the door of George Steinbrenner's office in Yankee Stadium yesterday, there were two trays of bite-sized roast beef, turkey, and ham sandwiches, each with a toothpick in it. As soon as fourteen invited newsmen entered his office for the execution of Dick Howser as manager and the transfer of Gene Michael from general manager to dugout manager, the Yankees' principal owner looked around.

"Anybody want any sandwiches?" he asked. "We've got a lot of sandwiches here."

Gene Michael had piled four little roast beef sandwiches on a small plastic plate, and he had a cup of coffee. But as he sat against the far wall, under a huge Yankee top-hat insignia and several enlarged photos of memorable Yankee Stadium moments, he was the only one eating when Dick Howser suddenly appeared and walked quickly to a chair in front of the table with the sandwiches.

"Nobody wants a sandwich?" George Steinbrenner asked. "Nobody wants a drink?"

One of the newsmen ordered a glass of white wine from the bartender, but that was all. Then there was a momentary silence as George Steinbrenner, husky in a soft-blue shirt with a navy-blue-and-green-striped tie, sat at a big tan vinyl chair behind his shiny round desk. On the desk was a gold numeral one, maybe several inches high, and a small sign announcing, "Lead, Follow or Get the Hell Out of the Way," and a miniature brass ship's telegraph.

"During the season it's always pointed to full speed ahead," he would explain later. "But in the off-season it's on standby."

To the owner's right, about 10 feet away, Dick Howser sat stiffly. His legs crossed, he was wearing a beige shirt, a brown tie, brown pants, and brown cowboy boots. He was staring out away from George Steinbrenner, staring blankly at the white draperies that had been drawn across the huge window that overlooks the grassy geometry of the field where Dick Howser no longer would work. Most of the time he had his left index finger up against his left cheek, as if to keep from having to look at the Yankee owner, who now was discussing the managerial situation that had been simmering for several weeks.

"Dick has decided," George Steinbrenner began, "that he will not be returning to the Yankees as manager."

Dick has decided. That would be the premise of George Steinbrenner's explanation. Dick has decided. Ostensibly he suddenly decided to go into real estate development in Tallahassee, Florida, and be the supervisor of Yankee scouts in the Southeast after having been the manager for the Yankee team that won 103 games last season, after having been in baseball virtually all his life as a major-league infielder, major-league coach, college coach, and major-league manager of baseball's most famous franchise.

But baseball's most famous franchise also has baseball's most demanding owner. When the Yankees were swept in three games by the Kansas City Royals in the American League championship series, George Steinbrenner steamed. And now Dick Houser is in real estate and is a Yankee scouting supervisor.

"At no time," George Steinbrenner said yesterday, "did I lay down rules or commandments that Dick would have to live by if he returned as manager. The door was open for him to return, but he chose to accept this business opportunity. It took so long because he wanted to make sure he was doing the right thing."

All the while Dick Howser stared at the drawn draperies.

"But could Dick," somebody asked George Steinbrenner, "still be the manager if he wanted to be?"

"Yes."

"Dick, why don't you want to be here?"

"I have to be cautious here," Dick Howser said, staring straight ahead. "But the other thing popped up."

"Were you satisfied that you could have returned without conditions?"

"I'd rather not comment on that," Dick Howser said.

"If you had won the World Series instead of being eliminated in the playoffs," he was asked, "would you have taken this real-estate opportunity?"

"That's hard to say."

"Were you fired, Dick?"

"I'm not going to comment on that," the former manager said.

"I didn't fire the man," the owner said.

Maybe not, but it is reasonable to believe that George Steinbrenner suggested that Dick Howser look for employment elsewhere. That way George Steinbrenner could put Gene Michael, whom he considers a more combative manager, in the dugout. Perhaps to soothe his conscience, he disclosed yesterday that Dick Howser could be paid his reported $100,000 salary for each of the remaining two years on his three-year contract.

"I feel morally and contractually obligated to Dick and his wife, Nancy," the owner said. "I took him out of Florida State, where he was the baseball coach and where he could have stayed for life. If it hasn't worked out, maybe it's my fault."

If it hasn't worked out. Until then it had been "Dick had decided." But perhaps on a slip of the tongue it was "if it hasn't worked out." Anybody who knew George Steinbrenner knew that all along. And anybody who knew Dick Howser knew that, if given a choice, he would not decide to go into real-estate development rather than be the Yankees' manager.

But still George Steinbrenner persisted.

"I think it's safe to say," he said at one point yesterday, "that Dick Howser wants to be a Florida resident year round, right, Dick?"

Dick Howser didn't even answer that one.

Say this for Dick Howser—instead of going along with George Steinbrenner's party line yesterday, he declined to comment. By not answering questions, he answered them. Anybody could see that. And anybody could see through George Steinbrenner's scheme.

"What advice," Dick Howser was being asked now, "would you give Gene Michael?"

"To have a strong stomach," Dick Howser replied, smiling thinly, "and a nice contract."

Minutes later, the execution was over. Dick Howser got up quickly and walked out of the room without a smile. Behind his round desk, George Steinbrenner looked around.

"Nobody ate any sandwiches," the Yankee owner said.

This beautiful and now famous essay is the culmination of Angell's first baseball book, *The Summer Game* (1972). At the beginning of his baseball assignment for the *New Yorker*, Angell saw that he could not beat the beat reporters at their own game and so "would have to find some other aspect of the game to study," he wrote in the foreword to *The Summer Game*. "My main job, as I conceived it, was to continue to try to give the feel of things—to explain baseball as it happened to me, at a distance and in retrospect. And this was the real luck, for how could I have guessed then that baseball, of all team sports anywhere, should turn out to be so complex, so rich and various in structure and aesthetics and emotion, as to convince me, after ten years as a writer and forty years as a fan, that I have not yet come close to its heart?" Oh yes he has.

ROGER ANGELL

The Interior Stadium

Sports are too much with us. Late and soon, sitting and watching—mostly watching on television—we lay waste our powers of identification and enthusiasm and, in time, attention as more and more closing rallies and crucial putts and late field goals and final play-offs and sudden deaths and world records and world championships unreel themselves ceaselessly before our half-lidded eyes. Professional leagues expand like bubble gum, ever larger and thinner, and the extended sporting seasons, now bunching and overlapping at the ends, conclude in exhaustion and the wrong weather. So, too, goes the secondary business of sports—the news or nonnews off the fields. Sports announcers (ex-halfbacks in Mod hairdos) bring us another live, exclusive interview in depth with the twitchy coach of some as yet undefeated basketball team or with a weeping (for joy) fourteen-year-old champion female backstroker, and the sports pages, now almost the largest single part of the newspaper, brim with salary disputes, medical bulletins, franchise maneuverings, All-Star ballots, drug scandals, close-up biogs, after-dinner tributes, union tactics, weekend wrap-ups, wire-service polls, draft-choice trades, clubhouse gossip, and the latest odds. The American obsession with sports is not a new phenomenon, of course, except in its current dimensions, its excessive excessiveness. What *is* new, and what must at times unsettle even the most devout and unselective fan, is a curious sense of loss. In the midst of all these successive spectacles and instant replays and endless reportings and recapitulations, we seem to have forgotten what we came for. More and more, each sport resembles all sports;

17

the flavor, the special joys of place and season, the unique displays of courage and strength and style that once isolated each game and fixed it in our affections, have disappeared somewhere in the noise and crush.

Of all sports, none has been so buffeted about by this unselective proliferation, so maligned by contemporary cant, or so indifferently defended, as baseball. Yet the game somehow remains the same, obdurately unaltered and comparable only with itself. Baseball has one saving grace that distinguishes it—for me, at any rate—from every other sport. Because of its pace, and thus the perfectly observed balance, both physical and psychological, between opposing forces, its clean lines can be restored in retrospect. This inner game—baseball in the mind—has no season, but it is best played in the winter, without the distraction of other baseball news. At first, it is a game of recollections, recapturings, and visions. Figures and occasions return, enormous sounds rise and swell, and the interior stadium fills with light and yields up the sight of a young ballplayer—some hero perfectly memorized—just completing his own unique swing and now racing toward first. See the way he runs? Yes, that's him! Unmistakable, he leans in, still following the distant flight of the ball with his eyes, and takes his big turn at the base. Yet this is only the beginning, for baseball in the mind is not a mere returning. In time, this easy summoning up of restored players, winning hits, and famous rallies gives way to reconsiderations and reflections about the sport itself. By thinking about baseball like this—by playing it over, keeping it warm in a cold season—we begin to make discoveries. With luck, we may even penetrate some of its mysteries. One of those mysteries is its vividness—the absolutely distinct inner vision we retain of that hitter, that eager base runner, of however long ago. My father was talking the other day about some of the ballplayers he remembered. He grew up in Cleveland, and the Indians were his team. Still are. "We had Nap Lajoie at second," he said. "You've heard of him. A great big broad-shouldered fellow but a beautiful fielder. He was a rough customer. If he didn't like an umpire's call, he'd give him a faceful of tobacco juice. The shortstop was Terry Turner—a smaller man, and blond. I can still see Lajoie picking up a grounder and wheeling and floating the ball over to Turner. Oh, he was quick on his feet! In right field we had Elmer Flick, now in the Hall of Fame. I liked the center fielder, too. His name was Harry Bay, and he wasn't a heavy hitter, but he was very fast and covered a lot of ground. They said he could circle the bases in twelve seconds flat. I saw him get a home run inside the park—the ball hit on the infield and went right past the second baseman and out to the wall, and Bay beat the relay. I remember Addie Joss, our great right-hander. Tall, and an elegant pitcher. I once saw him pitch a perfect game. He died young."

My father has been a fan all his life, and he has pretty well seen them all. He has told me about the famous last game of the 1912 World Series, in Boston, and seeing Fred Snodgrass drop that fly ball in the tenth inning, when the Red Sox scored twice and beat the Giants. I looked up Harry Bay and those other Indians in the *Baseball Encyclopedia*, and I think my father must have seen that inside-the-park homer in the summer of 1904. Lajoie batted .376 that year, and Addie Joss led the American League with an earned run average of 1.59, but the Indians finished in fourth place. 1904. . . . Sixty-seven years have gone by, yet Nap Lajoie is in plain view, and the ball still floats over to Terry Turner. Well, my father is eighty-one now, and old men are great rememberers of the distant past. But I am fifty, and I can also bring things back: Lefty Gomez, skinny necked and frighteningly wild, pitching his first game at Yankee Stadium, against the White Sox and Red Faber in 1930. Old John McGraw, in a business suit and a white fedora, sitting lumpily in a dark corner of the dugout at the Polo Grounds and glowering out at the field. Babe Ruth, wearing a new, bright yellow glove, trotting out to right field—a swollen ballet dancer, with those delicate, almost feminine feet and ankles. Ruth at the plate, uppercutting and missing, staggering with the force of his swing. Ruth and Gehrig hitting back-to-back homers. Gehrig, in the summer of 1933, running bases with a bad leg in a key game against the Senators; hobbling, he rounds third, closely followed by young Dixie Walker, then a Yankee. The throw comes in to the plate, and the Washington catcher—it must have been Luke Sewell—tags out the sliding Gehrig and, in the same motion, the sliding Dixie Walker. A double play at the plate. The Yankees lost the game; the Senators go on to a pennant. And, back across the river again, Carl Hubbell. My own great pitcher, a southpaw, tall and elegant. Hub pitching: the loose motion; two slow, formal bows from the waist, glove and hands held almost in front of his face as he pivots, the long right leg (in long, peculiar pants) striding; and the ball, angling oddly, shooting past the batter. Hubbell walks gravely back to the bench, his pitching arm, as always, turned the wrong way round, with the palm out. Screwballer.

Any fan, as I say, can play this private game, extending it to extraordinary varieties and possibilities in his mind. Ruth bats against Sandy Koufax or Sam McDowell. . . . Hubbell pitches to Ted Williams, and the Kid, grinding the bat in his fists, twitches and blocks his hips with the pitch; he holds off but still follows the ball, leaning over and studying it like some curator as it leaps in just under his hands. Why this vividness, even from an imaginary confrontation? I have watched many other sports, and I have followed some—football, hockey, tennis—with eagerness, but none of them yields these permanent interior pictures, these ancient and precise excitements. Baseball, I must conclude, is intensely remembered because only baseball is so intensely watched. The game forces intensity upon us. In the ballpark, scattered across an immense green, each player is isolated in our attention, utterly visible. Watch that fielder just below us. Little seems to be expected of him. He waits in easy composure, his hands on his knees; when the ball at last soars or bounces out to him, he seizes it and dispatches it with swift, haughty ease. It all looks easy, slow, and, above all, safe. Yet we know better, for what is certain in baseball is that someone, perhaps several people, will fail. They will be searched out, caught in the open, and defeated, and there will be no confusion about it or sharing of the blame. This is sure to happen, because what baseball requires of its athletes, of course, is nothing less than perfection, and perfection cannot be eased or divided. Every movement of every game, from first pitch to last out, is measured and recorded against an absolute standard, and thus each success is also a failure. Credit that strikeout to the pitcher but also count it against the batter's average; mark this run unearned, because the left fielder bobbled the ball for an instant and a runner moved up. Yet, faced with this sudden and repeated presence of danger, the big-league player defends himself with such courage and skill that the illusion of safety is sustained. Tension is screwed tighter and tighter as the certain downfall is postponed again and again, so that when disaster does come—a half-topped infield hit, a walk on a close three-and-two call, a low drive up the middle that just eludes the diving short-stop—we rise and cry out. It is a spontaneous, inevitable, irresistible reaction.

Televised baseball, I must add, does not seem capable of transmitting this emotion. Most baseball is seen on the tube now, and it is presented faithfully and with great technical skill. But the medium is irrevocably two-dimensional; even with several cameras, television cannot bring us the essential distances of the game—the simultaneous flight of a batted ball and its pursuit by the racing, straining outfielders, the swift convergence of runner and ball at a base. Foreshortened on our screen, the players on the field appear to be squashed together, almost touching each other, and, watching them, we lose the sense of their separateness and lonesome waiting.

This is a difficult game. It is so demanding that the best teams and the weakest teams can meet on almost even terms, with no assurance about the result of any one game. In March 1962, in St. Petersburg, the World Champion Yankees played for the first time against the newborn New York Mets—one of the worst teams of all time—in a game that each badly wanted to win; the winner, to nobody's real surprise, was the Mets. In 1970, the World Champion Orioles won 108 games and lost 54; the lowest cellar team, the White Sox, won 56 games and lost 106. This looks like an enormous disparity, but what it truly means is that the Orioles managed to win two out of every three games they played, while the White Sox won one out of every three. That third game made the difference—and a kind of difference that can be appreciated when one notes that the winning margin given up by the White Sox to all their opponents during the season averaged 1.1 runs per game. Team form is harder to establish in baseball than in any other sport, and the 162-game season not uncommonly comes down to October with two or three teams locked together at the top of the standings on the final weekend. Each inning of baseball's slow, searching time span, each game of its long season is essential to the disclosure of its truth.

Form is the imposition of a regular pattern upon varying and unpredictable circumstances, but the patterns of baseball, for all the game's tautness and neatness, are never regular. Who can predict the winner and shape of today's game? Will it be a brisk, neat two-hour shutout? A languid, error-filled 12–3 laugher? A riveting three-hour, fourteen-inning deadlock? What other sport produces these manic swings? For the players, too, form often undergoes ter-rible reversals; in no other sport is a champion athlete so often humiliated or a journeyman so easily exalted. The surprise, the upset, the total turnabout of expectations and reputations—these are delightful commonplaces of baseball. Al Gionfriddo, a part-time Dodger outfielder, stole second base in the ninth inning of the fourth game of the 1947 World Series to help set up Lavagetto's game-winning double (and the only Dodger hit of the game) off the Yankees' Bill Bevens. Two days later, Gionfriddo robbed Joe DiMaggio with a famous game-saving catch of a 415-foot drive in deepest left field at Yankee Stadium. Gionfriddo never made it back to the big leagues after that season. Another irregular, the Mets' Al Weis, homered in the fifth and last game of the 1969 World Series, tying up the game that the Mets won in the next inning; it was Weis's third homer of the year and his first ever at Shea Stadium. And so forth. Who remembers the second game of the 1956 World Series—an appallingly bad afternoon of baseball in which the Yankees' starter, Don Larsen, was yanked after giving up a single and four walks in less than two innings? It was Larsen's *next* start, the fifth game, when he pitched his perfect game.

There is always a heavy splash of luck in these reversals. Luck, indeed, plays an almost predictable part in the game; we have all seen the enormous enemy clout into the bleachers that just hooks foul at the last instant and the half-checked swing that produces a game-winning blooper over second. Everyone complains about baseball luck, but I think it adds something to the game that is nearly essential. Without it, such a rigorous and unforgiving pastime would be almost too painful to enjoy.

No one, it becomes clear, can conquer this impossible and unpredictable game. Yet every player tries, and now and again—very rarely—we see a man who seems to have met all the demands, challenged all the implacable averages, spurned the mere luck. He has defied baseball, even altered it, and for a time at least the game is truly his. One thinks of Willie Mays, in the best of his youth, batting at the Polo Grounds, his whole body seeming to leap at the ball as he swings in an explosion of exuberance. Or Mays in center field, playing in so close that he appears at times to be watching the game from over the second baseman's shoulder, and then that same joyful leap as he takes off after a long, deep drive and runs it down, running so hard and so far that the ball itself seems to stop in the air and wait for him. One thinks of Jackie Robinson in a close game—any close game—playing the infield and glaring in at the enemy hitter, hating him and daring him, refusing to be beaten. And Sandy Koufax pitching in the last summers before he was disabled, in that time when he pitched a no-hitter every year for four years. Kicking swiftly, hiding the ball until the last instant, Koufax throws in a blur of motion, coming over the top, and the fastball, appearing suddenly in the strike zone, sometimes jumps up so immoderately that his catcher has to take it with his glove shooting upward, like an infielder stabbing at a bad-hop grounder. I remember some batter taking a strike like that and then stepping out of the box and staring back at the pitcher with a look of utter incredulity—as if Koufax had just thrown an Easter egg past him.

Joe DiMaggio batting sometimes gave the same impression—the suggestion that the old rules and dimensions of baseball no longer applied to him and that the game had at last grown unfairly easy. I saw DiMaggio once during his famous hitting streak in 1941; I'm not sure of the other team or the pitcher—perhaps it was the Tigers and Bobo Newsom—but I'm sure of DiMaggio pulling a line shot to left that collided preposterously with the bag at third base and ricocheted halfway out to center field. That record of hitting safely in fifty-six straight games seems as secure as any in baseball, but it does not awe me as much as the fact that DiMadge's old teammates claim they *never* saw him commit an error of judgment in a ball game. Thirteen years and never a wrong throw, a cutoff man missed, an extra base passed up. Well, there was one time when he stretched a single against the Red Sox and was called out at second, but the umpire is said to have admitted later that he blew the call.

And one more for the pantheon: Carl Yastrzemski. To be precise, Yaz in September of the 1967 season, as his team, the Red Sox, fought and clawed against the White Sox and the Twins and the Tigers in the last two weeks of the closest and most vivid pennant race of our time. The presiding memory of that late summer is of Yastrzemski approaching the plate, once again in a situation where all hope rests on him, and settling himself in the batter's box—touching his helmet, tugging at his belt, and just touching the tip of the bat to the ground, in precisely the same set of gestures—and then, in a storm of noise and pleading, swinging violently and perfectly . . . and hitting. In the last two weeks of that season, Yaz batted .522—twenty-three hits for forty-four appearances: four doubles, five home runs, sixteen runs batted in (RBIs). In the final two games, against the Twins, both of which the Red Sox *had* to win for the pennant, he went seven for eight, won the first game with a homer, and saved the second with a brilliant, rally-killing throw to second base from deep left field. (He cooled off a little in the World Series, batting only .400 for seven games and hitting three homers.) Since then, the game and the averages have caught up with Yastrzemski, and he has never again approached that kind of performance. But then, of course, neither has anyone else.

Only baseball, with its statistics and isolated fragments of time, permits so precise a reconstruction from box score and memory. Take another date—October 7, 1968, at Detroit, the fifth game of the World Series. The fans are here, and an immense noise—a cheerful, 53,634-man vociferosity—utterly fills the green, steep, high-walled box of Tiger Stadium. This is a good baseball town, and the cries have an anxious edge, for the Tigers are facing almost sure extinction. They trail the Cardinals by three games to one, and never for a moment have they looked the equal of these defending World Champions. Denny McLain, the Tigers' thirty-one-game winner, was humiliated in the opener by the Cardinals' Bob Gibson, who set an all-time Series record by striking out seventeen Detroit batters. The Tigers came back the next day, winning rather easily behind their capable left-hander Mickey Lolich, but the Cardinals demolished them in the next two games, scoring a total of seventeen runs and again brushing McLain aside; Gibson has now struck out twenty-seven Tigers, and he will be ready to pitch again in the Series if needed. Even more disheartening is Lou Brock, the Cards' left fielder, who has already lashed out eight hits in the first four games and has stolen seven bases in eight tries; Bill Freehan, the Tigers' catcher, has a sore arm. And here, in the very top of the first, Brock leads off against Lolich and doubles to left; a moment later, Curt Flood singles, and Orlando Cepeda homers into the left-field stands. The Tigers are down 3–0, and the fans are wholly stilled.

In the third inning, Brock leads off with another hit—a single—and there is a bitter overtone to the hometown cheers when Freehan, on a pitchout, at last throws him out, stealing, at second. There is no way for anyone to know, of course, that this is a profound omen; Brock has done his last damage to the Tigers in this Series. Now it is the fourth, and hope and shouting return. Mickey Stanley leads off the Detroit half with a triple that lands, 2 inches fair, in the right-field corner. He scores on a fly. Willie Horton also triples. With two out, Jim Northrup smashes a hard grounder directly at the Cardinal second base-man, Javier, and at the last instant the ball strikes something on the infield and leaps up and over Javier's head, and Horton scores. Luck! Luck twice over, if you remember how close Stanley's drive came to falling foul. But never mind; it's 3–2 now, and a game again.

But Brock is up, leading off once again, and an instant later he has driven a Lolich pitch off the left-field wall for a double. Now Javier singles to left, and Brock streaks around third base toward home. Bill Freehan braces himself in front of the plate, waiting for the throw; he has had a miserable Series, going hitless in fourteen at bats so far and undergoing those repeated humiliations by the man who is now racing at him full speed—the man who must surely be counted, along with Gibson, as the Series hero. The throw comes in chest high on the fly from Willie Horton in left; ball and base runner arrive together; Brock does not slide. Brock does not slide, and his left foot, just descending on the plate, is banged away as he collides with Freehan. Umpire Doug Harvey shoots up his fist: out! It is a great play. Nothing has changed, the score is still 3–2, but everything has changed; something has shifted irrevocably in this game.

In the seventh inning, with one out and the Tigers still one run shy, Tiger manager Mayo Smith allows Lolich to bat for himself. Mickey Lolich has hit .114 for the season, and Smith has a pinch hitter on the bench named Gates Brown, who hit .370. But Lolich got two hits in his other Series start, including the first homer of his ten years in baseball. Mayo, sensing something that he will not be able to defend later if he is wrong, lets Lolich bat for himself, and Mickey pops a foolish little fly to right that falls in for a single. Now there is another single. A walk loads the bases, and Al Kaline comes to the plate. The noise in the stadium is insupportable. Kaline singles, and the Tigers go ahead by a run. Norm Cash drives in another. The Tigers win this searching, turned-about, lucky, marvelous game by 5–3.

Two days later, back in St. Louis, form shows its other face as the Tigers rack up ten runs in the third inning and win by 13–1. McLain at last has his Series win. So it is Lolich against Gibson in the finale, of course. Nothing happens. Inning after inning goes by, zeros accumulate on the scoreboard, and anxiety and silence lengthen like shadows. In the sixth, Lou Brock singles. Daring Lolich, daring the Tiger infielders' nerves, openly forcing his luck, hoping perhaps to settle these enormous tensions and difficulties with one more act of bravado, he takes an excessive lead off first, draws the throw from Lolich, breaks for second, and is erased, just barely, by Cash's throw. A bit later, Curt Flood singles, and, weirdly, he, too, is picked off first and caught in a rundown. Still no score. Gibson and Lolich, both exhausted, pitch on. With two out in the seventh, Cash singles for the Tigers' second hit of the day. Horton is safe on a slow bouncer that *just* gets through the left side of the infield. Jim Northrup hits the next pitch deep and high but straight at Flood, who is the best center fielder in the National League. Flood starts in and then halts, stopping so quickly that his spikes churn up a green flap of turf; he turns and races back madly, but the ball sails over his head for a triple. Disaster. Suddenly, irreversibly, it has happened. Two runs are in, Freehan doubles in another, and, two innings later, the Tigers are Champions of the World.

I think I will always remember those two games—the fifth and the seventh—perfectly. And I remember something else about the 1968 Series when it was over—a feeling that almost everyone seemed to share: that Bob Gibson had not lost that last game and the Cardinals had not lost the Series. Certainly no one wanted to say that the Tigers had not won it, but there seemed to be something more that remained to be said. It was something about the levels and demands of the sport we had seen—as if the baseball itself had somehow surpassed the players and the results. It was the baseball that won.

Always, it seems, there is something more to be discovered about this game. Sit quietly in the upper stand and look at the field. Half close your eyes against the sun so that the players recede a little and watch the movements of baseball. The pitcher, immobile on the mound, holds the inert white ball, his little lump of physics. Now, with abrupt gestures, he gives it enormous speed and direction, converting it suddenly into a line, a moving line. The batter, wielding a plane, attempts to intercept the line and acutely alter it, but he fails; the ball, a line again, is redrawn to the pitcher, in the center of this square, the diamond. Again the pitcher studies his task—the projection of his next line through the smallest possible segment of an invisible seven-sided solid (the strike zone has depth as well as height and width) 60 feet and 6 inches away; again the batter considers his even more difficult proposition, which is to reverse this imminent white speck, to redirect its energy not in a soft parabola or a series of diminishing squiggles but into a beautiful and dangerous new force, of perfect straightness and immense distance. In time, these and other lines are drawn on the field; the batter and the fielders are also transformed into fluidity, moving and converging, and we see now that all movement in baseball is a convergence toward fixed points—the pitched ball toward the plate, the thrown ball toward the right angles of the bases, the batted ball toward the as yet undrawn but already visible point of congruence with either the ground or a glove. Simultaneously, the fielders hasten toward that same point of meeting with the ball, and both the base runner and the ball, now redirected, toward their encounter at the base. From our perch, we can sometimes see three or four or more such geometries appearing at the same instant on the green board below us and, mathematicians that we are, can sense their solution even before they are fully drawn. It is neat, it is pretty, it is satisfying. Scientists speak of the profoundly moving aesthetic beauty of mathematics, and perhaps the baseball field is one of the few places where the rest of us can glimpse this mystery.

The last dimension is time. Within the ballpark, time moves differently, marked by no clock except the events of the game. This is the unique, unchangeable feature of baseball and perhaps explains why this sport, for all the enormous changes it has undergone in the past decade or two, remains somehow rustic, unviolent, and introspective. Baseball's time is seamless and invisible, a bubble within which players move at exactly the same pace and rhythms as all their predecessors. This is the way the game was played in our youth and in our fathers' youth, and even back then—back in the country days—there must have been the same feeling that time could be stopped. Since baseball time is measured only in outs, all you have to do is succeed utterly; keep hitting, keep the rally alive, and you have defeated time. You remain forever young. Sitting in the stands, we sense this, if only dimly. The players below us—Mays, DiMaggio, Ruth, Snodgrass—swim and blur in memory, the ball floats over to Terry Turner, and the end of this game may never come.

Much of baseball's appeal is its apparent permanence, its resistance to the change that swirls about the rest of society. But even though the game seems to stop time and time seems to have forgotten baseball (it really isn't all that much different from the game played in 1893), change has indeed stealthily worked its mischief. Marty Appel was not asleep at the typewriter, however, and adds these updates: first "compensation player," Joel Skinner, going from Pittsburgh to Chicago for the loss of White Sox free agent Ed Farmer; first to turn down a million-dollar annual contract, Johnny Bench, who chose to retire after the 1983 season; and first teams to use computers extensively to chart the opposition, the White Sox and A's of 1983.

MARTY APPEL

Noting the Milestones

Ralph Darwin Miller of Cincinnati died on May 8, 1973, at the age of 100 years, 54 days. Few if any baseball people noted the death other than to observe that Ralph had pitched for Brooklyn and Baltimore in 1898 and 1899 with a 6–16 record.

What should have been noted was the passing of two milestones—Miller was the last nineteenth-century major leaguer and also the only major leaguer (out of some 12,000) to live to see his 100th birthday.

It's not surprising, of course, that these things should have passed unnoticed. So much happens each day in baseball, so many statistical milestones are approached or reached, that it becomes an impossible task to properly log everything.

For example, when Hank Aaron retired after the 1976 season, did anyone note that he was the last player to arrive in the majors from the old Negro Leagues? He had played in the Negro American League in 1952.

And what honor awaits Tony Perez or Bert Campaneris? One of them (or perhaps Luis Tiant with a recall) will be the last Cuban player in the majors, signed before such immigration was halted. *

Has anyone noted that Tug McGraw is the last major leaguer still active to have played for Casey Stengel?

Again, history sails before us all the time, but we don't always have the

---

* It turned out to be Perez, in 1986.

wisdom to jot it down. Some of the achievements in baseball's modern, or post–World War II, era have been in the appearance of the game, such as tight uniforms, instant replays, or batting helmets, while others have been individual achievements.

Ron Blomberg was baseball's first official designated hitter, stepping up to the plate for the New York Yankees in Fenway Park on April 6, 1973. But in 1978 Blomberg became the first player with a guaranteed, multiyear contract to be released and paid in full when the White Sox made such a decision. They were not the first club to have to make such a difficult financial choice.

The game-winning RBI became an official baseball statistic in 1980, and the very first one was recorded by Cincinnati's George Foster on April 9. He was an appropriate choice for the distinction, having led the National League in RBIs three times.

The "save rule" for relief pitchers became an official baseball statistic in 1969, and the first save was recorded by Los Angeles's Bill Singer on April 7 against the Reds.

The first player in the major leagues born in the 1950s was John Mayberry (born February 18, 1950), who debuted with Houston in 1968. The first player born in the 1960s was Tim Conroy (born April 3, 1960), who pitched for Oakland in 1978.

The last Brooklyn Dodger to remain active in the majors was Don Drysdale, who retired in 1969, twelve years after the club's final year in Brooklyn. The last New York Giant was Willie Mays, who concluded his career with the 1973 New York Mets.

The World Series itself has of course been full of subtle "firsts" and milestones in modern times, many unnoticed or unappreciated at the time.

For example, if you accept the fact that the Dodgers left behind many loyal New York (and Brooklyn) fans when they and the Giants moved West in 1958, one can review the yearly World Series between 1949 and 1966 to find that New Yorkers had a "stake" in the Series for eighteen consecutive years, between the Yankees, Giants, and Dodgers. It was uninterrupted until the St. Louis-Boston Series of 1967.

The Dodgers pennant in 1959 brought about the first World Series games on the West Coast, but it wasn't until 1974 (Los Angeles vs. Oakland) that the entire Series was played in the Pacific Time Zone.

The first World Series game to be played on artificial turf was in 1970 at Cincinnati; the first all-artificial turf Series was last year's Kansas City-Philadelphia one.

The Royals-Phillies matchup also produced the first Series in which both managers were rookies and the first in modern times in which both teams were seeking a first World Championship.

The Royals were the first American League expansion team to make it to the World Series, but the New York Mets of the National League got there first—in 1969, and again in 1973, winning it all in '69 against Baltimore.

When Ken Brett pitched for Boston in the 1967 World Series, he became the first teenager to take the mound in the Fall Classic in history, being only nineteen at the time. The first teenager to appear at a position other than pitcher goes all the way back to Fred Lindstrom of the Giants, who hadn't yet reached his nineteenth birthday in 1924.

Did you know that it wasn't until 1947 that anyone hit a pinch-hit homer in a World Series game? It was the Yankees' Yogi Berra, hitting for Sherm Lollar who accomplished it. And a year later, 1948, marked the last appearance to date of a playing manager in a World Series, when Lou Boudreau led the Cleveland Indians against the Braves.

The first World Series in which six umpires were used came in 1947 and gave the National League's George Magerkurth and the American League's Jim Boyer the distinction of being the first "foul-line" umpires in history.

Eddie Mathews, with the 1968 Tigers, was the last Boston Brave, while Phil Niekro, still active with Atlanta, is the last remaining Milwaukee Brave. Boston moved to Milwaukee in 1953, and Milwaukee moved to Atlanta in 1966.

The last St. Louis Brown was pitcher Don Larsen, whose major league career ended in 1967, fourteen years after the Browns moved to Baltimore to become the Orioles. The last Philadelphia Athletic was fancy-fielding Vic Power, who retired following the 1965 season, eleven years after Philadelphia moved to Kansas City. There is one remaining Kansas City Athletic in the majors—Reggie Jackson.

The "old" Washington Senators moved to Minnesota in 1961, and Jim Kaat, still pitching in 1981, was with them. The "new Senators," who existed from 1961 to 1971, had five still-active major leaguers in 1981—Toby Harrah, Del Unser, Len Randle, Jeff Burroughs, Larry Bittner, and Bill Fahey. (All are gone.)

The Seattle Pilots played for only one season—1969—before moving to Milwaukee. The last Seattle Pilot still playing in 1981 was Oakland infielder Fred Stanley, although Lou Piniella of the Yankees spent spring training of 1969 with the Pilots.

Two modern clubs underwent name changes in the 1960s. The Los Angeles Angels adopted California, and the last of the L.A. Angels was Jim Fregosi, who retired in 1978 to manage his old club. And who will be the last man to have worn the uniform of the Houston Colt .45s, prior to their becoming the Astros? Will it be Rusty Staub, Joe Morgan, or Jerry Grote, all active in 1981?

Ballparks have certainly undergone changes over the years, most dramatically with the introduction of indoor baseball through the construction of the Astrodome in Houston, which opened in 1965. That brought about the need for the first artificial turf, and a year later it was installed in the Astrodome following lengthy tests. Chem Strand, a division of Monsanto, designed the product, and it lasted twelve seasons before a new carpet was necessary.

It was Riverfront Stadium in Cincinnati that introduced cutout sliding areas around the bases on June 30, 1970, rather than a full dirt infield.

Dodger Stadium, opened in 1962, was the first to have different-colored seats in each section and the first to have an organist excite the crowd with a call of "CHARGE!" Dodger fans also brought a relaxed, casual style of dress to the ballpark, following an era when suit, tie, and hat were the norm for male fans.

Shea Stadium in New York was the first to do away with light towers in favor of rows of lights along the roof of the upper deck. The year was 1964.

The Giants, at Candlestick Park, were the first to have a so-called dugout at field level rather than dug out below the ground. It was Riverfront Stadium that first measured fence distances in meters and the Kingdome in Seattle that took it one better, measuring the distances in fathoms, in keeping with its nautical theme.

The first message board in a stadium was built by the Yankees in 1959 in the old Yankee Stadium, a simple board eight lines high, eight spaces wide. A year later, Bill Veeck introduced his exploding scoreboard in Comiskey Park, Chicago.

The Astrodome, in 1965, brought animation in lights to scoreboard art, opening the gates for complex message boards. The first instant-replay boards in baseball came along in 1976, in the new Yankee Stadium and in ol' Fenway Park.

The sight of banners parading through the stands were popularized by the "New Breed" of fans in New York's Polo Grounds, when the Mets played there in 1962–63.

Players used to leave their gloves on the field when they were at bat—even in fair territory—but that was outlawed in 1953. Many clubs used to have a dirt path between home plate and the pitcher's mound, but by the early 1950s, that had been eliminated for good, mostly for aesthetics.

The introduction of new teams in the 1960s and 1970s created the opportunity to recognize "firsts," such as the first player to belong to each team's major-league roster. The honorees, not necessarily products of the selection draft, were:

Los Angeles Angels—Eli Grba
Washington Senators—John Gabler
New York Mets—Hobie Landrith
Houston Colt 45s—Ed Bressoud
San Diego Padres—Ollie Brown
Seattle Pilots—Marv Staehle
Kansas City Royals—Roger Nelson
Montreal Expos—Manny Mota
Seattle Mariners—Dave Johnson
Toronto Blue Jays—Phil Roof

Charles O. Finley's Kansas City Athletics brought some changes to baseball style in the 1960s. First came the green-and-gold uniforms of 1963, ending the exclusivity of white at home, gray on the road. In 1965, the manager (Mel McGaha) and his coaches wore white caps to distinguish them from the players. In 1967 came white shoes for the entire team. And to proper color coordinate it all, of course, came green shin guards and chest protectors for the A's catchers.

Tight uniforms originated in 1960, when Willie Mays of the Giants had a tailor go to work on his. That started a trend still in use today, although, interestingly, the 1981 Texas Rangers loosened theirs up a bit to accommodate the high temperatures in Arlington.

The orlon-wool-blend uniforms, better known as "flannels," became history in 1973 when the Yankees and Giants, the last holdouts, moved to knit material. The first to don the new look was the Pittsburgh Pirates, on the day they moved into Three Rivers Stadium—July 16, 1970. And it was the Pirates—in 1976—who introduced and retained the old-fashioned square baseball caps.

Names on the uniform backs date back to 1960, when the White Sox introduced them, with the Z in Kluszewski backwards to guarantee photo coverage. Bill Veeck was running the White Sox.

Fans have always had a high interest in uniform numbers, so the wearing of 00 by Paul Dade of Cleveland in 1977 should get a place in history, as well as the 0 by Al Oliver of Texas the following year. And while Carlton Fisk's 72 is one of the highest numbers worn in many years, it's not a record. Bill Voiselle wore 96 during his National League pitching career of 1942–50.

And how about the last pitcher to wear a single-digit number? It was Dooley Womack of the Oakland A's in 1970, who wore number 3.

Even umpires have looked different with the passage of time. American League umpires went to gray pants in 1967 and two years later were permitted to work without ties and jackets on unusually hot days. In 1971, they received red blazers, but by 1980 the leagues standardized, and once again the "men in blue" were truly in blue.

Soon we will witness the last umpire to wear an outside chest protector, and it will be either Bill Haller, Marty Springstead, Russ Goetz, George Maloney, or Bill Kunkel, the last American League umpires employing them.*

Johnny Bench altered the catcher's chest protector by having one made that fastened at the neck and waist rather than forming a strap down the back. Steve Yaeger of Los Angeles introduced the flap on the mask to protect the neck after he'd been hit by a flying bat. The year of his gift to baseball equipment was 1977.

In 1958, Baltimore manager Paul Richards designed an oversize catcher's mitt for Gus Triandos to work with knuckleball pitcher Hoyt Wilhelm, a concept still used today. A six-fingered fielder's glove was used by third baseman Ken Boyer of St. Louis in 1962.

"Hawk" Harrelson brought a lot of cosmetic changes to baseball. He popularized the use of a batting glove in 1964 following a day of golf and resulting raw hands. (The glove was first introduced by golf pro Danny Lawler in 1949, when he gave one to Bobby Thomson, but it was in vogue only for batting practice and spring training before Harrelson.)

The Hawk also popularized wrist bands, lamp black under the eyes, and high

---

* It turned out to be Jerry Neudecker, in 1985.

stirrups, although San Francisco's Tito Fuentes was pulling the sock high around the same time.

Long hair seemed to become popular with Harrelson while other players were still in crew cuts. Reggie Jackson brought mustaches and beards into vogue with Oakland in 1972. After he grew his mustache, Charlie Finley offered any teammate who grew one a $300 bonus. By the '72 World Series—which the scruffy-looking A's won—nineteen of their twenty-five players had them.

Joe Pepitone used a hair dryer in 1968 amid much publicity, but eight years later, when the new Yankee Stadium opened, every locker had an electrical outlet to accommodate one.

Branch Rickey's own company, American Baseball Cap, brought helmets into use. Phil Rizzuto was the first player to wear one, dating back to 1951, but the following year, on September 15, the entire Pittsburgh Pirate team wore them both at bat and in the field.

The last player to wear only a hard liner in his regular cap was Boston's Bob Montgomery, who retired in 1979. Now every player wears the helmet, most of them with earflaps.

It was Brooks Robinson who first wore the earflap for added protection, and Brooks also had half the bill of his helmet removed for greater visibility.

Even bats have changed in appearance. In 1969, Frank Torre of Adirondack suggested that a 1-inch stripe be painted around the center of the bat so that his company's product might be better identified. In 1975, Hillerich and Bradsby, makers of Louisville Sluggers, turned out a black bat for Pat Kelly of the White Sox, duplicating a style used by Rogers Hornsby and others in the 1920s and 1930s. In 1981, Pete Rose used a rose-colored bat made by Mizuno, and Dave Winfield used a blue bat made by Adirondack, but both limited use to batting practice.

The cup-ended or hollowed-out bats were first introduced in Japan and admired there by Lou Brock. Jose Cardenal of the 1976 Cubs was the first American player to have his Louisville Sluggers so designed, feeling that it put more weight into the "meat" of the bat.

The "tape-measure home run" was born on April 17, 1953, when Mickey Mantle powered one 565 feet in Washington and Yankee public relations director Red Patterson actually borrowed a tape measure to count it off.

The baseballs themselves were made of horsehide until 1974, when Spalding switched to the more available cowhide, and in 1976, the Rawlings name first appeared on major-league baseballs.

Bat Day, the most popular of baseball's gift days, was originated by Rudie Schaffer, Bill Veeck's deputy in Chicago.

Old-Timers' Days were made annual events in 1947 by the New York Yankees' Larry McPhail.

The weighted "doughnut" used by hitters in the on-deck circle was invented in 1968 by Elston Howard, then with the Red Sox.

The last playing manager was Don Kessinger of the White Sox in 1979.

The first night All-Star Game was played in July 11, 1967 in Anaheim. The first Championship Series was played in 1969 after four divisions were created for baseball.

Instant Replay, now so commonly accepted, was first used at a local level, when WPIX-TV in New York replayed the ruin of a no-hitter on July 17, 1959, with announcer Mel Allen asking director Jack Murphy to run the tape right there rather than wait for the postgame show. It showed Ralph Terry's no-hitter go down the drain as a base hit by Chicago's Jim McAhany fell in front of Norm Siebern in the ninth inning.

The first color telecast was on August 11, 1951, with Brooklyn hosting Boston for a doubleheader in Ebbets Field, carried by NBC.

The first woman baseball announcer on a regular basis was Mary Shane with the 1977 White Sox.

The first black player was, of course, Hall of Famer Jackie Robinson, who broke in with Brooklyn in 1947.* There are other firsts worth noting along the way, as well—the first black coach, Jim Gilliam of Los Angeles in 1965, for example. The first black umpire was the American League's Emmett Ashford in 1966. The first black manager was Cleveland's Frank Robinson in 1975. The first black general manager was Atlanta's Bill Lucas in 1977.

An all-black lineup appeared for the Pittsburgh Pirates on September 1, 1971, with Al Oliver at first, Rennie Stennett at second, Jackie Hernandez at short, Dave Cash at third, an outfield of Willie Stargell, Gene Clines, and Roberto Clemente, Manny Sanguillen catching, and Dock Ellis pitching.

The Baltimore Orioles introduced a base sweeper named Linda Warehime in 1969, and Oakland introduced ball girls down the foul lines in 1971.

Players like to make "curtain calls" after dramatic home runs these days, but that all started in 1961 after two of the most dramatic home runs in baseball history—Roger Maris's sixtieth and sixty-first, both at Yankee Stadium. On both occasions, teammates forced the shy Maris to step out of the dugout to acknowledge the fans' cheers.

The first $100,000 "bonus baby" was pitcher Paul Pettit, who signed with the Pirates in 1950 and who wound up with one major-league victory.

The first free-agent draft was conducted in June 1965, and Rick Monday, taken by the Kansas City Athletics, was the first player selected. The first player selected in the first reentry draft (1976) was Reggie Jackson (by Montreal), but the first to sign out of that draft was Bill Campbell with Boston.

The first player to exercise the "10 and 5 Rule," stopping his own trade thanks to length of service with one club, was Ron Santo of the Cubs.

We'll probably see the first computer in a dugout before long or the first team to play in T-shirts and no caps or the first stadium to bring relief pitchers in by helicopter, as we head for the twenty-first century. But let's all vow to pay just a bit more attention to the "historic happenings," as they occur, lest they get lost in the dust of the ever-changing scene of baseball's history.

---

* In this century, that is. See the essay "Out at Home," below, by Jerry Malloy.

Joe DiMaggio as Ponce DeLeon? With a Mister Coffee as the Fountain of Youth? Why not—baseball makes the old young with its magical mix of echo and revelation. The cryogenic power of nostalgia freeze-dries both idyll and idol, perhaps unfairly: maybe DiMaggio doesn't like being trapped in Baker's 1936, or his own. This charming piece ran in the New York *Times* on December 1, 1984.

RUSSELL BAKER

Idylls of the Kid

Joe DiMaggio is seventy. His birthday was last Sunday. The papers made nothing of it and I would not have been aware of it if we hadn't seen him Tuesday night doing his Mister Coffee commercial on television. "Joe DiMaggio is old," Harry said.

"Joe DiMaggio can never be old," I said. This is true in a very important unfactual sense. Joe DiMaggio inhabits a world in which I am always eleven years old. In it I always wear corduroy knickers and brown knee-length stockings held up by rubber bands and move around on roller skates. There is a Philco radio in the parlor. Inside is the voice of Franklin D. Roosevelt.

"That hair is gray," Harry said.

"Joe looks terrific, Harry."

He did, too. The commercial he was doing, of course, was in color. That was all wrong. Joe DiMaggio looks truly natural only in black and white. This is because when I see him he is always nineteen or twenty or some age like that, much older than I on my roller skates but not really old as Carl Hubbell, say, is old.

Hubbell pitches for the New York Giants. So we are talking, obviously, about the age of black and white, and neither Hubbell, who seems old but oh so magically unbeatable with his fabulous screwball, nor DiMaggio, who seems young and gawky, can exist in the age of color.

I see them always where they belong, motionless yet mysteriously and beautifully fluid in grainy black-and-white newspaper pictures on the sports pages of the *Journal American* and the *Daily Mirror*, the papers built for kids, with plenty of comics, full coverage of the electrocutions at Sing Sing, and great action still photos of great achievers, the old great Hubbell, the young great DiMaggio.

"Harry," I said, "Joe DiMaggio cannot be seen authentically on color television. Or on television at all, for that matter. No wonder you think he's old. Did you ever see DiMaggio play on television?"

I certainly never did. A few times I may have seen him swing the bat in one of the grainy black-and-white newsreels accompanying the double-feature bill at the Capitol or Horn movie theaters. This is probably why I often associate Joe DiMaggio with skating up to the Horn to see a Charlie Chan and a Laurel and Hardy.

"Snap out of it," Harry said. "Nobody has seen a Charlie Chan and a Laurel and Hardy on a double bill since Mussolini was in his prime."

"And those were the real Charlie Chans starring Warner Oland," I said, "not the decadent later Charlie Chans with Sidney Toler."

"The truth is," said Harry, "that you, just like me, never saw DiMaggio play anywhere except in a newsreel, so don't give me that malarkey about Joe's gracefulness being too pure to be appreciated by today's ignorant TV audiences."

Harry is a good man, but there is no poetry in him. He is a believer in facts. It has never occurred to him that there might be a wide chasm between fact and truth. The truth of this particular matter is that I can see DiMaggio play whenever the mood is on me.

This is something I owe to radio. By turning on the Philco, besides getting the voice of Franklin D. Roosevelt, I can often get sounds from the Yankee Stadium, sounds with power to create pictures inside my head more spectacular than television can possibly convey.

When I am eleven years old, in corduroy knickers, skimming down Washington Avenue on roller skates, these radio sounds show me Joe DiMaggio loping across a beautiful field of grass in the faraway, exotic Bronx, to haul in the white ball whirling out of the sky. Then I can see Joe stepping into the batter's box, wearing those loose billowing knickers real ballplayers all wore until television spurred them to vanity and vanity drove them to skin-tight double knits, like so many cruising sex objects.

"Harry," I said, "I hope Joe retires before television corrupts the baseball uniform. I'd hate to see him prancing around the diamond like some common, run-of-the-mill uniformed sex object."

The conversation had become pointless, since Harry had gone home in some disgust, leaving me, as he had said at the door, free to "skate up to the Horn and catch the new Mister Moto movie starring Peter Lorre on a double bill with Randolph Scott driving the cattle to Abilene."

Aside from having no poetry in him, Harry also has a weakness for ham-handed sarcasm, but I let it pass and, since my lumbago had me almost prostrate, went early to bed. Next morning Harry, the eternal fact man, phoned early.

"I looked it up. DiMaggio turned seventy on November 25," he said. In corduroy knickers, on roller skates, I said, "Harry, do you think we'll ever make enough money to go to Yankee Stadium sometime and see a game?"

If a tree falls in a forest where there is no one to hear it, does it make a noise? This hoary philosophical gambit is recalled by the analysis of baseball through new statistics, or sabermetrics (Bill James's term in recognition of the Society for American Baseball Research, or SABR). Reliever Firpo Marberry didn't know he set a record with his fifteen saves in 1924, because saves weren't invented until 1960—but he saved those games all the same. This article from SABR's *The National Pastime* measures the production of clutch batters on weak-hitting teams. (You can't drive in base runners who aren't on base.) The results are surprising, especially to Mr. Colbert.

BOB CARROLL

Nate Colbert's Unknown RBI Record

Nate Colbert set a single-season RBI record in 1972; hardly anyone noticed. Even today—ten years after the fact—few fans and fewer record books are aware of the big right-handed slugger's accomplishment. In fact, if it hadn't been for his performance on August 1 of that year—the best single day ever enjoyed by a major-league hitter—he might not be remembered at all.

Some of Colbert's obscurity may be blamed on the season. Nineteen seventy-two was not the happiest of baseball years. It began with Gil Hodges's fatal heart attack at spring training and ended with Roberto Clemente's tragic death in an airplane crash. In between, a player walkout shortened the season by thirteen days.

Another strike against Colbert was his team. The '72 San Diego Padres weren't quite the worst club in the National League—the Phillies were .001 lower—but it was hard to get excited about anything that happened on a 58–95 team sporting a .227 team batting average. Unless you had a cousin on the roster, you probably wouldn't even read the Padres' box scores.

A third strike on Colbert was his habit of missing third strikes. He could hit home runs and keep his batting average higher than his weight, but he also fanned more often than Scarlett O'Hara during a Georgia July. On average, he struck out every fourth time he went to bat. Among ten-year men, only Dave Kingman has been easier prey.

All in all, Nate was the wrong player on the wrong team in the wrong year to be making his mark on history.

His record doesn't reveal itself by a cursory glance at his batting stats for 1972: a .250 average, with 38 home runs and 111 RBIs. Forget the 127 strikeouts and it's a good year. But great? Record setting?

Take a look at San Diego's team batting. During the whole season, the Padres managed a mere 488 runs. Why, it seemed like the 1927 Yankees had that many by Memorial Day!

Now put the figures together. Colbert batted in 22.75 percent of his team's runs! Think of it this way: each batter makes up 11.1 percent of his team's lineup; Colbert did the work of two and then some. No major-league batter has ever done more for his team.

"How Nate ever knocked in 111 runs that otherwise dismal season has puzzled the experts ever since," says Padre statistician Mil Chipp. "He usually batted behind Derrel Thomas, Dave Roberts, and Jerry Morales. And none of them were that adept at getting on base. Thomas's on-base percentage (OBP) in 1972 was 29 percent, Roberts's was 28 percent and Morales's 31 percent." Colbert himself led the team with his modest 34 percent OBP.

It was no contest in RBIs. Chipp points out: "The only Padre players 'close' to Nate . . . were Leron Lee (47) and Clarence Gaston (44). They were light-years away."

There is a certain element of controversy involved in any RBI record: is it the man or the opportunity? Ever since the ribbie was dreamed up, some fans have opposed it as a measure of individual achievement. At the end of the 1880 National League season, according to Preston D. Orem's *Baseball (1845–1881) from the Newspaper Accounts*:

> The Chicago *Tribune* proudly presented the "Runs Batted In" record of the Chicago players for the season, showing Anson and Kelly in the lead. Readers were unimpressed. Objections were that the men who led off, Dalrymple and Gore, did not have the same opportunities to knock in runs. The paper actually wound up almost apologizing for the computation.

Ernie Lanigan, patron saint of ribbies, in his 1922 *Baseball Cyclopedia*, observed:

> As far back as 1879 a Buffalo paper used to include the runs batted in in the summary of the box score of the home game. Henry Chadwick urged the adoption of this feature in the middle '80s and by 1891 carried his point so that the National League scorers were instructed to report this data. They reported it grudgingly and finally were told they wouldn't have to report it.

Lanigan took up the ribbie torch in 1907 for the New York *Press*, working up the figures annually. At last, on the request of the Baseball Writers' Association of America (BBWAA), the major leagues added RBIs to their 1920 averages.

Yet, even more than a hundred years after RBIs were introduced, many fans view the stat skeptically. If a man singles, goes the argument, he has performed an individual act. But, to get a ribbie on that same single, he must have a teammate in scoring position. Colbert's 111 is an excellent total, but how many more might he have driven home in 1972 had he played for heavy-hitting Pittsburgh? For the record, Pirate first baseman Willie Stargell drove in 112.

Looking at the *percentage* of a team's runs driven in somewhat circumvents the anti-RBI argument. In theory, at least, a player on a light-hitting team with fewer opportunities to drive in runs can show his mettle by knocking in a high percentage. Conversely, a player with a group of bombers clustered around him in the batting order must drive in a much higher number to achieve the same percentage.

When Hack Wilson set the major-league record with 190 ribbies in 1930 (soon to be revised upward, to 191 or 192), his team scored another 803. His percentage was 19.04. Lou Gehrig's American League mark of 184 accounted for "only" 17.24 percent of the '31 Yankees' 1,067 runs. The accompanying chart shows all those players since 1900 who have knocked in 150 or more runs in a season, along with their teams' runs and their percentages. It comes as no surprise that all the 150-plus boys played on teams that scored a ton. Colbert's Padres scored an ounce, but his percentage was three points better than the highest of the big RBI guys.

As a matter of fact, only eight men in major-league history—from 1876 on—have topped the 20 percent mark. More men have hit .400.

The first hitter to achieve the improbable 20 was, not surprisingly, Babe Ruth. What is indeed surprising is that the Babe did it before he became a Yankee. In 1919, his last season in Boston, he drove in 114 runs—a 20.13 clip—for the fifth-place Red Sox. Although he topped that RBI *total* eleven times in a Yankee uniform, he never again drove in so high a proportion. (Note: some sources credit Ruth with only 112 RBIs in 1919, a 19.8 percent.)

It took sixteen years before another player reached 20 percent. Then the Braves' Wally Berger chased home teammates at 22.61 (130 out of 575). Despite Berger's efforts, the Braves won only thirty-eight games and came in dead last on a stretcher. But Wally's mark stood as the record until Colbert's big year.

Swish Nicholson drove the Cubs up to fifth place in 1943 with his 20.25 percent (128 out of 632). The Cubbies were back in fifth place in 1959 when Hall of Famer Ernie Banks made the "20 Club" with 21.25 (143 out of 673). That performance earned Banks his second consecutive MVP Award. Interestingly, he's the only 20-percenter to be so honored by the BBWAA.

Jim Gentile became the fifth member of the society in 1961. His 20.41 percent (141 out of 691) was a big factor in lifting the Orioles into third place, but it went virtually unnoticed in the excitement over Roger Maris's asterisk pursuit. Maris was also crowned the RBI "leader" on the basis of one more ribbie than Gentile, but his percentage was only 17.17 (142 out of 827).

Big Frank Howard belongs in the 20-percenter Hall of Fame—he topped the magic mark *twice*. In 1968 with Washington, he knocked in 106 runs (out of

Players	Team-Lg-Year			RBIs*	Team Runs*	Pct. of Team Runs
Top Single-Season Run Producers						
Hack Wilson	Chi	N	1930	190	998	19.04
Lou Gehrig	NY	A	1931	184	1067	17.24
Hank Greenberg	Det	A	1937	183	935	19.57
Lou Gehrig	NY	A	1937	175	975	17.95
Jimmie Foxx	Bos	A	1938	175	902	19.40
Lou Gehrig	NY	A	1930	174	1062	16.38
Babe Ruth	NY	A	1921	171	948	18.04
Chuck Klein	Phi	N	1930	170	944	18.01
Hank Greenberg	Det	A	1935	170	919	18.50
Jimmie Foxx	Phi	A	1932	169	981	17.23
Joe DiMaggio	NY	A	1937	167	979	17.06
Sam Thompson	Det	N	1887	166	969	17.13
Sam Thompson	Phi	N	1895	165	1068	15.45
Al Simmons	Phi	A	1930	165	951	17.35
Lou Gehrig	NY	A	1934	165	842	19.60
Babe Ruth	NY	A	1927	164	975	16.82
Babe Ruth	NY	A	1931	163	1067	15.28
Jimmie Foxx	Phi	A	1933	163	875	18.63
Hal Trosky	Cle	A	1936	162	921	17.59
Hack Wilson	Chi	N	1929	159	982	16.19
Lou Gehrig	NY	A	1937	159	979	16.24
Vern Stephens	Bos	A	1949	159	896	17.75
Ted Williams	Bos	A	1949	159	896	17.75
Al Simmons	Phi	A	1929	157	901	17.43
Jimmie Foxx	Phi	A	1930	156	951	16.40
Ken Williams	StL	A	1922	155	867	17.88
Joe DiMaggio	NY	A	1948	155	857	18.09
Babe Ruth	NY	A	1929	154	899	17.13
Joe Medwick	StL	N	1937	154	789	19.52
Babe Ruth	NY	A	1930	153	1062	14.41
Tommy Davis	LA	N	1962	153	842	18.17
Rogers Hornsby	StL	N	1922	152	863	17.61
Lou Gehrig	NY	A	1936	152	1065	14.27
Mel Ott	NY	N	1929	151	897	16.83
Lou Gehrig	NY	A	1932	151	1002	15.07
Al Simmons	Phi	A	1932	151	981	15.39
Hank Greenberg	Det	A	1940	150	888	16.89

* RBI and Team Runs figures courtesy of David Neft.

	The "20-Percent Club"						Pct. of
Players	Team-Lg-Year			RBIs*	Team Runs*	Team Runs	
Nate Colbert	SD	N	1972	111	488	22.75	
Wally Berger	Bos	N	1935	130	575	22.61	
Ernie Banks	Chi	N	1959	143	673	21.25	
Jim Gentile	Bal	A	1961	141	691	20.41	
Bill Buckner	Chi	N	1981	75	370	20.27	
Bill Nicholson	Chi	N	1943	128	632	20.25	
Frank Howard	Was	A	1968	106	524	20.23	
Babe Ruth	Bos	A	1919	114	565	20.18	
Frank Howard	Was	A	1970	126	626	20.13	

* RBI and Team Runs figures courtesy of David Neft.

524) for a 20.23 percent. Two years later, he reached 20.13 (on 126 out of 626). Unfortunately, Washington finished last both years, but without Frank's bat they would have finished in Guam.

Another two years went by before Colbert set the record. Since then only one player has been able to break the 20 barrier, Bill Buckner with 20.27 percent for the Cubs in last year's [1981] strike-shortened season. Buckner's accomplishment is interesting in that it came on only seventy-five RBIs.

Most of the 20 percenters played on second-division teams not only in their big years but for the majority of their careers; most of them might also be characterized as underrated. The relationship is not coincidental.

The key to Nate Colbert's record occurred on August 1, 1972 in Atlanta, where the Padres met the Braves in a twilight doubleheader. Colbert was among the league leaders in home runs and RBIs, but a slump had plunged his batting average toward .200. He'd also been forced to miss a couple of games the previous week when he'd injured a knee in a collision at home plate.

On the plane from Houston, Padre manager Don Zimmer asked Nate if he'd prefer to sit out another day or two. The big slugger insisted it didn't matter how he felt. He wanted to play in the Braves' cozy park, and he was determined "someone was going to pay" for his recent slump.

Before all the Atlanta fans had even found their seats for the opener, Nate put San Diego in front in the first inning with a three-run homer off Ron Schueler. In the third frame he contributed to a four-run Padre outburst by singling home a teammate. Another single and a bases-empty homer off Mike McQueen in the seventh gave him four-for-five and five ribbies in the 9–0 Padre win.

The second game was even better. Tom Kelley opened for the Braves, and he was as wild as a *Penthouse* party. He walked Colbert in the first inning, and Nate came around to score. Pat Jarvis replaced Kelley in the second inning just in time to face Colbert with the bases loaded. Nate promptly cleared them with his third homer of the evening.

A two-run blast off Jim Hardin in the seventh made the score 9–1. But the shell-shocked Braves fought back to make it 9–7 going into the final inning. Colbert was due up fourth. Cecil Upshaw retired the first two Padres, but Larry Stahl got a ground single to right. And up came Colbert.

The sidearming Upshaw had always given him trouble, so Nate decided to just try to meet the ball for a hit. Upshaw threw a high fastball for the first pitch. Colbert met it. Home run.

"I was shocked when I hit it," Colbert recalled. "I couldn't believe it when I saw it go over the fence. It was unreal! When I rounded second base, Umpire Bruce Froemming said to me: 'I don't believe this.' I told him: 'I don't, either.' "

The next day, it took the New York *Times* three paragraphs just to explain the records Colbert had broken or tied:

> The 13 runs batted in erased the major league record of 11 for a double-header, which had been shared by three American League batters, Earl Averill of the Cleveland Indians (1930), Jim Tabor of the Boston Red Sox (1939) and Boog Powell of the Baltimore Orioles (1966). The National League record of 10 was established in 1947 by Enos Slaughter of the St. Louis Cardinals.
>
> The 6-foot-1½-inch 200-pound Colbert also broke the National League record of 12 runs batted in in two consecutive games by Jim Bottomley of St. Louis in 1924. The major league mark is 15, established in 1925 by Tony Lazerri of the New York Yankees.
>
> The five home runs in a double-header by Colbert equaled the major league mark set by Stan Musial of the Cardinals in 1954 and also broke Musial's record of 22 total bases in a twin bill.

Yet when 1972 ended and Colbert had racked up a record even more impressive than any of these, not a newspaper in the land gave it so much as an agate line.

Call it Catch-22.75.

The short, happy life of the Inter-American League (IAL): two and a half months in 1979, with far-flung franchises from Miami to Maracaibo and more former big leaguers than you could shake a maraca at; the league's official song could have been "Yes, We Have No Mañanas." Although nearly forgotten, the IAL should be remembered as a forerunner of the intercontinental baseball that is surely to come and for its champion, the Miami Amigos, which supplied the Mets' Davey Johnson with his managerial baptism.

BILL COLSON

The Over-the-Hill League

With their tongues planted firmly in their cheeks, the players were touting the game as the Cuban Death Match. Facing each other were forty-two-year-old Mike Cuellar and thirty-four-year-old Oscar Zamora. Cuellar, the masterful screwballer, was a three-time twenty-game winner for the Orioles a while back and in 1969 shared the American League Cy Young Award. The less renowned Zamora played for the Astros as recently as last season. He now has a thriving shoe business in Miami and finds time to pitch only every eighth day or so.

This Latin showdown didn't occur in an Old-Timers' Game in Baltimore or on a dusty diamond in San Juan but in Miami, where the Amigos were opening their second home stand of the year against the San Juan Boricuas. And who in the world are the Amigos and the Boricuas? Well, they are none other than the first- and fourth-place teams, respectively, in the fledgling Inter-American League. The Inter-American is different from other minor leagues not only because it is peopled largely by players with familiar and semifamiliar names but also because it has clubs in Panama City, Panama; Santo Domingo, Dominican Republic; and Caracas and Maracaibo, Venezuela, as well as in Miami and San Juan.

On this night a predominantly Latin crowd of 3,152—the Amigos' largest turnout of the season—came to see the new show in town, and they weren't disappointed. After giving up two runs in the first inning, Zamora settled down and beat San Juan on six hits, two of them by Bobby Tolan, late of the Cards, Reds, Padres, Phils, Pirates, and Nankai Hawks. Inspired by their cheerleaders, the Hot and Juicy Wendy's Girls, the Amigos shelled Cuellar in the fifth when first baseman Brock Pemberton, who played for the Mets in '75, hit a grand-slam home run. The loss was the first in five decisions for Cuellar, who has been pitching with a pulled hamstring since his third start.

Many of the Cuban expatriates in the crowd had seen Cuellar pitch for the Havana Sugar Kings in 1957 and '58, and the game had the same festive atmosphere that characterizes games in Cuba. The spectators beat out Latin rhythms on conga drums and cowbells and reacted vociferously to events both on and off the field. When a shapely young woman in hot pants and halter top left her seat, she got a rousing round of applause. Her return was greeted by a standing ovation that stopped the game.

Unfortunately, customs and immigration officials aren't as thrilled by the goings-on in the Inter-American League. When the Boricuas left Caracas for Miami, the authorities kept Cuellar from boarding the team's flight, and he barely made it to the game on time. Nobody knows exactly what the holdup was except that it concerned visas, which are a persistent problem for the Cuban-born players in the league. Miami backup catcher Jorge Curbelo hasn't made it into Venezuela in two tries. In addition, a few members of the Santo Domingo Azucareros failed to show for a game in Puerto Rico, reportedly because of visa difficulties. Visas aren't the Azucareros' only problems; the club's discombobulated management didn't send box scores to the league until the season was six weeks old.

Immigration and front-office foul-ups are just a few of the IAL's many growing pains. After only six weeks of the season, two owners, two general managers, and one manager have been replaced, and the Boricuas have moved some of their games from San Juan to various sites in the interior of the Commonwealth because they were drawing only about 200 fans a game. In fact, attendance has been poor everywhere except Caracas, where the Metropolitanos are attracting nearly 7,400 a game, 2,400 more than any other Triple A team and 3,500 more than the Oakland A's.

Traveling has also been rough, even by minor-league standards. In most places, the hotels and clubhouses have been decidedly second-rate, and the Amigos have yet to take a flight that wasn't at least an hour late. Because of the vagaries of Caribbean air travel, they have started one game at 10:00 P.M., had another suspended in the eighth inning, and had to fly to a third in two shifts, with the second group not arriving until minutes before game time.

Such troubles are not wholly unexpected considering that the infant IAL was hastily put together over the winter. It is the brainchild of Bobby Maduro, who owned the Sugar Kings in pre-Castro Cuba and from 1967 to '78 was Bowie Kuhn's assistant for inter-American baseball. To get the new league under way, Maduro had to overcome strong opposition from the Caribbean winter leagues, which view the Inter-American as a competitor for Latin players' services and Latin fans' affections, and from several major-league owners, who felt they had a corner on baseball talent in the Caribbean.

Unlike teams in Triple A leagues based solely in the United States and

Canada, those in the IAL are not affiliated with big-league organizations. As a result, Inter-American rosters are composed almost entirely of players who have been released or overlooked by major-league teams. And that's precisely what Maduro wanted.

"This league was desperately needed," he says, "and I wrote a letter to the commissioner ten years ago telling him so. When I started in baseball, there were fifty-six minor leagues. Now there are only eighteen. Today, if you're not good enough to make it to the majors in three years, you're eliminated from consideration."

Miami Manager—and sometime player—Dave Johnson, a three-time Gold Glove winner with Baltimore and a .262 lifetime hitter, sees a need for a league that welcomes older players.

"The system isn't conducive to breeding talent anymore," he says. "The real problem is that, as a rule, scouts and minor-league managers are incompetent judges of ability. Usually they were .220 hitters who couldn't get jobs outside of baseball.

"You can't imagine the number of talented players these guys have hurt or overlooked. The Yankees were using the best pitcher in baseball, Ron Guidry, as a reliever in the minors. Also, with expansion and the rush to get kids into the majors came the elimination from Triple A ball of the veteran player. Instead of being a tough educational step to the big leagues, Triple A has become nothing more than glorified Double A. Owners didn't really appreciate the value of having young prospects playing against veterans."

Veterans are one thing the IAL has plenty of. The league boasts such golden oldies as thirty-eight-year-old Cesar Tovar, thirty-five-year-old Dave May, thirty-five-year-old Clarence (Cito) Gaston, and thirty-six-year-old Adolfo Phillips. And most of them can still play. According to Santo Domingo manager Mike Kekich, who is best remembered for his spouse swap with Fritz Peterson when both pitched for the Yankees, "They're now reaching their outer limits"—that is, they are still good enough to be major leaguers but in another year or two will be over the hill.

The Amigos, whose average age is 27.5, have thirteen players with big-league experience, twice as many as any other club except Santo Domingo, which has eight. Among the better known are pitchers Bob Reynolds (Montreal, St. Louis, Milwaukee, Baltimore, Detroit, Cleveland), Mike Wallace (Phillies, Yankees, Cardinals, Rangers), and Hank Webb (Mets); designated hitter Hal Breeden (Cubs, Expos), who is in a slump—"I just went 0 for Puerto Rico"; and outfielder Danny (the Sundown Kid) Thomas, who won the Triple Crown in the Eastern League in 1976. He also hit .276 in thirty-two games that season for the Brewers but was released because, as a member of the World Wide Church of God, he was forbidden to play from sundown Friday until sundown Saturday.

Whether they have been up to the big leagues or only as far as Double A, all of these players know this is probably their final shot at getting another serious look by the majors.

"Baseball has said we're dead," says Wallace, who was 6–0 pitching out of the Yankee bull pen in 1974 and never had a losing record in four seasons in the majors. "We're all trying to prove them wrong. Ninety-five percent of us have eaten the pink slip. It's almost like a bond among us. Even the trainer has been released. My only hope was to come down here and win twenty, and even that may not be sufficent."

Wallace, now 6–1, may well get twenty wins the way the Amigos are playing. Because their front office got organized earlier than the other teams' and because Miami is the only IAL club based in the United States, the Amigos had an advantage when it came to signing players. Consequently, they have a 28–8 record and a 7½-game lead. When the players and managers are asked to assess the IAL, they invariably tell you that, on balance, the quality of the league's play is somewhere between Triple A and Double A but that the Amigos are in a class by themselves. "We are probably the best Triple A club in existence," says Johnson.

Miami has a team batting average of .296 and a team ERA of 2.45. The Amigos' best batters are outfielders Jim Tyrone (.357), who was hitting over .300 for Oakland in 1977 when Charlie Finley benched him, and Leon Brown (.346), who hit over .300 in three of his four years in Triple A and was with the Mets for most of the 1976 season. Miami also has a twenty-six-year-old reliever from Nicaragua named Porfirio Altamirano, who may throw as hard as anyone in the majors. This is his first year of pro ball, and he has a 0.91 ERA. Each of these players, says Johnson, could help a major-league club right now.

For the time being, they must be content with playing in what they have nicknamed the Mañana League. "Every time you need something in one of those countries, you always hear *mañana, mañana*," says Wallace, reviving a shopworn stereotype. Although the players don't like to admit it, it is they who make this the Mañana League, because without it, there would be no *mañana* for most of them.

By the time this model of a spot report appeared, the Philadelphia Phillies had rolled up a record of misery unmatched in the National League: since their inception in 1883, no world championships and only two pennants, plus a collapse of epic proportion in the closing weeks of 1964 as they lost ten games in a row and with them the flag. As recounted below, their collapse of October 7, 1977, was a comparative jewel of compactness, requiring only ten minutes. The phutile Phils were only one out away from taking a two-games-to-one lead in the League Championship Series, and then, with incredible swiftness, the Astroturf was swept out from under their feet.

BILL CONLIN

The Ten-Minute Collapse

Dusty Baker hit a tough chopper to third, and Mike Schmidt pounced on the wicked short hop like a jaguar running down a rabbit.

That was one out in the top of the ninth, seven straight ground balls thrown by Gene Garber. And 63,719 fans were on their feet, a shrieking chorus that all afternoon had roared with the blood lust of a Roman Coliseum mob rooting for the lion.

Rick Monday bounced out to Teddy Sizemore. The Vet throng was chanting "DEEEFENSE." Eight straight ground balls by Geno. Game three was history. One more out, Geno, baby, and this was a 5–3 Phillies' victory. The Dodgers had coughed up two eighth-inning runs to go with three the crowd and plate umpire Harry Wendelstedt had bled from starter Burt Hooton in the second.

The Dodgers were down to their suspect bench. Ancient Vic Davalillo hauled his well-traveled bones to the plate, more wrinkles on his leather face than there are base hits left in his bat.

On deck was Manny Mota, thirty-nine years old, one final straw for Tommy Lasorda to clutch at should Davalillo reach first base.

Thus began the shortest, most devastating nightmare in the history of a town steeped in an athletic tradition of flood, fire, and famine, a town where some seasons even down seemed like a long way up.

A funeral dirge would be appropriate at this point, Beethoven's *Eroica*, perhaps, or a few choruses from *Lohengrin*.

You thought the *Titanic* went down fast!

The 1964 Collapse took ten games. This one took ten minutes. It was like watching the shambles of 1964 compressed into an elapsed-time film sequence.

With two outs, the Phillies met the enemy, and it was them.

Davalillo legged out a superb bunt to Sizemore, as if that is the normal play for a thirty-nine-year-old man with just forty-eight at bats after the Dodgers picked him up for late-season insurance.

"If he had hollered, 'Hey, I'm gonna lay one down,' we still couldn't have stopped it," First Baseman Richie Hebner said after the incredible 6–5 loss. "It was just a perfect bunt, a great play on Vic's part."

Mota came up swinging for a home run. He hit one in the final regular-season game last Sunday, hadn't hit one before that since the 1972 season.

He fouled a pitch back, then fell behind 0 and 2 with a swing so lusty it almost dislodged his batting helmet.

"Two strikes I am trying to just protect the plate," Mota said over the joyous babble of the winner's clubhouse. "I'm not a power hitter; I try to hit line drives. He threw me an inside slider."

Mota jumped on the pitch like a Santo Domingo street urchin putting the touch on a well-heeled gringo tourist. "Thank you, *señor*, may God bless you for this gift."

The fly ball carried, driving Greg Luzinski back toward the bull-pen fence in left. There was enough controversy in this schizophrenic game to keep a Warren Commission busy for weeks, and this was one chapter.

Luzinksi leaped at the fence. The ball lodged briefly in the webbing of his glove, then jarred loose, hit the fence, and nestled back into Bull's grasp. Wouldn't it have been a much easier play for fleet-footed Jerry Martin, often Luzinski's defensive caddy?

"He was the third batter up in the ninth," Danny Ozark said, wearing the dazed look of a train-wreck survivor. "I wanted him in the lineup in case the game was tied."

Davalillo was being held at third when Luzinski threw to second. The ball skidded through Sizemore's legs. Davalillo scored, and Mota huffed to third on the second baseman's error.

The inning reached a ten on the Richter Scale of natural disasters when Davey Lopes roped a one-hop shot off the heel of Schmidt's glove, off his knee, deflecting to Larry Bowa at shortstop. Bowa made a brilliant pickup and gunned a strike to Hebner. First-base umpire Bruce Froemming double-clutched, then spread his hands palm down. Hebner shrieked and stamped. Ozark erupted from the dugout. The veins in Bowa's neck bulged like telephone cables.

"If he had called the play right, both me and Hebner would have been thrown out," Ozark seethed in his office after a calm performance in the mass interview room. "He didn't know what the bleep to call it, so he called it safe. He was stunned by Bowa's throw, as far as I'm concerned. He just anticipated Bowa couldn't make the throw. He's got his hands stuffed in his pockets half the bleeping time."

For the second time in the tense war, the unwavering eye of the TV replay cameras would show Lopes out by a narrow margin, just as they proved from two angles that Steve Garvey never touched the plate on Bob Boone's superb block in the second.

Garber unfurled a pickoff move that skidded past Hebner, and Lopes jetted to second. "It was a sinker that exploded," Hebner said. "I should have got more body in front of it."

The Phillies fiery Götterdämmerung was complete when Bill Russell bounced a single up the middle.

Mike Garman, sixth Los Angeles pitcher on an afternoon of baffling selection by Lasorda, retired Bowa and Schmidt, then drilled Luzinski with a high, tight fastball.

Hebner bounced Garman's first pitch to Steve Garvey, and the crowd stood in a collective silence reserved for the demise of a great matador in a jammed Plaza de Toros.

Death had come to the executioners. The Phillies had met the enemy, and it was them.

These profiles of Dickey Pearce and George Wright, the two great shortstops of baseball's Pleistocene era, were part of a fascinating series on "The Fifty Greatest Ball Players in History" that ran in the *New York Evening Journal* in 1911–12. What makes these profiles so interesting today is that the author, veteran sportswriter Sam Crane, was himself a major-league second baseman who formed a keystone tandem with Pearce back in 1877 and frequently opposed Wright. The latter was one of the first men installed in the Hall of Fame, while Pearce has an outstanding claim to induction, inasmuch as he was the first to play shortstop *as an infielder*—not restricting his scope to short fly balls and relaying throws from the outfield, as was the practice in the 1840s and early '50s.

SAM CRANE

The Men Who Invented Shortstop

In the days of the old games between the Mutuals of New York and the Atlantics of Brooklyn in the late sixties and early seventies, when the fans of those days were even more partisan than now when the Giants and Superbas cross bats, there was one player who was more feared by the New Yorkers than any other on the Atlantic team, and that was Dickey Pearce.

The little fellow was not bigger than a good-sized cruller, the only food product at the time that seemed to be available by fair means or foul in those days, but little, fat, pudgy Dickey Pearce was about the whole show in the Atlantic team and did more, possibly, in his own way to win games for the famous old Atlantic club than any other player on the old team.

At any rate, every lover of baseball in Brooklyn thought so at the time, and it is a matter of baseball history over in the neighborhood of the Union Grounds and Capitoline Grounds that Dickey Pearce's short, pudgy legs brought in more tallies for the Atlantics than all the slugging sprinters there were on the team.

And why? Simply because Dickey knew how to get on first base.

He was not a slugger like many of his fellow players, but he had so studied the science of batting as it was in vogue at the time that his "fair foul" hits often counted much more than the home-run wallop of his bigger and stronger teammates.

Dickey Pearce was the originator of the present bunt. And that was the hit that transformed batting in his day. It was not known as the bunt at that time, and Dickey himself had no idea that he was making baseball history. But he had the baseball instinct, and that was that a player had to get on first base before he became a factor in the run getting. He appreciated the fact that unless he could reach first there was no possibility of his spikes denting the plate.

When Dickey first began to play baseball, the score was kept by cutting notches on a pine stick and every notch meant a tally. A fence rail instead of a pine stick did just as well, and the fence rail in Dickey's day was the official press box. Anyhow, what those notches figured up meant the road to victory for his side, and no player was more frequent than little Dickey in crossing over the plate and shouting gleefully, "Tally Pearce one."

Dickey played on the many open lots around Brooklyn for many years before he got his first chance on a real team. He was considered too small.

But like all little men, Dickey was cocky. He saw the big fellows play, and as he peeked through the knotholes in the fences of the Union and Capitoline grounds for two innings and then "flashed" his ten pennies to get into the enclosure when the gates were opened to the kids after the second inning, as was the custom at the time, Dickey came to the conclusion that he could play as well as any of the stars. But how to "mingle" was the great question.

The first start he got was to carry water to the players, and when he got that job, he was the envy of all of his fellows.

Finally he was allowed to carry the bat of one of his idols, and from that advancement he was allowed to chase balls in the outfield while the "big fellows" were at practice. Then on one long-to-be-remembered day he was asked to bat against one of the pitchers, who was out alone for practice, and he made a base hit. The pitcher took notice of him and told his captain there was a promising youngster that would bear watching.

The regular nine was shy of one player one day in a "match," and Dickey was selected to take his place. The ambitious youngster was put in at right field, a position at the time that was considered only fit for the "scrubs." Any old player could play right field. But my bold Dickey was there with both feet—not in fielding, possibly, for nothing came his way—but at bat the youngster was in his element. He was a hard man to pitch to, as all midgets have been, since, from Davy Force to Billy Keeler, and Dickey showed up some of the regular members in getting to first and getting around the bases.

That accidental chance to play made Dickey Pearce. He was put on the regular team and placed at shortstop, for the reason that he was considered to be too short-legged to cover ground in the outfield. It was a fortunate selection, for Dickey took to shortstop like a duck to water, and in the first game he played in that position, he showed such ability that none of the old-timers on the team had a chance to beat him out of the job. And none did after that for years and years. Dickey Pearce's name at shortstop for the Atlantics was stereotyped, and the scorecards always had his name in that position as long as he played baseball with that club, and that was for many years.

In fact, Pearce was a close rival of the great and only George Wright for the supremacy in the position.

Against the Mutuals in the games the Atlantics played with their New York opponents, and when partisanship was at the highest pitch, Dickey Pearce was always a star. When he went to bat, it was more than two to one that the little bit of a "sawed-off" would get his first.

Dickey Pearce's first chance to shine as a star of national reputation was when he played with the Atlantics against the Red Stockings of Cincinnati when the latter famous team lost its first game after an uninterrupted string of victories for a season and a half. In that great and historical game, Pearce's work, both as shortstop and at the bat, was the feature of the victor's game.

In the eleventh inning it was Dickey Pearce who started the rally that enabled the Atlantics to win out 8–7.

Pearce was the first player to work the "fair foul," a ball that was hit by chopping down at the ball, making it hit on fair ground and then bounding off into foul ground. It is a hit that is foul now under the present rules, but in those days there was no rule that prevented it from being perfectly fair. I have seen both Dickey Pearce and Ross Barnes get three bases by working this foxy bit of batting.

I have heard of home runs being made on the same hit, but I never saw it done, and I doubt if Dickey ever did, simply because I do not imagine that his short legs could ever carry him the distance, but many is the game little Dickey sewed up by the shrewd stab.

There were lots of objections and protests made in those days on that hit, but no rules could be found to prevent it, and until the rules were altered, Dickey always was high up in the existing batting records.

Pearce, by reason of that "fair foul," has been credited with originating the now famous bunt, but as Dickey worked it the hit was never intended to be worked as we understand it now.

I am inclined to give John M. Ward the credit of discovering the bunt as now played. But that is a story for a future article.

Dickey Pearce made such a big reputation with the Atlantics that he was in demand by the best clubs in the country, and finally he cast his fortunes with the old Mutuals, of New York, his old rivals. Over in Brooklyn he was considered somewhat of a renegade at the time, but that was the dawn of professionalism that had been more or less under disguise at the time, but Dickey's fine work with the crack New York team enabled him to retain his reputation and popularity, and he was a star until he was obliged to quit on account of age bedimming his former grand abilities.

Dickey kept in touch with the game for a long time after he got out of active participation in it as a player. He still continued to retain his popularity with players young and old, by whom he was considered an oracle.

When the Players' League was formed, in 1890, Dickey was given the position of grounds keeper of the Brotherhood Grounds (the present Polo Grounds) and helped Buck Ewing to lay out the field. And as Dickey laid it out then, it stands today. Of course grounds keeper Murphy has made improvements since, with all the money that since has come into the local club's coffers, but still, Pearce has to be given the credit for putting the field in the condition that allowed of the present model field of the country.

Dickey did not die overburdened with wealth, but he was well cared for until he passed away, a little over a year ago. He had a daughter who became prominent on the stage, and she saw that he wanted for nothing in his declining years.

The last time I saw Dickey Pearce was at one of the "old-timers'" reunions at Paddock's Island in Boston Harbor, three years ago, and the veteran was there, the recipient of all the love and respect that was his due. It was veneration, because we all appreciated what he had done for baseball.

As honest as the day.

Baseball was bettered by Dickey Pearce's connection with it.

There have been many great shortstops, but for all-round ability there has been none who ever played the position who has been able to force George Wright from the top-notch rung of the ladder of fame.

The game has gone along for over forty years, too, since George first blossomed out as a star, and I have in mind when I give him this lofty record all of those grand players who have shone so brilliantly in the past and present.

There have been shortstops and shortstops. The Dickey Pearces, Davy Forces, Bob Fergusons, Jack Glasscocks, Ed Williamsons, Herman Longs, Jack Nelsons, Johnny Wards, and other old-time luminants, who have come and gone, leaving reputations and records a mile long.

The Tinkers, Doolans, Elberfelds, McBrides, Brashes, Bridwells, Barrys, and Turners of the present are also all in my mind, who are thought by the fans of today to be preeminent. I have known them all and have seen them all play, but to George Wright I give the credit of being the best ever.

It is difficult to make the admirers of the "speed boys" of today think that any of the old-time ball players could approach the players of the present for stops, ground covering, and throwing, but while I acknowledge that there are more fast players today, still there were individuals in the earlier days of the sport who excelled the best who are now exploiting the game.

The game is faster now and has progressed simply because there are more speedy players now than in the past.

George Wright is a brother of Harry Wright, that noble old veteran around whom my first article on famous ballplayers was written. The fame of the Wright brothers was countrywide forty years ago, and George was the real player of the two. George's reputation as the greatest player of his time has not been dimmed in the least.

He was born in upper New York City, Yorkville, in the fifties, and with his elder brother, Henry, naturally took to baseball after learning the rudiments of cricket, taught him by his father, Sam Wright, the old professional cricketer.

Baseball was born in George Wright. He was consequently a natural ballplayer. He first came into prominence in the national game with the Unions, of Morrisania, with which club he played shortstop, the position he always occupied afterward in his long and brilliant baseball career. I do not remember that he ever played any other position. It therefore became second nature to him, and the many, many plays he was called on to perform that brought victory after victory to his teams year after year at critical stages were from intuition, although at times they often took on the look of being uncanny.

George Wright was probably as quick thinking a player as ever wore a uniform. His wits were always about him. He was invariably upon his mental tiptoes, and whenever he would pull off one of those grand, unexpected plays that were so dazzlingly surprising as to dumfound his opponents, his prominent teeth would gleam and glisten in an array of white molars that would put our own Teddy Roosevelt and his famed dentistry establishment far in the shadow.

In a game between the Boston Red Stockings and Philadelphia Athletics in 1873, when the Quakers had three men on base and none out, George caught a fly ball in his cap, tossed the ball to the pitcher, thereby putting the ball in play again, according to the rules of that time, and a triple play resulted, but it was not allowed.

But it was in such critical times that George showed his great nerve and quick thinking abilities. He was always ready to grasp a point of play and never hesitated, no matter how many chances there were to take by missing the anticipated point.

From New York George went to Cincinnati in 1868 and joined the Cincinnati Red Stockings, of which his brother Harry was manager. George was the all-around star of that famous bunch of champions. He led the club in batting and run getting, and these departments of play at that time were of the most importance.

In the fifty-seven games the Red Stockings played George took part in fifty-two. He made 339 runs, 59 of which were homers. His batting average was .518, showing that he made a fraction over a base hit every two times he was at bat.

Wonder if Ty Cobb could have done any better with the underhand pitching in vogue in those days?

George went to Boston in 1871 with his brother, Harry, as manager, and in the Hub George more than lived up to the reputation he had made in Cincinnati. He was the star of the Boston Red Stockings until 1879, when he went to Providence to manage the Providence Grays, the team that won the championship that year, although by a very close call. That wound up his active career on the diamond.

In 1874 George was a member of the Boston club that accompanied the Athletics to England, and while the introduction of baseball to our English cousins was not a pronounced success, still the ballplayers taught the Britishers some few points about their own game—cricket. It was always eighteen ballplayers against eleven cricketers, but the Americans were never defeated at the English game, and George Wright was the crack batter of the American eighteen.

George was the first shortstop to play a deep field. He played forty years ago just as far back of the line as the players in the same position do today. It was George's strong throwing arm and deadly accuracy that allowed of his playing so deep, and he of course saw the advantage there was to be gained in covering ground by playing deep. He was the first to grasp that idea.

George Wright was about 5 feet 10 inches tall and weighed about 160 in his prime. I remember him; he had a thick crop of dark curly hair, a small mustache and a dab on either cheek for a bluff at "siders." He was slightly bowlegged, and I never knew a bowlegged ballplayer who was not a crackerjack—à la Hans Wagner.

George Wright is a millionaire, having gained wealth and prominence in the sporting-goods business in Boston. He started in a small way in 1872, the year after he went to Boston to play ball.

George is one of the Hub's most respected citizens and still keeps in touch with the national game that he has done so much to build up. He is the proud father of Beals Wright, the champion tennis player.

A new literary theory: it is sometimes noted that Casey Stengel's gift of gab was Joycean, but might not Joyce's stream-of-consciousness technique—the Molly Bloom soliloquy, for instance—have been inspired by the Ol' Perfesser? After all, both of these giants hit the big leagues at about the same time, found glory in the early 1920s, and were widely vilified and misunderstood in the following decade. Oh, well; never mind. Here, from Bob Creamer's splendid biography of "a man that's been up and down," in Stengel's marvelous phrase, is a portrait of the artist as an old man.

ROBERT W. CREAMER

Do Not Go Gentle: Talking, Talking, Talking

Stengel lived for ten years after his retirement from the Mets—ten years and a month, to be exact. He was out of baseball. The Mets made him a vice-president, gave him a nebulous assignment as overseer of scouting in California, invited him to spring training and to club affairs and continued to pay him, but after fifty-six years it was finally over. He was no longer a factor in the game.

He kept as close to it as he could. He went to the World Series in Los Angeles in 1965, barely two months after his operation, looking natty in a yellow shirt and a blue tie, "just in case they want me on television." He flew back to New York in midwinter for the baseball writers' dinner, and in the spring of 1966 he showed up with Edna at St. Petersburg to watch the Mets in training.

Dressed in a red-checked sport jacket and a red tie and swinging his crooked black cane, he talked in St. Petersburg about the Mets and many other things and joked about the cane. "I don't really need this," he said, "but I have to limp or I can't get into the Hall of Fame." There is a rule that says a man must be out of baseball for at least five years before he is eligible for election to the Hall of Fame. It's a foolish provision, put into effect because baseball is afraid of its own sentimentality; it worries that it might elect someone impulsively who really doesn't belong, disregarding the fact that there is a bull penful of men who were elected to Cooperstown *after* the waiting period who don't belong there, either. After his retirement from the Mets the seventy-five-year-old Stengel faced five years of waiting before he could even be considered for election. However, the Baseball Writers Association of America, which conducts the Hall of Fame elections, consulted feverishly but secretly and agreed to waive the rule in Stengel's case. An unpublicized ballot was taken, and Casey was voted in, not long before he reached St. Petersburg that spring, although he didn't know about it yet.

On March 8, a few days after he had arrived in Florida, the Mets asked Casey to come out to the spring-training field to take part in a ceremony. The sportswriters were giving a plaque to George Weiss, he was told, and they wanted Casey to make the presentation. They told him to bring Edna along, too. It was a coldish morning for Florida, with a little of what Jimmy Cannon called "New York" in the wind. Stengel, wielding his cane, limped onto the field and walked with surprising quickness toward the clubhouse. He had on street clothes but wore a Mets baseball cap. As he reached the clubhouse, he was surrounded by writers and photographers, and he saw TV cameras, and he began to suspect something. The commissioner of baseball, Gen. William Eckert, was on the field, and so was Ford Frick, Eckert's predecessor and a member of the Hall of Fame committee.

Casey looked around, wondering. Someone gave Edna a bouquet of flowers, and someone else guided Casey toward a microphone where Frick stood, waiting to speak. Casey leaned over to Edna and said, "I gotta find out what I'm doing here."

The Met players stopped practicing and gathered around. The small crowd of spectators who had come to watch practice crowded closer to the chainlink fence that kept them off the field. Frick began to speak. He explained the eligibility rule and the fact that it had been waived and said a special vote had been held and Stengel had been elected to Cooperstown.

Casey, holding his cap in his hand, bowed his head quickly, then waved his cap, and everyone applauded. Edna kissed him. Casey was grinning, his wrinkled face beaming, looking, as Cannon wrote, very young. He stepped to the microphone.

"Edna," he said, "I appreciate that kiss."

He spoke for a few minutes, saying, among other things, "It's a terrific thing to get in it while you're still alive." After the little ceremony ended, he went over to the fence beyond third base to talk to the spectators gathered there, most of them elderly.

"They just put me in the Hall of Fame," he said. He mentioned a formal breakfast he had been to that morning, saying, "I got one leg and a cane, and I thought they was giving me a doughnut at the breakfast, which is pretty good because they get fifteen, twenty cents for a doughnut now, but they give me the full course, very good. I walked over thirty feet without the cane on a carpet to make the speech at the breakfast. But a coach walks ninety feet and there ain't no carpet, so I can't be a coach." The crowd laughed and applauded, and Casey acknowledged the applause by bending over halfway to the ground in a long, low bow, sweeping his cap across the ground.

A Met official asked him if he could walk over and talk to the spectators in the little grandstand beyond home plate. "I can't make the same speech," he said, but he limped over and spoke for a while there and then sat down on the team bench, still holding his black cane. He said, "Being in the Hall of Fame is an amazing thing. I didn't expect it to be so quick." He paused, then said, "It's bigger than I thought it was. This Hall of Fame thing is bigger than anything I ever saw."

For the rest of his life, whenever Stengel signed an autograph, he'd add the Hall of Fame to his signature. Even his letters were signed that way. When Ira Berkow wrote Casey outlining a book they might do together, Casey replied: "Dear Ira: Your conversation's; and the fact you were the working writer were inthused with the Ideas was great but frankly do not care for the great amount of work for myself. Sorry but am not interested. Have to many proposition's otherwise for the coming season. Fact cannot disclose my Future affair's. Good luck. Casey Stengel, N.Y. Mets & Hall of Famer."

That summer he and Edna went to Cooperstown for his formal induction to the Hall of Fame. Ted Williams had been elected at the same time as Casey, and the two were honored together. Williams, often an arrogant and difficult man when he was playing, made one of the best speeches ever heard at Cooperstown, a sensitive, intelligent expression of what baseball meant to him, what it had done for him and what it could still do for others.

Stengel followed, and while for once in his life he was unable to top another speaker, he was fine, too. He said, "I want to thank everybody. I want to thank some of the owners who were amazing to me and those big presidents of the leagues who were so kind to me when I was obnoxious." He thanked his parents, and he thanked George Weiss, "who would find out whenever I was discharged and would reemploy me." Casting back over his half century in baseball, he encapsulated his career in one brief sentence: "I chased the balls that Babe Ruth hit."

Stengel returned to Cooperstown faithfully every year after that for the Hall of Fame ceremonies, a pilgrimage that took considerable effort for an old man: from Glendale through Los Angeles to the airport; a flight across the country to New York City; another flight on a smaller airline to an airport in central New York state; a forty-mile drive from the airport over country roads to the little village of Cooperstown. He'd almost always arrive a couple of days early so that he could move around town, visiting and talking with people, savoring the atmosphere of baseball, his hawklike walk and garrulous face, as Kevin Cunningham called it, recognized everywhere.

His energy and drive remained high, even into his eighties. He and Edna would fly East each spring to the Mets' training camp in Florida. He'd return to New York every summer for the Mets' Old-Timers' Day. He'd attend Dodger games in Chavez Ravine and Angel games in Anaheim. He dedicated a baseball field in Glendale that was named for him and said, "I feel greatly honored to have a ballpark named after me, especially since I've been thrown out of so many."

He'd go to the World Series. He'd fly to New York in January for the baseball writers' dinner there, and he'd go to other cities for dinners, luncheons, gatherings of almost any sort. He spoke at all of them. At them, before them, and after them. He never flagged. At one dinner, after talking glowingly about the Mets, he grabbed a broom that chanced to be near the speakers' table and marched off the dais chanting, "Metsies! Metsies! Metsies!" Asked not long before he died who was the best manager he ever saw, he said, "*I* was the best manager I ever saw, and I tell people that to shut 'em up and also because I believe it."

Early in 1973, a month or so after Roberto Clemente of the Pirates was killed in a plane crash off Puerto Rico, Stengel went all the way to Manchester, New Hampshire, for a sports dinner. He spoke at the dinner, as did Curt Gowdy, the broadcaster, who delivered an eloquent tribute to Clemente. After the dinner, broadcaster Ken Meyer of WBZ in Boston took Casey aside for a taped interview. It turned out to be a classic Stengel performance.

What follows is a nearly exact transcription of that half-hour interview, with bracketed annotations here and there that try to explain some of the things Stengel was talking about. He was eighty-two years old, he was 3,000 miles from home, he had attended several banquets and luncheons on his journey, and on this day he had been talking, almost without stopping, for hours. He talked over breakfast, talked through lunch, talked with small groups of friends and admirers over predinner drinks. During the banquet he talked with the people sitting on either side of him on the dais. He had made his customary rambling speech in his heavy, growling voice, seemingly without taking a

breath, charming and confusing his listeners, most of whom laughed automatically, not really knowing what they were laughing at.

Now, late at night, the banquet over, the long day done, he sits in a small
room and talks on. Rather, he flows on, a Mississippi of words, overwhelming,
unceasing. Meyer begins the interview by asking Stengel about Clemente and
about the 1960 World Series when Clemente and the Pirates defeated Stengel
and the Yankees.

"What," asks Meyer, "do you remember about that Series and Clemente?"

That's the petcock that opens the flows. Stengel starts talking, his voice
hurrying, one sentence running into the next without pause:

"Well, I tell ya, it's an amazing Series. I thought I was going to win the Series
easy when I went to Pittsburgh, and I was very, uh, uh—I blame myself on
the whole Series. I mean for the Yankees losing. Now here's the reason why
I make that statement was because I thought Ford was so good, and I thought
that my pitching staff was a little better than what they had in, uh, Pittsburgh,
and they had—the idea was I never pitch Ford in the first game in the World
Series, and that's why I'm blamin' myself in the Series in the long run. When
Ford did pitch the second game [*actually the third game*] he was never scored
on. He wasn't scored on in the second game he pitched, so the blunder I made
not stopping, *starting* him in the first game was because in the last of the
World Series I went to pitch Ford and Ford says, 'Why, I can't loosen up my
arm.' Now if I'da pitched him in the first game, he'da been in better shape to
go in the last game when I blow the Series. [*If Ford had started the first game,
he probably would have pitched the fifth game instead of the sixth, which
would have given him sufficient rest to come back as a relief pitcher in the
seventh game.*]

"Therefore was on carelessness, and as good as the club was [*Pittsburgh*], I
didn't think that they was gonna have much of a chance. But I found out the
longer I played in that Series, Clemente commenced being alive again. In other
words, I mean he was a right fielder and a right fielder—he's like Kaline. He
plays right field and a man that's a right fielder—uh, I was played many outfield
positions. [*This preoccupation with right field and right fielders is caused by
the slip Casey makes when he says Clemente "commenced being alive again."
He is talking about Clemente in the 1960 World Series, but the player's recent
death intrudes, and Casey is momentarily flustered. He gets back on the track
by taking a fix on right field: Clemente was a right fielder; so was Al Kaline;
so, too, was Stengel for part of his career.*] He has to throw to second base.
You run a ball out, and you run hard, and he's facin' throwin' to second, he's
facin' throwin' to first, and there, facin' there, but when you get to first base
and you go to third [*on a ball hit to right*] just thinkin' a man that hits the
ball down the right-field line the right fielder *has to turn around to throw to
third.* He's out of position, where a left-handed man on the foul line is *in*
position to throw to second, to throw to third on the hit-and-run plays from
first to third. [*A right-handed-throwing right fielder fielding a ball near the
foul line has to turn his body in order to throw to second or third base, whereas*

a left-hander does not.] And in his *hitting.* [*Stengel suddenly recalls Clemente's hitting, mentions it, and then drops it.*] In turning around, a left-handed man, you'd think he'd be better out in right field, but he [*Clemente*] displayed, he and Kaline, that it's an amazing thing how a right-handed thrower could be that great as they were in the outfield.

"So then—Clemente then got *better.* [*Better than what? It's not clear, but it's a compliment.*] Now when it comes to hitting, you'd—he's so *quick* with the *wrists* and, you know, with the bat. Every time we went to pitch different to him, we were supposed to throw at him, back of him, you know, or move him back from home plate, and then when we'd pitch the ball over the plate, why he could hit down on the ball, and he rubbed the balls out [*hyperbole: Clemente wore the imprint off the ball*], which they said the effort he put into his work is like Gowdy said [*at the banquet*]. The effort he puts into his work all through the Series showed up, and it showed up there that he beat out three of those balls on me in the infield and if he hadn't I woulda finally won the last Series. Except that I, uh, pitchin' Ford the second game insteada the first game I never got to pitch Ford in the third game [*a third time*] of the Series and he wasn't scored on in two games. Now he's an outstanding player [*Clemente again*]; he can do everything, and it's like Kaline did, and I studied outfielding so much I can't understand how a man where I can play the best or in center field why a man what's right-handed shouldn't be in left field because a left-handed man in left field and he's out of position so half the time himself, yessir?" [*Stengelese at its most indecipherable. I don't know what he means by "where I can play the best or in center field," although I suspect DiMaggio and Mantle are stirring in his subconscious. The inanity of the passage seems suddenly to weigh upon him, and he returns the lead to the interviewer with an abrupt "Yessir?"*]

Meyer says, "All right, you mentioned Ford, and it seems a logical question. Why did you choose to pitch Art Ditmar in the first game instead of Ford? What caused the change?"

"Well," Stengel says, "I told ya because they pitched their best pitcher. Who was their best pitcher? It's the man that lived out in Idaho, and he was, uh, was that, uh, wonderful pitcher. [*Vernon Law. Casey can't remember his name, but he remembers that Law was from Idaho.*] He pitched in the spots [*was used in the tough games*]. He's been a coach and so on and so forth. [*Law became a coach after his playing career ended.*] He was a terrific pitcher, and I figured why pitch Ford against him? I know Ford is good, and I thought I was gonna beat 'em the Series, anyway, and we did; we had fourteen to nothing and sixteen to two [*the Yankees won three games overwhelming, 12–0, 10–0, and 16–3; the Pirates won their four games by margins of one, one, two, and three runs*], but they commenced then. They had Virdon in center field, he commenced makin' good catches, and then I had Shantz that had a crippled arm and when the ball went through and hit Kubek in the jaw, see? [*Casey is talking now about the seventh game of the 1960 World Series, the loss of which still galls him more than ten years later.*] The main thing about that was there was just a double play, and my pitcher had to go out on the next thing, because we had a secret on the bench and he said, 'I am gonna pitch for ya but my arm is sore.' So every time he warmed up he'd give me a signal to go without changin'. I'd warm a man up every inning [*Ralph Terry said Casey had him warm up five times during that game*], but he pitched five innings until that play that happened to Kubek, in which he missed the ball on the double play. Then he told me, he says, 'I can't pitch anymore, my arm is sore.' I mean, he said it was hurting *more*. Each inning I made him go out and warm up. The pitcher. So he was—Shantz was all right while he was in there. [*Sore-armed Bobby Shantz pitched five innings of excellent relief in the seventh game of the 1960 Series until that potential double-play ball took a bad bounce and hit Tony Kubek in the throat, but each inning as he warmed up he'd glance at Casey on the bench and signal whether or not he could go on. Finally, after the abortive double play, Stengel took him out.*] Then I took him out, and there wasn't anybody that I picked was right. [*Jim Coates gave up a three-run home run, and Terry the game-winning homer.*] And then I asked Ford to go in, and Ford said, 'Well, I said I can't loosen up.' And that's true 'cause he pitched the day before, and I shoulda pitched him the first game and I'da had him to relieve in the last game."

Meyer abandons the question of why Stengel picked Ditmar to start and says, "Another guy that was paid tribute to and who was lost during 1972 was a guy you also played in World Series competition with five or six times: Jackie Robinson [*who had died a few months before, in October 1972*]. What reflections and memories do you have about a great athlete like this?"

"Well," says Stengel, "I think he was a great athlete. I think he was one of the best football men that ever played. So was other men out there, like Tipton [*Eric Tipton, a Duke University football star who was a major-league outfielder from 1939 to 1945*]. Both of them were amazing in the same things in the same league in the Pacific Coast. [*Tipton played against Southern California in the 1939 Rose Bowl, and Robinson was a halfback for UCLA at the same time, so Casey seems at least mildly justified in lumping them in the same league. On the other hand, he may also be thinking of Kenny Washington, a great black running back who played football with Robinson at UCLA.*] And Robi'son at first was great. But as I ask ya now, ya have Satchel Paige here [*Paige was another guest at the banquet*], and I think later he might say a few words for ya. Because I watched Satchel Paige play twelve years before Robi'son started. And when Robi'son played against us and when he hit the ball as he did to the infield, it was because no left-hander had ever completed a game in the Dodger stadium at Ebbets Field, and when I put in the relief pitcher that I put in, why, that's when they popped the ball up the— to the—catcher because a relief pitcher did not start a game he just relieved. Which the relief for me was left-handed as it made Robi'son pop the ball up like he did. [*The popup Robinson hit in the 1952 World Series off left-hander Bob Kuzava; Stengel starts to gloat a little but thinks better of it and switches to compliments.*] Robi'son was a very good base runner and stealer. He was sensational stealing. [*But he cannot go on praising this man he disliked so.*] And, aaah, he was not the greatest fielder in my position. [*He means "opinion" and he gets flustered again.*] I know four or five men and where everybody said he was, he was in for the Brooklyn club at that time, but when they played with the Monarchs in Kansas City—that was one of the many colored teams I ever saw—I thought that they had four or five men that were outstanding in their play." [*He gets off the subject by ending the last sentence with an abrupt downward intonation and waits for the next question.*]

Meyer says, "All right. After ten pennants in twelve seasons, et cetera, you came back [*to the majors*] with the Mets. What induced you to come back and start over with an expansion ball club?"

"Well," Stengel says, "I, uh, I was turned loose by the Boston club one year and I said, 'Why not lay out in the, uh, and see if you wanna go back into baseball?' [*Casey gets a little mixed up here between 1937, the year after he was fired by Brooklyn, and 1944, the year after he was fired by Boston.*] And at that time I was offered an opportunity to go to two clubs [*that was 1944*] and while I went out I was in the oil business [*that was 1937*]. I looked up and I was given a chance to go with the Boston Braves [*after 1937*]. So I said, 'Well, I laid out one year [*1937*] and got a job, so this time [*1961, after being fired by the Yankees*] I laid out another year and that statement of yours [*earlier, off microphone, Meyer had asked him about the job offer he had received from the Detroit Tigers*], that's true. Mr. Fetzer [*John Fetzer, the Detroit owner*] came to see me himself and two of the—well, I guess they had two of the men who run the higher office [*the Detroit front office*] also called on me and asked if I would consider allowing my name to be used after, I think, they got rid of—Scheffling, wasn't it? *No!* They *hired* Scheffling [*Bob Scheffing, who became the Detroit manager in 1961*] when I told them Scheffling, uh, would be hired [*Casey recommended Scheffing*] and they said Scheffling instead of hiring three or four men that they had in view. I did [*recommended Scheffing, apparently*]. I still laid out a year. And then they [*the Continental League?*] offered me the opportunity so that Branch Rickey came and offered me a chance to go, uh, uh, if I would go, uh, in with the college team before they decided on expansion [*I think Casey means "Continental," not "college"*], which two teams not to use, or what teams to use. Why, he gave me a chance that I coulda gone with a club if he got in charge of it for an expansion, see? I mean, I coulda gone with him [*Rickey? Fetzer?*] but insteada that I had, uh, had, uh, Mrs. Payshon [*Joan Whitney Payson*] and, uh, Mr. Grant [*M. Donald Grant*] called me on the phone out on the Coast twice and offered me a chance if I would go, and I said, no, I was gonna maybe lay out for the rest of the year. But insteada doin' that Mr. Weiss was down at a racetrack, or in the winter he was in New Orlins, and he was also down in Florida, and he talked to him [*Grant talked to Weiss*] and he says [*Weiss says*], 'I myself will take a position over here with the Mets.' So they made him president of the Mets at that time and allowed him to get in touch with me, and then he convinced me after a period that I would go. Well, I was known in Brooklyn and I played with the Giants in '21, '22, and '23, when we played against Ruth and the Yankees, and I had a feeling out there that everybody knew me, see? More so than I would say to pick some other team. And when they decided they would start in the expansion league out in New York that's why I accepted the task. When Weiss took the job, he convinced me that I could go there and do the best I could, and they've been very nice to me up there. Of course, we were what you could call a complete flop" [*voice lifting gently at the end*].

Meyer says, "But in 1949 you were not a complete flop. Your first year with the Yankees, seventy-four injuries, and you still won yourself a pennant. You were like a magical wizard. How did you do it?"

"Well," says Stengel, "I believe it was platooning like the latest thing they asked me [*at the banquet*], and I never talked about it tonight [*pause, as though wondering why he hadn't talked about it*] was why is it now that I hope for you to have pinch hitters. I was a platoon manager, and McGraw platooned me, so if he platooned me I found out he was right, because he win three pennants [*during the three years Casey was with the Giants*]. And I felt when I started in baseball that they were not the same [*the two players being platooned?*]. They got twenty-four clubs [*there were twenty-four big-league teams in 1973*] and they can't fill the rosters. And I say right now with twenty-four clubs, as good as their training and their schools are to educate players, they're not whatcha want [*said almost sadly*]. In other words there still is too many holes to fill or some man gets sick or gets injured on ya and, uh, uh, it's, uh, it—[*he's forgotten the question and can't find his way back to it*]. To me they *have* to have platooning, and that gives an old man a job. Or if you owned a ball club for fourteen million or twelve million or ten million, how would you like to go along and say, 'I won't pinch-hit?' [*Stengel is objecting to players who object to platooning, who don't want to sit on the bench to be used as pinch hitters.*] Now, like I would say, 'The National League and you wouldn't pinch-hit?' Well, let me give you a good tip about it. What if you're in last place and you got new pinch hitters there and you turned them loose? Or what do ya, what if, how many men can hit good that are *pitchers*? Like today they honored Wood out there. [*Joe Wood, the famous old Boston Red Sox pitcher, who was honored at the banquet, was an excellent hitter, but Casey doesn't dwell on that and goes off on a tangent.*] I saw that man play, Wood. He's eighty-four years old and I'm eighty-two, and I watched him and I saw him today, you know, talked to him. I went out with my father to see him [*Wood was a Kansas City boy*]; now think of that, though it's true. I, when I was seventeen years old and he was nineteen, and he was pitching when he was seventeen, so I was fifteen when I went out and saw him. I said, 'Oh my goodness.' I'm thinkin' then of maybe going in semipro ball. Later I worked up in the big league and, uh, so on and so forth [*Casey is trying to recall something*] and it's like—Waite Hoyt! Waite Hoyt come out [*to Ebbets Field for a tryout as a pitcher when Stengel was a player*] with, his mother made his trousers. And he pitched battin' practice when I was in a slump in the big league, and I got mad. Waite Hoyt is—I'm eighty-two, Waite Hoyt now must be seventy-one years of age, and when I saw him out there, fourteen or fifteen, I was mad that the ball club made me—give me him for batting practice, a young kid in town [*Hoyt was a schoolboy sensation*] that the pitcher brought up. But now that he's seventy and he been into Europe, been in a World Series. He shut out—in '21 he pitched for the Yankees and shut us out, twice, when I was with the Yankee ball—I mean the Giant ball club. Later on in life, just think, I went over to Europe and Asia with him. China, so forth. And he was an outstanding pitcher then [*when he was fourteen*] but he didn't *look* that way then, see? Now, now I'm seventy [*a slip of the tongue*], and I saw him in two of these meetings in the Hall of Fame, and he's, uh, just think, he's seventy years old! Retired. I'm eighty-two [*correcting himself*]. But when I was twenty-four and that guy was only fourteen years old—now when they brought him out to the park I thought I'd *kill* him, you know, when he was just—threw the ball up to the plate and the pitcher brought him out. We didn't have many men, and I was disappointed [*that I had to bat against a kid*]. But then in '21 in the World Series I saw what he could do. Then he got better different times. He was a fellow that took care of himself, changed his methods of living. [*Hoyt, a heavy drinker, stopped and became a success in Cincinnati as a play-by-play announcer.*] He was a young, wonderful kid, and a terrific kid, and a handsome kid. And he always went on the air, and he worked for, always, somebody that was on radio. And he was such a handsome kid he ought to a been working *television* when he started because he was, uh, uh, had, had beautiful looks and there's, uh, and he, uh, without going on very far, important to the team and a very good speaker. [*Stengel is trying to remember what he was talking about before he got off on the subject of Waite Hoyt. He can't regain the thread, and so he finishes talking about Hoyt in a confidential tone.*] He laughs when he tells the jokes but they say you shouldn't do it, but he enjoys his own jokes, and I guess [*chuckles*] that's why he laughs at them."

Meyer, going back to the topic Casey forgot, asks firmly, "How about your '49 club?"

"It was a very *good* club," Stengel says, welcoming the topic back, "and I had the best man on the club was, who? Joe DiMaggio. He's worked up to be. When I took over the ball club, they commenced losing some of their best players. Now I commenced then, and I had Rizzuto at shortshop, and that's terrific. Now at second base we had four or five men, that I would say during the year which one would you play? I like Coleman for a double play [*Jerry Coleman*]. Beautiful, wonderful fellow, great. Could throw straight overhand, and if it was an ordinary first baseman, he [*Coleman*] never threw bad, because he threw overhanded. If he threw sidearm, the ball would sink and sink into the ground. So he became a good double-play man. And I had Rizzuto, who was perfect there [*at shortstop*]. Then later on I had, uh, naturally I had Martin that I brought up [*Billy Martin, who joined the Yankees in Casey's second year as manager*]. And they had to fight it out. [*Martin and Coleman were both second basemen.*] Each one went away to the war and save me [*from picking one over the other*]. Like when Martin went into the service for a year, why I had McDougald to play for me [*Gil McDougald*], and a very awkward man, a wonderful man. And now he's coaching now, I guess it's—is it Fordham he's coaching, or New York University? *Fordham*, yeah, and he's gonna be, I bet he'll be a splendid coach. 'Cause his wife writes me very good letters. Every Christmas she writes they have four or five kids, and she writes what the four or five kids do almost every day of the year. And that's a terrific thing. We don't have any children. And I liked him and I liked her. We went to Europe [*he means a trip the Yankees made to the Orient after the 1955 season*], and she quit halfway over. I mean the Orient. She quit halfway on the trip because she was too excited and not having those children at home without her, see? So she left the club and went back there after a short trip over in the Orient. [*Mrs. McDougald went as far as Japan and then returned home.*] Then he became better than he looked. [*Not after his wife left; Casey means McDougald looked awkward when he arrived in the majors but proved to be a far better player than he appeared to be.*] And he always hit. And they used to say to me, 'Why do you play that man with that silly stance?' [*McDougald had an odd batter's stance.*] And I said, 'Al Simmons did it that way,' and Al Simmons [*now in the Hall of Fame*] did put his foot in the bucket, or bent over, you know? And this boy here [*McDougald*] with men on base was a terrific hitter, and he hurt his back the last year he played for me and he didn't tell me, or they shoulda told me [*the doctors?*]. And I played him then at third again [*McDougald was a third baseman, later became a second baseman and then a shortstop before ending up on third again*], but if he'da been better—with a bad back you can't play third base because you gotta dip too quick, see? And when you're playin' shortstop even— Amazing after Rizzuto went into television, he was amazing playing shortstop. [*McDougald, before he hurt his back, took over at shortstop when Rizzuto was released. Actually, he became the regular shortstop when Rizzuto was still with the team.*]

"And then he could, and I put him in there [*at shortstop*] without buying another shortstop [*to replace Rizzuto*] because for this reason: he said I could play it if I played a month. But he had a wonderful way of studying. He could *surmise* you're gonna hit it to your right or to your left when he played short. And he played deep and got rid of the ball quick. So he did an outstanding job where I could have blown, with the ball club being weak at short.

"I was so successful [*self-directed sarcasm*] after I found DiMaggio played for me. To think: there's a man played in a ballpark that wasn't fitted for him. He played in a park that wasn't built for him. [*Yankee Stadium with its enormous left field works against right-handed batters like DiMaggio.*] Williams [*Ted*] played in a park where he hit to right field [*Fenway Park with its long right field, where the left-handed Williams had a problem similar to DiMaggio's in Yankee Stadium*] and—he should have—a right-hand man hits to left field and it looks like a bandbox [*Fenway, with its short left field*]. I used to say, well, uh, there with, uh. [*A vague thought has distracted him; it's that Joe's brother, Dominic, a fine player and a right-handed batter, played for the Red Sox in Fenway without becoming a great hitter, and Stengel doesn't*] *want to criticize him, especially to a Boston broadcaster.*] I had to say with DiMadge that if DiMadge had played in Boston—I don't mean that his brother wasn't great—but he should have played for us [*Williams, that is, not Dominic*] and somebody should've had DiMaggio there [*Fenway*] for years and he musta— he would've had an *outstanding* career, I imagine, of just tapping that ball and playing with it against that fence and—but he was terrific on my ball club. When I came up to the big leagues he was so good that I found out I never had to watch the outfield [*that is, signal the outfielders where to play*], because DiMaggio, wherever he went—if he went to the left center, ya didn't have to yell at the right fielder or the left fielder. They shifted automatically. They were positive his judgment was right, and it was, too, and it saved me, too. Many a tight place where the ball was hit where this man was lodged out there in the proper position."

"Casey—" Meyer begins.

"I'd like," Stengel says, "the best pitchers. I'd like ya to ask about them sometime."

"Go ahead," Meyer says.

"Well, I tell ya why I liked the best pitchers. I—I never—the first pitcher I got there then I got stuck on was Reynolds. [*Allie Reynolds, who with Vic Raschi and Ed Lopat formed the big three of Stengel's pitching staff through his early pennant-winning years.*] Because I put him in and he could strike out [*opposing batters*] and then I put him in one game to relieve and, my goodness, he got 'em out, and [*chuckles*] I had six pitchers back there. And the best part about pitching in that pitching staff was this. He [*Reynolds*] could start and he could relieve, and when I had the Quiz Kids—we were playing them. [*The young Philadelphia Phillies, whom the Yankees played in the 1950 World Series, were nicknamed the Whiz Kids, but Casey got that name mixed up with the name of a popular radio quiz show of the late 1930s and early 1940s that featured precocious youngsters called the Quiz Kids.*] I had Ford pitch [*in the World Series against the Phils*] and people that never knew how to write a World Series with both ball clubs came from all over the United States just to get in on free tickets and write and never had sports editors. [*Casey sweepingly indicts the sportswriters who criticized his strategy in the 1950 Series.*] They wondered why I took Ford out in the seventh inning [*it was the ninth*], and it was true they hit some balls hard off Reynolds [*who relieved Ford*], and I know that he [*Ford*] always said, 'Well, that old man knows,' that I'm hired by the club when he [*Ford*] was in the Eastern League. Now the trouble with that [*the press criticism*] was this. That I went and put in Rey- nolds—when Reynolds went in there, they [*the Phillies*] put in a couple of their boys, sure they hit him, and they just *got* to make a *b-e-e-g* foul, you know? And *foul* and *foul*, and they were out. [*Casey has confused Reynolds's relief of Ford in the last game of the 1950 World Series—when he came in with two out in the ninth and struck out pinch hitter Stan Lopata, a power hitter who did hit a hard foul—with Reynolds's relief of Raschi in the last game of the 1953 World Series, when he took over after the seventh inning, was hit hard but won the game and, as in 1950, the Series.*]

"So," Casey goes on, "when I went in [*the clubhouse*] they quizzed me and said, 'Why'd you take that Quiz Kid out?' [*meaning Ford, who was only twenty-two*]. And they'd been writing the Quiz Kwids [*sic*] with the Philadelphia players, but that was *wrong*. The Quiz Kid was *Reynolds*, and he was the oldest fella I had on the club [*delivered in an ingenuous Mark Twain "There you are" tone*].

"So he became a two-way man. Reynolds. Berra was catchin' good, too, then and we had a terrific thing with, uh, with, uh, I'd say Raschi. He was, uh, he was, I thought Raschi was the best pitcher I had on the team for nine innings [*meaning as a starting pitcher, in contrast to Reynolds, who could start and relieve*]. Now I tell ya why. Every time he pitched in the seventh, eighth, and ninth he'd almost *die* out there, tryin' to throw a ball hard. He knew that he *tried* to put more on that ball now. If I'm *tired* [*great emphasis on "die" and "tried" and "tired," so that you hear the effort, hear the weariness*], my arm will have too many baseballs being called balls. That guy in the eighth and ninth inning he'd give me, he'd give me, I mean he was almost a sure bet, and Berra admits that now, too. Boy, he was the best on the club in the eighth or ninth inning. But if I relieved with him, you'd be surprised. I was shocked. He couldn't do it.

"Now, Joe Page. Joe Page was what you'd call, well, they called him the fireman. Go up to Boston and they'd say, they got 'em now, they got the Yankees done. And I'd just call him in from the bull pen, and when he went around there, they'd start in fainting in the stands. They'd say, 'Oh my God, putting in that fireman.' And he did a tremendous job. He had guts. I believe in platooning pitchers now, too. And now they want to know why you can't pitch nine innings. Like Satchel Paige. I watched him pitch, but he had to pitch every day where he went. And I watched him when he had to rub it [*his arm, not the baseball*]. And you take now how scientifically they can hurt your arm, you know, at the elbow, or guys that work— Well, we used to have to drive automobiles with a clutch. You'd get sore joints. [*From shifting gears?*] Like a hinge bad on a door, you can't close it. Nowadays the best thing that I saw in the great Case's opinion was, I think, is a—everybody has a doctor [*every team*]. Now the doctor don't mean very much—they do it for spring training. [*The doctor comes to Florida for a vacation.*] And here every club now has an outstanding doctor. It's wonderful, but they just do— I guess when they go and say— [*Casey decides not to go on criticizing doctors.*] Well, with my experience, football, baseball, basketball, they got ways of handling fellas."

"Casey," says Meyer, ending the interview, "I'm going to use another word from your own vocabulary and that's 'amazing.' That's what you've been for these last twenty-five minutes. Thanks so very, very much."

"Yes, it's very good," Casey says, not ending the interview. "I wanted just to ask you another question about some of the players that I had I told you about when I changed to those other clubs. I had people come around and say, 'Well why don't ya?' [?] I used to have an interest in minor leagues and each time I had an interest was—it was to take young fellas and start 'em out. I believe in young fellas. I believe right now in young fellas. I believe right now that it's almost impossible to have some of the men not fail with the rapid thing of seeing a man's weakness. It used to be they [*young players*] didn't believe ya when you're watchin' the ball come across the plate. They [*the coaches*] would say, 'I'm tellin' ya this and you stand there. Do this, see? Look right at home plate. *Now* if you don't hit the ball you understand?' All right. Say, 'Well, you leaned in.' They say, 'Naw, I didn't.' Then if you show them that quick replay now do they get it? 'Well, uh,' they say, 'I swore I did not.' [*A strong protesting "Naw, I didn't," a meek embarrassed "I swore I did not."*]

"Well," says Casey, "the pitcher watches the ball, and that's the reason why you lose what any other teacher would tell ya. And that's why if you lean in, there's six guys like Paige and he's watchin' ya, and if you lean in he goes around once more and he throw in here. How can you lean in and pull back and the distance is sixty feet? And that's why he [*Paige*] became great. I saw him when he could throw like lightning, and I asked him myself. Men interview him at times, you know. And semipro games. And he was great. And you know what he used to do? He used to go in under the hot shower and put the hot shower on him, you know? And this was his rub, because they never had the trainer. And then he'd pitch the next day because he was so well known in the small towns. Yeah, he did a big job.

"All right! [*Now he's finishing the interview.*] It was very nice to do it. Nice to see ya here. I hope sometimes I can meetcha around. Very much enjoyed it, and I think I'll do better next time.

"If you wanta know this here year and know what I'm doin' at any time, I've had five or six offers to do this and that, you call me in Glendale, California, and I'll give you all the answers. And that's what I do now with the Mets. And they ask me. Well, I'm workin' for a woman [*Mrs. Payson*], and they ask me, 'Well, what do you do for 'em?' And I said, 'Well, I'm very careful now that I don't disturb 'em, as they're doin' well without me.' I tell you what, I saw rapid advancement, rapid advancement. If you've got somebody and he says, 'Well, he's stupid, and he's laid up.' Half of the men that we used to get, they came in there and they— I mean they were good enough, but they *slowed* up for you. They had injury in their lives. Maybe trouble with—eye trouble. Maybe they'd say, 'I cannot see with one eye.' Maybe they had to say, 'Well, I tell you what; I can't pitch anymore, but I can pitch three innings.' But Satchel Paige even said tonight he was going to spring training. He wouldn't pitch Friday and Saturday, too. He never was a relief pitcher [*not in the Negro Leagues, but Paige was a relief pitcher in the American League*]."

"Casey," says Meyer, "thanks again."

"You bet." Casey snaps it off vigorously. "I'll, uh, I'll go, uh, I'll have you in mind, and anytime something comes up, ask me what. I told you about the pinch hitter and about the old man. The old man gets to play now, and if he plays— If you own the ball club and you get the receipts, most of it, you better do well at home. You play half your games at home, and if you don't have a pinch hitter at home and your club is green, why you better have to play those home games in— The older man gets to play two or three years longer in baseball where the young man in pinch-hitting doesn't do great, *but* if the pitcher knew, I'm gonna throw the ball over the plate, the young man goes up, says, 'I'm gonna kill that pitcher.' And then he hits at bad pitches. But the old fella gets hit with the ball or makes you nibble on it.

"Thank you very much. I'm glad you give me that interview, and someday if you're in a pinch call me up and I'll have a better answer."

And that did end the interview.

Alphabetical fortuity brings us, in close marching order, four of the more compelling figures of the game's early days: Pearce and Wright, just before, Candy Cummings and Jim Devlin to follow. But now some background on Mr. Cummings's perfidious pitch. Historians dispute whether this 120-pound pony deserves more credit as pioneer or publicist, but he is certainly a historical figure to reckon with. Others may have established competing claims of authorship, more or less convincing (those of Fred Goldsmith, Phonnie Martin, Bobby Mathews, Tommy Bond, and Jim White), but Candy's claim still seems the best, and he rode it—and in this 1908 reminiscence, wrote it—into immortality.

CANDY CUMMINGS

How I Pitched the First Curve

I have been asked how I first got the idea of making a ball curve. I will now explain. It is such a simple matter, though, that there is not much explanation.

In the summer of 1863 a number of boys and myself were amusing ourselves by throwing clam shells (the hard-shell variety) and watching them sail along through the air, turning now to the right and now to the left. We became interested in the mechanics of it and experimented for an hour or more.

All of a sudden it came to me that it would be a good joke on the boys if I could make a baseball curve the same way. We had been playing "three old cat" and town ball, and I had been doing the pitching. The joke seemed so good that I made a firm decision that I would try to play it.

I set to work on my theory and practiced every spare moment that I had out of school. I had no one to help me and had to fight it out alone. Time after time I would throw the ball, doubling up into all manner of positions, for I thought that my pose had something to do with it; and then I tried holding the ball in different shapes. Sometimes I thought I had it, and then maybe again in twenty-five tries I could not get the slightest curve. My visionary successes were just enough to tantalize me. Month after month I kept pegging away at my theory.

In 1864 I went to Fulton, New York, to a boarding school and remained there a year and a half. All that time I kept experimenting with my curve ball. My boyfriends began to laugh at me and to throw jokes at my theory of making a ball go sideways. I fear that some of them thought it was so preposterous that it was no joke and that I should be carefully watched over.

I don't know what made me stick at it. The great wonder to me now is that I did not give up in disgust, for I had not one single word of encouragement in all that time, while my attempts were a standing joke among my friends.

After graduating, I went back to my home in Brooklyn, New York, and joined the "Star Juniors," an amateur team. We were very successful. I was solicited to join as a junior member the Excelsior club, and I accepted the proposition.

In 1867 I, with the Excelsior club, went to Boston, where we played the Lowells, the Tri-Mountains, and Harvard clubs. During these games I kept trying to make the ball curve. It was during the Harvard game that I became fully convinced that I had succeeded in doing what all these years I had been striving to do. The batters were missing a lot of balls; I began to watch the flight of the ball through the air and distinctly saw it curve.

A surge of joy flooded over me that I shall never forget. I felt like shouting out that I had made a ball curve; I wanted to tell everybody; it was too good to keep to myself.

But I said not a word and saw many a batter at that game throw down his stick in disgust. Every time I was successful, I could scarcely keep from dancing from pure joy. The secret was mine.

There was trouble, though, for I could not make it curve when I wanted to. I would grasp it the same, but the ball seemed to do just as it pleased. It would curve, all right, but it was very erratic in its choice of places to do so. But still it curved!

The baseball came to have a new meaning to me; it almost seemed to have life.

It took time and hard work for me to master it, but I kept on pegging away until I had fairly good control.

In those days the pitcher's box was 6 feet by 4, and the ball could be thrown from any part of it; one foot could be at the forward edge of the box, while the other could be stretched back as far as the pitcher liked; but both feet had to be on the ground until the ball was delivered. It is surprising how much speed could be generated under those rules.

It was customary to swing the arm perpendicularly and to deliver the ball at the height of the knee. I still threw this way but brought in wrist action.

I found that the wind had a whole lot to do with the ball curving. With a wind against me I could get all kinds of a curve, but the trouble lay in the fact that the ball was apt not to break until it was past the batter. This was a sore trouble; but I learned not to try to curve a ball very much when the wind was unfavorable.

I have often been asked to give my theory of why a ball curves. Here it is: I give the ball a sharp twist with the middle finger, which causes it to revolve with a swift rotary motion. The air also, for a limited space around it begins to revolve, making a great swirl, until there is enough pressure to force the ball out of true line. When I first began practicing this new legerdemain, the pitchers were not the only ones who were fooled by the ball. The umpire also suffered. I would throw the ball straight at the batter; he would jump back, and then the umpire would call a ball. On this I lost, but when I started the spheroid toward the center of the plate, he would call it a strike. When it got to the batter, it was too far out, and the batter would not even swing. Then there would be a clash between the umpire and the batter.

But my idlest dreams of what a curved ball would do as I dreamed of them that afternoon while throwing clam shells have been filled more than a hundred times. At that time I thought of it only as a good way to fool the boys, its real practical significance never entering my mind.

I get a great deal of pleasure now in my old age out of going to games and watching the curves, thinking that it was through my blind efforts that all this was made possible.

The final weeks of the 1877 National League season witnessed a mysterious collapse of the Louisville club, permitting Boston to take the pennant rather handily. The suspicious Louisville directors soon caught on that four of their players had sold out to gamblers. Among these was star pitcher Jim Devlin, who had hurled every one of the club's 129 games over the previous two years. Distraught over his banishment by the league that winter, impoverished and penitent, the poor soul begged help from Boston manager Harry Wright and league president William Hulbert. His poignant letter to Wright is reproduced below, and the wrenching scene in Hulbert's office is described by one-time pitching ace and sporting goods magnate Albert Spalding, whose office adjoined Hulbert's.

JIM DEVLIN

"I Am Honest, Harry"

Phila   Feb 24th 1878
Mr Harry Wright
*   Dear Sir*
as I am Deprived from Playing this year I thought I woed [would] write you to see if you Coed [could] do anything for me in the way of looking after your ground or anything in the way of work   I Dont Know what I am to do   I have tried hard to get work of any Kind   But I Canot get it   do you Know of anyway that you think I Coed [could] get to Play again   I Can asure you Harry that I was not Treated right and if Ever I Can see you to tell you the Case you will say I am not to Blame   I am living from hand to mouth all winter   I have not got a Stich of Clothing or has my wife and child   You Dont Know how I am Situated for I Know if you did you woed [would] do Something for me   I am honest Harry   you need not Be afraid   the Louisville People made me what I am to day   a Begger   I trust you will not Say any-thing to anyone about the Contents of this to any one   if you Can do me this favor By letting me take Care of the ground or anything of that Kind   I Beg of you to do it   and god will reward you if I Dont   or let me Know if you have any Ide [idea] of how I Coed [could] get Back   I am Dumb Harry   I dont Know how to go about it   So I Trust you will answear this and do all you Can for me   So I will Close by Sending you & Geo and all the Boys my verry Best wishes   hoping to hear from you Soon   I am yours Trouly
*   James A Devlin*
No 908   Atherton St
*   Phila   Pa*

Spalding writes:

> His lips gave utterance to such a plea for mercy as might have come from one condemned to the gallows. . . . It was a scene of heartrending tragedy. Devlin was in tears, Hulbert was in tears . . . I heard Devlin's plea to have the stigma removed from his name. I heard him entreat, not on his own account—he acknowledged himself unworthy of consideration—but for the sake of his wife and child. . . . I saw the president's hand steal into his pocket as if seeking to conceal his intended act from the other hand. I saw him take a $50 bill and press it into the palm of the prostrate player. And then I heard him say, as he fairly writhed with the pain his own words caused him, "That's what I think of you, personally; but, damn you, Devlin, you are dishonest; you have sold a game, and I can't trust you. Now go; and let me never see your face again; for your act will not be condoned so long as I live."

An archetypal figure of legend and literature is the wise fool, who accepts the world's mockery and, secure in his special relationship with higher powers, keeps his counsel. In the early days of baseball, when superstition was more widespread than today, managers sought a competitive edge by taking on as mascots a range of misfits, from dwarfs and hunchbacks to dingbats like Charles Victor (Victory) Faust, whose luck rubbed off on John McGraw's Giants from 1911 through 1913. The aptly named Faust makes an appearance in *Ragtime*, the 1975 novel that also presented such historical figures as J. P. Morgan and Henry Ford and brought fame to its author. Here a father feels his grip on his family slipping away as an outsider, Coalhouse Walker, holds the reins. Enter baseball.

E. L. DOCTOROW

Family

It was clear the crisis was driving the spirit from their lives. Father had always felt secretly that as a family they were touched by an extra light. He felt it going now. He felt stupid and plodding, available simply to have done to him what circumstances would do. Coalhouse ruled. Yet he had been to the Arctic, to Africa, to the Philippines. He had traveled out West. Did that mean only that more and more of the world resisted his intelligence? He sat in his study. Everyone he thought about, even Grandfather, he saw in terms of his own failed concern. He had treated Grandfather with the arrogant courtesy one gives to the senile even before the condition had set in. From Younger Brother he was completely estranged. Toward his wife he felt drastically slipped in her estimation, an explorer in body only, the spirit trapped in his own father's prejudices. He was beginning to look like him, too, going dry and juiceless in everything, with a mad glint showing in the corner of his eye. Why did that have to be?

He condemned himself most for the neglect of his son. He never talked to the boy or offered his companionship. He had always relied on his presence in the child's life as a model for emulation. How smug that was, how stupid, as the tactic of a man who had acted in his life to distinguish himself from his own father. He looked for the boy and found him on the floor of his room reading in the evening paper an account of the successful play of the New York baseball nine under the masterful coaching of John J. McGraw. Would you like to see that team? he said. The boy looked up, startled. I was just thinking of it, he said. Father went to Mother's room. Tomorrow, he announced, I am taking the boy to see a game of baseball. He said this with such resolve in its rightness that she was checked in her response, which was to condemn him for an idiot, and when he left the room, she could only wonder that she had had that thought in the first place, so separated from any feeling of love.

* * *

The next afternoon, when father and son left the house, two reporters followed them part of the way on their brisk walk to the railroad station on Quaker Ridge Road. We're going to the Giants baseball game, Father advised them. That's all I will say. Who's pitching? one of the reporters asked. Rube Marquard, the boy said. He's won his last three chances.

Just as they reached Quaker Ridge, a train pulled in. This was the New York Westchester and Boston railway. It did not go anywhere near Boston, nor did it provide service all the way to New York. But it gave a smooth ride to the Bronx and left them with a trolley connection, the 155th Street crosstown, which went over the Harlem River to the Polo Grounds at Coogan's Bluff.

It was a fine afternoon. Large white clouds moved briskly under a clear blue sky. As the trolley came across the bridge, they could see on the bluff overlooking the wooden stands several huge trees that, lacking leaves even in this season, supported derbied figures of men who preferred not to pay to enter the park but to watch the game festooned in the branches like black flowers swaying in the wind. Father caught some of the boy's excitement. He was immensely pleased to be out of New Rochelle. When they reached the park, crowds were streaming down the stairs from the El, cabs were pulling up and discharging their passengers, newsboys were hawking programs of the game, and there was a raucous energy everywhere in the street. Horns blew. The overhead tracks of the El left the street mottled with sun. Father bought the expensive fifty-cent admission, then paid extra for a box, and they entered the park and took their seats behind first base in the lower of the two decks where the sun would for an inning or two cause them to shade their eyes.

The Giants were dressed in their baggy white uniforms with black pinstripes. The manager, McGraw, wore a heavy black cardigan over his barreled trunk with the letters "NY" emblazoned on the left sleeve. He was short and pugnacious. Like his team, he wore socks with thick horizontal stripes and the small flat cap with a peak and button on the crown. The opponents of the afternoon were the Boston Braves, whose dark blue flannels were buttoned to the neck with the collar turned up. A brisk wind blew the dirt of the field. The game began, and almost immediately Father regretted the seats he had chosen. The players' every ragging curse could be heard clearly by his son. The team at bat shouted obscene taunts at the opposing pitcher. McGraw himself, the paternal figure and commander of his team, stood at third base, unleashing the most constant and creative string of vile epithets of anyone. His strident caw could be heard throughout the park. The crowd seemed to match him in its passions. The game was close, with first one team, then the other, assuming the lead. A runner sliding into second base upended the Giant second baseman, who rose howling, limping in circles and bleeding profusely through his stocking. Both teams came running from their dugouts, and the game was stopped for some minutes while everyone fought and rolled in the dirt and the crowd yelled its encouragement. An inning or two after the fight the Giant pitcher Marquard seemed to lose his control and threw the ball so that it hit the Boston batsman. This fellow rose from the ground and ran out toward Marquard, waving his bat. Again the dugouts emptied, and players wrestled with each other and threw their roundhouse punches and beat clouds of dust into the air. The audience this time participated by throwing soda-pop bottles onto the field. Father consulted his program. On the Giant side were Merkle, Doyle, Meyers, Snodgrass, and Herzog, among others. The Boston team boasted a player named Rabbit Maranville, a shortstop who he noted roamed his position bent over with his hands at the end of his long arms grazing the grass in a manner that would more properly be called simian. There was a first baseman named Butch Schmidt and others with the names Cocrehan, Moran, Hess, Rudolph, which led inevitably to the conclusion that professional baseball was played by immigrants. When play was resumed, he studied each batsman: indeed, they seemed to be clearly from the mills and farms, rude-featured, jug-eared men, sunburned and ham-handed, cheeks bulging with tobacco chew, their intelligence completely absorbed in the effort of the game. The players in the field wore outsized flapping leather gloves that made them look like half-dressed clowns. The dry dust of the diamond was blotched with expectorant. Woe to the campaigns of the Anti-Spitting League in the example of these men. On the Boston side the boy who picked up the bats and replaced them in the dugout was, upon second look, a midget, in a team uniform like the rest but proportionately minute. His shouts and taunts were piped in soprano. Most of the players who came to bat first touched him on the head, a gesture he seemed to invite, so that Father realized it was a kind of good-luck ritual. On the Giant side was no midget but a strange skinny man whose uniform was ill fitting, who had weak eyes that did not align properly, and who seemed to shadow the game in a lethargic pantomime of his own solitude, pitching imaginary balls more or less in time to the real pitches. He looked like a dirt eater. He waved his arm in complete circles, as a windmill turns. Father began to watch the game less than he did this unfortunate creature, obviously a team pet, like the Boston midget. During dull moments of the game the crowd yelled to him and applauded his antics. Sure enough, he was listed in the program as mascot. His name was Charles Victor Faust. He was clearly a fool who, for imagining himself one of the players, was kept on the team roster for their amusement.

Father remembered the baseball at Harvard twenty years before, when the players addressed each other as Mister and played their game avidly, but as sportsmen, in sensible uniforms before audiences of collegians who rarely numbered more than a hundred. He was disturbed by his nostalgia. He'd always thought of himself as progressive. He believed in the perfectibility of the republic. He thought, for instance, there was no reason the Negro could not with proper guidance carry every burden of human achievement. He did not believe in aristocracy except of the individual effort and vision. He felt his father's loss of fortune had the advantage of saving him from the uncritical adoption of the prejudices of his class. But the air in this ballpark open under the sky smelled like the back room of a saloon. Cigar smoke filled the stadium and, lit by the oblique rays of the afternoon sun, indicated the voluminous cavern of air in which he sat pressed upon as if by a foul universe, with the breathless wind of a 10,000-throated chorus in his ears shouting its praise and abuse.

Out in center field, behind the unroofed or bleacher seats, a great display board indicated the number of outs and the inning and the hits and runs made. A man went along a scaffold and hung the appropriate marked shingles that summarized the action. Father sank into his chair. As the afternoon wore on, he entertained the illusion that what he saw was not baseball but an elaborate representation of his own problems, accounted, for his secret understanding, in the coded clarity of numbers that could be seen from a distance.

He turned to his son. What is it you like about this game, he said. The boy did not remove his gaze from the diamond. The same thing happens over and over, he said. The pitcher throws the ball so as to fool the batter into thinking he can hit it. But sometimes the batter does hit it, the father said. Then the pitcher is the one who is fooled, the boy said. At this moment the Boston hurler, Hub Perdue, threw a pitch that the New York batter, Red Jack Murray, swung at. The ball soared into the air in a high, narrow arc and seemed then to stop in its trajectory. With a start Father realized it was coming directly at them. The boy jumped up and held out his hands, and there was a cheer behind them as he stood with the leather-covered spheroid resting in his palms. For one instant everyone in the park looked in their direction. Then the fool with the weak eyes who imagined he was a player on the team came up to the fence in front of them and stared at the boy, his arms and hands twitching in his baggy flannel shirt. His hat was absurdly small for his abnormally large head. The boy held out the ball to him, and gently, with a smile almost sane, he accepted it.

An interesting note is that this poor fellow, Charles Victor Faust, was actually called upon to pitch one inning in a game toward the end of this same season when the Giants had already won the pennant and were in a carefree mood. For a moment his delusion that he was a big leaguer fused with reality. Soon thereafter the players became bored with him, and he was no longer regarded as a good-luck charm by Manager McGraw. His uniform was confiscated, and he was unceremoniously sent on his way. He was remanded to an insane asylum and some months later died there.

At the end of the ball game a great anxiety came over Father. He felt it had been stupid to leave his wife alone. But as they left the park, borne by the streaming crowd, he realized his son had taken his hand. He felt an uplift of his spirit. On the open trolley he put his arm around the boy's shoulders. Arriving in New Rochelle, they walked briskly from the train station, and when they came in the door, they gave a loud hello! and for the first time in days Father felt like himself. . . .

"Nice guys finish last," Leo Durocher once said when asked why he wasn't a nice guy like Billy Meyer of Pittsburgh. These immortal words became the title for his tough and splendid autobiography, written with Ed Linn. Leo managed for twenty-four years and finished last only once, the year he took control of a basket-case Chicago Cub franchise; the following year, he brought the Cubs in third. It's hard to be neutral about Leo the man or Leo the manager, but it's impossible to make light of his record: he may have claimed only three pennants in a career that spanned 1939 to 1973, but in the history of baseball only five men won more games. This nasty episode took place in 1971.

LEO DUROCHER with ED LINN

The Santo Explosion

It was one of Santo's slumps that led, indirectly, to the worst argument I ever saw in a clubhouse. The only thing that didn't fly was fists, and for a while there it was a very near thing. And it wasn't Santo's fault. I have nobody to blame but myself. As a bow to the modern ballplayer, I had formed the habit of holding open meetings. "Okay, boys," I'd say after I had spoken my piece. "Now we'll forget that I'm the manager, and let's hear what's on your mind." Keep asking for it, buddy, and you're going to get it.

The real culprits were Milt Pappas and Joe Pepitone, a pair of renegades we had picked up during the previous season. Pappas I will never forgive. All I did for Pappas was save his life after he had done everything but crawl on his knees to me. He started on me in Acapulco in the winter of 1969 while my wife and I were sitting in a restaurant. Pappas was a great friend of our traveling secretary, Blake Cullen, and he came over to our table to say hello. "Goddam, get me, Leo," he said. "I want to pitch for you."

Now, Milt could pitch, but he had a reputation everywhere he had ever been of being one of the great clubhouse lawyers of our time. That's why Baltimore, his original club, had let him go; it was, from everything I heard, why Cincinnati had let him go; and it was probably why he no longer felt he had a glowing future in Atlanta. That didn't bother me at all. I always felt that I could handle the renegades.

I didn't think Atlanta was going to give him up that easily, though, and I told him so.

80

The following summer he wooed me. Early in the season we played three games in Atlanta, and he came to me three different times. The first two times he came over while I was on the field watching batting practice to let me know Atlanta wasn't using him and he definitely could be had. Just what I needed. To begin with, there's an antifraternization rule. You're not supposed to even talk to a player in the other uniform, let alone be talking about making a deal for him. The last day, I was told that he was waiting for me at the bus outside our clubhouse. "Get him out of there," I yelled.

Same thing when Atlanta came to Chicago a week later. And all the time he kept telling Blake Cullen how much he would like to be with the Cubs, and Blake would come to me and ask whether I thought Pappas could help us.

There was no question that he could help us. We needed another starting pitcher bad, and you only had to look at the box scores to see that Pappas was right in feeling that his future did not lay in Atlanta. So I talked to John Holland about him. John wasn't crazy about the idea, but—lucky me—I finally was able to talk him into it.

The guy could pitch, all right. But he always wanted to spit the bit out; that was the other part of his reputation. He'd give you a great six, seven innings, and if he had a one-run lead, he was through. If he won it, fine, he got credit for the win. If you lost, he was off the hook. If he was a run behind, it was a different story; he'd really be bearing down. The time that tore it, he was pitching against Cincinnati after he had been with us about a month, and he was pitching just great. (A couple of weeks earlier he had shut the Reds out, the only time they were shut out all year.) This time, I made the mistake of sending Joe Becker, my pitching coach, over to ask him how he felt, "Aahh,

I'm all in," Milt said. "I'd get a new pitcher in there." I took him out. My fault.

Cincinnati tied the game in the eighth and beat us in the ninth. If that wasn't bad enough, he threw a temper tantrum in the clubhouse when he heard the score had been tied. My coaches came to me in a body to tell me that I should never do that with Pappas. "I know," I said. "I wanted to be sure."

I sat everybody down, and I said, "I want to apologize to the rest of the team. I screwed up today." And then I turned to Pappas and told him he was never going to do that to me again. "You're going to start, and you're staying in there until I take you out, and nobody's going to ask you. Quit looking over your shoulder at me. I blame myself, because I should know better."

From that day on, he never got to talk to me. He'd come into the dugout looking for me, and wherever he went, I'd go the other way. He'd look into the dugout from the mound, and I'd put my head down. It didn't matter what he said to the coaches. They were under instructions never to relay any of his complaints to me. I made him stay nine. *Pitch*, I'd say to myself. *You ain't going to get out of there today; you're pitching too good. They're going to get a couple of men on, and somebody's going to get a base hit before I take you out now. Tired or not, you're pitching too good.* The same year we had the blowup, he won more games for me, seventeen, than he had ever won before in his life. And pitched more innings.

But he was always agitating. He became the player representative when Randy Hundley quit, a job nobody else wanted and Milt always loved. He had also been the player rep at Baltimore, Cincinnati, and Atlanta. Worst thing that could have happened. Once he was the player representative, he was holding meetings all the time. Practically overnight, all harmony disappeared from the Chicago clubhouse.

And it wasn't that the players looked on him with any particular affection, either. There was one time during a road trip that we were going from some-place or other to Cincinnati. We had been playing horribly, and since the first day in Cincinnati was open, I had Blake Cullen reroute us to Chicago. And not to give the players a day with their loved ones! "We're going to work out at Wrigley Field," I told them, "and everybody is to be there."

Milt Pappas didn't show up. His wife called up to say he was sick. As soon as the other guys saw he wasn't there, they just stood around on the field hollering, "Where is Pappas? Where is Pappas?" I was so mad about it myself that I sent everybody back into the clubhouse and told them they could go home. "See you tomorrow in Cincinnati." That was our workout. That was what we had made the trip to Chicago for.

Milt showed up about three days later with a note from his family doctor.

Pepitone was another kettle of fish entirely. I knew exactly what I was getting when I got him. A couple of days before Ernie Banks went on the disabled list, Pepitone had left Houston, wailing that he couldn't stand (1) Harry Walker, the manager; (2) Spec Richardson, the general manager; (3) anybody else who tried to tell him what he had to do. "I can't stand a million rules," Peppy had said—and a beautiful example was the awful thing they were trying to do to Peppy in Houston. They had actually tried to assign him a roommate on the road, like everybody else. Pepitone had gone home to his hairstyling salon in Brooklyn to brood about man's inhumanity to man, and he was nothing if not available.

He didn't come cheap, either. Although it was announced as a straight sale, it wasn't. We had to agree to give up a minor-league player at the end of the season, and the player was going to be Roger Metzger, who we really hated to lose.

It was a calculated risk we were willing to take because we were fighting for the division title, and Peppy was another guy who could play. He was a good hitter, he could run, he had a good arm. He knew how to play ball. He was the best first baseman we had, and he was also the best outfielder. He could do everything. It was just a question of how much of it he was willing to give you on any particular day.

It was a crime, watching a guy like that wasting all that talent. Because basically Peppy was a lovable guy. He could charm the birds out of the trees. No matter how mad you might be when you started to talk to him, you'd go away thinking, He's his own worst enemy, poor fellow. Too bad. Which, I guess, was exactly what Peppy, poor fellow, wanted you to go away thinking. Training rules? Forget it. No training rules where Joe Pepitone was concerned. What were you going to do, fine him? He was in debt up to his eyeballs when he came to us. He always owed the club half of his year's salary before the year started. Gratitude? You're kidding. His attitude, like most of them, was "I'm entitled to it."

A shining example of the new breed. Mod all the way.

I came into the office one day, and right outside my door there's a Harley-Davidson motorcycle. I called Yosh to find out whose it was. Listen, it didn't have to be Peppy's. We had another nut there, Ray Newman, who used to ride to the park from the Executive House, 10 or 12 miles away, on his bicycle. That was my left-handed relief pitcher. One day he ran it right into a bus and almost killed himself. Had to get rid of the bicycle. Him, too, while we were at it.

Peppy couldn't understand why I would object to having a motorcycle in the clubhouse. It seemed reasonable enough to him. "Every time I try to get on it out on the parking lot, the kids bother me."

We tried to put him on a budget. See you later, pal. He'd go into Cincinnati and visit Dino's, a fancy haberdashery, and the next thing you knew, you'd walk into the clubhouse, and he'd be putting on a fashion show.

"Joe, who's paying for this?"

"They took a check."

If you're thinking that Pepitone was sent to me in just retribution and that somewhere the ghosts of Sidney Weil and Branch Rickey were laughing uproariously, I have to admit that the same thought occasionally crossed my own mind.

If you have picked up the impression somewhere along the line that Joey Amalfitano is very important to me, you are absolutely right. Joe came to me in the spring of 1954 as an eighteen-year-old bonus boy who had just been signed by the New York Giants. Just what I didn't need, an untried kid I had to keep on the roster. But he hustled all the time, was very bright, and he got 120 percent out of his talent. After I left the Giants, he was sent down to the minors, but I always stayed in contact with him and used whatever influence I had to get him back there. He lived with his parents in Long Beach, California, in the off-season, helping with the family fishing fleet. He is a good son, and he is highly religious. Or wouldn't you say that a man who has got up with the dawn a minimum of four times a week all his life to take communion is highly religious?

I will never forget one Sunday in Mexico when I took Joe and a couple of other people to the bullfights in Acapulco. It was a little after seven at night, and we had barely started to drive back to the Racquet Club when Joe said, "Let me out."

"Let me out for what?" I yelped. "We've got five miles to go yet. How are you going to get back?"

He'd take a cab.

"Wait a minute, where are you going?"

To church.

"What church? Where's there a church?"

Up in the hills, he said. There was an open-air church up there that had a seven-thirty evening mass. "I'll walk up."

Don't you know, we went up with him in the burning heat? Worst-looking church you ever saw in your life. All open air. Kids running in and out. Mosquitoes everywhere.

But Joey wasn't going to miss mass.

By a stroke of luck, Joey was playing for the Cubs when I got there. Right away, I made him one of my coaches. If I hadn't, we probably never would have got Jim Hickman, who also had a role to play in the explosion.

We were making a deal with Los Angeles for Phil Regan, the relief pitcher I needed, and as the deal was worked out, we agreed to send a pitcher from our minor-league club in Tacoma to their minor-league team in Spokane. To even it off, Bavasi was going to send someone from Spokane to Tacoma. He gave us a list of four players we could choose from, and Hickman, who had been one of the original members of the New York Mets, was on it. "Grab him," Joey said. "He always hit well in Wrigley Field." A year later he was up with us, and in 1970, the guy who had been one of four names thrown into a minor-league deal won the All-Star Game for the National League with a hit in the thirteenth inning. What a year he had for us! He played the outfield for us, he played first base in a pinch, and when he wasn't starting, he was hitting home runs as a pinch hitter. He hit 32 home runs and knocked in 115 runs. He won game after game for us to keep us in the pennant race.

A very quiet, soft-spoken young man from Hennings, Tennessee. "My hillbilly," I called him. During spring training the following year, he was sitting morosely at a table in the Pink Pony, having a drink and doing his best, in his polite way, to get rid of some girl who was bothering him. Yosh came over to where Lynne and I were sitting. "Better go over and talk to Hickman."

I went over to the table and told the girl to get lost. "Jim, what's your problem, buddy? Anything I can do? Anything you want to tell me about?"

"Well," he said. "I don't want to bother you. You've been so good to me."

I finally got him to tell me. He had asked for $46,000, because that was what he thought he deserved, and all Holland had wanted to give him was $40,000. "I wanted to play for you," he said, "and I don't like to hold out, so I signed for the forty thousand." He just didn't like to get into a big fight over money, it went against him, but that didn't mean he didn't feel he was being cheated.

I said, "I wish you'd have told me about it, Jim. I wish I'd have known about it before you signed." I didn't know if I could do him any good now that the contract was signed, I told him, but I sure as hell was going to try.

I bided my time until Holland was in a particularly good mood, and then I said, "You know we've got a very unhappy player on this club." I sketched in the background for him very quickly. "Couple of thousand one way or the other doesn't make any difference, but there's a six-thousand-dollar difference here. It's entirely up to you, John. But he's been a hell of a guy on the club. Cost us nothing and done a great job since he came here. Very popular with the fans. Drew people in the park. I think he's an outstanding player on our club. I hate to see him unhappy."

"What are you asking me to do?"

"That's an unfair question, John," I said, laughing it up a little. "I'll just leave it up to you."

"Send him in to see me," John sighed.

I sent him in, and Holland gave him the $46,000.

And Jim Hickman never forgot it.

Now you have the main cast of characters. Pappas, Pepitone, Amalfitano, and Hickman. And Santo.

The whole thing started, really, when we arrived in Atlanta late at night on the last stop of a road trip before returning to Chicago. Santo got on the elevator with me, just the two of us, and asked if he could talk to me in private. When we got to my suite, it developed that he wanted to talk about the Day they were giving him the second Sunday after we got back. "I never wanted a Day to begin with," he said. "And now I'm going so lousy that the fans are going to be on me. I just wish you'd talk to Holland about calling it off."

No way, Holland told me. Too much had already been done. It was a hell of a time for him to be asking that it be called off, John said, especially since it had been Ron himself who had asked for it. *Ron had asked for it!* Yeah, while they had been negotiating his contract, Ron had argued that since Banks and Williams had been given a Day, he was entitled to one, too. Now in fairness to Ron, I want to add very quickly that Ron was a diabetic, something he had kept entirely to himself up to then. The principal beneficiary of Santo Day, as

the plans were worked out, was to be not Ron himself but the Diabetic Association. In fairness to myself, I should say that I didn't know this—I'm not
sure anybody outside of the front office knew it—until it came out during the
actual ceremonies. I hadn't even known there was going to be a Day until Ron
told me about it in my suite in Atlanta.

In the course of that same talk, Ron had also asked if it would be all right
with me if he didn't take batting practice. Just, you know, to see if it might
help him shake his slump. Sure, Ron. Good idea. Might be just the thing. He
had done pretty well for two days, too. And then he had gone into an even
worse slump. When I called the meeting on August 23, we had been home for
three days, and Ron had not had a base hit in twelve times at bat. And he still
wasn't taking batting practice.

To complete the background, we were still very much in the pennant race:
4½ games behind Pittsburgh with thirty-seven games left to play. We had lost
two straight to Houston, though, the last loss coming when Doug Rader doubled off Pappas on an 0–2 pitch, the unforgivable sin for a pitcher.

That was one of the things I brought up in the course of the meeting. We
weren't hustling, I told them. We weren't bearing down. We were slipping
back into the sloppy, uncaring ways that had beaten us for three straight years
now. I said, "The guy in left field, Number twenty-six, I write his name in the
lineup every day and forget about him. He's out there taking batting practice.
He's out there early fielding and throwing." I said, "I got a guy over here,
Beckert, busting his rear end. He's having a super year. Challenging Clemente
for the batting title. He's out there every day. He works on his hitting, he
works on his fielding. He works on all his weaknesses. He made himself into
a hell of a player."

But there were some of them, I said, who didn't seem to care. "I'm out there
watching the workout, Ronnie, and you're not even there during batting practice. You're coming out late."

"Well, in my case," Ronnie said, "I don't care to hit some days."

"Well, that's what I'm trying to say, Ronnie. Maybe if you came out there
and practiced, you wouldn't get into these slumps you get into periodically."

And that's where Ronnie started to blow up. He was different from Beckert,
he said. I had given him permission not to take batting practice, and now I
was jumping all over him. "You say we're all the same to you, and we're not
all the same. It doesn't matter what I do, you're right on my ass. . . ."

Well, this wasn't what I wanted at all. "Wait a minute," I said. "The only
thing I'm trying to tell you is that you got to go on the field and practice. If
nothing else, the fans come out early to see you, and you don't hit, you're not
even there, and they're disappointed."

It might have ended right there except that Pappas had to open his mouth.
"The whole trouble in this locker room," he said, "is that you don't know
how to handle us."

I had to sit there for ten minutes and listen to Milt Pappas lecture me on the proper way to handle ballplayers, something Milt Pappas knew all about from never having managed.

"Listen, Pappas," I said, when he was finished. "I brought you here from Atlanta. I've given you the ball. I don't know what you've got to complain about. You've been winning more games the way I've been handling you than you ever won in your life."

Pepitone's locker was right next to Pappas's, which was a mistake right there. "I want to say something," Peppy said. "You know, I played for the Yankees with some very good clubs, and Ralph Houk is just a super guy. He lets you play. The trouble with this club is if a guy makes a mistake on the field you talk about him on the bench. Houk never did that."

He held the floor for about ten minutes, too, telling me what a great manager Ralph Houk was, what a super guy. The only thing he didn't tell me was why Houk had finally thrown up his super hands and practically given him away. At the end, Peppy yelled at the top of his voice, "Hell, I can take it. Hell, I've been down that road before. But Ronnie can't take it. You got to rub Ronnie. You got to pat him."

"Are you through?" I asked him. Yes, he was through. "Okay, now I'm going to speak. Nobody wanted you, Pepitone. We took a chance and brought you here. Who in the hell sets any rules for you? You can come and go as you please. Do you mean to tell me that when you screw up in the ballgame I don't have the right to criticize you? Who the hell are *you*?" Now Joe started to pipe up again, and I had to remind him that I had asked him whether he had finished. "I'm going to do the talking now," I said.

Oh, no, I wasn't. Santo was yelling again. They had got him all worked up, and as emotional as Ronnie is, he was accusing me of all kind of things. And he wasn't alone. I had lost control of the meeting; it was out of hand. They had me backed against the wall, and when my back is against the wall, I hit back. "Wait a minute," I said. "Let me ask you something, Ronnie. Isn't it true that you came to my room in Atlanta to talk to me about calling off this Day that's coming up Sunday?"

Yes, it was.

"Didn't I tell you we couldn't do that, Ron?"

Yes, I had.

"Isn't it also true that you had a problem signing a contract this year and wanted a stipulation that the Cubs would have a Day for you because they gave one to Billy Williams and Ernie Banks? You told me you never wanted the Day, and that was an erroneous statement on your part, wasn't it?"

The room was absolutely quiet. "That's a lie!" Ron screamed, and took a leap across the room at me. I thought he was going to belt me one, that's how mad he was. If he had, there would have been a fight for sure, and I'd have probably been killed. He didn't swing at me, though. He just stood nose to nose with me and kept yelling.

"Do you want me to get Mr. Holland down here to clear that up, Ron?" I finally asked.

Yeah, why didn't I just get Mr. Holland down and clear it up?

I went over and picked up the phone. "John, we got a bit of a problem. I think you should come down here."

To keep things cooled down while we were waiting, I went up to my office to get some cigarettes. The office was up a little flight of stairs and through the equipment room. I'd hardly got there before I heard a racket. Santo had started after me. My guess is that he wanted to ask me to call Holland back or, possibly, to intercept Holland before he got to the locker room. There's no way of knowing. Some of the other players had grabbed him at the top of the steps, and I could hear Milt Pappas yelling, "Let him go. Let him do what he has to do. Let him go get him."

And Jim Hickman, who had just got out of the hospital, was yelling back, "Why don't you sit down, Pappas, and shut up. Just for once in your life, shut up!"

Holland was there within the minute. Without saying a word to him, I took him back down the steps into the dressing room. "I just want you to answer one question for me," I told him. "Yes or no. Isn't it true that the idea for this Day for Santo was brought up by Ron?" I put him on the spot, no question about it. "Didn't it enter into your discussion when you were trying to sign his contract? That's all. Just yes or no."

"Well, yes," he said. "In a way he did. When he signed his contract."

Santo blew up again. A lie. It was a goddam lie!

And poor John said, "Well, it seems to me that it did enter into your conversation that you desired to have a Day, Ron. It was so long ago that you probably don't remember. It was brought up casually, but you did bring it up. Not that you're not deserving of it, Ron."

Ron let out a scream. "Ooooohhh, my God! Ohhh, Jesus Christ." And then he was back at me. "I heard about you, but I didn't want to believe it."

Now Pepitone piped up again. "That's the most horseshit thing I've ever seen. You see what you've done! You've destroyed him. What kind of a manager are you?"

And Pappas is right in there agreeing with him. My heavenly twins. Look what I had done. I had destroyed Ron Santo.

Holland was trying to quiet them down. But I was burning. "Wait a minute," I yelled. "Let me say something." I told them I was sorry this had all come about. "I didn't know there was this much hatred for me on this ball club. So I've got a solution to the whole thing. *I'll see you later!*" I turned to Holland. "You can take the uniform and shove it up your ass. Just get yourself another manager."

I was stalking through the equipment room, with my shirt already off, when I thought of something else and came running back down the stairs. "One more thing," I said. "And all I need is a yes or no on this, too, John. Is there a player on this club that I didn't fight with you and Mr. Wrigley to get more money? Every player on this club. Didn't I always fight with you when you asked me? More money, more money, more money. Fighting for the player when I should have been on the executive side?"

"That's right. You were in the middle of it, always fighting for the player."

"Yeah," I said. "I think we've all done pretty well since I been here." I went back upstairs, took off the uniform, and went into the shower.

What was happening down in the clubhouse while I was showering I heard about later. Holland talked to the players and told them if they let me walk out of there under these conditions they were going to go down in history with the Cleveland Crybabies, who had petitioned the front office to fire their manager, Ossie Vitt, for being so mean to them. Well, that had happened in 1940, before most of our players had been born. Holland had to explain to them how the Cleveland players had become the laughingstock of the whole country.

After Holland was through, Jim Hickman said, "We've gotten this far with him, we can't let him go. He's helped us all, and we need him."

When some of the others, who had previously been silent, began to express the same sentiments, Pappas jumped up and yelled, "Let's take a vote on it."

Holland didn't say a word. It was Joey Amalfitano who jumped up on the equipment trunk and took over. Addressing himself specifically to Santo, Pappas, and Pepitone, he said, "I'm asking each one of you, has anybody ever told you three guys what to do in your careers? You think you're going to tell that man what to do? Leo's a personality all to himself. He's been here before you, and he'll be here after you're gone. This isn't a guy that walked off the street. He knows what he's doing. And you think you're going to change him? Mr. Holland can't even change him. If you think we got a chance to win the pennant without him, you're crazier than I think you are."

With nobody saying a word, Joey looked straight at Santo. "You want him to come back, Ron?"

And Santo said, "Yeah."

"Then get your ass up there with me." Which is strong language for Joey Amalfitano.

I had taken my shower and put on my street clothes when Amalfitano came in with Santo. The first thing he said to me was that Ron hadn't meant it. "What you said, Leo, I don't think you should have said. And the names you called him, Ron, you shouldn't have said, either. Now if you're two adults, like I think you are, you got to apologize to each other and shake hands."

"Ronnie," I said, "I haven't got a thing in the world against you." As we shook hands, Ronnie, who was just emotionally drained, threw his arms around me. "I didn't mean to say the things I said, Leo," he said. "You know how I get. How hot-tempered . . ." I had a cigarette in my hand, and I was shaking so bad I could hardly hold it. "Ronnie," I said, "I'm not mad at you. Hell, you got a right to your feelings. You had a right to pop off. It was an open meeting. So did I. Forget it. But those other two bastards . . ." I was never going to forgive them.

And I wasn't going to put the uniform back on, either.

"No, no," Joey said. "You've preached all your life you can't stand a quitter. And you're going to quit? You're just going to walk out of here and leave us by ourself?"

"I've had enough, Joe. I'm tired."

"Bullshit!" It was a swearing day for Joey.

Nothing he could say was going to change my mind. I was through. After Joe and Santo had left, Peanuts Lowrey, my other coach, came in to plead with me. And then, to my surprise, Ernie Banks, who was a player-coach by then, came up. "Please, Leo," he said. "Don't quit. We want you here. We need you. Don't go doing something you might regret."

"Well, I think I've had enough, Ernie. I've had enough of this."

While all this was going on, Jim Hickman had taken charge in the clubhouse. He started by telling Pappas and Pepitone what ungrateful bastards they were, and then he ate the rest of them out for the way they had turned on me. I guess it was the longest speech my hillbilly ever made in his life. There were three or four of them who never spoke to Jim Hickman again. What really surprised me when I heard about it was that J. C. Martin, my reserver catcher, and Chris Cannizzaro, who had just joined the team, were supporting him. "I've been around for a long time," Martin told them, "and this is the worst thing I've ever seen."

As for John Holland, he had come up to my office right behind Ernie Banks. Same plea. Same answer. "All right, then," he said. "If you won't do it for me, do it for Mr. Wrigley." After everything Mr. Wrigley had done for me, there was nothing I could say to that. And John knew it. I looked at my watch; the game was starting in seven minutes. I put the uniform back on and walked through the locker room as if nothing had happened. We won, 6–3. Santo had two doubles and a single and knocked in three runs.

The story broke all over the papers the next day. Which was to be expected. Everything that happened in the locker room was always all over the papers the next day. Dick Dozer of the *Tribune* told me straight out, "I don't care whether I ever go into your clubhouse or not, Leo. I don't have to. Ten minutes after the door opens, I know every word that was spoken in there."

So what else was new? Every writer who covered the Cubs had his private source among the players. Sometimes their information was even accurate.

The controversy continued to swirl around our heads for more than a week. Durocher was through again. You can't fire twenty-five players, but you can fire the manager. When Mr. Wrigley finally let it be known that he was standing solidly behind me, he did it, with his customary flair for the unusual, not by calling a press conference but by taking out a paid advertisement in all of the Chicago papers.

What follows are some selected excerpts from that advertisement:

Many people seem to have forgotten, but I have not, that after many years of successful seasons . . . the Cubs went into the doldrums and for a quarter of a century were perennial dwellers of the second division in spite of everything we could think of to try. . . .

We figured out what we thought was needed to make a lot of potential talent into a contending team, and we settled on Leo Durocher, who had the baseball knowledge to build a contender and win pennants, and also knowing that he had been a controversial figure wherever he went, particularly with the press because he just never was cut out to be a diplomat. He accepted the job at less than he was making because he considered it to be a challenge, and Leo thrives on challenges. . . .

In his first year we ended in the cellar, but from then on came steadily up, knocking on the door for the top. . . .

Each near miss has caused more and more criticism, and this year there has been a constant campaign to dump Durocher that has even affected the players. . . .

All this preamble is to say that after careful consideration and consultation with my baseball people, Leo is the team manager and the "Dump Durocher Clique" might as well give up. He is running the team, and if some of the players do not like it and lie down on the job, during the off season we will see what we can do to find them happier homes.

(signed) Phil Wrigley

P.S. If only we could find more team players like Ernie Banks.

I have my own P.S. I kept handing Milt Pappas the ball. I never will forgive him. Pepitone? Ahhh, Pepitone. Peppy is like me. He has made a career of being forgiven.

He had this little bar, called Peppy's Thing, only a block from where I lived. (The bar went under like everything else. I heard that Santo lost some money on it, too.) I dropped in one morning a couple of weeks later, just as I had been in the habit of doing earlier. Yosh and a couple of the other players were there, and so Peppy called me in back so that he could tell me how sorry he was. "I wish I had a knife," he said, "so I could cut my tongue out."

Peppy's always sorry. Ten seconds after I walked up the steps that day, he was buttonholing my coaches to tell them that he was sorry. In the newspaper stories the next day, Joe Pepitone was my greatest defender. He didn't get around to apologizing directly, of course, until after Wrigley's ad had appeared.

But if he was conning me, he did a magnificient job at it. Over the winter, Bill Wrigley wanted to know whether I'd give Peppy a two-year contract if I was the owner of the club. It was another way, you understand, of helping him to work out his debts by giving him a guaranteed income over a period of time. Work out his debts? The combined resources of the Bank of England and the Bank of America couldn't get him out.

After everything that had happened, I went to bat for him again. Yeah, he had the talent. Yeah, he could do it all. "Yeah," I said. "I would."

They did.

He appreciated it so much that he came down to Scottsdale for spring training with this eighteen-year-old girl he was living with. As soon as Holland heard about it, he ordered me to tell Pepitone to get her out of there. "We can't stand that kind of thing! Can't have that on this club!"

Peppy was already half into his salary by then, and we hadn't got out of Scottsdale. "If she leaves," he told me, "I leave."

I said, "That's probably the way it's going to be. Because I was told by Mr. Holland to tell you."

Immediately, he changed his tune. "Leo, I got this girl down here with me because I'm in love with her. I'm so much in love with her I'm home with her every night. If she wasn't here, I'd be out with some broad tonight. And every night I'd be out with some broad."

Which did make sense. Isn't it better that I'm going home every night instead of chasing around? Isn't that what you want from me? Stability. You've got to admit that it made better sense.

Guys like that always make sense. Once that kind of guy sees he can get around you, he'll con you right out of your shoes.

It was out of my hands, I told him. She had to leave. "But," I said, taking the first step backward, "if you want to talk to John, go ahead. I won't stand in your way."

I guess he gave John the same treatment, because when he came out, he was able to hand me the glad news that John was leaving it entirely up to me. "You're the boss, Leo. Whatever you say."

And *again* I let him. I let him keep the broad down there, and it was wrong. Wrong, wrong, wrong . . .

Right to the end. Leo the Lamb. I'm tough to play for, huh? If you couldn't play for me, you couldn't play for anybody.

Pepitone? He lasted about a month into the season, and then we traded him to Atlanta for a minor-league first baseman. A couple of months later, he was playing in Japan. The last I heard he wasn't happy there, either. The Japanese people were very inconsiderate. They insisted upon speaking Japanese.

Give Peppy a couple of hours with the emperor and the country will go bilingual.

When fans talk about phenoms and flashes in the pan, the names that crop up include Hurricane Hazle, Gene Bearden, and Bobo Holloman. When the talk turns to unquestioned stardom cruelly nipped in the bud, they think of Addie Joss, Ray Chapman, Herb Score—and Tony Conigliaro. Others have fallen victim to the beanball, among them Mickey Cochrane, Joe Medwick, Frank Chance, and Dickie Thon; but only Tony C. accomplished so much so young—56 homers before his twentieth birthday, 160 before his twenty-fifth, despite missing a year and a half. Then, as if the failing eyesight and flattened career weren't enough, he suffered a major heart attack at age thirty-seven. The late Ray Fitzgerald, a Boston institution, felt for him.

RAY FITZGERALD

Tony C, as in Courage, Comebacks, Coronary

January 12, 1982—Tony Conigliaro, fighting for his life at Massachusetts General after suffering a serious heart attack last Saturday, was the No. 1 maker of headlines during his short career with the Red Sox. Not even Carl Yastrzemski had as much flair for the dramatic as this former St. Mary's of Lynn All-Scholastic.

Whether it was for hitting a game-winning home run or dating glamorous Hollywood actress Mamie Van Doren or writhing at home plate in agony or making a courageous comeback or calling a press conference at three in the morning to announce his retirement, Tony C. had no peer as a sports newsmaker in Boston.

From the time the teenaged Conigliaro put on such a batting show at Scottsdale, Arizona, in the spring of 1964 that the Red Sox promoted him from Class D to the starting lineup on Opening Day to his final futile days of trying to see a baseball well enough to hit it in 1975, he was one of a kind.

Conigliaro's latest adversity has brought back a bunch of memories for a Red Sox baseball writer—me—who was new to the beat during Tony's years on the team. Some of those years were thrilling, some poignant, and a couple still bring a lump to the throat.

The days and years and games run into one another, but I especially remember two particularly dramatic home runs. On a warm June night in 1967, with the White Sox ahead, 1–0, in the bottom of the eleventh, Conigliaro hit a two-out, three-and-two pitch over the Fenway screen. Sometimes I have trouble remembering my middle name, but almost fifteen years later I *know* without looking it up that a right-handed Chicago pitcher named John Buzhardt gave up the homer.

In 1969, in a grueling night game that seemed as though it might last forever, Conigliaro slammed a home run to deep left-center field in Chicago off Joel Horlen to beat the White Sox again, this time by 7–6.

Conigliaro had the perfect Fenway Park stroke. Many a left fielder watched helplessly as a lazy Conigliaro fly ball—a poke that would have been an easy out in every other American league park—barely made the net. But he could hit prodigious homers, too. If he had been a major leaguer until he was thirty-six, and thus had played for seventeen seasons, there is little doubt he would have hit at least 500 home runs.

He was a fearless hitter and never backed away from a fast ball. Once, when sidearmer Fred Lasher of Detroit hit Conigliaro on the leg with a pitch, Tony dropped his bat, raced to the mound, and attempted to nail the pitcher with a karate kick.

But the very characteristic that made him a great hitter was the one that shortened his career on that hot August night when a Jack Hamilton fastball crashed into the side of Conigliaro's face. A smoke bomb thrown on the field had held up the game for several minutes, and I've always felt the delay might have taken away some of Conigliaro's concentration.

He was out the rest of that season and all of 1968 and then made two dramatic comebacks. He tried pitching in the Instructional League early in 1969, but that didn't work out, so he went to spring training determined to make it again as a hitter. For a while his swings were so bad that it was painful to watch him in the batting cage.

But gradually the stroke returned and with it the confidence, and I remember him saying one day after getting a couple of line-drive hits in an exhibition game at Sarasota that he no longer doubted his ability to hit big-league pitching again.

In his first regular-season game back, on April 9 in Baltimore, Conigliaro hit a tenth-inning homer with a man on base that put the Red Sox ahead. He returned to Fenway Park a few days later and got the most prolonged ovation this side of Bobby Orr.

In 1970 Conigliaro hit thirty-six homers, an amazing total for someone who had been considered all done two seasons previously. He was traded to California that winter, and in 1971 his vision began to deteriorate again. And one night, after he'd struck out several times in an extra-inning game, he called a press conference to announce his retirement.

Four seasons later he came back one more time with the Red Sox. After another tumultuous ovation on Opening Day in Fenway, he singled to right in his first at bat after being away almost four years.

However, although he had a few key hits early in the season, he had been away too long. He went to the minors in Pawtucket in an attempt to recapture the graceful swing, but this time he couldn't do it.

Conigliaro, Hollywood handsome, with soft Italian eyes and a quick smile, was often controversial and might not always have been the easiest player to manage. But nobody could ever accuse him of giving less than his best on the field.

Tony C. was a headline maker who had more talent in his line of work than most of us are given in ours, but he was seldom at the head of the line when good luck was being handed out.

He could use what fate owes him right now.

G. H. Fleming, professor of English literature and specialist in Victoriana, has created a genre of baseball books patterned after Akira Kurosawa's film masterpiece *Rashomon*. Fleming's first book-length collage was *The Unforgettable Season*, a kaleidoscopic newspaper reconstruction of the unparalleled events in the National League of 1908; then came *The Dizziest Season*, a similar approach to the 1934 National League race; and finally *Murderers' Row*, a look at how the Yankees tore up the American League in 1927. Here Fleming focuses on the central play in the 1908 season, the most famous and costly blunder in baseball history: Fred Merkle's "bonehead play" that cost the New York Giants the pennant.

G. H. FLEMING

The Merkle Blunder

On September 23, 1908, as I wrote in The Unforgettable Season, *"the Giants and Cubs played the most celebrated, most widely discussed, most controversial contest in the history of American sports. The game was declared a 1 to 1 tie." This was, of course, the game of the "Merkle blunder." As Kurosawa's film masterpiece* Rashomon *beautifully illustrated, the same event may be seen in different ways by different people; and so it was with what took place at the Polo Grounds on that momentous day. What is the truth, and what is illusion? You be the judge. As in* The Unforgettable Season, *everything below is presented exactly as it appeared in the original accounts of 1908.*

Monday, September 21

Here is something for the fans to consider. Suppose Fred Tenney should be crippled. That would be a calamity, wouldn't it? Yes, it would in one way, but it wouldn't keep the Giants from winning the pennant. There is a young fellow on the bench named Fred Merkle who can fill that job better than nine-tenths of the first basemen in the league. He is crying for a chance to work, but with Tenney playing like a youngster just out of college, it would be silly to take him out of the game.

BOZEMAN BULGER, Chicago *Tribune*

Wednesday, September 23

There were rumors afloat last night to the effect that Mr. Tenney had injured his back and might not play today.

Chicago *Tribune*

"Take nothing for granted" is the motto that hangs over the desk of President Pulliam. Evidently McCormick has never seen it. When he cracked a grounder to center in the fifth inning of the second game [of a doubleheader which the Giants lost to the Cubs] he loafed a little, thinking it a sure hit. Evers went over for a fine stop, and his throw just nailed McCormick. It should have been an infield hit.

New York *Globe*

Thursday, September 24

Censurable stupidity on the part of Merkle yesterday placed the Giants' chances of winning the pennant in jeopardy. His unusual conduct in the final inning perhaps deprived New York of a victory that would have been un-questionable had he not committed a breach in baseball play that resulted in Umpire O'Day calling the game a tie.

With the game tied in the ninth inning and two outs and New York having a runner, McCormick, on third base waiting for an opportunity to score and Merkle on first, looking for a similar chance, Bridwell hit into center field, a fair ball sufficient to win the game had Merkle gone on his way down the base path while McCormick was scoring. But instead of going to second base, Merkle ran toward the clubhouse, evidently thinking his share in the game had ended when Bridwell hit the ball into safe territory.

Manager Chance quickly grasped the situation and directed the ball be thrown to second base, which would force out Merkle.

Manager Chance ran to second base, and the ball was thrown there, but immediately Pitcher McGinnity interfered in the play, and a scramble of players ensued, in which, it is said, McGinnity obtained the ball and threw it into the crowd before Chance could complete a force play on Merkle, who was far from the baseline. Merkle said he had touched second base, and the Chicago players were equally positive he had not done so.

Chance then appealed to Umpire O'Day for a decision. The crowd, thinking the Giants had won, swarmed on the playing field in such a confusion that none of the fans seemed able to grasp the situation, but finally their attitude toward O'Day became so offensive that the police ran into the crowd and protected the umpire.

Umpire O'Day finally decided the run did not count, and inasmuch as the spectators had gained such large numbers on the field the game could not be resumed, O'Day declared the game a tie. Although both Umpires, O'Day and Emslie, it is claimed, say they did not see the play at second base, Umpire O'Day's action was based upon the presumption that a force play was made on Merkle.

The singular ending of the game aroused intense interest throughout the city, and everywhere it was the chief topic of discussion.

New York *Times*

Hofman threw the ball to Evers, but before the latter could step on second base, McGinnity, who had been on the coaching line and was on his way to the clubhouse, took a hand and grabbed the ball away from Evers. Evers and Tinker then grabbed McGinnity and wrestled with him, trying to get the ball. They weren't successful, for the next minute the ball was sailing over toward the left-field bleachers. Some Chicago player rescued it and brought it in. Merkle in the meantime had been trying to go back to second base before the ball could be brought there, and two or three Chicagoans were hanging on to him, trying to keep him from the bag.

There were excited cranks surging around the grouped and tussling players and many more swarming around the umpires, on their way to the exit beneath the stand. The Chicago players chased the umpires to find out what ruling had been made, and the cranks gathered around both, jostling, elbowing, and rubbering. The police jumped in quickly and scattered the crowds right and left as the umpires slowly made their way to the exit, the players following at their heels. The umpires made their escape finally, and then a crowd tagged on to the heels of Captain Chance and other Cubs who had been in the wrangling and turmoil. The police blocked off the crowd as the players moved across the field.

Everywhere in the stands and on the field spectators were all at sea as to what had happened and as to the status of the game. The cops were too active for anything in the way of violence to break loose. It was the general impression, too, that New York had won, and there was a feeling of satisfaction over that. Herzog, who had made the first run for the Giants, was carried off the field on the shoulders of a shouting string of admirers.

Charles Murphy, president of the Chicago club, came down from his box in the upper stand to find out what the umpire's decision had been. When O'Day was asked how the game stood, he replied: "Emslie says he didn't see the play at second base, and it's no game, I suppose."

New York *Sun*

When Bridwell slammed his hit in the ninth, Merkle, instead of starting promptly for the second bag, made a move toward the clubhouse. Warned by the yells of Little Johnnie Evers, the boy orator, who was entreating Hofman to chuck the ball to the infield, Merkle changed his course and waddled toward second base. The crowd, at this time, was surging out onto the field, and exactly what happened no man can say. But this much is certain: Hofman threw the ball to the infield; it bounced off Evers's back, rolled toward King, and was finally corraled by Joe McGinnity. When three or four frantic Cubs tried to tear the ball from Joseph's grasp, it disappeared from the scene and plays no further part in the interesting narrative.

Merkle, when he had touched second base, wanted to stay and see the fight out as Frank Chance, Evers, Steinfeldt, and a few other invaders were making frantic protests to Emslie and O'Day, but Mathewson dragged him away, and they went on a run to the clubhouse.

The writer wishes to assure the fans that neither Emslie nor O'Day saw the play at second base, and neither Emslie nor O'Day knows whether Merkle went to second base ahead of or behind the ball. As a matter of fact, the ball never got there.

The moment that both umpires started for their little coop and the crowd started for the El and surface cars, members of the visiting club rushed toward Emslie and shouted, "Merkle hasn't touched second base." Emslie kept on going, remarking in reply, "I didn't see any such play." O'Day also hurried to the shelter of the stand, though Chance tried nobly to get within slugging distance and the gathering thousands from stands and bleachers began to threaten the impetuous Chicago leader in rather ugly fashion.

Hank O'Day and Robert Emslie stayed in that little coop for many moments, talking it over. Emslie, seeing that he has a wig, was the judge, and Hank was the attorney. Many and learned were the arguments going back and forth, because neither of the worthy arbitrators had seen the play, and they were to make up in talk what they lacked in vision. When they finally came out of the gloom and were braced by a gathering of baseball scribes, Emslie declined to be interviewed, and O'Day muttered something about "no game."

WILLIAM F. KIRK, New York *American*

Never was a victory more cleanly won. The Giants and Cubs gave one of the most brilliant exhibitions of baseball in the history of the game, and all the way the Giants had just that shade of superiority that wins games and pennants. First of all, credit must go to Mathewson, who outpitched Pfiester, the southpaw who has bothered the Giants all season, but there was brilliant work all around, and McGraw's men fully justified the confidence of the crowd that went up to the Polo Grounds sure that New York would hold the lead so splendidly earned.

No matter what the ultimate decision as to the game may be, and that decision may determine the ownership of the pennant, yesterday's was a glorious victory.

New York was without the services of Tenney, who has a bad leg, and Merkle, who was to acquire notoriety soon enough, took his place. He played well, but Mathewson dominated the struggle and pitched a game that he has never surpassed in his wonderful career.

New York *Tribune*

The facts gleaned from active participants and survivors are these: Hofman fielded Bridwell's knock and threw to Evers for a force play on the absent Merkle. But McGinnity cut in and grabbed the ball before it reached the eager Trojan [Evers, who came from Troy, New York]. Three Cubs landed on the Iron Man from as many directions at the same time and jolted the ball from his cruel grasp. It rolled among the spectators who had swarmed upon the diamond like an army of starving potato bugs.

At this thrilling juncture "Kid" Kroh, the demon southpaw, swarmed upon the human potato bugs and knocked six of them galley-west. The triumphant Kroh passed the ball to Steinfeldt after cleaning up the gang that had it. Tinker wedged in, and the ball was conveyed to Evers for the force-out of Merkle. . . .

Some say Merkle eventually touched second base, but not until he had been forced out by Hofman to McGinnity to six potato bugs to "Kid" Kroh to some more Cubs and the shrieking, triumphant Mr. Evers, the well-known Troy shoe dealer. There have been some complicated plays in baseball, but we do not recall one like this in a career of years of monkeying with the national pastime.

Peerless Leader Chance ran at O'Day to find out what Hank had to say, but the sparrow cops, specials, 200 cops, and Pinks—slang for Pinkertons—thought Chance was going to bite Hank on the ankle. Half a hundred men in uniform surrounded the Peerless Leader, and thousands of bugs surrounded them. Bill Marshall [the utility player usually known as Doc], who is an expert on bacteria, and Del Howard rushed in to help the Peerless Leader. Another squad of cops had O'Day in tow some yards away.

Hank didn't know Chance wanted to converse with him, and they couldn't get together, anyhow. Finally the cops got O'Day into a coop under the stand and tried to slam the door in the face of the Peerless Leader. He jammed his robust frame in the opening and defied the sparrow chasers. Chance later got to O'Day, who said Emslie, working on the bases, did not see the second-base play because of the crowd, but Hank informed Chance that McCormick's run didn't count.

Still later, Hank submitted gracefully to an interview by war scribes. He said Merkle was forced at second and the game ended in a tie. None of the Giants remained to make public statements. Part of the crowd lifted a player in white to their shoulders and bore him to the clubhouse. The Giant thus honored was not Mr. Merkle. He left long before the trouble started.

CHARLES DRYDEN, Chicago *Tribune*

Merkle lost his head. He started for the clubhouse but only took a few steps when Matty, waiting his turn at bat, yelled to him. Chance was watching Merkle and frantically called to Hofman to field the ball to second. Hofman was also in the air and began to hunt for the ball. Evers ran down the field, waving his arms and legs at Hofman like a guy gone daffy.

The crowd, thinking the game was won, poured over the stands in a surging mass that swept some of the players off their feet.

Just then Chance and Steinfeldt got to second on the run, and those two, with Evers, surrounded McGinnity and began to wrestle with him for possession of the ball. Seeing he was outnumbered and getting wise to why they wanted the ball, Joe threw it into the left-field bleachers.

Where that ball is now no one knows, except perhaps the fan who captured it and has it in a frame over his pillow.

One thing is certain: it never got to second. Merkle got to second. He started late, but he got there. The ball never did.

Chance tore after Emslie, but the crowd blocked his way, not really knowing why they did it but blocking him all the same.

Chance fought like a real bear, and a grizzly at that, to get to the umpires. He's a husky guy, that Chance, and from the way he almost got through, he'd do well on a football team. But you can't buck a line of thousands, and Chance was stalled. He had his lungs with him, however, and did some yelling. This was partly drowned by the yells of the crowd, which had become a mob.

It began to look ugly. Chance was packed in the center of a push that didn't even give him elbow room. And O'Day was in a like predicament.

The near cops were spectators on the outside fringe of affairs. Then the real blue boys got busy. They formed a flying wedge and got to the center of the maelstrom. It took a few pokes with their nightsticks to do it, but when did a cop hide his stick when it was handy?

They rescued Chance, and the umpires were locked up behind the grandstand for safekeeping until such time as the crowd could be scattered to their homes.

GYM BAGLEY, New York *Evening Mail*

The Cubs are right, under every rule of baseball law and common sense, and entitled to win their protest. Rules are rules, and clubs having boneheaded mutts on the base paths deserve only to be penalized.

All honor to Hank O'Day. There has been much roasting of Hank, both on account of the exactly similar Pittsburgh affair some weeks ago [on September 4] and because he seemed to be handing the lemons to the Cubs in all close decisions. But Hank has shown the genuine goods and has put himself on record as an honest umpire and a game man—all honor and praise to Hank O'Day!

W. A. PHELON, Chicago *Journal*

It is high time that the league took a decided stand on the rules that are not specific enough for the controversial play of yesterday. It has long been an unwritten baseball law that as soon as a home player crossed the plate with a run that breaks a tie after the eighth inning the game is over that instant. A batter runs out his hit, and that is all. If a batter singles and scores a runner from second base, it is necessary for him to touch only first base.

If a game does not end when the winning run scores, then, pray, why does not a batter who makes a long hit get full credit for it? If it is a three-bagger and a man scores from third, why does not the batter get as many bases as he can take? If a ball is lifted into the bleachers, thereby scoring a runner ahead of the batter, no credit is given for a home run. [Since 1920, a ball thus hit has been ruled a home run.] Then why should base runners be compelled to run around the sack after the winning run has been scored?

If the National League throws out the game on such a technicality, the organization does not deserve any more of the splendid patronage it has had in this city. When games are played in an office with technicalities by politicians of the game, it is time for Ping-Pong to be chosen for the great American game.

SID MERCER, New York *Globe*

"When I saw Merkle leave the base path," declares Christy Mathewson, "I ran after him and brought him back to second base so as to make our lead unquestionable. He was on second base after McGinnity tossed away the ball, following his tussle with the Chicago players. Maybe Evers got the ball and touched the base afterward. If he did, it didn't prove anything. I can state positively that no force play was made before Merkle got to the base. He wanted to stick there when he saw the scrapping on the diamond, but I pulled him away, and we went to the clubhouse." [A myth later developed, and continues to receive support in print, that because Mathewson, unable to tell a lie, informed National League President Pulliam that Merkle had not touched second base, Pulliam ruled the game a tie.]

New York *Globe*

Friday, September 25

Following a sleepless night of agony throughout the length and breadth of Manhattan, haggard bugs waited all morning for President Pulliam's decision on the riotous windup of Wednesday's game. War scribes from far and near assembled in Pulliam's outer office, where he conversed on general topics in his usual affable manner. Then he retired to the inner sanctum and sent out a neatly typewritten ruling, which in effect ruled the game a 1–1 tie.

Barring himself within the inner precincts, Mr. Pulliam declined to see anybody; nor would he come forth to reveal the future. Questions sent in by scribes came back in the original state—unanswered. Nothing was said about playing off the tie game, as provided by the league constitution, which says such games shall be played. As this is the last day the game could be played, the Giants are subject to a fine. It rests with the home club to arrange such matters, but McGraw announced last night the contest would not be played over.

Umpires O'Day and Emslie were present in Pulliam's office when the decision was rendered. Secretary Williams of the Cubs notified these officials the Chicago team would be at the Polo Grounds at 1:30 today [September 24], the regular hour for starting doubleheaders. Hank and Bob were dumb as clams. All they did was do a looking, listening part.

Thinking the Giants might assemble on the field at 1:30 and attempt to put something over, the Cubs swallowed a quick lunch and hiked to the scene of combat. A dozen Giants were there in uniform, with a crowd pouring in, but the locals made no effort to line up in battle array. At 1:30 the Peerless Leader put a complete team on the field, with Coakley pitching and Kling behind the bat. Tom Needham kindly stood at the plate with a pestle in his hand while Coakley pitched four balls. There were no umpires to tell Needham whether he struck out or got a pass.

The bugs howled derision, but Chance had made his little play and will claim the game by forfeit.

CHARLES DRYDEN, Chicago *Tribune*

I have never seen local lovers of the game so fairly boiling over with anger as they were yesterday when President Pulliam's decision was announced. Eddie Tolcott voiced the opinion of all true lovers of the game when he said to me yesterday: "There was never a more hideous outrage committed. It is a slur on the great national game, the sport we all love and admire above all others for its heretofore absolute cleanliness and absence of all taints of dishonesty or unfairness.

"That the foundation of the sport should be undermined by such a contemptible trick is shameful. If the Cubs win the pennant by that one game they stole from the Giants, the streamer would amount to nothing but a dirty, dishonored dishrag. The Cubs' title to the championship would be discredited, and the name Champions would be an empty honor. It is simply a disgrace that any gentleman connected with the national game should stoop to such unsportsmanlike methods as I understand President Murphy has. If the Giants are robbed of their fair victory, I shall be ashamed to say I was ever connected with baseball."

SAM CRANE, New York *Evening Journal*

One of the remarkable things in this baseball race is the attitude of Mr. Fan and all his family and friends toward the late disaster at the Polo Grounds.

Truly, John McGraw should feel grateful for the sympathy of almost the entire baseball world in the controversy over that memorable battle with the Cubs.

For doing what is right, Umpire Hank O'Day and President Pulliam are being condemned all over the country, while Frank Chance and his Cubs are everywhere being branded as poor sportsmen because, forsooth, they acted with intelligence and took advantage of the rules to gain an edge in a race that is so close that every fraction counts.

The game of baseball takes nothing for granted. Because the play happened to be a final one does not make it excusable to slur the rule. It is just as much a crime against the baseball code to fail to complete a play at the end of a game as in the middle. Merkle was asleep and worked his little dab of gray matter very poorly. He paid the penalty of thoughtlessness, just as he must have paid the penalty had he been caught asleep off base.

Frank Chance was a man on his job. He saw the mistake and took advantage of it, and for this he deserves not condemnation but praise for his watchfulness and thoughtfulness.

As a matter of fact, the Giants deserved not merely to have the game declared a tie but to forfeit it. McGinnity's effort to stop the play by throwing away the ball is distinctly interference, the penalty for which is loss of the battle. And if you probe that cautious mind of John J. McGraw, you will probably find him secretly satisfied that no worse result followed the indiscretions of Merkle and McGinnity.

JOHN E. WRAY, St. Louis *Post-Dispatch*

Saturday, October 10

During the last few days many veteran ballplayers have come to the front and spoken in behalf of Fred Merkle, the young Giant who has been unmercifully roasted by many fans for his alleged failure to touch second base at the finish of the memorable September 23 contest. Seasoned ballplayers like Joe Kelley, Bill Dahlen, Billy Gilbert, Willie Keeler, Frank Bowerman, and Manager Billy Murray of the Philadelphia Club are among them. They call attention to the fact that ever since the rule was adopted under which a game ends when the team last at bat scores the winning run, players have run for the clubhouse as soon as the runner crossed the plate, without advancing to the next base.

New York *World*

How good was Roger Maris? During his playing days the largely antagonistic New York press portrayed him as a home-run-hitting automaton, in the current manner of Dave Kingman and Ron Kittle. In the wake of his recent death, many observers now cite his superb right-field play, his astute baserunning, seven World Series appearances in a nine-year span, and his winning character; some have gone so far as to suggest him for the Hall of Fame. The view from this corner is that Maris was a solid player, a ballplayer's ballplayer who for three years, 1960–62, was as good as anyone. And if the Yankees hadn't wrecked his body, as detailed in this passage from Peter Golenbock's *Dynasty*, he might have gone on to merit a plaque in Cooperstown, after all.

PETER GOLENBOCK

Roger Maris

With the pennant race virtually over, everyone concentrated on the Mantle-Maris home-run derby. In every park where the Yankees played, attendance records were set as people flocked to see whether Mantle and/or Maris would break Babe Ruth's single-season home-run record.

At Yankee Stadium the booing of Mantle had ceased. It was as though the Yankee faithful were apologizing to him for the harsh treatment he had been receiving all those years, and to make up for any past hurts, the Stadium fans were making a concerted effort to understand his temperament, overlook his imperfections, and shower him with huzzahs of love. In one game in which Houk had kept Mickey on the bench because of his sore arm, he went into the game for defensive purposes and received a standing ovation. A few nights later when he hit his fifty-second home run, the Stadium crowd rose as one and applauded and stomped wildly as he trotted slowly around the bases. Mantle was deeply moved. The applause did not stop until after he had crossed home plate and returned to the dugout.

On September 10 Mickey hit his fifty-third home run. It was a long home run in the first inning against Jim Perry. His arm was aching, and his legs pained him chronically—but still he played. The home-run derby had caught him up in something that didn't permit rest.

Then a head cold further deteriorated his physical condition, and on September 11, just before the Yankees left for a long road trip, Yankee announcer Mel Allen, worried about Mantle, took him to his personal physician for a penicillin shot. For the next week Mantle's physical condition did not improve, but Mickey kept playing. His home-run total stayed at fifty-three, while Maris hit his fifty-seventh home run against Frank Lary of the Tigers on September 16. On September 17 Bill Skowron made an error to send a game into extra innings, thus giving Maris two extra at bats. In the twelfth Maris hit his fifty-eighth home run off Terry Fox to win the game.

The next day Mantle arrived at the ballpark drawn and sweating badly. He had a temperature of 103 degrees and was developing an infection and rash where he had been given the penicillin shot. There were only three games remaining before the Yankees played their 154th ball game of the season, Commissioner Frick's Midnight Hour to break Ruth's record. Mantle could not play anymore. He was too weak. His challenge to the Babe was over.

Now only Maris remained, and the mounting pressure on the young right fielder was choking him in a viselike stranglehold. The publicity was increasing in quantum jumps. Reporters hounded his every footstep, recording what he was eating at every meal and following him to the movies. "The only time

I'm by myself is when I'm taking a crap," Maris said. Life was becoming increasingly more unpleasant for the man in the goldfish bowl.

Before and after every game the reporters and cameramen were lined up three deep in front of Maris's cubicle. One afternoon Maris listened to and answered a series of questions cabled to New York from a wire service in Tokyo. From halfway around the globe they were asking the same questions he had been answering for the last two months. "No wonder I'm going nuts," Maris said when he was finished. Writers who never covered sports before were covering Maris, and some of their questions bordered on the absurd. He was getting questions like "How does it feel to be hitting so many home runs?" and "Does all of this make you excited?" and "Do you still sleep well at night?" There were also questions like "What's a .260 hitter like you doing hitting so many home runs?"—to which Maris answered, "You've got to be a fucking idiot." That Roger was hitting .260 was discussed often. "Would you rather hit sixty home runs or bat .300?" he was asked. "No comment," Roger said. Obviously if it meant more to him to hit .300, he would have cut down on his swing and tried to hit .300. The reporter persisted. "Well, which would you?" he was asked. "What would you rather do?" Roger asked him. "I'd rather hit .300," the reporter said. Maris exhaled. "You do what you want, and I'll do what I want."

Away from the ballpark anyone who saw Maris on the street or in a restaurant wanted his autograph. He was not afforded five minutes of peace and quiet. "Some people want autographs on demand no matter what you're doing," Maris said. "They think they have a right to order me around. It's just a matter of courtesy." Maris shook his head. Too often there was no courtesy.

Only on the field was he afforded refuge from reporters, photographers, and autograph seekers. On the diamond, however, some of the fans, seeing that Roger was a man with a temper who reacted adversely to criticism, constantly reminded him that they thought Mickey Mantle should be the one breaking Ruth's record. Others reminded him that they thought that Ruth's record never should be broken at all. At the Stadium he took a frightful booing, and though the people applauding far outnumbered those booing, the ferocity of the minority made a strong impact on Maris. He was not used to being booed, but it was especially weird, since he was being booed for doing something extraordinary. "Give me the Kansas City fans anytime," Maris said. "There's no place that can compare with the people there." While at Kansas City, Roger during one streak was 6 for 110. Never once was he booed. But Roger's criticism of the New York fans didn't make him any more popular.

On the road Maris was the target of vicious verbal abuse and bottle throwing. After a doubleheader in Detroit during which Roger spent the entire day dodging garbage thrown at him from the right-field stands, he was so upset that he hid from reporters in the trainer's room for forty minutes after the game. "It's pretty tough to have to listen to it all through two games and then come in and have to answer a lot of questions I've answered a hundred times." Most of the reporters were not very sympathetic. Maris was causing them to miss their deadlines. The next day in the New York papers Maris was labeled a boor, a crybaby, and worse.

On September 19 the Yankees flew to Baltimore for a series with the Orioles. Maris needed three home runs in three games to break the record within Frick's deadline. Baltimore was the hardest park in the league in which to hit a home run. The day before, Hurricane Esther had skirted the city, and a powerful wind was still blowing in from right field as the Yankees and Orioles prepared to play a Sunday doubleheader. Before the games Maris as usual was surrounded by reporters. "My daughter, Susan," Maris said, "is four, and she's getting to an age where she wants her daddy home. She can't understand why the other kids her age have their daddys home and hers isn't. That's what I'm thinking about. Everybody thinks all I have on my mind are home runs." One reporter wanted to know if it was true the Yankees were having him trailed by private detectives. He denied it. The rumor was not allowed to die, though. In gossip columns Maris's name was appearing alongside names of renowned starlets, making him even less receptive to writers of the press. "How can they write shit like that?" he kept asking.

The Yankees split the doubleheader. Maris did not hit a home run. Steve Barber, a left-hander, was sharp in the first game. Skinny Brown and Hoyt Wilhelm, two knuckleball pitchers, stopped him in the second.

One more game to go. The 154th of the season. Maris needed two home runs to tie the record, three to break it. The pressure was causing Maris excruciating inner pain. Maris was a stoic individual, but he was human, though few accepted his frailties. Before the game Roger was sitting silently in front of his locker. It was very early. Most of the reporters had not yet arrived to stampede him. Maris's face was haggard; his eyes were red. Shaking, Maris walked from his locker. He went into manager Ralph Houk's office. Tears began streaming down his face. The shakes became worse. "I need help," Roger said to Houk. "I need help. I can't stand it anymore. All those goddam questions. I'm at the end of my rope. I just can't take it anymore." He buried his head in his hands. Houk was surprised at the intensity of Maris's distress, but the Yankee manager was able to convince his hitting star that with just a little more patience the season would be over. When the two men finished talking, Maris was once more in complete control and before the game answered the questions of reporters with outward calm. Only the constant tapping on the floor with his spiked shoes indicated this game was any more important than any other.

Baltimore manager Paul Richards didn't want Maris to break the record against his club. To stop Maris, he pitched another of his fast, young arms, twenty-two-year-old right-handed flamethrower Milt Pappas. Pappas had a further advantage. With Mantle still out, he could pitch around Maris.

Maris, batting in the first inning, hit a long fly ball to right field. There was a gasp, then a groan. Maris had gotten a little too far under it and flied out to

Oriole right fielder Earl Robinson. In the third, when Maris batted again, he said to Oriole catcher Gus Triandos, "If you don't think my ass is tight, you're crazy." Pappas threw, and Maris hit a rising line drive far above the outstretched glove of the second baseman that quickly rose until it landed out of reach in the Baltimore bleachers. It was Maris's fifty-ninth home run, tying Ruth for the second most ever hit in a 154-game season. Hank Greenberg and Jimmy Foxx each had hit fifty-eight home runs in a season.

In the ninth inning, with the Yankees safely ahead and one inning from winning another pennant, Maris again batted. There were two outs. Facing him was Hoyt Wilhelm, the toughest relief pitcher in the history of baseball, a knuckleball pitcher with more wins, more saves, more innings pitched, more strikeouts, and the lowest earned run average of any reliefer ever. It was said that trying to hit Wilhelm's knuckler was like trying to swat a fly in midair with a pencil. The ball darted so erratically that neither Wilhelm nor the catcher ever knew where or how it would break, one reason catcher Gus Triandos led the league in passed balls year after year. In the 112 innings Wilhelm had pitched this year to this game, he had allowed but five home runs.

Wilhelm, a quiet man, was more than willing to throw Maris a fastball or two to give him a chance, but Richards, the crusty manager, told Wilhelm, "If you throw him anything but knuckleballs, it will cost you $5,000." Obviously too dear a price to pay for being a nice guy. On Maris's final chance for immortality, Wilhelm threw Maris knuckleballs. The first one hit his bat and glanced off foul. It was deadly silent in the Baltimore ballpark. In homes across the country all activity ceased while Maris batted. The second pitch was again a flutter ball, and again Maris took a half swing at the elusive, darting pitch. This time, however, the ball hit the bat, and while Roger stood in the batter's box, the ball bounded 10 feet down the first-base line, in fair territory. Wilhelm ran over to field the ball, and it was easy for him to tag Maris, who had barely left the plate. The chase to catch the Babe as defined by Ford Frick was over.

There was a noisy Yankee clubhouse after the game. The Yankees had won the game 4–2, clinching the pennant. The players were celebrating with champagne. Everyone was drenched with the bubbly—except Maris. The players knew that he did not engage in that sort of hijinks. They respected him for it and left him alone. Reporters surrounded him admiringly. His eyes were strange, wild and crazy. He was breathing strenuously, trying to catch his breath. "I tried," he said. He took several more swallows of air. "I tried." Everyone could feel the deep respect for Maris in that clubhouse. The other players shook his hand and congratulated him for his effort. They gazed at him in awe. "I felt," one reporter said, "like I was in church."

Despite Frick's ruling, there were still nine games left in the season for Maris to hit more home runs, nine more games of answering endless questions, nine more games of pressure. When Maris talked, his right leg jiggled nervously. In the fourth game of the Baltimore series he went oh for four and after the game discovered his blond hair was falling out in clumps. Bald spots were appearing on the back of his head. He was frightened, and he ran to Dr. Gaynor, the team physician, to find out why. It was the result of nervous tension.

With five games left in the season, on September 26 the Yankees returned to the Stadium for two games against Baltimore and three against the Red Sox. Everyone was still interested in Maris, but the tension had lifted perceptibly after the 154th game. In game 158 versus Baltimore, against twenty-two-year-old Jack Fisher, another Baby Bird with great promise, Maris swung at a curveball that Fisher threw a little too high. After Maris swung, he remained at the plate, leaning on his bat, watching the flight of the ball. The vocal crowd of less than 20,000 people, many of whom were packed into the lower right-field stands where Maris hit most of his home runs, rose, baseball gloves ready to retrieve the souvenir, and when the ball fell into the upper-deck stands, the crowd sent up a deafening roar. Maris nonchalantly tossed the bat away and circled the bases in a jog, savoring the moment. The Oriole right fielder retrieved the ball after it bounced back onto the field and tossed it back in as the Yankees waited for Maris to return to the dugout. When Maris crossed the plate and disappeared into the dugout, every Yankee walked over to him to shake his hand. The crowd continued to cheer, and it would not to stop until Maris reappeared to take a bow, something he was extremely reluctant to do. "I didn't know what to do," Roger said, "I never was in a spot like that." His teammates knew what to do. They pushed him back out onto the field where Maris doffed his cap and waved to the appreciative fans. Maris was even with the Babe. Fisher, who had given up Ted Williams's final home run the day Ted retired, was philosophical. "I'm out there to win," Fisher said. "It doesn't matter to me whether it's Maris's sixtieth or someone else's first. I don't care who hits home runs as long as I win." Fisher lost 3–2.

The next day, exhausted and harried, Maris took the day off. He sat on the bench and watched the game. Mantle, his infection worse, stayed home.

Maris played in games 160 and 161 and was shut out. Again most of the fans who came sat in the three decks of right-field box seats, trying to capitalize on a $5,000 reward offered for home-run number 61. It was like "Let's Make a Deal" where Monte Hall innocently asks, "Who wants to win some money?" and everyone in the audience shouts, "Me, me, me, me, me."

That left game 162. There was tension, because it was Maris's final opportunity, but at this game much of the attraction was of instant riches for the person who caught the ball.

Only one run was scored in the ball game. The Boston pitcher, twenty-four-year-old Tracy Stallard, a fastball-pitching rookie, threw his finest game of the year, a slick five-hitter. One of those hits came in the fourth inning. Maris, waiting patiently in the batter's box, took an outside fastball and a curve inside as the fans booed Stallard loudly. Maris banged his spikes with the end of his bat and set himself again. The pitchers in the Yankee bull pen were all peering in from their right-field vantage point, hoping Maris would hit the ball to them. Before the game Maris had told them, "If you catch it, don't give it to me. Take the five thousand dollars." With the count 2 and 0, Stallard threw a fastball out over the plate. Roger swung smoothly, and a joyous roar followed the crack of the ball on bat as the ball rose high and carried over the head of right fielder Lu Clinton, backed against the stands. It fell into the lower-right-field stands for a home run, the sixty-first home run of the season for Maris. When the ball descended, the rush of fans to catch it was frenzied. "Holy cow!" yelled Yankee announcer Phil Rizzuto. "Look at the fight for that ball!" Even when the lucky fan caught it, others punched him and tried to take it away from him. He was ultimately rescued by the Stadium police.

Maris circled the bases, as usual not showing any emotion, but in the stands, apart from the fighting for the ball, the rest of the fans were screaming in absolute ecstasy, so pleased that Maris had overcome the forbidding odds against him over the excruciatingly drawn out season. As Maris rounded third, a young fan jumped out of the lower stands and raced to shake his hand. Maris shook it, as he did the hand of third-base coach Frank Crosetti. After Maris crossed the plate, the entire Yankee team was waiting for him. When they returned to the dugout, Maris's teammates would not let him in. While the crowd continued its wild, spontaneous cheering, the players kept pushing Maris back on the field, where he sheepishly waved his cap. Four times he tried to reenter the dugout. Four times he was rebuffed. Even when he was finally allowed back in, the cheering continued. It was a magic moment in baseball history.

Stallard, who each time he batted received an ovation for having the guts to pitch to Maris when he could have more safely walked him, was not upset by the home run. "I have nothing to be ashamed of," Stallard said. "He hit sixty others, didn't he?" Maris's home run was the Yankees' 240th of the season, a new record. Previously the record was 221 set by the 1947 Giants and 1956 Reds. The home run also gave Maris the RBI crown as he finished the year with 142, one more than Baltimore first baseman Jim Gentile.

The Yankees won the pennant by eight games over a strong Detroit team. Whitey Ford finished the year with a remarkable 25–4. Ralph Terry finished second in winning percentage to Ford with a 16–3 record. Bill Stafford, losing many close games and not getting credit for a number of other excellent performances, finished 14–9, and Jim Coates and rookie Rollie Sheldon both finished 11–5. Luis Arroyo completed one of the finest relief performances in baseball history with a 15–5 record and twenty-nine saves.

At the bat there was never a team with as much power throughout the entire batting order. Richardson and Kubek were not power hitters, but they were adept at getting on base, to be driven in by the others. Behind them were Maris, who finished with 61 home runs and 142 RBIs, Mantle with 54 home runs and 128 RBIs, first-baseman Bill Skowron, injury-free for most of the season, finishing with 28 home runs and 89 RBIs. Yogi Berra hit 22 home runs, Ellie Howard hit 21, and the third-string catcher, John Blanchard, also hit 21. Clete Boyer, the third baseman, had 11. It was a year for home runs, as opposing players were hitting them, too. Gentile hit 46. Harmon Killebrew hit 46. Rocky Colavito hit 45, and Norm Cash, 41. It was an exciting year, a year in which

Roger Maris, complete with asterisk, became the Home-Run King of baseball.

Before the advent of television and of the "new journalism," an athlete to be idolized needed only to be proficient on the field. The guy could have been the meanest, nastiest son of a bitch since Simon Legree, but if he could hit consistently with men on base or pitch with lightning speed, he was a hero, and how he treated his fellow man was quite irrelevant.

By 1961, however, television made Roger Maris visible and instantly recognizable even to those people who didn't know a stolen base from a stolen car. To the fan, the personality of the athlete had become as important as his statistics, and Maris's isolationist philosophy served to make him look both belligerent and nasty. In truth, toward most people he was neither of these. To most he was an honest, outspoken, unsophisticated man who was kind and considerate to his friends and warm and loving to his family. To those who infringed upon his privacy, especially to newspaper reporters who dogged his every step during his home-run chase, he was irritable, unfriendly, and distant. As a result, the reporters wrote what they observed: that Maris was irritable, unfriendly, and distant. Thus the fans who read the papers saw Maris in this light, and when they came to the ballpark, they believed that to boo Maris was to boo a Snidely Whiplash in pinstripes, a man who would tie Little Nell to the railroad tracks and watch the train run over her. This image of Maris made the equally closemouthed Mickey Mantle in comparison look like Dudley Dooright, the man who would ride in and save Little Nell. Neither characterization was accurate, but the fans saw these two men this way, and to this day their respective images have remained.

Maris's problems with the press and the fans really began the day in December 1959 when it was announced that George Weiss had obtained him from the Kansas City Athletics. To most players, going to the Yankees was an honor and a privilege. It was a chance for World Series loot. To Maris, a devout family man, it meant being separated from his wife and children, since he didn't want to uproot them from their Kansas City home.

When the trade was announced, the New York reporters immediately called Maris for a comment. They expected to hear how thrilled he was to be coming to New York. Instead, Maris said that he liked it in Kansas City and didn't want to leave. "I know that financially I can do much better in New York," he said. "Therefore I will go." It was not a diplomatic answer, but it was honest, consistent with his basic philosophies of life: "To thine own self be true" and "Don't bullshit me." It was his strict adherence to his own principles that caused Maris to be labeled a malcontent and a troublemaker.

In 1953, when Roger signed with the Cleveland Indians, the club wanted him to start at Daytona Beach, Florida, in Class D. Maris insisted on playing for Fargo, a Class C team in his hometown, where he could play in front of friends and be with his girl. The Indians said no. Roger refused to accept no for an answer and said that he wouldn't play. He'd go out and work for a living. Roger got his way, played at Fargo, and hit .325. This stubbornness nevertheless began his reputation as a troublemaker. Maris, however, felt he knew what was best for Maris and figured that what was best for him was also going to be best for whoever was paying his salary.

In 1954 Cleveland wanted Maris to spend another year at Fargo. This time Roger demanded to be promoted. He was, to Keokuk in Class B, where he hit .315 with thirty-two home runs and twenty-five stolen bases. In '55 he was promoted to Tulsa in Class AA. Early in the season, after Maris overthrew third base from right field and cost the team a game, the Tulsa manager, Dutch Meyer, ordered a special practice for Maris. Meyer hit fly balls to right field, and the embarrassed and enraged youngster practiced his throwing to third. After a number of long throws, Maris, steaming at what he felt to be an unjust humiliation, tucked his glove under his arm and walked off the field while Meyer stood at home plate with his fungo bat, screaming, "Get back out there." Maris resolutely continued to the dugout and into the locker room.

"I'll never take abuse from anybody, big or small, important or unimportant, if I think it's undeserved," Maris said. "You've got to have enough pride to stand up for yourself." Maris was immediately demoted to Reading. Meyer was fired shortly thereafter.

In 1956 Maris starred for Reading, where Yankee general manager George Weiss first noticed the youngster, and in 1957 he starred at Indianapolis, the top minor-league team in the Cleveland organization. Weiss followed Maris's progress.

In 1957 he finally was brought up to the Indians. Weiss told Kansas City A's owner Arnold Johnson that if he could trade for Maris, the Yankees would trade the A's for him and then make an offer Johnson would not be able to refuse. Weiss knew that Cleveland general manager Frank Lane would never trade Maris to the Yankees. Injuries and another Maris feud made it possible for Johnson to acquire Maris in mid-1958. Weiss, true to his word, acquired Maris from the A's in the winter of 1959. It is said that when Weiss acquired Bob Turley and Don Larsen in the winter of 1954, he set the rest of the American League back five years. When he acquired Maris in the winter of 1959, he set it back another five years.

The Yankees in 1959 had finished a dismal third. In 1960 Maris helped return the franchise to its winning tradition. In 1960 he hit thirty-nine home runs, in '61 he hit sixty-one to break Babe Ruth's record, in '62 he hit thirty-three, and in '63, though he was out half the season with injuries, he still managed to hit twenty-three home runs. In 1964 Maris hit twenty-six home runs, and then in '65 he broke his hand and played sparingly as the Yankees plummeted. For five years Roger Maris was one of the great home-run hitters in the game, and teamed with Mantle, they were the most fearsome one-two punch since Ruth and Gehrig.

Casey Stengel, who managed him in 1960, didn't completely understand the closemouthed Maris. "That's Maris," Casey said. "You tell him something, and he'll stare at you for a week before answering," but Casey nevertheless appreciated his excellence as a complete ballplayer. "I give the man a point for speed," Casey said. "I do this," he said with unassailable logic, "because Maris can run fast. Then I can give him a point because he can slide fast. I give him another point because he can bunt. I also give him a point because he can field. He is very good around the fences—sometimes on top of the fences. Next I give him a point because he can throw. A right fielder has to be a thrower or he's not a right fielder. So I add up my points," Casey concluded, "and I've got five for him before I even come to his hitting. I would say this is a good man."

Maris was far better than a good man. Back-to-back in 1960 and 1961 he won the Most Valuable Player award in the American League. In '61 he won the Hickok Belt for the best professional athlete of the year. He was named the Top Catholic Athlete of the Year. He won the Sultan of Swat award, the Bill Corum award from the New York City B'nai B'rith. What he never won was a sympathetic press. At banquets he was criticized for mumbling "thanks" and sitting down. The Yankees kept getting letters complaining that he didn't speak. It was reported that the Yankees tried to explain to Maris the value of public speaking and that they even wrote a speech for him. "I'm no speaker," Maris protested.

When spring training of 1962 began, Maris figured that the pressures the media placed on him would cease. He was wrong. From the start of spring training there was a new set of standard questions, the most prevalent one being "Will you hit sixty-two home runs in 1962?" Maris became angry whenever someone asked him that. "This was the first time in thirty-four years that someone hit sixty home runs. Anybody who expects me to do it again must have rocks in his head," he replied.

In March his worst public-relations problems began when a reporter from the Fort Lauderdale *News* wrote that when one youngster asked Maris for an autograph, Maris wrote an *X* on the ball. It was a malicious, false accusation, making Maris appear cruel to children. Maris was livid. He had made an *X*, but Maris, who liked kids, was only making a joke and afterward signed a personal inscription and his signature. Maris vowed not to talk to any reporters from the local Florida papers. The next day a Miami reporter asked Maris, "How do you think you'll do this season?" "No comment," growled Maris. "How much do you weigh?" "No comment," Maris answered. "Do you think we should sign a nuclear-disarmament treaty with the Russians?" "No fucking comment," Maris growled. Maris then explained that his new policy was not to give interviews. "Let 'em write what they want," said Roger. "Ted Williams was right. Go your way and let the writers go theirs."

A few days later, the day after St. Patrick's Day, Oscar Fraley, the author of the "The Untouchables," the TV show starring Robert Stack as Eliot Ness, wrote an article for UPI about Maris that was prominently displayed at the top of the Fort Lauderdale sports page. Fraley had never met Maris or even talked to him, but he knew he didn't like him, anyway. Fraley criticized Maris for his refusal to be courteous with newspapermen and submit to interviews. "If either of my two sons has a hero," Fraley concluded in his article, "I hope it's a modest fellow named John Glenn, who went for the circuit when it really counted. Because guys like Maris bat a round zero with me."

When the fighting-mad Maris finally caught up with Fraley, Roger called him every name in the book, publicly, to his face. "If you weren't so old," Maris told him, "I'd knock you right on your ass." He stormed into the clubhouse. Following behind him was Jimmy Cannon, the highly respected journalist from the New York *Journal-American*. "Can I talk to you?" Cannon asked the shaken Maris. "Not now," Maris said. "Later." Cannon shot back, "Go fuck yourself."

Two days later Cannon began a two-part series. The headlines of the two columns read: "Maris—'The Whiner'—a Threat to Yank Pennant" and "Maris Envies Mantle's Prestige Among Yankees." It was another distorted piece by an irate journalist who should have controlled his temper and been more objective. "The community of baseball feels Mantle is a great player," Cannon wrote. "They consider Maris a thrilling freak who batted .269 . . . but his reputation is demolished when they compare him to Mantle. This apparently irritates Maris, who gives the impression that he inhabits a league filled with enemies. Obviously Maris considers Mantle a competitor instead of a partner on a team."

By this time Maris was ready to pack his bag and go home. His character had suffered such assassination that if he had discovered a cure for cancer he still would have been thought of as an arrogant and aloof scientist. "Rude Roger," some writers were calling him in the papers. Cannon continued to call him the Whiner.

There was yet another ugly scene. A photographer asked Maris to pose with New York Mets coach Rogers Hornsby, one of the game's great hitters. Maris, still seething at the beating he was taking, did not want to pose. During the 1961 season Hornsby had said that there was only one thing Maris could do as well as Babe Ruth, and that was run. In his agitated state, Maris saw Hornsby as another critic who had been taking potshots at him. The headlines in the papers the next day read, "Hornsby Calls Maris 'Little Punk Ball Player!' " "I've posed with some real major leaguers, not bush leaguers like he is," Hornsby said.

Before the end of spring training Roger was so agitated that he didn't know his friends from his enemies. He even offended the elderly Dan Daniel of the *World-Telegram*, one of Maris's strongest supporters. "Maris will have to learn to laugh, even while bleeding internally," Daniel wrote. "If he continues to be the Angry Man, may the Lord have mercy on him. The customers won't."

And the customers didn't. When Roger did not hit sixty-two home runs in 1962, he was booed. When he responded to the booing by giving the finger to the fans, the booing increased. By the end of 1962 Maris had hit thirty-three home runs, an excellent total for anyone else but unsatisfactory to the fans. The booing upset the Yankee management. If Manager Houk had not insisted that Maris remain with the Yankees, General Manager Roy Hamey would have traded him at the end of '62. The booing continued. He was a marked man.

"Some kids feel they're big shots if they boo me," Maris said. "I don't have to explain why I don't like certain fans. Would you like it if someone threw a beer can at you? How 'bout if someone threw a bottle at you?

"What the hell," Maris said philosophically, "as long as I stay in New York, it's going to keep on. They're on my back, and they're never going to get off. There's no use letting it bug me." Maris was right. They never did get off his back, even after he helped lead the Yankees to five straight pennants. The booing did, however, bug him.

The writers never got off his back, either. It was never written that Maris was surly because he was bitter. "Charm is not his strong suit," wrote writer Charles McCabe. "He is said to feel he should be paid to smile. And maybe even breathe. It is believed that in his sleep he intones the stirring shibboleth of the professional athlete, 'What's in it for me?' He is a redneck. He ain't bright. He's about as lovable as a tarantula. And he ain't even hitting .300 these days." "What would the New York writers say," said Maris, "if they knew my uncle was Adolph Eichmann?"

His teammates, traveling with him every day, felt that Maris was a straightforward, no-nonsense person. They admired him for his courage, marveled at his sixty-one home runs in the face of intense pressure, and respected him for what he was: the best right fielder in the American League. Around his teammates Maris did not have to pick and choose every word. He had a cutting, Billy Martin type of humor, so that when Ellie Howard got on the bus, Martin would say, "Ellie, get in the back," and everyone would laugh. "Hey, Mick," Maris would say, "I'm not talking to you today. I'm jealous of you." Roger, contrary to what McCabe wrote, was not a dumb guy. He was, in fact, quite articulate around his friends—only around his friends. He had been burned too often to trust any strangers.

In 1964 Maris's hitting was the key factor in the Yankees' winning the pennant, his last great Yankee hurrah. In June 1965 Maris, playing despite a pulled hamstring muscle, tried to score from second base on a base hit. When he slid home, he dislocated two fingers on his right hand when they caught on the spikes of umpire Bill Haller, who had been standing too close to the plate. Several days later, batting against Washington, he felt something pop in the palm of his right hand while swinging the bat. There was no official diagnosis of what had happened to him, but throughout the season the Yankee bulletins kept saying Maris was almost ready to play. When the season ended, Maris had not played one inning after the June injury. The hand was so badly injured he was unable to turn a doorknob with it. It was broken. Maris played again in 1966 but was only a shadow of his old self. The fans still booed him, the press still picked on him, and his performance suffered terribly. He hit .233 with thirteen home runs and only drove in forty-three runs. The Yankees finished last. In December 1966 Yankee general manager Lee MacPhail traded Maris to the St. Louis Cardinals for Cardinal third baseman Charlie Smith, the ex-Met, White Sox, Phillie, and Dodger who never hit too well and wasn't much of a fielder, either. It was the final insult from the Yankees. Roger Maris for Charlie Smith. When Maris led the Cardinals to pennants in 1967 and 1968 it was Maris who had the last laugh. In his first time at bat in a Cardinal uniform Maris hit a double and went flying into second. The Cardinal fans gave him a standing ovation. He was made. He was promised a beer distributorship by Gussie Busch, the Budweiser beer baron who owns the Cardinals. In 1968 he retired to his Gainesville, Florida, home to run that beer distributorship.

I was aware of Maris's antipathy toward the media when I wrote him a letter asking him if I could talk to him. When he didn't write back, I assumed that he wished to continue his anonymity. Then, while driving through the Southeast, on a hunch I detoured through Gainesville, Florida, hoping to find him working at his beer distributorship, located near the Gainesville airport. When I arrived, he wasn't there, and I waited two hours for him. All the employees, including his brother, said that they did not know where he was or how he could be reached. The only evidence that Roger Maris was associated with the operation was a Sultan of Swat trophy, awarded for his home-run hitting, and a Most Valuable Player Award, tarnished mementos that sat alone, unexplained, on the bottom shelf of a drab brown glass-enclosed case, the silver bowls uncared-for symbols of an uncherished past.

After waiting fruitlessly, I went to visit with Bill Skowron in Dunnellon, Florida, about 75 miles south of Gainesville. Skowron and Maris were close friends, and Bill generously offered to call Roger and ask him if he would have breakfast with us. "I'd love to see you, Moose," Maris said, "but leave the other guy home." After writing Maris another letter, I gave up.

Months later, when I was arranging to see Clete Boyer in Atlanta, I called Clete to tell him when I was coming. Clete said, "I got a buddy of mine down here with me. Roger Maris."

"Will he talk with me?" I asked.

"I don't know," Clete said. "You'll have to see."

We met at Boyer's nightclub, the Golden Glove, where a live band was playing very loud rock music in the darkly lit, low-ceilinged bar. Boyer, Maris, and I sat down at a table, ordered drinks, and made small talk for a minute or two. Clete then excused himself to go to the bar and talk business. I was left alone at the table with Maris, who hasn't changed much since his playing days. He still looked like the son of Odin, a sandy-haired Viking with piercing eyes and broad shoulders. I told him about some of his Yankee teammates I had seen, but I didn't come right out and ask him if he would talk. I didn't want to ask, because if he said no, it would have spoiled everyone's evening. Maris and I sat over our drinks, minutes of deadly silence hanging heavily while the blaring of the raw rock music was drowning out coherent thought. I was groping for a comfortable topic when Roger looked up from his drink. "This noise is really brutal," he said. "Let's go out into the parking lot. We can talk there." He got up to go. I followed.

The air outside was fresh, and though the music was still audible, it was no longer piercing. I sat on one of the parked autos while Maris stood alongside, sipping his drink. Seeing my tape recorder, Roger nodded toward the music. "You'll get some good background music." He smiled. Already I was saying to myself, *Is this the Roger Maris who kicks dogs and hates children?*

"I guess," I said, choosing my words carefully, "the thing I want to ask you about most is that after 1961, when you hit all those home runs, your relationship with the Yankees deteriorated. You had problems with newspapermen, the fans were really lousy, and it was just a bad thing." Now I had to phrase the question properly. "What are your feelings today about all the things that happened to you in New York?" I asked.

Maris sipped his drink. "Actually," he said, "I don't really feel that bad about it. It's something that happened, something that I had no control over. It was the writers' control. Sure, things could have been handled a lot differently by the Yankees. But they weren't. And it was just something that . . ." He paused and shrugged his shoulders. "Who knows how they happened or why they happened? It's stuff that's gone behind me, and really, it hasn't bothered me a lick." He paused again. "It would have been a lot nicer had it been the other way around, but . . ." A shrug.

"It almost seemed that everyone was holding this tremendous feat that you had performed against you," I said.

"Well," Maris said, "you might call it that. I guess I came along and did something that evidently was sacred, something that nobody was supposed to do. Especially me."

"Did this feeling against you affect your play?" I asked.

"There's no question about it," Maris said. "You don't go out there and play one hundred and sixty-two ball games and have people on your back continuously day in and day out and not have it affect your play. It took a lot away from the game as far as I personally was concerned. Naturally you're trying to do your best, but when all the elements are somewhat against you, I don't really feel that I got the best out of me."

"You were under a great deal of pressure," I said.

"Well, like I said before, and I'll say again, as far as playing the ball game, there was no pressure. Playing was probably the easiest part of it. Well, mentally it got pretty strong, the press before and after the ball games, the continuous questions, continuously trying to be on your guard because there were a certain few looking for you to maybe make a slip. I'm not trying to knock anybody, you understand, but when you're trying to answer one question, someone else butts in with another thing, and another guy comes in on half of what you said, and they misinterpret, and through all the continuous questions being fired at you, the pressure was quite strong. Mentally it was tough. I needed time off, and in the last week I took a day off."

"In the spring of the next year, the spring of '62, it was one incident after another."

"Yeah," Roger said. "There were a lot of things I didn't understand. There are a lot of things I won't ever understand. But," he said, again shrugging, "these things happen. They have happened to other ballplayers before me, a certain few. But like I say, unfortunately I was one of those few who had that type of publicity, and you just somewhat have to live with it. The Fraley article, for instance," he said. "After I read that, I was burning, and I just didn't want to talk with anyone. And Jimmy Cannon came over and asked me if he could talk to me, and I said, 'Jimmy, not right now. I'm not in the mood to talk with anyone.' And we were close friends, I thought. Every morning we had breakfast together. And Jimmy said to me, 'If that's the way you feel, the hell with you.' And that was the end of our friendship." There was a look of hurt and disappointment on Roger's face. "I really thought our friendship was worth more than that," Roger said. "To me it's all over and done with, what happened with the Yankees, and the people I got to know, I let them judge me for themselves. I just let it go at that."

"Any number of your teammates," I said, "told me that there was one season when you had a broken wrist, and the doctor didn't even tell you it was broken."

"It was a broken hand," Roger said. "Someone was told not to tell me; I can't say it was the doctor."

"Ralph Houk certainly must have known that the X rays showed it to be broken," I said.

"Well, I'm sure Ralph knew about it," Maris said. "It's sort of a peculiar thing. I didn't feel that I was just the ordinary run-of-the-mill ballplayer, and to break a hand in May and not find out about it until a week before the season was over in September . . . you know? And it just sort of seems strange, because the whole time they kept saying it was a day-to-day proposition. I felt personally that there were a few people who made me look like I didn't *want* to play, that I was just there to draw a salary. And I really didn't think that was too right, either.

"Once I broke the hand in '65, though," he said, "really, it was all over for me, because even today I don't have the gripping strength in two fingers of my right hand. I would swing the bat and have that hand slip right out there.

"It was sort of a disappointing thing," he continued, "because the ball club had taken X rays. We took X rays in Washington. We took them in Minneapolis. We took them in New York, and there was never any mention of a break. At first it started out I could go out in the field and take infield, throw the baseball. Then the ball club every four or five days asked me to take batting practice, so I'd go ahead and try a few swings, and it didn't work, and it got to the point where I couldn't even throw a baseball, 'cause I couldn't hold the baseball in my hand. And yet they were asking me to continuously take the batting practice. Now I'm not going to knock Mr. Houk. I'm not going to knock anybody. Everybody's going to draw their own conclusions. There are just a lot of things that I don't understand, and I never will. A lot of things. I just don't want to get into knocking Ralph. I've got my own personal feelings. I feel that a lot of things could have been handled a lot differently than they were, and naturally I was quite disappointed in the way they were handled. I can turn around and say something in my defense, and that means nothing.

So you end up sitting back and saying, 'Let it quiet down.' I was more interested in just having things quiet down than continuously bringing up things from the past.''

"There reached a point," I said, "near the end of your Yankee career you told Lee MacPhail you weren't going to play in New York anymore."

"No," Roger said. "I really didn't say it that way. I said that I was not going to play anymore. Anywhere. I had plans to retire after the '66 season, and I told Ralph Houk that. I told Ralph that in July of '66, and when I came to the end of the season, rather than announce I was not going to play the following year, Ralph told me to wait till spring training before I announced it to make sure of what I was doing. So I said okay, and I went home after the season ended. Lee MacPhail called me up one day and asked me if I had changed my mind. I said, 'No, I haven't.' But just detecting the way he was talking, I thought he had something in mind, and I said, 'Lee, if you have any intentions of trading me, let me know now, and I'll announce my retirement.' He said, 'No, we have no intentions of trading you.' I said, 'Then let's just do it the way Ralph wanted to do it, wait till spring training, but I'm still not going to play.' And he said, 'Okay.' And a few days later I was traded. So I personally thought that they could have respected me a little bit by letting me retire if I wanted to retire instead of doing things the way they did them. If I wanted to retire, I think I should have had that much courtesy from the ball club. But when this came up the way it did, I had voiced to only a couple of people that I was retiring, and the writers would have made me look bad again. They'd say, 'Well, he's not going to play because he was traded away from the Yankees.' They would have jumped on me like it was a big news story. So I finally agreed to go ahead and play the year." Roger ultimately played two more years, an integral number of the 1967 and '68 pennant-winning Cardinals.

"Will you ever come back to New York?" I asked. "You never come back to the Old-Timers' Games."

"Oh," Maris said, "one day I'll come back. When, I don't know. Right now I just don't have the desire to do a lot of those things. Like this year I had many people writing letters to me, asking me to come back to the Old-Timers' Games in New York, and from what I understand, the ball club put out the word through the announcers that the reason I'm not coming back to New York for the Old-Timers' Game is because I'm afraid the people are going to boo me." Roger smiled and shook his head. "I've been booed by the best of them for many years," he said. "The ball club is trying to push off, 'Well, bad ole Roger again, he's not going to come out because the poor boy is afraid of boos.' That's not the case. I have had other reasons why I have not wanted to go up there. The ball club knows what they are. Ralph Houk knows what they are. Lee MacPhail knows what they are."

"But aren't Ralph and Lee gone?" I asked.

Roger grimaced slightly and nodded, but his silent response indicated that though the two men were not Yankee executives any longer, the wounds they caused him still remained. There was something heroic in Maris's stoicism, in his insistence in not verbally retaliating against the men who helped sully his image.

"You've got to understand me," Maris said. "I've never believed in knocking people. Never. It's not my nature. I really don't even care to get into those kinds of things, 'cause all you do is reopen wounds. Right now Roger Maris is in Podunk. Nobody knows he's around. You know? Half of us haven't heard of him in the last five years, and it's beautiful. I really hate to reopen old wounds. No news is good news. This is basically what it amounts to."

Clete Boyer joined us in the parking lot, and following him was an older woman, tottering slightly, and in her hand was a Polaroid camera. "Can I take your picture?" she asked Boyer, a hometown Atlanta favorite. "Why, sure you can," Clete said graciously. "Roger Maris is here, too. You can get both of us together." The lady didn't register any surprise or delight that Clete's friend Maris was there, too. "You know who Roger is, don't you?" Clete asked the woman.

"No, ah don't," she said.

Roger, posing with Boyer, smiled. "That's just the way I like it."

This is the opening of *The Celebrant*, a novel little noted upon its publication in 1983 but one that has since steadily risen in stature. Greenberg's agreeably archaic style combines with an evident appetite for the game—he gets the baseball *right*, as no contemporary novelist has except perhaps Mark Harris—to produce what is, in this editor's opinion, the most satisfying of all baseball novels. In the following passage, Greenberg fillets that curious phenomenon of hero worship and exposes its cannibalistic core: the hope and dream of the fan for merged identity and transference of powers.

ERIC ROLFE GREENBERG

Hero

Our family came to New York in the winter of '89, and in the spring I saw my first game of baseball. I was eight. My mother's brother, a jeweler, had preceded us across the Atlantic; Uncle Sid's family was small—only four children—but the crowding was awful, and in April my father thought to find a place of our own across the river in Brooklyn. He inquired of a German-speaking landlord near Prospect Park, who asked if there were children; my father answered "nine," the German nodded, and the two men shook hands. The following Sunday we stacked all we owned onto a rented dray and, daunted by the spectacular height of the new bridge, crossed the river by ferry. We returned before nightfall, much abashed. The German had understood my father to say he had no children, and when he arrived with nine, the door was slammed in his face.

I missed this famous encounter. I'd run off to the park after my older brother Eli and discovered there clay diamonds cut into an immense field of grass, an expanse so generous that half a dozen ball games were under way at once, some so distant that they appeared contests between toy miniatures. But toy players could hardly have amazed me more than these—adults! grown men playing games!—and many in uniforms complete with gaudy striped stockings. Far away a bat struck a ball; seconds later I heard the sound. This phenomenon was a great excitement, and I ran back and forth, altering the time lapse until I was nearly trampled by an outfielder in furious pursuit of a fly ball. I dodged as he sprang, and as he stretched out in full flight, the side of his shoe caught

my cheek. I reeled and fell down. The ball bounded on, and the man who'd kicked me spat dirt from his mouth, looked up, and said, "Well, *shit!*"—the first words ever spoken to me on a ball field.

The family stayed in Manhattan. We found the game everywhere, in every imaginable variation. There were large lots along both rivers that allowed the full exercise, and each street and alley had its own rules and exceptions. First by imitation, then by practice, we learned the game and the ways of the boys who played it, the angle of their caps, the intonations of their curses and encouragements. Our accents disappeared; our strides became quick and confident. My left-handedness, regarded by my parents as a devil's curse, turned to my advantage in the pitcher's box. I threw a submarine ball, my knuckles grazing the dirt as I released it. "Get those knuckles dirty, Jackie!" my infielders would shout—Jackie, not Yakov.

The new fashion of overhand pitching soon threatened my eminence. When the National League legalized the pitch, the neighborhood clubs followed suit; I tried the style but had trouble keeping the ball low, and it's the high pitch that's hit a distance. Our team enlisted a big fellow who could throw the overhand pitch with mustard, and to counter his advantage, I attempted to learn the curve. It was accounted a disreputable pitch, the refuge of a trickster who had not the honest strength to power the ball over the plate. I found it difficult, for my fingers were too short to give the ball sufficient spin. Soon I was in the outfield, not liking the change; pitching is the core of the game. Vowing to master the curve, I threw to Eli for an hour every evening in the narrow alley behind our tenement. The youngsters on the block would come out and carry on as if I were pitching for the Giants against the Orioles for the Temple Cup: "Keeler's up, Jackie; watch it now! Ball one—come on, put it over! The curve, the curve! Oh, he hit it! Base hit! Now Jennings—better bear down, Jackie! McGraw's on deck!"

Finally, at fifteen, I made the curveball work. I threw it as hard as the fast one, and it broke just as it reached the plate, a small break but a sharp one, straight down. It was a ground-ball pitch, and it kept my infielders busy. In tandem with the big fellow I won a good many ball games and achieved something of a neighborhood celebrity.

At the close of the '97 season the league sponsored an awards dinner at a restaurant on Grand Street, and there I shook hands with a major-league player. His name was Jack Warner. I'd watched him play shortstop for an uptown semiprofessional club, marveling at his size and power, but he lacked speed, and the professional leagues had made him first an outfielder, then a catcher. His face showed the marks of that ignoble position. At the dinner, his eyes never leaving the page, he delivered a speech analogizing baseball and life. Practice, dedication, clean living, and fair play—these guaranteed success on and off the field. We froze in a handshake while a photographer immortalized the moment, and then I took a silver cup from him. He turned to the organizer of the event and asked for his fee.

In the spring I was asked to a professional tryout at Manhattan Field, far uptown. Men with leather faces and tobacco-stained teeth examined me microscopically and stood in at bat as I pitched. A week later a letter arrived, the first I'd ever received, offering a contract with the Altoona club of the New York–Pennsylvania League.

My parents wouldn't hear of it.

Prizefighters, jockeys, ballplayers: these were professional athletes. Most celebrated were the fighters at the championship level; heavyweight Corbett could get a room at most hotels, and it was said that the better people of San Francisco welcomed him to their salons. The exemplary Gentleman Jim thus crossed once-impregnable barriers, but the gulf between his status and that of the journeyman was vast. Club fighters were neighborhood heroes, yet the unspoken assumption was that they fought because they were unfit to do anything else; a man did not opt for the ring, he was condemned to it. Most jockeys were black, apprenticed to trainers or breeders; one thought of them as one thought of the horses they rode. Some professional ballplayers were locally bred, but an increasing number were itinerants from distant farmlands who lived out of cardboard suitcases in back-street boardinghouses. Annually they jumped from league to league and team to team for the sake of a few dollars' increase in salary. To bankers and landlords and shopkeepers they were suspect, disreputable; to a man with daughters they were dangerous. An underclass supported them. Ballpark crowds were mean and roistering.

I was seventeen and done with school; I'd stayed at it longer than most. All the pressure of a family's traditions, hopes, and plans pressed down upon me. I was the fifth son; the first had driven teams to put the second through college, and the third, Eli, sold my Uncle Sid's jewelry to see the fourth through his studies. I was obliged to provide for young Sam's higher education. I argued that I could do this on a ballplayer's salary, $20 a month, but though my parents came to believe that I'd actually be paid to play ball, the issue went far deeper than money. We had not crossed the ocean to find disgraceful employment.

I had not the wherewithal to resist my parents. Rather than be dead to them—for my father threatened to turn his back to me and say a kaddish for my soul—I put away the contract and assumed Eli's position at Uncle Sid's jewelry store, while Eli packed a case of samples and sought markets in faraway cities. I was no sales clerk, nor as proficient as my cousins in working the precious metals and stones, but I did show a flair for design. Should a customer find nothing on display to his liking, I'd inquire what he had in mind and quickly sketch a model; often enough, a sale would result. Once I turned this trick to delight a trio of sisters who were shopping for an anniversary present for their parents. When the piece was done, I delivered it to their home, far uptown in Turtle Bay—and what a home, a mansion with fantastic wrought-iron fencing at the doors and windows and an interior elegance that to my mind quite belied the small mezuzah posted at the entry. That Jews could achieve such grandeur was well nigh unbelievable.

The next week the youngest of the daughters returned to the shop to thank me and to order another piece. She was merry; she kept me so long at the sketch pad with her suggestions and alterations that Uncle Sid had to bustle us out of the store at closing time. I escorted her home by trolley and learned her name—Edith—while she learned of me everything I could babble in an hour. When our club played in Central Park the following Sunday, she was there with her sisters; they carried matching parasols that spun prettily in their gloved hands. I pitched well that day, breaking off the curveball time after time. Afterward we shared lemonade in the Ramble.

The next day I could hardly lift my arm. The curveball was proving too great a strain. I needed a week between turns, and soon that wasn't enough. In the end I was back in the outfield, where the dream of Altoona and the big leagues faded. Playing less, I found time for afternoons with Edith; often I had to choose between her company at a concert or museum and Eli's for a ball game. Once my brother had offered to escort all three Sonnheim girls to the Polo Grounds; the suggestion scandalized Edith's father, who coldly opined that baseball had ceased to be a gentleman's game after the Civil War, when it had been taken over by professional athletes. Might as well recommend a tour of the Tenderloin!

In deep summer, with Edith at her family's lodge on Lake George, I was ever at the ballpark—the new Polo Grounds, where the Giants were declining from their glory years of the early nineties, or more frequently the Atlantic Avenue park in Brooklyn to watch the Superbas, stocked with Baltimore veterans, driving to the championships of '99 and 1900. Eli would introduce me to his sporting friends as his "expert" and make a great show of consulting me in whispers before placing a bet. It seemed he required a wager to excite his interest, whereas for me the game was all.

As the spring of 1901 turned toward summer, Eli urged me to join him on his annual "big swing" west to the Mississippi, north to Chicago, and east along the Lakes. "Sport, we'll eat a steak and see a ball game in every city!" he swore. Uncle Sid accepted Eli's contention that my designs would be improved with a better knowledge of our markets, and Edith was away. I bought a suitcase—leather, not cardboard—and packed for my first excursion beyond the Hudson. Our first calls were in Philadelphia, where the steaks weren't much to speak of and the ball game worse. The National League club was on the road, and we decided to test the infant American League, which had no New York franchise. The great attraction was Napoleon Lajoie, whose batting average for the Americans was a hundred points above what he'd hit for Philadelphia's Nationals the year before. His outrageous success seemed proof of the new league's inferiority. Nap was one of several former collegians courted for the club by Philadelphia's gaunt manager, Connie Mack; another was Plank, who pitched that day and easily beat the Milwaukee entry. Lajoie had three hits and scored twice.

We caught up with the Philadelphia Nationals in Pittsburgh. They missed Lajoie; the home club beat them authoritatively to move further ahead in the race. In Cincinnati dwelt a cadet branch of the family, and we stayed nearly a week. A second cousin, whose face was a startling female approximation of my brother Sam's, took me on an outing along the river and somehow contrived a rainstorm, a sheltering toolshed, and a blanket, but she could not contrive a different face, and the matter came to nothing. To my joy, the Cincinnati Red Stockings arrived for the latter part of our visit, and with them our own wonderful Brooklyn club, Ned Hanlon and his boys, the defending World Champions. But the club was fading, the old Baltimore heroes further past their prime, and we sensed there would be no pennant flying over Atlantic Park at year's end.

On a Saturday morning in mid-July we stepped off the westbound train into the heat of St. Louis and proceeded to the Chase Hotel. My brother always put up at the best hotels, signing as "E. Kapp." The name Kapinski would not be welcome on those registers. As I unpacked, he searched out sheaves of the hotel's stationery and addressed invitations to the buyers of the town, requesting the honor of their presence at our "suite" on the Monday following. That done, he summoned an assistant manager to lay plans for breakfast, mid-morning, and luncheon service: oysters and champagne, deviled eggs, a variety of sausage to suit the Swiss and Germans among our clientele. (Later Eli would cadge some kosher delicacies for our coreligionists, some of whom would first set foot in the Chase at our invitation.) He would welcome them all; he would tell the latest tales and gags; he would profess that, had he a choice, he would visit them at their offices, but to carry his samples on the dangerous streets was to court dire attack; he would show his wares and write his orders. In such ways did Eli advance the family business as it increasingly turned from retailing to manufacture. A middle-range market was emerging between the jeweler's private customer and the mail-order public, and the avenue to it was the department store. Our product line was priced below the artisan's custom work and above the COD merchandise that Eli accurately described as cheap junk. His job was to secure outlets against the efforts of dozens of direct competitors, and he shared the rails with a gaggle of salesmen hawking hardware or hose or outrageous feathered wraps; together they were inventing the business of the new century. Not all stayed at the grand hotels, but my brother would have put up at the Chase (or Boston's St. James or Baltimore's Belvedere) had his suitcase carried sandstone or cement.

Yet for all this show, his delight was to invite guests to the local ballpark. He'd staked this out as his personal form of business entertainment, leaving the burlesques and bawdy houses to his fellows of the selling trade. Here professional calculation matched his personal inclination. For himself, Eli Kapinski of New York, no fancy out-of-town attraction could rival those of home, but a major-league ball game in any city carried a sort of guarantee. For his clients—what a disarming suggestion! An afternoon at the ballpark, so refreshing, so American!

Shortly before three o'clock on a cauterizing Monday we rented a hack, collected three buyers who'd breakfasted with us that morning, and set out for League Park. St. Louis in July was the hottest place on the circuit, the hottest place God ever made a city. Our guests blamed the heat for the team's sorry record in the National League; they'd never finished above fifth place. I pointed out that the city's entry had won four championships in the old American Association in the eighties. "Mildest summers on record," I was assured. This season their club had known early success, but now, beset by slump and injury, they were losing ground to Pittsburgh. Still the fans prayed for a cool summer and came to League Park in record number; more than 20,000, an unprecedented gathering, had encircled the field for the previous game of the current series with the New York Giants.

In the matter of rooting, a boy's first team is his team forever. I'd seen my first big-league game below Coogan's Bluff ten years before, and whatever Brooklyn's current success, the Giants were the club of my heart, their championships my own. But seven years' famine had followed the feast, and a dozen managers had come and gone under the club's owner, Tammany politico Andrew Freedman. A great war was waged between Freedman and my own idol, Amos Rusie, the huge right-hander who'd won thirty-six games in glorious '94. Rusie refused to sign a contract in '96, came back to win forty-eight games for a lesser club in '97 and '98, and then held out for two full seasons rather than throw another pitch for Freedman. He called the owner a liar, a chiseler, a welcher, and a cheat; Freedman called Rusie a Republican. They were both right. Without Rusie or any other player of great regard, the Giants finished last in 1900. They'd replaced most of their infield and half their mound staff, but their current fifth-place standing owed largely to the advent of a talented collegiate pitcher of their own, a right-hander who was scheduled to throw for New York.

Play had just begun when we arrived at League Park. We watched from the outfield as the Giants mounted an early attack. Sudhoff, the elfin St. Louis pitcher, began badly: a walk, a base hit, and then a drive that skipped under the right fielder's glove and rolled to our feet. The tallest of our clients, a thin man with merry eyes, kicked the ball back toward the fielder. Far away, in the middle of the diamond, the umpire threw up his hands and shouted, "Hold! Three bases!" Two Giants scored, and we moved with haste to the grandstand, a single-tiered wooden structure that rose along both foul lines. Having paid a quarter a head to enter the park grounds, we were now charged as much again to gain the grandstand and needed fifty cents more for box seats beneath the low, shading roof. But an attendant at the box-seat turnstile swore there was no room for us in the shade, and when Eli protested, he scolded us with Irish vigor: "You want to come out early these days, we're winning now, don't you know!" Finally we found room behind third base for three on one grandstand bench and for two more directly behind. The thin client and a bearded one flanked Eli, while the stoutest squeezed in next to me. We doffed our jackets and loosened our collars. The Giants had scored no more, and the teams had changed sides. Little Jess Burkett stood in for St. Louis, hands high on the bat, feet spread wide. Behind him, Patsy Donovan, who doubled as manager, picked at the tape around the handle of his bat. The sun burned down, the cries of the crowd floated in the humid air, and the umpire pointed a finger at the New York pitcher and bid him throw.

This pitcher was big—gigantic, compared to Wee Willie Sudhoff—yet his motion matched Sudhoff's for balance and ease until he pushed off the pitcher's slab with his right foot and drove at the plate with startling power. His follow-through ended in a light skip, and he finished on his toes, his feet well apart, his hands at the ready for a fielding play. I heard the umpire's call but didn't know if Burkett had swung and missed or taken the strike, for my eyes hadn't left the pitcher. He took the catcher's return throw and regained the hill in three strides. His broad shoulders and back tapered to a narrow waist; he wore his belt low on his hips, and his legs appeared taut and powerful beneath the billowing knickers of his uniform. A strong, muscular neck provided a solid trunk for a large head, and his cap was tipped rather far back on his forehead, revealing a handsome face and an edge of thick light brown hair. He bent for his sign, rolled into his motion, and threw; this time I followed the ball and saw Burkett top it foul.

The fat man moved against me, reaching for his kerchief. "Who's your pitcher?" he asked.

"It's Mathewson," I said. "Christy Mathewson."

"That's Mathewson? Big kid!"

"He is that. He's bigger than Rusie, that's for sure."

"Throws hard."

"Yes, he does."

"He's winning for you, isn't he?"

"Eleven games, best on the club."

"Not bad for new corn."

"Actually, he pitched a few last year," I said.

"Win any?"

"No. As a matter of fact, he lost two in relief. Then he went back to school."

Another fastball: Burkett's swing was late, and the ball bounced to first base. Ganzel gloved it and tossed underhand to Mathewson, who caught it in full stride and kicked the base for an out.

"He got over there in a hurry, too," the fat man observed.

"Hey, sport, take this and bring back some wieners and beer for us all, won't you?" said Eli, pushing a silver dollar into my hand. He winked and clapped my arm. "Hurry back, now; I'm going to need your advice."

I struggled to the aisle and headed along the walkway that divided the grand-stand benches from the box seats. As I reached the ramp, I paused to watch Donovan at bat. His red face was lined with a manager's web of worry. Patsy fought off the pitches with short, choppy swings, hitting several foul before earning a base on balls. Ganzel met him at first, and they exchanged a greeting. Ganzel was ancient, nearly forty, and Donovan beside him looked as old. I scanned the Giants in the field: Strang and Hickman, on either side of second base, were no striplings, and Davis, New York's playing manager at third, was older yet. They were all past thirty in the outfield. The catcher was Jack Warner, he of the awards dinner years before; already he was a veteran of years. Schriver, ready at the bat for St. Louis—enough to say that they called Schriver "Old Pop." At the center stood Mathewson, young as an April morning in that sweltering July, and I, small in the crowd at the top of the ramp, turned and walked down into the shadow beneath the grandstand.

The vendors at their sizzling grills cursed loudly as fat spattered on their aprons. All about, sports in checkered vests argued, passed money, and wrote betting slips. Every inning, sometimes every pitch, was worth a wager. With my dollar I bought five pigs-in-a-blanket and as many bottles of beer and pocketed two bits in change. I worked my way back up the ramp with some difficulty. Near our seats the fans came to my rescue, passing the food hand over hand to Eli with the efficiency of a fire brigade. I couldn't resist an urge to toss the quarter to my brother, who snared it backhanded. The section resounded with cheers, and the ballplayers on the field turned at the commotion.

"Still two–nothing, sport. Donovan was caught trying to steal. Hey, here we go again!" Eli cried as a base hit began the Giant second. But their game was all sock-and-run; after Strang's single, Warner flied out.

"They don't believe in the bunt, do they?" said the fat man.

"They won't win till they learn how," said Eli. "You've got to be able to lay it down, right, sport?"

"Here's Mathewson," I said. "He'll be bunting."

Eli looked at me. "A dollar says he brings off the sacrifice. All around?"

The clients accepted the wager. Sudhoff pitched, and Mathewson pushed the ball onto the grass and ran to first with the sprightly grace of a smaller man. He was narrowly out.

"He can bunt," the thin man conceded.

"Double or nothing that they score," said Eli.

Sudhoff walked a man, and the next nailed the first pitch on a low line over second base. Two Giants crossed home.

"Double or nothing they score again!" said Eli. I pushed my knee into his back, but he looked over his shoulder and winked. The three buyers took the bet and cheered when a fly ball ended the inning and wiped out their debts. Mathewson walked slowly to the pitcher's mound, dug at the slab with his toe, smoothed the dust, and worked into his warm-ups. Again his size and youth impressed. The bearded man beside Eli studied him.

"Mathewson, his name is?"

"College kid," said Eli. "Connie Mack signed him for Philly, but he jumped to New York."

"Where's he from?"

"Pennyslvania," said Eli at the same time that I said, "Bucknell College."

"Imagine a college man playing ball for a living!"

I mentioned Lajoie and Plank, whom we'd seen in Philadelphia, but the bearded man snorted that the new league would sign anyone, and while he knew Lajoie had played in a college uniform, he doubted the boy had ever seen the inside of a classroom. Nor had Mathewson, he'd wager.

The fat man turned to me. "But you said he went back to school after last season!"

"Quit the team in September to do it," I said.

"You've seen him before?"

No, I explained; in recent seasons the more talented Brooklyn club had caught my fancy, and I hadn't been among the few at the Polo Grounds when the rookie threw his first big-league pitches that summer or won his first victories in the spring. What I knew of Mathewson came from notes in the newspapers: his age, a year greater than my own, and his home, the farming country of the Susquehanna Valley; his fame as a Bucknell footballer. I knew he'd pitched in professional leagues in New England and Virginia and that while he'd put his name to a major-league contract with Connie Mack, he'd never worn a Philadelphia uniform. Instead, he'd come to New York, and now, in his first full year, he had a third of the club's victories. If his skills were the test, he belonged in the National League, but like the bearded client, I wondered why a true collegian would choose the life of a professional ballplayer.

The second inning ended quickly, and while Sudhoff hit his stride in the third, Eli began to orchestrate wagers with every batter. If I thought the proposition doubtful, I'd signal by pressing my knee into his back, but he ignored my advice as often as he accepted it, and I came to understand that a deeper game was in progress. Eli was selling jewelry, and it wouldn't do to take too much of his clients' money. Each time he won, he offered double or nothing on the next bet; at best he would finish little better than even, and at worst, far worse. I engaged in chatter with the partisans around us when the Giants batted or gazed over the Midwestern crowd dotted with wide-brimmed western hats among the standard derbies and occasional boater. Far down the right-field line was the only uncrowded grandstand section; there the coloreds sat in overalls and yellow straw hats. When St. Louis batted, I studied Mathewson. He could throw hard and with excellent control, shading the edges of the strike zone, mixing his fastball with a curve that seemed somehow erratic. Sometimes it fell an astonishing measure, while other times—what did it do? Certainly it behaved differently from the drop, but from our location I couldn't track the pitch. When St. Louis came to bat in the fifth inning, I excused myself and threaded my way to a spot close behind home plate. Now I could see the inner game, the fierce battle between pitcher and batter where power and control sought mastery over instinct and guess.

Mathewson began against Padden with a pitch that came in hard at belt level and dropped abruptly and dramatically, a superb overhand curve, and one that had wrenched my arm when I'd tried it. The second pitch was a fastball on the outside part of the plate, a second strike. Now another breaking ball, but so unlike the first, slower and breaking in reverse, in the nature of a left-hander's curve; I'd never seen a right-hander throw one. Nor had Padden, who swung late and was lucky to tip it foul. Padden stepped out of the box and shook his head like a man who'd just seen a rabbit leap out of his own hat. He took his stance a bit closer to the plate, leaning over to guard the outside corner. Then, in an instant, he was on his back in the dirt; comically, the bat landed on his head. Mathewson's fastball had reclaimed that disputed inside territory. Padden dusted off his knickers and took his stance farther off the plate. Mathewson stretched and threw another reserve curve, and Padden missed it badly. Strike three.

Mathewson worked through the St. Louis lineup just so. Always the first pitch was a strike, and usually the second; then a teasing pitch down low or that strange fading curve thrown where no batter could hit it squarely, if at all. His rhythm and motion were balletic: a high kick, a swing of the hips, a stride forward, and finally the explosive release of the ball. There was intelligence as well as power behind the pitches: he had a four-run lead and found it to his purpose to walk Kruger with two out in the fifth and then retire the light-hitting Ryan and to pass the dangerous Burkett in the sixth in favor of facing Donovan, who grounded out. When I rejoined Eli in the seventh inning, Mathewson had allowed three base runners but no hits.

"Think they'll get to him, sport?"

I'd never witnessed a no-hit game. I'd come close to pitching one four years before, as close as the eighth inning, but a swinging bunt that squiggled up the first-base line had foiled me, and in my disappointment I'd been racked for three runs. "He's doing pretty much what he wants," I said.

"A dollar says he gets by Schriver," Eli offered; the odds were heavily against a no-hitter, and betting with Mathewson seemed the safest way to protect the clients. Old Pop took a fastball for a strike, and the crowd booed. Its cries had taken on the anger of the heat and the temper of frustration. The fat man ground his cigar beneath his patent-leather boot and muttered something about Schriver; the club missed its injured sluggers. Mathewson pitched, and Pop grounded weakly to Strang at second base. One out in the seventh.

"Double or nothing, all around?"

Now Padden again, and the first pitch a high strike, the second higher yet— but Padden had no wish to wait for another curve and swung, lifting a fly to center field, where Van Haltren had hardly to move to glove it. Two outs now.

"Double or nothing?"

"It's a bet."

"What happens on a walk?" I asked.

"Do you think he'll pass him, sport?"

"He'll be careful with Wallace. It's his pattern."

Eli nodded. "I say he'll get him out. Double or nothing on an out." Mathewson's fastball flashed, and Wallace took it and jawed loudly at the umpire's strike call. Now that strange breaking pitch, and Wallace bounced it to third; he was out by two steps at first. The Giants came off the field as the crowd booed all the more, at Wallace, at the umpire, at the summer's merciless heat, at the cast of impending defeat.

The fat man tapped Eli on the shoulder. "It's four dollars now, right?"

"Two," said Eli.

"Four."

"No, the bet on Schriver brought us even."

"We were even before then. It's four."

"Well, if you insist," said Eli, laughing.

The Giants went down swiftly in the eighth, but New York's efforts at bat hardly mattered now; we wanted Mathewson pitching. In the St. Louis half he began with a strikeout, and the buyer's debts to Eli doubled to $8 apiece. The total was nearly a month's salary to me. Next was Ryan, hardly a threat; after taking two strikes, he chased a high fastball and lifted it to the center fielder's range. Van Haltren loped easily across the grass and reached out to cradle it, but the web of his glove seemed to fail him, and the ball dropped at his feet.

Twenty thousand roared, but the fat man shook his head. "An error," he said.

"It's all the same," said Eli, attempting a mournful expression. "We're even."

"No, as far as I'm concerned, it's an out."

"The man's on second base," said Eli.

"But the bet is on a no-hit game, isn't it? The pitcher against the hitter. The man should have been retired. Now, double or nothing?"

It seemed it was a matter of integrity, for which the fat man had a reputation; when Eli made to forgive the debts of the men flanking him, they proved no less upright than their colleague. They could play the inner game as well as my brother, for what might be lost in money was more than made in future favor. Word spread from the press benches that "error" was indeed the official call; the no-hitter was intact. Eli shifted ground: why not call the play "no bet"? The compromise was accepted, and the balance among the men reverted to $8 apiece.

While the party debated, I studied Mathewson. He showed no annoyance in the wake of the misplay. His team still led by four runs, the inning was late, and the weak-hitting Nichols was at bat, with pitcher Sudhoff to follow. Mathewson set, glanced at the base runner, and threw. Nichols's bunt was a surprise; the score, the inning, the pitcher on deck, all argued against it. Catcher Warner was slow to move after the ball, but Mathewson was upon it instantly, the ball in his glove, then in his hand, then at first base. Two outs, and $16 due to Eli from each of his clients.

"Double or nothing?"

Sudhoff, the little pitcher, hit the ball sharply, but Mathewson snatched it out of the air, and the inning was over. At the Giant bench Mathewson greeted center fielder Van Haltren with a forgiving slap on the rump. He was far more cheerful than Eli, a man due $96 of easy money. When Mathewson batted in the Giant ninth, he was applauded by the home fans, and I cheered. Mathewson tugged at the bill of his cap in acknowledgment. "Imagine, a college kid!" said the bearded client. Most of the crowd had conceded the game, and many would prefer a defeat of special regard to a spoiling single in the home ninth. For myself, I wanted three clean outs and a glorious end; our clients' purses were of no matter.

"Double or nothing?"

Burkett led off. Mathewson started with a fastball; for the hundredth time he took Warner's return throw and climbed the mound. On the right knee of his knickers was a round smudge of red clay, the emblem of a hundred strides and a hundred pitches launched. He bent, stretched, and pitched again, a fastball in on Burkett's hands; it ticked the bat and sailed past Warner, who walked slowly in the heat to retrieve it.

"Oh, college boy! Oh, you college boy!"

Mathewson stood on the hill, waiting for the catcher to return to position, his left leg slightly bent, his weight on the right. He gloved Warner's toss and bent for his sign, the ball resting in the pocket of his small brown glove. He seemed as fresh as when he had begun, and quite still: no heaving breath, no sleeve drawn across his face to clear the summer sweat. All question left me. This was Mathewson's place and moment; my whole being was with him. Burkett would not deny him, nor Donovan next or old Pop Schriver, that dark moving figure on the St. Louis bench.

"So young!" muttered the bearded man.

And I was old, I thought. I was older than Mathewson, older than Schriver, older than any of them in uniform. My youth had ended on a ragged lot by the Hudson when the curve ball had beaten my arm and my spirit—no, when I'd folded the contract into a drawer and reported for work at Uncle Sid's shop. I was on the road, yes, but as an old man, hawking samples in old men's hotels, learning how I might bet to keep old men happy. I watched Mathewson, and he became my youth; it was my fastball burning by Burkett, it was my curve that little Jess lifted to the outfield, and after the ball came back and around the infield, I felt it was my glove closing around it, my arm that launched the fastball at Donovan's knees and the next that cut the black of the plate on the outside. My youth made him chase a breaking ball in the dirt, and there were two outs; here was Old Pop, and I had the game and the no-hitter in my hand.

Curveball: Schriver lets it pass for a strike.

The other, fading curve: Schriver, off balance, swings and ticks the ball foul. Ganzel picks it up barehanded and throws it to me. Schriver is nervous; I see his hands moving on the bat, his heel twisting in the dirt.

I waste a pitch high, ball one. I take Warner's toss, wrap the ball in my glove, jam the package under my arm, reach for the resin, dust my hand. There is a lone, incomprehensible cry from the grandstand, then silence. I turn, I bend, I look for Warner's sign. I toe the slab. I stretch. I throw.

Ground ball.

I reach; it is past me—but Strang is there, he takes it on a high bounce, he waits for Ganzel, old Ganzel, to set himself at first, he snaps a sidearm throw, and the ball disappears into Ganzel's mitt.

The crowd's hoarse voice rises in the heat, the Giant bench empties, the fielders race to the mound, and the team leaps to touch and embrace—

Mathewson.

Those who know Zane Grey only for *Riders of the Purple Sage* and other purple-prose shoot-'em-ups may be surprised to learn of his connection with the national pastime. Not only did he publish three baseball books (including *The Redheaded Outfield*, in which this story appears), but he also was a star outfielder for the University of Pennsylvania, in 1896 making a spectacular catch that enabled the Quakers to defeat the New York Giants in an exhibition game. Moreover, he went on to play four seasons in the bush leagues (brother Reddy was a cup-of-coffee major leaguer) before finding his true vocation.

ZANE GREY

Old Well-Well

He bought a ticket at the twenty-five-cent window and, edging his huge bulk through the turnstile, laboriously followed the noisy crowd toward the bleachers. I could not have been mistaken. He was Old Well-Well, famous from Boston to Baltimore as the greatest baseball fan in the East. His singular yell had pealed into the ears of 500,000 worshipers of the national game and would never be forgotten.

At sight of him I recalled a friend's baseball talk. "You remember Old Well-Well? He's all in—dying, poor old fellow! It seems young Burt, whom the Phillies are trying out this spring, is Old Well-Well's nephew and protégé. Used to play on the Murray Hill team—a speedy youngster. When the Philadelphia team was here last, Manager Crestline announced his intention to play Burt in center field. Old Well-Well was too ill to see the lad get his tryout. He was heartbroken and said, 'If I could only see one more game!' "

The recollection of this random baseball gossip and the fact that Philadelphia was scheduled to play New York that very day gave me a sudden desire to see the game with Old Well-Well. I did not know him, but where on earth were introductions as superfluous as in the bleachers? It was a very easy matter to catch up with him. He walked slowly, leaning hard on a cane, and his wide shoulders sagged as he puffed along. I was about to make some pleasant remark concerning the prospects of a fine game when the sight of his face shocked me and I drew back. If ever I had seen shadow of pain and shade of death, they hovered darkly around Old Well-Well.

136

No one accompanied him; no one seemed to recognize him. The majority of that merry crowd of boys and men would have jumped up wild with pleasure to hear his well-remembered yell. Not much longer than a year before, I had seen ten thousand fans rise as one man and roar a greeting to him that shook the stands. So I was confronted by a situation strikingly calculated to rouse my curiosity and sympathy.

He found an end seat on a row at about the middle of the right-field bleachers, and I chose one across the aisle and somewhat behind him. No players were yet in sight. The stands were filling up, and streams of men were filing into the aisles of the bleachers and piling over the benches. Old Well-Well settled himself comfortably in his seat and gazed about him with animation. There had come a change to his massive features. The hard lines had softened, the patches of gray were no longer visible; his cheeks were ruddy; something akin to a smile shone on his face as he looked around, missing no detail of the familiar scene.

During the practice of the home team Old Well-Well sat still with his big hands on his knees; but when the gong rang for the Phillies, he grew restless, squirming in his seat and half rose several times. I divined the importuning of his old habit to greet his team with the yell that had made him famous. I expected him to get up; I waited for it. Gradually, however, he became quiet as a man governed by severe self-restraint and directed his attention to the Philadelphia center fielder.

At a glance I saw that the player was new to me and answered the newspaper decription of young Burt. What a lively-looking athlete! He was tall, lithe, yet sturdy. He did not need to chase more than two fly balls to win me. His graceful, fast style reminded me of the great Curt Welch. Old Well-Well's face wore a rapt expression. I discovered myself hoping Burt would make good; wishing he would rip the boards off the fence; praying he would break up the game.

It was Saturday, and by the time the gong sounded for the game to begin, the grandstand and bleachers were packed. The scene was glittering, colorful, a delight to the eye. Around the circle of bright faces rippled a low, merry murmur. The umpire, grotesquely padded in front by his chest protector, announced the batteries, dusted the plate, and, throwing out a white ball, sang the open sesame of the game: "Play!"

Then Old Well-Well arose as if pushed from his seat by some strong propelling force. It had been his wont always when play was ordered or in a moment of silent suspense or a lull in the applause or a dramatic pause when hearts beat high and lips were mute to bawl out over the listening, waiting multitude his terrific blast: "Well-Well-Well!"

Twice he opened his mouth, gurgled and choked, and then resumed his seat with a very red, agitated face; something had deterred him from his purpose, or he had been physically incapable of yelling.

The game opened with White's sharp bounder to the infield. Wesley had three strikes called on him, and Kelly fouled out to third base. The Phillies did no better, being retired in one, two, three order. The second inning was short, and no tallies were chalked up. Brain hit safely in the third and went to second on a sacrifice. The bleachers began to stamp and cheer. He reached third on an infield hit that the Philadelphia shortstop knocked down but could not cover in time to catch either runner. The cheer in the grandstand was drowned by the roar in the bleachers. Brain scored on a fly ball to left. A double along the right foul line brought the second runner home. Following that, the next batter went out on strikes.

In the Philadelphia half of the inning young Burt was the first man up. He stood left-handed at the plate and looked formidable. Duveen, the wary old pitcher for New York, to whom this new player was an unknown quantity, eyed his easy position as if reckoning on a possible weakness. Then he took his swing and threw the ball. Burt never moved a muscle, and the umpire called strike. The next was a ball, the next a strike; still Burt had not moved.

"Somebody wake him up!" yelled a wag in the bleachers. "He's from Slumbertown, all right, all right!" shouted another.

Duveen sent up another ball, high and swift. Burt hit straight over the first baseman, a line drive that struck the front of the right-field bleachers.

"Peacherino!" howled a fan.

Here the promise of Burt's speed was fulfilled. Run! He was fleet as a deer. He cut through first like the wind, settled to a driving stride, rounded second, and by a good, long slide beat the throw in to third. The crowd, which went to games to see long hits and daring runs, gave him a generous hand clapping.

Old Well-Well appeared on the verge of apoplexy. His ruddy face turned purple, then black; he rose in his seat; he gave vent to smothered gasps; then he straightened up and clutched his hands into his knees.

Burt scored his run on a hit to deep short, an infielder's choice, with the chances against retiring a runner at the plate. Philadelphia could not tally again that inning. New York blanked in the first of the next. For their opponents, an error, a close decision at second favoring the runner, and a single to right tied the score. Bell of New York got a clean hit in the opening of the fifth. With no one out and chances for a run, the impatient fans let loose. Four subway trains in collision would not have equaled the yell and stamp in the bleachers. Maloney was next to bat, and he essayed a bunt. This the fans derided with hoots and hisses. No team work, no inside ball for them.

"Hit it out!" yelled a hundred in unison.

"Home run!" screamed a worshiper of long hits.

As if actuated by the sentiments of his admirers, Maloney lined the ball over short. It looked good for a double; it certainly would advance Bell to third, maybe home. But no one calculated on Burt. His fleetness enabled him to head the bounding ball. He picked it up cleanly and, checking his headlong run, threw toward third base. Bell was halfway there. The ball shot straight and low with terrific force and beat the runner to the bag.

"What a great arm!" I exclaimed, deep in my throat. "It's the lad's day! He can't be stopped."

The keen newsboy sitting below us broke the amazed silence in the bleachers.

"Wot d'ye tink o' that?"

Old Well-Well writhed in his seat. To him it was a one-man game, as it had come to be for me. I thrilled with him; I gloried in the making good of his protégé; it got to be an effort on my part to look at the old man, so keenly did his emotion communicate itself to me.

The game went on, a close, exciting, brilliantly fought battle. Both pitchers were at their best. The batters batted out long flies, low liners, and sharp grounders; the fielders fielded these difficult chances without misplay. Opportunities came for runs, but no runs were scored for several innings. Hopes were raised to the highest pitch, only to be dashed astonishingly away. The crowd in the grandstand swayed to every pitched ball; the bleachers tossed like surf in a storm.

To start the eighth, Stranathan of New York tripled along the left foul line. Thunder burst from the fans and rolled swellingly around the field. Before the hoarse yelling, the shrill hooting, the hollow stamping, had ceased, Stranathan made home on an infield hit. Then bedlam broke loose. It calmed down quickly, for the fans sensed trouble between Binghamton, who had been thrown out in the play, and the umpire, who was waving him back to the bench.

"You dizzy-eyed old woman, you can't see straight!" called Binghamton.

The umpire's reply was lost, but it was evident that the offending player had been ordered out of the grounds.

Binghamton swaggered along the bleachers while the umpire slowly returned to his post. The fans took exception to the player's objection and were not slow in expressing it. Various witty encomiums, not to be misunderstood, attested to the bleachers' love of fair play and their disgust at a player's getting himself put out of the game at a critical stage.

The game proceeded. A second batter had been thrown out. Then two hits in succession looked good for another run. White, the next batter, sent a single over second base. Burt scooped the ball on the first bounce and let drive for the plate. It was another extraordinary throw. Whether ball or runner reached home base first was most difficult to decide. The umpire made his sweeping wave of hand, and the breathless crowd caught his decision.

"Out!"

In action and sound the circle of bleachers resembled a long curved beach with a mounting breaker thundering turbulently high.

"Rob-b-ber-r!" bawled the outraged fans, betraying their marvelous inconsistency.

Old Well-Well breathed hard. Again the wrestling of his body signified an inward strife. I began to feel sure that the man was in a mingled torment of joy and pain, that he fought the maddening desire to yell because he knew he had not the strength to stand it. Surely, in the years of his long following of baseball he had never had the incentive to express himself in his peculiar way that rioted him now. Surely before the game ended he would split the winds with his wonderful yell.

Duveen's only base on balls, with the help of a bunt, a steal, and a scratch hit, resulted in a run for Philadelphia, again tying the score. How the fans raged at Fuller for failing to field the lucky scratch.

"We had the game on ice!" one cried.

"Get him a basket!"

New York men got on bases in the ninth and made strenuous efforts to cross the plate, but it was not to be. Philadelphia opened up with two scorching hits and then a double steal. Burt came up with runners on second and third. Half the crowd cheered in fair appreciation of the way fate was starring the ambitious young outfielder; the other half, dyed-in-the-wool home-team fans, bent forward in a waiting, silent gloom of fear. Burt knocked the dirt out of his spikes and faced Duveen. The second ball pitched he met fairly, and it rang like a bell.

No one in the stands saw where it went. But they heard the crack, saw the New York shortstop stagger and then pounce forward to pick up the ball and speed it toward the plate. The catcher was quick to tag the incoming runner, and then snap the ball to first base, completing a double play.

When the crowd fully grasped this, which was after an instant of bewilderment, a hoarse crashing roar rolled out across the field to bellow back in loud echo from Coogan's Bluff. The grandstand resembled a colored cornfield waving in a violent wind; the bleachers lost all semblance of anything. Frenzied, flinging action—wild chaos, shrieking cries—manifested sheer insanity of joy.

When the noise subsided, one fan, evidently a little longer winded than his comrades, cried out hysterically, "O-h! I don't care what becomes of me—now-w!"

Score tied, three to three, game must go ten innings—that was the shibboleth; that was the overmastering truth. The game did go ten innings—eleven—twelve, every one marked by masterly pitching, full of magnificent catches, stops, and throws, replete with reckless baserunning and slides like flashes in the dust. But they were unproductive of runs. Three to three! Thirteen innings!

"Unlucky thirteenth," wailed a superstitious fan.

I had got down to plugging, and, for the first time, not for my home team. I wanted Philadelphia to win, because Burt was on the team. With Old Well-Well sitting there so rigid in his seat, so obsessed by the playing of the lad, I turned traitor to New York.

White cut a high twisting bounder inside the third base, and before the ball could be returned, he stood safely on second. The fans howled with what husky voice they had left. The second hitter batted a tremendously high fly toward center field. Burt wheeled with the crack of the ball and raced for the ropes. Onward the ball soared like a sailing swallow; the fleet fielder ran with his back to the stands. What an age that ball stayed in the air! Then it lost its speed, gracefully curved, and began to fall. Burt lunged forward and upward; the ball lit in his hands and stuck there as he plunged over the ropes into the crowd. White had leisurely trotted halfway to third; he saw the catch, ran back to touch second, and then easily made third on the throw-in. The applause that greeted Burt proved the splendid spirit of the game. Bell placed a safe little hit over short, scoring White. Heaving, bobbing bleachers—wild, broken, roar on roar!

Score 4–3—only one half inning left for Philadelphia to play—how the fans rooted for another run! A swift double play, however, ended the inning.

Philadelphia's first hitter had three strikes called on him.

"Asleep at the switch!" yelled a delighted fan.

The next batter went out on a weak pop-up fly to second.

"Nothin' to it!"

"Oh, I hate to take this money!"

"All-l o-over!"

Two men at least of all that vast assemblage had not given up victory for Philadelphia. I had not dared to look at Old Well-Well for a long while. I dreaded the next portentous moment. I felt deep within me something like clairvoyant force, an intangible belief fostered by hope.

Magoon, the slugger of the Phillies, slugged one against the left-field bleachers, but being heavy and slow, he could not get beyond second base. Cless swung with all his might at the first pitched ball, and instead of hitting it a mile, as he had tried, he scratched a mean, slow, teasing grounder down the third-base line. It was as safe as if it had been shot out of a cannon. Magoon went to third.

The crowd suddenly awoke to ominous possibilities; sharp commands came from the players' bench. The Philadelphia team was howling and hopping on the sidelines and had to be put down by the umpire.

An inbreathing silence fell upon stands and field, quiet, like a lull before a storm.

When I saw young Burt start for the plate and realized it was his turn at bat, I jumped as if I had been shot. Putting my hand on Old Well-Well's shoulder, I whispered, "Burt's at bat. He'll break up this game! I know he's going to lose one!"

The old fellow did not feel my touch; he did not hear my voice; he was gazing toward the field with an expression on his face to which no human speech could render justice. He knew what was coming. It could not be denied him in that moment.

How confidently young Burt stood up to the plate! None except a natural hitter could have had his position. He might have been Wagner for all he showed of the tight suspense of that crisis. Yet there was a tense, alert poise to his head and shoulders that proved he was alive to his opportunity.

Duveen plainly showed he was tired. Twice he shook his head to his catcher, as if he did not want to pitch a certain kind of ball. He had to use extra motion to get his old speed, and he delivered a high, straight ball that Burt fouled over the grandstand. The second ball met a similar fate. All the time the crowd maintained that strange waiting silence. The umpire threw out a glistening white ball, which Duveen rubbed in the dust and spat upon. Then he wound himself up into a knot, slowly unwound, and, swinging with effort, threw for the plate.

Burt's lithe shoulders swung powerfully. The meeting of ball and bat fairly cracked. The low driving hit lined over second a rising, glittering streak and went far beyond the center fielder.

Bleachers and stands uttered one short cry, almost a groan, and then stared at the speeding runners. For an instant, approaching doom could not have been more dreaded. Magoon scored. Cless was rounding second when the ball lit. If Burt was running swiftly when he turned first, he had only got started, for then his long sprinter's stride lengthened and quickened. At second he was flying; beyond second he seemed to merge into a gray flitting shadow.

I gripped my seat, strangling the uproar within me. Where was the applause? The fans were silent, choked as I was, but from a different cause. Cless crossed the plate with the score that defeated New York; still the tension never laxed until Burt beat the ball home in as beautiful a run as ever thrilled an audience.

In the bleak dead pause of amazed disappointment Old Well-Well lifted his hulking figure and loomed, towered over the bleachers. His wide shoulders spread, his broad chest expanded, his breath whistled as he drew it in. One fleeting instant his transfigured face shone with a glorious light. Then, as he threw back his head and opened his lips, his face turned purple, the muscles of his cheeks and jaw rippled and strung, the veins on his forehead swelled into bulging ridges. Even the back of his neck grew red.

"Well! Well! Well!"

Earsplitting stentorian blast! For a moment I was deafened. But I heard the echo ringing from the cliff, a pealing clarion call, beautiful and wonderful, winding away in hollow reverberation, then breaking out anew from building to building in clear concatenation.

A sea of faces whirled in the direction of that long-unheard yell. Burt had stopped, statuelike, as if stricken in his tracks; then he came running, darting among the spectators who had leaped the fence.

Old Well-Well stood a moment with slow glance lingering on the tumult of emptying bleachers, on the moving, mingling colors in the grandstand, across the green field to the gray-clad players. He staggered forward and fell.

Before I could move, a noisy crowd swarmed about him, some solicitous, many facetious. Young Burt leaped the fence and forced his way into the circle. Then they were carrying the old man down to the field and toward the club-house.

I waited until the bleachers and field were empty. When I finally went out, there was a crowd at the gate surrounding an ambulance. I caught a glimpse of Old Well-Well. He lay white and still, but his eyes were open, smiling intently. Young Burt hung over him with a pale and agitated face. Then a bell clanged, and the ambulance clattered away.

This scientific look at the game's tradition of chicanery comes from an intriguing collection entitled *Newton at the Bat*. When did cheating first rear its ugly head on a diamond? Probably at Hoboken's Elysian Fields, where Alexander Cartwright and his Knickerbocker comrades cavorted in the 1840s. However, the first documented instance of rule skirting was Jim Creighton's adding an underhanded wrist snap to his underhand pitching delivery, violating the rule that obtained in 1859 or so. The torch of deceit passed to King Kelly, John McGraw, Clark Griffith, on up through such moundsmen as Russ Ford, Lew Burdette, and Gaylord Perry. All were honored in their generation and were the glory of their crimes.

STEPHEN S. HALL

Baseball's Dirty Tricks

"The tradition of professional baseball has been agreeably free of charity," Heywood Broun noted back in 1923. "The rule is 'Do anything you can get away with.' "

Sixty years later, it may be added, charity still does not begin at home . . . or at first or on the pitcher's mound. Whether it is increasing friction at the grip of a moving object (i.e., using pine tar on the handle of a bat) or creating an aerodynamic irregularity on a moving sphere (i.e., throwing a scuffed-up or cut baseball), all players are amateur practitioners of applied physics when it comes to the tricks of the trade.

Batters, of course, believe they have the toughest job in the game. A variation of a millimeter or two at the point where bat meets ball can make the difference between a Rod Carew and a Rod Kanehl. A batter facing an 85-mile-per-hour fastball on its 56-foot journey from pitcher's hand to home plate has only about forty-five-hundredths of a second to decide if and when to swing.

That is also about how long the chalk lines of the batter's box remain intact at the beginning of the game. With the boundaries blurred, some batters stand farther from the mound, gaining perhaps 3 inches of patience. Those 3 inches translate into an extra two-thousandths of a second to look over the pitch. Two milliseconds.

To a few, that advantage is too slight to matter, and they step, figuratively, even farther over the line. Players have been known to drill a half-inch-diameter hole down from the fat end of the bat—anywhere from 8 to 14 inches—and cap it or fill it with cork. Some feel that if cork is stuffed into the core, the bat might transfer energy to the ball better—and also not sound too hollow if a suspecting umpire or opposing catcher decided to tap it on the ground. But the people at Hillerich and Bradsby, makers of the "Louisville Slugger" bat, say corking a bat doesn't do anything except make it more likely to break.

"They're wrong; I can guarantee you that," counters former Detroit Tiger first baseman Norm Cash. Thoroughly unrepentant, Cash admits using a corked bat en route to winning the 1961 American League batting title with a .361 average (along with 41 home runs and 132 RBIs). Cash, like most ballplayers a self-confessed nonphysicist, explains the advantage of corked bats with a layman's simplicity and clarity: "The faster you can swing the bat, the more you can hit the ball."

Cash has the law on his side in this case—Newtonian laws of motion, to be exact. "It's the same principle as when an ice skater wants to go into a spin and pulls the body in to spin faster," explains Peter Brancazio, a professor of physics at Brooklyn College. "The greater the distance of the mass from the axis of rotation, the harder it is to rotate." Top-heavy bats are harder to turn around. And bat speed, both hitters and physicists agree, is more important than mass when it comes to making good contact with the ball.

The trend in major-league baseball is toward lighter bats with thin handles and thick barrels—the type preferred by Rod Carew of the California Angels. It is also a nightmare for manufacturers, because thin-handled bats break easily. "The problem," says Rex Bradley of Hillerich and Bradsby, "is that the good Lord doesn't make timber that good." Yet the Carew-style bat is a step closer to the ideal baseball bat, which in fact would be a golf club—at least in an ideal world in which the ball was stationary. The head of a golf club, like the "sweet spot" of a bat (about 4 inches down from the end of the barrel), is where the best contact is made; the thin shaft is just there to move the head through the air. Likewise with Carew's thin handle.

There are also tales of bats with flattened sides (Nellie Fox reputedly used one), bats whose hollowed innards were filled with a free-floating dollop of mercury, bats fortified around the midsection with tacks, and even a bat stuffed like sausage with Super Balls. (Such a bat reportedly broke open on American Leaguer Graig Nettles in 1974.) According to Paul Kirkpatrick, a retired Stanford physicist, "That's going in the wrong direction. The harder the material, the more energy will be returned to the ball after a collision. If you put a bat in a vise and bang on it, it won't vibrate long; it absorbs the force. But a steel bar will ring a few seconds because very little of the collision is absorbed. If a bat were made entirely of cork, the only thing it would be good for is bunting."

A perfectly legal but vanishing tradition is the old clubhouse soup bone. Players used to expend considerable elbow grease rubbing the "sweet spot" of their bats on a soup bone to harden the surface. (Today's practitioners use soda-pop bottles.)

"Yeah, I used to bone 'em," says former slugger Frank Howard. "I'd spend two hours boning 'em and rubbing 'em, and then the first time up, I'd hit one off the end or on the handle and break the damn bat."

"You could do things with bats years ago that you can't do anymore," adds former Yankee shortstop Tony Kubek, now an announcer for NBC Sports. "We used to take an ice pick and carve out the dark grain, which was the softer part of the wood. Then you'd put pine tar in the grooves, let it harden, and resand it." This supposedly gave the bat a harder surface and put more sock into a swing, although even Kubek concedes that the main advantage may have been psychological.

Rex Bradley recalls hearing of cases where the grooves in a bat were carved out but never filled in—"like scoring on a golf club," he says. The idea is that a grooved bat, like a grooved golf club, imparts backspin when it makes contact with the bottom of the ball. Others maintain that the direction of the bat at impact is much more important in generating backspin than grooves in the bat. But there seems to be no question that backspin helps a fly ball. "I imagine it could add twenty to thirty feet to a three-hundred-fifty-foot hit," says Brancazio, and that could easily be the difference between a long out and a home run.

To take away that advantage, of course, the home team could always toss its supply of baseballs into the freezer. This is exactly what the good-pitch, no-hit Chicago White Sox used to do—according to Tony Kubek and others—when the Yankees and other hard-hitting teams came to town in the late 1950s. A frozen ball shows no spunk: The all-important coefficient of restitution—the ability of an object (such as a baseball) to rebound after a collision with another hard object (such as a bat)—goes down with temperature. This is because the core of each baseball is a combination of cork and rubber and rubber becomes less bouncy when the temperature is lowered.

Talk of resilience and spunk invariably provokes discussion of the ball's liveliness. There is quite a lively discussion going on right now, in fact, between Rawlings, which manufactures all major-league baseballs, and MacGregor Sporting Goods, which would like to. Like many corporate discussions these days, this one is taking place in court. In an antitrust suit against Rawlings, MacGregor charges, among other things, that the Rawlings ball fails to meet major-league specifications. Major-league baseballs, for example, are supposed to weigh between 5 and 5¼ ounces and have a coefficient of restitution of between .514 and .578 (this determined after a collision when the ball is traveling about 58 miles per hour). For a softball traveling at 55 miles per hour, by contrast, the coefficient of restitution is .400, while for a Super Ball it is .850.

MacGregor hired Richard Brandt, a physicist at New York University, to test about fifty Rawlings baseballs. He found that 20 percent of the balls had coefficients of restitution higher than the .578 limit—in one case as high as .607. Brandt adds, "The balls are supposed to have a circumference between nine and nine and one quarter inches, but almost half of the balls were too small." Both these factors individually contribute to a livelier baseball, and in combination they can make "a significant difference," according to Brandt. "If you compare today's baseballs with ones from the past, the old ones were twenty-five to thirty percent less lively. What that means is that if you went back to 1927, when Babe Ruth hit sixty home runs, and you used the modern ball, Ruth would have hit eighty home runs."

Rawlings maintains that Brandt uses an unorthodox method of measuring the coefficient of restitution, hitting the balls with a flat metal plate instead of shooting them out of an air cannon. Brandt responds that "any freshman physics student could tell you that the results will be the same." Brandt, in fact, tested the baseballs both ways and says the results were exactly the same.

Until they hear otherwise, Brandt's findings give pitchers one more reason to justify their time-tested mischief. In a sport where Hall of Famer Whitey Ford once admitted to throwing a doctored pitch in an Old-Timers' Game, it is obvious that choirboys and winners don't sit on the same bench. Baseball outlawed the spitball in 1920, but it is the sport's version of the 55-mile-an-hour speed limit: It has been estimated that one-third to one-half of all pitchers in the majors throw doctored balls.

And a pitcher doesn't have to go to his mouth to make the ball dance. Any irregularity in the cowhide surface—whether it is cut, scuffed, shined, or freighted with mud—changes the pattern of airflow around the baseball as it makes its journey to the plate. All that's needed is to make one side rougher than the other, and this can be accomplished by making one side smoother than usual.

"In the [1982] World Series we saw something that is technically legal: Bruce Sutter (the St. Louis relief pitcher) rubbing the ball on his pants," says Tony Kubek. "Well, that's what we used to call a 'shiner'—a dry spitball." Others, according to one American League veteran, will use the less legal sandpaper—often on the official label, where it is more difficult for umpires to pick up. A scuff ball is thrown somewhat like a whiffle ball: the pitcher puts the rough side away from the way he wants it to break. For example, to make the pitch curve right, the scuff is put on the left and thrown overhand.

There may be a tiny consolation in all this for hitters who face scuff balls and other ballistic indignities: if they make good contact, the ball may actually travel a bit farther. The boundary layer of a scuffed ball experiences turbulence, and this in turn reduces the size of the wake behind the ball, thus reducing drag. In short, a roughed-up ball is aerodynamically more efficient than a perfect sphere. "Is that right?" asked a wide-eyed Detroit slugger Darrell Evans when Brancazio passed on the good news. "Usually we try to get the scuffed ones out of the game, but . . ."

This is an excerpt from the 1953 novel *The Southpaw, by Henry W. Wiggen; Punctuation Freely Inserted and Spelling Greatly Improved by Mark Harris.* "Author" Wiggen, rookie pitcher of the New York Mammoths, anticipated by several years such real-life pitcher-authors as Jim Brosnan, Jim Bouton, Pat Jordan, and Sparky Lyle. Nature imitates Art.

MARK HARRIS

Henry Wiggen Goes Up

It is now 3 A.M. in the morning, and I am disgusted. It is a very cold winter night out, and I have got a fire in the fireplace.

I begun this book last October, and it is now January, and I doubt that I am halfway through. I will give 1 word of advice to any sap with the itch to write a book—do not begin it in the first place.

I got 12 chapters wrote on this blasted thing and it was not easy. My hand does not grip a pencil so good, for it is rather large, and I went and bought a couple big fat pencils called an Eagle number 4 from Fred Levine that does not make my hand so tired. Fred is still rather cool to me.

After I got through the 12 chapters I bumped into Aaron yesterday morning, and he said, "Well, Henry, I do not see much of you anymore. Ain't you afraid of putting on weight staying indoors like that?"

"I have wrote 12 chapters," I said, "and lost 12 pounds at the least."

"I admire your get up and go," he said.

"Get up and go hell," said I. "It is the sit down and stay that gets books wrote," and he got a great laugh out of that.

Well, like a fool I stood there gassing with him, and the next thing I knowed I promised him that if him and Pop dropped over tonight—that is, *last* night—I would read the works out loud. Then I went back and polished up number 12 a bit, and in the evening me and Holly slung sandwiches and coffee together, and about 7 Pop and Aaron come. I begun to read out loud, starting with chapter 1 and following through in order, though here and there I skipped over parts

147

that seemed too personal to mention. I did not read the pages concerning me and Thedabara that night, nor the pages concerning me and Holly. Holly knows it's there, though, and says okay, and Thedabara will never know the difference because I doubt that she ever looked at a book since Perkinsville High and ain't likely to take up the habit now. I left out the swear words, too, for Pop's sake. He gets all red when you swear around him around women.

Every so often they would laugh, and then again they would sit so still it was like if it would of been a book it would of been 1 of those that you can't lay it down. Sometimes when they laughed they would laugh in the wrong spot, though.

After number 6 Holly called the halt for food, and we all drifted in the kitchen, and afterwards I begun to read out loud again, burping most of the way through 7, and when I got through with number 12 I said that was all I done to date.

Nobody said a word. They all just sat there, and I said, "Do not be bashful. Say anything you want, pulling no punches," for to my mind it was all very good. I damn near broke my hand doing it. Finally Holly was the first to speak, and she said, "The first 11 chapters is just about right, but number 12 is too long."

Now, if that was not a dirty crack! Of all the chapters number 12 was the 1 I was proudest of, for it run 73 pages on both sides of the paper, and I done it in less then a week. If that is not some kind of a record I will be mighty surprised.

"Yes," said Aaron, "I think number 12 is too long."

"Have you ever wrote a book?" said I to him.

"No," said he.

"Well, then," said I, "why are you so quick to run down what another writer did?"

"That is not the proper attitude on your part, Henry," he said, "for we are gathered here for the purpose of being helpful. I agree with Holly that number 12 is too long. But we must take it apart and see *why* it is too long and how we might cut it down and aim it to the point."

"Well, then," said I, "half of it is wrote on yellow paper and half on white. Leave us throw out all the yellow," and I took all the yellow and tore it in 2. However, I tore it so as to be able to paste it up again, for I will be damned if I will write 73 pages front and back and take a week doing it and bust my hand besides and then just heave it out.

"No," said he, "that is not the way to go about it."

"Very well," said I, "then we might just as well forget the whole thing and skip number 12 and start in on number 13."

"In my opinion," said Aaron, "all that is wrong with the chapter is that it has got too much material that does not belong. It is up to us to try to decide what is good and what is too much."

And then it all begun, and the sum and total was this:

First off, I had wrote 9 pages front and back covering the time from when we broke camp at Aqua Clara to the time we arrived in Queen City in the Four-State Mountain League AA. I give an excellent picture of all the cities we went through, all the games, and the view that you got coming down off the slope of the mountains into Q. C., and then I told a good bit about the type of a place Q. C. is and the Blue Castle Hotel, which was the headquarters of the club when we was at home. "That is too much space to give to things of such little importance," said Aaron.

"That is a lot of rubbage," said I. "If you have got the sense to think back on chapter 11 you will remember that it run 9 pages front and back between the time Sid Goldman hit the home run, about 3 o'clock, until midnight. That is 9 pages covering 9 hours, while this is 9 pages covering 3 *weeks*, so it seems to me that you are the slightest bit cockeyed in your calculations."

"But the things that happened in number 11," said he, "was important things concerning important people such as the remarks of Mr. Moors. I actually think that the whole exhibition trip could be knocked off in 1 page." Well, I finally agreed.

Then I done 9 pages front and back about Mike Mulrooney, telling about his family which I met in Q. C. and his whole life history. Part of it I copied out of a book called "Forty-One Diamond Immortals," but mostly it was my own writing. I give him a great build-up, for he is 1 of the grandest men that ever lived. That is what nobody liked. Holly said, "About 1 dozen times you said Mike Mulrooney is 1 of the grandest men that ever lived. That is not saying anything."

"The hell it ain't," said I, "for if you knowed Mike you would say the same."

"I do not say that Mike is not all you say," said she, "but you must tell us why."

"Because he *is*," said I. "Because he does not wish to run the whole show but just live an easy going life and not worry you ragged about setting the whole world on fire. Because if you make a mistake he will not eat you out in front of all the rest nor give you the icy glare every time he runs into you in the hotel. He will stand by you and not go about talking behind your back. He will treat you all the same, no matter if you are on the way up or the way down, for he takes the attitude that if you are not the greatest ballplayer in the world still and all you are a human being. He is not a frog," said I, "that goes about kissing the ass of every writer and every club official and everybody else that he thinks can do him any good. Mike says if they do not like the way he runs his club in Q. C. he will go back to his ranch in Last Chance, Colorado, but he will never stoop down to where his head is lower than his shoulders for the purpose of getting a brown nose."

"Excellent, excellent," said Holly, and up she jumped. "You have told us more about Mr. Mulrooney right there then you done in the 9 pages of Chapter 12 concerned with him."

"Rats," I said.

Then Pop throwed in. "Here is what they mean," said he. "It is like a baseball game. If you was to pitch a ball game and win it by a score of 1–0 would you tell me how it went inning by inning, every foul ball and every little detail along the way? No, the main thing is how was the run scored and what particular scrapes you was in."

"Very well," said I, "out goes the 9 pages on Mike."

"Then there is the description of all the cities of the league," said Aaron.

I done 16 pages front and back on the different towns of the Four-State Mountain League, and I thought I done a fine job, and Aaron said, "Yes, you done a fine job. Yet it is like your pa says. It is not to the point. You do not need to tell us about the cities, for we know all about them. I have never seen a 1 of them, yet I know what they are like. They are like Perkinsville. They are all the same."

"They are all different," said I. "In some you have got the mountains, and in others you have not, and in 1 place you will have a fine and modern ball park while elsewhere it will be an old park."

"But they are talking about building a new 1," said he.

"Why yes," said I. "Naturally."

"And in every town you was in you walked about on the main street," said he, "and then you got tired and went back and laid in the hotel. You and Coker and Canada and Perry."

"Yes," said I. "You guessed it."

"You said to 1 another, 'This is a dull town and there is nothing to do until game time,' and you laid on your bed in your shorts, and you talked about everything, baseball mostly, and you told each other over and over again your whole life history."

"Why, yes," said I.

"In Salt Lake you went and seen the big tabernacle, for that was where everyone told you to go. In Denver you went and seen the capitol with the big gold dome on top, and you also took a trip through the mint, for that was where everybody told you you must go in Denver. In all the cities you admired such places as these, though as a matter of fact you thought they was rather a bore. So after awhile you went over and laid in the park, and you fed the squirrels and birds and looked at the girls, and after awhile even *that* become a bore. There was the railroad station and the hotel, and each was the same as the next and it got so you could not hardly tell them 1 from the other."

"Yes," said I, "that is about the way it was. Yet they was all different."

"No," said he. "No, they were not. For they was all about like Perkinsville. There was a Legion club in Wichita, and you hung at the Legion club, and they made a big fuss over you. Maybe they even give you a dinner."

"They did not," said I. "It was the Chamber of Commerce of Queen City that give me the dinner."

"They sung songs to you," said he. "They sung For He Is a Jolly Good Fellow, For He Is a Jolly Good Fellow, and they give you a wrist watch."

"They give me a traveling bag," I said.

"With your name in silver," said he.

"With my name in silver," I said.

"They are all the same," said he. "There is no need to have so many pages concerning the cities."

I give in. Out they went.

There was a long letter waiting at the hotel when I hit Q. C. the second summer from Thedabara Brown, broke in Sacramento and wishing she could see me in Q. C. I copied it down, 5 pages front and back, and nobody could see the sense in putting it in. "There will be nothing left," I said. "You are blasting away my chapter until there is nothing left but air. It was 2 whole summers. You cannot skip over 2 whole summers in a couple pages."

"I am after the high spot," said Aaron. "Never mind the mail of little Miss Brown. What was the very biggest thing about the 2 summers at Q. C.?"

"I guess," said I, "the big thing is that I shook off my greenness and got myself ready for the big-time."

"Ah," said Aaron, "now we are getting somewheres."

"If so," said I, "we are getting there in reverse gear. It took up 4 days of my time to write the 39 pages that you have just throwed out like it was so much wrapping off a load of fish. It took me 1 whole afternoon alone to put my hands on the letter from Thedabara Brown and then copy it down, plus a whole morning copying out the material on Mike Mulrooney from "Forty-One Diamond Immortals," holding the book in 1 hand and writing it all down with the other. That is how you do everything—backwards and in reverse." I would not of stood for it, but we had another break for coffee and sandwiches, and Pop said he thought they was right in connection with Chapter 12.

"You take that business with Lindon Burke," said he. "That is too much on that."

I had give 12 pages to Lindon. He is a fine fellow. In July of the first summer Mike got a telegram from New York, asking for Lindon right away. The Mammoths was flagging at the time, and Dutch was of the opinion that they needed a righthander for relief, maybe for a starter, though it was my opinion then and still is that the Mammoths have always had *too goddam many* righthanders. Nonetheless we was all glad for Lindon. We had a big celebration before he went. We was in Denver, and we beat Denver that night, and Lindon's train was not until morning, and we stood him a dinner at Boggio's. We all made speeches. I wrote down what I could remember of each 1, for each and every 1 was a dandy. Then I copied down the menu, for I swiped 1. It was signed by everybody who was there that night. The last speech of all was that of Mike Mulrooney, and after he finished he give Lindon the present we bought, consisting of a silver bracelet with his name. Then we all started in to sing, "Stand up, stand up, stand up and show us your ugly face," and he stood up and begun to speak. But he could not speak, for he was bawling, and the tears was racing down his cheek. Then Mike got back up, and he was laughing, and he said, "Lindon need not make no speech. Instead of that, he must win the first game he gets to pitch up there in the big-time, for after all he is a pitcher and not an after-dinner speaker." Lindon shook his head, meaning he would do it, and sure enough he done it, beating Washington the first full game he pitched, and that night we got a wire saying "I done it, and I am thinking of all you boys," signed Lindon Burke.

"Very well," said I to Pop, "I will trim that down."

"You could also chop out the amusement park," said he.

I done 8 pages concerning 1 afternoon me and Perry and Coker and Canada went to Mountaineer Park in Q. C. For a dime you could throw 3 baseballs at wooden bottles stood up on a barrel, and if you knocked them all off you got a prize. "If I cannot knock them bottles off," said I to the boys, "I will turn in my suit and go home and pump gas," and I got up close, and I throwed, and I will be damned but I could not knock them off.

Then Perry give the man a dime. He did not get up close but went off to the side a bit, and he bent down like he was fielding a ground ball, and then, still in the bending position, he flipped in with that little snap throw a good second baseman knows how to make, and he clubbed the bottle dead center, and off they all went. The man give him a prize, consisting of a raggedy doll.

Then I said to the man, "Give me 3 more, and here is your dime," and I took the balls, and I said, "How far is it from that barrel to this here counter?" meaning the place you was to throw from.

"About 6 feet," said the man.

"Well then," said I, "I will pace off 54 more and make it an even 60," and back I went. There was people passing back and forth up and down the midway, and I said, "Out of the way, folks, unless you wish to be beaned," and the people lined up to see what was going on. I throwed from the 60 feet, which is the regular pitching distance, and I tagged the center bottle on the nose, and off they all went, and Canada collected my raggedy doll and I come down and flipped the man a dozen dimes or more and went back to the 60 feet. About 2 throws in 3 I turned the trick. There was a quite a big crowd gathered around, and the bigger the crowd the hotter I am, and Perry and Canada and Coker gathered up my prizes. I must of spent 4 dollars in dimes, and we had about 50 dolls and wind-up toys and candy canes and balloons and circus masks and glass jugs and a little red fire engine and a bowl of goldfish, and I give it all away to the kids except a couple candy canes that It ate myself. It warmed me good. That night I shut out Omaha.

"Why," said I to Pop, "it was a good time and ought to be in."

"Son," said he, "as long as you are doing it you might as well do it in a straight line. Aaron and Holly have read many books and know how they ought to be wrote."

"They do not know center field from the water fountain," I said. "They make me dizzy. What is the sense of writing a chapter for them to tell me chuck it out the door?"

"Now," said Aaron, "we was saying that the big thing about the 2 summers in Q. C. was that you shook off your greenness and was getting ready to go up to the big-time." He never forgets what he was saying. He will meet you and pick up the conversation he was snarled up in 3 weeks before, after you had forgot all about it.

"Right," said I.

"Just what is left?" said he.

I shuffled through the pages, and there was nothing left but 14 pages front and back regarding Coker and Canada and Perry. We was the closest of buddies in Q. C. If someone was to come looking for 1 all they need do is find the other 3. We was either in Perry and my room or Coker and Canada's, or else the coffee shop, or else we was somewheres out on the town, whatever town it may be, walking along and seeing the sights.

The only other place we could be was at the park, and we always went there together, and we had our lockers 1 next to the other, and we would dress and then go out on the field together. If it was not my day to work I might take a turn at first base during the infield drill, for squarehead Flynn would leave me do so. He is a prince of a fellow but still with Q. C. He will be there till he is old and gray.

When I worked it was a pleasure to have that infield behind me. Ground balls was sure outs. Then, too, Coker and Perry was a grease of lightning on double plays, and Canada down at third had no little hand in double plays himself. They set a record for the Mountain League in that department the first summer, and they busted their own record the summer after.

After the ball games, in the clubhouse, the 4 of us sung together in the shower. I wrote out all the songs we sung, such as "I Love You As I Never Loved Before," "Some Enchanted Evening," "Going to Wash That Man Right Out of My Hair," "The Good Old Summertime," "Sweet Adeline," "Down by the Old Mill Stream," "Meet Me In St. Louis," "Goodnight, Irene," "White Christmas," "God Bless America," "A Bicycle Built for 2," "Old Black Joe," "My Old Kentucky Home," and some songs that Coker sung back in the coal mines of West Virginia, and it took up 7 pages front and back. That was a good deal of work.

Nonetheless Aaron said it had no place in the book. "For God's sake," said I, "they was the best infield the Mountain League ever seen and if it was up to you they would be slid over without hardly a mention."

"Just exactly what *is* a double play?" said Holly.

I leaned forwards and put my head down on my arms.

"Go ahead and tell her, Hank," said Pop, and I lifted up my head and begun to explain.

"The most usual type is when you have a man on first," I said. "Then the batter hits a ground ball to the infield, and the infielder scoops it up and tosses to second. That gives you a force on 1 man. Then the second baseman or the shortstop, whichever took the throw, he rifles it down to first base. If it gets to first base ahead of the runner you have worked the play. You have got 2 men out on the 1 pitch."

"That does not sound hard," said Aaron.

"It is a beautiful play when done right," said I. "It is harder than it sounds. The average ballplayer can get from home plate to first base in 3 seconds. A fast man can do it in less. So you have got 3 seconds to field the ball clean, fire it to second, make the play there, keep clear of the runner, pivot and throw to first. That is a lot of work to do in 3 seconds. The shortstop and the second baseman have got to be like a fine machine, working together to the split of a second. They have got to know each other like a book. It is like they was 1 and the same man, not 2 different men. That is how Perry and Coker works, like they was 1 and the same man. It is beautiful. Then, too, it is a great help to any pitcher. It saves wear and tear on him. A good double play combination around second base will save you many a ball game. It can win a pennant for you or lose it."

"All this brings us to the very point of the whole discussion," said Aaron.

"I must say it is about time," said I, "for it is now 2 o'clock in the morning and we have jawed away at this thing for 7 hours. There is nothing left."

"There is still the main point left," said Aaron. "You have jammed it all in 1 sentence, but it is the main point," and he picked up 1 half of the last page that I had tore in 2, and he read what I had wrote. He read: "Well, the outcome was that I went up to the Mammoths in September of the second summer, and I pitched 1 inning in relief against Boston."

"You might just as well throw that out, too," said I, "for you cannot have a chapter that has got only 1 sentence in it."

"Yet that is the big point," said he, "for that is what you were aiming at from the time you first took a baseball in your hand. The rest of the chapter is full of dead matter that leads you nowheres."

"I will not write it over," said I. "I should of never begun it. It is chapter 12 and that is a bad number for me and always was."

"That is up to you," said he. "If you wish to leave number 12 out of your book it is your right to do so. However, it seems to me that whatever chapter follows 11 ought to be about when you was sent up to the Mammoths."

"Tomorrow," I said. "I will do it tomorrow. I thank you all for your wonderful goddam help."

Aaron and Pop went home, and I was tired, and yet I could not calm down and sleep. I lit the fire in the fireplace and shaved a new point on an Eagle #4. I thought I would write a few minutes and then turn in. Yet when you get to writing you run on and on, and it is hard to stop, and I have wrote 14 more pages front and back and *still* not got into the main point, which is when I went up to the Mammoths. I will do it tomorrow—that is, tonight. It is now daylight and I must first get some sack.

Well, the outcome was that I went up to the Mammoths in September of the second summer, and I pitched 1 inning in relief against Boston.

The word come on a hot afternoon. Me and Perry was laying on our beds in our room in the Blue Castle Hotel in Queen City in the Four-State Mountain

League when in come Coker and Canada in their shorts and bare feet. Canada said it was so hot he had took 4 showers since noon. Coker said you would never know what hot was until some summer's day you was down in a coal mine in West Virginia, and then you would know.

"I will tell you what hot is," said Perry. "If you was ever to be in the Ford Rouge plant of a summer's day you would know what hot is. When I lay me down here and I think it is hot I say to myself be thankful you are laying here in your under drawers with this pitcher of ice water in your hand and be glad you are not back in the Ford plant." He took a drink from the pitcher, and he passed it to me, and I drunk and I give it to Canada. "I only hope I can save my money and never go back to the factory," said Perry.

Just then in come Mike Mulrooney, manager of the Queen City Cowboys and 1 of the grandest men you will ever meet. He taught me more baseball then any man before or since. Pop set me up and Mike put the finish on. When I went to Q. C. the summer before I was a fair enough country ballplayer, and when I come away I was big-time, and Mike said, "Well boys, leave us phone down and have them send up some steam heat." This give us all a big laugh, for Mike was always ready with a joke. He flopped down in a chair and begun to fan himself with the newspaper. We sat, and we waited for him to say what he come to say, for Mike seldom come just for the visit. He always come for a purpose. Maybe he would come to tell of a fault he seen in 1 of us, or he would come and wise us up on some trouble another fellow was having. He might say, "Now boys, I want you to help me out with Squarehead Flynn," meaning Squarehead Flynn the first baseman. "I do not think it is kind to Flynn to call him by the name of Squarehead, so if you boys will just call him Flynn or Bob it will be a big favor to me." We done it when we remembered, though "Squarehead" seemed to fit perfect. But if Mike Mulrooney was to ask it you could never refuse. Still and all he never jumped right into the business of his visit, and we always waited, and he would talk about the weather or last night's ball game or some old-time remembrance, and on this day he said, "I do not call this hot. Nowadays the ballplayer has got things better. It is cool at night, and we play so much at night nowadays, and the trains and the hotels is air-condition. I will tell you what I call hot. I remember double-headers in St. Louis when it was 110 in the shade."

"What would you say is the hottest city of all?" said Canada.

"St. Louis," said Mike. "Washington is close. All of them is hot. I remember hot days everywhere. Yet I was always a good hot weather ballplayer."

"The hotter it is the better Pop likes it," said I.

"I have played ball in cold and snow in Boston and wet and dry and thunder and lightning. I once played ball in the flood in Cincinnati. But the worst of all is heat," said Mike. "However, I did not drop in for story hour. The reason I come is because I just heard from Dutch." He took a wire out of his pocket and handed it to me. It was the wire I was waiting 20 years to see. It said:

R. DVA 165 SER PD WUX NEW YORK 12 1158A
MICHAEL J. MULROONEY
BLUE CASTLE HOTEL
QUEEN CITY
SHIP ME WIGGEN FASTEST

DUTCH

I have got the wire yet, and I could not believe my eyes, and the other boys come around behind me and looked, and Canada give a whoop and shot out the room and spread the news around. I sat froze to my bed, and the first 1 I saw was Pop in my mind, and I said, "I must send a wire to Pop."

"I have sent 1," said Mike.

"I better get moving," I said, and I begun to cram things in my bags.

Mike laughed. "Do not be in such a hurry, Hank. I have got your plane reservations for 11 tonight," and I sat back down, and Mike said, "I hope it is the right thing."

"I am ready," said I.

"Yes, you are ready," said he. "But you have still got many things to learn." He fussed and fidgeted, and finally he said, "I will tell you the truth, for you will hear nothing but lies from now on. You are a natural ballplayer. You have won 21 games this year. You are a regular horse for work. Yet you have got things to learn. When you get up to the Mammoths there will be 1 man that will be no end of help to you."

"That is Sad Sam Yale," said I.

"No," said he, "it is not Sam. Do not listen to a single word said by Sam Yale. Do not play cards with him. Do not drink with him. Do not lend him money nor borrow any. If you see him with a woman put that woman down in your book as a tramp, for if she is not a tramp at the start Sad Sam will make her 1. Everything that Yale touches will turn to shit. Except only 1 thing, and that is a baseball. When he is pitching you must glue your eyes to him and never take them off. You must learn to watch him and never listen to him, and you will learn much about baseball and much about life."

"Then who is the man that will help me?" said I.

"That is Red Traphagen," said he, meaning the Mammoth catcher. "When he says something that has got to do with playing baseball you must hang on his every word like it was the word of God. He is the smartest ballplayer in baseball today. If he did not have so much respect for his own personal self-respect he would be in line to be a manager. But he will not brown-nose. On the ball field he will talk only about baseball, and you must listen. If you can remember to do it write it down afterwards and study it once in a while. But when you are off the field do not pay him no more mind then if he was a pillar or a post. He is all full of chatter and nonsense. He does not believe in God." Mike was quite religious himself and went almost every Sunday. I did not know if I believed in God or not. I rather suppose I did not, but I said nothing.

I said, "It is sad to me to hear what you say of Sad Sam Yale."

"Yes," said he, "it is sad. It is always sad when a great ballplayer goes wrong as a man. I am not telling you these things out of anything personal. I am telling them to you because I want you to be a great and immortal ballplayer. You have all the makings. You learn fast and never forget. But never listen to Sam nor the men that is his pals. If they was once good in their heart they are good no longer, for Sam Yale has did them in. Steer clear of Knuckles Johnson and Goose Williams and Swanee Wilks." Mike grabbed the water pitcher and took a swig, and then he took some ice from the tray and dumped it in the pitcher and sloshed it around. "There is nothing more to tell," said he. "Remember that the parks will be bigger than in the Mountain League. But do not let this make you over-confident. Do not relax too much at first. When you are in trouble rely on your curve and forget the fast 1. Do not forget that the boys you will be throwing against will be hitting harder than any you have ever faced. Remember that you will be throwing against the very best ballplayers in the world. True, some of the best ballplayers in the world will be on your side, too.

"Henry, I will tell you the damn truth. The damn truth is that I can tell you no more about baseball. You are already a fine young pitcher. When you are up there you will be playing the same game you been playing all your life. The ball will be the same, and the bases will be the same 90 feet apart, and there will be 9 men to a side, and the game is still decided by who scores the most runs. The main thing is not half so much the other teams but your own men that you will be playing with and traveling with and be close to every hour of the day from February to October. I have told you what I know about the men. The rest I do not know so well. They are young men. Let me see," and he leaned back and begun to reel off the men on his fingers. "The Carucci brothers, they are Roman Catholics of the Italian race, and good boys, and they stick together. I do not know them, nor I do not know Lucky Judkins, for he is young and new. Scotty Burns and Sunny Jim Trotter is the rest of the outfielders. They do not mix in with the rest. They stay to theirselves and sometimes I think this is best.

"Ugly Jones and Gene Park are steady hands. You can depend on them. I do not know Goldman or Gonzalez. Gonzalez does not speak the language, and he is just as well off. They are the kind of young men that Dutch is trying to build a club around. That is your infield, for the rest will be cut loose." Mike looked at Coker and Perry and Canada. "Here is the rest of your infielders right there in their underwear if they show up good in Aqua Clara in the spring. That is a secret amongst us 5, but it is the straight dope from Dutch.

"Red Traphagen will catch about 135 games a year. I have spoke about him and Goose. Bruce Pearson is your other catcher. He was big-time when I sent him up, but he does not get enough work. This has knocked his spirits all to hell.

"The pitching is young. If the pitching comes through you will have a winner up there in New York in the next year or 2. It all depends. Sam and Knuckles and Horse Byrd is your only veterans. Carroll I do not know. Castetter was sent down today, and he will never go back up. That leaves Sterling and Gil Willowbrook and Macy, plus Lindon Burke and yourself. Tell Lindon that if he gives himself 10 seconds between pitches he will help his control." Mike kept looking off in the distance, like he was in a dream. There was more he had on his mind to say, and we knowed it, and we waited, and he did not say it. I always wonder what it was, and I wonder to this day. Yet he said nothing but only rose and said, "I will see you boys at the park tonight," meaning Coker and Canada and Perry.

"I will be there, too," said I, "for my plane does not leave till 11."

Mike laughed, and he said, "There is no need, but it is up to you." Then he left, and we begun to dress for supper.

I got in uniform that night and worked out. The crowd give me a fine hand when I come on the field, for they had by now read it in the paper, and I tipped my hat and played pepper with some of the boys. Then I moved down to first base and took a hand in the drill and kept pretty loose.

After the drill I ducked back through the dugout and into the clubhouse, and I was alone. I showered and dressed, feeling sad. I cleaned out my locker. The 4 of us had lockers together, 1 right after the other, and I stuck a note in their lockers, and it said, "I will see you in Aqua Clara in the spring, and we will be in the Series next October. Good luck. Your friend, HENRY WIGGEN."

Then out I went, catching a cab on Rocky Mountain Avenue. We heard about 2 innings along the way, the Cowboys pasting the hell out of Denver. Perry hit a home run with 2 on in the third. The cabbie asked me if I had ever saw the Cowboys play. He said it was the best club they had in Q. C. in quite some years. I said I had saw them play once or twice and thought particularly high of that fellow by the name of Wiggen. He told me that Wiggen was signed on by the Mammoths and had went off that very day to New York by air. "What is your line of work?" said he to me.

"I am a heaver in the horsehide plant," said I. That was a joke that me and Coker and Perry and Canada played on people. We would run into some people in a restaurant or a bowling alley or somewheres and get to talking, and they would say, "What do you boys do?" Then Coker would speak up. "We work in the horsehide plant," he would say. "This here is Henry, and he is a heaver, and this here is Perry, and he is a scooper. I work alongside of Perry. This here is Canada, and he works the far throw."

They would say, "What is the far throw?"

"Why," said Coker, "everybody knows what a far throw is. Only a particularly pinheaded person would not know."

"Oh," they would say. "A *far* throw. I did not hear you right at first."

The cabbie said, "You are a what in a what?"

"A heaver in the horsehide plant," said I. "Sometimes I am a swatter, but mostly I am a heaver."

"Where is that?" said he, "for I seem to forget."

"Why, it is over there near the ball park. Do you mean to say you are a cabbie and do not know where the horsehide plant is?" said I.

"Oh," said he, "the *horse*hide plant. Why do you not speak up when you speak?"

At the airport I picked up my tickets and weighed my bags through and bought some insurance out of a machine, 50,000 dollars made out to the New York Mammoths. What a simple soul! Then I read some magazines while they dillied and dallied until finally they left us on the plane. The last I heard we beat Denver 15–3, but I could not get the details, and I have never been back to Q. C. since.

It took me about 10 minutes to get past the clubhouse guard. Naturally they post a guard there, for you have got any number of these kids that in the course of a year tries to worm through and tell Dutch Schnell what a great ballplayer they are. The guard gripped me like I was some sort of a crook and led me in the clubhouse. We seen Sid Goldman sitting on a bench putting laces in his shoes, and he looked up, and at first he did not recognize me, and I said, "Sid, why do you not tell this fellow just who I am?"

The cop said, "Do you know this boy?" and Sid squinted at me and said, "Yes, he is the new pitcher," and the cop left go of my arm. Sid stretched out his hand. "I hit a home run off you 1 time in Aqua Clara," he said, and he give me a smile.

"And last spring I struck you out twice in Jacksonville," I said, for we had played a couple exhibitions there. Q. C. and the Mammoths, and we shook hands and he said, "Boy, if you will pull us out of this slump you are my friend for life."

The Mammoths at the time was 6 games behind Brooklyn, which was in second, and only 2 games ahead of Cleveland, with Washington behind Cleveland, about 1½ games. There was the danger of falling back to fourth and maybe out of the first division money altogether. They had give up all idea of climbing higher. What they wanted now was to fight off Cleveland.

"Well," said I, "you have just shook hands with the best lefthander this town has ever saw," and he laughed, and just then Dutch Schnell come up behind me, and he said, "If you are 1 half so good as you say you are I will be 1 happy old man." Then he took me down the line and give me the locker Bub Castetter had before he was sent down. Dutch tore off Castetter's name and said they would put up mine, and I said he might as well paint it with paint that would last forever, for I had a mind to stay up in the big time for 20 or 25 years, and he said he was highly encouraged by my remarks, and he turned and walked back through the door to his office.

The boys begun to gather. Sid introduced me to them as they come in, and some of them shook my hand and chatted, and some of them shook it but never said a word. The gloom hung heavy. The 1 who spoke the most was George Gonzalez, and he blabbered away for 2 minutes in Spanish, and I never understood a word, and I said, "Do you remember when I struck you out on

3 pitches at Aqua Clara?" and he said, "Up yours, up yours," which is the only 2 words of English that he seems to know. It was the only time anybody in the clubhouse laughed all day. Me and Lindon Burke dressed side by side, and he asked me how everybody was back in Q. C., and I told him they was all fine and running away with the flag, and somebody said, "It is nice to hear that somewheres there is a Mammoth club that is winning a flag."

"Buck up your courage," said I, "for the tide is changing now that I am here."

"Shut up," said the voice.

"No, sir," said I. "I will not shut up."

But just then Lindon nudged me with his elbow, and he said, "You had best shut up."

In come Bradley Lord with a suit over his arm, and he brung it down to me. It smelled all fresh and clean like it just been took out of the moth balls, and I looked at the number on the shirt, and it said "48" and I said, "I cannot wear such a shirt."

"Why not?" said he.

"Because of the number," said I. "I cannot wear no number that has got 12 in it."

"That is ridiculous," said he.

Then the same voice come again, and it said, "Bradley Lord, God damn you, go back and get that boy a shirt with a number like he likes it or I will break your f——ing back between my 2 f——ing hands." The boys all call him Bradley Lord, for nobody likes him well enough to call him Bradley, and yet nobody would ever call him Mr. Lord, and then I knowed whose voice it was. It was Sad Sam Yale's, for I could tell by the way he said it—"God damn you"— which was the first thing he ever said to me at Aqua Clara that time. His voice was like thunder, and it rolled like thunder rolling in across the mountains, and you could feel it in your belly, for it made you shiver and shake, and Bradley Lord scampered off and come back with a different shirt, number 44, and he said real soft, "Is that a better number?"

"Yes it is," said I, and I took it, and away went Bradley Lord. I shouted out, "Thank you, Sam."

"F—— you too," said he.

Cleveland was in town, finishing up on a 3-game series. We had beat them the first day, and they beat us the next, which was the day before I come, and the day I come they not only beat us but massacred us as well, winning 9–1 and drawing up to 1 game behind. The scoreboard showed Washington beating Chicago, and that made us feel no better, and the clubhouse afterward was quieter than hell.

Generally the Mammoth clubhouse will be full of writers. But when we hit the slump that year Dutch give the order not to let a single 1 of them donkeys in. You cannot blame him. They are like the plague. There is not a 1 of them that has got the guts and gumption to get out there and play ball theirselves, yet they know just exactly how the game should be played. They will get the fatigue from climbing 6 steps, yet they know how Perry Simpson should steal a base. They will get a cramp in their arm from writing a few words down on paper, yet if a ballplayer pitches 7 innings and poops out they are as libel as not to decide he is a quitter. They tell Dutch how to manage the club, and if he does right they will crow in their column for 2 weeks, saying it was all their idea to begin with. They are like fans. Red says the only difference between the writers and the fans is that the fans have at least got the honesty to pay their own way in the park.

Yet ballplayers read the papers day and night, mostly buying "The News" in New York. Red Traphagen will buy "The Star-Press," but I can't see it. I only buy it on Sunday when they run the pitching records and batting averages.

Cleveland lost the day after to Boston, Boston turning the trick again the following night whilst we was taking 2 in a row from Chicago. That give us our 3-game edge again and things begun to be more tolerable around the clubhouse. I got to know some of the boys, and half the club was my personal friends before the week was out. The west went back west, and Brooklyn moved in at the Stadium beginning on a Sunday, and a hot 1, with Sad Sam slated to work. There was a good crowd, for Brooklyn always draws well against the Mammoths, besides which they was still hopeful of overtaking Boston, which they finally done 2 days before the end, as you know. I was down in the bullpen as usual but I did not throw a ball all afternoon, just sitting and watching while Sam turned in a neat job. We scored 3 in the third and 2 in the fifth and that was enough. 5–0.

We still had the 3-game edge on Cleveland when Boston come in in the middle of the week with the flag hot in their nose and dumped us 2 straight, and we lost ground. Things was back to where the clubhouse was like a museum, so silent and still, the boys watching their third-place money about to float away, and maybe fourth as well, and I dared not speak above a whisper, for the tension was so high it was like you was sitting on thin ice and the least little rustle would crack it and down you would go in the drink.

Friday Dutch pitched Sam, hoping to beat Boston and hang on, Sam grumbling from overwork, but he had it that day, and the guts to go with it. I was in the bullpen again. He got in trouble in the fifth, and I got up and took off my jacket and begun to throw down to Bruce, and then he pulled out of his trouble and I sat down again. Then he was in trouble in the sixth, and then out of it again, and in the eighth Boston had 2 on and 2 down when a young kid name of Hillhouse, now no longer with Boston, hitting for the pitcher, clubbed a drive into right-center that Pasquale Carucci went halfway up the fence and pulled down or it would of went for a triple at least. It was 1 of the finest fielding gems that I ever seen, and I am lucky to have had the chance. Pasquale got a great hand from the crowd. It was still 0–0 and anybody's ball game.

In the last of the eighth Gene Park and Red Traphagen singled, and Dutch played the gamble and lifted Sam and sent Swanee Wilks up to hit. I knowed my turn had come, for there was only me and Lindon in the bullpen, and Dutch would not send a righthander in against Boston if he could help it at a time like now.

I warmed up hard. I was really throwing, and Swanee lined a single into right, and Gene scored, and I knowed it was now my ball game to win or lose for Sam, and when the signal come from the dugout Lindon said to me, "You will do it, boy," and I started across the field. Pasquale Carucci, on his way out to right, he give me a slap on the rump, and then it come over the speaker. I will never forget it: *"Your attention please. Now pitching for New York. Wiggen. Number forty-four. Now pitching for New York."*

Down around second base Gene Park give me a cluck-cluck with his mouth, meaning good luck, and Sid Goldman and George Gonzalez was waiting at the hill with Red and Dutch, and they said words to me, though I forget them, and then Red went down behind the plate and I throwed a few, and Dutch headed back for the dugout and Sid and George back to their spots, and Ugly come in from short and said something and then turned and went back, and then I was alone.

I remember. I remember I seen Sad Sam standing at the dugout door, and I seen Dutch on the bench with his legs crossed, and I seen the club all leaned forward with their elbow on their knees like they do, waiting and waiting to see if I was a man or just another boy, and down in the coaching boxes the Boston coaches was roaring insults out my way, saying did I happen to know I was now in the big-time and did I not know this and that, usually things of a rather low-down nature, and Red called down from behind the plate, "Give me what I call for and we will be back in the showers in 5 minutes," and I said to myself, "I will try. Yet at this particular moment I am not sure that I could hit the side of a barn with a basketball." I looked down at the ball in my hand, and it did not seem like my hand a-tall but like the hand of a stranger attached to my wrist, and the arm was not mine and I did not believe I could trust it. I wished I was anywhere but where I was, maybe down in Borelli's in Perkinsville, relaxed, *listening* to this ball game. And then I thought of Borelli's, and it flashed like a vision through my brain that probably this very minute Pop was down in Borelli's, and there was a silence amongst the men, and the barbers was standing with razors in mid-air, and I could just see old Borelli running out in the street and setting up the cry.

Then I wound and pumped and throwed. It was a ball, slightly wide, and just about then a cheer went up, and I did not know why. For an instant I thought Dutch was lifting me, and I looked around, puzzled, and Ugly Jones laughed and pointed to the scoreboard, and I looked, and it showed 5 runs in the second inning for St. Louis at Cleveland, and I knowed that if we won now we would be breathing easier again.

The batter was Black. I remembered the knee-high curve Sad Sam had throwed when me and Pop come down that day for the Opener, and Black had connected by sheer luck, and Red called for that kind of a pitch now, and it cut the corner, as clean a strike as you ever seen, and Hunt Glidden, the umpire, called it a ball, and I stormed down towards the plate and made a few remarks about how it was my belief umpires ought to be pensioned off once they went blind, and Glidden said to me, "You have throwed 2 pitches in the big time and already you are a hot head. Now get back out there and pitch," and I offered a few further bits of advice about the knack of being an umpire, and he turned his back. George shouted down from third, "Up yours, up yours," and Ugly and Gene come in and give Glidden a piece of their mind, and Dutch come up off the bench and told Glidden several things more or less harsh in tone. It seemed to bring the club to life, I think it was the first time in several days that it showed any life, and I went back out and throwed the same pitch again, and this time it was a strike and no mistake.

Then it was a fast ball, letter high, and Black never seen it, and the count was 2 and 2. Then I struck him out with the screw.

The crowd give me a good hand, and they give the razzberry to Granby, the next Boston batter, for he was not popular in New York since 1 time he spiked Ugly Jones in a play at second. He tried to cross me up by bunting down the third base line. I seen him shift when the ball left my hand, and I went down fast, and Red yelled "Wiggen, Wiggen," meaning for George to get out of the way, and I fielded it clean and whirled and fired to Sid Goldman at first, and Granby was out by a full step.

Now I was relaxed. It was like I was always up there, like I was there all my life, with the Mammoths, and I went back to the hill and scrubbed around with my toeplate, and I fingered the resin bag, and I looked up at the scoreboard and out at the fielders, and I was no more nervous then if I was back in the Legion League in Perkinsville.

Fielding stepped in. Casey Sharpe, the Boston clean-up man, was kneeling in the on-deck circle. "Get on," shouted he to Fielding, "and I will drive you home," and then he shouted something out at me that I will not repeat, and I shouted down to him, "Go back to the dugout, Casey, for number 3 is at the plate." Fielding must of liked those shoulder balls I throwed him, for he went after 2. He did not have the good fortune to get wood on them, however, and then Red called for the screw, and Fielding got a slice of it, and he skied it up behind third base. Ugly and George both went for the ball, and Ugly called "George" and George took it on the lope, a very easy play, and that was the ball game.

You would of almost thought we clinched the pennant. The clubhouse was downright cheerful. We got a later score on Cleveland, and Cleveland was losing, and Dutch come by, and he said to me, "Good work," and then he went back in his office. That was the game we needed, and we knowed it.

Patricia Moors was all smiles. Bradley Lord give us the warning, and she come through on the way to the office. She stopped near the door, and she said, "Sam Yale, nice game," and he told her he thought so himself, considering that he was more overworked then a nigger, and she said, "Where is Pasquale Carucci?" and he come forward, and she said, "That was a fine catch. I never saw DiMaggio make a better 1," DiMaggio being Pasquale's hero since he was a kid, and Pasquale said "Thank you, ma'am," and then she looked around some more, and her eyes lit on me, and mine on her.

"1-2-3 they come up and 1-2-3 they went down," I said, and she laughed, and when she laughed all the diamonds jiggled on her ears, and she brushed back her hair with 1 arm, and I think there was about 4 pounds of bracelets on the arm, and she stood looking at me.

"You set them down fine," she said.

"I rather thought the same," said I.

And still she stood there and looked at me, and I at her. "The trouble with you," she said, "is that you do not have enough confidence in yourself," and she laughed and turned and went off towards the office, and I watched her go, and a fine sight it was.

That day we dressed slow, me and Lindon, and in the days after. We made the last tour of the eastern clubs, and I worked just about every day down in the bullpens, yet Dutch did not use me. He said he would pitch me the last game, which was Sunday in Boston, and we beat them Friday and Saturday and knocked them out of the top spot, Brooklyn taking 2 from Washington in Brooklyn, and then it rained on Sunday and I never got the chance. I guess nobody give a damn but me, the race already settled, Brooklyn, Boston, New York and Cleveland finishing 1-2-3-4.

We had a meeting in the hotel that afternoon, and the boys voted shares of the third-place money. They voted me 100 dollars, which was good enough pay for 1 inning of work, and then we broke up, and it was sad because you knowed there was some amongst us that had played their last games in the big time. Next year they would be on their way down, down and down to nowheres.

Yet I was happy, for I was on the way up, and I said to Lindon, "I guess we are sitting on top of the world, away up in the clouds, and the gate is open and the music is playing," and Lindon said the same.

This first-person recollection is from one of the outstanding books of oral history that appeared in the mid-1970s: John B. Holway's *Voices from the Great Black Baseball Leagues*. That book, along with Robert Peterson's *Only the Ball Was White*, sparked a new interest in black baseball that predated Jackie Robinson and led to further study of those dimly documented days. Perhaps the most neglected of the "invisible men" playing professional baseball in the shadow of the major leagues was Hilton Smith, Satchel Paige's other—and some would dare to say better—half.

JOHN B. HOLWAY

Hilton Smith Remembers

Hilton Smith was the invisible man of black baseball. For years he toiled behind the glare of an almost blinding star known to the world as Satchel Paige, but who in reality was a hyphenated pitcher named Paige-Smith. After Satchel had pitched three innings to draw a crowd (and incidentally earn his 15 percent of the gate), Hilton Smith would trudge in from the bull pen and finish the game. And there are many black hitters who declare that of the two, when Smith appeared, the hits became even tougher to collect.

Ironically, Smith had been the star on the Monarchs before Paige arrived. Indeed, even for a while afterward Smith continued to be the ace of the staff. In 1941 Paige-Smith went barnstorming against Bob Feller and Ken Heintzelman of the white big leagues, and, wrote Bob Burnes, sports editor of the St. Louis Globe-Democrat, *"Smith showed the best speed and sharpest curve of the quartet."*

Even the New York Yankees learned to respect Smith. He beat them in Caracas, Venezuela, in the spring of 1947, and while most U.S. papers ignored the game, John Drebinger of the New York Times *didn't. "For the first five innings," he reported, "the Bombers ran into quite a Tartar in Hilton Smith, a right-hander, who gave up only one hit, a single to Phil Rizzuto, and two passes."*

I met Smith in 1969 in his handsome brick house on a terraced lot in one of Kansas City's best black neighborhoods. Although somewhat heavier than in his playing days, he does not look a bit like the grandfather he is. He talks in a high-pitched, rapid voice about the particular burden he carried for years as Satchel Paige's other half.

Hilton Smith Speaks . . .

I played twelve years with the Kansas City Monarchs, 1937–48, and I won twenty games or more every year. Not counting exhibitions, I won 161 league games and lost 22, but most people have never heard of me. They've only heard of Satchel Paige. That's because I was Satchel's relief.

Every Sunday I'd start, then Monday night come on in relief, start on Wednesday and maybe Friday, according to how Satchel was feeling. It was my turn to relieve him in all big games. He'd go two or three innings; if there was a big crowd and we had to win it, I'd go in there and save it. Then the next day I'd look in the paper and the headline would say: "Satchel and Monarchs Win Again."

I just took my baseball serious; I just went out there to do a job. But Satchel was an attraction; he could produce, and he'd clown a lot. I guess it really hurt me. I tried to get away, but there wasn't anything I could do about it.

Now Satchel never did pitch much here in Kansas City. Oh, no, he never did a lot of pitching here. But ooh, when he left here, my goodness, they'd eat him up all those other places, because he was an attraction, but these people here, they never did. He never was able to produce here. Some little old team would be able to hit on him, like Memphis and a lot of the teams like that. I remember '41 we opened up here against Memphis, and they got to him in about the second inning, and I relieved him. I shut them out the rest of the game, and we went on and beat them. So they never did book him in here hardly, I mean advertise him as a star pitcher. He played with us all those years, but he didn't do too much pitching here. I pitched all Sunday games.

Satchel was a great pitcher, I don't take anything away from him. I'd like to have seen him in his early age, back in '29 and the early thirties. Good God, he could throw that ball! And perfect control; he never walked anybody. He could throw it. But he hurt his arm in '37, and it didn't come back until '41. His arm was sore all those years, and he played with the Monarchs' "small team," while I was with the "big team." In '39 he came and played us over in Kansas City, and I shut him out 9–0. We just wore Satchel out. So I was the star.

But in '41 Satchel suddenly got his arm back, and that was the worst break I got. I guess in '42 Satchel was as great a pitcher as you want to see. He had a good curveball, and he always had that good fastball, and in '42 he just had everything on the ball. That's when he hit his peak.

I actually hit my peak, too, in '41. I was to the place then that I could just do anything, I felt that good. I thought I could go out there and get *anybody* out. I won twenty-five games and lost one that year. A semipro team in Dayton, Ohio, beat me, 1–0, after I had relieved Satchel. We struck out eighteen between us; they got one hit off Satchel and none off me but beat me on an error. It was the only game I lost that year.

In 1941 I pitched one game against Bob Feller's All-Stars. Walker Cooper was catching. Johnny Hopp was at first base—he had a good year that year, hit about .300; oooh, that guy could hit! The outfield was Ival Goodman, Stan Musial, and somebody else. They hit Satchel pretty hard in the first four innings, and I came in and relieved him in the fifth. I held them, struck out six of them in five innings, didn't give but one hit, but they beat us 4–3. Bobby Feller pitched three innings, and Kenny Heintzelman of Philadelphia pitched the last six. He really broke off some jugs that day, because I doubled with nobody out and didn't score. It would have been the tying run, but the guy struck out all the rest of them.

One of my greatest thrills was beating Dizzy Dean in Wrigley Field, Chicago, in 1942. We had a turnout of 30,000 people that day. Yeah, boy, you're talking about some good baseball, there was some that day. You remember big old Zeke Bonura, used to play with the White Sox? He played first base. Buddy Lewis of Washington played third and Cecil Travis short. All of them were major-league ballplayers who were in the service, and they came up for that game. Dizzy Dean pitched the first three innings. We "carried" Dizzy; because he wasn't too good, we kind of carried him along. I beat him 3–1. Satchel pitched the first five innings for us and came out with the score 1–1. He had struck out three, walked one, gave up two hits and one run. I struck out three, didn't walk anybody, gave up one hit and no runs. Big Joe Greene, our catcher, got a hit with two men on around the seventh inning, and I held 'em. In the ninth Travis came up with one on. Barney Serrell, our shortstop, said, "Make him hit it on the ground," and that's just what it was, a double play, and the ball game was over.

Jackie Robinson used to tell me, "Hilton, you're going under the same thing with Satchel that I went under with Kenny Washington at UCLA." See, at UCLA Jackie had to play second to Kenny. Kenny was a great football player; we all heard about him, but I never heard about Jackie until I went to the Coast in 1942.

In fact, I'm the one who signed Jackie to a Monarchs' contract. I had met him in '42 when Red Ruffing had a team in the service out there on the Coast. Jackie asked me about getting him a job, so I wrote to Mr. Wilkinson, the owner of the Monarchs, and he wired back to keep in touch with Jackie, so I did. In 1944 he got out of the service and joined the Monarchs.

Actually, Jackie didn't look that good. He was a little old to be a major-league rookie—twenty-seven—but there weren't any good young ballplayers then. Jackie's arm was weak at shortstop; Willie Wells was better than Jackie at that position. But the Dodgers picked him on account of he'd played college baseball; he'd played with white boys before.

I was born in 1912 in Giddens, Texas, a little town between Austin and Houston. Rube Foster came from about 25 miles from my house, a little town right above me.

I patterned myself after my uncles. I had two uncles that my mother would let me play with. They were powerful good ballplayers. I guess I inherited my ability from them. They were good, but they played out in the country there, played for fun. I just loved it, and that was what started me off. I just made myself, didn't have a teacher. I kept picking up and looking and learning as I went up.

I started out playing with my dad, who was a schoolteacher. I played for my dad's team when I was in the tenth grade. I guess I was about fifteen. During the summertime I played with older boys—they were all grown men. I pitched against the town high school team and shut them out 2–0.

Austin had a team, the Austin Senators, a semipro team that played Houston and all the towns down there. They had a pitcher named Willie Owens who had played with Birmingham in the Negro Leagues. In 1931, when I was nineteen, I went down and pitched against him one Saturday and beat 'em, I just beat 'em good. He went back to Austin and said, "My goodness, there's a little kid there, he's something else." So when the Chicago American Giants came down there to play Austin the next weekend, Austin came down and got me to pitch for them. I beat 'em 5–4 in eleven innings.

So Austin picked me up to play in Mexico. Mexico had an awful good ball club; they were good enough to play the major leaguers when they went down there that fall. Ramon Bragana was there pitching. They had Chili Gomez, who had been there and played with Washington. I'm telling you, we had a lot of trouble beating those guys. Well, we started another boy, and they ran him out. Then I went in and relieved him and got them out. So they started me Sunday again. The manager told me just to go out there and throw hard. But my arm was so sore—I wasn't nothing but a kid, and I hadn't been pitching that much baseball—I couldn't get anybody out. I don't think I got anybody out the first inning.

Next Thursday they started me again. The manager said, "Listen, I want you to go out there and try to get by the first inning." I said, "Yes, sir." I asked him, "Can I throw some curveballs today?" He said, "Yeah, I guess so."

I beat 'em 5–1, and I hit in all five runs. I struck out so many of them, they didn't think I was the same pitcher.

Monroe, Louisiana, had a real good Negro team then. They were champions of the Southern Conference, had beaten everybody. They had Red Parnell out of Houston; a little old guy name of Ducky Davenport; and Barney Morris and Goose Curry out of Memphis pitching. They had a tremendous ball club. They came to Austin and played us two games. They were talking about they heard of this little schoolboy up there and said, "Well, we came up here to work him over." But we had a great big ballpark, and I beat 'em 2–1. They couldn't believe it. They said, "Well, this big old park, no wonder you won. When you come to Monroe"—Monroe had a small park—"we'll hit so many home runs off you . . ." So I went to Monroe the following Sunday and beat 'em 4–2.

Monroe picked me up to play with them and carried me to Pittsburgh. That was the first time I saw Satchel Paige. I played with Monroe for the next three years. I had a great year in '32; won thirty-one games, didn't lose a ball game.

When the Pittsburgh Crawfords came down to Monroe to play us, I opened up against them. With Josh and them it was one of the best teams of all time: Oscar Charleston, Pee Wee Stephens, Ted Page, Double-Duty Radcliffe. I led them, 2–0, in about the sixth inning, when Boojum Wilson came up and got a hit. Then Josh Gibson hit a home run off me to tie the game 2–2. I came out the next inning. I was only twenty years old then. I was nervous, I'd never faced those kind of ballplayers before.

I pitched against the American Giants in '33. They beat the Crawfords out that year, beat Satchel and them. Yep, they won the championship and came to New Orleans. Chicago had Mule Suttles, Willie Wells, Jack Marshall, Alex Radcliff; outfield was one of the best outfields I ever saw—major league or anybody else: Steel-Arm Davis, Turkey Stearns, and Nat Rogers. They were a *tremendous* ball club.

We beat them three out of five ball games. Sure did, 'cause I remember now. They beat us the first ball game, Sunday—I think it was about 5–1. They stayed over till Saturday, and Bill Foster pitched against me—I'm strictly a rookie now—and I beat him 6–1. We came back and beat 'em again Sunday, 3–2, in twelve innings. George Giles tripled with a man on base and beat 'em. Bill Foster came back Monday and beat us—that guy pitched three ball games in a week's time. Then I beat Cornelius. I think they got four hits, and all the hits were the infield variety; they never hit the ball out of the infield. And it was just natural stuff; I didn't know how to pitch to those guys. Curveball and fastball were all I threw.

I went to Bismarck, North Dakota, in 1935. The league broke up down South, and Monroe went on a tour all around the Midwest. We weren't making any money, just touring around, but we were playing good ball, beating just everybody we met. I didn't know what it was to lose a ball game; I hadn't lost a ball game. We got into Bismarck the fifth of July—I never will forget that. A guy named Churchill was mayor of the city and had a ball club. Barney Morris, who played with Monroe, had gone to Bismarck earlier that spring. Satchel was pitching for them, too. They were getting ready to go to this Wichita semipro tournament, and they needed another pitcher. Churchill asked me about staying, and I said I didn't know. He offered me $125 a month. I wasn't making a quarter, but I told him no, I didn't want to, so he said, "How about $150?" I told him okay.

I didn't lose a ball game with Bismarck the whole year, but I didn't pitch much. I played right field on that club most of the time and batted third or fourth.

When we went to Wichita, to the semipro tournament, we didn't lose a ball game. I pitched the first game and shut somebody out 2–0; I don't remember who it was. I played outfield the rest of the games and hit fourth. Satchel and Chet Brewer did all the pitching.

The next year, when I went back to Bismarck, Satchel had gone East, so I did all the pitching down there in Wichita. I won four games, and all four of them were shutouts. Last time I saw the records on that, about six years ago, my record was still holding. I had more shutouts than any pitcher who had ever been in the tournament. I don't know if anyone's broken it or not. Satchel had the strikeout record.

Actually I didn't really learn how to pitch until I came to the Monarchs that fall. I just had natural stuff before that. I learned by having such guys for teachers as Frank Duncan, Bullet Rogan, and Andy Cooper.

Rogan. . . . He played with us in '38, and then he was through. He was a guy who, if you didn't know him, you'd think he was kind of a snob like, but he was a nice guy, and he used to get on you if you didn't do your job. He was umpiring, and I'd be pitching, and right after the ball game he'd come out and he'd tell me, "You've got a lot of stuff, but why'd you do such and such a thing?" I'd say, "Well, I don't know." He'd say, "Well, from now on, you *know*." I'd answer, "Okay, I'll do it." Next time he was umpiring and I got in the ball game, he'd say, "Un-huh, I see you're picking up."

Andy Cooper was a smart manager, and he was a great teacher—great teacher! A student of baseball. He would take me aside and just sit there and talk to me, and I'd watch how he'd pitch. And my owner, Wilkinson, would talk to me. He was a doll, that guy. He had played a little semipro ball himself, and he really knew baseball. He said, "Look, you've got everything, but use your wrist a little more, see if you can't get a little more hop on your ball." I took him at his word, and sure enough it worked.

So I'd watch and observe and listen.

The first ball game I pitched in this park out here in Kansas City was a no-hitter. I beat the Chicago American Giants 4–0. Nobody got on first base—I mean a perfect game. The Giants had Sug Cornelius pitching, Larry Brown catching, Alex Radcliff. They were *hard* to beat.

I didn't lose many games that year. I probably lost three the whole season.

The Monarchs used to play Texas League teams all the time. We played Oklahoma City when they were in the Texas League in '37. They had a good team, too; they had finished way up in that league, Double A baseball. We wanted to find out how good we were. Shoot, I pitched two ball games against them, and they haven't scored yet. I beat 'em Friday night, and we played 'em two games Sunday. We beat them the first ball game, and the second game they kind of started hitting our pitching, and Cooper brought me in there. A boy named Clay Touchstone—he was a great pitcher—I had beat him. He said, "What is this, the World Series, you bring that man back in here! Doggone, let us win *something!*" But I beat them. We beat them three straight. But we wanted to prove a point, see. We didn't have a chance to play in those leagues. We wanted to prove a point that we were good enough to.

We played the major leaguers about seven games that fall, too, and I pitched three of them. I pitched eighteen innings in all, and they never got a score off me. They had Johnny Mize on first, Lonnie Fry on second. Outfield had Ivy Goodman, Vince DiMaggio, and Gus Suhr. Pitchers were Mace Brown, Lou Fette—he won twenty games that year—Mike Ryba and Bob Feller.

I pitched three innings in Rock Island in relief and didn't give up any hits or runs. Bob Feller started for them, and we beat 'em, but I don't think we scored on Bob that day; he only pitched three innings. Lou Fette came on next, and we beat him. Next day I pitched six innings and didn't give up any runs. And then I beat Fette in a nine-inning game. I shut them out 10–0 in Oklahoma City.

Mize didn't get a hit off me the whole series. He was hitting everybody else, but he didn't hit me. How could that man hit that ball standing way back from the plate? I kept a-looking at him. I guess I had a curveball as good as anybody's in baseball at that time. My fastball ran; it just jumped. I bet I only struck him out twice that whole series, but he would hit the ball weakly back to me. I just kept it on the outside; the curveball would break in, and the umpire would call it. He'd try to pull it, and he never was able to pull it.

In 1937 I was on Martin Dihigo's team in Cuba. Josh was down there with Havana. Early Wynn was playing with Springfield in Triple A ball, and he only won one game down there that year. And he was going to the majors the next year! He could not win down there. Boy, it was tough.

That was 1937. In '37, '38, and '39 I had tremendous years. I could pitch and hit, both. Andy Cooper'd pinch-hit me for his fourth-place hitters just as quick. Several years I hit over .400 pinch-hitting, outfield, first base, and pitching.

I was pitching about four times a week, because we were playing six or seven games a week, and we only carried about four pitchers. Maybe sometimes we'd have five; that was the most. We didn't know what it was to relieve. When you went out there, you didn't look at the bull pen; you were expected to go the whole route.

They knew I wasn't wild; they knew I threw strikes. We didn't hardly walk anyone. The curve, we'd just slice it off, pfffft. And everybody threw hard. Good curveballs, and that live fastball moved. Today you see a lot of these guys' fastballs, just straight. But our fastballs *moved*. We had to have two curveballs, a big one and a small one. Now they call it a slider, but those guys were throwing it years and years back. It kind of just darted over the corner like that. Good control.

We were tremendous rivals with the Washington Homestead Grays. Tremendous rivals. A lot of those guys could have got in the majors, they were such good ballplayers. And gentlemen—Buck Leonard and them were such nice guys. We'd set and talk and jolly one another. My goodness! I pitched against them one night in New Orleans in 1939. They had Leonard, Josh, and all of them, and I struck out so many that night ol' Josh came up to me, said, "Say, fellow, look, you doctoring the ball or something?" I said, "Here it is; look at it."

Up until '42 I had more trouble with Josh than I did any other ballplayer. Gibson had those great big old muscle arms, weighed about 205, 6 foot 1. He would swing flatfooted, wouldn't stride. The first time I faced him, he hit a home run off me. But in '42 I didn't have any trouble with him at all. No, from then on I really began to get him out.

I learned how to get Buck Leonard out, too. I'd slow the ball up on him, screwball him, and slow curveballs. He'd ground out—oh, he'd get hits sometimes, but I mean I could get him out.

In 1942 I remember we played the Homestead Grays in Washington. Boston had played a day game against the Senators that day and drew 3,000; we played the Grays that night and drew 28,000. That's the year we beat the Grays four straight for the Negro World Championship.

We had a tremendous ball club that year. A lot of the boys had jumped to Mexico, and they all came back in '42. We had Joe Greene catching, John O'Neil first base, Jesse Williams short, Newt Allen second. Outfield we had Ted Strong, Willard Brown, and a boy named Bill Simms—he was a ballplayer never got much publicity, but he could do anything; he could hit, oooh, he could hit. Ted Strong was just as good a ballplayer as there was in baseball, but he kind of laid on the bottle. That got him in his late years.

We had a tremendous pitching staff in '42. We had Satchel, Jack Matchett, a boy named Connie Johnson, who played in the majors. And Lefty LaMarque and a boy named Booker McDaniels. Nobody hardly beat us. That particular year, '42, I don't think I lost maybe one or two ball games the entire year.

This kid Connie Johnson was awful good, too. He had hurt his arm when he went in the majors. I'd like to have seen *him* go in there before he hurt his arm. You talking about Satchel and me—Johnson and I would team up and beat anybody. I remember Baltimore came here with Campanella and all those good ballplayers. I beat them 3–1. He came back the second game and beat them 3–1. I mean we didn't lose—he and I didn't lose. Johnson—ooh, that guy could throw that ball. He wasn't but about nineteen or twenty years old. He hurt his arm in '42. He went into the service and came back. His arm came back to him, but nothing like it had been.

That '42 World Series. We opened up against the Grays in Washington. I think Satchel pitched the first game, and Jack Matchett relieved him. I started the second game; Satchel relieved me. We changed around. He said, "Hilton, you've been relieving me all this year. Let me relieve you; just see what we can do." I pitched five innings; he pitched four. When I left, the score was 5–0. They scored four runs off Satchel, and we beat 'em, 8–4. Then we went over to New York. Satchel started, and Matchett relieved him, and we beat 'em, 9–3. Then we went to Philadelphia and beat 'em 9–5, and I beat 'em the last ball game in Portsmouth, Virginia; I think it was 14–2. We just silenced them, just whipped 'em. I mean we killed their pitchers, and they didn't do anything with our pitching.

My arm went dead in 1943. I hurt it, and I played first base and outfield for two years. In '44 I began working back into shape, so I went out on the Coast that fall and played baseball against Bob Lemon, who's right down here as manager of Kansas City now. They had a good ball club. All those guys were in the service. They had an All-Star Game, and I beat them that evening.

Biz Mackey caught me. Oooh, my goodness, I didn't know he was such a catcher! I think I struck out fifteen of those guys. That guy was a marvelous catcher! I just—ooh, I just was on *edge,* and it looked like all my stuff was just working. Had the hitters looking like they didn't know what to do. Mackey told me, "I don't see how in the world you *ever* lose a ball game."

My arm came back in 1945 or '46, and in 1946 we played Newark for the Negro World Championship. They had Larry Doby and Monte Irvin, and I beat them two games. I beat them in Chicago, 5–1, and I beat them in New York, 2–1. No, that's wrong, I didn't beat them, I had them 1–0 going into the sixth inning, and Satchel came in. We had a guy from the Coast named Hamilton to replace Jackie Robinson—a good hitter, a good-looking boy. A big boy from Newark slid into second on the double play and broke his leg. Hamilton just laid there, and before we could resume play, it was almost an hour. So I cooled off, got stiff, and walked a man, and Satchel came in and relieved me. They tied it up, but he went on and beat them 2–1.

Monte Irvin played shortstop for Newark, and he looked awful good. Yeah, he was a *good* ballplayer. There's one guy I was really pulling for when he went to the majors.

But Doby didn't look too good. Three straight times I struck him out in Chicago, and he started jawing with the umpire. I asked him, "Doby, why do you want to jump on the umpire?" And he said, "Man, do you see my owner sitting up there in the stands? I've got to look good for her."

Roy Campanella didn't show me anything, either. Campanella and I were very good friends. I used to pitch against old Campy when he was seventeen years old. I'd strike him out all the time. In the All-Star Game one year I struck that boy out two times.

Campanella came down to the Polo Grounds one night when we were playing Newark in the World Series and asked me what did I think about playing with the Dodgers. He said the front office had told him to talk to me. He asked how old I was, and I told him thirty-four. Actually, they were wondering about Jackie [Robinson]. Jackie was around twenty-seven when he went up there, and they were debating whether he was too old. They knew he had to make it within one year, because if he didn't, he would be too old.

I figured I was too old at thirty-four. See, we were getting a pretty good salary, and we were afraid to go down to the minors and take a pay cut. With the Monarchs I was making $800 a month, and I felt like $400 would have been the best I could have got in Triple A baseball. Don Newcombe went down to the minors from Newark and stayed for three years, and I don't think he was getting over $250 a month.

Had it been opened up—had there been some other team beside the Dodgers—I probably would have taken a chance. I knew the Dodgers were pretty well loaded and I'd have to sit around in the minors and they'd be slow about bringing me up, and at my age that was too much. I wouldn't have minded going down to the minors for one year, then come back up. But at that particular time I felt I was too old to have a comeback with the Monarchs if I didn't make it with the Dodgers right away. Campanella said, "Well, think it over and let me know." But I couldn't see going down there for them.

That fall I went with Satchel to play against Bob Feller's big-league All-Stars. I remember they had Sam Chapman, Jeff Heath, and Charlie Keller in the outfield; Mickey Vernon, who won the batting championship, was on first; Phil Rizzuto and Kenny Keltner in the infield; pitching was Feller, Bob Lemon, Johnny Sain, Dutch Leonard, and Spud Chandler. I never *saw* so many good pitchers. Boy! Bob Feller said, "I wish I had this ball club all year to play with!" They had a powerhouse. Man!

We played fifteen or sixteen games, and I relieved in two and pitched two complete games. I broke even with them. They beat me 6–3, and I beat Feller 3–2. I gave up four or five hits. Vernon gave me the most trouble; he got two doubles.

What messed us up was Jackie Robinson had an All-Star team that fall— Monte Irvin went with him, and that left us with no outfielders. We had a pickup outfield—and Sam Jethroe had to catch when Quincy Trouppe got hurt. That really weakened our ball club defensively; we picked up a boy named Gene Benson to play center field. Artie Wilson played short, Hank Thompson played second, Buck O'Neill first. Catching, Quincy Trouppe started off; then he got his finger hurt.

We started off in Pittsburgh and went to Youngstown, played in Cleveland, Cincinnati, Chicago—just overflow crowds. We really lost a lot of money in Chicago. We had 30-some thousand there and thought we'd get ten or fifteen. They weren't expecting so many people, and Bob Feller himself had to go and try to help the ticket taker. They just rushed us. The policemen were taking up tickets and taking up money. My goodness. I don't know how much money we lost. Everywhere we went, just overflow crowds. They really poured out to see us that year. And we played some great baseball.

Hank Thompson just wore out that Bob Feller on that tour. I mean he just wore him out! He hit a home run and a double in Wichita, another home run off him somewhere else. Hit a home run in New York, because we beat Bob Feller 4–0 in New York. We had around 40,000 people, and our cut was $300 that day, each player.

Bob Feller's people made around $6,000 apiece for that trip. Ken Keltner said, "Hilton, my goodness!" I think his salary was $12,000 that year, and he cleared $6,000 for that trip.

But that was the end of it. They broke it up after that; the commissioner stopped it. Stan Musial was supposed to be on that club from the start, but that's the year St. Louis played Boston in the World Series in those little bandboxes they had for parks. Musial got in the World Series instead of coming with us, and he must have made a little over $2,000 for winning the Series. My goodness, he raised all kind of heck about it. Some of those players said, "The heck with the World Series when we can make this kind of money here." And that was the end of it.

I guess one of my greatest thrills was pitching against the New York Yankees in 1947—March 17—in Caracas, Venezuela. That was the first time I pitched against a whole major-league ball club. And they had quite a club, too, believe you me. Dr. [Bobby] Brown was about as good a hitter as I've seen. Boy! He was playing third base. Rizzuto was at shortstop, Stirnweiss was playing second, first base was Tommy Henrich and Nick Etten. Outfield was Keller, big Cliff Mapes, Johnny Lindell, and Yogi Berra. I think Ralph Houk was catching. Pitching they had Allie Reynolds. They had quite a ball club. I pitched six innings, didn't give up any runs, and gave up one hit, to Rizzuto. We won 4–3.

So I pitched against enough major leaguers to see if I was on the level. You know, naturally if you never compete with those people, you're always in doubt in your mind whether you're good enough to play against them. But I played against them enough, and they never did hit me. So I feel that had I had a chance, I could have pitched in the big leagues.

All our source of guys being developed was through the Negro League. Yeah, they were taking them, and I don't think any of the clubs got much out of it— Doby, Irvin, Newcombe, Campanella, Ernie Banks. And they were great attractions. You could see it in '46, the first year Jackie went to Montreal. Then in '47 Negro baseball began to go back. All the people started to go Brooklynites; everybody who had never known anything about baseball. Even if we were playing here in Kansas City, everybody wanted to go over to St. Louis to see Jackie. So our league really began to go down, down, down.

It looked like it was dead, so I played in Fulda, Minnesota, in '49, and in '50 I went out to Armco-Sheffield Steel here in Kansas City. They had a ball club, and they wanted me to manage it. So I said, "Well, maybe I better get on out of here." So I gave it up. I could have pitched a little more. But I'd seen so many ballplayers that just kept a-hanging around when they were over the hill, so I'd always made up my mind when I got to the place where I was going down, I'd just give it up. I'm a supervisor with Armco now. I'm lucky; I got a real good job.

A young girl asked me one day, "Did you ever play ball? I've heard my father and a lot of them talk about you. How did you get started?" and one thing and another. I told her, and she said, "Funny, there's no literature or anything. We would like to read about some of the older ballplayers so we'd know something about them." I said, "Well, maybe eventually there will be a book or something." She said, "If you ever run across one, let us know."

It was a rough life—ride, ride, ride, and ride. I remember many a day, ride a bus, get out and get you a little bit to eat, go to the ballpark, go out there and pitch nine innings, play a doubleheader, play outfield the second game. But I enjoyed baseball; I really did. It was spoiling me. I loved it, and it was sweet. We had some great moments. I enjoyed every bit of it.

Here's the thing of it: I know we were playing better ball than some of the lower teams in the big leagues. The only difference was, they had a better bench, more people sitting on the bench. See, if we had one shortstop, we had one shortstop, and our guys just played day in and day out. The majors had more replacements, more pitchers and reserves. Just man-for-man, we were tremendous. We'd put our ball club on the field and something's got to give; those guys could hit that ball, I don't care who was pitching. And we had pitchers could get anybody out and could throw the ball over the plate.

I look at these eighteen- and nineteen-year-old kids today—wild, can't get the ball over to save their lives. They have good coaches who talk to 'em, tell 'em things, but one thing, I don't think they have that desire to want to play, to *want* to develop, to want to learn. They just take it for granted: "Oh, I can go out and play golf." A lot of them quit. All this opportunity they've got. But we played because we loved it. I didn't care if I never got a dime, I just loved it that well. I just used to eat and sleep baseball. And I always had a desire.

I enjoyed baseball; I really did. I tell those kids, "You wouldn't believe I made my living for thirteen or fourteen years at baseball." They say, "You did!" I say, "Yeah, that's the only job I had. And here you all are just monkeying around here." See, I always wanted to win, and it's hard, you know—I just can't hardly take it the way these kids play ball. I always wanted to win, and I gave it my best.

I'd pick Buck Leonard as the best first baseman I ever saw. Martin Dihigo at second. Willie Wells shortstop. At third base I'd pick Kenny Keltner of Cleveland. In the outfield I'd put Sam Chapman, and Charlie Keller of the Yankees. Catcher of course is Josh Gibson. Pitching staff? I'd have to go with Lon Warneke of the Cubs. Ooh, that boy could *pitch!* And Bobby Feller, of course, and Bob Lemon, and Raymond Brown of the Homestead Grays. And yeah, oh, yeah, I'd put Satchel in there, too.

From the marvelously titled *Baseball When the Grass Was Real*, the first of Don Honig's four oral histories, comes this flavorful reminiscence of baseball in the storm-tossed 1940s. Max Lanier's major-league career actually began in 1938 and ran through 1953, and today fans may know him principally as the father of Astros' manager Hal Lanier, but Max was a fine southpaw with a colorful *curriculum vitae*. Read on.

DONALD HONIG

Max Lanier Remembers

Looking back on it all, I can tell you that it happened too quick. It doesn't seem like it could be that long ago. Time really flies. I know when I signed that first contract, it looked as big as this room.

I was pitching a high school game, down home in North Carolina. I won it 2–0. When I came out of the ballpark later, this guy was standing there waiting for me.

"Hi, Max," he said.

"Hi yourself," I said. I didn't know who he was.

"Can I give you a ride back to the school?" he asked.

"Well, I don't know you," I said.

He pulled out his identification and showed it to me. Frank Rickey, Branch's brother. Representing the St. Louis Cardinals.

"You interested in playing pro ball?" he asked.

"Yes, indeed," I said. That was one of my dreams. I was already playing semipro ball while I was still in high school. We had a pretty good semipro club there in Denton, North Carolina. This was around 1934.

Frank Rickey signed me to a contract when I was sixteen years old. My family wasn't too enthused about the idea. You see, I'd been offered a scholarship by Duke University, and my parents wanted me to accept it, but I turned it down to play pro ball.

I signed right out of high school, with a Class B club. I stayed there a week and then they wanted to send me to a D club, Huntington, West Virginia, for $70

177

a month. I didn't go for that, and I quit and came home. That was my first money dispute with the Cardinals. It didn't take long, did it? One week.

I started playing semipro ball again, in Ashbury, North Carolina. In 1936 I won sixteen straight games. That's against no losses. One day I walk out of the ballpark, and there's Frank Rickey standing there.

"Back again, are you?" I asked.

"How would you like to go to Columbus in the American Association?" he asked.

"Why should I?" I asked.

"It would be a great opportunity for you," he said. "That's Triple A ball."

"I might consider it," I said. "Under one condition—that you guarantee I'll be on the ball club the whole year."

I guess you talk that way when you've got a 16–0 record, no matter who you've won them against.

"How do you know you can pitch in Triple A?" he asked.

"I think I can," I said, "because we've got a lot of ballplayers right here who are that good, and I'm doing all right against them."

He went along with it. I was talking tough, but to tell you the truth, you couldn't afford to bargain too much with the Cardinals back then, because they had so many ballplayers. They were way ahead of everybody else in that respect. At one time they had about thirty farm clubs. And they kept us hungry. That was Branch Rickey's philosophy: a hungry ballplayer was a better ballplayer. I'll tell you one thing about him: he could tell you how much he paid you for each pitch, not how many games you won or lost.

The competition was murder. When I was coming up, they had, just in left-hand pitchers, fellows like Howie Pollet, Al Brazle, Harry Brecheen, Ernie White, Preacher Roe. That was pretty stiff competition. Why, Preacher Roe couldn't even make the club!

I got lucky at Columbus and won ten and lost four. The next year I went up to the Cardinals. Frisch was managing then. He was tough on young ball-players. I didn't appreciate it then, but I did later. He'd find faults no matter what you did, but if you paid attention to him, you'd find yourself learning something. He was a good baseball man and a full-fledged character at the same time. I remember one time Paul Waner was wearing us out with line drives. Finally Frisch stood up in disgust and yelled, "Who on this ball club can get that Waner out?" Max Macon was sitting on the bench—this was before he went to the Dodgers. Well, Max liked to pop off a little, anyway, and he said, "I can get him out." Frisch was delighted to hear that. He clapped his hands and said, "Atta boy. Get down there and warm up." Waner comes up again. Frisch brings in Macon. The first pitch Waner hits a line drive and breaks Macon's little finger. Frisch couldn't help but lie down on the bench and laugh himself silly.

Pepper Martin was on that ball club. I'd say he was the most colorful ball-player I ever saw. He was a real fun lover. He'd come into the clubhouse and tie your uniform into knots or nail your shoes to the floor. Sometimes during a game you'd be out there pitching, and he'd walk over from third base to talk to you and slap a wad of chewing gum onto your wrist.

One day, I think it was in Chicago, he pulled a beauty. He was great at throwing paper sacks full of water out the window. Well, there was a mezzanine in the lobby of this hotel, with a staircase leading up to it from the ground floor. Pepper got himself a paper sack full of water and hung around by the mezzanine window with a newspaper in his hand. He was waiting for Frisch. When Frisch came along, Pepper dropped his water bomb right on Frank's head, then tore back down the stairs, threw himself into a big chair, crossed his legs, and opened the newspaper and looked as though he'd been sitting there all day.

Frisch came storming in, wringing wet. He ran up to Pepper and said, "Damn you, if I wasn't seeing you sitting there, I'd swear it was you that did it!"

Pepper brought his paper down, looked at him as innocent as a baby, and said, "Did what, Frank?"

Another time, we lost a doubleheader in the Polo Grounds. That's pretty rough going when you lose two. You don't hear a voice in the clubhouse, much less see anybody smile. So we trudged into the clubhouse, and it's like a tomb. Buzzy Wares, our first-base coach, goes to light up a cigar. Well, Pepper had switched matches on him, and the matches were loaded. Buzzy strikes a match, and it explodes. Buzzy exploded right along with it.

"Damn you guys!" he yells. "Lose a doubleheader and you're still pulling pranks."

He went and got another book of matches. But Pepper had loaded the cigar, too. Everybody's sitting there watching Buzzy light it. When twenty-five guys are sitting stone still, watching you light your cigar, you ought to suspect something. But I guess Buzzy was too mad to take notice. Boy, he took notice a second later. The damn thing blew up in his face, and he had tobacco in his eyes, his ears, his nose. Twenty-five guys turned around and looked into their lockers, their shoulders shaking. You wouldn't want to be caught laughing then, would you?

Pepper kept you loose, all right.

Joe Medwick was in his heyday when I joined the ball club. So was Johnny Mize, one of the greater left-hand hitters. He and Medwick were as good a pair of hitters as I've seen. Of course, after Joe took that beaning, he seemed to lose some of his edge. That was in 1940, at Ebbets Field, soon after he'd been traded over to the Dodgers. I've heard stories that there was some bad blood, that we were throwing at him, but I never believed it.

I was rooming with the fellow that hit him, Bob Bowman, and I didn't know of any reason for Bob to be throwing at him. Here's what I think happened. Charley Dressen was coaching third for Brooklyn, and he always tried to call the pitches. He was skilled at that, but sometimes he called them wrong. Bowman was wrapping his curveball, and then he wrapped a fastball the same way, and it faked Dressen. Medwick stepped right into it, thinking it was going to be the curve. I think that's what happened. And Joe got hit hard.

Bowman was upset about it, I know. He never showed up in the room that night. He was supposed to be in at twelve, and he didn't come in. I thought, gosh, maybe something's happened to him. I didn't want to call the manager, because there was the chance Bob might be out having a couple of drinks, and I didn't want to get him in dutch. So I called Pepper, and he told me that they'd sent Bowman on to Boston. They wanted to get him out of town because they were afraid some of those very rabid Dodger fans might try something the next day. But I wished somebody had told me about it.

We had some pretty good throwing contests with the Dodgers in '41 and '42. Guys like Whitlow Wyatt and Mort Cooper would come close to you when they wanted. Of course, we never threw to hit anybody, but we'd brush them back. We had some great battles with the Dodgers.

Somebody would start throwing close, or there would be some jockeying from the dugout, and that would start it off. Durocher was a great one for that. You could hear him in the dugout: "Stick it in his ear. Knock him down." Stuff like that. You never knew when he meant it. You take that kind of thing, some mean pitchers, a great rivalry, and put it in the middle of a tense pennant race, and you're going to have some fun out there.

I remember this one time Marty Marion was taking a throw at second and Medwick slid into him pretty high. I guess Marty didn't like spikes up in his face, so he just flipped Joe. The next thing you knew, the whole gang was out there. I was pitching that day. Dixie Walker ran right by me and made a diving tackle into Kurowski, and then Jimmy Brown and me went after Walker. Oh, it was a great one. Players rolling and scrambling and wrestling all over the grass. Nobody got hurt. Nobody ever gets hurt in those things. Safest place to be in a baseball fight is right in the middle of it.

Another time, in St. Louis, in 1942, I saw Stan Musial get mad. It was the only time I ever saw Musial really get mad. Les Webber was pitching for the Dodgers, and he threw four pitches behind Musial's head. That's the worst place to throw, because a guy's instinct is to jerk back from a close pitch.

Musial was steaming. The whole ball club was steaming. You just knew something was going to happen. Walker Cooper was the next hitter. He hit a ground ball, and when he went across first, he jarred Augie Galan. Augie was playing first that game. Mickey Owen was backing up the play, and he didn't like what Cooper had done. What does Mickey do but jump right up on Cooper's back. Mickey was a scrapper, but he wasn't too big, and Cooper was like an ox. I remember looking at that sight and thinking, *What in the world is he doing up on Cooper's back, how's he going to get off, and what's going to happen when he does get off?*

Well, Cooper, he was so strong, he just threw Mickey right over on the ground and held him there. Next thing you knew, we were all out there again.

I had particularly good luck against the Dodgers. One of the reasons, I think, was Durocher. He'd sit in that dugout and holler at me and get me mad. He thought he was going to upset me, but the madder I got, the better I could pitch.

I believe there was more pressure in '42 than in '41. We were 10½ games behind the Dodgers in August. Then we went on the road and won something like twenty-three out of twenty-six ball games. Finally we got within two games of the Dodgers and went into Ebbets Field. Mort Cooper pitched the opener, and he beat Whitlow Wyatt a close game. That put us just one back.

I was scheduled for the next day, but I'd been having a little trouble with my elbow. Billy Southworth came up to me in the clubhouse.

"Max," he said, "I believe I'll pitch Beazley today and let you rest that elbow."

"No, sir," I said. "I've beaten them four times already, and I think I can beat them once more."

He thought about it for a moment, then handed me the ball.

I beat Max Macon 2–1 that day. Kurowski hit a home run in the second inning with one on, and then they got one run in the second inning. And that was it.

I can tell you who was the last hitter I faced. Billy Herman. One of the best. I threw him a fastball, and he took it. Well, I knew Billy—when he takes a pitch, he's looking for something else. So I wasted my curve and threw him another fastball for a strike. He was a guess hitter, and I figured he was guessing on the curve. So I threw him another fastball, right down the middle, and he took it for strike three. And we were tied with the Dodgers for first place.

We went on from there to Boston. Naturally you're not supposed to look at the scoreboard, and naturally you do. We were behind late in the game, and when we saw the Dodgers had lost, we went and came up with a big inning and won the game. We took over first place, and from then on they never caught us.

We played the Yankees in the Series that year. The Yankees had been in a lot of World Series, and they were a little bit cocky, though any ball club that had won as many pennants as they had had a right to be. I think we were kind of nervous in the first game. They beat us 7–4, but something happened in that game that took away our nervousness and gave us confidence. We were behind 7–0 going into the last of the ninth. We scored four runs and had the tying run at the plate. Musial was the hitter, and he flied out to deep right.

Well, that rally made us feel better, even though we lost the game. It showed we could throw a scare into the Yankees. And then we did more than scare them. We beat them four straight. I think that was one of the biggest World Series upsets ever.

I'll tell you, beating the Yankees in '42 will always be the highlight for me, more so than winning in '44 against the Browns, even though I beat them in the sixth game for the championship.

I went into the service in 1945 and missed most of that year. I came back in '46. I reported to the club in St. Pete. I was rarin' to go, but I hadn't signed my contract yet, so they wouldn't let me work out. The reason I hadn't signed was that old bugaboo, money. I'd won seventeen in 1944, plus the big game in the Series. I was making $10,000 and was holding out for more.

Eddie Dyer was the manager then, and he was anxious for me to start working out. I was hanging around the clubhouse, waiting to get the thing settled. Eddie saw me there.

"Come into my office," he said.

I followed him into the office, and he closed the door.

"I'm going to call Mr. Breadon in St. Louis," he said.

"Think it'll do any good?" I asked.

"I don't know," he said. "We can try. You get on the other phone."

So I listened to the conversation.

"Mr. Breadon," Eddie said, "this boy is worth more money than what you've offered him."

"Do you think so?" Breadon asked.

"Yes, I do think so," Eddie said.

"Well," Breadon said, "I'll give him five hundred more. He can take it or go home."

So I had to take it. I wasn't satisfied, but I took it. I felt I'd been dealt with unfairly, but there wasn't much I could do about it.

When the season started, it seemed I couldn't do anything wrong. In the first month I had six starts, six complete games, six wins. I was pitching great ball, but I still wasn't entirely happy, because of the way I'd been treated by Breadon.

One night I was leaving the ballpark in Philadelphia, and a couple of guys approached me. One of them was Bernardo Pasquel. He was the brother of Jorge Pasquel, a multimillionaire Mexican who owned a league in Mexico.

They were offering a lot of money to big leaguers who were willing to jump. Some guys, like Mickey Owen and Sal Maglie, had already gone.

That first conversation didn't amount to much, but he said he would contact me in New York, which was our next stop. I didn't say much to him one way or the other at that time.

When we got into New York, I found out that Lou Klein, our second baseman, and Fred Martin, a pitcher, had already agreed to go to Mexico. They started talking to me about going with them. Then Pasquel contacted me, and we all met at the Roosevelt Hotel. I was a little hesitant; after all, it was quite a big move to be contemplating. But I'll tell you something. I'd had some trouble with my elbow the last few games. Nobody knew about it but me. I wasn't letting on to anybody, but I was getting concerned. I knew if that elbow went, I'd be in trouble. I'd be nowhere then. You know what a pitcher with a bad elbow is worth.

So I began to get receptive. Pasquel's first offer wasn't good enough, but finally he made me the right offer. I got a bonus of $25,000 to sign and $20,000 a year for five years. I couldn't turn it down. I said, shucks, I'll pitch the rest of my life for the Cardinals and come out with nothing. I think the highest-paid guy on the ball club at that time was $14,000, and I'm talking about a ball club that had won three out of the last four pennants and had a lot of top stars on it.

After the meeting I went back with Klein and Martin to the Hotel New Yorker, where the Cardinals were staying. After thinking it over, I let Pasquel know the next day. We didn't tell anybody, not the Cardinals, not anybody. We went to St. Louis and from there drove to Mexico City.

I thought I was making the right move at the time. Remember, I'd just received this shabby treatment from Breadon. In the long run, though, I think that whole business probably didn't help us as much as it did some of the rest of the players, because I do know the Cardinals started paying more money.

When I got down there, Jorge Pasquel told me just to run and work out for a couple of days to get used to the high altitude. But my third day there I got into a ball game. It was the damnedest thing. I was sitting on the bench, watching the game. In the ninth inning the other team got the bases loaded with nobody out. All of a sudden the game stops. I look around to see what's happening, and Jorge Pasquel is coming out of his box. He walks across the field and comes to our dugout and says to Mickey Owen, who was managing the team, "I want Max to go in." Mickey didn't say anything; he just looked over at me and shrugged, as if to say, "It's his money."

So they stopped the game long enough for me to warm up. And I went out there and threw nine pitches and struck the side out. Pasquel came into the clubhouse after the game and patted me on the back and said, "Max, I won this game, didn't I?"

Pasquel owned the whole league, you see. They said he was worth something like $70 million. He used to sit up in his box during the game and eat off silver trays.

Conditions down there weren't too good. Half the time you couldn't play, you were so sick. You know, problems with the water. Mexico City was the only place where you didn't have to boil the drinking water; they had artesian wells there. And I got to where I was eating out of cans most of the time; I was afraid to eat the food.

I couldn't believe there was that much difference between two countries that were so close together. The conditions in the smaller cities were terrible. Tampico. San Luis Potosí. Puebla. Gosh, that Tampico was hot. I'd be so tired after pitching a game there that I couldn't talk above a whisper. There was no air conditioning, for one thing. Didn't even have screens in the windows. They had these overhead fans with the big black blades that used to go around and around very slowly and not do a damn thing.

Sometimes we traveled by plane, sometimes by bus. Those bus rides through the mountains were hell. They'd drive on either side of the road, didn't make any difference. The one that had the loudest horn had the right-of-way, I'll tell you.

The whole thing didn't last very long. I stayed in Mexico about a year and a half. We found out later why the Pasquel brothers were after the big leaguers to come down there. At that time Alemán was running for president, and I think there was some family relationship between him and Jorge Pasquel. Now the people in Mexico loved baseball. It was worked out so Alemán got the credit for us coming down there. They figured he'd get some votes out of it. And he did get elected. So I think the whole thing was strictly a political deal. After the election Pasquel started cutting everybody. He cut me from $20,000 a year to $10,000. That's when we started jumping back to the States.

Of course, everybody who went to Mexico was suspended from the big leagues for five years. I thought that was a little stiff. Heck, we didn't go down there to hurt anybody. We just didn't think we were making enough money.

After I got back, this was in '48, I formed an All-Star team, and we went on the road and played about eighty ball games against college and semipro teams. We played all over, Kansas, Iowa, Nebraska, Wisconsin, Indiana, Louisiana. But do you know, we got to where we couldn't get a ball game. I'm not especially against Happy Chandler—I suppose he had his job to do—but he tried to stop us from playing. We knew we couldn't play in professional ball-parks against professional ballplayers, but he shouldn't have tried to stop us from playing against colleges and semipro clubs. But he did.

We were supposed to be suspended for five years, but in '48 we started a lawsuit against baseball, and that's how we got back. We had them by the tail then because the suspension was illegal.

I went up to Drummondville, Canada, in '49 and was playing ball there. Around the end of June I got a phone call from Fred Saigh, who now owned the Cardinals.

"You've been reinstated," he said. "You ready to come back?"

"Sure," I said. "If the price is right."

"Look," he said, "you did the club an injustice when you went to Mexico, and we can't give you any more money."

"You don't have any reason to say that," I told him, "because you didn't even own the ball club then. You can forget about it if you think I'm going to come back for the same amount of money I was getting before I left. I'm making more money here in Drummondville than you're offering me."

Eddie Dyer got on the phone then.

"Max," he said, "we sure would like to have you back. We think we can win the pennant, and the fellows would like to have you back."

"Eddie," I said, "if you were managing in the minor leagues, making more money than the major leagues offered, what would you do?"

"I'd probably stay where I was," he said.

"Well," I said, "those are exactly my circumstances right now."

Saigh called me back the next day.

"We'll double your salary," he said. "And we'll give you expense money if you can get to St. Louis by the Fourth of July."

Well, that sounded just great to me. As a matter of fact, I was there on the second of July.

I pitched for the Cardinals for a few more years and then in '52 was traded to the Giants. The next year I went back to St. Louis, but this time it was with the Browns. Bill Veeck owned the ball club, and what a great guy he was. Veeck was a generous and good-natured man and a real hell raiser when he wanted to be. Of course, we didn't have a very good ball club, but that didn't seem to dampen his spirits any. One time we'd lost eight straight, and he decided to give a party, to loosen us up.

This was in Cleveland, at the Aviation Room in the Carter Hotel. It was a pretty fancy place, decorated with a lot of airplane stuff, and had a big, glass-framed picture of Eddie Rickenbacker on the wall. Veeck told the whole ball club to be there, every man. He hired a piano player, and he had plenty of food and drink laid out. It was a great time; we were singing songs and laughing and telling stories. You'd have thought we had just won the World Series instead of riding an eight-game losing streak.

Around one o'clock in the morning a few of us started getting ready to leave. But Veeck got by the door and said, "Nobody can leave until I say they can leave." Then he started opening champagne and squirting it at everybody. Vic Wertz and myself, we caught him and poured a bottle of it right down his back. He was laughing so hard we could hardly hold him. Then there was one bottle of scotch left, and Veeck grabbed it and threw it at Eddie Rickenbacker's picture and smashed the glass frame into a thousand pieces.

It was a great party. Cost him $1,850, Veeck said. We went out the next day, nice and loose, and lost our ninth straight.

The land of baseball is one: a man may be lonely though in a crowd, but no one is alone at a ball game. In the poet's words, "That each of us was a player for a moment": this is the satisfying feeling of unity, of connection, that each of us craves.

ROLFE HUMPHRIES

Night Game

Only bores are bored,—wrote William Saroyan—
And I was a bore, and so I went to the ball game;
But there was a pest who insisted on going with me.
I thought I could shake him if I bought one ticket,
But he must have come in on a pass. I couldn't see him,
But I knew he was there, back of third, in the row behind me,
His knees in my back, and his breath coming over my shoulder,
The loud-mouthed fool, the sickly nervous ego,
Repeating his silly questions, like a child
Or a girl at the first game ever. *Shut up*, I told him,
For Christ's sweet sake, shut up, and watch the ball game.
He didn't want to, but finally subsided,
And my attention found an outward focus,
Visible, pure, objective, inning by inning,
A well-played game, with no particular features,—
Feldman pitched well, and Ott hit a couple of homers.

And after the ninth, with the crowd in the bleachers thinning,
And the lights in the grandstand dimming out behind us,
And a full moon hung before us, over the clubhouse,
I drifted out with the crowd across the diamond,
Over the infield brown and the smooth green outfield,

So wonderful underfoot, so right, so perfect,
That each of us was a player for a moment,
The men my age, and the soldiers and the sailors,
Their girls, and the running kids, and the plodding old men,
Taking it easy, the same unhurried tempo,
In the mellow light and air, in the mild cool weather,
Moving together, moving out together.
Oh, this is good, I felt, to be part of this movement,
This mood, this music, part of the human race,
Alike and different, after the game is over,
Streaming away to the exit, and underground.

Here is Bill James at his considerable best: asking the questions few have thought to ask and fewer still to pursue the answers. James does all the tedious spadework to get to the bottom of things, not just rearranging the terrain and shouting, "Eureka!"

BILL JAMES

A History of Platooning

Who invented platooning? Where does it come from? When did it become common? What was said about it when it began? Who was the first manager to platoon extensively?

One of the things I had wanted to do with this book was to answer those questions. Platooning existed prior to 1910 but was rare; by 1920 it was common. It is curious that baseball has, really, not even a myth to explain the origins of platooning; its beginnings are not shrouded in a haze but blanketed in utter darkness. This is atypical for baseball, for as historian David Voight has pointed out, baseball men love myths of creativity and have spun birth-in-a-thunderclap legends about the inception of almost everything connected with the game. Of platooning, though, one sees only an occasional suggestion that "some say it was John McGraw" who first realized that a left-handed batter might have an advantage against a right-handed pitcher, and vice versa.

It was not John McGraw who first realized this. For one thing, there is the matter of switch-hitting. The fact that one would switch-hit, bat right-handed against a left-hander and left-handed against a right-hander, implies clearly a recognition of the platoon advantage. The first man to switch-hit—and thus, in one sense, the inventor of platooning—was Bob "Death to Flying Things" Ferguson, whom we have encountered several times in the early history of the game. Ferguson played in the major leagues from the time they were organized (1871; he was twenty-six then and a well-known "amateur" player) until 1884;

188

he was switch-hitting before McGraw was born. Ferguson was more noted as a glove man and manager, but he did hit .351 in 1878.

His experiment with switch-hitting was not widely imitated at first, in part perhaps because nobody wanted to be like Bob Ferguson, but in the 1880s it became the fashion, and there were quite a number of switch-hitters. Will White, the bespectacled pitcher, was a switch-hitter (1877–86). The first outstanding switch-hitter was Tommy Tucker (1887–99), who won the American Association batting title in 1889 with a .372 mark. After him there were a bunch of them. There were at least four outstanding switch-hitters in the 1890s. John Montogmery Ward experimented with switch-hitting in 1888, plus, of course, you have the famous switch-pitcher, Tony Mullane. Actually, according to Al Kermisch, at least three right-handed pitchers of the 1880s pitched a few innings left-handed—Mullane, Larry Corcoran, and Icebox Chamberlain.

So the platoon advantage was something they were thinking about, but when did they start platooning? In *The Glory of Their Times*, Al Bridwell (a left-handed batter) was discussing the play on which Merkle failed to touch second in 1908:

> I stepped back into the box. Jack Pfiester was pitching for the Cubs, a left-hander. We didn't platoon in those days. The fact that Pfiester was a lefty and I was too didn't bother anybody. I was supposed to be able to hit left-handed pitching just as well as right-handed.

Let us use 1908, then, as the back boundary of platooning; it started sometime after then.

The boundary of platooning on the other end is 1920, when the strategy had its first big vogue. I have heard a number of baseball people say in the last few years that Casey Stengel was the first man to platoon extensively. This is completely false; Tris Speaker platooned at four positions in 1921, and platoon arrangements at two or three positions were quite common at that time. A few years later platooning fell out of favor and was not widely used for many years until Stengel revived it—but by no stretch of the imagination did he initiate it or even raise it to new levels.

If platooning was being done at three and four positions in 1920, then it must have begun sometime before 1920, but when? Jim Baker and I attempted to answer this question by "walking it backward," starting at 1920. Pardon me; I intend to describe that process here in some detail. In the 1920 World Series, both managers used platoon arrangements. In Game One, with Marquard (a left-hander) starting, Tris Speaker started Joe Evans in left field, George Burns at first base, and Smokey Joe Wood in right field, all right-handed batters; when a right-hander (Al Mamaux) relieved Rube, the left-handed hitting Charlie Jamieson pinch-hit for Evans, and left-handers Doc Johnston and Elmer Smith came into the game to play first base and right field. Speaker continued to make strict platoon moves with these six players throughout the series, in which Brooklyn split its innings almost equally between left-handed and right-handed pitchers. For his part, Brooklyn's Wilbert Robinson used the right-handed Bernie Neis in right field against the Duster Mails, the only left-hander to pitch for Cleveland, but Tommy Griffith (a left-handed hitter) against all the other pitchers.

What about 1919? In the 1919 World Series, Cincinnati's manager used Bill Rariden as catcher against Chicago's two left-handed pitchers (Williams and Kerr) but used Ivy Wingo against the right-handers. That's a platoon arrangement. For his part, Kid Gleason of the White Sox used Nemo Leibold in right field against Cincinnati's right-handers and Shano Collins against the left-handers.

In short, platooning is strong in 1919; it's easy to find. In the 1918 World Series—I'm using World Series because the box scores are available—the Cubs did not platoon themselves and started left-handers in all six games, so Boston didn't platoon, either. In the 1917 Series, the White Sox again used the Leibold/Collins platoon arrangement in right field—sort of. All five of Leibold's at bats in the Series did come against right-handed pitching, but Collins played all of the time against left-handers and half of the time against right-handers.

For his part, John McGraw did not have an option to platoon in that Series, and that could be significant. Chicago had basically a five-man pitching staff, with two right-handers and three left-handers, but the two right-handers (Faber and Cicotte) did all the pitching in the World Series. If you look at the Giants' lineup, it's basically a right-handed-hitting lineup—so that may imply that Pants Rowland, in 1917, was selecting his starters with recognition of the platoon advantage.

In 1916 Boston platooned Tilly Walker in center field with Chick Shorten. Brooklyn platooned Casey Stengel in right field with Jimmy Johnston. In 1915 Philadelphia (National League) used only one left-hander in the Series, Eppa Rixey, who was brought into the game in the third inning. When Rixey entered, the Red Sox made a response move, bringing Del Gainor off the bench to play first base instead of Hoblitzell. A trip to the microfilm room at the library to find some more box scores confirms that this was, indeed, a platoon arrangement. However, Philadelphia did not platoon; they used exactly the same lineup to face the left-handed Dutch Leonard in Game Three that they had used the first two games.

It's growing weaker; we're down to one team and one position here. The 1914 Series is the same cities—Philadelphia against Boston—but a switch of leagues. This is the Braves against the Athletics. Philadelphia started a right-hander in Game One and a left-hander in Game Two; Boston made two response moves, starting the right-handers Les Mann and Ted Cather in place of the left-handers Joe Connolly and Herbie Moran. In Games Three and Four, the A's went back to right-handers, and the Miracle Man, George Stallings, went back to Moran and Connolly. When a left-hander relieved in Game Four, Mann came back in, but Moran stayed in right field, as Stallings played to preserve the lead. Connie Mack did not platoon in the Series.

Two things about this, I would later decide, were significant. Number one, it was the first time that a manager had platooned at two positions in a World Series. And number two, it was the first time that a National League manager had platooned in the World Series—and quite possibly the first time that a National League manager had platooned, period.

Let's continue to walk it back. In the 1913 World Series (Connie Mack vs. John McGraw), neither team made any platoon changes, although both teams used both left-handed and right-handed pitching. In the 1912 World Series (Jake Stahl vs. John McGraw), neither team made any platoon changes. In the 1911 World Series (Mack vs. McGraw again), neither team made any platoon changes. Significantly, Connie Mack used a left-handed catcher and a right-handed catcher all year, but did not use them in a platoon arrangement, choosing instead to rotate them on some other basis. He started the left-handed Lapp against the left-handed Marquard in one game and the right-handed Thomas against the right-handed Mathewson in another.

Christy Mathewson put his name on a book written during that 1911 World Series, the book *Pitching in a Pinch*. On page 44 of that book, he says that Josh Devore "has improved greatly against all left-handers . . . so much so that McGraw leaves him in the game now when a southpaw pitches, instead of placing Beals Becker in left field as he used to." This would be evidence of early platooning on the part of John McGraw, except for one thing. Beals Becker was also a left-handed batter. In taking Devore out against a left-hander, McGraw was not platooning, but reacting to a weakness on the part of the player—a weakness that many other players must have had before 1910.

With platoon combinations in the World Series drying up, I started looking for evidence of platooning in the rest of the league. If a manager platoons at a position and sticks with it, this is fairly easy to recognize in the statistics; you'll have a left-handed batter with 60–80 percent of the at bats (50–70 percent in our own time), and a right-handed batter who plays the same position with 20–40 percent of a full season's at bats. The problem, of course, is that with platooning in an embryonic state, you're not going to get that kind of commitment to it; a manager might platoon a man in left field for a few weeks, then play him regularly for a month at third base to cover an injury, then bench him entirely, or any number of other options. You can recognize possible platoon combinations, but you have to get into the box scores to know for sure whether they were or were not.

Jim Baker and I spent a good many hours checking out those possible platoon combinations. We found no evidence that any National League manager was platooning prior to 1914. This certainly does not mean that there isn't, anywhere between 1876 and 1914, any platoon combination in that league; there may well be. We didn't find it. With platoon combinations stopping sharply before 1914, it seemed appropriate to look more closely at what happened that year.

The account of the 1914 World Series in the *Reach Guide* runs to many thousands of words but makes only two brief references to this matter. The first occurs in the discussion of Game Two, the second in the discussion of Game Four:

> In accordance with his season-long policy, Manager Stallings shifted his outfield to meet southpaw pitching, and Mann and Cathers acquitted themselves creditably. . . .
>
> When Pennock relieved Shawkey, Manager Stallings followed his season custom and substituted right-handed Mann for left-handed Connolly in the sixth inning but allowed Moran to remain in the game when his turn at bat arrived in the seventh inning.

Stallings's handling of his outfield that year deserves an essay in itself. He used eleven outfielders in 1914, several of them interesting people but none of them terrific ballplayers, giving each of those at least two weeks in the outfield to impress him. It is not strictly true that he alternated on a left/right basis all season; for one thing, the right-handed-hitting Mann had 389 at bats, and if you count the number of left-handed pitchers in the National League in 1914, you quickly realize that that ain't right. At one point in the season Boston went about three weeks without seeing a left-hander. But he did platoon when he saw a left-hander; one of the people he platooned with, incidentally, was Josh Devore.

Anyway, that is not this essay. For this essay, the key point is that Stallings was "The Miracle Man," the media hero of the 1914 season. As best you can tell, he deserved to be; what he did that season is like winning the pennant by coming up with a handful of Hurricane Hazles. His cleanup hitter for much of the season was Rabbit Maranville; Maranville led the team in RBIs, too. The *Reach Guide* gave him a two-page spread: Boston's Miracle Man. So what you have here is a manager who is (1) following a new and experimental policy, (2) having remarkable resuilts, and (3) receiving extensive praise. Although no one that I can find cited his platooning as the key to his accomplishment, it is a fact that the popularity of the strategy grew rapidly, as we have seen, after 1914. For example, the other Boston manager, Bill Carrigan, who was not platooning in 1914, began platooning in 1915.

George Stallings was a smart man. He graduated from the Virginia Military Institute in 1886 at the age of seventeen; whether or not that is unusual I don't know. He then began to study medicine, but Harry Wright, then managing the Phillies, saw him catching a game and offered him a contract. He went to spring training with the Phillies in 1887, but Wright cut him. Ten years later, Stallings was managing the Phillies. He was the bright guy who buried the wire into the third-base coach's box.

But he did not, as best I can ascertain, invent platooning. He apparently imported it to the National League from the American. In 1911, Hughie Jennings, manager of Detroit, platooned in left field—not all year, but most of it—with Davy Jones and Delos Drake. Jones, also interviewed in *The Glory of*

Their Times, makes no reference to this. But it happened, and for a time I thought this would stand as the first identifiable case of platooning. Note the distinction; we are down now to trying to find the first, isolated instance of platooning.

I missed one for a while because I was looking for left/right combinations. But because we knew that Hughie Jennings was platooning in 1911, I thought I'd better look a little more carefully at his earlier teams, particularly his pennant-winning teams of 1907–09. In the 1909 World Series, I noticed that Boss Schmidt, a switch-hitter, did not play in one game, the one game that a left-hander had started. In the 1908 World Series, again, there was one game that Schmidt had not played and one game that a left-hander (Jack Pfiester, the man who just weeks earlier had surrendered the single to Al Bridwell, providing the back boundary for platooning) had started for the opposition. They were, again, the same game. In the 1907 Series there was, again, one game started by a lefty—and again, it was the one game in the series that Schmidt did not play.

The three Series games that Schmidt missed were started by Freddie Payne, Ira Thomas, and Oscar Stanage—all three of them right-handers. Though Schmidt was listed as a switch-hitter, he was, in effect, a left-handed platoon player. The microfilm quickly confirmed this.

Schmidt was, obviously, a left-handed hitter who couldn't hit left-handed pitching, and tried to switch-hit in desperation. But unlike McGraw, who replaced Devore with another left-hander, McGraw's old teammate Jennings had evolved a series of platoon combinations—Schmidt and Payne, then Schmidt and Thomas, then Schmidt and Stanage. It is interesting to note that Thomas, as a platoon player in 1908, hit .307. He was traded to Philadelphia after that season, and in Philadelphia, not platooning, he hit .223.

These were the only platoon combinations I found that Jennings was using; I never found any instances of his generalizing the principle and platooning at another position. In the time that he was using this arrangement in Detroit, one of his rivals was the New York Highlanders, who were lifted briefly out of the basement and into the pennant race during a period in which they were, quite by coincidence, I'm sure, managed by George Stallings. Stallings had a bad New York club in the pennant race in 1910, and it is during that period that I find the first instance of platooning on any team other than Detroit. The Miracle Man experimented for a time with platooning Charlie Hemphill and Bert Daniels in center field.

It seems, in short, to have been Stallings who first formulated the idea of platooning as a weapon rather than as a possible response to a player's weakness.

I wish that we could let it rest there, because that makes a creditable story. Hughie Jennings was a famous and successful (1) ballplayer and (2) manager. He was a lawyer, an educated man, but also a part of the Old Orioles with McGraw and Wee Willie, a running mate and later a coach of little Napoleon. That's a good story—the lawyer/manager thought up the idea of platooning sometime while he was playing, implemented it when he became a manager in 1907, and immediately won a pennant with it. This spread the idea at least as far as George Stallings, and Stallings's success attracted the attention of others, and platooning became popular. That makes perfect sense; if Hughie Jennings didn't invent platooning, he should have.

It makes sense, and it fits. If you were to draw a schematic of baseball history and you were to say, "Where *should* platooning begin?" you would come up with the answer that an American League team should have begun platooning at the catcher's position sometime about 1905.

Platooning should have begun at the catcher's spot, obviously, because that was the one spot at which few teams (very few teams) used regular players prior to 1920; almost every baseball team from 1876 to 1920 consists of a pitching staff, seven regulars and two or three catchers. (Sometimes the seven regulars change in a season, but rarely would any manager alternate.) Platooning should have begun about 1905 because (1) we know it was common by 1920 and (2) it would have been very difficult to platoon prior to 1900.

There are two reasons why it would have been difficult to platoon prior to 1900. Number one, the rosters were too small. The National League teams in the 1890s used a varying number of people, but seventeen is about the median, and with the game under severe economic pressure, the crunch was to reduce it even lower. When baseball became popular again after the turn of the century, the rosters swelled rapidly in size, reaching twenty-five by the end of the decade. That makes it a lot easier to platoon.

Number two, there weren't enough left-handers. Of the fifty-two National League pitchers listed in the 1900 *Spalding Guide* (1899 season), only nine were left-handed. My guess is that that ratio represented a big increase from the earlier part of the decade. Let me ask you: if you were playing with a sixteen-man roster, in a twelve-team league with only nine left-handed pitchers in it, do you think you would platoon?

Platooning should have started in the American League, because that's where the left-handers were. For some reason, or probably no reason, the American League from 1901 through 1915 had many more left-handed pitchers than the National; a spot check of 1905 shows that American League left-handers accounted for 316 decisions, 26 percent of the league total; National League left-handers accounted for only 178 decisions, 15 percent of the total. You can start considering platooning at 26 percent; it's very difficult to do at 15 percent.

It's a good story, and it fits, but it isn't exactly true. We had walked it back now to 1907, before the Bridwell line, and I was ready to declare that the start of it. But I felt compelled to check out the rest of Boss Schmidt's career, and guess what. Jennings did not invent a platoon arrangement. He inherited it.

Schmidt came to the majors in 1906. I had Jim check out a forty-eight game sample of the Tiger's schedule for 1906. Here's what he found:

Schmidt started:	19 games
Against left-handers	1
Against right-handers	18
John Warner started:	17 games
Against left-handers	5
Against right-handers	12
Freddie Payne started:	12 games
Against left-handers	10
Against right-handers	2

John Warner was a left-handed batter—and that's a platoon arrangement; the Tigers started the catcher who would give them the platoon edge (considering Schmidt a left-hander) in forty of the forty-eight games.

Well, what about 1905?

No major-league team was platooning in 1905, at any position. I state this with some confidence, as we made a real effort to nail it down.

What I did is, I developed the idea of a "platoon scan." To make a platoon scan, you divide a team's starts into games against right-handed starters and games against left-handed starters. Then you go through that team's box scores, game by game, and you count the number of left-handed batters (or right-handed batters) in the lineup. If they have three left-handed batters in the lineup against a right-handed pitcher, you write down a "3" under "Right." Boston's platoon scan for one twenty-two-game sample in 1905 looks like this:

	Right	Left
Boston	3322223333333	432222233

Using this method, if a team is platooning, it very quickly becomes obvious, even if there is some shifting around in the lineup that might tend to disguise it. Full-scale platooning would look like this:

	Right	Left
Boston	3322223333333	321111122

While the inconsistent, spotty platooning that you might otherwise miss would look something like this:

	Right	Left
Boston	3322223333333	312211231

If they're *really* platooning, the average of the "Right" column and the average of the "Left" column will differ by 1.00 (or 2.00 if platooning at two positions). But even if they're just kind of experimenting, a separation of .40 or .50 should appear quickly.

We took samples of at least fifty games for every American League team in 1905, and quite simply, there was no platooning in that league. We didn't do the platoon scans in the National League, but we did do a thorough job of checking out player usage patterns that could have resulted from platooning, and I am 99 percent certain that no National League team was platooning in 1905.

It makes a terrible story, you see. The first known platoon arrangement was operated by some guy named Bill Armour, who nobody knows anything about, who thought it up and implemented it in his fifth and final season as a major-league manager, had a poor year, and was fired?

I don't know that. I know this: no one was platooning in the major leagues in 1905, and Bill Armour was platooning in 1906. I still get the feeling, somehow, that somebody did platoon, sort of, sometime in the nineteenth century. It would have been awkward as hell, but they could have done it. I fully expect some other baseball researcher to take an interest in this subject and find an earlier platoon arrangement.

The other thing that we didn't find was the discussion of the issue. What I had expected to find, somewhere in this process of walking it backward—and what I still know must exist, somewhere—is a whole bunch of essays by journalists of the period discussing the issue, talking about who started it and what the idea is and who else is doing it and where's it all going to end. It's a funny business, doing this kind of research. One time Baker and I were talking about general managers over lunch, and we got to wondering who the first general manager was. We decided it was our job to find out that kind of stuff, so we got up and went back to the office and decided to dig into it. The first book I picked up was the 1928 *Reach Guide*, and I flipped to page 23, and it said, "William Evans, famous American League umpire, [was] chosen general manager of the [Cleveland] club. This is a new office in a ball club." So we found the answer to that question, I swear, inside of twenty seconds after specifically setting out to look for it.

Well, this time we weren't lucky. We never could find that article saying that "Alfred Smartguy has a new strategy this year of playing his left-handed hitters against right-handed pitchers." We could never find Fred Lieb telling us what he thought about the idea in the New York *Press*, with Grantland Rice answering the next day in the *Tribune* and Damon Runyon the third day in the *American*. Maybe that's why platooning has no myth of creativity, like everything else; it just sort of snuck up on everybody, and it was fifteen years old before anybody realized it was here to stay.

Well, let's go forward with it. Tris Speaker, like Jennings, inherited a platoon arrangement and improved upon it. In mid-season, 1919, he took over a Cleveland team that was platooning at two positions. He extended that arrangement to three positions in 1920 and occasionally to four positions in 1921, as discussed before, making him the first manager to use extensive platooning.

As platooning grew, John McGraw was never ahead of the pack at any time; he was not the first man to platoon or the first to platoon at two positions or three or four or anything. He was never the last one to adapt, either, but so

---

A CAPSULE HISTORY OF PLATOONING
(For those of you who are too "busy" to read the whole thing)

1871—First professional league opens with Bob Ferguson, the first switch-hitter.

1889—Tommy Tucker, first outstanding switch-hitter, wins American Association bat title at .372.

1906—First known platoon arrangement, involving Detroit catchers Boss Schmidt, John Warner, and Freddie Payne.

1914—First known National League platoon arrangement; first platooning at more than one position helps Boston win World Series title.

1920—First extensive platooning, by Tris Speaker in Cleveland.

1930—Platooning falls into disfavor.

1949—Platooning revived by Casey Stengel's success in New York.

1968—Earl Weaver hired by Baltimore, adds batter/pitcher record keeping and evolves personal style in platooning.

---

far as I can tell, he never used a strict platoon arrangement. He used more of a platoon recognition in alternating players.

As the American League had more left-handed pitching, platooning, as it developed, was always more of an American League thing. The American League champions platooned at at least one position every year between 1915 and 1925, with the possible exception of 1922. The major proponent of platooning in the National League in this period was Bill McKechnie, who had extremely good success with platoon combinations at Pittsburgh, including his 1925 combinations of George Grantham (.326) and Stuffy McInnis (.368) at first base and Earl Smith (.313) and Johnny Gooch (.298) behind the plate.

After about 1930, platooning fell into some disfavor. Even McKechnie, who had been so successful with it at Pittsburgh, abandoned the practice, though there were always a few who kept a candle burning for it. Casey Stengel, a player when platooning was in its heyday, was one of those—and if you look at his records as a player, it isn't hard to understand why. As a platoon player in 1922 and 1923, Stengel hit .368 and .339, the lower figure being fifty-five points above his career average.

Casey would eventually breathe new life into platooning. One reason for this was that he took some criticism for platooning through much of his career and he became defensive about it; he spoke about it as "my platooning," particularly after his platooning was vindicated in New York. For those of us in my generation, Stengel stands at the border of our memory, and only records exist before him. But through those records you can walk platooning backward a long, long way before 1949.

Pat Jordan was a pitching prodigy whose glorious big-league career seemed assured: he threw four consecutive no-hitters in Little League; he starred in high school; he was a bonus baby of the Milwaukee Braves in 1959; and then he was nothing. Of course, Jordan soon saw that life is more than baseball and became a fine writer. *A False Spring* is an anomaly in baseball writing: it is a book about failure and the self-knowledge that failure sometimes brings; and in that is its success.

PAT JORDAN

A False Spring

I see myself daily as I was then, framed in a photograph on the desk in my attic room. The picture was taken on June 27, 1959, at County Stadium in Milwaukee, Wisconsin, a few minutes before the Milwaukee Braves were to take the field against the Chicago Cubs, to whom they would lose that day 7–1.

I am standing midway between the first-base line and the home team's dugout. To my back I see the stadium's half-filled bleachers. I am wearing a Braves' uniform. Although the photograph is black and white, I see all the colors. My cap has a navy crown, a white M, and a red bill. My flannel uniform is the color of cream. It is trimmed—shirt and pants—with a half-inch-wide tricolored stripe of black-and-red-and-black satin. The word "Braves" is scripted in red and outlined in black at a slight upward angle across the front of the shirt. The script is underlined by a black-and-gold tomahawk. Below the tomahawk, in the left-hand corner of the shirt, is "24" in large block numerals, also red and outlined in black. Unseen in the photograph but clearly in my mind's eye is the small gold patch stitched onto the shirt-sleeve below my left shoulder. It is the face of an Indian of indeterminate tribe, the face contorted by a war cry no less menacing for being inaudible.

To my right is Whitlow Wyatt, the Braves' fifty-two-year-old pitching coach. Wyatt is smiling at me. My gaze, however, is directed to my left toward Warren Spahn, the Braves' great left-handed pitcher. Both Spahn and I are perspiring. We have just finished running wind sprints in the outfield and are apparently on the way to the clubhouse to change our shirts when we stop to pose for this photograph. . . . For whom? For some faceless fan leaning over the dugout roof, imploring, "Please!" whose good fortune it was to catch us in an obliging mood? So we stop, strike a pose, so casual, and wait for the camera's click. To pass this moment, as he has innumerable others like it, Spahn, hands on hips, turns to me with some bit of small talk, a phrase, meaningless, meant only to fill the instant. And I listen. Nonchalantly, hands on hips also, I listen to Spahn. To Spahnie. To Spahnie, who is talking to me, so much younger and yet with my amused smile looking so at ease—today amazed at how truly at ease I do appear, at how naturally I did fit, in that uniform, between those men, with Spahn, Spahnie and I, the best of friends, I, too, having done this small thing so often, having struck this obliging pose for so many fans, waiting only for the camera's click before tossing off a remark at which Spahnie and I would laugh on the way into the clubhouse to change our shirts.

I was eighteen years old that day, and the photograph had been arranged by the publicity department of the Milwaukee Braves, with whom I had just signed my first professional baseball contract. Of all the major-league uniforms I wore that summer—and I wore many—none was so gaudy and none so impressive as the uniform of the Braves. That was one reason I signed with them rather than with one of the other fifteen major-league teams that had also offered me a contract. There were other reasons. The Braves had agreed to pay for my college education, to pay me a salary of $500 per month during each baseball season, and to deposit in my savings account every June 27 for the next four years a certified check for $8,750. All told, my bonus amounted to more than $45,000, distributed over a four-year period. It was one of the largest bonuses— if not *the* largest—any young player received from the Braves in 1959. For my part, I promised to leave Milwaukee the following morning on a flight to McCook, Nebraska, where I would begin my professional career as a pitcher with the McCook Braves of the Class D Nebraska State League.

I pitched in the minor leagues for three years, at towns like McCook, Davenport, Waycross, Eau Claire, and Palatka, before I was given my unconditional release by those same Milwaukee Braves. I never did pitch a game in Milwaukee County Stadium, nor did I ever again speak to Warren Spahn. I did, however, keep the cash.

As I write this, confronted on my desk by that reminder of unfulfilled promise, thirteen years have elapsed since I posed with Warren Spahn and ten years since my last professional game. I was married the year I left baseball (the phrase I always use) and now have five children. I also returned to college and graduated in 1965 with a bachelor of arts degree in English. I taught English at a parochial all-girls high school for five years (the only male in a world of nuns and teenyboppers) and finally turned to writing. I have had little to do with baseball since my release by the Braves. Except for an abortive comeback attempt at twenty-two (at twenty-two?), I have not pitched a game.

That "comeback" was a disaster. It had been urged on me by my brother, George, a lawyer, thirteen years older than I, who had had so much to do with my career, with my having had a career, that he could never reconcile himself to my having lost it. Years after I left baseball, he still kept on the wall of his law office that photograph of me at County Stadium. It was a constant embarrassment to me. Yet he never tired of explaining to his clients who that young player next to Spahn was or what his promise had once been. I think he did this from a sense of loyalty to me, a brotherly duty not to abandon, and also because he remembered me only as I had been before that publicity shot. He never saw me pitch in the minor leagues, especially that last year, and so never saw the roots of my failure, a failure that has always bewildered him. George remembered me only as I had been in high school, when there was little I could not do on a pitcher's mound. Or in Little League, when my successes, which he shared, were close to total. In those days I often pitched to him on the sidewalk in front of our house. Our parents sat on the front porch and watched. They applauded my efforts. After a fastball that cracked in his catcher's mitt, my brother would yank his hand out of the glove and shake it fiercely as if to shake off the hot pain. And they would applaud. My brother, tall, gangling, wearing a white button-down shirt, the sleeves rolled up past his elbows, would grimace in both mock and very real pain as he shook his burning hand. How I responded to that gesture!

One day when George couldn't "work with me," as he used to call it, I badgered my father into catching me. I was eleven, I think, and already threw quite hard. My father, a lefty, had never been much of an athlete. He had been an orphan, and in his teens he turned to gambling for his satisfactions, and in later years for his livelihood. His interest in sports was less fervid than that of the rest of us. My mother was passionately devoted to Joe DiMaggio, and George and I were just as passionately devoted to my pitching, which we thought of even then as potentially a career. For my father, sports were never something to be played, but something to lay 9–5 on. He was in his early forties then, and although he'd ceased to gamble full-time, he was still a betting man. And occasionally he would deal cards in a late-night poker game. He was an excellent dealer and was paid handsomely for his efforts. It was in the hands, he said. His fingers were small and soft and plump; my mother said they were like the link sausages she threw in the spaghetti sauce. But how they flashed when dealing cards! He used only his left hand. His fingers were pressed together in the shape of a trowel. They supported the deck. He dealt with a flick of his wrist, his thumb shooting cards around the table with such speed and precision one listened for clicks.

My father began to catch me with reluctance. He had to wear the catcher's mitt—meant for one's left hand—on his right hand. His little finger fit into the glove's fat thumb, which stuck out ridiculously. He grumbled as I threw. His mind was on the card game at which he would deal later that evening at a local Italian athletic club. "Fellow athletes," my mother used to say, and we'd all laugh. All except my father. He took his sport seriously, too. To impress him, I cut loose with a fastball without telling him. Startled, he caught it on the middle finger of his left hand, the one without the glove. The finger split open, and blood spurted out, spotting his shirt and pants. For just a second he looked at his finger in disbelief. Then he ran bellowing into the house. I was too terrified to follow. When I finally did get up the courage to go inside, I found him sitting at the kitchen table, his hand wrapped in a blood-soaked handkerchief. He was trying to deal a poker hand to my white-faced mother. With a glance she warned me to silence. The cards slipped in his bleeding hand. They began to spill, slide down his wrist. He tried to pin them to his side with his elbow. They scattered across the floor. He glared at them. Cursed their ancestry. Snatched them up with his good hand and tried to deal again.

Years later we would laugh at that scene—my mother and I terrified, my father dealing, the cards spilling, curses and blood-stained kings. It became one of those anecdotes for which families invent a significance that eluded them but in retrospect grows to mythical proportions. The point became—my speed! I threw *that* hard! Hard enough, at eleven, to break a grown man's finger, pink and vulnerable as it might have been. It seems, even then, we were attuned to such small evidences of my destiny. My parents, brother, and I always had more than a premonition that my talent was something beyond the ordinary. It was a gift, we knew, and so it must be cultivated with the greatest care. For instance, my mother never asked me to do chores on a day I was to pitch, while my father spent all his spare money on the best equipment for me. (At eleven I had a $30 glove and $27 kangaroo-skin baseball spikes.) George, a struggling lawyer then, spent most of his lunch hours working out with me at the park near home. He would catch me for about twenty minutes, then make me run wind sprints from home plate to first base and back again. All the while I ran, he would remind me in long monologues just how badly I wanted a baseball career and how hard I must work at it. This way, the entire family shared in the development of my talent. From the very first I was aware that this talent I possessed must be treated with reverence, because it was only partly mine, and partly my family's. My talent united my family in a way we have never been since I lost it.

When I was twelve years old and in my final season of Little League baseball, my name appeared regularly in headlines in the sports section of the Bridgeport, Connecticut, *Post-Telegram*. The stories varied only slightly. Another no-hitter. More strikeouts. My third consecutive no-hitter. My fourth. And so it went. A season of six games in which I allowed two hits and struck out 110 of the 116 batters retired when I was on the mound. I had been almost perfect. Just two hits all year. And in my last two games every single out made was, in fact, a strikeout (thirty-six in a row, since Little League games last only six innings), with scarcely a walk, an error, or a foul ball in between. After the fourth consecutive no-hitter, my parents were called by a reporter for Ripley's *Believe It Or Not*. He wanted to verify certain facts. Possibly I would appear in one of their columns, he said. Where, I wondered? Alongside some Zulu tribesman who could fit an entire watermelon, lengthwise, in his mouth?

One night we received a call from Dick Young, the sportswriter for the New York *Daily News*. He interviewed my parents and me over the telephone. A few days later he wrote a column about me. In August the New York Yankees, with whom we were all enamored, invited my parents and me to appear on Mel Allen's television show prior to a Yankee–Red Sox doubleheader. We arrived at the Stadium properly awed—my mother wearing a corsage and my father and I dressed uncomfortably in suits and ties. We were treated royally. Pinstripes everywhere. Pictures of Ruth and Gehrig and DiMaggio. My mother swooned. Yankee executives hovered over me, smiling. "So this is our little pitcher? Does he want to be a Yankee when he grows up?"

Needless to say, I did not think of myself as "a little pitcher." Nor did I think I had to "grow up" before I could pitch for the New York Yankees. I was ready then, and to prove it I had brought my glove in a brown paper bag. I expected Mel Allen to turn to me in mid-interview and say, "Well, Pat, why don't you throw a few? Show the fans your stuff." And I would step on to the field and proceed to astonish all the viewers and fans, but most importantly, the Yankees, with my blazing fastball. What an embarrassment it would be for Vic Raschi! How he would envy me, throwing in my suit and tie with more speed than he ever dreamed of having!

We sat in box seats along the third-base line. Television cameras were aimed at us from the field. The signal was given. Mel Allen, turning to his right, asked my parents a question. His lips peeled apart like an open wound. My father fidgeted; my mother touched her corsage. One of them answered. More questions. Nervous smiles. Quick glances at the cameras and then back to Mel Allen. I sat at the end of the row, farthest away. I could barely hear. It did not matter. I just sat there waiting, my heart pounding, the brown bag at my feet. And when it was almost over and I knew it was too late for me to throw, Mel Allen leaned across my parents and asked me a question. I was so disheartened I couldn't answer. He repeated it. I mumbled something, and he returned to my parents. I sat there, glaring across the field at Vic Raschi, warming up with his pathetic fastball.

My brother remembered this. The no-hitters, the headlines, Dick Young, Mel Allen. He remembered it all so well that when I told him what I'd written about that day at Yankee Stadium, he said, "But you forgot Casey Stengel! Remember what he said when he found out about the strikeouts?" I didn't remember. "He said, 'I guess your fellas don't need no gloves when you pitch.'"

What I had been is still clear to my brother. It is a picture whose lines have been redrawn so often, retracing identical successes year after year, that it has become etched in his memory. He never saw those lines erased during my years in the minor leagues and then somehow redrawn, without his knowledge, until what they defined when I was released by the Braves in 1962 was something unrecognizable to him. That was why he urged me to make a comeback so soon after I had left baseball. He would not accept the fact that I had lost it all in only four years. It would take only a little practice, he said. We could work out on his lunch hour. He would have me throwing like my old self again. That was the phrase he used: throwing like my old self. Then, when I was ready, he would pick some Sunday afternoon and some team in the Senior City League and would inform the newspapers and the scouts he knew that I would pitch that day. And after the game, after I had struck out thirteen or fourteen batters, the scouts would be only too eager to sign me again. "Maybe even another bonus," my brother said, only half kidding. "But smaller, naturally."

The high school field where we threw was always deserted at noon. I would arrive first, to claim the field, then wait for George. I passed those agonizing minutes pacing from the pitcher's mound and back again, praying that no one else would show up, would intrude on this routine, our ritual, wishing my brother would hurry so we could get it over with and I could flee. He would then pull up in his new air-conditioned car. A successful lawyer now, approaching forty, with a touch of gray in his wiry hair, which he still wore in a crew cut. He had fleshed out a lot and was no longer gangling. Still, he was 6 feet 4 inches tall and very sturdy looking. Unbreakable is the word that perhaps best described him, still describes him. He played sports mechanically, as if by memory but not instinct. He moved stiffly, his back a poker that seemed incapable of bending. *He* seemed incapable of bending, of ever breaking— as I had in the minor leagues. (His argument for my attempting this comeback was brief: "You aren't going to quit, are you?") He wore dark-rimmed glasses and a snazzy bow tie. He would take off his jacket, some Scottish plaid from the racks of J. Press in New Haven, and fold it neatly over a bench. Then he would roll up the sleeves of his shirt. Very carefully, fold after even fold, past his elbows, that same white button-down shirt, the gesture suddenly calming me, reassuring me. Then we would begin throwing as we had so many times before.

But my comeback did not work out as my brother had planned. I have never again thrown like my old self. And on the day I finally took the mound in the same semipro league in which five years before I had struck out batters at will, I was unable to retire a single man. The fans loved it. They laughed and hooted each time my poor catcher (some high school boy I have never seen again) scrambled back to the screen to retrieve another of my wild pitches. I wore my Braves' uniform that day, a further affront to those fans, many of whom had seen me pitch before and who had been burdened too long with my past successes. I left the game in the first inning. So many runs were scored, so many batters walked or hit, so many wild pitches bounced in front of the plate or flung over my catcher's up-stabbing mitt, that I have retained only fragments from that day. Jagged little pieces . . . the shouts of "has-been," "washed-up," "always a bum." The look of pity on my catcher's face as he walked out to reassure me for the tenth time. A look he is not easy with at his age. And I, feeling bad for him, too. He senses that something is eluding him besides my fastballs. The fans *so* vicious at this meaningless game? It frightens him. This exorcising of private devils. He crouches for another pitch. I begin my windup, rear back, and catch him shooting a look over his shoulder at the fans. The ball rattles the home-plate screen. The runner on third trots home and with a little jump lands on the plate with both feet. I sigh, exhausted, feeling empty. Truly empty. Without insides. Filled only with air. Floating above things for a change. Not caring now. Untouchable. Not a bad feeling. Nice, really. New to me. At ease now, I wait for the ball. Look around. Catch sight of my brother. All else dissolves—fans, players, noise, heat, exhaustion, time—is gone. I see only him. Standing beneath a tree along the first-base line. Wearing dark glasses. Watching and not seeing. He clenches his fist, makes a short, pistonlike punch into an invisible gut. Mine! He still believes! Amazing! It doesn't matter if I don't believe. He does. In spite of me, it can still be done. Merely by an act of his will. Another punch. But the niceness remains. I shrug.

I think often about that day. And about the others, too, the good ones. Baseball was such an experience in my life that ten years later I have still not shaken it, will probably never shake it. I still think of myself not as a writer who once pitched but as a pitcher who happens to be writing just now. It's as if I decided at some point in my life, or possibly *it* was decided, that of all the things in my life only that one experience would most accurately define me. It hardly matters whether this is a fact or a private delusion. It matters only that I devoted so great a chunk of my life to baseball that I believe it's true. I believe that that experience affected the design of my life to a degree nothing else ever will. Yet it never seemed to end properly, neatly, all those bits and pieces finally forming some harmonious design. It just stopped, unfinished in my memory, fragmented, so many pieces missing. Over the years I have begun sorting and resorting those bits and pieces—delicately, at first—finding every now and then a new one to further flesh out that design, finally discovering the pieces had always been there and that what had been missing was in me. This book, then, is an attempt not to relive that experience but to resee it, once and for all, as it truly was, somehow frozen in time, unfragmented, waiting only for me to develop the perception needed to see it whole.

The bird dogs came first. They appeared one spring day in my sophomore year of high school, drawn by the odor of fresh talent and sweet young grass. I knew about bird dogs even then, at fifteen, and had been waiting impatiently for them to appear. It was a sign. On that day baseball ceased to be just a game for me; it also became my career.

They were called bird dogs because they sniffed out talent, although the name does not do justice to the men. They were kindly, stooped old men in plaid shirts and string ties. They had once owned taverns or hardware stores and in their youth had possibly played ball with Kiki Cuyler or Georgie Cutshaw. Now, retired, they measured out their weekday afternoons at a succession of high school baseball games. They were always easy to spot, even from the pitcher's mound, since few adults ever bothered to attend the meaningless games my coach let me pitch as a sophomore; and because they always stood behind the home-plate screen, as if they were ill at ease unless viewing life through a maze of wire triangles. Their job was to unearth talent for the major-league team with which they were affiliated. It was a loose affiliation, really. In most cases it consisted simply of their friendship with some organization's full-time scout. Most bird dogs never got paid a cent for their efforts, although occasionally one might be slipped $100 if his discovery reached the major leagues. But they were so old (in their seventies and eighties) and the gestation period of a professional ballplayer so long (often more than six years in the minor leagues) that few bird dogs lived long enough to see their judgments confirmed. That wasn't the reason they spent the time and effort, anyway. They did it to pass the time, for one thing, and because they loved the game. But most of all they did it because they appreciated talent. Just discovering it and watching it develop was satisfaction enough for these old men.

One day in my sophomore year at Fairfield Prep, a Jesuit-run high school in Fairfield, Connecticut, I struck out nineteen apprentice plumbers, bricklayers, and carpenters from nearby Bullard-Havens Technical High School. That night, Johnny Barron, an aged Cincinnati bird dog, telephoned our house. He spoke first with my father and then my mother, as if, like some Victorian suitor, he was seeking permission to court me—which, in a way, he was. Finally, I took the receiver with trembling hands. His voice surprised me. It was ragged and halting, yet somehow at ease, as if we were old friends. And in his mind we were old friends since he'd just seen me pitch.

Johnny did most of the talking that night. He took much for granted. He detailed my strengths and weaknesses (weaknesses?) with a familiarity that would have annoyed me were it not for the warmth in his voice. He said of my fastball, "And when you do make the big leagues, it'll be your fastball that takes you there. It's a beautiful fastball!" It was a strange word to use, I thought, one reserved for a painting or statue or some other work of art. He was a strange man, too. He took such delight in just talking to me that it embarrassed me, even though I'd been aware from the first that my talent, with which I was so familar as to be no longer awed by it (just as I was no longer awed by my ability to walk), was to others so extraordinary as to inspire a respect that approached adoration. Its presence could lead a dignified old man like Johnny Barron to lose his composure when merely talking to its possessor, a fifteen-year-old boy. However, the fact that this respect was for the talent, not its possessor, escaped me then.

Johnny concluded his talk a little breathlessly, saying, "I wish we could sign you now. But we can't until you graduate high school. By that time most of the other clubs will be bidding a lot of money for you. I'll be out of the picture then. Our scouts and front-office people will have taken over. But I hope you'll remember me, that I was the first to appreciate your gift. It will mean a lot to me." Although I was not sure what he wanted or why, I promised, and he hung up satisfied. I seldom pitched a game that year without spotting him behind the backstop. Often I would not feel comfortable on the mound until spotting him and would spend long moments rubbing up a baseball until I did. Strangely enough, I never talked to Johnny again, although he often spoke with my parents during the games I pitched. When I did sign a professional baseball contract in 1959, it was with the Braves, however, not the Reds. But I kept my promise and had the local newspaper insert a small paragraph near the bottom of the article that told of my signing. The paragraph mentioned how John Barron, Sr., of Haddon Street, Bridgeport, Connecticut, had been the first bird dog to notice me.

I pitched four one-hitters in my sophomore year of high school, and the following year my reputation as a major-league prospect was firmly established. The bird dogs, like Johnny, were gone by then. They had been replaced by full-time scouts who moved in quickly, like carpetbaggers, to take advantage of the friendships cultivated by the bird dogs. The scouts were younger men, in their fifties usually, and their appreciation of talent was more professional than aesthetic. They were not unkind men, although they were certainly not so lovable as the bird dogs. But maybe when I caught my first whiff of that bonus money I was not so lovable, either, and perhaps it was a good thing that bird dogs like Johnny Barron could not see me then.

When my brother, George, was twelve years old, my father took him along on a gambling foray into Canada. In Montreal my father won $10,000 in an all-night poker game. The game broke up after dawn, and my father went directly to a bank where he exchanged the large bills for singles, which he stuffed into an old valise. He returned to the hotel as my brother was waking. He made him sit up in bed and put his hands over his eyes. Then he emptied the contents of the valise over his head. The bills fluttered about my brother like falling leaves. They both began to laugh idiotically and to toss the bills into the air until the room was littered with them. For the rest of the day, while my father slept, my brother counted and stacked the bills. And he played with them daily over the next few weeks, although each day their number diminished until finally none were left. Then he and my father returned to Connecticut. If George and I inherited any legacy from our father, who in a lifetime of gambling let over a million dollars slip through his fingers, it was this ironic disregard for money. Money was never something one saved in our home (there were no piggy banks), nor was it something one learned the value of (no stern lectures on lost dimes). Nor was it an evil. It was simply something one needed a minimum of in order to live. Any amount beyond that should be acquired as effortlessly as possible and consumed just as effortlessly. My father was a master at both, although his mastery of the former was surpassed by the latter. My brother and I still cherish this legacy, however, and it has greatly affected our lives. Yet during 1958 and 1959 the anticipation of a large amount of money became our common obsession in a way it never has before or since.

It began during my junior year of high school. I had won twelve consecutive games over a two-year period and had averaged almost two strikeouts per inning. I'd been equally successful pitching in the Senior City League, a nearby semiprofessional circuit filled with ex-minor leaguers in their twenties and thirties. In my first appearance with them, at the age of fifteen, I pitched a one-hit shutout. But beyond such achievements and my obvious physical talent, I had the look of a finished pitcher. I was big for my age. At sixteen I stood six feet tall and weighed 175 pounds. My pitching delivery, so painstakingly cultivated by my brother, was smooth and natural and all of a piece, unlike other young pitchers whose deliveries are composed of distinct and conscious stages. My mannerisms on the mound were those of a professional. My brother had taught me how to shake off a catcher's sign with a flick of my glove; how to landscape the dirt on the mound with my spikes; how to hold a runner to first base with the barest of peeks over my left shoulder; and how to receive my catcher's return throw with such a disdainful snap of the glove that the batter could not help but feel my contempt for him. My brother and I left no detail unperfected. We discussed the proper way for a pitcher to wear his uniform, and we decided that a fastball pitcher, like myself, should let his pants' legs fall well below his knee before fastening them. Only infielders and pitchers without "stuff" wore their pants' legs fastened at the knees. "Besides," my brother said, "it'll make you look taller in the eyes of the scouts."

I'd been able to master these peripheral details because for ten years I'd done little else but pitch. I had never really liked the rest of the game, for it was filled with too much dead time. Only the pitcher, isolated on a small rise, seemed constantly in motion. He was the catalyst about whom the fans, the players, and the game itself revolved. I liked this feeling of power, of being the center of the action, of controlling things. When not pitching, I had no desire to play shortstop or left field or even take my turn at bat. I was solely a pitcher—and in my mind's eye I am still one today. I often go to the small park near home and, when the field is deserted, take the mound and begin to pitch baseballs into the screen behind home plate. It relaxes me. The pump, the kick, the follow through. No longer the center of the action, no longer controlling things, feeling often powerless, I take comfort only in the act as it has finally become for me, divorced from all externals. I am at home with it because it was the first thing in my life that I could do well and others couldn't. At eight, this discovery was my first hint that I was a distinct and separate entity with potentials and abilities entirely my own. I stood out, both in my own eyes and to those around me. Because I owed my first distinctness to this talent, I mistook it for the only distinctness I would ever have. I *was* my talent. Its loss would be a loss of self. So I played to it. I polished it at the expense of everything else. And I could do it so well, naturally, almost without effort, that it became increasingly easy for me to neglect any other potential whose luster would have demanded a strenuous effort.

But at sixteen I knew none of this. I knew only that I loved to pitch. And it was this strong affection for my talent as much as the talent itself that drew the dozen or so major-league scouts to each game I pitched as a high school junior. Unlike the bird dogs, who had appeared alone and inconspicuously, the full-time scouts entered the park in garrulous clusters. They carried aluminum deck chairs in one hand and fat little black notebooks in the other. They were always deeply tanned from their recent spring training with "the big club" in

Florida or Arizona, while we in New England were not even pink from our faint and fleeting spring sun. They dressed with the flamboyance of traveling men who seem always to be anticipating warmer climates. They wore bright Banlon jerseys and golf sweaters and gold slacks and black-and-white loafers with tiny tassels and, even on the most sunless of days, dark glasses. And yet, despite this flamboyance, their clothes were in a way quite nondescript, of indefinable origin, a wardrobe of brand names that could have been pieced together anywhere across the country. Those Haggar slacks might have been picked up in a Sears Roebuck in Stockton, California, on the hot, dusty day they saw that farm boy strike out seventeen, or at a J. C. Penney's in Fayette-ville, North Carolina, on the muggy evening they watched that good Nigra boy hit four home runs. The scouts' origins were as indefinable as their clothes'. Those men had been worn thin by years of travel, then rewoven with remnants from all their stops so that even a native New Yorker might now chew tobacco and speak with faint threads of a southern drawl.

The scouts unfolded their deck chairs in the grass behind the home-plate screen and watched the game with what seemed to be barely passing interest. They talked mostly among themselves. Their conversation seldom touched on what was happening before their eyes. They paused only infrequently to pull out a stopwatch and time a runner to first base or maybe to ask a neighbor about that last putout, which they then recorded in the notebooks they had to turn in to the front office as proof they were doing their job. But these pauses were merely interruptions in their perpetual talk about good restaurants nearby where they would meet after this, their third game of the afternoon; or about too much bourbon consumed last night in a motel room in Naugatuck, Con-necticut, and how they couldn't handle it like they used to, or women, either, for that matter, and they'd all laugh; or finally about that good Polack boy they'd given a $40,000 bonus a few years ago and was now hitting .227 in the Three I League but still was saving their hide with the front office by showing a little power, and thank God for small blessings. Their conversation touched rarely on the progress and doings of "the big club" for which they worked— that world, although in the same universe, was just too many light-years removed from their own, from this moment and the high school game they were only half watching. Inevitably, during the course of these games, their talk drifted to mutual friends in baseball, old friends who were doing well financially or physically, or maybe not so well, who were actually broke, or maybe sick, or dying even of the Big C, or worse than that, who were out of baseball. There was nothing worse than being out of baseball for men who'd spent their lives in it. It was like being out of the mainstream of all that really mattered in life, the good life. And it was so unnecessary, stupid even, to be out of baseball. There was always a place for those who kept their noses clean. "Don't ever make enemies," they were taught on becoming professionals. "You never know who you might be playing for someday." The scouts had listened and survived. They had played for fifteen years in the minor leagues and never moved higher than the Sally League. And when they got hurt one day and kept on playing for the good of the organization and in so doing had sacrificed their careers (a smart sacrifice really, for by then they had no careers), they were rewarded on their fortieth birthday with a job as manager of Mayfield, Texas, in the Kitty League. And at fifty, when they could no longer take the pressure of the six-hour bus rides from Mayfield to Corpus Christi, which had begun to get to their kidneys, they were rewarded further with a job of full-time scout for the Eastern Seaboard, or maybe the West Coast or the Southwest Territory. They breathed easily now, a little more easily, anyway. As long as they didn't do anything foolish, they would never be out of baseball. They would never have to join that "lunch-bucket brigade" that they feared and that they joked about as they watched from their deck chairs behind the home-plate screen.

But it wasn't all the good life for the scouts. There were hazards. And in those days before the advent of the free-agent draft, they could be treacherous.* It was easy for the bird dogs. They simply pointed to the talent. It was the scouts who had to then bring it down on the wing. They needed good reflexes and strong insides and a quick mind and plenty of endurance, even at their age. Without these qualities, too much talent might escape them, and they'd find themselves out of baseball, just as they might if they got trigger-happy and bagged too many $100,000 bonus babies who never made it past the Three I League. And always there was the competition squatting right there beside them, eating and drinking and laughing with them, but nevertheless scheming against them, just as they, too, were scheming. It was a risky business, and that's what appealed to them. It was exciting; it kept them young. To do it well they had to retain at least remnants of those physical attibutes that had meant so much to them in their playing days. They had been physical men in their youth, and their values and pleasures had remained physical beyond middle age. As long as they remained in baseball, no matter how peripherally, they would never completely lose that physicality, would never grow too old to

---

* The free-agent draft was initiated by the major leagues in 1965. Prior to it, all amateur players were free to sign with any club of their choice the moment their high school class was graduated. By the 1950s, when baseball, like most sports, had become a vastly more lucrative business than ever before (thanks primarily to television), major-league teams began offering large sums of money to untried youngsters in order to outbid their rivals for his services. The result was a bidding war that reached its peak when Rick Reichardt, a Madison, Wisconsin, teenager, was given a $175,000 bonus by the California Angels. The free-agent draft eliminated such excesses by eliminating the open market on players. It made all free agents susceptible to two major-league drafts, one held in June and the other in January. If a player was drafted by a club in one phase, he was unable to sign with any club but that one for six months. Then, if still unsigned, he was returned to the draft pool and could be drafted by a new club in the next phase. The process repeated itself until a player either signed with a club that drafted him; enrolled in a four-year college, in which case he could not be drafted until his class was graduated or he had turned twenty-one; or was no longer drafted. At no point, however, was a player free to bargain with or sign with any club other than the one that owned his current draft rights. Players could no longer auction themselves off to the highest bidder, so bonus demands plummeted. Now, in order to sign a draft choice, a major-league club had only to make its offer tempting enough to convince a player it would be foolish to waste six months hoping he might be drafted by a new club that would offer him more money. In fact, usually when a player was redrafted, he was offered less money than before.

function in the only way that had ever mattered. Even approaching sixty, it would still be possible for them to consume large quantities of bourbon or have an occasional woman in their motel room, while other men their age were going on errands for their wives or tending an orange tree in the backyard of their home in St. Petersburg, Florida.

But the competition *was* fierce. The scouts needed all the weapons they could carry. Money was the most powerful. If they were sufficiently impressed with a prospect, they simply offered him more money than anyone else. Few prospects could refuse. But such offers were rare and a little too risky for most scouts, who treated bonus money as if it were fished dollar by dollar from their own pockets. It was safer for them to equal a rival's offer and then bring up other weapons. A scout for the Yankees, for instance, might inform a prospect, some thickly muscled outfielder from Sioux City, that Mickey Mantle's legs were starting to go. The Yankees would need someone soon to carry on that pin-striped tradition of great outfielders that began with Babe Ruth and continued through DiMaggio and Mantle. If the prospect still wavered, the scout had only to point to those World Championship pennants flying above Yankee Stadium. There was a great deal of money to be made playing for the Yankees in New York, money that no ballplayer, no matter how talented, would ever see in Pittsburgh.

That may have been true once, a scout for the Milwaukee Braves might say to that same prospect, but don't forget, the Braves defeated the Yankees in the 1957 World Series and were forging a new and more powerful dynasty of their own. Ah, yes, a scout for the lowly Washington Senators might say, the Yankees and Braves are powerful teams. They have extensive farm systems loaded with much talent. The Senators, however, have finished in last place three years running, and their farm system is a mere skeleton of most clubs' and sorely lacking in talent. Of course, this means that a young prospect signing with the Senators would move rapidly through their system to the major leagues, whereas he might languish unnoticed in the more corpulent systems of the Yankees and Braves. That's all very nice, a scout for the recently transplanted Dodgers might respond, but what happens when a ball game is over? A ballplayer has to live in the city in which he plays. After a strenuous day at the ballpark he needs to fall back on a life-style conducive to relaxation. Such a life-style can be found only on the Coast. The West Coast. L.A. And that scout would spin tales of eager starlets and perpetual sunshine that few boys from Sioux City ever dreamed existed, except between the covers of *Playboy*, and which few could resist. But some did. And if a scout could not bring down a prospect with money or such arguments, he brought him down with the force of his own personality. Or what purported to be a personality. Most scouts had discovered early in their careers that they possessed certain attributes useful in capturing young talent. And so they traded on them, just as in their playing days they had traded on their hustle, which for a while had obscured their inability to hit. They traded so heavily on these attributes that eventually they became vivid parts of themselves, which, like their clothes, drew one's attention but revealed nothing of the man.

With each new success my junior year, the scouts lavished more and more attention on my parents, my brother, and myself until there was barely a moment when their presence was not felt. On a night before I was to pitch, for instance, a scout would telephone our home. Once he had identified himself as a scout, he would be turned over to my brother, to whom we had entrusted my career. (I was not allowed to talk to scouts.) While he gave directions to the ballpark or accepted or refused a dinner invitation, I would be upstairs sleeping, trying to sleep, anyway, actually just lying perfectly still, catching bits of the conversation below—the names of famous men like Paul Richards or George Weiss, who were making a special trip from New York or Baltimore to see me pitch.

In school the next day as I daydreamed through my classes, strange men in bright clothes wandered the corridors in search of my classroom or waited for me in the school parking lot when I went outside to eat lunch. Those same men reappeared later in the afternoon as I warmed up far down the left-field foul line. At first I could distinguish them only as middle-age men carrying deck chairs and black notebooks, but as the year progressed and I saw the same faces game after game, I began to distinguish one scout from another. I never really got to know them personally, except for one or two, and so I remember them only vaguely as possessors of a certain eccentricity. And yet, to this day, I *see* them quite clearly, as in snapshots that have been perfectly preserved. I retain a memory filled with such snapshots taken at various moments as I paused on the mound between pitches.

Has there ever been a more motley crew of ballplayers? Not even the Miami Amigos or Santo Domingo Azucareros (see Bill Colson's piece on the Inter-American League) had more "hope junkies." Steve Howe, Mike Norris, Ken Reitz, Derrel Thomas—why would these exiles from the Show play for peanuts in the Class A California League with a team that had no major-league affiliation? Easy: no one else would have them, and the dream of return still gripped them. Ex-dopers, head cases, rebels, but overridingly, ballplayers and human beings—presenting the 1986 San Diego Bees, in a fine portrait from *Rolling Stone*.

NEAL KARLEN

Bad-Nose Bees

The Rebel Cave

It's three in the morning in the subterranean cement training room below the San Jose Bees ballpark. The 10-by-20 windowless bunker is as musty and cluttered as Bruce Wayne's Bat Cave. Though the airless cell with the low ceiling is the size of a Bowery flop, the three professional athletes who actually live here call it the Stadium Hilton.

The Hilton sports no bathroom, so Ken Reitz is outside peeing in the dark beneath the grandstand. Down below, Mike "Stash" Bigusiak and Darryl Cias are half out of their uniforms, lounging on their greasy mattresses and trying to forget the last three days on the road. It's been a long night. Earlier in the evening the Bees were two-hit by the Fresno Giants, a collection of peach-faced, cocky teenagers wearing the sparkling uniforms of a bush-league team with major-league connections. After the game, the unshowered Bees were treated to a fifteen-minute dinner at a roadside Burger King. Then it was back on the bus for a rickety four-hour ride home, up California's desolate Central Valley and over the Pacheco Pass road, a suicide run to the South Bay.

Such is life for the lowliest team in the lowly California League. You ride a bus with a million miles under the hood, hang your one uniform on a locker-room hook, sleep in cheap motels, draw $11 a day meal money, and pay for whatever pleasure you can find on the road. Average California League salary: $750 a month.

It sure ain't the Show. That's what baseball players call the major leagues. When you're part of the Show's cast, you ride first-class on chartered airplanes, sleep in fancy big-city hotels, play ball in air-conditioned domed stadiums, and have your pick of some of the finest groupies in the country. Average Show salary: $431,521 a year.

Team captain and third baseman Ken Reitz, catcher Darryl Cias, and six other San Jose Bees have already played the Show, many in starring roles. But somewhere along the line, most were labeled—incurable drug addict, head case, or rebel—and banished, probably forever, from the major. They all want back.

But on this late San Jose night, the bunker beneath the third-base line will have to do. The denizens have redecorated the place: rug remnants lifted from the dumpster of nearby Carpet City, U.S.A. now line the bare cement floor. There's a refrigerator, a beer sign, and three broken bleacher seats for guests. Cias, a devoted painter who bears a striking resemblance to Jimmy Buffett, has recently finished a huge, madly grinning portrait of a green-faced Charles Manson on the inside door. "I am *not* a fan of the man," says the laid-back twenty-nine-year-old. "I painted Charles Manson as a conversation piece."

Cias's winding road through Organized Baseball began hours after his high-school prom. That was when the Oakland A's signed the promising catcher for $15,000. He made slow but steady progress through the minors, finally getting called up at the beginning of the 1983 season. He batted a solid .333 with the A's, then headed to South America, where he starred in winter ball. He thought he was a shoo-in to start for Oakland in 1984.

Over the winter, however, the team had hired a new general manager, Karl Kuehl. A strict disciplinarian who liked to lecture his troops on the psychology of victory, Kuehl apparently couldn't come to terms with Cias's Gomer Pyle attitude toward the diamond wars. "He was a real Nazi," remembers Cias. "He believed that you couldn't have fun and work at the same time. To me the game was always fun. I played because I loved the game."

After the first few games of spring training, Kuehl told Cias he was sending him back to the minors. Cias, convinced he could catch for someone else in the majors, asked for his outright release. The A's refused; Cias asked louder. The A's finally relented, and Cias suddenly found himself unemployable. "Anytime a new team wants to sign you," he explains, "they call your last team and ask why you were released. Now if the general manager is any kind of human being, he says, 'There just wasn't any room on the team.' But Kuehl said, 'Cias is a problem; he doesn't want to work.' That was a lie—Karl Kuehl is the only guy in my entire life I didn't get along with."

Kuehl, still with the A's, pish-poshes the notion that personality played any part in the decision to get rid of Cias. "We *like* people who have fun," he insists. "Darryl was a good guy to have on a ball club—he kept guys loose and had a positive attitude. It's unfortunate when you run into a numbers problem. With younger guys moving up, sometimes you just have to make room. No major-league ball club is going to let someone go who they feel can help them."

Kuehl professes disbelief when he learns Cias thinks he personally blackballed the catcher. "Oh my God, not at all!" he says. "You know, at one point a couple months after Darryl left, we had some injuries, and our manager wanted to have him back. We tried to reach him—and no one knew where to find him."

Meanwhile, Stash Bigusiak, who has been listening to Cias lament from his mattress, chuckles, shakes his head, and flips on the Hilton's battered black-and-white TV. Footage of bombed-out buildings from the U.S. raid on Libya flashes on the screen. "Shit," he says, shaking his head again. "And we think we've got problems."

Unlike Cias, Stash never even made it to the Show. Signed three months after his high school graduation for $25,000, he made good progress through the Los Angeles Dodgers organization. But in 1976, shortly after he was named minor-league player of the month for his work with the Clinton, Iowa, farm club, Stash's career screeched to a halt. He says his manager, Bob Hartsfield, called him a "dumb Polack." Stash then told the skipper he would deck him if he repeated the slur. The manager said it again. Moments later, says Stash, the manager was on the floor, and Stash was out of baseball. "I was a punk," says Stash. "That's one of the bad things about baseball—it takes young, immature kids and puts them in the limelight. And ten years later you end up like this." (Hartsfield, now a scout with the Houston Astros, says the incident never took place. "Forget it," he scoffs. "I never had any problems with Mike. He just couldn't throw the ball real hard. He couldn't get anybody out.")

Stash spent the next decade away from baseball. For the past two years he'd been working as a gumshoe for an Atlanta, Georgia, detective agency. But even while videotaping adulterous couples from behind motel hedges, he couldn't forget his aborted career. When his girlfriend, a producer for the Cable News Network, gave him his walking papers, he signed with the Bees and headed West. Though he now spends a lot of time trashing his ex-girlfriend's memory, he keeps two framed snapshots of her prominently displayed in the Hilton. "She'll be back," he says as he adjusts the TV's coat-hanger aerial, "just as soon as I hit the Show."

Ken Reitz has finished his predawn piss under the grandstand and returns to the Hilton wearing only his underwear, black-and-white checked tennis shoes, and sunglasses. Cias holds up a clipping he's been handed and laughs. "Hey, Reitzy," says the catcher, "we were just reading about you. In The New York *TIMES*!!" Reitz, thirty-five, yawns, pulls out a slimy mattress from the closet, and lies down. Cias reads aloud:

"Dateline St. Louis, April 23, 1979. 'The St. Louis Cardinals third baseman, Ken Reitz, said today that his temper had cost him $1,250. The penalty stemmed from an incident that occurred April 11 during a ten-hour rain delay at Lambert Airport here while the team was waiting to fly to Pittsburgh. Reitz said the amount represented damages he and two teammates caused to a Trans World Airlines waiting room, plus a fine of undisclosed amount. . . .'"

"We were sitting in this airport VIP lounge for *ten hours*," Reitz says. He laughs, takes off his shades, and settles back on the mattress. "Everybody was loaded—the players, the sportswriters, everybody. Keith Hernandez and I started to play football. I went out for a pass and crashed through a plate-glass partition. Then everybody went wild. I started throwing chairs, and some phones got ripped out of the wall."

"A twelve hundred and fifty dollar fine," marvels Cias.

Reitz folds his arms behind his head and stares at the concrete ceiling. "Twelve hundred and fifty dollars, shit," he says with a laugh. "I made *two million dollars* playing baseball, and I don't know where a *fucking cent* is." Cias stares dumbfounded and says, "Reitzy, you're laughing. How the hell can you laugh?" Stash barks, "What else is he supposed to do?" Reitz yawns, turns out the light, and giggles, "Yeah, what else am I supposed to do?" Cias returns the giggle. "Christ, Reitzy, you know I used to have a picture of you from the cover of the *Sporting News* on my wall?"

Reitzy is already asleep.

Most of the Bees dispersed that night as soon as the bus wheezed to a wee-hour halt in front of San Jose Municipal Stadium. Hank Wada—a Zen master, former star catcher with the Nishetetsu Lions, and the Bees' acupuncturist and pitching coach—mysteriously vaporized from the parking lot like Kane in *Kung Fu*. Meanwhile, the five Japanese youngsters on the squad headed home to their boardinghouse across the railroad tracks from the stadium. Outfielder Mickey Yamano probably had gotten the most out of the torturous trip back from Fresno. Before he boarded the bus, he had known only two American phrases: "thank you" and "hamburger." Now, after a midnight tutorial offered by team captain Reitzy, Mickey could hum "Jingle Bells" and say "cow," "six-pack," "Hulk Hogan," and "blow job."

A few Bees near the bus tried to round up a proper quorum for an after-hours booze jaunt. "Hey, Howser," one yelled to the most notorious Bee of all. "You want to go drinking?" But infamous wild man Steve Howe, the 1980 National League Rookie of the Year, passed. Someone told Howe what L.A. sportswriters—the very men who'd hounded him out of their town in 1985 after portraying him as John Belushi in a jockstrap—were calling his new team. "The Bad-*Nose* Bees?" laughed the rowdy, personable Howe. "I've got a *great* nose. The son of a bitch could suck an egg through a garden hose." But not tonight, not this year, no more.

Steve Howe is on a mission. And although he has not turned into a wimp—it was *his* idea to paint the team bus black with a huge logo reading EAT ME—Howe has informed everyone that he has taken a vow of sobriety worthy of a Hank Wada disciple. He, too, headed into the dark alone, back to the San Jose Hotel where he lives under an assumed name.

The Blackball

The Encyclopedia of Baseball gives no clue as to why so many ballplayers with big-league talent are spending their summers playing ball for the barrel-bottom Bees. The team's lineup of ex-big-league stars, each still in what should be his prime, is impressive: besides Reitz, Cias, and Howe, there is pitcher Mike Norris, thirty-one, who won twenty-two games and was runner-up for the Cy Young Award with the Oakland A's in 1980; and Daryl Sconiers, twenty-six, a power-hitting first baseman who was knighted by the California Angels as Rod Carew's heir apparent. Then there is Derrel Thomas, who in fifteen respectable years in the majors set the all-time record for most nicknames denoting a walking time bomb. Thomas's monikers include Hot Dog, Minute Man, Farmer John, and Junkyard Dog.

Somewhere along the line, each of these Bees blew a promising major-league career and was banished from the Show. For Howe, Norris, Thomas, and Reitz it was drugs. Reitz, a twelve-year major-league veteran who holds the single-season record for fewest errors committed by a third baseman, said he was so hooked on pills that by the time the Pittsburgh Pirates cut him, "I was functionally psychotic." Reitz's number came up on a Chicago expressway a few years back. Convinced a stranger was lurking in his backseat, Reitz pulled over, took out a shotgun, and blew his car to bits.

Substance abuse among baseball players is a tradition older than the seventh-inning stretch. Ever since the *Sporting News* reported in the 1880s that St. Louis Browns outfielder Curt Welch habitually hid cases of beer behind the billboards lining Sportsman's Park, it has been common knowledge that baseball players enjoyed getting high before, after, and sometimes *during* games. In 1903, a Cincinnati newspaper went so far as to publish the following advice to the city's constantly besotted Reds: "Whenever a ball looks like this—ooo—take a chance on the middle one."

Later, Babe Ruth, Mickey Mantle, and many of the innocently cast Brooklyn Dodger "Boys of Summer" did much of their best work either plastered or hung over. Pete Rose admitted he used to enjoy an occasional pregame upper; pitcher Dock Ellis even said he was tripping on acid when he threw a no-hitter for the Pittsburgh Pirates in 1970.

Still, the game retained its squeaky-clean image. For the public, baseball players were working-class heroes who, like most of their fans, were paid little money for a lot of work and who suffered at the hands of their employers. Sportswriters, paid as poorly as the players, served the players as friends and propagandists. Even well-paid superstars were treated with kid gloves, and their images remained as shiny and vacuous as a smile on a Wheaties box. Hence, Ty Cobb was not even fined when he was accused in the 1920s of fixing a game years earlier. Hence, when Babe Ruth allegedly came down with a vicious dose of the clap that caused him to miss part of the 1925 season, the press reported that the Bambino had simply eaten too many hot dogs and come down with "the bellyache heard around the world."

The first real dent in the public's one-dimensional perception of ballplayers came with the publication in 1970 of *Ball Four*, pitcher Jim Bouton's locker-room journal of life in the big leagues. Though the book seems quaint by today's tell-all standards, it created a scandal. Here, for the first time, were players as they really were—painfully human. They drank, they fought, and they whored.

The next blow came in 1976 when baseball's reserve clause was lifted and players were allowed to market themselves to the highest bidder. During the next ten years, fans watched as average salaries went up almost 900 percent and their favorite players heedlessly shuttled from team to team. At the same time, a new breed of sportswriter emerged. Unwilling to act as sycophants for the game, they increasingly portrayed both owners and players as they often were: greedy and stupid. In other words, as people.

In the past, the owners burnished the game's image by pridefully booting out chance screwups. Except, that is, when the jugheads turned out to be superstars who filled the owners' stadiums and bankbooks. No longer. With the public calling for the heads of its former heroes, not even stars like Mike Norris and Steve Howe could keep messing up. "Knowing what I know now," says Howe with a sigh, "I would never have come forward [with my addictions]. I would have kept my mouth shut and not said a word to anybody." Howe's statistics were great even when he was addicted—and he realizes that if he had not gone public with his problems, he would have saved a couple of the strikes that baseball allows its premier players.

The Rebel Leader

Last spring, thirty-year-old Harry Steve found himself in the role of president, general manager, and field boss of the sorry San Jose Bees. Harry, a slight, chain-smoking man in an almost constant state of agitation, had already been running the club for two years as a salaried employee. But when the team's owner, businessman Peter Kern, refused to raise his $1,000-a-month salary, Harry came up with an offer that even Kern couldn't turn down. Harry would run the team for free, keep any profits the never-before-profitable Bees made, and pay for any losses out of his own pocket. Kern agreed, and Harry got what he had always dreamed of, his own baseball team. Never mind the fact that he was broke and there was virtually no way the Bees could make any money.

Harry Steve's gamble was insane. Of the 150 teams that compose the country's eleven minor leagues, only three have no affiliation with a major-league organization and, as a result, get no free players or financial help. Without that big-league umbilical, an independent club is doomed to suck, both on the field and at the cash register. All the good young players are already owned by major-league teams with minor-league affiliates, and it's almost impossible to turn a profit solely on gate receipts.

As fate would have it, the team Harry got for free was one of those doomed independents. For the last three years, the San Jose Bees have finished last in the California League, averaging a dismal 752 fans a game. The Bees were so bad that no one ever complained when the San Jose *Mercury News* barely mentioned the team.

Harry's first move upon arriving in San Jose was to try and lure a major-league team to associate itself with his team. No one would touch the dreck franchise or the unorthodox general manager. The only deal Harry could strike was with the Seibu Lions of Japan's Pacific League. That's how he came by Hank Wada and his five samurai.

Finally, at the end of his wits and bankbook, Harry got an idea. Instead of making do with young, talentless minor-league castoffs, he would try using genuine major-league athletes branded as untouchables by the men who run the Show. He would hire every talented dope fiend or head case who had been thrown a blackball by the majors. He would pay them peanuts, win some games, draw some fans, and maybe make some money; in return, the pariahs would get another shot at showing the world they had learned their lesson. So Harry got out a phone book and tracked down the twenty-eight-year-old host of a radio show called "Steve Howe's Rock and Roll Revue" in Whitefish, Montana.

The Rebel Reliever

In 1980, Steve Howe brought his 95-mile-per-hour fastball to the Los Angeles Dodgers. In his first year, Howe became the ace of the Dodgers relief staff, winning seven games and saving seventeen more. He finished with a 2.65 earned run average and was named National League Rookie of the Year. In the next two years, he won or saved dozens, had a minuscule ERA, and was named to the National League All-Star Team. The Dodgers won the World Championship, and Howe won a World Series game.

Howe, drawing an $800,000-a-year salary, was quickly buttered up as the toast of baseball-crazed L.A., whose sycophants rate personal access to Dodger stars on a par with lunch at Spago with Quincy Jones. Steve Howe, a twenty-two-year-old son of an auto worker from Pontiac, Michigan, wandered unaware into the dangerous sludge of Hollywood hangers-on. To put it mildly, he began to party.

At the end of the 1982 season, he publicly announced he was a cocaine addict and checked into an Arizona clinic for five and a half weeks. He went in again the following May, at which time the Dodgers fined Howe one month's salary—$53,867. He briefly fell off the wagon in September and told management of his problem. They suspended him for the entire 1984 season. Manager Tommy Lasorda's advice to Howe: "You sleep with dogs, you're going to wake up with fleas."

"It was brutal in L.A.," he now says. "I found out one thing—the difference between real people and phony people. Everyone wanted something from me. I was fun at first—and then I got in trouble." After he came forward with his addiction, the local press began hounding him. "Baseball is a great part of my life, but it was tedious to go to the park. I reached the point where I didn't want to pick up the newspaper because I was afraid of what someone was writing about me."

Determined to get out of Los Angeles, Howe asked for his release and last year signed with the Minnesota Twins. Eager to please his new bosses, Howe rushed himself back from arm surgery. His fastball still hummed, but his elbow ached. Not wanting to let down his teammates, he took the pitching mound secretly stoned on painkillers. "Needless to say," says Howe, "I wasn't too effective. I was taking three hundred to eight hundred milligrams of Darvocet, and I never knew whether to throw a slider or go to sleep."

At the end of last season, Howe went back to Montana to prepare for the coming year. He fielded phone calls from several other major-league teams interested in his still-hopping fastball, and it looked as if the Twins might re-sign him. He headed down to spring training in Florida, confident that a number of teams would be bidding for his arm. But when he got there, no one would even let him throw batting practice. Word was out—newly installed, hard-guy commissioner Peter Ueberroth was not happy with Howe's past or the fact that his name had come up, along with those of several other major leaguers, at last year's heavily publicized trial of a Pittsburgh cocaine dealer. With Ueberroth frowning, no team dared touch Steve Howe. After it became obvious that no one was going to sign him, he went back to Montana and a part-time job as a DJ for a local radio station. And then Harry called. Howe doesn't mind that he isn't living the life of a Show star. "First-class is in the mind," he says. "If you're happy, you can have fun in the desert. And I'm finally happy."

The deal with the Bees was simple. Howe would get about $2,000 a month, a chance to play, and a constant supply of urinalysis bottles to fill. If and when Howe's contract was purchased by a major-league team, Harry would get almost 50 percent of the buy-out action. In today's bull market for relief pitchers who can throw 95-mph fastballs, Harry could make a few hundred thousand dollars.

Steve Howe also brought Harry Steve's team much-needed publicity. As soon as word got out that he was negotiating with Howe, it seemed that every outcast ex-big leaguer in the country was calling San Jose. Harry is quick to point out that he wasn't on any moral crusade. "As long as they're ready to play," he said, "I don't care what they do. I'm not going to be a baby-sitter— these guys know this is their last chance around." The players didn't care that Harry was refusing the role of Mother Teresa. "Shit," says Reitz, "he was the only one in all of baseball willing to give me a fourth second chance."

While all the other teams in the league sported spiffy pro-model warm-up jerseys, Harry printed up T-shirts for his players that read THE BAD NEWS BEES. The team—which hadn't had new uniforms in several seasons—got freshly minted on-field apparel. "I bought them on credit," says Harry. "Buy now, worry later, I figured. The creditors will get their money; maybe not on time, but they'll get it."

Opening Day

The team was a mess. Harry couldn't afford to send the Bees to Arizona for spring training, and there was barely enough time to get the new guys fitted for uniforms, let alone *practice*. Then there was a slight problem with Derrel Thomas. Upon arriving in San Jose, Thomas decided that he, not Harry, should be the manager. Secretly gathering the players, Thomas outlined a bizarre plan for a dugout coup. The Bees said no; when Harry caught wind of the plot, he fired Thomas. The Junkyard Dog cleaned out his locker in five minutes and was last seen speeding his sports car up Highway 101.

And then there was the erratic behavior of Mike Norris. "When I was a kid," Norris told a reporter while he was still with the A's, "I used to scribble on pieces of paper that I was going to be the greatest pitcher ever." Five years ago, that seemed possible. But with the good life came the bad. Since his 1981 All-Star year, Norris has reportedly been in two drug-treatment centers and was recently placed in a two-year counseling program as a result of his 1985 arrest for possession of cocaine. Last winter, he spent four days in a Dominican Republic jail cell for allegedly carrying marijuana into the country. Even though the charges were later dropped, they didn't help Norris's growing reputation as a player who had blown his shot at greatness.

This spring, Roger Angell devoted his annual *New Yorker* baseball preview to the topic of drugs in baseball. The best baseball writer ever wrote:

> Anyone who has been involved with the sports world can easily bring to mind a particular athlete whose shining, wonderfully promising career was cut down by drug addiction. (For me, this will always be Mike Norris, the angular and elegant right-handed pitcher . . . with the A's. . . . I can still see the unique little flourish of his trailing leg as he finished his delivery, and his comical, hot-dog mannerisms on the mound, and recall the charm and intelligence of his interviews. . . .)

Norris arrived in camp with a permawear grin and a Willie Mays "sayhey-heyhey" for anyone in earshot. After casing out his new teammates, Norris opined, "I feel like I'm at an AA meeting," But he quickly announced that he would not be one to judge. "I'm in the Fun Hall of Fame"—he giggled—"and now I gotta start acting like a member of society, not like Jimi Hendrix." Unbothered by references to his several convictions for cocaine possession, Norris says he was so confident of his willpower that he recently tested himself with a visit to his favorite Oakland dealer. The dealer laid out ten grams of coke and invited Norris to sample. Instead of inhaling, Norris says, he blew the coke over the entire room. "I can still see the stuff floating through the air," he says with a laugh.

The reason he's with the San Jose Bees? "There's an unspoken law in the majors about not hiring me," Norris snaps. "There's got to be. I'm too good to be here. Except, I guess, that I fucked myself and *put* myself here." But he has no intention of showing up his fellow Bees. "I've got a Jaguar and a Mercedes sitting pretty in my garage. But I ain't going to be big-leaguing my teammates." There was another reason for Norris keeping his automobiles where they were— the California Department of Motor Vehicles had suspended his license.

Norris misses several practices his first week. His excuses include missed rides and command performances with the IRS and DMV. Harry is worried but not surprised. "I knew who Mike Norris was before I signed him. He is just someone who is very irresponsible in his personal life. But he is sincere, he means well, and he has a good heart." Does Norris plan to be around for the season opener? "Heyheyhey," says Norris, "I'll be there."

Opening Day finally arrives at San Jose Municipal Stadium; Steve Howe warms up on the sidelines. The stands are overflowing with 4,911 fans, lured by the appeal of Harry Steve's geek show. He has gone all out for the opener, investing $51 in rock tapes that boom over the stadium's scratchy public-address system. A local grocery clerk sings "The Star-Spangled Banner," and John Novak, an almost totally deaf, one-legged, seventy-one-year-old retired railroad baggage handler, throws out the first ball. ("They could have gotten a president," Novak told reporters, "but they chose me.") Finally, and to loud cheers, Steve Howe takes the mound.

Howe blows the first Salinas Spur away on three straight major-league strikes. Several beefy major-league scouts are in the stands, chomping cigars and taking careful notes. Howe goes on to toy with the Spurs for five innings, giving up only one hit and no walks. "Most of these guys have no idea what it means to be set up by a major-league pitcher," he later says gleefully. "They're just out there hacking."

The Bees lose their next two games at home and head to Fresno for the season's first road trip. "I'm not worried," says Harry, "because there's *no* way this team is not going to be in first place at the end of the season. We just haven't had any practice." Harry is exicted about Fresno; he has scheduled Norris to start and has told several scouts to show up—with their checkbooks.

The Bees' team bus pulls up in front of the Tropicana Inn, an ugly motel splayed on the ugliest concrete strip in Fresno, which was ranked two years ago as the worst American city in which to live. Across the street, loitering in the parking lot of a furniture-rental store, are four of what must surely be the fattest hookers in the Central Valley. "All the teams stay at the Tropicana," says Fern, who says her *real* job is working the legalized chicken ranches of Nevada. On most game days, however, she can be found right here, bird-dogging the Tropicana.

Norris is not on the bus ride from the motel to the Fresno stadium. He shows up minutes before game time in a dented green Buick, nicknamed Bess, owned and driven by his pal Ken Foster, a journeyman bush-league outfielder. "Hey-heyhey," yells Norris, several pairs of cleats slung over his shoulder. Norris explained later that Bess had stalled on the way to Fresno. "I was sitting out there with the cows, thinking, *They ain't never going to believe this one.* I thought I'd miss this game and Mike Norris's days with the Bees would be history." Harry decides to hold Norris out until the team gets back to San Jose.

The first game is a fiasco. Some 1,500 fans have shown up for the Fresno Giants' Opening Day; the rain starts twelve seconds after the national anthem. The showers intensify, the Bees and Giants boot half a dozen balls in the mud and the umpire doesn't stop the game. By the seventh inning the deluge has whittled the paid audience to 23, including 8 bare-chested drunks doing a mambo in the aisles. It starts to hail, and the leader of the pack wanders behind the backstop and quiets the stadium by waving his arms. "Hey, Howe," the young drunk screams toward the Bees' dugout 15 feet away, "you're a douche bag! A real douche bag! Yeah, a real fucking douche bag!" With that, he dumps a beer over his head. In the dugout, Howe and Harry listen impassively, both with cigarettes cupped in their hands. The Bees lose 6–4.

Back at the motel, Captain Reitz hosts a midnight party in his motel room. Nine players jam inside with cases of beer; Reitzy turns on the tube and blasts MTV. "Springsteen, you like Springsteen?" he asks the Japanese players. Three nod their heads, jump from the bed, and air-guitar an accompaniment to a blasting "Born in the U.S.A." Harry observes it all, silently sucking up ciggies. At two-thirty, the party breaks up.

The Bees lose the next night, getting only two hits and making six errors. After the game, the team moves right from the dugout to the waiting team bus that will take them back to San Jose. Everyone, that is, except Mike Norris and Ken Foster, who have sped off in Foster's green bomber. Five minutes later, the bus pulls up to a Burger King at the edge of Fresno. Across the street, in the parking lot of Rep's House of Ribs, are the four hookers from outside the Tropicana. "Come on," yells Fern from across the road, "we'll do you right here. Twenty-five bucks." Howe walks across the road, and the girls begin preening. When the pitcher comes within 10 feet, he makes a wide veer to the left. He trundles off into the dark, returning with a pack of cigarettes. "I'm amazed," says Harry Steve, "by how many women want to drop their drawers for Steve Howe. Just because he's Steve Howe!"

Munching fries, the team quietly reboards the bus for the midnight ride back to San Jose. The silence is shattered as soon as the bus hits the highway. Reitz, sipping from a flask of vodka, decides it's time to introduce the Japanese kids to the sing-along. As the bus careens through the pitch-dark flatlands, he leads the team in boisterous choruses of "New York, New York" and "We Are the World." The smiling Japanese join in, mouthing "heyheyhey" for lyrics.

Howe says this team has the best spirit of any he's ever been on. "You have to be close. This is our last chance," he says. Even Harry allows a tad of sentiment to creep in. "I never went into this as a moral thing," he says. "I did it to win ball games and make some money. But once I got to know these guys, I took a real personal interest. I'd like to see these guys beat the system and forget about their pasts and go on from here. This rebel image is great. Some of those major-league teams that were laughing when we signed Howe will begin standing in line when they see how he can still pitch. Now there's a part of me, the adventurous part, that says I never want a development deal."

An hour out of Fresno a burning car is spotted on the side of the road. It is green, a bomber, and empty. "Bess!" shout several players. A mile on, two black men in baseball uniforms are standing on the side of the road with their thumbs out. In this part of California it is not safe to be a black man hitchhiking on the highway at midnight. Even if they are carrying baseball bats.

The bus pulls over, and Howe runs out the door to welcome Norris and Foster with high fives. Norris, delighted, wanders back to the bus with a mock-arthritic Fred Sanford waddle. "I am *so* happy to see you guys," he yells. "I was about to call up a bitch and tell her to get her ass down to this fucking exit." Harry is silent, barely listening to explanations about the broken radiator that led to Bess's cremation.

In the back of the bus muted conversations are held regarding the fates of the team's stars. All agree, Ueberroth allowing, that Howe should be up in the majors within weeks—his fastball is popping, his head is centered. But no one is betting on Norris. "He's lost thirty pounds," ventures one. "His strength is all gone. He looks like Kunta Kinte."

As the bus throttles through the darkness, Jim Bolt, an innocent-looking first-year infielder, excitedly quizzes seatmate Daryl Sconiers. "So what's it like up in the Show?" he whispers. "I hear there are guys whose whole job is to keep track of your luggage." Sconiers, veteran of three full major-league seasons, nods. "Your luggage. Your plane ticket. Your check. All you have to do is play." The bus rumbles on, over the Pacheco Pass, home.

The Bad News Bees

Two nights later, Norris and Foster are two hours late to the San Jose ballfield. More car problems, they say. Harry shakes his head, looks in their eyes, and fires them both. All three chat for a few seconds, then shake hands. Norris and Foster clean out their lockers and hand back the last pro-baseball jerseys they will probably ever wear. Both know there are no more Harry Steves in Organized Baseball, but there are smiles on their faces as they head to the parking lot and Foster's new old car. At last sight, they were burning rubber toward Oakland.

"I knew this wasn't going to be some fantasy where this all worked out perfect," Harry later told reporters. Howe reflected pragmatically: "The public doesn't care if your car broke down. They just see you're late. I'm at the ballpark an hour before I'm supposed to be because of that. I'm not going to let anything get in the way of me getting back to the majors. Too much money to be made."

Finally playing together as a team, the Bees catch fire in the coming weeks. They win seven out of eight and pull from last place to within three games of the league lead. Howe is magnificent, clocking in with another win, some saves, a 1.97 ERA, and only three walks in thirty-two innings. More important, he passes four drug tests—three administered by Harry and one by the California League under the auspices of Peter Ueberroth's office. (That the league subjected Howe to a test is not unusual—under order from Ueberroth, all minor-league players are now subject to random urinalysis.) With Howe's fastball humming and his specimens clean, the cigar-chomping scouts in the stands are replaced by major-league executives with buffed nails. When it comes down to actually signing someone like Steve Howe, the big boys who sign the checks make the final call.

In mid-May, the Fresno Giants pull into town. Howe is scheduled to pitch the last game of the series. In attendance, he and Harry know, will be Al Rosen, president of the San Francisco Giants, and Pat Gillick, vice-president of the Toronto Blue Jays. Two hours before game time, John Johnson, president of the National Association, which governs minor-league baseball, calls Harry with news that he has been informed by Ueberroth's office that there is a "discrepancy" in a fifth drug test administered to Howe thirteen days before. Refusing to say exactly what that discrepancy is, the California League temporarily suspends its best pitcher.

Harry Steve is infuriated. "*Thirteen* days to get drug-test results?" he mutters. "Shit, I could test him myself in a day. There was a mistake." He ignores the suspension—something that is just not *done* in Organized Baseball—and goes with his scheduled pitcher. Howe throws five strong innings and is put on the ineligible list the next day by Johnson. "I know I'm going to get fined and suspended myself," says Harry, "but it just wasn't fair." A week later, California League president Joe Gagliardi announces Harry's penalty: a two-week suspension and a $500 fine.

Howe, banned from even suiting up, says, "It's like what was said in *North Dallas Forty*—we say it's a game, and the owners say it's a business. So we say it's a business, and they say it's a game. The owners' attitude is 'We say it, you believe it, or you're gone.' I'll be back. Count on it."

With Howe gone, the team sputters, falling back into last place. Harry, who has been keeping in touch with Norris, gives him a call and asks him to come back. He says he re-signed the erratic player "because we were into a losing streak and had some pitchers that weren't doing the job. I know he can pitch in our league. Hopefully he can win games for us."

Meanwhile, the residents of the Stadium Hilton ponder their future. Reitz, batting only .231 a month into the season, realizes he will probably never play back in the Show. But he has some other plans. He recalls his time in the drug hospital, after he got straight, when he stayed on as a counselor. Staying up all night with violent runaway teenagers tripping on angel dust, he got a new idea. "I realized how much I liked working with young people," he says. "It made me think I could be a good coach. But first I have to prove to people that I'm not insane."

Cias, batting a strong .306, spouts nothing but hope. "I have something to prove to myself," he says. "I can still play. I don't want to be one of those sour guys who quits and then years later tells everybody how he could have played major-league baseball." Cias is willing to bide his time; until he gets the call, he will busy himself airbrushing billboards out in the Bees' outfield. "You should see what I'm going to do to the TraveLodge sign," he says.

There is a void, however, down in the Stadium Hilton. A couple of weeks into the season Harry made a painful decision regarding Mike Bigusiak. "He stunk," says Harry. "He just plain stunk." So Stash is now gone for good from the Stadium Hilton, and he is sorely missed by his cave mates. Upon getting fired, he took away the few things he brought to San Jose—his cleats, his glove, and the two framed pictures of the woman who he was sure would be back "just as soon as I hit the Show."

Heading south on 101, Stash passed near Monterey, home of John Steinbeck's Cannery Row. Like the Stadium Hilton, like Harry Steve's gamble, like the unknown futures of Steve Howe, Derrel Thomas, and Mike Norris, Cannery Row, wrote Steinbeck, "is a poem, a stink, a grating noise, a quality of light, a tone, a habit, a nostalgia, a dream." Like those who tried one last time at San Jose Municipal Stadium, "its inhabitants are, as the man once said, 'whores, pimps, gamblers, and sons of bitches,' by which he meant Everybody."

Lake Wobegon, Minnesota (1418 alt., 942 pop.) sits plunk in the middle of the author's imagination and, by now, square in the heart of America. This excerpt is taken from *Lake Wobegon Days*.

GARRISON KEILLOR

Old Hard Hands

It took me a long time to learn to read. I was wrong about so many words. *Cat, can't. Tough, through, thought. Shinola.* It was like reading a cloud of mosquitoes. Donna, in the seat behind, whispered right answers to me, and I learned to be a good guesser, but I didn't read well until Mrs. Meiers took me in hand.

One winter day she took me aside after recess and said she'd like me to stay after school and read to her. "You have such a nice voice," she said, "and I don't get to hear you read in school as much as I'd like."

No one had told me before that I had a nice voice. She told me many times over the next few months what a *wonderful* voice I had as I sat in a chair by her desk reading to her as she marked work sheets. "The little duck was so happy. He ran to the barn and shouted. 'Come! Look! The ice is gone from the pond!' Finally it was spring."

"Oh, you read that so well. Read it again," she said. When Bill the janitor came in to mop, she said, "Listen to this. Doesn't this boy have a good voice?" He sat down, and I read to them both. "The little duck climbed to the top of the big rock and looked down at the clear blue water. 'Now I am going to fly,' he said to himself. He waggled his wings and counted to three. 'One, two, three.' And he jumped and—" I read in my clear blue voice. "I think you're right," Bill said. "I think he has a very good voice. I wouldn't mind sitting here all day and listening to him."

One word I liked was *popular*. It sounded good, it felt good to say, it made lights come on in my mouth. I drew a rebus: a bottle of Nu-Grape + U + a Lazy Ike. *Pop-u-lure.* It didn't occur in our reading book, where little children did the right thing, although their friends scoffed at them, and where despised animals wandered alone and redeemed themselves through pure goodness and eventually triumphed to become Top Dog, the Duck of Ducks, the Grand Turtlissimo, the Greatest Pig of Them All, which, though thrilling, didn't appeal to me so much as plain *popular*. "The popular boy came out the door, and everybody smiled and laughed. They were so glad to see him. They all crowded around him to see what he wanted to do."

Morning and afternoon, school recessed and we took to the playground; everyone burst out the door except me. Mrs. Meiers said, "Don't run! Walk!" I always walked. I was in no hurry, I knew what was out there. The girls played in front. Little girls played tag and stoopball, hopscotch, skipped rope; big girls sat under the pine tree and whispered. Some girls went to the swings. Boys went out back and played baseball, except for some odd boys who lay around in the shade and fooled with jackknives and talked dirty. I could go in the shade or stand by the backstop and wait to be chosen. Daryl and David always chose up sides and always chose the same people first, the popular ones. "Let somebody else be captain!" Jim said once. "How come you always get to choose?" They just smiled. They were captains; that was all there was to it. After the popular ones got picked, we stood in a bunch looking down at the dirt, waiting to see if our rating had changed. They took their sweet time choosing us; we had plenty of time to study our shoes. Mine were Keds, black, though white ones were more popular. Mother said black wouldn't show dirt. She didn't know how the wrong shoes could mark a person and raise questions in other people's minds. "Why do you wear black tennis shoes?" Daryl asked me once. He had me there. I didn't know. I guessed I was just that sort of person, whether I wanted to be or not. Maybe not showing dirt was not the real reason, the real reason was something else too terrible to know, which she would tell me someday. "I have something to tell you, son." She would say it. "No! No!" "Yes, I'm afraid it's true." "So that's why—" "Yes. I'm sorry I couldn't tell you before. I thought I should wait." "But can't I—" "No, I'm afraid not. We just have to make the best of it."

Nine boys to a side, four already chosen, ten positions left, and the captains look us over. They chose the popular ones fast ("Brian!" "Bill!" "Duke!" "John!" "Bob!" "Paul!" "Jim!" "Lance!"), and now the choice is hard, because we're all so much the same: *not so hot*—and then they are down to their last grudging choices, a slow kid for catcher and someone to stick out in right field where nobody hits it, except maybe two guys, and when they come to bat, the captain sends the poor right fielder to left, a long, ignominious walk. They choose the last ones two at a time, "You and you," because it makes no difference, and the remaining kids, the scrubs, the excess, they deal for as handicaps. ("If I take him, then you gotta take *him*.") Sometimes I go as high as sixth, usually lower. Just once I'd like Daryl to pick me first. "Him! I want him! The skinny kid with the glasses and the black shoes! You! Come on!" But I've never been chosen with any enthusiasm.

I think that if Wally ("Old Hard Hands") Bunsen were here, things would be different for me; he and I would be close friends. He was a true champion, a man among men, known for his kindness as well as athletic prowess. He saved a boy from drowning once, and another time he brought a crippled kid to the ball game to see him hit a double off Carl Hubbell. That was in the season he spent with the Chicago Cubs.

Born, Lake Wobegon, August 1, 1910. Died, Lake Wobegon, June 11, 1936. I know those dates by heart. The year 1933 he was with the Cubs and batted .348 from April to July and then came home. He died while batting for the Lake Wobegon Volunteers (who later became the Whippets), versus Albany, bottom of the seventh inning, with men on first and third (later known as "The Dead Man's Spread"). He batted left, threw right, was 6 feet 2 inches and weighed 181 pounds. His golden hair was parted down the middle, and he wore a gold ring on his right hand. The little finger of his right hand was cut off in a corn picker, 1931. The little white house next door to the Dieners' was his house; he slept on the back porch, even in winter, and his dog's name was Buddy. His parents' names were Clara and Oscar. He was smart as a whip, and if he hadn't played ball, he would have been an inventor. He made a gasoline-powered sled, an automatic apple corer, and an electric water fountain for his mom's rock garden.

Two pictures of him hang in the Sidetrack Tap: one in his Cubs uniform, his bat cocked, and the other with Jack Dempsey, who is kissing him on the cheek, a great tribute when you think about it. What sort of man would the Heavyweight Champion of the World kiss? A man's man, of course. I wasn't allowed in the Sidetrack as a boy, but I went in—just to have a look at the pictures, and they were permanently imprinted in my mind, and from his wonderful grin I began to imagine him as a personal friend.

Wally Krebsbach: "He had wings on his feet and a whip for an arm. He ran, he threw, he came to bat, and it was all play to him. He just laughed out there, it was so natural to him. A beautiful ballplayer. God gave him the talent, and he had no trouble with it. The outfield was his home, and any ball hit near him just naturally belonged in his hand. He came to bat and had no trouble in his mind; he was meant to hit."

His trouble with the Cubs lay in his glove. Growing up in Lake Wobegon, being poor, he learned to play without one, and by the time he could afford to have it, he was such an excellent bare-handed fielder he didn't bother with a glove. Thus the nickname "Old Hard Hands." His palms were like leather. In 1931, a Cubs scout went to look at a prospect in Duluth, and the hotel clerk said "Dobbins? Hell, you ought to see a guy in this little town near St. Cloud; he could put Dobbins in his back pocket." So the scout came to town, in his gabardine suit with a bottle of rye in his valise, and took one look at Wally shag flies and waved $500 in his face as if he were trying to wake him up. "One thing, kid, you gotta get a glove," he said. Wally was about to leave for spring training the next January, but his father got sick, so he stayed until he recovered, which wasn't until May, and the year after that he went to Florida and put on the uniform.

"Dear Folks," he wrote. "Arrived this morning and went straight to the park for practice. The grass is brown, and the ground is hard as cement, but guess it will do. Tried on so many gloves and none felt just right, so just picked the smallest one and hoped for the best. Ran for an hour and felt better, then lunch. Food here is all fried. Felt queasy after but swung the bat okay and then came back to the hotel, which is small but clean. The others went to a movie. Miss you all."

He begged the Cubs to let him play bare-handed, but they said it was against the rules. "You will get accustomed to it," they said. He was so good in every department, they figured it would be easy for him to learn this one little thing. A man who stood at the plate so relaxed and easy, then cocked his hip, lifted his foot, and the next you saw was him trotting slowly toward first—a man who if he did have to leg it cruised on the base paths so deceptively fast, the center fielder trotted in and picked up Wally's single and went to lob it to the cutoff man and saw Wally ambling into second—a man whose eye in the field was so keen, he was momentarily distracted by a pigeon gliding into the grandstand or a shooting star—a man whom people would have paid just to watch him throw a ball home, so hard it hummed, so true the catcher never moved his feet—surely a man so talented could learn to wear a glove on his left hand and catch with it.

"He could've, but his heart wasn't in it," says Wally Krebsbach. "It didn't feel right to him. It threw him off balance. It took the fun out of the game. He actually got headaches from it. And then he dropped a couple, and that made him ashamed, and then he came home. They offered him more money, but he just laughed. It wasn't worth it to him.

"If they'd let him play the way he wanted to, bare-handed, he would've been the greatest they ever saw, but they wouldn't, so he came home.

"He wasn't the same. He looked forty. His hand shook. Then he had a run of bad luck. His dad passed away. That was hard on him. And then his girl told him she didn't love him anymore—that took all the spirit out of him. Nobody could cheer him up after that. He told me—he said, 'Buddy, she says to me, she says, "My daddy says you're nothing but a ballplayer and you'll never hold down a regular job, but that doesn't matter to me. I could love you, anyway." She says, "It's your hands being so hard. I just can't get used to it." Can you believe that, Buddy?' he says. He couldn't believe it. He said, 'A man is *supposed* to have hard hands, ain't he? Who has soft hands? Nobody but fruitcakes and bank clerks.' He was broken up over her for weeks.

"And then he got the idea from the way people talked that he'd been a failure, that if he was any good he'd be in Chicago. And that just killed him. He knew it wasn't true; it was that they thought it that killed him. He knew how good he was; he didn't have to prove it by going someplace else. A man is just *good*; he can be good anywhere. This was his own family who looked down on him, though, so it tore him apart. Clarence's dad, that's Wally's brother, he gave him a hard time about quitting the team and embarrassing the family, as if he had any right to talk about it. Well, Wally didn't have a job; he was living off what he'd earned from the Cubs, and he was lying around in that sleeping porch, thinking too much, just living from Sunday to Sunday for the Volunteers games. One Saturday night he comes down here and asks for a drink. My old man was bartending; he says no. So Wally left. Where he found it I don't know, but he found enough to last him all night, because when he came to the game next day, he was suited up, and that was about all. He looked like death on toast.

"He never should have played. Dutch and me, we argued with Henneman to send him home, but there was naturally a big crowd to see him play, so play he did. I never saw a man sweat so much. His eyes bugged out. He flopped on the bench and almost passed out. Then he dropped one in the top of the seventh. It wasn't important, we were up by six runs, there were two outs, we said, 'Shake it off,' but it bothered him so that when he come up to bat, he was set to kill one. And instead it killed him.

"It was the bottom of the seventh, Roy on first and me on third, no outs, a count of two-and-two, and he stepped out of the box and looked down toward me, but he wasn't looking *at* me, because his eyes wouldn't focus. He was clearing his throat, and I thought he was choking, so I called time and ran in, but he wasn't choking; he was crying. He says, 'I'm no good.' I said, 'You're the best. You're the best there ever was.' And then I went back to the bag."

Wally stops. He can't finish the story. He shuts his eyes, and tears squeeze out from his eyelids and fall down his poor old face. Up and down the bar, old guys look away and touch their eyes. The alarm clock ticks by the cash register, and you can hear the electric clock hum in the Cold Spring beer sign. The big fan above the door hums. Everything else stops at the Sidetrack when he comes to the point in the story everybody has heard him tell so often.

The rest is: Wally Bunsen swung at the next pitch, an inside fastball across the letters, and fouled it off into his own head and fell across home plate and died. They said he never knew what hit him. Some of his family said that was what comforted them in this terrible tragedy, that he hadn't had to suffer, but of course he had suffered a great deal more than they knew.

When I thought of him, I imagined him as my best friend and him and me taking off to go fishing together. I even practiced what we would say. He'd say, "Nothing beats fishing." And I'd say, "*You're* not just talking."

Nearly seven decades later, the Black Sox Scandal retains its strong, strange hold on the imagination. Novelists have reveled in the ripe characters and mock-profound implications of the "fix." The sordid tale becomes baseball's equivalent of the Fall, with Shoeless Joe Jackson cast as the fig-leafed Adam, Arnold Rothstein as the serpent, and Chick Gandil as—think about it—Eve. Abe Attell might even be the worm in the apple; and Judge Landis, Moses the deliverer. . . . One could go on. But casting a cold eye on the actual events, Byzantine though they were, turns up no martyrs, no heroes: not Jackson, not Eddie Cicotte, not even Buck Weaver. He who would know the true story, or as near as we can get it, must put the novels aside and first read Lardner's *Remember the Black Sox?*, written in 1938. Here, the lowdown on the legendary 1919 World Series.

JOHN LARDNER

Remember the Black Sox?

The first of October 1919 was the Fourth of July all over again in Cincinnati. Most of the big stores were closed for the day. Flags draped the business section of town, and newsboys yelled themselves hoarse. Senator Warren Gamaliel Harding and party had the bridal suite at the Sinton Hotel. Barney Oldfield held court at the Gibson.

Tickets? You could still get a block of three for a hundred bucks from that operative over there in the corner of the lobby, if you liked to do business with Sitting Bull on a strictly Custer basis. The face value of a block was $16.50—first, second, and sixth games, Cincinnati at home.

Everybody who was anybody would be at the ball game that afternoon. Anybody who was everybody would do the best he could. They were setting up direct-wire connection, follow it play-by-play on the scoreboard, getcher official lineup here, getcher autograph picture of Eddie Roush!

Big-league baseball had boomed in its first season after the World War. Every year the magnates cleared their throats and said, "Baseball, the national pastime, has enjoyed a banner year," and this time, in the autumn of 1919, they never spoke a truer word. The fever was soaring. Lotteries or pools, selling tickets on total scores for the week, had done a million-dollar business from Oregon to Virginia since May. Batting averages were familiar to the country, and players heroic, as they never had been before.

And now, at the end of the bobtailed—140 games—but lively season, the fans were sitting down, unglutted, to a World Series that was a World Series.

Or, rather, to an exhibition of skill and science by the greatest ball club of all time, complete with human foils. For the White Sox, of Chicago, were like John L. Sullivan in the days when the Strong Boy toured the country offering $100 to the local volunteer who could go three rounds with him.

Cincinnati, the critics said, would last five rounds anyway—the series was five games out of nine. The Reds were simply the survivors of a National League dogfight. But the Sox . . .

Take the testimony of an expert witness, Edward Trowbridge Collins.

"They were the best," says Eddie, their captain and second baseman. "There never was a ball club like that one, in more ways than one. I hate to say it, but they were better than the Athletics I played with from 1910 through 1914.

"Offensively, from top to bottom, there wasn't a breather for an opposing pitcher in the lineup; and when it came to pitchers, Cicotte, Williams, Kerr, and Faber were tops as pitchers in the American League at the time—all on one club."

Shano Collins or Nemo Liebold in right field; your witness, Eddie Collins, the peer of Lejoie, Hornsby, and Gehringer, second base; Buck Weaver, natural ballplayer of natural ballplayers, third base; Shoeless Joe Jackson, forerunner of Ruth , left field; Hap Felsch, great thrower and dangerous hitter, center field; Chick Gandil, a slick genius, first base; Swede Risberg, sure-handed fielder and tidy batsman, shortstop; Ray Schalk, the fastest and smartest catcher of his generation, behind the plate; and Cicotte, Williams, Kerr.

The Reds were just a pretty good team, and their best friends did not claim more for them at the time. The Redlegs who survive today—Greasy Neale, for one, whose brain, working on the sideline of the Yale Bowl every fall, can be heard to purr like a dynamo as far away as Bridgeport—will not contradict you when you classify them as the short-enders of the century. On paper, they were 5 to 1.

But October first brought high carnival to Cincinnati just the same. Thirty-one thousand squeezed into the grandstand and bleachers, and hundreds of thousands stood outside by the scoreboards.

This was the first postwar World Series, the crowning glory of baseball's renaissance, and it was Shineball Eddie Cicotte pitching for the White Sox—the greatest right-hander, next to Walter Johnson, in the game.

Cicotte's second pitch of the day hit the batter, Maurice Rath, Red second baseman, in the small of the back. It wasn't the first pitch, as generally believed. The first was a called strike.

In the last half of the fourth inning, Cicotte took the mound with the score 1–1 and looked nervously around at his fielders. Something about his manner had been puzzling the inmates of the press box from the start, from the time he hit Rath. Now they muttered, "What the hell?" Those men behind Eddie Cicotte could field their positions in their sleep.

Then boff! boff! boff! A run was in, and there were Reds on second and third. Dutch Ruether, Cincinnati pitcher, came to the plate. He whaled a terrific triple between Felsch and Jackson.

A few minutes later, five Red runs were in, and Cicotte was out. Kid Gleason, tough, gray little manager of the White Sox, was on the playing field, yanking his arms around, crazy with rage and grief.

The Reds won the ball game 9–1, as the Sox batsmen, each a sharpshooter, waved gently at Ruether's delivery.

Cincinnati went solidly nuts that night. But some of the folks from out of town—ballplayers who watched from the grandstand, certain Chicago baseball writers, and a small percentage of Chicago fans—were mumbling and shaking their heads. This wasn't any part of the ball club they'd been seeing.

Something Rotten in Denmark

Kid Gleason went into conference that night with his employer, the Old Roman, Charles A. Comiskey. And up in a double room at the Sinton Hotel, where the telephone rang every sixty seconds, a fellow called Bennett, from Des Moines, became very irritable.

"This thing is beginning to smell," he said to his roommate, a fellow from New York. "The dogs in the street know it."

If, by dogs in the street, Mr. Bennett meant smart gamblers, he was absolutely correct. But the country at large didn't know for another twelve months that the fix was in—the biggest, sloppiest, crudest fix of a sporting event that ever was known to man. It was a makeshift job; compounded in equal parts of bluff and welsh and cold gall, with no contributor or agent-contributor knowing what the man next to him was up to, and very seldom bothering to find out.

The series was fixed on the strength of a fake telegram, with the help of a pair of go-betweens who lost their shirts on it. Three quarters of the bounty money was withheld from the players who threw the series. Arnold Rothstein, widely accused of being the Judas-in-chief of the stratagem, could sit back and deny the charge blandly and securely, because, after coming up and telling him what they were going to do and insuring him a handsome betting profit, the fixers went through with the thing without him.

It was a haphazard business, all right, comical in some of its aspects, but it nearly wrecked baseball for all eternity. Those who followed its unraveling in 1920 remember that it touched off a rash of scandal rumors that spread across the face of the game like measles. A hundred players and half a dozen ball clubs were involved in stories of sister plots. Baseball was said to be crooked as sin from top to bottom.

And people didn't take their baseball lightly in those days. They threw themselves wholeheartedly into the game when the war ended, so much so that the sudden pull-up, the revelation of crookedness, was a real and ugly shock. It got under their skins. You heard of no lynchings, but Buck Herzog, the old Giant infielder, on an exhibition tour of the West in the late fall of 1920, was slashed with a knife by an unidentified fan who yelled: "That's for you, you crooked such-and-such!"

Buck's name had been mentioned by error in a newspaper rumor of a minor unpleasantness in New York that John J. McGraw had ironed out ruthlessly a few years before. Buck was innocent as a newborn pigeon, but rumors were rumors, and the national temper was high.

"Too high," says Mr. Herzog, looking back. "I never want to see the like again."

It's a fact that some of the White Sox, after the scandal hearings, were unwilling to leave the courtroom for fear of mobs.

Well, that was the business that nearly forestalled the careers of Joe Di-Maggio, Jerome H. Dean, Carl Hubbell, Lou Gehrig, Mickey Cochrane, William (Terrible) Terry, and Paul Waner. The public came within a whisker's width of never seeing another box score, never heckling another umpire, never warming another hot stove. It was close—too close for comfort. And though the baseball magnates of 1938 like to think of 1919 as a tightly sealed chapter, and though the Hall of Fame at Cooperstown is closed, actually if not officially, to Joe Jackson, Buck Weaver, and Eddie Cicotte—well, we're wallowing in baseball luxury now. We can afford to look back at the abyss after eighteen years of hard, steady climbing.

To a loosely knit group of technicians on the fringe of baseball, the news of the scandal, when it broke, was no complete surprise. It took the country by storm, but Jack Doyle remembers that there were rumors of something off-key several days before the series began, which means a full year before the story became public property.

"You couldn't miss it, if you were doing important betting," says Mr. Doyle, Broadway's price maker. "The thing had an odor. I saw smart guys take even money on the Sox who should have been asking five to one. Those Sox, may they rest in peace, should have been the shortest-priced favorites that ever started a World Series."

The series was scheduled to open on the first of October. On September twenty-ninth, in Boston, well-known professionals began to grab all the 4-to-1 money they could lay their hands on, and backed the price down to even money. Similar movements started simultaneously in Pittsburgh, New York, St. Louis, Des Moines, and Philadelphia. The Red wave seemed senseless, but Nat Evans and Nick the Greek were not senseless fellows when it came to laying their funds on the line. Nor were Rachel Brown and Sport Sullivan and Joe Gedeon.

The fix had been clumsy. It's small wonder that sharp-eared characters like Nicholas Dandolos were "wised up and kicking the market to hell," in the subsequent bitter words of Abe Attell. They were even wised up in Wall Street, where bets of $1,000 were placed on Cincinnati at even money.

The series began with Cicotte's strange defeat. It grew stranger. In the second game, Lefty Claude Williams—"the best pitcher in this league," said Gleason—yielded three walks and two hits in the fourth inning, for three runs. The Reds picked up another run in the sixth. The final score was 4–2.

In the Bag

"The game was given to Cincinnati on a platter," said Gleason. It was a thing any manager might say under the circumstances, and when Wee Dickie Kerr, former bantamweight prize-fighter, shut out the Reds in the third game, the fans of Chicago took heart. But the small-time professionals of the city were going around hotel lobbies with sheaves of folding money in their hands, offering 5 to 2 on Cincinnati, begging to be covered. The market was dead, for the moment.

Eddie Cicotte's second start, in the fourth game of the series, produced an eerie development. Cicotte, a good fielding pitcher, managed to turn in two errors before three men were out. For one, he made an atrociously bad throw to Chick Gandil on first. The other came after Pat Duncan, young Red outfielder, had reached second. Larry Kopf singled into Joe Jackson's territory. Joe's great arm rifled the ball ahead of the runner, toward home. Cicotte made the technically proper play—when he saw that Duncan was not going to try to score, he intercepted the throw, apparently to make sure that Kopf would not try to take two bases while the ball was going all the way to the plate. But instead of completing the interception, Cicotte's gloved hand batted the ball to the grandstand. Duncan scored. Then Kopf did, too, on Greasy Neale's double off Cicotte. The Sox supporters were not alone in expressing their chagrin over Cicotte's performance when the Reds won, 2–0.

"In all his life he never pulled two like that before," said Gleason to reporters.

On October seventh, trailing by four games to one, the Sox rallied behind a failing Kerr and won the hard way, in the tenth inning, on hits by Weaver and Gandil. Cincinnati businessmen lost $60,000 in bets that day.

The Sox won again behind Cicotte, next afternoon.

And then, on October ninth, with Chicago fans yelling for a stretch finish, and the Reds seemingly on the run, the greatest ball team on earth collapsed like a parasol. The generous Williams gave up three runs before two were out in the first inning. In Chicago's half of the first in this game, with Liebold and Eddie Collins on base, and no one out, Weaver and Felsch went down in order, on two swinging strikeouts. And the mighty Jackson finished the inning by fouling out.

"If they'd shut their eyes, they couldn't 'a' done it," said Kid Gleason. The Kid seemed to have aged ten years in nine days. The furrows in his face were deeper, and his feet moved with a drag.

Rumors soared like kites in the breeze off Lake Michigan on October tenth, the day after the series ended. They were rumors strong enough to demand public attention. Charles A. Comiskey offered a reward of $20,000 for "a single clue" to evidence that his "boys" had been to the tank. No clues were forthcoming, and the rumors subsided. Chicago did not know that Commy was hiring private detectives to carry on the investigation undercover, or that the paychecks of eight White Sox players were held up—Jackson, Cicotte, Williams, Gandil, Felsch, Weaver, Risberg, and the utility infielder and pinch hitter, Fred McMullin.

Christy Mathewson spoke of the rumors at the time. He said it was ridiculous to question the honesty of the series. To be sure, Matty was a National League booster and the recently retired manager of the Cincinnati club (1918), and talk of a fix was hard for him to stomach.

The Hard Way to Deception

His arguments were irrefutable:

1. Too many players would have to be approached and bribed. One man can't throw a series.

2. A manager can't throw a series. The team will hustle in spite of him.

3. A pitcher can't do it. He would be yanked at the first sign of weakness.

4. You can't fix several players on one club and be sure your secret is safe.

5. No player would want to risk everything—his career, his future, his income—for a bundle of quick cash.

"And besides," said Matty, summing up, "it's just unthinkable, generally."

It was unthinkable, all right, and the way they worked it, it was grotesque. The dizziest wonder of all is that the whole house of marked cards did not topple about the ears of Sleepy Bill Burns and Billy Maharg and Abe Attell and Bennett, of Des Moines, and the boys on the field, long before Jake Daubert planted his shoe on first base for the final put-out of the series.

Before we examine the gamblers and their methods, though, let's have a look at the boys on the field. Unthinkable, said Matty. But this was a ball club unique in baseball history. Eddie Collins tells you it was the greatest club of all time and the greatest trouble club.

"That's what made its greatness so hard to understand," Eddie says. "As a rule, the chief requirement for a great team is harmony and cooperation on and off the field. That was an important thing about Connie Mack's teams. The White Sox? They were night and day to the Athletics. They seethed with discord and bitterness. Time after time they were close to open fighting with fists among themselves. And still they won going away."

It was a team of cliques, conspiracies, headaches, and fights. Collins and Chick Gandil, playing side by side in the infield, hadn't been on speaking terms since 1917, following a queer episode in which Gandil raised a pool among the players to reward the members of another club which had helped them win the pennant. Ray Schalk, the catcher, spoke to only three of the pitchers between games, Faber, Kerr, and Lowdermilk.

Gandil was known around the league as a gambler and a troublemaker. Cicotte used to say, "Chick was raised with low characters. He ain't got no ethics." Ethics or not, Chick had a strong influence over Cicotte and the happy-go-lucky Jackson.

Was the ball club underpaid? That's the excuse which many critics give for what happened in 1919. Commy was a powerful, upright man, a baseball pioneer, but his best friends could not call him a lavish spender—not with the hired help. The salaries of the "takers," or Black Sox, excepting McMullin, the utility man, ranged from $5,000 to $10,000. Jackson got a little more, $12,000. And they were the stars of the team—some of them the stars of all baseball.

This was before a fellow named Ruth revolutionized the game and nudged the wage scale upward with the blows of his mighty bat. Few ballplayers had five-figure incomes prior to 1920. But Commy's scale was lower than most, and his players were better than any. It's not hard to understand that the prospect of making the equivalent of a year's salary—"all in one whack, all green," as Jackson said—would dazzle the boys.

Throwing a ball game—"It's easy," said Cicotte later. "Gee, how easy! And you can make it look good." There was a lot of talk like that in the summer of 1919, among some of the players, especially in the later months, when it became obvious that the Sox were a shoo-in for the pennant. The talk was mostly in hotel rooms. One of the hotels was the Ansonia, in New York. They were talking there one day, Gandil and Cicotte, and a couple of outsiders were with them—a former ballplayer and a former fighter.

Sleepy Bill Burns had pitched here and there in both major leagues, with the White Sox and the Reds among other clubs. He moved from team to team, not sticking long with any. Bill had a habit of going to sleep on the bench, which won him his nickname. He was a guy who had been around. He admitted it.

Treason From Within

Billy Maharg, from Philadelphia, was an old-time lightweight who had fought some of the good ones, including Freddie Welsh.

Gandil and Cicotte and Burns and Maharg sat talking in the hotel room, with the door shut and the window open and a hot breeze and the smell of asphalt sifting in. Presently Burns and Maharg went away. A couple of days later, Sleepy Bill went out to the racetrack. They were running at Jamaica then.

"Where's Rothstein?" he asked of a fellow he knew.

"Over on the rail."

Bill went over. Arnold Rothstein, the "real-estate operator" and sportsman, a pale-faced pouter pigeon of a man, said, "Hello."

"The series can be fixed," said Bill. "It's ripe. But it'll take financing. They'd want a hundred grand."

Rothstein shook his head.

"They'll do business," urged Burns. "It's strictly an investment."

"No, not me," said Rothstein. "It's not the money. It's the details. It's too risky. It can't be done."

Burns took "no" for an answer. At least, he swears up and down that he did, and Rothstein's intimates of the time swear he did, and while one man's oath is another man's succotash, the thing is altogether logical. For Rothstein had his ear to the ground. He knew the mood and temper of some of the White Sox. One way or another, he thought, the fix would be in, and there was no sense in tying up money that could otherwise be bet.

This thought occurred later to other minds, to the mortification of the White Sox who threw the series. The bankrolling of the scheme—the payoff—was a department which gripped the interest of almost nobody.

Rothstein used to say, in the years that followed, that he never made a nickel betting on the series of 1919, but people close to him put the figure now at closer to $60,000.

It was Abe Attell who next tuned in on the eloquence of Sleepy Bill Burns. Bill was eloquent still, but a trifle discouraged, and even shocked, by the nearsighted reluctance of business leaders to invest in a sure-fire scheme. Bill was like Fulton, peddling his steamboat. It seemed to him sometimes that he had been born too soon. These were backward times.

But Abe Attell gave him hope. Abe was another fellow who had been around. One of the greatest small fighters of all time—former featherweight champion of the world, a miracle of speed, skill, and science—he had taken to living by his wits when he left the ring. Abe's wits were in first-class condition. "I think maybe Rothstein has changed his mind," he said.

That was good enough for Burns.

It was at the Sinton, a couple of days before the series began, and not until then, that Attell showed Burns, Maharg, and Gandil "proof" that Rothstein was financing the deal. The proof was a telegram signed with Rothstein's name.

It was all the proof that Gandil, now ringmaster of the players' side of the circus and chief go-between, ever saw. Would the boys be paid off? Chick didn't know, and he didn't much care. He had money. He was betting it.

An Open Secret

And so, it seemed to Attell and Bennett, was everybody else. Bennett, Des Moines gambler, was working with Abe, digging up money and getting it down at the best odds possible, but the best odds were none too good by the morning of October first. It was most annoying. Those thieves in Boston, New York, Pittsburgh, St. Louis, and elsewhere were butchering the price. Even dumb ballplayers around the leagues were on the line for Cincinnati and getting rich.

"Kind of an open secret, eh, pal?" said Mr. Attell.

"It smells," grumbled Mr. Bennett.

"Well, keep punching," said Abe. "Get it down."

The ballplayers, tipped off by Gandil that the promised fee was $100,000, to be paid in installments of $20,000 after each of the five losing games and split among them, were getting restless and uneasy in their hotel rooms and around the clubhouse. Cicotte's nerves were close to breaking.

"You can't bluff me," he told Burns, Maharg, and Gandil. "I got to have $10,000, and have it now."

He got it after the first game, which he lost. But he and the rest of the boys were drifting around in a heavy mist.

"We didn't know nothin'," says Joe Jackson. "Not a thing."

Burns and Maharg, calling at Attell's room on the morning of the second game, got $10,000 for Cicotte, and no more. Eddie said later that he found the money half hidden under his pillow—two or three $1,000 bills and several hundreds in the pile.

A total of $25,000 was paid up, divided among three players. The rest say they never touched a dime, and the facts seem to bear them out. The payoff department, as noted above, was not popular with any of the gamblers involved in the deal. It was office work, drudgery, giving no scope to the soaring qualities of the intellect.

And out on the ball field, the Sox went blindly through their paces. They were cutting their own throats on the strength of a fake telegram, and they were doing a thorough job. The fix of the series was a hit-or-miss business by the gamblers, who seemed to be making up the plot as they went along, but the players' work was well done.

Cicotte lobbed the ball to the plate "so you could read the trademark on it." Williams, "the best control pitcher in the league," gave out passes like a drunken press agent. Risberg's foot missed the bag by twelve inches on an easy double-play ball. Felsch played his position for Neale as though Greasy, a long hitter, were a crippled schoolgirl.

"It's too terrible to watch," shuddered Gleason, on the bench.

But the lighthearted Joe Jackson, now confused and shaken, could not pass up all that appetizing Cincinnati pitching. Joe was the leading batsman of the series, with .375. He hit the only home run. And when he walked to the plate, he carried his lucky hairpins with him. Hairpins were always lucky for Joe. He took them along up there even when he knew that Lady Luck had gone to Cain's Warehouse for the duration of the series.

Burns and Maharg were moaning in close harmony with the players. Thinking that the third game was also in the bag for Cincinnati, they had lost all their funds betting against Dickie Kerr. And they felt they had reason enough to do so.

"If we can't win for Cicotte and Williams," Gandil had said a few days before, "we're not gonna win for no busher."

The sixth game, won by Chicago the hard way, was a betting counterstroke. Cincinnati businessmen, supporting their home team heavily by now, were milked at odds which favored the Reds. On the last game, when the White Sox seemed to be coming back, a group of Texas oil men admitted later that they were taken for $82,000. Gambling experts all over the country were sitting in on the game by then, and business was good.

The series ended, and the boys went home to hunt, fish, and loaf—and to grumble and chew their nails, for there was trouble about the delivery of those series paychecks, and friends in Chicago wrote some of them that Commy's detectives were up to their noses in hot scents.

As the winter wore on, Gandil made a fuss—for publication—about his next season's salary, and dropped quietly from the club. When the scandal broke, the following September, Chick was in a hospital in Lufkin, Texas, having his appendix removed. He lost this spare part the same day, September twenty-eighth, that Eddie Cicotte lost his nerve and talked to the grand jury of Cook County.

The White Sox, racked by internecine strife, nobody talking to anybody, were still a good enough ball club at the time to be fighting with Cleveland for the pennant—one game behind, three games to go. Comiskey, with his world breaking about him, sent seven copies of one telegram to seven men:

> You and each of you are hereby notified of your indefinite suspension as a member of the Chicago American League baseball club.
>
> Your suspension is brought about by information which has just come to me directly involving each of you in the baseball scandal now being investigated by the present Grand Jury of Cook County resulting from the world series of 1919.
>
> If you are innocent of all wrongdoing, you and each of you will be reinstated; if you are guilty, you will be retired from organized baseball for the rest of your lives if I can accomplish it.
>
> Until there is a finality to this investigation, it is due the public that I take this action, even though it cost Chicago the pennant.

Actually, the information had not "just come" to Commy. It was all in his hands when the scandal suddenly went off in scattered pops, like a string of firecrackers. The grand jury had subpoenaed Bill Burns, Abe Attell, Arnold Rothstein, and others on September twenty-fourth. Billy Maharg had told his side of the case to Jimmy Isaminger, Philadelphia's alert baseball writer, and the story was circulated nationally. There was nothing for Commy to do but break up his ball club, and, in fairness to him, it should be said that he did a thorough and relentless job of it. Offers from Colonel Jake Ruppert and other club owners of "your choice of players" were rejected with thanks. Cleveland clinched the pennant.

Shoeless Joe's Exit Line

In a queer set of semiformal talks with the grand jury, Cicotte, Jackson, Williams, and Felsch told their stories. The shock hit the baseball public between the eyes, but the hearing fathered two phrases which promptly became paid-up members of the American language. There is nothing bogus about the origin of these phrases; just a little juggling. Three local writers and a news-service man were on hand when a kid stepped out of a group of kids and said to Jackson, just leaving the confessional:

"It ain't true, is it, Joe?"

"Yes, boys, I'm afraid it is," said Shoeless Joseph.

The authenticity of this incident seems pretty well established by the fact that four different men mentioned it in four different stories within three hours of the time that Jackson left the hearing. The capsule, cross-section version of the kid's remark was, "Say it ain't true, Joe," and if he didn't actually put it that way, he leaves himself open to a charge of untidy rhetoric.

As for Cicotte, Eddie "did it for the wife and kiddies" three times in the presence of the court stenographer, who took his words down in shorthand.

The grand jury and prosecuting staff of Cook County were seriously seeking indictments for conspiracy against the eight Sox. The magnates weren't. Not when they thought it over. They would handle this thing in their own way. They did.

There is a Napoleonic bee in the bonnet of nearly every baseball magnate, owing, probably, to the fact that he has the power of buy-and-sell over his employees; the power—it has been called unconstitutional—of auctioneering in terms of men, of blacklisting and suspending without hearing, of writing and signing contracts which guarantee the rights of the owner, but not the chattel.

It would prick the vanity of many a club owner today to see his affairs—baseball affairs—settled in a court of law. Commy and his colleagues wanted to keep this thing in the lodge. They had their own way of dealing with it—more effective and ruthless, when you consider the facts, than any judgment a criminal court could pass.

The trial of the eight Sox, in July and August 1921, was a little on the hollow side. The signed confessions taken by the grand jury the year before had "disappeared"—certain of the magnates advancing the theory, which would have been funnier in dialect, that Rothstein had made a secret trip to Chicago and bribed an aide of the district attorney's to burn them.

These confessions were the backbone of the case for conspiracy, although Sleepy Bill Burns testified for twelve hours, and went to sleep in the box before he had finished. The night of the acquittal, the Sox held a celebration party at an Italian restaurant near the Loop. The jurors held a celebration party in the same restaurant the same night. There was no prearrangement about this joint revel, and though their private rooms adjoined, the two parties kept sternly to themselves.

Then the magnates went to work. Kid Gleason had taken the stand in defense of his players in the "kangaroo" court, but when the state acquitted them the Kid turned cold as steel. He had little vitality left in his small, tough body after 1910, but all there was of it he directed against the men who had sold him out. He never spoke to one of them again.

The retrial of the Black Sox by baseball's own tribunal was a star-chamber affair. The decision was foregone, and the action swift. The eight men—Gandil, Cicotte, Jackson, Felsch, Weaver, Risberg, Williams, and McMullin—were barred from the game for life. This meant organized baseball, which meant everything but the frayed fringes of the professional game—semipro ball, sandlot ball, twilight-league ball. Within a few months, most of the outlaws were skimming those fringes for what they could find.

Where Are They Now?

The boys, all of them, pleaded their innocence for years afterward, to anyone who would listen. Eddie Cicotte came back from the semipro honky-tonk to Detroit, to argue his case on street corners. Joe Jackson buttonholed patrons in his barbecue hutch in South Carolina. Hap Felsch harangued the customers at his Milwaukee beer parlor.

It's obvious today that some of them, fix or no fix, were never paid money to throw a game. That all of them are serving life sentences without trial. That, with one or two exceptions, none of them belongs in the same league with Arnold, Tarquin, Cesare Borgia, or Guy Fawkes.

Where are they now? Shoeless Joe keeps his clippings and talks his baseball in his West Greenville, South Carolina, liquor store. Joe is a hero among the textile workers of the community. He says he gets more fan mail now than when he was in the big leagues. The scandal drove him from baseball before he piled up much money at it. But the publicity the scandal gave him has enabled him to parlay a successful barbecue stand into a prospering liquor store. He manages a successful semipro team.

Cicotte went into the automobile industry in Detroit and stayed there. He is a paymaster.

Up till recently, Gandil was playing Sunday ball in Shreveport and minding his own business.

Happy Felsch has been selling bottled conviviality across the bar in Milwaukee for fifteen years. Hap steadfastly refused to handle the hard stuff, though, until repeal.

Buck Weaver's home address is Chicago, and he dabbles in softball, and spends his winters on the Coast, where major-league scouts still take his tips occasionally on promising ballplayers. Some years ago, 10,000 Chicagoans signed a petition for Buck's reinstatement. No answer.

Horsehide Exile

Risberg, now a San Franciscan and a part-time fruit picker in Southern California, plays semipro games now and then. Williams, a Missourian born, was last heard of in Springfield, where he tried his hand at a softball league. The mysterious Fred McMullin used to live in Pasadena—no forwarding address.

If they never did anything else, the outlawed Sox—black or white, take your pick—were responsible for the presence of that snow-haloed, hawk-faced gentleman who hangs over the edge of his field box at the World Series, chewing the brim of his hat. Judge Kenesaw Mountain Landis once fined the Standard Oil Company $29,000,000, a tidy assessment. When the scandals broke in 1920, there was a cry for a high commissioner to replace the three-man commission at the head of baseball, and the judge was elected, and if you hear eight strong voices joined some evening in the strains of We Made Him What He is Today, those are the outlaws serenading Judge Landis.

There's another matter which calls the Sox of 1919 to mind these days. Up in Cooperstown, New York, where Abner Doubleday experimented with balls and bats some nine-and-ninety years ago, there is a Hall of Fame.

The names of great ballplayers have been or will be inscribed there—Ruth, Cobb, Wagner, Johnson, Mathewson, Speaker, Young, Lajoie, and Alexander. Which of the Black Sox, on playing merit alone, deserve mention in the same breath? Well, Jackson, Weaver, and Cicotte, by general agreement among the people, especially the ballplayers, who saw them in action. There is no ruling which says that the baseball writers cannot vote the Sox to the Hall, if they feel in their hearts that they belong there. There never will be a ruling until some outlaw collects enough votes to qualify him for the holy tablets, and the magnates hope very earnestly that no such emergency will arise.

The Spalding Guide, the voice of the magnate, said editorially in 1921:

> The gambler has done his worst again. He is the respecter of no game. He would as quickly buy the youth in the lot as the professional in the arena, if he could. He has tried both. He will try again. The honest ballplayer need have no fear of any gambler. There are thousands and thousands of honest ballplayers. There is another small group—they were ballplayers once—to be immured in the Chamber of Oblivion. There let them rest.

That seems to be official.

The lot of the official scorer is not a happy one. If he has any sense of personal integrity, he will call 'em as he sees 'em. If he has any sense of self-preservation and job security, he will, now and then, tilt the table homeward—preserving no-hitters, boosting the averages of batting-title contenders, sustaining errorless streaks. But controversies and scandals of a historic magnitude are few: the six bunt "hits" allowed Nap Lajoie on the final day of the 1911 season; the dubious hit that denied Howard Ehmke a double no-hitter; and the questionable third and final .400 season by Ty Cobb. Fred Lieb began as an official scorer in the year he first covered baseball, 1911. Sixty-six years and millions of words later he told his story in a captivating memoir, *Baseball as I Have Known It.*

FRED LIEB

"Hits Are My Bread and Butter"

In my first year in the press box and my first year at official scoring, Frank Farrell, president of the Highlanders, called me up and said, "What does a player have to do to get an error in our park?" I said, "Make an error." And he said, "Then why don't you put some errors in our box scores? Yesterday Jack Knight made two errors that you scored as hits for Ty Cobb."

"Well," I said, "about those hits, I thought one of them was too hot to handle. The other one was hit to deep short, Knight had a long throw, and maybe the throw pulled Chase a little off the bag, but I thought Cobb had it beaten, anyway. So I marked them both hits."

"Listen," Farrell retorted, "when my players make errors, I want you to give errors. I pay Jack Knight forty-five hundred dollars a year [supposedly a lot of money in 1911] for playing shortstop, and when he makes errors, I want you to give 'em to him."

That telephone conversation I will let stand as a fair measure of this not untypical franchise owner of the period. I knew enough about the relations between Farrell and Knight to know that Farrell was looking for statistical support to help him knock down Knight's salary when contract time came around. The statistical game can be played by owners as well as by players.

Criticism for a scoring decision can also come from parties with no financial interest in it. I once drew about my head the unleashed sarcasm of Bill Hanna, then of the New York *Sun-Herald.* It was in 1919, and I was substituting as official scorer for Bill Farnsworth. It involved a not-hit game pitched by a

Cleveland pitcher, Ray Caldwell, a former Yankee. It happened that my wife and Mrs. Caldwell were very friendly, and the Caldwells and Liebs frequently visited each other's houses. But this had nothing to do with my judgment of the play that gave Ray his no-hitter. In the middle of the game Frank Baker, Yankee third baseman, hit a smash toward right field. Bill Wambsganss, the Cleveland second baseman, who would make an unassisted triple play in the World Series in 1920, was playing Baker deep in the hole, on the grass. As I saw the play, Wamby made a good play to knock it down but then cuffed it around enough to let the slow Baker beat his throw. I thought this added up to an error, I so scored it and didn't give any further thought to it. The next morning Hanna started his story of the game in this manner: "A no-hit game was credited to Slim Caldwell at the Polo Grounds yesterday. It was so scored by the official scorer, but I will insist till my dying day that it was not an error but a hit for Frank Baker."

Bob Shawkey, who pitched thirteen years for the Yankees, also reproved me for that scoring decision. "I think you took a hit away from Bake yesterday," he told me through the screen before the next day's game. I laughed. "Bob, I think it's funny for a pitcher to be grousing at my scoring another pitcher with a no-hitter. And Caldwell was your pitching teammate here until last year." Then I closed the door on him by telling him what is the essential truth about any "score" a scorer makes: "It was my judgment that it was an error; that's the way I scored it, and that's the way it goes into the official records."

Most controversies over a scoring decision burn themselves out quickly, but a decision I made in August 1922 had repercussions for several months and kept popping up years later. It is the story behind Cobb's .401 batting average in 1922. In brief, a hit I scored for Cobb—and I wasn't even the official scorer—made it possible for Cobb to hit .400 for the third time. Without that hit he would have finished at .399.

A bit of background is necessary to understand the tangle. First, a man named Irwin Howe, who was the American League statistician, also ran a baseball statistics bureau and sold unofficial hitting, pitching, and fielding records to a lot of newspapers. Now, Howe took his figures day by day from the AP box scores, and I was scorer for the AP, but not the official scorer.

On the day of this particular play it had started to rain, and I moved back into the stands from the uncovered press box. But Jack Kieran, then of the *Tribune* and that year the official scorer, stayed at his post despite the rain. When Cobb came to the plate on the disputed play, it was raining fairly hard, and the infield was getting gooey. Cobb hit a grounder toward Everett Scott, the Yankee shortstop. It rolled close to the ground, and in going over a soggy field, a ball picks up a lot of wet soil. Scott had just a little trouble handling the muddy ball, and he didn't get Cobb by a full step. Considering the condition of the field and Cobb's speed, I gave it a hit. I wasn't near Kieran and gave no further thought about it. Neither did Kieran, who sent in an official score for the game, showing Scott had made an error.

Meanwhile, Howe, using my AP score, fed "hit" into his computations, and at the end of the season Howe's unofficial statistics showed Cobb at .401 (his third season batting over .400), and the official figures in due course showed him at .3995. Now if the difference had been between Cobb's hitting .348 and .346, Howe would have thought no more about it. It was very common for unofficial and official averages to vary a point or two. But here the question was whether this immortal had or had not again hit the magic .400 figure. If Howe had just given out his 1922 official American League averages—with Cobb hitting .401—without comment, I feel no one would have challenged. Neither the public, nor the baseball writers knew anything about the August incident. However, perhaps from a sense of guilt, Howe sent out a brief explanation along with the figures to explain Cobb's .401 average. It went: "I noted that the averages reached from my official scoring sheets had Cobb hitting .3995. With the unofficial averages giving him .401, I felt how can we deprive this great player of a third .400 average over a fraction of a point?

"It was then that I compared Cobb's official sheets with the unofficial figures we had in the office, game for game, until we reached the August game in the New York Polo Grounds in which Kieran had scored as an error for Scott and Fred Lieb's Associated Press showed a hit for Cobb. I took into consideration Lieb's long experience as a scorer. Since Kieran was scoring officially for the first year, I felt I was justified in using Fred Lieb's score."

In the meantime, Ban Johnson, American League president, got into the act. Ban was a stickler for supporting his umpires, and now he stood behind his designated statistician, Howe, 100 percent. Johnson and I exchanged some vitriolic telegrams, which appeared in the national press. He said he always had regarded me as a competent scorer, and he was dismayed that in the Cobb case I did not have the guts to stand up for my score. My reply was that my scoring was not an issue. I was standing up for a principle, that the official scorer is official. The fat was now in the fire. In no time at all the situation was splashed across the sports pages, and the fans for the most part were on Cobb's side. The New York writers, I'm happy to say, argued that the official scorer should have the final decision, and there wasn't any point in having official scorers if they'd throw out one of his decisions just to give a man a .400 batting average.

So the case came up at our Baseball Writers Association meeting the following winter. I was in an awkward position, as I was both national president and chairman of the New York chapter. Speaking as chairman in behalf of John Kieran, who felt concerned that his score had been tossed out and mine accepted, I told the members that I felt the same way: Kieran was the official scorer, and if the situation had been reversed and my official score had been tossed out, I'd have been incensed.

Some of the chapters, particularly Detroit and Philadelphia, were strongly in favor of Cobb. After I had made my statement, several writers asked, "Don't you like Cobb? Are you penalizing him for something he may have done in New York or to you? Why would you deprive Cobb of a .400 average for a fraction?" There were other chapters that stood behind Kieran loyally. They were bascially defending the official scoring system and trying to make other writers see that their turn at official scoring could come to them sometime and also that to change something for Cobb opened the door to protests by some Joe Blow backed by a few friends.

When it came time to vote, two of the chapters, Brooklyn and Washington, decided to abstain. Then by a narrow 5–4 vote, the association upheld Kieran's official score. Furthermore, it added a statement to the resolution to the effect that the 1923 *Baseball Guides* should be instructed to carry an asterisk after the .401 figure, the footnote reading, "Not recognized by the Baseball Writers Association."

John Kieran was not at all satisfied with the decision and I fully understand why. He had been supported at the end, when the vote was taken, by only five of the eleven chapters—a minority—counting the abstainers as nonsupporters. They had let an "unofficial" hit carry the day. They had undercut the official scoring system. It took some years before the kettle stopped simmering in the association over this one. And as an aftermath of the controversy, the Baseball Writers Association changed its bylaws so that no one could hold the position of national president and chapter chairman at the same time.

The next year, in 1923, I became more personally involved in a different kind of controversy with Cobb. It happened this way: the managers of the teams playing each day always gave the evening papers the starting lineups about ten minutes before game time, which then was 3:30. This enabled the writers to telegraph them downtown and catch one of the early editions. We were consistently having trouble getting the lineup of the Detroit Tigers when they came to town. Cobb by this time was player-manager. Somebody complained to Jack Lenz, the announcer. Jack blamed Cobb: "Cobb doesn't give us his lineup until just the minute the game starts." (In those days, before public address systems, an announcer with a big cheerleader's megaphone would read off the lineups, facing the stands from behind home plate.) We persuaded Lenz to complain to Cobb, whose response was "Why should I give a damn about those twenty-five- and thirty-dollar-a-week sons of bitches?"

The next day in the *Evening Telegram* I took a whack at Cobb for his high-handedness toward the press and wrote that he had done pretty well over the years and that a lot of us "twenty-five- and thirty-dollar-a-week" boys had probably given him a lot of doubtful hits. I had in mind the two I had given him in 1911 that Frank Farrell had complained to me about.

The next day Cobb sent the Tigers' trainer up to the press stand with a message: "Mr. Cobb wants to see you after the game." So when I saw Cobb, he began, "I don't like what you wrote about me yesterday; that wasn't very nice." I said, "Well, I don't like the way you acted when Lenz asked you to send the lineups a little earlier." We got to jawing at each other, and he said, "Do you believe that stupid SOB over me?" I said, "I have no reason to think that Jack would lie." Cobb said, "Well, we may have to have this out man-to-man." I well knew Cobb's reliance on fisticuffs to settle arguments, so grinning weakly, I said, "You probably weigh one hundred eighty-five, and I weigh one hundred sixty-five, and you're in shape and I'm not, so I guess I'm not in your class.''

Oddly enough, my lack of interest in a fight didn't rouse him further, and he soon calmed down. Out of this came a good friendship between us. I remember especially an all-day conversation with him in 1931 as I stopped over in San Francisco after my arrival from Japan at the end of a tour with an All-Star team. Cobb, then in retirement, was living in the suburb of Atherton. Ty was on a talking jag that day—he had an old acquaintance to talk baseball with and wouldn't let me go. During the evening he pumped me about his chances of getting the general manager's position with the Philadelphia Phillies; he thought he could put some guts into the team and get it out of its rut in the second division. I remember recommending that he buy the Phillies, a franchise he could have picked up for perhaps $300,000 at the time. But Ty, perhaps the prudent investor, wasn't interested in financial control or ownership. Nor did he want another job as field manager. He wanted front-office managerial control, a salary commensurate with his baseball name, and a return to baseball. As it turned out, he never did get back inside.

Equal in importance, in the realm of baseball statistics, to my scoring the hit that ultimately gave Ty Cobb his .401 batting average in 1922 was the decision I made against Howard Ehmke of the Red Sox the next year. This was, in retrospect, perhaps the saddest decision I ever made, for it prevented Ehmke from becoming the first pitcher ever to throw two successive no-hitters. (Johnny Vander Meer of Cincinnati would do it for the first and only time in 1938.) Ehmke was then with the last-place Red Sox of 1923, and the Yankees were winning an easy pennant, their third in a row. Ehmke had had a great season: he would wind up winning twenty games with a bad ball club. It was in September, on what I believe was the last swing around the East for the eastern teams. The first batter for the Yankees was Whitey Witt, a fast little leadoff man who got a good jump from the plate and was quick getting down the line. So he hit a chopper down the third-base line to Howard Shanks, a former outfielder who was playing third. The ball took an odd hop, and Shanks muffled it against his chest. By the time he was ready to throw, he saw there was no chance to get Witt, and so he didn't throw. Considering all these things—the ball took a strange hop and Witt was the fastest man, I think, in the American League at that time in getting down to first base—I decided it was a hit, however scratchy. There was no murmuring over my "score" in the press box at the time.

Strange as it may seem, that was not only the only Yankee hit that day but Witt was the only Yankee to reach first base. After that, Ehmke retired twenty-seven men in order. As early as the sixth inning some of the Boston writers said, "Don't you think you ought to change that, Fred? This man has a chance to be the first two-no-hit man." "No," I said, "I scored it a hit then, and it's a hit in the early edition of my paper, and it's a hit in my score book."

As the innings progressed and Ehmke went one-two-three, one-two-three, the pressure on me became heavier, and even the New York writers, Boyd of the *Evening World* especially, said, "Oh, Fred, you *must* change that!"

I said, "No, it's a one-hit game in my book, and it's going to stay that way." So it went in as a one-hitter. Of course, it *was* a doubtful call on my part, and if it had happened later in the game I just might have scored it as an error for Shanks. My obstinacy about not changing my score stemmed from a talk I had in 1912 with Tom Lynch, president of the National League, best known as "king of the umpires." The day before our talk, Jeff Tesreau of the New York Giants had been given a no-hitter by the official scorer in Philadelphia under pressure after the game from Sid Mercer. Mercer was backed up by the Giants first baseman, Fred Merkle, who told the scorer that the one hit charged against Tesreau was really his (Merkle's) error. The scorer let himself be swayed and between games of a doubleheader reversed himself. Lynch was angry at such scoring and told me never, never change a scoring decision once I had made it. "Be like an umpire," he said. "He can't be influenced by anyone to change a decision he made in the second inning. Whether right or wrong, it was his honest judgment. As a scorer, hold your ground the same way. I don't like no-hitters that are scored in the clubhouse."

My ruling against Ehmke caused quite a rumpus, for the game was taken to the American League headquarters, and the editor of *Baseball Magazine* had four hundred signatures on a petition sent to Ban Johnson, American League president, protesting this scoring decision. The umpire, Tom Connally, was asked about the play, and he said, "If that wasn't an error, I never saw one." That made me feel even worse. So there was quite an aftermath to it.

In the year after I had been Yankee official scorer, Ossie Vitt, then second baseman for the Detroit Tigers, came to the chicken screen in front of the press box and said, "How many hits did I get yesterday?" I looked in my score book and said, "Two." And he said, "Well, I made three." And I said, "Well, my score book says that you had two, and the other time you got on base by an error by Ward, our second baseman." Vitt said, "I got *three!*" Then I said, "What I say doesn't count, anyway, because I'm not the official scorer." Vitt said, "Sam Crawford says you are." I said, "Well, I'm not."

So Vitt went back to the bench, and his teammate Sam Crawford repeated I was the official scorer. "You are the official scorer." Vitt then shouted, "And I want you to know that when I make hits I want you to give them to me. *Hits are my bread and butter!*" Vitt's phrase made a good title for a *Saturday Evening Post* article I wrote a few years later. But it took a while for the players to understand I was no longer robbing them of hits as official scorer.

In 1920, as a nonvoting member of the Rules Committee of organized baseball (serving on behalf of the Baseball Writers Association), I introduced a rule whereby a batter knocking the ball out of the park in the bottom of the ninth inning or in a succeeding extra inning would receive credit for a home run, even after the winning run was scored. The batter would also be credited with all the runs that crossed the plate on the hit, exactly as he would be if he had hit the home run in the first or eighth inning.

Up to that time if the score was, say, 1–1 in the bottom of the ninth (or tenth or eleventh) inning and a batter hit a ball into the bleachers with a man on third, the batter received credit for only a single on the theory that the game ended when the man on third scored and it took only a single to bring him in. Furthermore, the home-run hitter in this case received credit for only 1 RBI.

My suggestion was hotly criticized by Hank O'Day, a veteran umpire who was one of three representatives of the National League on the committee. Hank insisted vociferously to the last that no run could be scored after the winning run had crossed the plate. This particular rule he regarded as sacred and untouchable. Hank also charged me with trying to get more home runs for Babe Ruth, whom the Yankees had bought from Boston a few weeks earlier.

In the final vote, however, my measure won, 5–1, with Hank still beating his fist on the table and shouting, "I'm telling you, it is illegal. You can't score runs after a game is over!" By now my amendment has been in the rules for over half a century, and hundreds of players have me to thank for additional home runs and RBIs credited to them under such last-inning circumstances.

In 1977 Sparky Lyle was the top reliever in baseball and led the New York Yankees to the World Championship. In 1978 Goose Gossage came over from the National League, and Lyle went to long relief, or in Graig Nettles's memorable phrase, "from Cy Young to Sayonara." He also went the way of Henry Wiggen, from pitcher to author, keeping a log of the tumultuous 1978 season. Shaping it with the considerable aid of Peter Golenbock, Lyle created *The Bronx Zoo*, probably the biggest-selling baseball book ever. This passage ends just before the firing of Billy Martin (who said of Reggie Jackson and George Steinbrenner, "One's a born liar, the other's convicted") and the Yankees' incredible climb to the pennant under Bob Lemon.

SPARKY LYLE with PETER GOLENBOCK

The Bronx Zoo

Tuesday, July 11 Lake George, New York

I'm really glad I didn't go to the All-Star Game. Mary and I have been camping out in the woods, and we're having a wonderful time away from the madness. Goose went to the game, Billy brought him in, and he ended up getting his ass kicked and losing the game. Just like what happened to me last year.

You can pitch during the regular season and not have your good stuff and get by, but in the All-Star Game you have no chance. I don't care who goes out there. If you have the good stuff, you'll be all right. But if you don't when you're facing one tremendous hitter after another, boy, it's very scary. Goose still hasn't gotten sharp, and he didn't have a prayer out there in San Diego this evening.

I remember my first All-Star Game. It was in '73, and I was very happy to have made that team, because I never dreamed I'd get a chance to play in one. I thought I should have been named after some of the years I had had before that, but I wasn't, so I really hadn't counted on ever playing in one. Managers rarely pick relief pitchers, anyhow. Ordinarily they use starters in relief. The game was in Kansas City, and I remember pitching to Willie Mays, who had announced that it would be his last year. I struck him out on three pitches.

The writers asked me if I felt bad striking Willie Mays out in his last All-Star Game. I said, "Hell, no. Why should I feel bad?" They said, "It was his last All-Star Game." I said, "I don't know what you're getting at, but I felt real good about striking him out. Real good. I'm sorry I didn't get the chance to strike him out twice."

I went to the All-Star Game three times, in '73 and the last two years, but I don't want to go again. The All-Star Game is a popularity contest, a matter of being in the right place at the right time. Take Mark Belanger, for instance. He played for years before he got into an All-Star Game, and he's been the top fielding shortstop every year. He plays as well as anybody, but the fans don't even look at him. The ballplayers should pick the players. We play against the guys. We know who's hitting the best and who's having the best years. Some of the best guys sometimes don't even get on the ballot because they're rookies or they got traded, and another guy who's on the ballot, he may be having a lousy year, but he's going to get votes. It's so ridiculous.

Graig hurt his toe in our last game against Boston and, as a result, missed the last couple of games before the All-Star break. Graig had been elected to be the starting third baseman for the American League in the All-Star Game, but the Yankee management called him up and told him he couldn't go, which made him mad as hell. They said it was for his own good, which made him even madder. The game was played in San Diego, Graig's hometown, and he wanted to play in front of his family and friends. Jeez. How could they do that to him after the way he's played for the New York Yankees?

Graig has been jerked around more than anyone on this team. He had a contract problem last year, which they could have taken care of in a matter of minutes, but no, they had to mess with his mind for three-quarters of a season before straightening it out. The front office gave him a lot of grief about his contract, and they didn't give a damn about him. You know, the old "You play third base and shut your goddam mouth" sort of thing. It's unbelievable what George did to him.

When Graig signed a contract in July 1976, George and Graig agreed that Graig would get some deferred compensation. Graig asked George the best way to do it, and George set it up in such a way that Graig would be able to take the money anytime he wanted. The only problem with that was that the IRS doesn't see it as deferred compensation if you can take it anytime you want. George had given him the worst possible advice.

What made things complicated was that in August the owners and players agreed to a new contract, one that gave the players the right no longer to be bound to the reserve clause after a certain number of years, and when Graig discovered last spring that he had tax problems, when he went to George and asked him to change the contract to get him a better tax break on his deferred compensation, George refused to do it. George was afraid to change it because he didn't want Graig under a new contract. When Graig got mad, as he had every right to be, and walked out of camp, George made him look bad in the press. George came out with this: "If Graig realizes he made a mistake by leaving this team and he learns from it, I'm willing to sit down and help him. But he has to stand up like a man and admit he made a mistake." The next day Graig handed in a printed statement saying he was sorry.

And now all of a sudden the tide has turned where they need him. They're afraid he's going to hurt himself worse by playing in the All-Star Game, so now it's "For your own good, Graig, we feel . . ." They're acting real concerned. And what really pissed him off was that they weren't concerned about him as a person at all. All they cared about was a void that they might not be able to fill. It just proves one more time how management dicks you around, dicks you around until they need you, and all of a sudden they turn around and look you in the eye and act real sincere and expect you to believe them and buy what they say. It's like a guy sticking you in the back with a knife and then turning around and putting a bandage on and fixing you up. Graig just said, "Go screw yourself. I'm playing."

The only way Graig got to play was that the day before the game Reggie called and said he had a temperature, and they put Graig on in Reggie's place.

The second half of the season began today, and before the game George held a meeting. I knew he wouldn't be able to go through an entire season without jumping in. He couldn't stand it. He's done everything he could to stay in the background, but he can no longer stand by and watch this crap. It's not his nature. I will say this for him: when he makes up his mind to do something, he'll do it come hell or high water. He'll get a lot of flack for this after his promise not to interfere, but he won't give a damn. That's what makes him so interesting.

You can usually tell when George holds a meeting. When it's Billy's meeting, it's "Meeting in five minutes." When George holds a meeting, it's "The guys better get over here. We're having a meeting." This afternoon George was in Billy's office, and Billy came out and started to say, "Will you gather round here, please," and right in the middle of the sentence, we heard, "Can I have your attention? Can I have your attention?" It was George. He said, "We've done it your way for the first half of the season, and it didn't work, and now we're going to do it my way. I still believe we can win the pennant, but we're going to have to try harder. I've had a talk with Billy, and there are going to be some changes made, and if you don't like them, come and see me and I'll try to accommodate you."

He said, "There are going to be some changes made in the lineup; some players aren't going to play as much, but there's no sense in getting mad. This is the way it's going to be. It's my ball club. I sign the checks, and I'll do what I want."

Under George's lineup, Thurman will play right field, rookie Mike Heath will catch, Reggie will DH, and Gary Thomasson will be in left. George is also bringing in Clyde King to help coach the pitchers. Lou and Roy end up on the bench, or Lou may end up DHing against lefties, which means that Reggie's the DH against righties and nothing else.

It wasn't one of those "Rah rah, you have to have balls" meetings that George likes. It was short and sweet. Still, you can shuffle the guys around all you want, and you still can't play Randolph and Dent, 'cause they're out, and you can't start Messersmith or Clay or Cat or Gullett, 'cause they're out. We have exactly three starters left: Guidry, Dirt, and Figgie, and Figgie's forearm has been hurting. That leaves Beattie and this kid Rajsich. They're good prospects. Plus, nobody's going to make any trades with us, 'cause Rosen refuses to trade unless it's a steal for the Yankees. I do not mind telling you that we are in a shitload of trouble.

After George left the clubhouse, Billy finished the meeting. He told us we are going to get a list of dos and don'ts, and he brought up the tie thing again. He said he was now going to enforce the tie rule. It's going to be $25 for the first time, and it escalates up. I just can't see bringing this up time and again. Just fine me and get it over with. Saying, "We're going to do this, we're going to do that," that's half the trouble. They set down rules, and when we break them, nothing's said. Everybody's guilty of not wearing ties, not just one or two guys. But not wearing ties isn't why we're not winning.

After the meeting was over, Mickey Rivers was talking about George's moves. He feels they're horseshit. "He shouldn't be screwing around with a team that won the World Championship," he said. "It ain't right to panic. All Steinbrenner has to do is wait until the hurting guys get healthy. Then we would have started to win. There isn't any need for this crap." Mickey's right about George, but George doesn't have the patience to wait for the guys to get well. He wants to start winning now.

To me the worst part of George's shuffling the lineup is with Thurman in right field, they have to alternate Thomasson and Lou in left. I don't agree with that, because I don't give a damn who's pitching, when Lou gets hot, he can hit anybody. All they're going to do now is screw up Lou's stroke. And I don't know why Thurman's not catching anymore, unless his legs are hurting so much he can't catch. I'd rather see him behind the plate, Thomasson in left and Lou in right, with Reggie DHing. That's our best ball club. Thomasson's good. He's an aggressive ballplayer. He wants to play. He's hit a couple of home runs that have helped us, and he's a steady outfielder. One game he slid into the fence and caught the ball to save the game. That's what we need. A couple of more plays like that could turn this club right around. It happened last year. We came from behind a couple of times, and it fired up the whole team, and there we were, playing good all of a sudden. Right now, we're far from that. It's going to be a long, hard road. Today Garcia made an error that let in two unearned runs, and we lost to the White Sox, 6–1. Fortunately, the Red Sox also lost. We're eleven games out, and we're going to have to play better ball to have a chance at catching the Sox.

Friday, July 14   New York

Gid's arm finally may be tired. He gave up six runs in the nine innings he pitched, but he didn't lose because Cliff hit a pinch-hit home run in the bottom of the ninth inning to tie it. Goose won it in relief in the eleventh when Graig drove Reggie home with a single. Willie Randolph played his first game since mid-June, and it was great to see him back. It's nice to win every once in a while when you're playing poorly.

There haven't been many funny things happening. It's been very quiet. I didn't think I would ever see this on the ball club, but it has a lot to do with what Billy's going through. He looks awful, and he hasn't slept much, and George is giving him a rough time 'cause we're so far back, and nobody wants to intimidate him any more than he has been already. Billy doesn't like us to carry on, especially after we lose, so we haven't been. Not that anybody really feels like carrying on. We're getting tired of losing. This may sound like the players want to keep Billy, and I believe they do. After you play for him awhile, off and on you hate him and like him, but that's his way of sparking a ball club. Some of the guys have been saying, "Maybe they should fire him," but when they start to talk about who would replace him, they say, "Christ, keep the man."

I saw Catfish today for the first time in a couple of weeks. He's been through so much this year, and a lot of people think he may be finished. He even might think that. If he does, he's not going to hang on. He'll just say, "Screw it. See ya." He has too much pride to hang on.

As a last resort Cat was put under anesthesia, and the Yankee orthopedist, Dr. Maurice Cowen, stretched his pitching arm back farther than Cat could have by himself. By doing this, Dr. Cowen broke the adhesions in his arm that were causing him pain and keeping him from throwing naturally. What's hard for me to understand is how they know just the right amount to bend the son of a bitch. Do they bend it this far? or this far? or this far? How do you know that when you wake up your arm won't fall off?

Saturday, July 15   New York

George has been saying all along that he would call me up to his office when he was ready to talk about my contract, and today he made the call. I told Mary, "If he offers me close to what I want, I'll sign." I'm not the type of guy who harps on something and fights and then at the very end, when the other guy makes an offer, says to himself, "Well, hell, if he'll give me this much, I'll try and get a little bit more." When I arrived at George's office, he said he would give me $200,000 a year for the next three years, and it's their option whether they want to pick me up for the 1981 season. I agreed to that because if I can't pitch by 1981, what the hell, nobody's going to want me, anyway.

It's a fair offer, and I'm satisfied. I really hadn't been expecting anything like that from George. I had learned to cope with my depression over the money and was at peace with myself. I had lost my fire and had quit trying to piss George off. I just accepted what was as what was. If he had called me and said tough shit again, I probably wouldn't have said a thing. I might very well have said, "Okay, screw it," and been satisfied with my $135,000 a year.

Figgie made his first start since July 3 and gave up eight runs in four innings. Dennis Leonard beat us 8–2. In the second, Figgie had Pete LaCock 0 and 2, and threw him a curve. It was the same sort of thing that happened with Ron Fairly. LaCock hit it out, and the Royals had a 5–0 lead. Me and Kammeyer mopped up.

For the second game in a row Billy had Reggi DHing and batting sixth. The way he's been hitting, he's lucky he isn't lower in the order. We're a better team when Reggie's not playing the outfield, and we're a better team when he's not hitting in the number-four spot, because he strikes out too much. Billy has known this all along. Unfortunately for Billy, George puts pressure on Billy to bat Reggie fourth and play him in right. When Reggie's in a slump like he is now, he strikes out a hell of a lot with runners on base. We lost a lot of games 'cause of that this year, and as long as he does this, I guess we're going to lose a lot more. And what makes it bad is that when he strikes out, he doesn't put any pressure at all on the opposing pitcher. The pitcher just throws the ball anywhere. That's all, just throw it up there, 'cause he's not going to touch it. With men on base, it's important to put pressure on that pitcher, to make him throw a wild pitch or make him pitch in and out, up and down to tire him out. If they would put someone who doesn't strike out a lot in there, you're gonna have a different ball game. Some of those runners would score.

Billy batted Munson third, Chambliss fourth, and Nettles fifth. It's a smart move on Billy's part.

Sunday, July 16   New York

We were losing 3–1 with the bases loaded. Lou Piniella got up against Larry Gura, and he hit a ball 430 feet—where it was caught by Amos Otis in the deepest part of Death Valley. Lou couldn't believe it! He thought he had a home run for sure, that he had won the ball game, and all he ended up with was a long out. After the game he was moaning and groaning about Yankee Stadium. Piniella was saying, "To hit a home run here you need help from Superman, Batman, Robin, Spiderman, Wonder Woman, Godzilla, King Kong," and he kept naming more and more comic-book characters. We've lost eight out of ten, Boston is thirteen games in front, and the way things are going, we'll be watching the play-offs this fall on Channel 4.

Gura, who's now 7–2 for Kansas City, played for the Yankees, but one morning last spring Billy saw him and Rich Coggins in their whites going to play tennis. Billy, who calls tennis a pussy game, went right up a tree.

You have to understand, Billy was seeing this guy who hadn't been pitching well going out to play tennis. Billy said to himself, *What the hell is he playing tennis for when he isn't pitching worth a crap? Swinging that racket can't be doing his pitching any good. No wonder he's horseshit.* Gura, on the other hand, is thinking, *I'm keeping in shape playing tennis.* They're looking at it from different standpoints. But the manager, of course, is going to win out. Billy said, "I'll get rid of them fuckers." And that's just what he did.

Reggie didn't play tonight. Gura's a lefty, and Billy benched Reggie in favor of right-handed Cliff Johnson, who is making the situation worse by going 0 for 4 every time he plays. These days when Reggie plays, it's only to DH, which I know he doesn't like. Even so, Reggie hasn't said very much. He told reporters, "I'm not talking anymore." Who knows what's lurking in the heart of Mr. October? I'm sure we'll find out soon.

On the surface it seems that Billy's sitting Reggie down against lefties is bad on Billy's part, and yet Billy isn't treating Reggie any different from the way he treats anyone else. A number of guys like Piniella, Thomasson, and Roy White were even hitting the ball and found themselves sitting. Spencer was one of the hottest hitters on the team for a little while, and all of a sudden he stopped playing. When you're struggling like we are, you have to try things, and Reggie hasn't been swinging the bat very well, and that's the reason Billy takes him out. Not for any other reason.

It's hard to tell what's running through Reggie's mind. Billy has finally been allowed to keep Reggie out of the outfield because he hurts us too much out there, but any time a manager does that to a ballplayer, especially a ballplayer with an ego as big as Reggie's, the ballplayer is going to go into a tizzy. No ballplayer likes to be told he sucks, even if he knows it's true, and what makes it worse is that because it's New York, the Yankees, the team of controversy, Reggie Jackson, Billy Martin, George Steinbrenner, it gets magnified way out of proportion, and everyone makes a big deal out of it. The writers are now going to run over to Reggie and ask him provocative questions like "Is Billy deliberately showing you up?" or "Do you think you're good enough to play right field?"; questions like that, and Reggie's going to say something bitchy, and then the writers will go back to Billy, and after the writers get finished with them, there's going to be some shit flying.

Billy didn't want Reggie on the Yankees. Billy wanted Joe Rudi, a right-handed batter who hits in the clutch and who's an excellent defensive out-fielder. Rudi, however, isn't very colorful, and he isn't a draw. Reggie, with his big mouth and his big swing, puts people in the park. Plus he's a home-run hitter, and he makes a good play in the field every once in a while. George knew this and spent almost $3 million to sign him. What George didn't know was that this guy is a real piece of work.

After George signed him, when he told the papers, "I didn't come to New York to become a star. I brought my star with me," right then I knew. I said to myself, *This guy is going to be trouble.* He's always telling everybody how great he is, and you never know whether he believes the stuff he says or not. This spring he told a TV reporter how important it was that people respect him. Then he said, "But to be respected, you have to be godly." Godly? Is he kidding? I respect plenty of people, but not one of them looks like the pope, or Charlton Heston even.

Reggie's a mystery to me. He's a very intelligent guy. I've watched him on TV when he announces for ABC's Superstar competition during the off-season. He ad-libs, jokes around, uses the right words, and you can see that Reggie's a really smart person. If you listened to Reggie, you'd think he was the only intelligent guy on the whole Yankee team. That's what Reggie says—over and over. He told that to Carlos May once. May didn't give a damn what his IQ was and told him so. Reggie said, "You can't even spell IQ." Another time Reggie was giving Mickey Rivers the same jive. "My IQ is 160," he told Mickey. Mickey looked at Reggie and said, "Out of what, Buck, a thousand?" Cracked everybody up. Reggie's always trying to show Mickey how much smarter he is. One day he asked Mickey, "What am I doing arguing with someone who can't read or write?" Mickey replied, "You oughta stop reading and writing and start hitting."

Another thing I noticed about him. When Reggie was taking so much heat after his article in *Sport* magazine, he told a reporter, "The guys don't like me 'cause I'm black." The guys didn't like him 'cause he came to our team, and he wasn't here three months when he attacked Thurman in a magazine article and told everybody how great he was. Then we got pissed, and he said it was because he's black! Why did he have to say a thing like that?

Reggie isn't one personality. He's several. Some days he's real happy and friendly and nice, and other days he's nasty and surly and always growling at everybody. Then on other days he sits by himself and doesn't talk.

Reggie doesn't usually talk much with the other players, anyway. Mostly it's with the press. We get to read the bull he says in the papers the next day. I don't pay attention to anything the guy says, never, and I'll tell you why. We were in Oakland for a game, and after it was over, Reggie was being interviewed on the radio. Radios were on in the clubhouse, and we could hear what he was saying. Reggie's talking away, and he says, "You can't believe most of what the New York writers are saying about this team." Well, the New York writers are listening to him say this, and when he comes back to the clubhouse, they are pissed. They ask him exactly what he meant by that. Reggie for a few seconds didn't know what to say, and then he said, "You guys heard that? If I knew you were listening, I wouldn't have said it."

When Reggie started playing with the Yankees last year, Billy discovered that Reggie wasn't nearly as good as Reggie thought or said he was. Billy started batting Reggie fifth instead of fourth, where he was used to batting, and George went crazy. George ordered Billy to bat him third or fourth. Billy told the press, "It's no big deal. Reggie's just not used to playing the way other people want him to." But it was a big deal, because Reggie's George's boy, and for the two years Reggie's been here, Billy rarely can play Reggie the way he wants to, which is frustrating for Billy, 'cause he feels a team should do everything it can to win, regardless of whose feelings get hurt.

Billy almost got fired last year over Reggie. We were getting our ass kicked by Boston, and George was on Billy's back because we weren't in first place, and in the middle of the game Jim Rice hits a pop fly to right field. The ball fell in, and Reggie trotted after it like it didn't matter at all, and he took forever to throw it back in. Billy walked out to the mound to take out the pitcher, Mike Torrez, and as I was walking in from the bull pen to relieve him, Billy also sent Paul Blair out to right to replace Reggie, who had without a doubt loafed after that ball. Billy was so angry he wanted to embarrass Reggie. If you lose, Billy always wants you to go down fighting, and Billy had been pissed off because even though Reggie had been winning some games for us, he was costing us a lot of ball games with his fielding.

Let's face it, Reggie's a bad outfielder. He has good speed to get to the ball, but the catching part is shaky. Before the game, Billy had wanted Reggie to shag fly balls during batting practice, but Reggie had refused. See, if Reggie had done that, I don't think Billy would have been as angry as he was. And Billy's taking Reggie out of the game embarrassed him in front of all the people in the park and all the people watching on national television, which really hurt Reggie a lot. Reggie hates to be embarrassed, especially in front of 50 million people. So when Reggie came in to the dugout, Reggie said, "What did I do? What did I do?" Billy said, "You know what you did." Reggie said, "You have to be crazy to show me up in front of all those people," and then Reggie made the mistake of calling Billy an old man.

When Reggie said that, something in Billy snapped. Billy hates to be embarrassed as much as Reggie does, and when he said that, Billy went for his throat. Ellie, Howser, and Yogi had to wrestle him to the bench to keep him from reaching Reggie. Reggie was yelling at Billy, "You better start liking me," as if to say, "If one of us is going to go, it isn't going to be me."

George had not been at the game. He was at a funeral someplace, and he had watched the game on TV, and he saw the whole thing. A couple of days later he decided to fire Billy for losing his temper, but when Milt Richman of UPI leaked the story, the reaction of the fans was so hostile, George changed his mind.

When I heard that Billy was going to get fired, I went to him and told him, "I want you to know something. If you get fired because of this incident, I'm going home. I'm going to pack my bags and go back to New York for the rest of the road trip, and I'll show up when the team gets back." What I would have been saying was, if you fire Billy over an incident like that, where Reggie was loafing and Billy was punishing him for it, then you might as well have made Reggie the manager. "I can't see the manager taking the consequences when he's right," I told Billy. Not so much that it was Reggie and Billy. If it had been any manager and player, I would have felt the same way.

Monday, July 17   New York

Before the game tonight Reggie met with George for more than an hour, and they must have discussed Reggie's bitch that Billy's been batting him low in the order and has been DHing him—against righties—because tonight Paul Splittorff, who's a lefty and a good one, started for Kansas City and Reggie played. Splittorff had been the opposing pitcher when Billy benched Reggie in the final game of the play-offs last year. Tonight against Splittorff, Reggie DHed and batted fourth in the lineup. Reggie ripped Billy about that before the game. He told the reporters, "One day I won't play. The next day I'm the cleanup hitter." The way he's been hitting, he's lucky he's ever the cleanup hitter.

Billy really burned my ass tonight, too. Billy told me I was going to pitch the sixth and seventh innings and then he was going to bring Goose in. In other words, it was Long-Man Lyle again. It didn't matter how well I pitched. He wasn't going to leave me in there. Billy keeps telling me he understands how I feel about going into games early, and yet it keeps happening again and again. So tonight Catfish made his first start since May, and he pitched well. He left with a 5–3 lead after five innings and a third. Billy sent me in, and I got out of the inning, and I shut them out in the sixth, too. I walked in from the mound, went into the dugout, and said, "That's it, my two innings," and I left. I walked up the runway to the clubhouse to get dressed. When Fowler came after me to pitch the seventh, I told him, "I'm not a long man, and you're not going to put me in that job. Two innings are two innings, and now the other guy can take over." I showered, dressed, and went home.

He's made me the long man, and now, when I go out there to pitch, I can see Goose behind me in the bull pen warming up. If I give up one or two hits, the manager's walking out to the mound to take me out. Leave me out there, for Christ's sake. I'll get out of it. I got in it, I'll get out of it. But Billy doesn't do that anymore. With Goose back there, he doesn't feel he has to.

After I left the park, I was driving home in my van, listening to the game on the radio. Goose had given up two runs in the top of the ninth to tie it, and in the bottom of the tenth Thurman leads off with a single. Phil Rizzuto then starts talking about Reggie bunting. The first time Reggie tried to bunt, I thought, *That's good. Reggie's trying to move the runner over.* After he fouled off another bunt for strike two, I said, *Well, hell, at least he tried. Now he'll have to hit away.* But when he bunted with two strikes and struck out, I thought, *Holy shit. I can't believe this. There is going to be hell to pay.* Just listening to the radio and knowing how the game is played, I knew Reggie wasn't bunting to move the runner. He was bunting to get back at Billy.

I don't know. But I didn't feel it was entirely my fault that we lost. Thurman dropped a fly ball in right to help load the bases in the eleventh. With two outs, Goose went to 3 and 2 on Willie Wilson, and on the next pitch Heath and Goose both started walking off the mound, knowing it was strike three. Umpire Marty Springstead, however, called it a ball, the winning run came in, and Goose got so mad he got thrown out of the game. Kammeyer came in, gave up a two-run single to Patek and another run to make it 9–5, and when we scored two in the bottom of the eleventh, it was too little too late.

Tuesday, July 18   New York

It's too bad Reggie and Billy had to clash, but the way both of them are, that's something that's going to go on forever. Neither one of them is going to let a dead dog die. No way, and neither one of them is gonna get any good out of it.

I can see why Billy got so goddam mad at Reggie. Reggie was telling everybody, "I bunted because I thought that was the best thing to do since I wasn't swinging the bat so good." To me that's a weak excuse for doing what he did. He got himself into trouble he didn't count on, and now he's trying to get himself out of it. When a manager gives a sign and the third-base coach tells you, "Reggie, swing away. Don't bunt," and he bunts, anyway, you might as well not have a manager.

And what gets me is that Reggie can make a statement like "I bunted because I thought it was right to bunt" and the reporters accept it. They don't give it a second thought that "Hey, wait a second. Is this guy bullshitting us or putting us on?" They don't force him into a corner. Why doesn't Steve Jacobson ask him the type of question he asks everyone else, where you have to give an answer: "You mean to tell us, Reggie, you honestly weren't mad at Billy? You expect us to believe you really were interested in moving the runner over?" But they don't do that 'cause why should they? This way they go over to Billy and tell him what Reggie says, and it gives Billy an opportunity to call Reggie a liar, and they go back to Reggie and tell Reggie what Billy says, and Reggie says something nasty back, and it is on.

The Yankees have announced that Reggie has been suspended for five games, which is right. Mickey Rivers, though, was angry that he was suspended. Mickey thought they should have just fined him and let him play. "We need a big bat in the lineup right now," Mickey said. But Reggie's been 2 for 16 since the All-Star break.

We needed the day off today, but Boston won again and is sixty-one and twenty-eight, fourteen games in front of us. Forget this season. The rest of the year is just playing out the string.

When Jackie Robinson opened the 1947 season with the Brooklyn Dodgers, most base-ball fans and writers believed that he was the first black to play in the major leagues. (Robinson himself believed that at the time.) He was the third. (Who were the first two? Read on.) For a few years in the 1880s, with slavery dead and Jim Crow not yet ascendant, a spirit of racial tolerance prevailed in America that permitted black and white to rub shoulders without strife. Many black players performed at all levels of Organized Baseball into the 1890s, but the color bar that Jackie Robinson broke was erected in the International League in 1887. How and why it happened makes com-pelling reading; from *The National Pastime*.

JERRY MALLOY

Out at Home

Baseball is the very symbol, the outward and visible expression of the drive and push and rush and struggle of the raging, tearing, booming nineteenth century.

MARK TWAIN

. . . social inequality . . . means that in all the relations that exist between man and man he is to be measured and taken not according to his natural fitness and qualification, but [by] that blind and relentless rule which accords certain pursuits and certain privileges to origin or birth.

MOSES F. WALKER

It was a dramatic and prophetic performance by Jackie Robinson. The twenty-seven-year-old black second baseman opened the 1946 International League season by leading the Montreal Royals to a 14–1 victory over Jersey City. In five trips to the plate, he had four hits (including a home run) and four RBIs; he scored four runs, stole two bases, and rattled a pitcher into balking him home with a taunting *danse macabre* off third. Branch Rickey's protégé had punched a hole through Organized Baseball's color barrier with the flair and talent that would eventually take him into the Hall of Fame. The color line that Jackie Robinson shattered, though unwritten, was very real indeed. Baseball's exclu-sion of the black man was so unremittingly thorough for such a long time that most of the press and public then, as now, thought that Robinson was making

the first appearance of a man of his race in the history of Organized Baseball.

Actually, he represented a return of the Negro ballplayer not merely to Organized Baseball but to the International League, as well. At least eight elderly citizens would have been aware of this. Frederick Ely, Jud Smith, James Fields, Tom Lynch, Frank Olin, "Chief" Zimmer, Pat Gillman, and George Bausewine may have noted with interest Robinson's initiation, for all of these men had been active players on teams that opened another International League season, that of 1887. And in that year they played with or against eight black players on six different teams.

The 1887 season was not the first in which Negroes played in the International League, nor would it be the last. But until Jackie Robinson stepped up to the plate on April 18, 1946, it was the most significant. For 1887 was a watershed year for both the International League and Organized Baseball, as it marked the origin of the color line. As the season opened, the black player had plenty of reasons to hope that he would be able to ply his trade in an atmosphere of relative tolerance; by the middle of the season, however, he would watch helplessly as the International League drew up a written color ban designed to deprive him of his livelihood; and by the time the league held its off-season meetings, it became obvious that Jim Crow was closing in on a total victory.

Yet before baseball became the victim of its own prejudice, there was a period of uncertainty and fluidity, however brief, during which it seemed by no means inevitable that men would be denied access to Organized Baseball due solely to skin pigmentation. It was not an interlude of total racial harmony, but a degree of toleration obtained that would become unimaginable in just a few short years. This is the story of a handful of black baseball players who, in the span of a single season, playing in a prestigious league, witnessed the abrupt conversion of hope and optimism into defeat and despair. These men, in the most direct and personal manner, would realize that the black American baseball player soon would be ruled "out at home."

I

The International League is the oldest minor league in Organized Baseball. Founded in 1884 as the "Eastern" League, it would be realigned and renamed frequently during its early period. The league was not immune to the shifting sands of financial support that plagued both minor and major leagues (not to mention individual franchises) during the nineteenth century. In 1887 the league took the risk of adding Newark and Jersey City to a circuit that was otherwise clustered in upstate New York and southern Ontario. This arrangement proved to be financially unworkable. Transportation costs alone would doom the experiment after one season. The New Jersey franchises were simply too far away from Binghamton, Buffalo, Oswego, Rochester, Syracuse, and Utica in New York, and Hamilton and Toronto in Ontario.

But, of course, no one knew this when the 1887 season opened. Fans in

Newark were particularly excited, because their "Little Giants" were a new team and an instant contender. A large measure of their eager anticipation was due to the unprecedented "colored battery" signed by the team. The pitcher was George Stovey, and the catcher was Moses Fleetwood Walker.

"Fleet" Walker was born in Mt. Pleasant, Ohio, on the route of the Underground Railroad, on October 7, 1857. The son of a physician, he was raised in nearby Steubenville. At the age of twenty he entered the college preparatory program of Oberlin College, the first school in the United States to adopt an official admissions policy of nondiscrimination by sex, race, or creed. He was enrolled as a freshman in 1878 and attended Oberlin for the next three years. He was a good but not outstanding student in a rigorous liberal arts program. Walker also attended the University of Michigan for two years, although probably more for his athletic than his scholastic attainments. He did not obtain a degree from either institution, but his educational background was extremely sophisticated for a nineteenth-century professional baseball player of whatever ethnic origin.

While at Oberlin, Walker attracted the attention of William Voltz, former sportswriter for the Cleveland *Plain Dealer*, who had been enlisted to form a professional baseball team to be based in Toledo. Walker was the second player signed by the team, which entered the Northwestern League in 1883. Toledo captured the league championship in its first year.

The following year Toledo was invited to join the American Association, a major-league rival of the more established National League. Walker was one of the few players to be retained as Toledo made the jump to the big league. Thus did Moses Fleetwood Walker become the first black to play major-league baseball, sixty-four years before Jackie Robinson. Walker played in forty-two games that season, batting .263 in 152 at bats. His brother, Welday Wilberforce Walker, who was two years younger than Fleet, also played outfield in five games, filling in for injured players. Welday was 4 for 18 at the plate.

While at Toledo, Fleet Walker was the batterymate of Hank O'Day, who later became a famous umpire, and Tony Mullane, who could pitch with either hand and became the winningest pitcher, with 285 victories, outside the Hall of Fame. G. L. Mercereau, the team's batboy, many years later recalled the sight of Walker catching barehanded, as was common in those days, with his fingers split open and bleeding. Catchers would welcome swelling in their hands to provide a cushion against the pain.

The color of Walker's skin occasionally provoked another, more lasting kind of pain. The Toledo *Blade*, on May 5, 1884, reported that Walker was "hissed . . . and insulted . . . because he was colored," causing him to commit five errors in a game in Louisville. Late in the season the team traveled to Richmond, Virginia, where manager Charley Morton received a letter threatening bloodshed, according to Lee Allen, by "seventy-five determined men [who] have sworn to mob Walker if he comes on the ground in a suit." The letter, which Morton released to the press, was signed by four men who were "determined" not to sign their real names. Confrontation was avoided, for Walker had been released by the team due to his injuries before the trip to Richmond.

Such incidents, however, stand out because they were so exceptional. Robert Peterson, in *Only the Ball Was White*, points out that Walker was favorably received in cities such as Baltimore and Washington. As was the case throughout the catcher's career, the press was supportive of him and consistently reported his popularity among fans. Upon his release, the *Blade* described him as "a conscientious player [who] was very popular with Toledo audiences," and *Sporting Life*'s Toledo correspondent stated that "by his fine, gentlemanly deportment, he made hosts of friends who will regret to learn that he is no longer a member of the club."

Walker started the 1885 season with Cleveland in the Western League, but the league folded in June. He played the remainder of 1885 and all of 1886 for the Waterbury, Connecticut, team in the Eastern League. While at Waterbury, he was referred to as "the people's choice" and was briefly managed by Charley Hackett, who later moved on to Newark. When Newark was accepted into the International League in 1887, Hackett signed Walker to play for him.

So in 1887 Walker was beginning his fifth season in integrated professional baseball. Tall, lean, and handsome, the thirty-year-old catcher was an established veteran noted for his steady, dependable play and admired, literally, as a gentleman and a scholar. Later in the season, when the Hamilton *Spectator* printed a disparaging item about "the coon catcher of the Newarks," the *Sporting News* ran a typical response in defense of Walker: "It is a pretty small paper that will publish a paragraph of that kind about a member of a visiting club, and the man who wrote it is without doubt Walker's inferior in education, refinement, and manliness."

One of the reasons that Charley Hackett was so pleased to have signed Walker was that his catcher would assist in the development of one of his new pitchers, a Negro named George Washington Stovey. A 165-pound southpaw, Stovey had pitched for Jersey City in the Eastern League in 1886. Sol White, in his *History of Colored Base Ball*, stated that Stovey "struck out twenty-two of the Bridgeport [Connecticut] Eastern League team in 1886 and lost his game." The *Sporting News* that year called Stovey "a good one, and if the team would support him they would make a far better showing. His manner of covering first from the box is wonderful."

A dispute arose between the Jersey City and Newark clubs prior to the 1887 season concerning the rights to sign Stovey. One of the directors of the Jersey City team tried to use his leverage as the owner of Newark's Wright Street grounds to force Newark into surrendering Stovey. But as the *Sporting Life* Newark correspondent wrote, ". . . on sober second thought I presume he came to the conclusion that it was far better that the [Jersey City] club should lose Stovey than that he should lose the rent of the grounds."

A new rule for 1887, which would exist only that one season, provided that walks were to be counted as hits. One of the criticisms of the rule was that in an era in which one of the pitching statistics kept was the opposition's batting average, a pitcher might be tempted to hit a batter rather than be charged with a "hit" by walking him. George Stovey, with his blazing fastball, his volatile temper, and his inability to keep either under strict control, was the type of pitcher these skeptics had in mind. He brought to the mound a wicked glare that intimidated hitters.

During the preseason contract dispute, Jersey City's manager, Pat Powers, acknowledged Stovey's talents, yet added:

> Personally, I do not care for Stovey. I consider him one of the greatest pitchers in the country, but in many respects I think I have more desirable men. He is headstrong and obstinate, and, consequently, hard to manage. Were I alone concerned I would probably let Newark have him, but the directors of the Jersey City Club are not so peaceably disposed.

Newark planned to mute Stovey's "headstrong obstinance" with the easy-going stability of Fleet Walker. That the strategy did not always work is indicated by an account in the Newark *Daily Journal* of a July game against Hamilton:

> That Newark won the game [14–10] is a wonder, for Stovey was very wild at times, [and] Walker had several passed balls. . . . Whether it was that he did not think he was being properly supported, or did not like the umpire's decisions on balls and strikes, the deponent saith not, but Stovey several times displayed his temper in the box and fired the ball at the plate regardless of what was to become of everything that stood before him. Walker got tired of the business after a while, and showed it plainly by his manner. Stovey should remember that the spectators do not like to see such exhibitions of temper, and it is hoped that he will not offend again.

Either despite or because of his surly disposition, George Stovey had a great season in 1887. His thirty-five wins is a single-season record that still stands in the International League. George Stovey was well on his way to establishing his reputation as the greatest Negro pitcher of the nineteenth century.

The promotional value of having the only all-Negro battery in Organized Baseball was not lost on the press. Newspapers employed various euphemisms of the day for "Negro" to refer to Newark's "colored," "Cuban," "Spanish," "mulatto," "African," and even "Arabian" battery. *Sporting Life* wrote:

> There is not a club in the country who tries so hard to cater to all nationalities as does the Newark club. There is the great African battery, Stovey and Walker; the Irish battery, Hughes and Derby; and the German battery, Miller and Cantz.

The Newark correspondent for *Sporting Life* asked, "By the way, what do you think of our 'storm battery,' Stovey and Walker? Verily they are dark horses and ought to be a drawing card. No rainchecks given when they play." Later he wrote that "Our 'Spanish beauties,' Stovey and Walker, will make the biggest kind of drawing card." Drawing card they may have been, but Stovey and Walker were signed by Newark not for promotional gimmickry but because they were talented athletes who could help their team win.

Nor were other teams reluctant to improve themselves by hiring black players. In Oswego, manager Wesley Curry made a widely publicized, though unsuccessful, attempt to sign second baseman George Williams, captain of the Cuban Giants. Had Curry succeeded, Williams would not have been the first, nor the best, black second baseman in the league. For Buffalo had retained the services of Frank Grant, the greatest black baseball player of the nineteenth century.

Frank Grant was beginning the second of a record three consecutive years on the same integrated baseball team. Born in 1867, he began his career in his hometown of Pittsfield, Massachusetts, then moved on to Plattsburg, New York. In 1886 he entered Organized Baseball, playing for Meriden, Connecticut, in the Eastern League until the team folded in July. Thereupon he and two white teammates signed with the Buffalo Bisons, where he led the team in hitting. By the age of twenty Grant was already known as "the Black Dunlap," a singularly flattering sobriquet referring to Fred "Sure Shot" Dunlap, the first player to sign for $10,000 a season and acknowledged as the greatest second baseman of his era. Sol White called Frank Grant simply "the greatest ballplayer of his age," without reference to race.

In 1887, Grant would lead the International League in hitting with a .366 average. Press accounts abound with comments about his fielding skill, especially his extraordinary range. After a series of preseason exhibition games against Pittsburgh's National League team, "Hustling Horace" Phillips, the Pittsburgh manager, complained about Buffalo's use of Grant as a "star." The Rochester *Union* quoted Phillips as saying that "this accounts for the amount of ground [Grant] is allowed to cover . . . and no attention is paid to such a thing as running all over another man's territory." Criticizing an infielder for this excessive range smacks of praising with faint damns. Grant's talent and flamboyance made him popular not only in Buffalo but also throughout the International League.

In 1890 Grant would play his last season on an integrated team for Harrisburg, Pennsylvania, of the Eastern International League. His arrival was delayed by several weeks due to a court battle with another team over the rights to his services. The Harrisburg *Patriot* described Grant's long-awaited appearance:

Long before it was time for the game to begin, it was whispered around the crowd that Grant would arrive on the 3:20 train and play third base. Everybody was anxious to see him come and there was a general stretch of necks toward the new bridge, all being eager to get a sight at the most famous colored ball player in the business. At 3:45 o'clock an open carriage was seen coming over the bridge with two men in it. Jim Russ's famous trotter was drawing it at a 2:20 speed, and as it approached nearer, the face of Grant was recognized as being one of the men. "There he comes" went through the crowd like magnetism, and three cheers went up. Grant was soon in the players' dressing room and in five minutes he appeared on the diamond in a Harrisburg uniform. A great shout went up from the immense crowd to receive him, in recognition of which he politely raised his cap.

Fred Dunlap should have been proud had he ever been called "the White Grant." Yet Grant in his later years passed into such obscurity that no one knew where or when he died. (Last year an obituary in the New York *Age* was located, revealing that Grant had died in New York on June 5, 1937.)

Meanwhile, in Binghamton, Bud Fowler, who had spent the winter working in a local barbershop, was preparing for the 1887 season. At age thirty-three, Fowler was the elder statesman of Negro ballplayers. In 1872, only one year after the founding of the first professional baseball league, Bud Fowler was playing professionally for a white team in New Castle, Pennsylvania. Lee Allen, while historian of baseball's Hall of Fame, discovered that Fowler, whose real name was John Jackson, was born in Cooperstown, New York, in about 1854, the son of itinerant hops pickers. Thus, Fowler was the greatest baseball player to be born at the future site of the Hall of Fame.

As was the case with many minor-league players of his time, Fowler's career took him hopscotching across the country. In 1884 and 1885 he played for teams in Stillwater, Minnesota; Keokuk, Iowa; and Pueblo, Colorado. He played the entire 1886 season in Topeka, Kansas, in the Western League, where he hit .309. A Negro newspaper in Chicago, the *Observer*, proudly described Fowler as "the best second baseman in the Western League."

Binghamton signed Fowler for 1887. The *Sportsman's Referee* wrote that Fowler ". . . has two joints where an ordinary person has one. Fowler is a great ballplayer." According to *Sporting Life*'s Binghamton correspondent:

> Fowler is a dandy in every respect. Some say that Fowler is a colored man, but we account for his dark complexion by the fact that . . . in chasing after balls [he] has become tanned from constant and careless exposure to the sun. This theory has the essential features of a chestnut, as it bears resemblance to Buffalo's claim that Grant is of Spanish descent.

Fowler's career in the International League would be brief. The financially troubled Bings would release him in July to cut their payroll. But during this half season, a friendly rivalry existed between Fowler and Grant. Not so friendly were some of the tactics used by opposing baserunners and pitchers. In 1889, an unidentified International League player told the *Sporting News*:

> While I myself am prejudiced against playing in a team with a colored player, still I could not help pitying some of the poor black fellows that played in the International League. Fowler used to play second base with the lower part of his legs encased in wooden guards. He knew that about every player that came down to second base on a steal had it in for him and would, if possible, throw the spikes into him. He was a good player, but left the base every time there was a close play in order to get away from the spikes.

I have seen him muff balls intentionally, so that he would not have to try to touch runners, fearing that they might injure him. Grant was the same way. Why, the runners chased him off second base. They went down so often trying to break his legs or injure them that he gave up his infield position the latter part of last season [i.e., 1888] and played right field. This is not all.

About half the pitchers try their best to hit these colored players when [they are] at the bat. . . . One of the International League pitchers pitched for Grant's head all the time. He never put a ball over the plate but sent them in straight and true right at Grant. Do what he would he could not hit the Buffalo man, and he [Grant] trotted down to first on called balls all the time.

Fowler's ambitions in baseball extended beyond his career as a player. As early as 1885, while in between teams, he considered playing for and managing the Orions, a Negro team in Philadelphia. Early in July 1887, just prior to his being released by Binghamton, the sporting press reported that Fowler planned to organize a team of blacks who would tour the South and Far West during the winter between 1887 and 1888. "The strongest colored team that has ever appeared in the field," according to *Sporting Life*, would consist of Stovey and Walker of Newark; Grant of Buffalo; five members of the Cuban Giants; and Fowler, who would play and manage. This tour, however, never materialized.

But this was not the only capitalistic venture for Fowler in 1887. The entrepreneurial drive that would lead White to describe him as "the celebrated promoter of colored ball clubs and the sage of baseball" led him to investigate another ill-fated venture: the National Colored Base Ball League.

II

In 1886 an attempt had been made to form the Southern League of Colored Base Ballists, centered in Jacksonville, Florida. Little is known about this circuit, since it was so short-lived and received no national and very little local press coverage. Late in 1886, though, Walter S. Brown of Pittsburgh announced his plan of forming the National Colored Base Ball League. It, too, would have a brief existence. But unlike its southern predecessor, Brown's Colored League received wide publicity.

The November 18, 1886, issue of *Sporting Life* announced that Brown already had lined up five teams. Despite the decision of the Cuban Giants not to join the league, Brown called an organizational meeting at Eureka Hall in Pittsburgh on December 9, 1886. Delegates from Boston, Philadelphia, Washington, Baltimore, Pittsburgh, and Louisville attended. Representatives from Chicago and Cincinnati also were present as prospective investors, Cincinnati being represented by Bud Fowler.

Final details were ironed out at a meeting at the Douglass Institute in Baltimore in March 1887. The eight-team league consisted of the Keystones of Pittsburgh, Browns of Cincinnati, Capitol Citys of Washington, Resolutes of Boston, Falls City of Louisville, Lord Baltimores of Baltimore, Gorhams of

New York, and Pythians of Philadelphia. (The Pythians had been the first black nine to play a white team in history, beating the City Items 27–17 on September 18, 1869.) Reach Sporting Goods agreed to provide gold medals for batting and fielding leaders in exchange for the league's use of the Reach ball. Players' salaries would range from $10 to $75 per month. In recognition of its questionable financial position, the league set up an "experimental" season, with a short schedule and many open dates.

"Experimental" or not, the Colored League received the protection of the National Agreement, which was the structure of Organized Baseball law that divided up markets and gave teams the exclusive right to players' contracts. *Sporting Life* doubted that the league would benefit from this protection, "as there is little probability of a wholesale raid upon its ranks even should it live the season out—a highly improbable contingency." Participation in the National Agreement was more a matter of prestige than of practical benefit. Under the headline "Do They Need Protection?" *Sporting Life* wrote:

> The progress of the Colored League will be watched with considerable interest. There have been prominent colored baseball clubs throughout the country for many years past, but this is their initiative year in launching forth on a league scale by forming a league . . . representing . . . leading cities of the country. The League will attempt to secure the protection of the National Agreement. This can only be done with the consent of all the National Agreement clubs in whose territories the colored clubs are located. This consent should be obtainable, as these clubs can in no sense be considered rivals to the white clubs nor are they likely to hurt the latter in the least financially. Still the League can get along without protection. The value of the latter to the white clubs lies in that it guarantees a club undisturbed possession of its players. There is not likely to be much of a scramble for colored players. Only two [sic] such players are now employed in professional white clubs, and the number is not likely to be ever materially increased owing to the high standard of play required and to the popular prejudice against any considerable mixture of races.

Despite the gloomy—and accurate—forecasts, the Colored League opened its season with much fanfare at Recreation Park in Pittsburgh on May 6, 1887. Following "a grand street parade and a brass band concert," about 1,200 spectators watched the visiting Gorhams of New York defeat the Keystones, 11–8.

Although Walter Brown did not officially acknowledge the demise of the Colored League for three more weeks, it was obvious within a matter of days that the circuit was in deep trouble. The Resolutes of Boston traveled to Louisville to play the Falls City club on May 8. While in Louisville, the Boston franchise collapsed, stranding its players. The league quickly dwindled to three teams, then expired. Weeks later, Boston's players were still marooned in Louisville. "At last accounts," reported the *Sporting News*, "most of the Colored Leaguers were working their way home doing little turns in barbershops and waiting on table in hotels." One of the vagabonds was Sol White, then nineteen years old, who had played for the Keystones of Pittsburgh. He made his way to Wheeling, West Virginia, where he completed the season playing for that city's entry in the Ohio State League. (Three other blacks in that league besides White were Welday Walker, catcher N. Higgins, and another catcher, Richard Johnson.) Twenty years later he wrote:

> The [Colored] League, on the whole, was without substantial backing and consequently did not last a week. But the short time of its existence served to bring out the fact that colored ballplayers of ability were numerous.

Although independent black teams would enjoy varying degrees of success throughout the years, thirty-three seasons would pass before Andrew "Rube" Foster would achieve Walter Brown's ambitious dream of 1887: a stable all-Negro professional baseball league.

III

The International League season was getting under way. In preseason exhibitions against major-league teams, Grant's play was frequently described as "brilliant." *Sporting Life* cited the "brilliant work of Grant," his "number of difficult one-handed catches," and his "special fielding displays" in successive games in April. Even in an 18–4 loss to Philadelphia, "Grant, the colored second baseman, was the lion of the afternoon. His exhibition was unusually brilliant."

Stovey got off to a shaky start, as Newark lost to Brooklyn 12–4 in the team's exhibition opener. "Walker was clever—exceedingly clever behind the bat," wrote the Newark *Daily Journal*, "yet threw wildly several times." A few days later, though, Newark's "colored battery" performed magnificently in a 3–2 loss at the Polo Grounds to the New York Giants, the favorite National League team of the Newark fans (hence the nickname "Little Giants"). Stovey was "remarkably effective," and Walker threw out the Giants' John Montgomery Ward at second base, "something that but few catchers have been able to accomplish." The play of Stovey and Walker impressed the New York sportswriters as well as New York Giants' Captain Ward and manager Jim Mutrie, who, according to White, "made an offer to buy the release of the 'Spanish battery,' but [Newark] Manager Hackett informed him they were not on sale."

Stovey and Walker were becoming very popular. The Binghamton *Leader* had this to say about the big southpaw:

> Well, they put Stovey in the box again yesterday. You recollect Stovey, of course—the brunette fellow with the sinister fin and the demonic delivery. Well, he pitched yesterday, and, as of yore, he teased the Bingos. He has such a knack of tossing up balls that appear as large as an alderman's opinion of himself, but you cannot hit 'em with a cellar door. There's no use in talking, but that Stovey can do funny things with a ball. Once, we noticed, he aimed a ball right at a Bing's commissary department, and when the Bingo spilled himself on the glebe to give that ball the

right of way, it just turned a sharp corner and careened over the dish to the tune of "one strike." What's the use of bucking against a fellow that can throw at the flag-staff amd make it curve into the water pail?

Walker, too, impressed fans and writers with his defensive skill and base-running. In a game against Buffalo, "Walker was like a fence behind the home-plate. . . . [T]here might have been a river ten feet behind him and not a ball would have gone into it." Waxing poetic, one scribe wrote:

> There is a catcher named Walker
> Who behind the bat is a corker,
> He throws to a base
> With ease and with grace,
> And steals 'round the bags like a stalker.

Who were the other black ballplayers in the International League? Oswego, unsuccessful in signing George Williams away from the Cuban Giants, added Randolph Jackson, a second baseman from Ilion, New York, to their roster after a recommendation from Bud Fowler. (Ilion is near Cooperstown; Fowler's real name was John Jackson—coincidence?) He played his first game on May 28. In a 5–4 loss to Newark he "played a remarkable game and hit for a double and a single, besides making the finest catch ever made on the grounds," wrote *Sporting Life*. Jackson played only three more games before the Oswego franchise folded on May 31, 1887.

Binghamton, which already had Bud Fowler, added a black pitcher named Renfroe (whose first name is unknown). Renfroe had pitched for the Memphis team in the Southern League of Colored Base Ballists in 1886, where "he won every game he pitched but one, averaging twelve strikeouts a game for nine games. In his first game against Chattanooga he struck out the first nine men who came to bat," wrote the Memphis *Appeal*; "he has great speed and a very deceptive down-shoot." Renfroe pitched his first game for Binghamton on May 30, a 14–9 victory over Utica, before several thousand fans.

"How far will this mania for engaging colored players go?" asked *Sporting Life*. "At the present rate of progress the International League may ere many moons change its title to 'Colored League.' " During the last few days in May, seven blacks were playing in the league: Walker and Stovey for Newark, Fowler and Renfroe for Binghamton, Grant for Buffalo, Jackson for Owsego, and one player not yet mentioned: Robert Higgins. For his story, we back up and consider the state of the Syracuse Stars.

IV

The 1887 season opened with Syracuse in a state of disarray. Off the field, ownership was reorganized after a lengthy and costly court battle in which the Stars were held liable for injuries suffered by a fan, John A. Cole, when he fell from a grandstand in 1886. Another fall that disturbed management was that of its team's standing, from first in 1885 to a dismal sixth in 1886. Determined to infuse new talent into the club, Syracuse signed seven players from the defunct Southern League after the 1886 season. Although these players were talented, the move appeared to be backfiring when, even before the season began, reports began circulating that the Southern League men had formed a "clique" to foist their opinions on management. The directors wanted to sign as manager Charley Hackett, who, as we have seen, subsequently signed with Newark. But the clique insisted that they would play for Syracuse only if Jim Gifford, who had hired them, was named manager. The directors felt that Gifford was too lax, yet acquiesced to the players' demand.

By the end of April, the Toronto *World* was reporting:

> Already we hear talk of "cliqueism" in the Syracuse Club, and if there be any truth to the bushel of statements that team is certain to be doomed before the season is well under way. Their ability to play a winning game is unquestioned, but if the clique exists the club will lose when losing is the policy of the party element.

Another off-season acquisition for the Stars was a catcher named Dick Male, from Zanesville, Ohio. Soon after he was signed in November 1886, rumors surfaced that "Male" was actually a black named Dick Johnson. Male mounted his own public relations campaign to quell these rumors. The Syracuse correspondent to *Sporting Life* wrote:

> Much has been said of late about Male, one of our catchers, being a colored man, whose correct name is said to be Johnson. I have seen a photo of Male, and he is not a colored man by a large majority. If he is, he has sent some other fellow's picture.

The *Sporting News'* Syracuse writer informed his readers that "Male . . . writes that the man calling him a Negro is himself a black liar."

Male's performance proved less that satisfactory, and he was released by Syracuse shortly after a 20–3 drubbing at the hands of Pittsburgh in a preseason game, in which Male played right field, caught, and allowed three passed balls. Early in May he signed with Zanesville of the Ohio State League, where he once again became a black catcher named Johnson.

As the season began, the alarming specter of selective support by the Southern League players became increasingly apparent. They would do their best for deaf-mute pitcher Ed Dundon, who was a fellow refugee, but would go through the motions when Doug Crothers or Con Murphy pitched for the Stars. Jim Gifford, the Stars' manager, not equal to the task of controlling his team, resigned on May 17. He was replaced by "Ice Water" Joe Simmons, who had managed Walker at Waterbury in 1886.

Simmons began his regime at Syracuse by signing a nineteen-year-old left-handed black pitcher named Robert Higgins. Like Renfroe, Higgins was from Memphis, and it was reported that manager Sneed of Memphis "would have signed him long ago . . . but for the prejudice down there against colored men." Besides his talents as a pitcher, Higgins was so fast on the base paths that *Sporting Life* claimed that he had even greater speed than Mike Slattery of Toronto, who himself was fast enough to steal 112 bases in 1887, an International League record to this day.

On May 23, two days after he signed with the Stars, Higgins pitched well in an exhibition game at Lockport, New York, winning 16–5. On May 25 the Stars made their first trip of the season to Toronto, where in the presence of 1,000 fans, Higgins pitched in his first International League game. The Toronto *World* accurately summed up the game with its simple headline: "DISGRACEFUL BASEBALL." The Star team "distinguished itself by a most disgusting exhibition." In a blatant attempt to make Higgins look bad, the Stars lost 28–8. "Marr, Bittman, and Beard . . . seemed to want the Toronto team to knock Higgins out of the box, and time and again they fielded so badly that the home team were enabled to secure many hits after the side should have been retired. In several instances these players carried out their plans in the most glaring manner. Fumbles and muffs of easy fly balls were frequent occurrences, but Higgins retained control of his temper and smiled at every move of the clique. . . . Marr, Bittman, Beard, and Jantzen played like schoolboys." Of Toronto's twenty-eight runs, twenty-one were unearned. Higgins's catcher, Jantzen, had three passed balls, three wild throws, and three strikeouts, incurring his manager's wrath to the degree that he was fined $50 and suspended. (On June 3 Jantzen was reinstated, only to be released on July 7.) The *Sporting News* reported the game prominently under the headlines "THE SYRACUSE PLOTTERS; The Star Team Broken Up by a Multitude of Cliques; The Southern Boys Refuse to Support the Colored Pitcher." The group of Southern League players was called the "Ku-Klux coterie" by the Syracuse correspondent, who hoped that player Harry Jacoby would dissociate himself from the group. "If it is true that he is a member of the Star Ku Klux Klan to kill off Higgins, the negro, he has made a mistake. His friends did not expect it. . . ."

According to the Newark *Daily Journal*, "Members of the Syracuse team make no secret of their boycott against Higgins. . . . They succeeded in running Male out of the club, and they will do the same with Higgins." Yet when the club returned to Syracuse, Higgins pitched his first game at Star Park on May 31, beating Oswego 11–4. *Sporting Life* assured its readers that "the Syracuse Stars supported [Higgins] in fine style."

But Bob Higgins had not yet forded the troubled waters of integrated baseball. On the afternoon of Saturday, June 4, in a game featuring opposing Negro pitchers, Syracuse and Higgins defeated Binghamton and Renfroe 10–4 before 1,500 fans at Star Park. Syracuse pilot Joe Simmons instructed his players to report the next morning to P.S. Ryder's gallery to have the team portrait taken. Two players did not comply, left fielder Henry Simon and pitcher Doug Crothers. The Syracuse correspondent for the *Sporting News* reported:

The manager surmised at once that there was "a nigger in the fence" and that those players had not reported because the colored pitcher, Higgins, was to be included in the club portrait. He went over to see Crothers and found that he was right. Crothers would not sit in a group for his picture with Higgins.

After an angry exchange, Simmons informed Crothers that he would be suspended for the remainder of the season. The volatile Crothers accused Simmons of leaving debts in every city he had managed, then punched him. The manager and his pitcher were quickly separated.

There may have been an economic motive that fanned the flames of Crothers' temper, which was explosive even under the best of circumstances: he was having a disappointing season when Simmons hired a rival and potential replacement for him. According to the *Sporting News'* man in Syracuse, Crothers was not above contriving to hinder the performance of another pitcher, Dundon, by getting him liquored up on the night before he was scheduled to pitch.

Crothers, who was from St. Louis, later explained his refusal to sit in the team portrait:

> I don't know as people in the North can appreciate my feelings on the subject. I am a Southerner by birth, and I tell you I would have my heart cut out before I would consent to have my picture in the group. I could tell you a very sad story of injuries done my family, but it is personal history. My father would have kicked me out of the house had I allowed my picture to be taken in that group.

Crothers's suspension lasted only until June 18, when he apologized to his manager and was reinstated. In the meantime, he had earned $25 per game pitching for "amateur" clubs. On July 2, he was released by Syracuse. Before the season ended, he played for Hamilton of the International League, and in Eau Claire, Wisconsin, all the while threatening to sue the Syracuse directors for $125.

Harry Simon, a native of Utica, New York, was not punished in any way for his failure to appear for the team portrait; of course, he did not compound his insubordination by punching his manager. The Toronto *World* was cynical, yet plausible, in commenting that Simon "is such a valuable player, his offense [against Higgins] seems to have been overlooked." The sporting press emphasized that Crothers was punished for his failure to pose with Higgins more than his fisticuffs with Simmons.

Thus in a period of ten days did Bob Higgins become the unwilling focus of attention in the national press, as the International League grappled with the question of race. Neither of these incidents—the attempt to discredit him with intentionally bad play nor the reluctance of white players to be photographed with a black teammate—was unprecedented. The day before the Stars' appointment with the photographer, the Toronto *World* reported that in 1886 the Buffalo players refused to have their team photographed because of the presence of Frank Grant, which made it seem unlikely that the Bisons would have a team portrait taken in 1887. (Nonetheless, they did.) That Canadian paper, ever vigilant lest the presence of black ballplayers besmirch the game, also reported, ominously, that "the recent trouble among the Buffalo players originated from their dislike to [sic] Grant, the colored player. It is said that the latter's effective use of a club alone saved him from a drubbing at the hands of other members of the team."

Binghamton did not make a smooth, serene transition into integrated base-ball. Renfroe took a tough 7–6 eleven-inning loss at the hands of Syracuse on June 2, eight days after Higgins's 28–8 loss to Toronto. "The Bings did not support Renfroe yesterday," said the Binghamton *Daily Leader*, "and many think the shabby work was intentional."

On July 7, Fowler and Renfroe were released. In recognition of his consid-erable talent, Fowler was released only upon the condition that he would not sign with any other team in the International League. Fowler joined the Cuban Giants briefly, by August was manager of the (Negro) Gorham Club of New York, and he finished the season playing in Montpelier, Vermont.

On August 8, the Newark *Daily Journal* reported, "The players of the Bing-hamton base ball club were . . . fined $50 each by the directors because six weeks ago they refused to go on the field unless Fowler, the colored second baseman, was removed." In view of the fact that two weeks after these fines were imposed the Binghamton franchise folded, it may be that the club's investors were motivated less by a tender regard for a social justice than by a desire to cut their financial losses.

According to the Oswego *Palladium*, even an International League umpire fanned the flames of prejudice:

It is said that [Billy] Hoover, the umpire, stated in Binghamton that he would always decide against a team employing a colored player, on a close point. Why not dispense with Mr. Hoover's services if this is true? It would be a good thing for Oswego if we had a few players like Fowler and Grant.

There were incidents that indicated support for a color-blind policy in base-ball. For example:

A citizen of Rochester has published a card in the *Union and Advertiser* of that city, in which he rebukes the Rochester *Sunday Herald* for abusing Stovey on account of his color. He says: "The young man simply discharged his duty to his club in whitewashing the Rochesters if he could. Such comments certainly do not help the home team; neither are they creditable to a paper published in a Christian community. So far as I know, Mr. Stovey has been a gentleman in his club and should be treated with the same respect as other players."

But the accumulation of events both on and off the field drew national attention to the International League's growing controversy over the black players. The forces lining up against the blacks were formidable and deter-mined, and the most vociferous opposition to integrated baseball came from

Toronto, where in a game with Buffalo on July 27, "the crowd confined itself to blowing their horns and shouting, 'Kill the nigger.' " The Toronto *World*, under the headline "The Colored Ball Players Distasteful," declared:

> The *World*'s statement of the existence of a clique in the Syracuse team to "boycott" Higgins, the colored pitcher, is certain to create considerable talk, if it does not amount to more, in baseball circles. A number of colored players are now in the International League, and to put it mildly, their presence is distasteful to the other players. . . . So far none of the clubs, with the exception of Syracuse, have openly shown their dislike to play with these men, but the feeling is known to exist and may unexpectedly come to the front. The chief reason given for McGlone's* refusal to sign with Buffalo this season is that he objected to playing with Grant.

A few weeks later the *World* averred, in a statement reprinted in *Sporting Life*:

> There is a feeling, and a rather strong one, too, that an effort be made to exclude colored players from the International League. Their presence on the teams has not been productive of satisfactory results, and good players as some of them have shown themselves, it would seem advisable to take action of some kind, looking either to their nonengagement or compelling the other element to play with them.

Action was about to be taken.

V

July 14, 1887, would be a day that Tommy Daly would never forget. Three thousand fans went to Newark's Wright Street grounds to watch an exhibition game between the Little Giants and the most glamorous team in baseball: Adrian D. (Cap) Anson's Chicago White Stockings. Daly, who was from Newark, was in his first season with the White Stockings, forerunners of today's Cubs. Before the game he was presented with gifts from his admirers in Newark. George Stovey would remember the day, too. And for Moses Fleetwood Walker, there may have been a sense of déjà vu—for Walker had crossed paths with Anson before.

Anson, who was the first white child born among the Pottawattomie Indians in Marshalltown, Iowa, played for Rockford and the Philadelphia Athletics in all five years of the National Association and twenty-two seasons for Chicago in the National League, hitting over .300 in all but two. He also managed the Sox for nineteen years. From 1880 through 1886, Anson's White Stockings finished first five times and second once. Outspoken, gruff, truculent, and

---

* John McGlone's scruples in this regard apparently were malleable enough to respond to changes in his career fortunes. In September 1888 he signed with Syracuse, thereby acquiring two black teammates—Fleet Walker and Bob Higgins.

haughty, Anson gained the respect, if not the esteem, of his players as well as opponents and fans throughout the nation. Cigars and candy were named after him, and little boys would treasure their Anson-model baseball bats as their most prized possessions. He was a brilliant tactician with a flair for the dramatic. In 1888, for example, he commemorated the opening of the Republican national convention in Chicago by suiting up his players in black swallow-tailed coats.

In addition to becoming the first player to get 3,000 hits, Anson was the first to write his autobiography. *A Ball Player's Career*, published in 1900, does not explicitly delineate Anson's views on race relations. It does, however, devote several pages to his stormy relationship with the White Stockings' mascot, Clarence Duval, who despite Anson's vehement objections was allowed to take part in the round-the-world tour following the 1888 season. Anson referred to Duval as "a little darkey," a "coon," and a "no-account nigger."

In 1883, when Walker was playing for Toledo, Anson brought his White Stockings into town for an exhibition. Anson threatened to pull his team off the field unless Walker was removed. But Toledo's manager, Charley Morton, refused to comply with Anson's demand, and Walker was allowed to play right field. Years later *Sporting Life* would write (mistaking Walker's position):

> The joke of the affair was that up to the time Anson made his "bluff" the Toledo people had no intention of catching Walker, who was laid up with a sore hand, but when Anson said he wouldn't play with Walker, the Toledo people made up their minds that Walker would catch or there wouldn't be any game.

But by 1887 times had changed, and there was no backing Anson down. The Newark press had publicized that Anson's White Stockings would face Newark's black Stovey. But on the day of the game it was Hughes and Cantz who formed the Little Giants' battery. "Three thousand souls were made glad," glowed the *Daily Journal* after Newark's surprise 9–4 victory, "while nine were made sad." The *Evening News* attributed Stovey's absence to illness, but the Toronto *World* got it right in reporting that "Hackett intended putting Stovey in the box against the Chicagos, but Anson objected to his playing on account of his color."

On the same day that Anson succeeded in removing the "colored battery," the directors of the International League met in Buffalo to transfer the ailing Utica franchise to Wilkes-Barre, Pennsylvania. It must have pleased Anson to read in the next day's Newark *Daily Journal*:

THE COLOR LINE DRAWN IN BASEBALL.

The International League directors held a secret meeting at the Genesee House yesterday, and the question of colored players was freely discussed. Several representatives declared that many of the best players in the league are anxious to leave on account of the colored element, and the board finally directed Secretary White to approve of no more contracts with colored men.

Whether or not there was a direct connection between Anson's opposition to playing against Stovey and Walker and, on the same day, the International League's decision to draw the color line is lost in history. For example, was the league responding to threats by Anson not to play lucrative exhibitions with teams of any league that permitted Negro players? Interestingly, of the six teams that voted to install a color barrier—Binghamton, Hamilton, Jersey City, Rochester, Toronto, and Utica—none had a black player; the four teams voting against it—Buffalo, Oswego, Newark, and Syracuse—each had at least one.

In 1907, Sol White excoriated Anson for possessing "all the venom of a hate which would be worthy of a Tillman or a Vardaman* of the present day. . . ."

> Just why Adrian C. Anson . . . was so strongly opposed to colored players on white teams cannot be explained. His repugnant feeling, shown at every opportunity, toward colored ballplayers, was a source of comment throughout every league in the country, and his opposition, with his great popularity and power in baseball circles, hastened the exclusion of the black man from the white leagues.

Subsequent historians have followed Sol White's lead and portrayed Anson as the *meistersinger* of a chorus of racism who, virtually unaided, disqualified an entire race from baseball. Scapegoats are convenient, but Robert Peterson undoubtedly is correct:

> Whatever its origin, Anson's animus toward Negroes was strong and obvious. But that he had the power and popularity to force Negroes out of organized baseball almost single-handedly, as White suggests, is to credit him with more influence than he had, or for that matter, than he needed.

The International League's written color line was not the first one drawn. In 1867 the National Association of Base Ball Players, the loosely organized body that regulated amateur baseball, prohibited its members from accepting blacks. The officers candidly explained their reason:

> If colored clubs were admitted, there would be in all probability some division of feeling, whereas, by excluding them no injury could result to anybody and the possibility of any rupture being created on political grounds would be avoided.

This 1867 ban shows that even if blacks were not playing baseball then, there were ample indications that they would be soon. But the NABBP would soon disappear, as baseball's rapidly growing popularity fostered profession-

---

* Sen. Benjamin R. ("Pitchfork Ben") Tillman, of South Carolina, and Gov. James K. Vardaman, of Mississippi, were two of the most prominent white supremacists of their time.

alism. Also, its measure was preventive rather than corrective: it was not intended to disqualify players who previously had been sanctioned. And since it applied only to amateurs, it was not intended to deprive anyone of his livelihood.

Press response to the International League's color line generally was sympathetic to the Negroes—especially in cities with teams that had employed black players. The Newark *Call* wrote:

> If anywhere in this world the social barriers are broken down it is on the ball field. There many men of low birth and poor breeding are the idols of the rich and cultured; the best man is he who plays best. Even men of churlish dispositions and coarse hues are tolerated on the field. In view of these facts the objection to colored men is ridiculous. If social distinctions are to be made, half the players in the country will be shut out. Better make character and personal habits the test. Weed out the toughs and intemperate men first, and then it may be in order to draw the color line.

The Rochester *Post-Express* printed a shrewd and sympathetic analysis by an unidentified "old ball player, who happens to be an Irishman and a Democrat":

> We will have to stop proceedings of that kind. The fellows who want to proscribe the Negro only want a little encouragement in order to establish class distinctions between people of the white race. The blacks have so much prejudice to overcome that I sympathize with them and believe in frowning down every attempt by a public body to increase the burdens the colored people now carry. It is not possible to combat by law the prejudice against colored men, but it is possible to cultivate a healthy public opinion that will effectively prevent any such manifestation of provincialism as that of the ball association. If a negro can play better ball than a white man, I say let him have credit for his ability. Genuine Democrats must stamp on the color line in order to be consistent.

"We think," wrote the Binghamton *Daily Leader*, "the International League made a monkey of itself when it undertook to draw the color line"; and later the editor wondered "if the International League proposes to exclude colored people from attendance at the games." Welday Walker used a similar line of reasoning in March 1888. Having read an incorrect report that the Tri-State League, formerly the Ohio State League, of which Welday Walker was a member, had prohibited the signing of Negroes, he wrote a letter to league president W. H. McDermitt. Denouncing any color line as "a disgrace to the present age," he argued that if Negroes were to be barred as players, then they should also be denied access to the stands.

The sporting press stated its admiration for the talents of the black players who would be excluded. "Grant, Stovey, Walker, and Higgins," wrote *Sporting Life*, "all are good players and behave like gentlemen, and it is a pity that the line should have been drawn against them." That paper's Syracuse correspondent wrote "Dod gast the measly rules that deprives a club of as good a man as Bob Higgins. . . ." Said the Newark *Daily Journal*, "It is safe to say that Moses F. Walker is mentally and morally the equal of any director who voted for the resolution."

Color line or no color line, the season wore on. Buffalo and Newark remained in contention until late in the season. Newark fell victim to injuries, including one to Fleet Walker. Grant's play deteriorated, although he finished the year leading the league in hitting. Toronto, which overcame internal strife of its own, came from the back of the pack, winning twenty-two of its last twenty-six games; they may have been aided by manager Charley Cushman's innovative device of having his infielders wear gloves on their left hands. On September 17, Toronto swept a doubleheader from Newark at home before 8,000 fans to take first place. One week later they clinched their first International League title. To commemorate the triumphant season, the Canadian Pacific Railway shipped a 160-foot-tall pine, "the second tallest in America," across the continent. Atop this pole would fly the 1887 International League pennant.

Before the season ended, there was one further flare-up of racial prejudice that received national attention. On Sunday, September 11, Chris Von der Ahe, owner of the St. Louis Browns, canceled an exhibition game that was scheduled for that day in West Farms, New York, against the Cuban Giants. Led by its colorful and eccentric owner and its multitalented manager-first baseman, Charles Comiskey, the Browns were the Chicago White Stockings of the American Association. At ten o'clock in the morning Von der Ahe notified a crowd of 7,000 disappointed fans that his team was too crippled by injuries to compete. The real reason, though, was a letter Von der Ahe had received the night before, signed by all but two of his players (Comiskey was one of the two):

> Dear Sir: We, the undersigned members of the St. Louis Base Ball Club, do not agree to play against negroes tomorrow. We will cheerfully play against white people at any time, and think by refusing to play, we are only doing what is right, taking everything into consideration and the shape the team is in at present.

The Cuban Giants played, instead, a team from Danbury, New York, as Cuban Giant manager Jim Bright angrily threatened to sue the Browns. Von der Ahe tried to mollify Bright with a promise to reschedule the exhibition, a promise that would be unfulfilled. The Browns' owner singled out his star third baseman, Arlie Latham, for a $100 fine. Von der Ahe did not object to his players' racial prejudice. In fact, he was critical of them not for their clearly stated motive for refusing to play but for their perceived lack of sincerity in pursuing their objective:

> The failure to play the game with the Cuban Giants cost me $1,000. If it was a question of principle with any of my players, I would not say a word, but it isn't.

Two or three of them had made arrangements to spend Sunday in Philadelphia, and this scheme was devised so that they would not be disappointed.

VI

There was considerable speculation throughout the off-season that the International League would rescind its color line or at least modify it to allow each club one Negro. At a meeting at the Rossin House in Toronto on November 16, 1887, the league dissolved itself and reorganized under the title International Association. Buffalo and Syracuse, anxious to retain Grant and Higgins, led the fight to eliminate the color line. Syracuse was particularly forceful in its leadership. The Stars' representatives at the Toronto meeting "received a letter of thanks from the colored citizens of [Syracuse] for their efforts in behalf of the colored players," reported *Sporting Life*. A week earlier, under the headline "Rough on the Colored Players," it had declared:

> At the meeting of the new International Association, the matter of rescinding the rule forbidding the employment of colored players was forgotten. This is unfortunate, as the Syracuse delegation had Buffalo, London, and Hamilton, making four in favor and two [i.e., Rochester and Toronto] against it.

While the subject of the color line was not included in the minutes of the proceedings, the issue apparently was not quite "forgotten." An informal agreement among the owners provided a cautious retreat. By the end of the month, Grant was signed by Buffalo, and Higgins was retained by Syracuse for 1888. Fleet Walker, who was working in a Newark factory crating sewing machines for the export trade, remained uncommitted on an offer by Worcester, as he waited "until he finds whether colored players are wanted in the International League [sic]. He is very much a gentleman and is unwilling to force himself in where he is not wanted." His doubts assuaged, he signed, by the end of November, with Syracuse, where, in 1888, he would once again join a black pitcher. The Syracuse directors had fired manager Joe Simmons and replaced him with Charley Hackett. Thus, Walker would be playing for his third team with Hackett as manager. He looked forward to the next season, exercising his throwing arm by tossing a claw hammer in the air and catching it.

After a meeting in Buffalo in January 1888, *Sporting Life* summarized the International Association's ambivalent position on the question of black players:

> At the recent International Association meeting there was some informal talk regarding the right of clubs to sign colored players, and the general understanding seemed to be that no city should be allowed more than one colored man. Syracuse has signed two whom she will undoubtedly be allowed to keep. Buffalo has signed Grant, but outside of these men there will probably be no colored men in the league.

Frank Grant would have a typical season in Buffalo in 1888, where he was moved to the outfield to avoid spike wounds. For the third straight year his batting average (.346) was the highest on the team. Bob Higgins, the agent and victim of too much history, would, according to *Sporting Life*, "give up his $200 a month, and return to his barbershop in Memphis, Tennessee," despite compiling a 20–7 record.

Fleet Walker, catching seventy-six games and stealing thirty bases, became a member of a second championship team, the first since Toledo in 1883. But his season was blighted by a third distasteful encounter with Anson. In an exhibition game at Syracuse on September 27, 1888, Walker was not permitted to play against the White Stockings. Anson's policy of refusing to allow blacks on the same field with him had become so well-known and accepted that the incident was not even reported in the white press. The Indianapolis *World* noted the incident, which by now apparently was of interest only to black readers.

Fowler, Grant, and Stovey played many more seasons, some with integrated teams, some on all-Negro teams in white leagues in organized baseball, some on independent Negro teams. Fowler and Grant stayed one step ahead of the color line as it proceeded westward.

Fleet Walker continued to play for Syracuse in 1889, where he would be the last black in the International League until Jackie Robinson. Walker's career as a professional ballplayer ended in the relative obscurity of Terre Haute, Indiana (1890), and Oconto, Wisconsin (1891).

In the spring of 1891 Walker was accused of murdering a convicted burglar by the name of Patrick Murphy outside a bar in Syracuse. When he was found not guilty, "immediately a shout of approval, accompanied by clapping of hands and stamping of feet, rose from the spectators," according to *Sporting Life*. His baseball career over, he returned to Ohio and embarked on various careers. He owned or operated the Cadiz, Ohio, opera house and several motion picture houses, during which time he claimed several inventions in the motion picture industry. He was also the editor of a newspaper, the *Equator*, with the assistance of his brother Welday.

In 1908 he published a forty-seven-page booklet entitled *Our Home Colony; A Treatise on the Past, Present and Future of the Negro Race in America*. According to the former catcher, "The only practical and permanent solution of the present and future race troubles in the United States is entire separation by emigration of the Negro from America." Following the example of Liberia, "the Negro race can find superior advantages, and better opportunities . . . among people of their own race, for developing the innate powers of mind and body. . . ." The achievement of racial equality "is contrary to everything in the nature of man, and [it is] almost criminal to attempt to harmonize these two diverse peoples while living under the same government." The past forty years, he wrote, have shown "that instead of improving we are experiencing the development of a real caste spirit in the United States."

Fleet Walker died of pneumonia in Cleveland at age sixty-six on May 11,

1924, and was buried in Union Cemetery in Steubenville, Ohio. His brother Welday died in Steubenville thirteen years later at the age of seventy-seven.

VII

In *The Strange Career of Jim Crow*, historian C. Vann Woodward identifies the late 1880s as a "twilight zone that lies between living memory and written history," when "for a time old and new rubbed shoulders—and so did black and white—in a manner that differed significantly from Jim Crow of the future or slavery of the past." He continued:

> . . . a great deal of variety and inconsistency prevailed in race relations from state to state and within a state. It was a time of experiment, testing, and uncertainty— quite different from the time of repression and rigid uniformity that was to come toward the end of the century. Alternatives were still open and real choices had to be made.

Sol White and his contemporaries lived through such a transition period, and he identified the turning point at 1887. Twenty years later he noted the deterioration of the black ballplayer's situation. Although White could hope that one day the black would be able to "walk hand-in-hand with the opposite race in the greatest of all American games—base ball," he was not optimistic:

> As it is, the field for the colored professional is limited to a very narrow scope in the base ball world. When he looks into the future he sees no place for him. . . . Consequently he loses interest. He knows that, so far shall I go, and no farther, and, as it is with the profession, so it is with his ability.

The "strange careers" of Moses Walker, George Stovey, Frank Grant, Bud Fowler, Robert Higgins, Sol White, et al., provide a microcosmic view of the development of race relations in the society at large, as outlined by Woodward. The events of 1887 offer further evidence of the old saw that sport does not develop character—it reveals it.

He caught his first major-league game at the age of seventeen and his last at the age of thirty-seven. He played for four decades, with four teams, and put mind over batter for at least four hundred pitchers. Today he is a rising star of television broadcasting as the urbane voice of the Mets and ABC's Monday Night Baseball. And as if all that weren't enough, he even writes well. Presenting James Timothy McCarver and what are laughably termed the tools of ignorance.

TIM McCARVER

How a Catcher Calls a Game

If I had ever had a doubt that catching was my calling, it was wiped away during the 1973 season, when I made an attempt at playing first base. Joe Torre was the third baseman on that Cardinals team (with catchers at the corners and one behind home plate, I'm amazed we didn't win it all that year), and he warned me right away about the dangers of first base.

"Your biggest problem," Torre said, "will be to keep your mind in the game. You're going to find it wandering and wandering and wandering."

Sure enough, I'm looking in the stands, I'm looking everywhere, I don't know what to do with myself. All you have to worry about at first base is catching a ball if it's hit to you on a line—what a bore. I wanted to be back in the action, where every pitch is racing through your mind.

For too long catchers have been measured in baseball along the same lines as the rest of the players. And not just by the fans, either. When I argued contract, the front office would judge me by comparing my numbers from year to year. "Well, the guy is a .275 hitter," they'd say, "and maybe we'll add ten extra points on to that because of the grueling position behind the plate." But that's all. It didn't matter if I caught 150 games or handled the league's best pitching staff, because they didn't understand that stuff—and they weren't going to deal with it, either.

What they were really doing was getting their priorities backward. They'd look at a guy as a hitter who caught instead of as a catcher who hit. As a matter of fact, on August 5, 1967, I was hitting .355 and leading the league ("You can look it up," as Casey said), and I ended the season as the runner-up to Orlando Cepeda for the MVP Award. Well, the next year I hit .253, but we won the pennant by nine games. The pitching staff had a record thirty shutouts, and I felt I made more of a winning contribution that year than in any of my previous five. But even so, I didn't get a raise.

Montreal's Gary Carter is going through the same thing right now. Gary was criticized after last season because his numbers were declining. But when Gary first came up, he was very easy to read behind the plate. A lot of catchers have a tendency to call pitches that they can't hit, so Gary would fall behind with the breaking ball by calling for it too often and too early and then he'd be forced to come in with the 2 and 1 or 3 and 1 fastball. He couldn't come in with more breaking balls when he was behind on the hitter, and as a result they were all sitting back and waiting for the fastball. (A guy like Rusty Staub, who may be the best hitter I've ever seen at working a guy into a hole where he has to throw him one pitch, can eat up a catcher like that.) Today, though, Carter is more valuable to his team than he ever was because he is no longer an easy catcher to read. He has learned to keep the ball off of the fat part of the bat—and that is the catcher's ultimate task.

People just don't take these things into consideration when they talk about a catcher's value to a team. They don't understand that contrary to the axiom that you hit off of, or read, the pitcher, the game's best hitters hit off of the catcher. The catcher is out there every day, not every four days, and very few pitchers want to constantly shake off their catcher. So, if you can get into the mind of a catcher, you can be a better hitter. The common talk about catching will inevitably revolve around a guy's arm or how many passed balls he's allowed, not in what situations the guy calls for certain pitches or his success in getting a pitcher to hit certain locations or his ability to communicate successfully with a staff. These hidden elements are the backbone of a baseball game but are rarely discussed. They will be now.

Calling Pitches
(Or, Is That Finger Tentative?)

Dave Cash, the former Phillies second baseman, used to tell me that he couldn't wait until he could call a game from second base someday. Talk about megalomania; the guy actually thought he could do a better job *from second base* than I was doing from behind the plate. Well, that's just indicative of how much a catcher is second-guessed. And what this has done is make many catchers tentative. They're more afraid of failure than excited by success.

How can you tell if a catcher is not giving the signs with conviction? Usually, if he is too deliberate behind the plate. Now, there's a difference between deliberate and tentative (Carlton Fisk is the most deliberate catcher in the game; he prefers to work slowly), but if a catcher gets down into a crouch and then gets back up, he's not sure what to call.

The Padres' Terry Kennedy seems to be a guy who's caught in the middle, thinking much too long about the perfect pitch. You see, he's an example of a guy who has been second-guessed instead of instructed in the proper technique. Who knows what the perfect pitch is? It hasn't been thrown. These guys should let their instincts take over and just fire that signal down there. The point is, if you're tentative, you're going to get a tentative fastball or a doubt-ridden curveball, to coin a phrase. And sometimes the way a pitcher goes about throwing a pitch is more important than the particular pitch. The Astros' Alan Ashby is a guy who doesn't get much credit, but he certainly isn't tentative. The Braves' Bruce Benedict and the Dodgers' Mike Scioscia are guys who also seem secure behind the plate.

Once you understand the importance of getting that finger down with conviction, there are some rules to remember as you call for the first pitch. Generally speaking, it's much easier to work a good hitter than it is a poor hitter. Poor hitters have no idea what you're going to throw to begin with, so why try to outthink them? You go after them with stuff, rather than with pitch selection. But there's beauty in working a good hitter. There's really no formula for doing it; there's feel. What can your pitcher do? Can he get the breaking ball over behind on the count?

Pitchers *definitely* should start more hitters off with breaking balls. That doesn't mean you're going away from the fastball. On the contrary. It means you're keeping the fastball fresh. By throwing the fastball all the time, you're making your best pitch, in effect, your worst pitch. So how do you keep the fastball fresh? By calling things your pitcher doesn't ordinarily throw. As an example, if a left-handed hitter is facing the Pirates' Kent Tekulve—and his fastball away is certainly his best pitch—you have to find a way to keep that as his best pitch. One way is to get ahead and then use the fast ball in, off the plate, to move the hitter back. This will give the outside of the plate back to Tekulve.

To be successful, a pitcher has to be able to throw a breaking ball for a strike when he's behind on the count, because a batter ahead on the count will sit on one pitch, usually the fastball. So if a catcher can call for that breaking ball, the percentages go down dramatically that the pitch will be met with damaging results. (Remember, though, we're talking about fastball pitchers. If a guy like the Giants' Mike Krukow, who may throw 70 percent breaking balls, is pitching, a hitter will be more inclined to sit on the breaking ball behind in the count.)

Now, let's set up a confrontation. We'll put a great thinker up at the plate, like the Mets' Keith Hernandez, and match him against the Reds' hard-throwing right-hander Mario Soto. On the first two pitches, Hernandez has guessed fastball and seen two sliders, one of which was called a strike. On an even count a pitcher has got to come in with the pitch that he can get over best. To me, Soto's got the best straight change-up in baseball, so on a 1 and 1 or 2 and 2 count, I might just call for three in a row (*this* time, and three straight fastballs the next time—every at bat is different with a thinker up there). But a lot depends on where you came from, too. If you came from 2 and 0 to run the count to 2 and 2, the hitter's thinking defensively. If you came from 0 and 2 to 2 and 2, the hitter's on the offensive. With each ball a pitcher throws when he's ahead in the count, the hitter fills up the hole a little bit; he's not as deep in trouble as he was, and he's not protecting the outside part of the plate as much as he's looking for a pitch on the inside part of the plate—fertile ground for a good hitter.

If Hernandez has waited me out and worked out a walk, the strategy shifts. With Soto pitching, a man on first base and a left-handed batter at the plate, I'm much less inclined to go to the off-speed pitch. A hitter is more likely to pull an off-speed pitch, and with the second baseman cheating toward second for the double play and the first baseman holding the runner on, there's a big hole over there—and the good hitters shoot for that hole. So the better the hitter, the less inclined I am to call for the off-speed stuff.

So, I've now called for two fastballs to the Mets' next hitter, Darryl Strawberry. If both pitches were strikes, what *must* be done now is to call for a pitch out of the strike zone. It continually amazes me that pitchers are not patient enough to make a hitter swing at a bad ball with the count at 0 and 2. A 1 and 2 pitch is different. That is the count, more than any other count, where you want to polish a guy off. But on 0 and 2, why throw a strike? Bob Gibson was impatient that way, as are most strikeout power pitchers: they just don't want to finesse hitters. So what if a hitter bloops a flair over the shortstop after you've jammed him? You've done all that you can do.

But sometimes that's just not enough. I remember a situation back in 1963 when Ron Taylor was pitching for the Cardinals in a 2–1 game at Wrigley Field. There were two men out in the ninth, a runner at second and pinch-hitter Ken Aspromonte at the plate when our manager, John Keane, decided to take a walk to the mound. When a manager comes to the mound in that situation, what he immediately does is plant the seed of doubt in your mind. And that's what Keane did on this day. He comes out for a conference and says, "You know, we've had good luck with this guy when he hits the ball hard."

Now I'm young at the time, but not that young. I just can't put together what he's saying. "When we make good pitches on this guy," Keane goes on, "he has a tendency to get jammed and slap a flair for a hit."

"What are you talking about, Johnny?" I said. "What you're saying makes no sense. Are we supposed to try and get him to hit the ball hard?"

Sure enough, on the first pitch Taylor jams Aspromonte, who hits a flair to left center to tie the game. In the eleventh inning Aspromonte wins the game with a flair to right center. It was the most incredible thing, but the incident taught me a valuable lesson. And that is: if you think long enough about a guy doing a certain thing, eventually he'll do it. It all goes back to conviction; you've got to believe in what you're doing, and you can't let anyone—including the manager—flip-flop your thinking. As Jim Kaat used to say, "If you think long, you think wrong."

Communication
(Or, How to Be a Pitcher's Friend)

I think the first thing I learned in the big leagues was never to hang out with a pitcher, because for them every four days was either a wake or New Year's Eve. It can kill you.

Honestly, I don't think there was ever a good pitcher I didn't have a disagreement with. When Bob Gibson was on the mound and Johnny Keane demanded that I go out there and talk to him, I dreaded it.

"God dammit, go out there and slow him down," Keane would say.

"He doesn't want me out there," I'd answer.

"Well, I'm running this club, and I don't give a damn what he wants."

So I'd just sort of go out there about halfway to the mound and stand there, trying to appease everybody.

But Gibby was this snarling, raging competitor, and he wanted me nowhere near him. "Keep your ass away from me while I'm working," he'd scream. "I like to work fast, and I don't want any help from you. You just put those goddam fingers down as fast as you can, and if I don't like it, I'll shake them off."

The great pitchers tend to be like that, though, and a catcher has to be something of a diplomat. The key ingredient in communicating with a pitcher is to get him to trust you. You can't walk out to the mound and tell a guy, "What you have to do is throw strikes," or "Don't give him anything good to hit, but don't walk him." What's he going to say? "Okay, sure"? It's incredible how many times a pitcher will hear that and how many meetings on the mound are just pure rubbish as a result. And the more often you go out there—like Mike Scioscia of the Dodgers does—the less effective your advice will be. So what you have to do is work on his confidence. "Here's what you're going to do tonight, and you will do it because I have caught you a lot of times and I have confidence in you."

Once a pitcher trusts you, you've cleared a big hurdle. You've taken the heat off him, and now that he doesn't have to worry about making the decisions, he can concentrate on pitching. A pitcher has enough trouble trying to do what you want him to do out there without having to worry about pitch selection.

Of course, there's a lot of anger (overt and otherwise) that exists in a pitcher-catcher relationship. And a catcher's job is to cut away all of the other crap and make sure you get down to the issues. You have to keep a pitcher honest and aware of his limitations, for the more honest the pitcher, the better the chance for the outcome. Sometimes it takes going toe-to-toe to make it work. I remember in spring training of 1965 I had a little confrontation with Steve Carlton. Lefty was twenty at the time, and the Cardinals were world champions. I had never caught Carlton before this game, and he had kind of a lackluster performance. Not terrible, mind you (two runs in three innings), just kind of typical for the first outing of the spring. Anyway, after the game I'm showering, and Carlton comes over to me with this kind of "you dummy" look on his face and says rather flippantly, "You're going to have to call for more breaking balls behind in the count."

I said, "What? First of all, how many pitches have I ever called for you? Are you basing this on three innings? You're going to start telling me what I'm supposed to do when we don't even know each other?"

We got involved in a very heated conversation, and I backed Steve against the wall to the point where he was swallowing a lot, if you know what I mean. We were both sorry later, of course, but incidents like this one took place for about the first four years that we knew each other. It is only once a pitcher trusts you, that you can deal with him in a two-way relationship.

Once you've established a relationship with a pitcher, there are times you'll find that he needs you. Not during a six-game winning streak, when he's on top of the world (in fact, you may need to be intentionally aloof toward the guy to bring him back down to earth), but when he's going bad. That's when pitchers start groping and taking advice from everybody. "Hey, my mailman told me I'm not coming over the top with my curveball; what do you think?" These are the times when you have to comfort the guy, get him to turn the page. Steve Carlton has always been able to put a home-run ball out of his mind immediately, and that's a vital trait for a successful pitcher. What a catcher must do is help him work on it.

I first realized that I had reached the point of ultimate trust with Lefty during the 1973 season. He had been traded to Philadelphia the year before, and we were playing the Phils out in St. Louis. Steve was knocked out of the box early and was in the midst of a bad streak. He phoned me in the Cards' dugout during the game and asked me to meet him under the stands. He wasn't getting good pop on his fastball, he explained—it was flat and just gliding in. I told him I thought he was dropping his hand down and pushing the ball. That was the only technical point I could help him with that day, but I knew that I had gained his trust, even though now we were on different clubs.

Location
(Or, Stay in Your Lanes)

When Steve Carlton and Fernando Valenzuela pitch, they help illustrate a staggering epidemic in baseball today. Major-league hitters simply do not know the strike zone. Look at the Pirates when they were going good—Dave Parker, forty walks a year, Willie Stargell maybe fifty. The best-kept secret in all of baseball is Steve Garvey's poor pitch selection; two years ago, in 625 at bats, he walked just twenty times, ten times intentionally.

Carlton and Valenzuela illustrate this point so well because their out pitches (Carlton's slider and Valenzuela's screwball) are rarely strikes. They simply give the illusion of being strikes, and by the time the hitter realizes that, he's already decided to swing. When those two guys are pitching, I'd bet that close to 90 percent of their strikeouts come on pitches out of the strike zone. So when you're talking about location, the first point to remember is that the illusion of a strike can do as much damage to a hitter as will a strike.

Carlton, in fact, concentrates on location before every start. He sits in the training room, closes his eyes, and concentrates on the lanes of the plate. His idea is to divide the plate into three sections, the outside width of the ball, the inside width of the ball, and the fat part of the plate. Gibson taught Lefty a lot about this. Gibson used to say, "The plate's seventeen inches; the middle twelve belong to the hitter; the inside and outside two and a half are mine. If I hit my spots, he's not going to hit it."

Before Gibson would pitch, he'd concentrate on the fertile lanes: "Inside and outside," he'd say. "The more I think about them, the more I'll hit them. There's no such thing as the middle twelve; it just doesn't exist." That's all he'd think about, and before long he had eliminated the idea of bad pitches, because all he was thinking about were the channels.

Now that your pitcher is thinking about his lanes, you get him ready to work the hitter inside and out. How many times have you heard someone say that a pitcher just has to keep the ball down to be successful? Well, that one statement shows how many baseball people continue to say what their predecessors have said without giving it any thought. Carlton never mentioned the lane from the knees to the letters. There's no lane there, and you can be dangerously close to the middle of the plate where the fat part of the bat lies. The lanes where you get a guy out are those two to three inches inside and outside. (Of course, sinkerball pitchers like Tekulve or the Angels' Doug Corbett must keep the ball down to be successful, but they're different animals— they rotate the plate so that their lane is the low road.)

Once you've made the decision to pitch in and out, there are no hard-and-fast rules dealing with where you can be most effective. (Remember, it is not the pitch itself that is most important, but how you got there.) But Gibson used to say, "If you make a mistake away, it's a single; if you make a mistake inside, it's a home run."

A catcher, knowing that his pitcher is set to work the hitter in and out, will move his target accordingly. (Pittsburgh's Tony Peña, who, by the way, I feel is the best defensive catcher in baseball because of his uncanny ability to get to balls in the dirt, gets a lot of attention for getting into his crouch with one leg sticking straight out. It's wonderful that he can do that, but technically it's not correct because he should be working both sides of the plate.) However, he must be careful not to set that target up too early, because a lot of guys peek. What a catcher has to do is give the pitcher the signal, watch him go into his windup and then, while the hitter's waiting for the pitch and too intent to notice, move either to the inside or the outside part of the plate by the time the pitcher releases the ball.

If you're seated outside, the umpire is inclined to give you that outside pitch. While the catcher is off the plate, the umpire has moved with him—he's working the slot between the batter and the catcher—and the pitcher has hit the mitt perfectly. Even though the pitch may not be a strike, it's too close to take, so the umpire will ram his arm up there for a strike.

Catchers are a smart breed, of course, so once a hitter figures out that you're setting up outside, you occasionally decoy. Hitters are attuned to where a catcher is sitting by the pounding on the glove, so a lot of times a catcher will go boom, boom, boom inside; and then bang, the pitch is made, and he's sitting on the outside with the ball in his mitt.

Playing Catch
(Or, Putting It All Together)

When I've tried to put together all the do's and don'ts of pitch selection and location, I've found that Steve Carlton puts it best. What you must do is ignore the batter, Carlton says, and think of the pitcher and catcher as having an elevated game of catch.

What any pitcher who hopes to succeed in the major leagues must learn is to throw through the batter and to the catcher. Too many young pitchers may be overly impressed with the way a big-league hitter puts his jock on. They throw to him and not through him. It's the same when a catcher throws the ball down to second base. If he throws *to* second base, his ball is more likely to go into the dirt than if he's throwing to the outfield grass (with the shortstop or second baseman cutting it off before it gets there). That's what you call throwing through the bag, and a catcher must have his pitcher do the same thing when a hitter is in the box.

It's always been a great frustration of mine that the hidden aspects of a catcher's performance have never been adequately explained. I've tried to do that in this story, and hopefully I've shed some light on the subject. At the very least, the next time you see a manager take a slow walk to the mound, you'll be able to guess what he's talking about. He'll probably be telling his pitcher to keep the ball down (and warning him not to give the batter anything good to hit—but not to walk him). And you'll know exactly what the pitcher will answer. Thanks very much for the advice, but I'm pitching to my catcher, and we're going to work in and out. And by the way, we think you're making far too many trips to the mound.

If it hadn't been for the intrusion of Messrs. Malloy and McCarver, we could have moved neatly from the Bronx Zoo to Yazoo, the Mississippi city that raised Willie Morris. This chapter from his autobiographical *North Toward Home* is about growing up with baseball, about recreation and re-creation, and about a memorable bit of oneupmanship.

WILLIE MORRIS

The Phantom

Like Mark Twain and his comrades growing up a century before in another village on the other side of the Mississippi, my friends and I had but one sustaining ambition in the 1940s. Theirs in Hannibal was to be steamboatmen; ours in Yazoo was to be major-league baseball players. In the summers we thought and talked of little else. We memorized batting averages, fielding averages, slugging averages; we knew the roster of the Cardinals and the Red Sox better than their own managers must have known them, and to hear the broadcasts from all the big-city ballparks with their memorable names—the Polo Grounds, Wrigley Field, Fenway Park, Yankee Stadium—was to set our imagination churning for the glory and riches those faraway places would one day bring us. One of our friends went to St. Louis on his vacation to see the Cards, and when he returned with the autographs of Stan Musial, Red Schoendienst, Country Slaughter, Marty Marion, Joe Garagiola, and a dozen others, we could hardly keep down our envy. I hated that boy for a month and secretly wished him dead, not only because he took on new airs but because I wanted those scraps of paper with their magic characters. I wished also that my own family was wealthy enough to take me to a big-league town for two weeks, but to a bigger place even than St. Louis: Chicago, maybe, with not one but two teams, or best of all, to New York, with three. I had bought a baseball cap in Jackson, a real one from the Brooklyn Dodgers, and a Jackie Robinson Louisville Slugger, and one day when I could not even locate any of the others for catch or for baseball talk, I sat on a curb on Grand Avenue with the most dreadful feelings of being caught forever by time—trapped there always in my scrawny and helpless condition. *I'm ready, I'm ready,* I kept thinking to myself, but that remote future when I would wear a cap like that and be a hero for a grandstand full of people seemed so far away I knew it would never come. I must have been the most dejected looking child you ever saw, sitting hunched up on the curb and dreaming of glory in the mythical cities of the North. I felt worse when a carload of high school boys halted right in front of where I sat and they started reciting what they always did when they saw me alone and daydreaming: *Wee Willie Winkie walks through the town, upstairs and downstairs in his nightgown.* Then one of them said, "Winkie, you *gettin'* much?" "You bastards!" I shouted, and they drove off, laughing like wild men.

Almost every afternoon when the heat was not unbearable, my father and I would go out to the old baseball field behind the armory to hit flies. I would stand far out in center field, and he would station himself with a fungo at home plate, hitting me one high fly, or Texas Leaguer, or line drive after another, sometimes for an hour or more without stopping. My dog would get out there in the outfield with me and retrieve the inconsequential dribblers or the ones that went too far. I was light and speedy and could make the most fantastic catches, turning completely around and forgetting the ball sometimes to head for the spot where it would descend or tumbling head-on for a diving catch. The smell of that new-cut grass was the finest of all smells, and I could run forever and never get tired. It was a dreamy, suspended state, those late afternoons, thinking of nothing but outfield flies as the world drifted lazily by on Jackson Avenue. I learned to judge what a ball would do by instinct, heading the way it went as if I owned it, and I knew in my heart I could make the big time. Then, after all that exertion, my father would shout, "I'm whupped!" and we would quit for the day.

When I was twelve I became a part-time sportswriter for the Yazoo *Herald*, whose courtly proprietors allowed me unusual independence. I wrote up an occasional high school or Legion game in a florid prose, filled with phrases like "two-ply blow" and "circuit ringer." My mentor was the sports editor of the Memphis *Commercial Appeal*, whose name was Walter Stewart, a man who could invest the most humdrum athletic contest with the elements of Shakespearean tragedy. I learned whole paragraphs of his by heart and used some of his expressions for my reports on games between Yazoo and Satartia, or the other teams. That summer, when I was twelve, having never seen a baseball game higher than the Jackson Senators of Class B, my father finally relented and took me to Memphis to see the Chicks, who were Double A. It was the farthest I had ever been from home and the largest city I had ever seen; I walked around in a state of joyousness, admiring the crowds and the big park high above the River, and best of all, the grand old lobby of the Chisca Hotel.

Staying with us at the Chisca were the Nashville Vols, who were there for a big series with the Chicks. I stayed close to the lobby to get a glimpse of them; when I discovered they spent all day, up until the very moment they left for the ballpark, playing the pinball machine, I stationed myself there, too. Their names were Tookie Gilbert, Smokey Burgess, Chuck Workman, and Bobo Hollomon, the latter being the one who got as far as the St. Louis Browns, pitched a no-hitter in his first major-league game, and failed to win another before being shipped down forever to obscurity; one afternoon my father and I ran into them outside the hotel on the way to the game and gave them a ride in our taxi. I could have been fit for tying, especially when Smokey Burgess tousled my hair and asked me if I batted right or left, but when I listened to them as they grumbled about having to get out to the ballpark so early and complained about the season having two more damned months to go and about how ramshackle their team bus was, I was too disillusioned even to tell my friends when I got home.

Because back home, even among the adults, baseball was all-meaning; it was the link with the outside. A place known around town simply as the Store, down near the train depot, was the principal center of this ferment. The Store had sawdust on the floor and long shreds of flypaper hanging from the ceiling. Its most familiar staples were Rexall supplies, oysters on the half shell, legal beer, and illegal whiskey, the latter served up, Mississippi bootlegger style, by the bottle from a hidden shelf and costing not merely the price of the whiskey but the investment in gas required to go to Louisiana to fetch it. There was a long counter in the back. On one side of it, the white workingmen congregated after hours every afternoon to compare the day's scores and talk batting averages, and on the other side, also talking baseball, were the Negroes, juxtaposed in a face-to-face arrangement with the whites. The scores were chalked up on a blackboard hanging on a red-and-purple wall, and the conversations were carried on in fast, galloping shouts from one end of the room to the other. An intelligent white boy of twelve was even permitted, in that atmosphere of heady freedom, before anyone knew the name of Justice Warren or had heard much of the U.S. Supreme Court, a quasi-public position favoring the Dodgers, who had Jackie Robinson, Roy Campanella, and Don Newcombe—not to mention, so it was rumored, God knows how many Chinese and mulattoes being groomed in the minor leagues. I remember my father turned to some friends at the Store one day and observed, "Well, you can say what you want to about that nigger Robinson, but he's got *guts*," and to a man the others nodded, a little reluctantly, but in agreement nonetheless. And one of them said he had read somewhere that Pee Wee Reese, a white southern boy, was the best friend Robinson had on the team, which proved they had chosen the right one to watch after him.

There were two firehouses in town, and on hot afternoons the firemen at both establishments sat outdoors in their shirt-sleeves, with the baseball broadcast turned up as loud as it would go. On his day off work my father, who had left Cities Service and was now a bookkeeper for the wholesale grocery, usually started with Firehouse No. 1 for the first few innings and then hit No. 2 before ending up at the Store for the postgame conversations.

I decided not to try out for the American Legion Junior Baseball team that summer. Legion baseball was an important thing for country boys in those parts, but I was too young and skinny, and I had heard that the coach, a dirt farmer known as Gentleman Joe, made his protégées lie flat in the infield while he walked on their stomachs; he also forced them to take 3-mile runs through the streets of town, talked them into going to church, and persuaded them to give up Coca-Colas. A couple of summers later, when I did go out for the team, I found out that Gentleman Joe did in fact insist on these soul-strengthening rituals; because of them, we won the Mississippi State Championship, and the merchants in town took up a collection and sent us all the way to St. Louis to see the Cards play the Phillies. My main concern that earlier summer, however, lay in the more academic aspects of the game. I knew more about baseball, its technology and its ethos, than all the firemen and Store experts put together. Having read most of its literature, I could give a sizable lecture on the infield-fly rule alone, which only a thin minority of the townspeople knew existed. Gentleman Joe was held in some esteem for his strategical sense, yet he was the only man I ever knew who could call for a sacrifice bunt with two men out and not have a bad conscience about it. I remember one dismaying moment that came to me while I was watching a country semipro game. The home team had runners on first and third with one out when the batter hit a ground ball to the first baseman, who stepped on first and then threw to second. The shortstop, covering second, stepped on the base but made no attempt to tag the runner. The man on third had crossed the plate, of course, but the umpire, who was not very familiar with the subtleties of the rules, signaled a double play. Sitting in the grandstand, I knew that it was not a double play at all and that the run had scored, but when I went down, out of my Christian duty, to tell the manager of the local team that he had just been done out of a run, he told me I was crazy. This was the kind of brainpower I was up against.

That summer the local radio station, the one where we broadcast our Methodist programs, started a baseball quiz program. A razor-blade company offered free blades, and the station chipped in a dollar, all of which went to the first listener to telephone with the right answer to the day's baseball question. If there was no winner, the next day's pot would go up a dollar. At the end of the month they had to close down the program because I was winning all the money. It got so easy, in fact, that I stopped phoning in the answers some afternoons so that the pot could build up and make my winnings more spectacular. I netted about $25 and a ten-year supply of double-edged, smooth-contact razor blades before they gave up. One day, when the jackpot was a mere $2, the announcer tried to confuse me. "Babe Ruth," he said, "hit sixty home runs in 1927 to set the major-league record. What man had the next-highest total?" I telephoned and said, "George Herman Ruth. He hit fifty-nine in another season." My adversary, who had developed an acute dislike of me, said that was not the correct answer. He said it should have been *Babe* Ruth.

This incident angered me, and I won for the next four days, just for the hell of it.

On Sunday afternoons we sometimes drove out of town and along hot, dusty roads to baseball fields that were little more than parched red clearings, the outfield sloping out of the woods and ending in some tortuous gully filled with yellowed paper, old socks, and vintage cow shit. One of the backwoods teams had a fastball pitcher named Eckert, who didn't have any teeth, and a fifty-year-old left-handed catcher named Smith. Since there were no catcher's mitts made for left-handers, Smith had to wear a mitt on his throwing hand. In his simian posture he would catch the ball and toss it lightly into the air and then whip his mitt off and catch the ball in his bare left hand before throwing it back. It was a wonderfully lazy way to spend those Sunday afternoons—my father and my friends and I sitting in the grass behind the chicken-wire backstop with eight or ten dozen farmers, watching the wrong-handed catcher go through his contorted gyrations and listening at the same time to our portable radio, which brought us the rising inflections of a baseball announcer called the Old Scotchman. The sounds of the two games, our own and the one being broadcast from Brooklyn or Chicago, merged and rolled across the bumpy outfield and the gully into the woods; it was a combination that seemed perfectly natural to everyone there.

I can see the town now on some hot, still weekday afternoon in midsummer: ten thousand souls and nothing doing. Even the red water truck was a diversion, coming slowly up Grand Avenue with its sprinklers on full force, the water making sizzling steam clouds on the pavement while half-naked Negro children followed the truck up the street and played in the torrent until they got soaking wet. Over on Broadway, where the old men sat drowsily in straw chairs on the pavement near the Bon-Ton Café, whittling to make the time pass, you could laze around on the sidewalks—barefoot, if your feet were tough enough to stand the scalding concrete—watching the big cars with out-of-state plates whip by, the driver hardly knowing and certainly not caring what place this was. Way up that fantastic hill, Broadway seemed to end in a seething mist—little heat mirages that shimmered off the asphalt; on the main street itself there would be only a handful of cars parked here and there, and the merchants and the lawyers sat in the shade under their broad awnings, talking slowly, aimlessly, in the cryptic summer way. The one o'clock whistle at the sawmill would send out its loud bellow, reverberating up the streets to the bend in the Yazoo River, hardly making a ripple in the heavy somnolence.

But by two o'clock almost every radio in town was tuned in to the Old Scotchman. His rhetoric dominated the place. It hovered in the branches of the trees, bounced off the hills, and came out of the darkened stores; the merchants and the old men cocked their ears to him, and even from the big cars that sped by, their tires making lapping sounds in the softened highway, you could hear his voice, being carried past you out into the delta.

The Old Scotchman's real name was Gordon McLendon, and he described the big-league games for the Liberty Broadcasting System, which had outlets mainly in the South and the Southwest. He had a deep, rich voice, and I think he was the best rhetorician, outside of Bilbo and Nye Bevan, I have ever heard. Under his handling a baseball game took on a life of its own. As in the prose of the *Commercial Appeal*'s Walter Stewart, his games were rare and remarkable entities; casual pop flies had the flow of history behind them, double plays resembled the stark clashes of old armies, and home runs deserved acknowledgment on earthen urns. Later, when I came across Thomas Wolfe, I felt I had heard him before, from Shibe Park, Crosley Field, or Yankee Stadium.

One afternoon I was sitting around my house listening to the Old Scotchman, admiring the vivacity of a man who said he was a contemporary of Connie Mack. (I learned later that he was twenty-nine.) That day he was doing the Dodgers and the Giants from the Polo Grounds. The game, as I recall, was in the fourth inning, and the Giants were ahead by about 4–1. It was a boring game, however, and I began experimenting with my father's shortwave radio, an impressive mechanism a couple of feet wide, which had an aerial that almost touched the ceiling and the name of every major city in the world on its dial. It was by far the best radio I had ever seen; there was not another one like it in town. I switched the dial to shortwave and began picking up African drum music, French jazz, Australian weather reports, and a lecture from the British Broadcasting Company on the people who wrote poems for Queen Elizabeth. Then a curious thing happened. I came across a baseball game—the Giants and the Dodgers, from the Polo Grounds. After a couple of minutes I discovered that the game was in the eighth inning. I turned back to the local station, but here the Giants and Dodgers were still in the fourth. I turned again to the shortwave broadcast and listened to the last inning, a humdrum affair that ended with Carl Furillo popping out to shortstop, Gil Hodges grounding out second to first, and Roy Campanella lining out to center. Then I went back to the Old Scotchman and listened to the rest of the game. In the top of the ninth, an hour or so later, a ghostly thing occurred; to my astonishment and titillation, the game ended with Furillo popping out to short, Hodges grounding out second to first, and Campanella lining out to center.

I kept this unusual discovery to myself, and the next day, an hour before the Old Scotchman began his play-by-play of the second game of the series, I dialed the shortwave frequency, and, sure enough, they were doing the Giants and the Dodgers again. I learned that I was listening to the Armed Forces Radio Service, which broadcast games played in New York. As the game progressed, I began jotting down notes on the action. When the first four innings were over, I turned to the local station just in time to get the Old Scotchman for the first batter. The Old Scotchman's account of the game matched the shortwave's almost perfectly. The Scotchman's, in fact, struck me as being considerably more poetic than the one I had heard first. But I did not doubt him, since I could hear the roar of the crowd, the crack of the bat, and the Scotchman's precise description of foul balls that fell into the crowd, the gestures of the base coaches, and the expression on the face of a small boy who was eating a lemon popsicle in a box seat behind first base. I decided that the broadcast was being delayed somewhere along the line, maybe because we were so far from New York.

That was my first thought, but after a close comparison of the two broadcasts for the rest of the game, I sensed that something more sinister was taking place. For one thing, the Old Scotchman's description of the count on a batter, though it jibed 90 percent of the time, did not always match. For another, the Scotchman's crowd, compared with the other, kept up an ungodly noise. When Robinson stole second on shortwave, he did it without drawing a throw and without sliding, while for Mississippians the feat was performed in a cloud of angry, petulant dust. A foul ball that went over the grandstand and out of the park for shortwave listeners in Alaska, France, and the Argentine produced for the firemen, bootleggers, farmers, and myself a primitive scramble that ended with a feeble old lady catching the ball on the first bounce to the roar of an assembly that would have outnumbered Grant's at Old Cold Harbor. But the most revealing development came after the Scotchman's game was over. After the usual summaries, he mentioned that the game had been "re-created." I had never taken notice of that particular word before, because I lost interest once a game was over. I went to the dictionary, and under "re-create" I found, "To invest with fresh vigor and strength; to refresh, invigorate (nature, strength, a person or thing)." The Old Scotchman most assuredly invested a game with fresh vigor and strength, but this told me nothing. My deepest suspicions were confirmed, however, when I found the second definition of the word—"To create anew."

So there it was. I was happy to have fathomed the mystery, as perhaps no one else in the whole town had done. The Old Scotchman, for all his wondrous expressions, was not only several innings behind every game he described but was no doubt sitting in some air-conditioned studio in the hinterland, where he got the happenings of the game by news ticker; sound effects accounted for the crack of the bat and the crowd noises. Instead of being disappointed in the Scotchman, I was all the more pleased by his genius, for he made pristine facts more actual than actuality, a valuable lesson when the day finally came that I started reading literature. I must add, however, that this appreciation did not obscure the realization that I had at my disposal a weapon of unimaginable dimensions.

Next day I was at the shortwave again, but I learned with much disappointment that the game being broadcast on shortwave was not the one the Scotchman had chosen to describe. I tried every afternoon after that and discovered that I would have to wait until the Old Scotchman decided to do a game out of New York before I could match his game with the one described live on shortwave. Sometimes, I learned later, these coincidences did not occur for days; during an important Dodger or Yankee series, however, his game and that of the Armed Forces Radio Service often coincided for two or three days running. I was happy, therefore, to find, on an afternoon a few days later, that both the shortwave and the Scotchman were carrying the Yankees and the Indians.

I settled myself at the shortwave with notebook and pencil and took down every pitch. This I did for four full innings, and then I turned back to the town station, where the Old Scotchman was just beginning the first inning. I checked the first batter to make sure the accounts jibed. Then, armed with my notebook, I ran down the street to the corner grocery, a minor outpost of baseball intellection, presided over by my young Negro friend Bozo, a knowledgeable student of the game, the same one who kept my dog in bologna. I found Bozo behind the meat counter, with the Scotchman's account going full blast. I arrived at the interim between the top and bottom of the first inning.

"Who's pitchin' for the Yankees, Bozo?" I asked.

"They're pitchin' Allie Reynolds," Bozo said. "Old Scotchman says Reynolds really got the stuff today. He just set 'em down one, two, three."

The Scotchman, meanwhile, was describing the way the pennants were flapping in the breeze. Phil Rizzuto, he reported, was stepping to the plate.

"Bo," I said, trying to sound cut-and-dried, "you know what I think? I think Rizzuto's gonna take a couple of fast called strikes, then foul one down the left-field line, and then line out straight to Boudreau at short."

"Yeah?" Bozo said. He scatched his head and leaned lazily across the counter.

I went up front to buy something and then came back. The count worked to nothing and two on Rizzuto—a couple of fast called strikes and a foul down the left side. "This one," I said to Bozo, "he lines straight to Boudreau at short."

The Old Scotchman, pausing dramatically between words as was his custom, said, "Here's the windup on nothing and two. Here's the pitch on its way— There's a hard line drive! But Lou Boudreau's there at shortstop, and he's got it. Phil hit that one on the nose, but Boudreau was right there."

Bozo looked over at me, his eyes bigger than they were. "How'd you know that?" he asked.

Ignoring this query, I made my second prediction. "Bozo," I said, "Tommy Henrich's gonna hit the first pitch up against the right-field wall and slide in with a double."

"How come you think so?"

"Because I can predict anything that's gonna happen in baseball in the next ten years," I said. "I can tell you anything."

The Old Scotchman was describing Henrich at the plate. "Here comes the first pitch. Henrich swings, there's a hard smash into right field! . . . This one may be out of here! It's going, going— *No!* It's off the wall in right center. Henrich's rounding first, on his way to second. Here's the relay from Doby . . . Henrich slides in safely with a double!" The Yankee crowd sent up an awesome roar in the background.

"Say, how'd you know that?" Bozo asked. "How'd you know he was gonna wind up at second?"

"I just can tell. I got extravision," I said. On the radio, far in the background, the public-address system announced Yogi Berra. "Like Berra right now. You know what? He's gonna hit a one–one pitch down the right-field line—"

"How come you know?" Bozo said. He was getting mad.

"Just a second," I said. "I'm gettin' static." I stood dead still, put my hands up against my temples and opened my eyes wide. "Now it's comin' through clear. Yeah, Yogi's gonna hit a one–one pitch down the right-field line, and it's gonna be fair by about three or four feet—I can't say exactly—and Henrich's gonna score from second, but the throw is gonna get Yogi at second by a mile."

This time Bozo was silent, listening to the Scotchman, who described the ball and the strike, then said: "Henrich takes the lead off second. Benton looks over, stretches, delivers. Yogi swings." (There was the bat crack.) "There's a line drive down the right side! It's barely inside the foul line. It may go for extra bases! Henrich's rounding third and coming in with a run. Berra's moving toward second. Here comes the throw! . . . And they *get* him! They get Yogi easily on the slide at second!"

Before Bozo could say anything else, I reached in my pocket for my notes. "I've just written down here what I think's gonna happen in the first four innings," I said. "Like DiMag. See, he's gonna pop up to Mickey Vernon at first on a one–nothing pitch in just a minute. But don't you worry. He's gonna hit a three-hundred-eighty-foot homer in the fourth with nobody on base on a full count. You just follow these notes and you'll see I can predict anything that's gonna happen in the next ten years." I handed him the paper, turned around, and left the store just as DiMaggio, on a one–nothing pitch, popped up to Vernon at first.

Then I went back home and took more notes from the shortwave. The Yanks clobbered the Indians in the late innings and won easily. On the local station, however, the Old Scotchman was in the top of the fifth inning. At this juncture I went to the telephone and called Firehouse No. 1.

"Hello," a voice answered. It was the fire chief.

"Hello, Chief, can you tell me the score?" I said. Calling the firehouse for baseball information was a common practice.

"The Yanks are ahead five to two."

"This is the Phantom you're talkin' with," I said.

"Who?"

"The Phantom. Listen carefully, Chief. Reynolds is gonna open this next inning with a pop-up to Doby. Then Rizutto will single to left on a one–one count. Henrich's gonna force him at second on a two-and-one pitch but make it to first. Berra's gonna double to right on a nothing-and-one pitch, and Henrich's goin' to third. DiMaggio's gonna foul a couple off and then double down the left-field line, and both Henrich and Yogi are gonna score. Brown's gonna pop out to third to end the inning."

"Aw, go to hell," the chief said, and hung up.

This was precisely what happened, of course. I phoned No. 1 again after the inning.

"Hello."

"Hi. This is the Phantom again."

"Say, how'd you know that?"

"Stick with me," I said ominously, "and I'll feed you predictions. I can predict anything that's gonna happen anywhere in the next ten years." After a pause I added, "Beware of fire real soon," for good measure, and hung up.

I left my house and hurried back to the corner grocery. When I got there, the entire meat counter was surrounded by friends of Bozo's, about a dozen of them. They were gathered around my notes, talking passionately and shouting. Bozo saw me standing by the bread counter. "There he is! That's the one!" he declared. His colleagues turned and stared at me in undisguised awe. They parted respectfully as I strolled over to the meat counter and ordered a dime's worth of bologna for my dog.

A couple of questions were directed at me from the group, but I replied, "I'm sorry for what happened in the fourth. I predicted DiMag was gonna hit a full-count pitch for that homer. It came out he hit it on two and two. There was too much static in the air between here and New York."

"Too much *static*?" one of them asked.

"Yeah. Sometimes the static confuses my extravision. But I'll be back to-morrow if everything's okay, and I'll try not to make any more big mistakes."

"Big mistakes!" one of them shouted, and the crowd laughed admiringly, parting once more as I turned and left the store. I wouldn't have been at all surprised if they had tried to touch the hem of my shirt.

That day was only the beginning of my brief season of triumph. A schoolmate of mine offered me $5, for instance, to tell him how I had known that Johnny Mize was going to hit a two-run homer to break up one particularly close game for the Giants. One afternoon, on the basis of a lopsided first four innings, I had an older friend sneak into the Store and place a bet, which netted me $14.50. I felt so bad about it I tithed $1.45 in church the following Sunday. At Bozo's grocery store I was a full-scale oracle. To the firemen I remained the Phantom, and firefighting reached a peak of efficiency that month, simply because the firemen knew what was going to happen in the late innings and did not need to tarry when an alarm came.

One afternoon my father was at home listening to the Old Scotchman with a couple of out-of-town salesmen from Greenwood. They were sitting in the front room, and I had already managed to get the first three or four innings of the Cardinals and the Giants on paper before they arrived. The Old Scotchman was in the top of the first when I walked in and said hello. The men were talking business and listening to the game at the same time.

"I'm gonna make a prediction," I said. They stopped talking and looked at me. "I predict Musial's gonna take a ball and a strike and then hit a double to right field, scoring Schoendienst from second, but Marty Marion's gonna get tagged out at the plate."

"You're mighty smart," one of the men said. He suddenly sat up straight when the Old Scotchman reported, "Here's the windup and the pitch coming in. . . . Musial *swings!*" (bat crack, crowd roar). "He drives one into right field! This one's going up against the boards! . . . Schoendienst rounds third. He's coming on in to score! Marion dashes around third, legs churning. His cap falls off, but here he *comes!* Here's the toss to the plate. He's nabbed at home. He is *out* at the plate! Musial holds at second with a run-producing double."

Before I could parry the inevitable questions, my father caught me by the elbow and hustled me into a back room. "How'd you know that?" he asked.

"I was just guessin'," I said. "It was nothin' but luck."

He stopped for a moment, and then a new expression showed on his face. "Have *you* been callin' the firehouse?" he asked.

"Yeah, I guess a few times."

"Now, you tell me how you found out about all that. I mean it."

When I told you about the shortwave, I was afraid he might be mad, but on the contrary; he laughed uproariously. "Do you remember these next few innings?" he asked.

"I got it all written down," I said, and reached in my pocket for the notes. He took the notes and told me to go away. From the yard, a few minutes later, I heard him predicting the next inning to the salesmen.

A couple of days later, I phoned No. 1 again. "This is the Phantom," I said. "With two out, Branca's gonna hit Stinky Stanky with a fastball, and then Alvin Dark's gonna send him home with a triple."

"Yeah, we know it," the fireman said in a bored boice. "We're listenin' to a shortwave, too. You think you're somethin', don't you? You're Ray Morris's boy."

I knew everything was up. The next day, as a sort of final gesture, I took some more notes to the corner grocery in the third or fourth inning. Some of the old crowd was there, but the atmosphere was grim. They looked at me coldly. "Oh, man," Bozo said, "*we* know the Old Scotchman ain't at that game. He's four or five innings behind. He's makin' all that stuff up." The others grumbled and turned away. I slipped quietly out the door.

My period as a seer was over, but I went on listening to the shortwave broadcasts out of New York a few days more. Then, a little to my surprise, I went back to the Old Scotchman, and in time I found that the firemen, the bootleggers, and the few dirt farmers who had shortwave sets all did the same. From then on, accurate, up-to-the-minute baseball news was in disrepute there. I believe we all went back to the Scotchman not merely out of loyalty but because, in our great isolation, he touched our need for a great and unmitigated eloquence.

Joe's American Legion Junior team actually amounted to an All-Star squad from all the country towns surrounding ours; it was easier to make the high school team first. On Tuesday and Friday afternoons we would ride in our red-and-black bus through the heavy green woods to the small crossroads towns to play the locals. The crowds would sometimes be in a foul frame of mind, especially if the farmers had got hold of the corn gourd early in the day. Since we were the "city boys," with our pictures in the Yazoo *Herald* every now and again, we were particularly ripe for all that boondocks venom. The farmers would stand around the field shouting obscenities at the "slickers," sometimes loosening up their lungs with a vicious organized whoop that sounded like a cross between a rebel yell and a redneck preacher exorcizing the devil and all his family. More often than not, to compound the injury, we got beat. Yet far from being gracious in victory, those sons of dirt farmers rubbed our noses in our own catastrophes, taunting us with threats to whip us all over again in the outfield pasture, while their elders stood around in a group as our coach chased us into the bus and shouted, "You ain't such hot stuff, slickers!" or "Go on back to town now, boys, and get your *photos* took some more." One afternoon when I ruined the no-hitter the best pitcher in the county had going (he later made Double A), with a broken-bat fluke into right field in the eighth inning, I thought those farmers might slice me in pieces and feed me to the boll weevils. "You proud of that little skinny hit?" one of them shouted at me, standing with his nose next to mine, and his companion picked up the broken bat that had done the evil deed and splintered it apart against a tree trunk. When we beat the same team two or three weeks later on our home field, I ran into their shortstop and catcher, two tough hard-noses, on Main Street the following Saturday. They sidled right up to me and waited there glowering, breathing in my face and not saying a word for a while. We stood nostril to nostril until one of them said, "You think you're somethin', don't you, bastid? Beat us at home with your crooked umpires. Next time you come see us we'll whup you till the shit turns green." And they did.

The next summer, when I made the Legion team, I finally came under the tutelage of Gentleman Joe, a hard taskmaster of the old school despite his unfamiliarity with "stragety," as he called it. Gentleman Joe would always have us pray before a game and sometimes between innings when the going got rough. He was a big one for church and began to remind me more and more of my old fourth-grade teacher. But his pep talks, back behind the shabby old grandstand of our playing field, drew on such pent-up emotions, being so full of Scriptures and things of God's earth, that I suspected we were being enlisted not to play baseball but to fight in the Army of the Lord.

That was the team that won the Mississippi championship, beating almost everybody without much trouble. Before the final game for the championship in Greenwood, with 4,000 people waiting in the stands, Gentleman Joe delivered the best speech of all. *"Gentlemen,"* he said, using that staple designation that earned him his nickname, "I'm just a simple farmer. Fifteen acres is all I got, and two mules, a cow, and a lot of mouths to feed." He paused between his words, and his eyes watered over. "I've neglected my little crop because of this team, and the weevils gave me trouble last year, and they're doin' it again now. I ain't had enough rain, and I don't plan to get much more. The corn looks so brown, if it got another shade browner, it'd flake right off. But almost every afternoon you'd find me in my pickup on the way to town to teach you gentlemen the game of baseball. You're fine Christian gentlemen who don't come no finer. But I saw you gettin' a little lazy yestiddy, showin' off some to all them cute little delta girls in the bleachers. We didn't come way up here to show off; we come up here to *win!*" Then, his pale blue eyes flashing fire, half whispering and half shouting, he said: "Gentlemen, I want us to pray, and then . . . I want you to go out there on that field and win this Miss'ippi championship! You'll be proud of it for the rest of your lives. You'll remember it when you're ole men. You'll think about it when you're dyin' and your teeth are all gone. You'll be able to tell your grandchildren about this day. Go out there, gentlemen and *win this ball game for your coach!*" After we prayed and headed for that field like a pack of wild animals, the third baseman and I shouted in unison, and we meant it: "Boys, let's get out and win for our *coach!*" That fall they gave us shiny blue jackets, with "Miss. State Champions" written on the back; I was so happy with that jacket I almost wore it out. And when my old dog Skip died of a heart attack trying to outflank a flea that had plagued him since the Roosevelt administration, looking at me with his sad black eyes and expiring in a sigh as old as death, that is what I wrapped him in before I took him in my arms and put him in the ground.

Two or three years later, when we were past the age for Legion competition, I had my last confrontation with baseball. The owner of the tire store organized a semipro team, made up of college and high school players from around the state. There was a popular tire that year called the "Screaming Eagle," and thus we were the Yazoo "Screaming Eagles," the pride of the delta. Out of a roster of fourteen, one made it to the major leagues, one to a Triple A league, and two to Double A. That team won the Deep South Championship, and at the national tournament in Wichita beat the U.S. Navy and ended up close to the top.

The state league we played in, making $25 or $30 apiece a game, was composed of both delta and hill-country towns, and we played to big Saturday night crowds who had heard about the Screaming Eagles, under lights so faulty that it was difficult to see a ball coming at you in the outfield. Insects bigger than fifty-cent pieces caromed off the bulbs and zoomed around us in our isolated stations in the field, and the ground was full of holes, ruts, and countless other hazards. Playing center field one night in one of the hill towns, I went back to examine a sloping red mound of earth that served as the outfield fence; I discovered a strand of barbed wire 8 or 10 feet long, an old garbage can full of broken beer bottles, and a narrow hole, partially covered with Johnson grass, that looked as if it might be the home for the local rattlers. The most indigenous field of all was near a little delta town called Silver City. It was built right on a cotton field and was owned by the two young heirs to the plantation on which it sat, one of whom later made it all the way to the New York Yankees. The grandstand would seat close to 2,000 people, but the lights were so bad you had to exert all your finer perceptions to discriminate between the bugs and the balls; this took genius and tested one's natural instincts. It was here, in the state finals, that a sinking line drive came toward me in right field, with the bases loaded and two out in the first inning; I lost track of that ball the moment it came out of the infield. A second later I felt a sharp blow on my kneecap, and then I saw the ball bouncing 30 feet away over by the bleachers. "*Get* it, boy! Stomp on it! Piss on it!" the enemy bleacher section shouted gleefully, and by the time I could retrieve it, three runs had scored. Between innings our pitcher, who soon would be pitching in the major leagues for the Pittsburgh Pirates, looked at me wordlessly but with a vicious and despairing contempt. Right then, with the world before me, I promised myself that if I ever made it to those mythical cities of the North, the ones I had dreamed about in my Brooklyn cap, it would have to be with a different set of credentials.

This 1898 newspaper clipping turned up in a dusty scrapbook kept by turn-of-the-century star Cy Seymour. It is a strange story, to be sure, but replete with unexpected pleasures: the refreshingly matter-of-fact (if, to modern sensibilities, brutal) attitude toward disability; the post-playing-career whereabouts of Hugh "One Arm" Daily (here spelled Daly), previously unknown; and the stunningly offhand solution to one of the game's most perplexing mysteries—the origin of the epithet "yannigan," reserved for scrub or second-rate players.

NEW YORK *WORLD*

Armless, Legless Baseball Pitchers

Herbert Van Cleef, of Trenton, N.J., is the baseball wonder of the age. He is a legless pitcher and has as many curves, shoots, drops, snake twisters, and raise curves as even "Si" Seymour, of the Giants, can untangle from his celebrated left "whip."

There have been one-legged catchers, one-armed twirlers, and wooden-headed players galore during the long history of the national game, but Van Cleef tops all the baseball freaks who ever came down the pike.

The most famous cripple who ever played the game was Hugh Daly, better known to patrons of the sport fifteen years or so ago, when he was in his prime, as "One Arm Daly," and "Fin Daly." Daly's left arm was cut off just below the elbow, and when he was pitching, the stump was covered with several layers of chamois skin, topped with hard leather. Daly was a very prominent professional player for many years. He pitched for the Cleveland League Club and many other prominent clubs in both the National League and American Association. He is best remembered by New Yorkers as a pitcher for the old Metropolitans in 1882. He was a star player of that famous band known as "Mutrie's Indians."

Although having just but one hand, Daly was a fair batter and made in his career many long hits. He was one of the wildest Indians of the Mutrie "push." He was a great poker player and could shuffle cards as deftly as the best, and when playing the "paper" with his fellow players, seldom got up from the table without having most of their salaries in his pockets.

309

"Tom" Deasley was "Fin's" catcher and they were a great pair when they did the battery work. "Tom" was about as crazy as they make 'em—"nutty" his associate players said, but "Tom" was as good and game a catcher as ever donned a mask and could handle Daly's terrific speed and curves to the "Queen's taste." The two were the best of friends, and yet they were continually squabbling during a game, only to "blow the froth" amicably together when the game was over.

One incident that happened during a game in Baltimore that the writer witnessed will serve to illustrate the peculiar eccentricities of the pair. Daly's stump was somewhat tender, although well protected, and he was never over anxious to face a hot hit or hard throw. Deasley knew this weakness of his partner and, when not feeling in the best of humor, would throw the ball back to Daly on a line and hard. In this particular game the two had some unusually hot words, and "Tom," to get even, threw several swift balls back to his pitcher. "Arch them, 'Tommy,' arch them!" shouted Daly, but Deasley paid no attention to this plaintive appeal, but continued to send them back on a line. At last Daly held up his finger and, motioning to Deasley, said: "Come here, 'Tommy.' I want to show you a new sign."

The two met midway between the plate and the pitcher's box, and as Deasley leaned forward to hear the instructions, Daly, with a terrific uppercut, landed the stump on the point of Deasley's jaw. Poor "Tom" got the cleanest knockout of his career. The game was played out after "Tom" had been revived, but he "arched" them during the balance of the contest.

Deasley is now in some asylum in Philadelphia, having "gone nutty for fair," and Daly is back at his old business as a scene shifter in a Baltimore theater.

Another cripple who was famous as a ballplayer was "Con" Yannigan, who made a big reputation around Hartford, Connecticut, several years ago. He was a first baseman and had a cork leg. Yannigan was brought out by "Steve" Brady, of the "Old Mets." "Steve" considered him one of the best first basemen he ever saw. A great play of his was to block off base runners with his game leg. Opposing players could sharpen their spikes to a razor edge, but "Con" didn't scare for a cent.

"Charlie" Bennett, the great catcher of the Detroit and Boston champion teams, has both of his legs off, as the result of a railroad accident, but has done no catching since.

So that Van Cleef is, without doubt, the star wonder of the age as a baseball pitcher. He lost his legs in a railroad accident two years ago. Before that unfortunate occurrence Van Cleef was a pitcher of merit. He was captain of a local team in Trenton and acknowledged to be its best player. In fact, he had professional aspirations and no doubt would have become a league player. "Mike" Tiernan, who is a native of Trenton, knew Van Cleef well and had promised to push him forward.

The accident to Van Cleef did not dampen his ardor or enthusiasm as a ballplayer. Just as soon as he had recovered from his injuries, he attended a game. It was between his old team and another local club for the city championship. His team was defeated by reason of the poor work of the pitcher. This was gall and wormwood to Van Cleef. He immediately issued a challenge for a return game, saying he would pitch for his side the next time—and would win, too. He was laughed at and derided, but when the second game came off, Van Cleef was there and in uniform ready to pitch. He was not on his old legs, however, but in a small carriage pushed by his brother.

As the game progressed, it was seen that Van Cleef had retained all of his old curves and speed, and he also worked several new tricks on his opponents. He never pitched a better game, even when he was whole, and his side won, as he said it would. His reputation has become national.

Van Cleef will make his first appearance in this vicinity this afternoon at Standard Park, Fair View, Hudson County, New Jersey. He will pitch for the Standard Athletics against the second team of the Englewood Field Club. Standard Park is 9 miles from the city, on the line of the Northern Railroad of New Jersey. The game is for the benefit of the legless pitcher, and his pluck and gameness are surely entitled to recognition.

The Dean of American Sportswriters was a mere tad when the first three of these Casey sequels were published in *Base-Ball Ballads* (1910). The first he wrote in 1906 and published the following year under the pseudonym James Wilson; the second, Rice declared, was rivaled for pathos only by Goldsmith's *Deserted Village*; the third is a delightful parody of Eugene Field's "The Man Who Worked with Dana on the Noo York Sun"; and the fourth was written years later in amazed response to a letter to the newspaper editor inquiring what exactly *was* "Casey at the Bat." There are many sequels to Ernest Lawrence Thayer's classic original, first published in the San Francisco *Examiner* on June 3, 1888. These include such implausible efforts as "Mrs. Casey at the Bat," "Casey's Daughter at the Bat," and even "Casey—Forty Years Later"!

GRANTLAND RICE

That Man from Mudville

CASEY'S REVENGE

There were saddened hearts in Mudville for a week or even more;
There were muttered oaths and curses—every fan in town was sore.
"Just think," said one, "how soft it looked with Casey at the bat,
And then to think he'd go and spring a bush-league trick like that!"

All his past fame was forgotten—he was now a hopeless "shine."
They called him "Strike-Out Casey," from the mayor down the line;
And as he came to bat each day his bosom heaved a sigh,
While a look of hopeless fury shone in mighty Casey's eye.

He pondered in the days gone by that he had been their king,
That when he strolled up to the plate they made the welkin ring;
But now his nerve had vanished, for when he heard them hoot
He "fanned" or "popped out" daily, like some minor-league recruit.

He soon began to sulk and loaf, his batting eye went lame;
No home runs on the scorecard now were chalked against his name;
The fans without exception gave the manager no peace,
For one and all kept clamoring for Casey's quick release.

The Mudville squad began to slump, the team was in the air;
Their playing went from bad to worse—nobody seemed to care.
"Back to the woods with Casey!" was the cry from Rooters' Row.
"Get someone who can hit the ball and let that big dub go!"

The lane is long, someone has said, that never turns again,
And Fate, though fickle, often gives another chance to men;
And Casey smiled; his rugged face no longer wore a frown—
The pitcher who had started all the trouble came to town.

All Mudville had assembled—ten thousand fans had come
To see the twirler who had put big Casey on the bum;
And when he stepped into the box, the multitude went wild;
He doffed his cap in proud disdain, but Casey only smiled.

"Play ball!" the umpire's voice rang out, and then the game began.
But in that throng of thousands there was not a single fan
Who thought that Mudville had a chance, and with the setting sun
Their hopes sank low—the rival team was leading "four to one."

The last half of the ninth came round, with no change in the score;
But when the first man up hit safe, the crowd began to roar;
The din increased, the echo of ten thousand shouts was heard
When the pitcher hit the second and gave "four balls" to the third.

Three men on base—nobody out—three runs to tie the game!
A triple meant the highest niche in Mudville's hall of fame;
But here the rally ended, and the gloom was deep as night,
When the fourth one "fouled to catcher" and the fifth "flew out to right."

A dismal groan in chorus came; a scowl was on each face
When Casey walked up, bat in hand, and slowly took his place;
His bloodshot eyes in fury gleamed, his teeth were clenched in hate;
He gave his cap a vicious hook and pounded on the plate.

But fame is fleeting as the wind, and glory fades away;
There were no wild and woolly cheers, no glad acclaim this day;
They hissed and groaned and hooted as they clamored: "Strike him out!"
But Casey gave no outward sign that he had heard this shout.

The pitcher smiled and cut one loose—across the plate it sped;
Another hiss, another groan. "Strike one!" the umpire said.
Zip! Like a shot the second curve broke just below the knee.
"Strike two!" the umpire roared aloud; but Casey made no plea.

No roasting for the umpire now—his was an easy lot;
But here the pitcher whirled again—was that a rifle shot?
A whack, a crack, and out through the space the leather pellet flew,
A blot against the distant sky, a speck against the blue.

Above the fence in center field in rapid whirling flight
The sphere sailed on—the blot grew dim and then was lost to sight.
Ten thousand hats were thrown in air, ten thousand threw a fit,
But no one ever found the ball that mighty Casey hit.

Oh, somewhere in this favored land dark clouds may hide the sun,
And somewhere bands no longer play and children have no fun!
And somewhere over blighted lives there hangs a heavy pall,
But Mudville hearts are happy now, *for Casey hit the ball.*

L'envoi

There is no sequel to this plot—except in Mudville's square
The bronze bust of a patriot—arms crossed—is planted there.
His cap is cocked above one eye—and from his rugged face
The sneer still curls above the crowd—across the marketplace.

And underneath, in solid bronze, these words are graved in flame—
"Here is a man who rose and fell—and rose again to fame—
He blew a big one in the pinch—but facing jeering throngs
He came through Hell to scramble back—and prove a champ belongs."

MUDVILLE'S FATE

I wandered back to Mudville, Tom, where you and I were boys
And where we drew in days gone by our fill of childish joys;
Alas! the town's deserted now, and only rank weeds grow
Where mighty Casey fanned the air just twenty years ago.

Remember Billy Woodson's place, where, in the evening's shade,
The bunch would gather and discuss the home runs Casey made?
Dog fennel now grows thick around that "joint" we used to know,
Before old Casey whiffed the breeze some twenty years ago.

The grandstand, too, has been torn down; no bleachers met my gaze
Where you and I were wont to sit in happy bygone days;
The peanuts which we fumbled there have sprouted in a row
Where mighty Casey swung in vain just twenty years ago.

O how we used to cheer him, Tom, each time he came to bat!
And how we held our breath in awe when on the plate he spat;
And when he landed on the ball, how loud we yelped! But O
How loud we cursed when he struck out some twenty years ago!

The diamond is a corn patch now; the outfield's overgrown
With pumpkin vines and weedy plots; the rooters all have flown—
They couldn't bear to live on there, for nothing was the same
Where they had been so happy once before that fatal game.

The village band disbanded soon; the mayor, too, resigned.
The council even jumped its graft and in seclusion pined;
The marshal caught the next train out, and those we used to know
Began to leave in flocks and droves some twenty years ago.

For after Casey fanned that day the citizens all left,
And one by one they sought new lands, heartbroken and bereft;
The joyous shout no more rang out of children at their play;
The village blacksmith closed his shop; the druggist moved away.

Alas for Mudville's vanished pomp when mighty Casey reigned!
Her grandeur has departed now; her glory's long since waned.
Her place upon the map is lost, and no one seems to care
A whit about the old town now since Casey biffed the air.

THE MAN WHO PLAYED WITH ANSON ON THE OLD CHICAGO TEAM

Thar showed up out in Mudville in the spring of '83
A feller evidently just recoverin' from a spree.
He said his name was Casey, and he wuz a sight to view
As he walked into the ballpark and inquired for work to do.
Thar wuzn't any openin', for you should understand
That wuz the time when Mudville had a bunch of stars on hand;
But the stranger lingered, tellin' Mickey Nolan and the rest
What an all-fired battin' av'rage he possessed when at his best,
Till finally he stated, quite by chance, as it would seem,
That he had played with Anson on the old Chicago team.

Wal, that was quite another thing; we owned that any cuss
Who'd played with old Pop Anson must be good enough for us;
So we took Casey at his word and signed him while we could,
Well knowin' if we didn't that some other ball club would,
For Kankakee wuz lookin' round for people that could play,
And Pikeville wouldn't overlook this feller any day;
And we give him quite a contract, tho' it made the others swear,
Sayin' we had done 'em dirty and it wuzn't on the square;
But we laid back and cackled, for the pennant warn't no dream
With the man who'd played with Anson on the old Chicago team.

It made our eyeballs nigh pop out and pop back in again
To hear that Casey tellin' of old Anson and his men;
Why home runs wuz so common that nobody waved a hat,
With Williamson, King Kelly, or Fred Pfeffer at the bat;
A man who didn't hit above .500 couldn't stick
With that old bunch, for Anson would release him mighty quick;
They handled ground balls with their teeth and often shut their eyes

While in the act of pullin' down the longest, hardest flies;
And after all the "fannin' bees" each night we used to dream
Of the man who played with Anson on the old Chicago team.

But somehow this feller Casey never felt like goin' in;
He spent his time at Wilson's shakin' poker dice for gin.
Whenever he wuz needed he wuz always sure to shirk,
Remarkin' he would have to wait before he started work.
If any other gent had loafed the way he used to do,
We'd have fined him fifty dollars every day, and benched him too;
But you see the fans respected him and backed him to the last
On account of his connections with the diamond in the past,
For no one felt like knockin' or handin' out a call
To the man who'd played on Anson's team, the greatest of 'em all.

Wal, finally the climax came—the big test of the year—
And the fans wuz there in bunches from the country far and near,
Especially attracted by the statement made that day
That, having rounded into shape, big Casey wuz to play.
The other nine wuz lookin' kinder worried and upset,
And they wouldn't even listen to an even-money bet.
We kidded 'em and joshed 'em, but no wagerin' wuz done,
Till at last they placed a thousand at the odds of ten to one;
But even at these odds it looked an easy-money scheme,
With the man who'd played with Anson on the old Chicago team.

But Casey never drew a chance to shine in any way;
They handed him a base on balls without the least delay;
The pitcher didn't seem to care to put one over straight
While the man who'd played with Anson was a-standin' at the plate.
He only had one fly in left, which bounded off his head
(It seems the sun was shinin' in his countenance, he said);
And so the people waited in much anger and suspense
For Casey's opportunity to drive one through the fence;
And it came—O yes—it landed with a nauseating rap
For the man who'd played with Anson and referred to him as "Cap."

Old Mudville was a run behind when that last inning came;
The bases full and two wuz out—a hit would win the game.
"He's got to put it over now," each rooter waved his hat,
And shouted in delirium as Casey stepped to bat.
The first two inshoots jumped across the center of the plate,
As Mr. Anson's college chum found out a bit too late;
The next looked good and Casey swung—there came a mighty crack—
But the noise originated from the spine in Casey's back.
In reaching for that outshoot he had wrenched the spinal beam
Of the man who played with Anson on the old Chicago team.

That night we wired Anson to discover if he knew
A man by name of Casey, as we felt we ought to do;
And when the answer came next day it stirred up quite a fuss:
"Yes, I remember Casey well—he carried bats for us."

We hunted for him quite a spell, but he had gone away,
Else the daisies would be bloomin' over his remains today.
But if you land in Mudville on the lookout for some fun,
Don't ever mention Casey's name unless you wear a gun.

HE NEVER HEARD OF CASEY!

I knew a cove who'd never heard of Washington and Lee,
Of Caesar and Napoleon from the ancient jamboree,
But, bli'me, there are queerer things than anything like that,
For here's a cove who never heard of "Casey at the Bat"!

He never heard of Mudville and its wild and eerie call,
"When Flynn let drive a single, to the wonderment of all,"
Nor the stormy roar of welcome that "recoiled upon the flat
As Casey, mighty Casey, was advancing to the bat."

"There was ease in Casey's manner," from the Ernest Thayer style,
"There was pride in Casey's bearing," and his tanned face wore a smile,
And when they thundered "Attaboy!" of course he tipped his hat,
But here's a cove who never heard of "Casey at the Bat"!

"Who is Casey?" Can you beat it? Can a thing like this be true?
Is there one who's missed the drama that ripped Mudville through and through?
Is there a fan with soul so dead he never felt the sway
Of these famous lines by Thayer in the good old Thayer way?

"Ten thousand eyes were on him as he rubbed his hands with dirt;
Five thousand tongues applauded as he wiped them on his shirt;
Then while the writhing pitcher ground the ball into his hip,
Defiance gleamed in Casey's eye, a sneer curled Casey's lip."

The drama grew in force and flame, and berserk went the mob,
With Casey representing more than Hornsby, Ruth, or Cobb;
And as the pitcher cut one loose as if fired from a gat—
Say, here's a guy who never heard of "Casey at the Bat"!

"The sneer is gone from Casey's lip, his teeth are clenched in hate;
He pounds with cruel violence his bat upon the plate."
And as the pitcher shot one through to meet the final test,
There's one low and benighted fan who never heard the rest.

Ten million never heard of Keats, or Shelley, Burns, or Poe;
But they know "the air was shattered by the force of Casey's blow";

They never heard of Shakespeare, nor of Dickens, like as not,
But they know the somber drama from old Mudville's haunted lot.

He never heard of Casey! Am I dreaming? Is it true?
Is fame but windblown ashes when the summer day is through?
Does greatness fade so quickly and is grandeur doomed to die
That bloomed in early morning, ere the dusk rides down the sky?

Is there nothing left immortal in this somber vale called Earth?
Is there nothing that's enduring in its guarding shell of worth?
Is everything forgotten as the new age stumbles on
And the things that we once cherished make their way to helengon?

Is drifting life but dust and dreams to fade within a flash,
Where one forgets the drama of the Master and the Ash?
Where one has missed the saga with its misty flow of tears,
Upon that day of tragedy beyond the tramping years?

"Oh! Somewhere in this favored land the sun is shining bright;
The band is playing somewhere, and somewhere hearts are light;
And somewhere men are laughing, and somewhere children shout,
But there is no joy in Mudville—mighty Casey has struck out!"

Rise, De Wolf Hopper, in your wrath, and cut the blighter down!
Although Wang may be forgotten in the passing of renown,
There's a graver crime committed which should take you to the mat,
For here's a cove who never heard of "Casey at the Bat"!

I had an epic written which I thought would never die,
Where they'd build a statue for me with its head against the sky;
I said "This will live forever"—but I've canned it in the vat,
For here's a guy who never heard of "Casey at the Bat"!

In 1969 the city of Duddy Kravitz became major league, with the expansion of the senior circuit into Montreal (and San Diego). But Montreal and Quebec had long ago shown themselves to be big league in heart with their welcome of black players in first the Provincial League and then the International League, with the Royals. Now if only the Big O could be completed and the team name changed (who remembers the 1967 Exposition, anyway?), there would be no more complaints about this lovely city being bush league.

MORDECAI RICHLER

Up from the Minors in Montreal

Pronouncing on Montreal, my Montreal, Casey Stengel once said, "Well, you see they have these polar bears up there, and lots of fellows trip over them trying to run the bases, and they're never much good anymore except for hockey or hunting deer."

Alas, we have no polar bears up here, but kids can usually heave snowballs at the outfielders at the opening game of the season, and should the World Series ever dare venture this far north, it is conceivable that a game could be called because of a blizzard. Something else. In April, the loudest cheers in the ballpark tend to come when nothing of any consequence seems to have happened on the field, understandably baffling the players on visiting teams. These cheers spring from fans who sit huddled with transistor radios clapped to their ears and signify that something of importance has happened, albeit out of town, where either Guy Lafleur or Pierre Mondou has just scored in a Stanley Cup play-off game.

Baseball remains a popular game here in spite of the Expos, but hockey is the way of life.

Montreal, it must be understood, is a city unlike any other in Canada. Or, come to think of it, the National League. On the average, 8 feet of snow is dumped on us each winter and, whatever the weather, we can usually count on three bank robberies a day here.

This is the city of wonders that gave you Expo in 1967, the baseball Expos a couple of years later, and, in 1976, the Olympic Games, its legacy, among other amazing artifacts, a stadium that can seat or intern, as some have it, 60,000 baseball fans. I speak of the monstrous Big O, where our inept Expos disport themselves in summer, their endearing idea of loading the bases being to have two of their runners on second. Hello, hello. Their notion of striking fear into the heart of the opposition being to confront them with muscle, namely one of their pinch-hitting behemoths coming off the bench: group average, .135.

Major-league baseball, like the Olympics and the Big O itself, was brought to this long-suffering city through the machinations of our very own Artful Dodger, Mayor Jean Drapeau.

Bringing us the Games, he assured Montrealers that it would be as difficult for the Olympics to cost us money as it would be for a man to have a baby. He estimated the total cost of all facilities at $62.2 million but, what with inflation and unfavorable winds, his calculations fell somewhat short of the mark. Counting stationery and long-distance calls, the final cost was $1.2 billion. Never mind. To this day our ebullient mayor doesn't allow that the Games were run at a loss. Rather, as he has put it to the rest of us, there has been a gap between costs and revenue. And, considering the spiffy facilities we have been left with, it would be churlish of us to complain.

Ah, the Big O. The largest, coldest slab of poured concrete in Canada. In a city where we endure seven punishing months of winter and spring comes and goes in an afternoon, it is Drapeau's triumph to have provided us with a partially roofed-over $520 million stadium, where the sun never shines on the fans. Tim Burke, one of the liveliest sportswriters in town, once said to me, "You know, there are lots of summer afternoons when I feel like taking in a ball game, but I think, hell, who wants to sit out there in the dark."

"Shivering in the dark" might be more accurate, watching the boys lose line drives in the seams of the artificial turf.

"The outfield," another wag remarked, "looks just like the kind of thing my aunt used to wear."

Furthermore, come Cap Day or Bat Night ours is the only park in the National League that fills a social office, letting the poor know where to get off, which is to say, the scruffy kids in the bleachers are beyond the pale. They don't qualify.

It's a shame, because the Expos, admittedly major league in name only, came to a town rich in baseball history, and, to begin with, we were all charged with hope. In their opening game, on April 9, 1969, the Expos took the Mets 11–10 at Shea Stadium, collecting three homers and five doubles. Five days later, the 29,184 fans who turned up for the home opener were electrified by an announcement over the public address system. "When the Expos play a doubleheader," we were informed, "the second game will go the full nine innings, not seven."

Those of us old enough to remember baseball's glory here, the Montreal Royals of the old International League, nodded our heads, impressed. This was the big time. "Montreal," said Warren Giles, president of the National League, "is a growing and vibrant city." Yessirree. And we hollered and stamped our feet as our champions took to the field under the grim gaze of manager Gene Mauch, who had the look of a marine drill sergeant.

I still have that incomparably bubbly Opening Day program. *Votre première équipe des ligues majeures.* Vol. 1, No. 1. *Publié par Club de Baseball Montréal Ltée.* "The Expos believe they landed a real prize when they snatched Gary Sutherland from the Philadelphia Phillies. Big things are expected from John Bateman, the former Houston Astros' fine receiver. Bob Bailey impressed everybody with his tremendous hustle. Ty Cline is a two-way player. 'In the field,' said Larry Shepard, manager of the Pittsburgh Pirates, 'Don Bosch can be compared with none other than Willie Mays.' Larry Jaster has youth on his side. This may be the year Don Shaw comes into his own. Angel Hermoso is one of the fine young Expo prospects the scouts have hung a 'can't miss' label on. On a given day, Mike Wegener, only twenty-two, can throw with the best. Don Hahn was a standout performer during spring training. Bob Reynolds's main forte is a blistering fastball. Expansion could be 'just what the doctor ordered' for Coco Laboy."

To be fair, the original Expos included Rusty Staub, sweet Mack Jones, and Bill Stoneman, a surprisingly effective player who pitched two no-hitters before his arm gave out. Manny Mota, another original draft choice, was one of the first to be sent packing by a management that was to become celebrated for its lame-headed dealings, its most spectacular blunder being a trade that sent Ken Singleton and Mike Torrez to Baltimore for a sore-armed Dave McNally and a totally ineffective Rich Coggins. It should also be noted that the Expos did take their home opener, defeating the Cardinals 8–7, and that tiny Parc Jarry, where they were to play, futile in their fashion, for another eight years, was a charming, intimate stadium with the potential to become another Fenway Park.

Opening day, I recognized many of the plump faces in the box seats on the first-base line. Among them were some of the nervy kids who used to skip school with me on weekday afternoons to sit in the left-field bleachers of Delormier Downs, cheering on the Royals and earning nickels fetching hot dogs for strangers. Gone were the AZA windbreakers, the bubble gum, the scuffed running shoes, the pale, wintry faces. These men came bronzed to the ballpark from their Florida condominiums. Now they wore foulards and navy blue blazers with brass buttons; they carried Hudson's Bay blankets in plastic cases for their bejeweled wives; and they sucked on Monte Cristos, mindful not to spill ashes on their Gucci sandals. Above all, they radiated pleasure in their own accomplishments and the occasion. And why not? This was an event, and there they were, inside, looking out at last, right on the first-base line. Look at me. "Give it some soul, Mack," one of them shouted.

An article in that memorable Opening Day program noted that while the province of Quebec had never been known as a hotbed of major-league talent, we had nevertheless produced a few ballplayers, among them pitchers Claude Raymond and Ron Piché, and that three more native sons, Roland Gladu, Jean-

Pierre Roy, and Stan Bréard, had once played for another ball club here, the Montreal Royals.

Oh, I remember the Royals, yes indeed, and if they played in a Montreal that was not yet growing and vibrant, it was certainly a place to be cherished.

Beta Dodd, "The Girl in Cellophane," was stripping at the Gayety, supported by 23 Kuddling Kuties. Cantor Moishe Oysher, the Master Singer of his People, was appearing at His Majesty's. The Johnny Holmes Band, playing at Victoria Hall, featured Oscar Peterson; and a sign in the corner cigar-and-soda warned Ziggy Halprin, Yossel Hoffman, and me that

LOOSE TALK COSTS LIVES!
Keep It Under
Your
STETSON

I first became aware of the Royals in 1943. Our country was already seventy-six years old, I was merely twelve, and we were both at war.

MAY U BOAT SINKINGS EXCEED REPLACEMENTS;
KING DECORATES 625 CANADIANS ON BIRTHDAY

Many of our older brothers and cousins were serving overseas. Others on the street were delighted to discover they suffered from flat feet or, failing that, arranged to have an eardrum punctured by a specialist in such matters.

R.A.F. HITS HARD AT COLOGNE AND HAMBURG
2,000 Tons of Bombs
Rain on Rhine City

On the home front, sacrifices were called for. On St. Urbain Street, where we served, collecting salvage, we had to give up American comic books for the duration. Good-bye, Superman, so long, Captain Marvel. Instead, we were obliged to make do with shoddy Canadian imitations printed in black and white. And such was the shortage of ballplayers that the one-armed outfielder, Pete Gray, got to play for the Three Rivers club on his way to the Browns, and French Canadians, torn from the local sandlots, actually took to the field for our very own Royals: Bréard, Gladu, Roy.

Even in fabled Westmount, where the very rich were rooted, things weren't the same anymore. H.R., emporium to the privileged, enjoined Westmount to "take another step in further aid of the Government's all out effort to defeat aggression!"

HOLT RENFREW ANNOUNCE THAT BEGINNING
JUNE FIRST <u>NO DELIVERIES</u> OF MERCHANDISE
WILL BE MADE ON <u>WEDNESDAYS</u>

This forethought will help H.R. to save many gallons of gasoline . . . and many a tire . . . for use by the government. Moreover, will it not thrill you to think that the nondelivery of your dress on Wednesday will aid in the delivery of a "block-buster" over the Ruhr . . . Naples . . . Berlin . . . and many other places of enemy entrenchment?

Our parents feared Hitler and his panzers, but Ziggy, Yossel, and I were in terror of Branch Rickey and his scouts.

Nineteen thirty-nine was not only the date we had gone to war; it was also the year the management of the Royals signed a contract with Mr. Rickey, making them the No. 1 farm club of the Brooklyn Dodgers. This dealt us young players of tremendous promise, but again and again, come the Dodgers' late-summer pennant drive, the best of the bunch were harvested by the parent team. Before we had even reached the age of puberty, Ziggy, Yossel, and I had learned to love with caution. If after the first death there is no other, an arguable notion, I do remember that each time one of our heroes abandoned us for Ebbets Field, it stung us badly. We hated Mr. Rickey for his voracious appetite. "There has been no mention officially that the Dodgers will be taking Flowers," Lloyd MacGowan wrote in the *Star* on a typical day, "but Rickey was in Buffalo to watch the team yesterday. The Dodgers can't take Flowers without sending down a flinger, but chances are the replacement for the burly lefty will hardly be adequate."

The International League, as we knew it in the forties, its halcyon years, was Triple A and comprised of eight teams: Montreal, Toronto, Syracuse, Jersey City, Newark, Rochester, Baltimore and Buffalo. Newark was the number-one farm team of the Yankees and Jersey City filled the same office for the Giants. But Organized Baseball had actually come to Montreal in 1898, the Royals then fielding a team in the old Eastern League, taking the pennant in their inaugural year. In those days the Royals played in Atwater Park, which could seat 12,000, and from all accounts was a fine and intimate stadium, much like Parc Jarry. During the twenty-one years the Royals played there, they offered Montreal, as sportswriter Marc Thibault recently wrote, *"du baseball parfois excitant, plus souvent qu'autrement, assez détestable,"* the problem being the troubled management's need to sell off their most accomplished players for ready cash. Be that as it may, in 1914, long before we were to endure major league baseball in name only here, George Herman Ruth came to Atwater Park to pitch for the Baltimore Orioles. Two years later, the team folded, a casualty of World War I, and another eleven years passed before the Royals were resuscitated.

It was 1928 when George Tweedy "Miracle Man" Stallings bought the then-defunct Syracuse franchise and built Delormier Downs, a stadium with a 22,000 capacity, at the corner of Ontario and Delormier streets. An overflow crowd of 22,500, including Judge Kenesaw Mountain Landis, was at the opening game, which the Royals won, defeating the fearsome Reading Keystones 7–4. Twelve months later Stallings died. In 1929, not a vintage year for the stock market, the Royals finished fourth. Two years later, Delormier Stadium, like just about everybody, was in deep trouble. There were tax arrears and a heavy bank debt to be settled. The original sponsors resigned.

In the autumn of 1931 a new company was formed by a triumvirate that included a man who had made millions in gas stations, the rambunctious, poker-playing J. Charles-Emile Trudeau, father of our present prime minister. Another associate of the newly formed club, Frank "Shag" Shaughnessy, cunningly introduced the play-off system in 1933 and two years later became the club's general manager. In 1935, fielding a team that included Fresco Thompson, Jimmy Ripple, and Del Bissonette, the Royals won their first pennant since 1898. However, they finished poorly in '37 and '38, and, the following year, Mr. Rickey surfaced, sending in Burleigh Grimes to look after his interests.

Redemption was at hand.

Bruno Betzel came in to manage the team in 1944, the year the nefarious Branch Rickey bought the Royals outright, building it into the most profitable club in all of minor-league baseball, its fans loyal but understandably resentful of the head office's appetite, praying that this summer the Dodgers wouldn't falter in the stretch, sending down for fresh bats, strong arms, just when we needed them most.

The Royals finished first in 1945, and in '46 and '48 they won both the pennant and the Little World Series. They were to win the pennant again in '51 and '52, under Clay Hopper, and the Little World Series in '53, when they were managed by Walter Alston. The Royals fielded their greatest team in 1948, the summer young Duke Snider played here, appearing in seventy-seven games before he was snatched by Mr. Rickey. Others on that memorable team included Don Newcombe, Al Gionfriddo, Jimmy Bloodworth, Bobby Morgan, and Chuck Connors. The legendary Jackie Robinson and Roy Campanella had already come and gone.

Sam Jethroe was here in 1949, and two years later Junior Gilliam was at third, and George Shuba hit twenty home runs. In 1952, our star pitcher was southpaw Tommy Lasorda, the self-styled Bob Feller of the International League. Lasorda pitched his last game for the Royals on July 4, 1960, against Rochester, which seemed to be hitting him at will. Reminiscing recently, Lasorda recalled, "I knew I was in trouble when I saw our manager's foot on the top of the dugout step. If the next guy gets on base, I'm going to be out of there. I turned my back to the hitter and looked up toward the sky. Lord, I said, this is my last game. Get me out of this jam. I make the next pitch, and the guy at the plate hits the damnedest line drive you ever saw. Our third baseman, George Risley, gets the tips of his fingers on it but can't hang on. The ball bloops over his hand, and our shortstop, Jerry Snyder, grabs it. He fires it to Harry Shewman at second base, who relays it to Jimmy Korada at first. Triple play."

A year later the Royals were dissolved, and in 1971 the Delormier Stadium was razed to make way for the Pierre Dupuy School.

*   *   *

On weekday afternoons kids were admitted free into the left-field bleachers, and by the third inning the more intrepid had worked their way down as far as the first-base line. Ziggy, Yossel, and I would sit out there in the sun, cracking peanuts, nudging each other if a ball struck the Miss Sweet Caporal sign, hitting the young lady you-know-where. Another diversion was a porthole in the outfield wall. If a batter hit a ball through it, he was entitled to a two-year supply of Pal Blades. Heaven.

Sunday afternoons the Royals usually played to capacity crowds, but come the Little World Series, fans lined up on the roof of the adjoining Grover Knit-To-Fit Building, and temporary stands were set up and roped off in center field. Consequently, as my cousin Seymour, who used to sit there, liked to boast, "If I get hit on the head, it's a ground-rule home run." After the game, we would spill out of the stadium to find streetcars lined up for a half mile, waiting to take us home.

In 1945, the Royals acquired one of ours, their first Jewish player, Kermit Kitman, a William and Mary scholarship boy. Our loyalty to the team was redoubled. Kitman was a center fielder and an Opening Day story in *La Presse* declared, *"Trois des meilleurs porte-couleurs du Montréal depuis l'ouverture de la saison ont été ses joueurs de champ: Gladu, Kitman, et Yeager. Kitman a exécuté un catch sensationnel encore hier après-midi sur le long coup de Tores à la 8e manche. On les verra tous trois à l'oeuvre cet après-midi contre le Jersey-City lors du programme double de la 'Victoire' au stade de la rue Delormier."*

In his very first time at bat in that opening game against the Skeeters, Kitman belted a homer, something he would not manage again until August. Alas, in the later innings he also got doubled off second. After the game, when he ventured into a barbershop at the corner of St. Catherine and St. Urbain, a man in another chair studied him intently. "Aren't you Kermit Kitman?" he asked.

"Yeah," he allowed, grinning, remembering his homer.

"You son of a bitch, you got doubled off second; it cost me five hundred bucks."

Leadoff hitter for the Royals, Kitman was entitled to lower berth one on all their road trips. Only twenty-two years old but a college boy, he was paid somewhat better than most: $650 monthly for six months of the year. And if the Royals went all the way, winning the Little World Series, he could earn another $1,800. On the road, his hotel bill was paid, and he and the other players were each allowed three bucks a day meal money.

There was yet another sea change in the summer of 1946. After scouting what were then called the Negro Leagues for more than a year, Mr. Rickey brought the first black player into Organized Baseball. So that spring the Royals could not train in the regular park in Daytona, which was segregated, but had to train in Kelly Field instead.

Actually, Jackie Robinson had been signed on October 23, 1945, in the offices of the Royals at Delormier Stadium, club president Hector Racine saying, "Robinson is a good ballplayer and comes highly recommended by the Brooklyn Dodgers. We paid him a good bonus to sign with our club."

The bonus was $3,500, and Robinson's salary was $600 monthly.

"One afternoon in Daytona," Kermit Kitman told me, "I was leadoff hitter and quickly singled. Robinson came up next, laying down a sacrifice bunt and running to first. Stanky, covering the sack, tagged him hard and jock high. Robinson went down, taking a fist in the balls. He was mad as hell, you could see that, but Rickey had warned him, no fights. He got up, dusted himself off, and said nothing. After the game, when he was resting, Stanky came over to apologize. He had been testing his temper, under orders from Rickey."

Kitman, a good glove man, was an inadequate hitter. Brooklyn born, he never got to play there. Following the 1946 season, he was offered a place on the roster of another team in the Dodger farm system but elected to quit the game instead.

The 1946 season opened for the Royals on April 18, with a game in Jersey City. The AP dispatch for that day, printed in the Montreal *Gazette*, ran:

> The first man of his race to play in modern organized baseball smashed a three-run homer that carried 333 feet and added three singles to the Royals' winning 14–1 margin over Jersey City. Just to make it a full day's work, Robinson stole two bases, scored four times and batted in three runs. He was also charged with an error.

Robinson led the International League in hitting that year with a .349 average. He hit 3 home runs, batted in 66 runs, stole 40 bases, scored 113 runs, and fielded .985 at his second-base position. And, furthermore, Montreal adored him, as no other ballplayer who has been here before or since. No sooner did Robinson reach first base, on a hit or a walk, than the fans roared with joy and hope, our hearts going out to him as he danced up and down the base path, taunting the opposing pitcher with his astonishing speed.

We won the pennant that year and met the Louisville Colonels, another Dodger farm club, in the Little World Series. The series opened in Louisville, where Robinson endured a constant run of racial insults from the Colonels' dugout and was held to a mere single in two games. Montreal evened the series at home and returned to Delormier Downs for the seventh and deciding game. "When they won it," Dick Bacon recently wrote, recalling that game in the 200th anniversary issue of the *Gazette*, "Jackie was accorded an emotional send-off unseen before or since in this city.

"First they serenaded him in true French Canadien spirit with '*Il a gagné ses Epaulettes*' and then clamored for his reappearance on the field.

"When he finally came out for a curtain call, the fans mobbed him. They hugged him, kissed him, cried, cheered, and pulled and tore at his uniform while parading him around the infield on their shoulders.

"With tears streaming down his face, Robinson finally begged off in order to shower, dress, and catch a plane to the States. But the riot of joy wasn't over yet.

"When he emerged from the clubhouse, he had to bull his way through the waiting crowd outside the stadium. The thousands of fans chased him down Ontario Street for several blocks before he was rescued by a passing motorist and driven to his hotel.

"As one southern reporter from Louisville, Kentucky, was to write afterward:

" 'It's probably the first time a white mob of rioters ever chased a Negro down the streets in love rather than hate.' "

That was a long time ago.

I don't know whatever became of Red Durrett. Marvin Rackley, of whom Mr. Rickey once said, "I can see him in a World Series, running and hitting," has also disappeared. Roland Gladu, who got to play twenty-one games with the old Boston Braves, failed to sign the major-league skies with his ability. Robinson died in 1972, and last season a plaque to his memory was installed in the chilly Big O. Jean-Pierre Roy now does the French-language broadcasts for the Expos, and a graying but still impressive Duke Snider is also back, doing the color commentary for Expo games on CBC-TV, trying his best to be kind to an uninspired bunch without compromising himself.

The Expos have yet to play .500 ball or, since Mack Jones's brief sojourn here, come up with a player that the fans can warm to. But there is hope. Next year, or maybe five years from now, the Big O will be completed. The retractable roof will be set in place. And, in this city of endless winter and short hot summers, it will be possible to watch baseball played under a roof, on artificial grass, in an air-conditioned, possibly even centrally heated, concrete tomb.

Progress.

Before the advent of free agency, the ironclad reserve clause made the baseball player a chattel, to be bought and sold regardless of his wishes and denied access to any potential employer but his current one. When it came time to negotiate a salary, the owner's ultimate bargaining position was to say, "Play for me at the wage I offer or play for no one"; the only leverage the player had was to (1) jump his contract and hook on with a rival league—which in this century was only briefly a real option, (2) hold out and hope to pressure management, or (3) play for no one. Edd Roush, a hardheaded and independent man, on separate occasions did all three. This is a chapter from the incomparable *The Glory of Their Times.*

LAWRENCE S. RITTER

Edd Roush Remembers

"Who is he, anyhow, an actor?"

"No."

"A dentist?"

". . . No, he's a gambler." Gatsby hesitated, then added coolly: *"He's the man who fixed the World Series back in 1919."*

"Fixed the World Series?" I repeated.

The idea staggered me. I remembered, of course, that the World Series had been fixed in 1919, but if I had thought of it at all I would have thought of it as a thing that merely happened, *the end of some inevitable chain. It never occurred to me that one man could start to play with the faith of fifty million people—with the single-mindedness of a burglar blowing a safe.*

"How did he happen to do that?" I asked after a minute.

"He just saw the opportunity."

"Why isn't he in jail?"

"They can't get him, old sport. He's a smart man."

F. SCOTT FITZGERALD, *The Great Gatsby*

Yes, I knew at the time that some finagling was going on. At least that's what I'd heard. Rumors were flying all over the place that gamblers had got to the Chicago White Sox, that they'd agreed to throw the World Series. But nobody knew anything for sure until Eddie Cicotte spilled the beans a year later.

We beat them in the first two games 9–1 and 4–2, and it was after the second game that I first got wind of it. We played those first two games in Cincinnati, and the next day we were to play in Chicago. So the evening after the second game we were all gathered at the hotel in Cincinnati, standing around waiting for cabs to take us to the train station, when this fellow came over to me. I didn't know who he was, but I'd seen him around before.

"Roush," he says, "I want to tell you something. Did you hear about the squabble the White Sox got into after the game this afternoon?" And he told me some story about Ray Schalk accusing Lefty Williams of throwing the game, and something about some of the White Sox beating up a gambler for not giving them the money he'd promised them.

"They didn't get the payoff," he said, "so from here on they're going to try to win."

I didn't know whether this guy made it all up or not. But it did start me thinking. Later on in the Series the same guy came over to me again.

"Roush," he says, "you remember what I told you about gamblers getting to the White Sox? Well, now they've also got to some of the players on your own ball club."

That's all he said. Wouldn't tell me any more. I didn't say anything to anybody until we were getting dressed in the clubhouse the next day. Then I got hold of the manager, Pat Moran, just before the pregame meeting.

"Before you start this meeting, Pat," I said, "there's something I want to talk to you about."

"Okay," he says, "what is it?"

"I've been told that gamblers have got to some of the players on this club," I said. "Maybe it's true, and maybe it isn't. I don't know. But you sure better do some finding out. I'll be damned if I'm going to knock myself out trying to win this Series if somebody else is trying to throw the game."

Pat got all excited and called Jake Daubert over, who was the team captain. It was all news to both of them. So at the meeting, after we'd gone over the White Sox lineup, Moran looked at Hod Eller, who was going to pitch for us that day.

"Hod," he said, "I've been hearing rumors about sellouts. Not about you, not about anybody in particular, just rumors. I want to ask you a straight question, and I want a straight answer."

"Shoot," says Hod.

"Has anybody offered you anything to throw this game?"

"Yep," Hod said. Lord, you could have heard a pin drop.

"After breakfast this morning a guy got on the elevator with me and got off at the same floor I did. He showed me five thousand-dollar bills and said they were mine if I'd lose the game today."

"What did you say?" Moran asked him.

"I said if he didn't get damn far away from me real quick he wouldn't know what hit him. And the same went if I ever saw him again."

Moran looked at Eller a long time. Finally, he said, "Okay, you're pitching. But one wrong move and you're out of the game."

Evidently there weren't any wrong moves. Because ol' Hod went out there and pitched a swell game. He won two of the games in that Series.

I don't know whether the whole truth of what went on there among the White Sox will ever come out. Even today nobody really knows exactly what took place. Whatever it was, though, it was a dirty rotten shame. One thing that's always overlooked in the whole mess is that we could have beat them no matter what the circumstances!

Sure, the 1919 White Sox were good. But the 1919 Cincinnati Reds were *better*. I'll believe that till my dying day. I don't care how good Chicago's Joe Jackson and Buck Weaver and Eddie Cicotte were. *We* had Heinie Groh, Jake Daubert, Greasy Neale, Rube Bressler, Larry Kopf, myself, and the best pitching staff in both leagues. We were a very underrated ball club.

I played center field for that Cincinnati club for eleven straight years, 1916 through 1926. I came to Cincinnati from the Giants in the middle of 1916, along with Christy Mathewson and Bill McKechnie.

Of course I started playing ball long before that, around 1909 or so, right here in Oakland City, Indiana. In those days every little town had an amateur club, and so did Oakland City. Never will forget it. I was only about sixteen at the time. Oakland City had a game scheduled with a neighboring town this day, and one of Oakland City's outfielders hadn't shown up. Everybody was standing around right on the main street of town—only a small town, you know—wondering what to do, when one of the town officials says, "Why not put that Roush kid in?"

I was kind of a shy kid, and I backed away. But the manager says, "Well, that's just what we'll do if he don't show up in five more minutes."

We waited for five minutes, and the outfielder never did show, so they gave me a uniform and put me in right field. Turned out I got a couple of hits that day, and I became Oakland City's regular right fielder for the rest of the season.

The next year, of course, I was right in the middle of it. We reorganized the team—the Oakland City Walk-Overs, that's what we called ourselves—and had a pretty good club. In those days, you know, I used to throw with *either* hand. I'm a natural lefty, see, but when I was a kid, I never could find a lefty's glove. So I just used a regular glove and learned to throw righty. Batted lefty but got so I could throw with my right arm almost as well as with my left.

The year after that we got in quite a hassle. That would be 1911. Seems as though some of the Oakland City boys were getting $5 a game, and I wasn't one of them. So I started raising Cain about this under-the-table business and treating some different than others.

Wound up we had such an argument that I quit the hometown club and went over and played with the Princeton team. Princeton is the closest town to Oakland City, about 12 miles due west. And don't think that didn't cause quite a ruckus. Especially when Princeton came over to play Oakland City *at* Oakland City, with me in the Princeton outfield. A fair amount of hard feelings were stirred up, to say the least. I think there are still one or two around here never have forgiven me to this very day.

I played with Princeton about a year and a half, and then a fellow connected with the Evansville club in the Kitty League asked me would I like to play for them in professional baseball. Well, Evansville's only about 30 miles from Oakland City, almost due south, and the idea of getting paid for playing ball sounded real good to me. And Dad thought it was terrific. He'd played semipro ball himself, when he was young. William C. Roush was his name. A darn good ballplayer, too. So I signed with Evansville and finished the 1912 season with them.

I bought a lefty's glove when I started playing with Evansville, figuring I might as well go back to the natural throw. From then on I always threw left-handed, 'cause it didn't carry quite so well when I threw with my right. Wasn't really a natural throw.

After that, things moved quick. Evansville sold me to the Chicago White Sox—of all teams, considering what happened later—in the middle of the following season. I stayed with them a month—Cicotte was there then, and Buck Weaver and Ray Schalk—and then they optioned me to Lincoln, Nebraska, in the Western League.

The next year the Indianapolis club in the new Federal League got in touch with me and offered me $225 a month, almost twice what I was getting at Lincoln. So I jumped to the Federal League for the next couple of years. That Federal League wasn't a bad league. Too bad it only lasted two years. Ran into a lot of financial troubles and folded in December of 1915. Of course, it was an outlaw league, you know, raiding the other leagues for its players. The established leagues threatened that anybody who jumped to the Feds would never be allowed back in organized ball, but once the Feds broke up, they were glad to get us.

We had some good players there the two years the Federal League lived. A lot of old-timers jumped over, like Three-Fingered Brown, Chief Bender, Eddie Plank, Davy Jones, Joe Tinker, Jimmy Delahanty, Al Bridwell, and Charlie Carr, the old Indianapolis first baseman. They didn't care if Organized Ball never took them back, 'cause they were near the end of the trail, anyway.

But there were also a lot of younger players, like Benny Kauff, Bill Mc-Kechnie, and myself. All three of us were sold to the New York Giants when the Federal League collapsed, and that's where we reported in the spring of 1916.

Me, I didn't like New York. I'm a small-town boy. I like the Midwest. Well, it wasn't *exactly* that. Not entirely, anyway. It was really McGraw I didn't like. John J. McGraw. I just didn't enjoy playing for him, that's all. If you made a bad play, he'd cuss you out, yell at you, call you all sorts of names. That didn't go with me. So I was glad as I could be when he traded me to Cincinnati in the middle of the '16 season. I couldn't have been happier.

McGraw traded Mathewson, McKechnie, and me to Cincinnati for Wade Killefer and Buck Herzog, who had been the Cincinnati manager. Matty was to replace Herzog as the new manager. I still remember the trip the three of us made as we left the Giants and took the train to join the Reds. McKechnie and I were sitting back on the observation car, talking about how happy we were to be traded. Matty came out and sat down and listened, but he didn't say anything.

Finally I turned to him and said, "Well, Matty, aren't you glad to be getting away from McGraw?"

"I'll tell you something, Roush," he said. "You and Mac have only been on the Giants a couple of months. It's just another ball club to you fellows. But I was with that team for sixteen years. That's a mighty long time. To me, the Giants are 'home.' And leaving them like this, I feel the same as when I leave home in the spring of the year.

"Of course, I realize I'm through as a pitcher. But I appreciate McGraw making a place for me in baseball and getting me this managing job. He's doing me a favor, and I thanked him for it. And by the way, the last thing he said to me was that if I put you in center field, I'd have a great ballplayer. So starting tomorrow you're my center fielder."

Well, we got to Cincinnati, and sure enough, right off Matty puts me in center field. Greasy Neale was the right fielder. It was his first year with the Reds, too, but he'd been there since the start of the season and, of course, I was a newcomer. The first game I played there, about three or four fly balls came out that could have been taken by either the center fielder or the right fielder. If I thought I should take it, I'd holler three times: "I got it, I got it, I got it." I'd holler while I was running for it, see.

But Greasy never said a word. Sometimes he'd take it, and sometimes he wouldn't. But in either case he never said a thing. We went along that way for about three weeks. What I finally did was watch *both* him and the ball. If it looked to me like I could catch the ball and get out of his way, I'd holler and take it. But if it looked like it was going to be a tie, I'd just cut behind him and let him take it. He still never hollered and didn't have too much else to say to me, either. So I didn't have too much to say to him.

You see, I could watch both him and the ball at the same time because I didn't really have to watch the ball. As soon as a ball was hit, I could tell where it was going to go, and I'd just take off and not look at it anymore till I got there. So I'd take a quick glance at him while I was running.

Finally, one day Greasy came over and sat down beside me on the bench. "I want to end this, Roush," he says to me. "I guess you know I've been trying to run you down ever since you got here. I wanted that center-field job for myself, and I didn't like it when Matty put you out there. But you can go get a ball better than I ever could. I want to shake hands and call it off. From now on, I'll holler."

And from then on Greasy and I got along just fine. Grew to be two of the best friends ever. In fact, I made a lot of good friends those years I played in Cincinnati, still my close friends to this day. I think that Cincinnati club from 1916 to 1926 was one of the nicest bunch of fellows ever gathered together.

We even had Jim Thorpe there one year, you know. By thunder, there was a man could outrun a deer. Beat anything I ever saw. I used to be pretty fast myself. Stole close to 300 bases in the Big Leagues. And I had a real long stride, for the simple reason that in the outfield if you don't take a long stride your head bobs up and down too much and makes it hard to follow the flight of the ball. But Jim Thorpe would take only two strides to my three. I'd run just as hard as I could, and he'd keep up with me just trotting along.

One day I asked him, "Jim, anybody in those Olympic Games ever make you really run your best?"

"I never yet saw the man I couldn't look back at," he says to me. I believed him.

Well, sir, I really hit my own stride those years in Cincinnati. Led the league in batting twice, hit over .350 three years in a row—'21, '22, and '23—and generally had a ball. The lowest I ever hit while I was there was .321 in 1919, and that was good enough to lead the league that year. We won the pennant and the World Series in 1919 and finished either first, second, or third in seven of the eleven years I was there. Good teams—very much underrated. Like I say, *better* than the 1919 White Sox.

Of course, I hit very different from the way they hit today. I used a 48-ounce bat, heaviest anyone ever used. It was a shorter bat, with a big handle, and I tried to hit to all fields. Didn't swing my head off, just snapped at the ball. Until 1921, you know, they had a dead ball. Well, the only way you could get a home run was if the outfielder tripped and fell down. The ball wasn't wrapped tight, and lots of times it'd get mashed on one side. I've caught many a ball in the outfield that was mashed flat on one side. Come bouncing out there like a jumping bean. They wouldn't throw it out of the game, though. Only used about three or four balls in a whole game. Now they use sixty or seventy.

Another thing that's different now is the ballparks. Now they have smooth infields and outfields that aren't full of rocks, and they keep them nice. Back in the old days there were parks weren't much better than a cow pasture. Spring training was the worst. Some of those parks they'd want you to play exhibition games in had outfields like sand dunes, and others were hard as a cement sidewalk. The hell with that! I wouldn't go to spring training, that's all.

I used to hold out every year until the week before the season opened. That's the only time they ever had any trouble with me, contract time. Why should I go down there and fuss around in spring training? Twist an ankle or break a leg. I did my *own* spring training, hunting quail and rabbits around Oakland City.

After eleven years with the Reds, they traded me to the Giants for George Kelly. That was after the 1926 season. Well, I figured that was it. I was around thirty-four, and I wasn't about to start taking abuse from McGraw that late in life. However, I figured I had one chance: maybe I could get McGraw to trade me.

So in January of '27, when the Giants sent me a contract for $19,000, same as I'd been getting in Cincinnati, I sent it right back and wrote them I wouldn't play in New York. A couple of weeks later another one arrived, calling for $20,000. I figured they hadn't gotten the point. So I wrote a letter telling them I wouldn't play with the Giants for *any* kind of money. And wouldn't you know it, two weeks after that another contract arrived, calling for $21,000. I didn't even bother to send that one back.

Since they didn't seem to get the point the way I was doing it, I finally wrote and said I wanted $30,000. I figured that would sink in and they'd get the idea. Send me to another club.

Well, spring training started—and ended—and the team began to move up north, playing exhibition games along the way. I was still busy hunting quail right here around Oakland City. Then one day I got a call from McGraw. Would I meet him in Chattanooga next week? After thinking it over, I decided I might as well.

I arrived at the hotel in Chattanooga at eight o'clock on a Thursday morning, and when I registered, the clerk said to me, "Mr. McGraw left a message for you to come up to his room as soon as you arrive."

Well, it was eight o'clock, and I hadn't had any breakfast. So I went into the dining room and ordered a good meal. About nine o'clock a bellboy comes over and says, "Mr. McGraw would like to see you in room 305."

"All right," I says, "tell him I'll be there."

About that time the ballplayers started to drift in, so I visited with them awhile. One of them gave me a good cigar, so I sat down in a comfortable chair in the lobby and talked to some of the boys while I enjoyed it. About eleven o'clock one of the coaches came over. "McGraw wants to know why you're not up there yet?"

Finally, by about twelve-thirty or so, after I'd finished visiting with the ballplayers, completed a detailed reading of three newspapers, and had a haircut and a shoeshine, I decided to go upstairs and see Mr. John J. McGraw.

"What the devil's the matter with you, Roush?" he says. "Don't you want to play ball for me?"

"Hell, no," I said. "I don't want to play ball for you. Haven't you figured that out by now?"

"Why not?"

" 'Cause I don't like the way you treat your players, that's why. First time you call me a damn so-and-so, somebody's going to get hurt."

"Listen, we'll get along fine. Don't you worry," he says.

"Yeah. I've heard that one before."

"Sit down," he says, "and listen to me. You know this game as well as I do. You play your own game and I'll never say anything to you."

"That's another one I've heard before."

"Well," he says, "it's the truth."

"The first time something happens out there and you start on me," I said, "I'm taking off for Oakland City, Indiana. Why don't we stop all this horsing around and you just send me to another ball club?"

"I won't do it," he says. "I've been trying to get you back ever since I traded you away a long time ago. Now you're either going to play for me or you're not going to play ball at all. I'm sure not going to let you go a second time."

"Okay," I said, "if that's the way you feel about it. If you give me my salary, I'll try it. But I still say I'll be back in Oakland City, Indiana, in ten days."

"How much do you want?"

"Twenty-five thousand dollars."

"I can't pay it."

Well, I took my hat and started for the door. "Where do you think you're going?" he says.

"Back to Oakland City, Indiana. Why?"

"Now hold on," he says. "Come back and sit down. I'll tell you what I'll do. I'll give you a three-year contract for seventy thousand."

"All right," I said, "I'll take it."

I signed the contract, went out to the ballpark, got into a uniform, and played six innings that afternoon. Got two hits out of three times up, too.

I played that three-year contract out, and after that I quit and finally did come back to Oakland City, Indiana. McGraw kept to his word and never bothered me. But it wasn't like playing in Cincinnati. I missed my teammates, and I missed the Cincinnati fans.

I've read where as far as the Cincinnati fans are concerned I'm the most popular player ever wore a Reds' uniform. I don't know about that. It's not for me to say. But—assuming it's true—I'll tell you one thing: the feeling is mutual.

I have included this essay only to demonstrate how an always entertaining and otherwise enlightened writer can overcome a glaring perceptual disability and achieve national standing as a pundit. Mr. Rooney might benefit from reading George Will's contribution to this volume.

ANDY ROONEY

Real Men Don't Wear Knickers

David Fisher has made me mad . . . not angry, mad. Angry isn't a strong enough word for what I am at David Fisher.

David Fisher, who writes baseball books, wrote an article saying the Super Bowl is only important because it means the baseball spring training season is four weeks away.

The time has come for football fans to face baseball fans . . . face-to-face. We might as well come out with it. The taste and mentality of the average baseball fan—and there is no more average group of people anywhere—is best expressed in the old song:

"Buy me some peanuts and Cracker Jack
I don't care if I never get back."

Baseball is a pleasant little game, but to compare it to football is to compare tiddlywinks with chess. Baseball is known as "the national pastime," and that's fitting. It appeals to people on whose hands time hangs heavy. (I can't help noting here that our last several presidents have been calling the winners' locker room after the Super Bowl in place of throwing out the first ball on opening day of baseball.)

Fisher, referring to football, asks, "What kind of ball game is it that allows most of the players to go through an entire season without ever touching the ball?"

Football is not handball, Mr. Fisher. The game's tactility involves people touching people and moving them from one place to the other or to the ground.

Football is a game that employs every physical and mental attribute known to man and a few known to woman.

It would be interesting if the National Football League and major-league baseball could organize an off-season contest between all the players in both sports that would allow us to compare the IQ of all baseball players with that of all football players. Or perhaps it could be limited to the coaches and managers. Any game in which Billy Martin is hired to tell the players what to do because he's smarter than they are must have a lot of dumb players.

Baseball fans are often Democrats who voted for Ronald Reagan. They are people whose idea of a good time is to sit out in the hot sun, drinking warm beer from a paper cup while watching grown men in baggy knickers try to hit a ball with a stick. A player who hits the ball three out of every ten times he tries is said to be "hitting .300." He's hitting .300 what? I suppose it doesn't sound like enough to say a player is "hitting thirty percent."

Fisher notes that Phil Niekro, a pitcher, will be playing the game again this year at age forty-seven. It's nice for Niekro, and I approve of being nice to the elderly, my peer group, but if a man forty-seven years old can still play the game at the highest level, it cannot be a very demanding game. There is no other sport in which that happens. If it were possible, Muhammad Ali would still be heavyweight boxing champion at forty-four; Joe Namath would still be the Jets quarterback at forty-two; and Swaps would be running in the Derby again this year.

The two baseball leagues have different rules. One of them lets a tenth player try to hit the pitched ball in place of one of the regular players. He's called "the DH," meaning "designated hitter." Last year the designated hitter for Seattle, Gorman Thomas, came to bat 484 times and missed the ball 380 times. It seems to me he's more like a DM, designated misser.

What they call a baseball "glove" bears about as much relationship to a human hand as snowshoes bear to a man's feet. It's not a glove; it's a leather basket. Of course they can catch a ball that comes anywhere near them with it.

I do not hate baseball fans. Pity I feel, yes, but not hate. Quite the contrary. I believe the federal government should make every effort to see that baseball fans are accorded equal rights with the more fortunate among us. It's not their fault that they got in with a bad crowd when they were young.

The novel that supplies this exciting passage won the 1984 Edgar Allan Poe Award for best first mystery. The struggling Providence Jewels have a killer in the clubhouse. Relief pitcher Rudy Furth has been found dead in the whirlpool, leaving whispers about underworld entanglements and violently lovesick groupies. Center fielder Harvey Blissberg, playing private eye, has figured out that Rudy—at the behest of Frances, his mob-connected lover—was dumping games that pitcher Bobby Wagner started. Here Blissberg confronts Wagner in the locker room and tells him a thing or two he knows about Frances.

R. D. ROSEN

Strike Three, You're Dead

". . . She's smart, Wags. She knows you're a streak pitcher. Most of those streaks have been winning ones, but she knew that—when was it, Wags, three years ago?—she knew that even when you went something like twenty and thirteen that season, eight of those losses were in a row. She realized that you only knew how to win, not how to lose. She knew that if she got Rudy to throw a few games, you might do the rest of the damage yourself. That was one of the reasons your old manager didn't like you, wasn't it? You didn't bounce back when you lost.

"And Rudy was only a decent relief pitcher, so he could come in and throw a few pitches just fast enough to cost you the game, and no one would ever think he was in the tank. But Frances didn't know when to stop. She gave you a chance to prove you were a little smarter than she gave you credit for. She threw Rudy in the tank once too often, and you smelled it."

Harvey watched the minute hand on the clock over Bobby's shoulder twitch from 5:29 to 5:30.

"What do you care about any of it?" Bobby said evenly. "He was a punk, Professor. He was trash. Why didn't you leave it alone? What did it matter to you?"

"It mattered."

"I never did anything to him."

"That's not how it works."

"He screwed with my career. He screwed with the biggest thing I've got."

"Frances did, not Rudy. Frances did it to you."

"And you were about to screw me even more, Professor." Bobby came two steps closer and stopped, 6 feet away.

Harvey pushed away from the desk in his chair. "I didn't know what I was going to find. I was just looking."

"I wish I could help you, Professor."

"Don't be a fool. Put that bat down."

"He hit me first." Bobby's voice was unnervingly soft. "He wouldn't tell me. Then I found the money, and I couldn't believe it. It was sitting in his pocket, and he still wouldn't admit anything. He just sat in the whirlpool with that shit-eating grin and said he always carried a lot of cash. You get that, Professor? He always carried around a few big bills like that. That's when it got serious." He tapped the head of Harvey's bat against the indoor-outdoor carpeting. "He got out of the whirlpool and shoved me."

"Put the bat down, Wags."

"I didn't have the bat with me then." Bobby appeared almost hypnotized. "Just wanted to talk it out. Then he came at me, and we mixed it up, and he shoved me against the bat rack and—"

"It's going to be all right, Wags." Harvey felt his heart pounding in his neck.

Bobby came forward another step. "It's too late," he said. "It's much too late. I thought you'd understand about the rat. That was strike one." He now held the bat in front of him horizontally, one hand on each end. "Then I left you a message in Yankee Stadium. Why didn't you pay attention? Strike two, Professor."

He slid the hand that was on the head of the bat down to join the other on the handle. "Now this." He looked down at the thick book of statistics on Felix's desk. "Now you know too much. And you know what they say. Strike three you're dead."

"Goddam it, you—"

Bobby swung the bat back over his head like an ax and brought it down.

Harvey grabbed the statistics book just in time and held it up with both hands in front of his face, twisting his head as far to the side as he could. The force of the bat flattened the book against his shoulder and carried Bobby's body forward on top of Harvey.

Before Bobby could recover his balance, Harvey speared him in the groin with an outstretched leg, leaped from the chair, and dashed for Felix's door. He ran across the locker room toward the runway that led to the dugout.

The metal door swung outward, and Harvey jumped down the three cement steps to the runway. Ahead of him, a square of morning light showed the dugout and a section of the left-field stands against pink sky.

Bobby came down the steps after him. For an instant, Harvey thought about running up onto the field, but it was Bobby's running shoes against his penny loafers, Bobby's bat against his bare hands. Halfway down the runway, Harvey took a left and pushed open the door to the unused network of tunnels that ran under the stands. He kicked off his loafers in stride and took off into the darkness.

The floor of the tunnel was damp, and Harvey's socks were soaked through within a few steps. The tunnel was about 6 feet wide, dark green walls with rashes of rust, but then the light from the runway faded, and Harvey was running in total darkness. Behind him, Wagner's shoes slapped soddenly, too infrequently to be a run.

"Take your time, Professor. There's nowhere to go." The voice surrounded him.

Harvey slowed, lowering his feet into the cool puddles on the cold concrete. He reached out with his right hand, felt for the oily wall, and followed its gentle curve. They were behind home plate somewhere, and the tunnel followed the contour of the stands. He had never been in the catacombs. He knew there were connecting tunnels but couldn't be sure they weren't dead ends. The main tunnel had to feed out somewhere, probably near the visitors' clubhouse under the stands on the third-base line. That still wouldn't do him any good; the door to the clubhouse would be locked from the outside. He had been stupid not to run onto the field when he had the chance; there, at least, he could have seen what his chances were.

With his left hand, he reached out for the other wall, hoping to find an alcove, a doorway, anything. The tunnel wasn't narrow enough for him to feel both walls at the same time. For all he knew, he had already missed a connecting tunnel. Maybe he could crouch down against one side of the tunnel and hope that Wagner would walk right past him. Then he could run back to the clubhouse and out to the street.

His foot came down on a piece of paper.

"There you are," Wagner's voice said close behind him, and Harvey broke into a run again, dragging a hand along the wall.

"He was just a punk, Professor. He never belonged in the big leagues." The voice was soft and deep as it reverberated down the passage. "Your roomie was a nothing."

After every two slaps of Wagner's feet came a harder noise, the bat tapping against the concrete.

Abruptly, there was no wall at Harvey's right hand. He moved quickly into the opening and saw a hairline of light ahead. After 10 or 12 yards, he found a doorknob that turned, but not easily; it felt as if it would squeak if he twisted it too far. He leaned against the corner of the passageway and caught his breath in a series of silent heaves. He heard Wagner walk past the opening, his bat clicking.

The door probably connected the catacombs to the near end of the visitors' dugout. In that case, the central tunnel would have to end soon, where it met the runway that ran from the far end of the dugout to the clubhouse. Seventy, maybe 80 feet. Wagner would know shortly that he had lost Harvey.

Wagner's footfalls suddenly became faster and louder. Harvey turned the doorknob and pulled on the heavy door. It let out a thin screech. Light flooded the passageway. Harvey found himself where he had expected, at the end of the dugout between the end of the bench and the water cooler against the wall. Just below eye level was Rankle Park's grass. The sky was as soft as tissue, infused with pink over the stands.

Harvey leaped onto the end of the bench by the door and pressed himself against the back wall of the dugout. Wagner appeared suddenly, carelessly, in the doorway. He took a step toward the dugout steps, where he stopped, like a man whose peripheral vision was burdened. He turned and raised the bat. Harvey jumped off the bench and grabbed the shaft of the bat with both hands and brought his knee up into Wagner's gut. Wagner vomited air and doubled over. When he straightened up, Harvey had the bat and was standing on the grass at the lip of the dugout.

"You tried to kill me, you bastard." Harvey, panting, held the bat over his head.

Below him, Wagner clasped his hands over his stomach. His black hair was matted in wild curls on his forehead. "What happens now, Professor?" he said between gasps.

"Just go home."

"There's nothing in it for me."

"There's nothing in it for you here."

"There's you, Professor."

"The bat's mine now," Harvey said, but Wagner had seen the ball bag near his feet. It was the size of a bowling-ball bag, made of canvas, and it was filled with baseballs for batting practice. The Yankees must have left it in the dugout after Saturday's game. Wagner picked it up in his left hand, reached in for a baseball with his right, and started up the steps.

"I used to be pretty good at this," Wagner said, squeezing the ball.

Harvey retreated a few steps, waving his bat. "You're crazy, Wags," he screamed. "I'll hurt you if I—have to."

"You just had your chance."

Harvey backpedaled on the grass in foul territory. "I'll hurt you."

"No, you won't." Wagner bounced the baseball lightly in his right hand. "I'll take this bag of balls against your bat."

Harvey turned and ran toward the infield. From a distance of 60 feet, 6 inches, any major-league pitcher could nail a target the size of a human head; Bobby Wagner could put it right in your ear. There were two ways to go after a batter. If you only wanted to scare him, you aimed the ball directly at his head, because he would instinctively fall away from the pitch. But if you really wanted to hurt him, you would throw your best fastball a foot or so behind his head, and he would fall back into it. As Harvey ran, he saw it happening again and again— the batter involuntarily throwing himself, as if magnetized, into the path of a perfectly aimed beanball. If the batter was lucky enough to get his batting helmet between his cranium and the ball, he'd be able to get up and play ball again. If he wasn't, it was a most unnpleasant way to end a baseball career.

Harvey was not wearing a batting helmet. Of course, he was a moving target. But then, he only had 30 feet on Wagner, and Wagner had a bagful of baseballs. Harvey bobbed and weaved as he ran to give Wagner less to throw at.

He was about to look to see where Wagner was when the first ball combed his hair above his left ear. He heard it sizzle as it flew by and rolled out to right field. Now he looked back and saw Wagner 40 feet behind him, running, dipping into the bag for another ball. Harvey veered right. Wagner had to stop to throw again, and by the time he released the ball, Harvey was 60 feet away, near second base.

The ball struck him in the meat of his deltoid behind his left shoulder, and his entire arm went numb. He stumbled forward, managing to keep his balance, and switched the bat to his right hand. He cut to his right, toward the Jewels' dugout along the first-base line. It gave Wagner the angle on him, but he had to chance it now; his best hope was to make the dugout, then the runway, the clubhouse, the street, his car. The electric tingling in his left arm was going away, and it hurt like a bitch; as he ran, he carried it dead at his side. The 90 feet between second base and the foul line had never been so endless. As he tore across the infield, he could see Wagner winding up out of his right eye.

He turned his head, and the ball was coming at it, bearing down, a 95-mile-an-hour Bobby Wagner rising fastball. For a split second that went on too long, Harvey felt transfixed, almost attracted to the ball. He had seen the pitch countless times before, under better circumstances, when Wagner was with Baltimore—the red seams reduced to streaks in the blur of the backspin, less than half a second from mound to plate, the ball taking off in the last 20 feet.

This time the ball was rising toward his head. In that split second, Harvey felt that he and the ball were fated to meet. That was the thing about a good beanball, not a brushback pitch but one meant to change your idea of batting forever: it seemed to pursue you.

Harvey fell forward onto the damp infield grass, and the ball whistled furiously over him. It caromed off the top concrete edge of the dugout and bounced ineffectually into right. He clambered to his feet. There were still 40 feet between him and the dugout. He couldn't find enough traction in his socks, and the dugout was not getting any closer.

He was 10 feet from the top step of the dugout when the back of his right thigh exploded in pain. His leg gave, and he crumpled to the ground. He heard Wagner breathing coarsely behind him. Harvey tried to get up, but the feeling had gone out of his leg, and he fell back on his seat.

Wagner had caught him just above the back of the knee, and as Harvey clutched his leg in pain, he wondered why Bobby had not simply gone for his head again; it would have been quicker. He was just toying with him now.

Wagner walked slowly toward him off the mound, the ball bag dangling from his left hand. His right hand was caressing another baseball. He came in short heavy strides, looking right at Harvey, and stopped past the first-base line, 20 feet away. The two of them were surrounded by 37,000 empty seats. Harvey did not even try to get up. He still had the bat, though, and from a sitting position, he wound up awkwardly and heaved it at Wagner. It missed him by 3 feet and skidded along the grass.

The pitcher looked at him. "Nice try, Professor."

"Please," Harvey said.

"It wouldn't take much from here, would it?" Wagner said. "What do you think—one pitch, maybe two?"

"Please," Harvey said again.

"They'd never know it was me."

"Of course they would," Harvey panted. "I've told Linderman everything I know. I've told Mickey. Don't be stupid." Propelling himself with one hand, he inched helplessly away from Wagner. "If you kill me, it'll be murder. It's only manslaughter now. You didn't mean to kill Rudy. Anyway, it was the whirlpool that finished him, not you. He provoked you, didn't he? It's man-slaughter, but if you kill me, they'll really put you away."

Wagner looked down at him, chewing his gum. Harvey couldn't tell if he even heard what he was saying. Wagner kept turning the ball over in his hand, like a madman mindlessly practicing his tic.

"You made one mistake," Harvey called out. "Are you listening? You made one mistake. Frances has been making mistakes all summer. Rudy, too. Com-pared to them, I'd say you look like a prince. Go home. Go home and it's between you and me. It won't do you any good if they know you even came after me, so just go home. You've got to trust me, Wags. I never saw you this morning. You're going to be all right."

Wagner lifted his right hand and wiped his brow with the back of it.

"Go home," Harvey pleaded.

Wagner dragged his forearm across his face, and it made Harvey think of the famous photo of him, after he had no-hit Kansas City in 1978. Bobby was on his stool in front of his locker at Memorial Stadium in Baltimore, his uniform drenched with beer poured over him by jubilant teammates; he had his arm over his face, and he was weeping with joy.

Now his arm fell away, and there was no expression at all. "You're through, Professor," he said.

Harvey felt his bowels begin to loosen.

Wagner put the ball bag at his feet and cocked his arm.

There was a kind of mechanical fluttering noise and then a great whooshing sound. Harvey looked up.

The entire system of sprinklers set into Rankle Park's outfield turf had gone on. Twelve jets of water rose simultaneously into the air behind Wagner and began twirling slowly in the morning sunlight.

Wagner turned for an instant, and when he did, Harvey scrambled the 10 feet to the dugout and dropped onto the wooden duckboards.

Three hundred fifty feet away, a maintenance door in the left-field fence opened, and a member of the grounds crew, a tiny figure pushing a wheelbarrow, came out. He spotted Wagner, put the wheelbarrow down, placed his hands on his hips, and yelled, "Hey! You!" at the top of his voice.

Wagner looked at the baseball in his right hand as if it were the first one he had ever seen, fixed Harvey with his eyes, then looked over his shoulder at the figure with the wheelbarrow.

He walked in toward the dugout another 10 feet, until he could see Harvey cowering on his knees on the dugout floor. He stopped and threw the ball as hard as he could up into the upper deck along the first-base line.

Harvey listened to it rattle briefly among the wooden seats.

Then Wagner went past Harvey into the dugout runway and was gone.

A boy wrestles with his insecurities and wonders, *What does it mean to be a man?*
What does a man do? (Lots of us old boys continue to wonder about this, as well.) It
is easy to get lost in the wide world with its thickets of ambivalence; the imperatives
in baseball, on the other hand, are few and unequivocal—either you do or you don't—
and, as in center field, one stands always in the clear. When real life overwhelms,
thinking about baseball is particularly a comfort. From *Portnoy's Complaint.*

PHILIP ROTH

Center Field

So I ran all right, out of the hospital and up to the playground and right out
to center field, the position I play for a softball team that wears silky blue-
and-gold jackets with the name of the club scrawled in big white felt letters
from one shoulder to the other: S E A B E E S, A.C. Thank God for the Seabees
A.C.! Thank God for center field! Doctor, you can't imagine how truly glorious
it is out there, so alone in all that space. . . . Do you know baseball at all?
Because center field is like some observation post, a kind of control tower,
where you are able to see everything and everyone, to understand what's happening the instant it happens, not only by the sound of the struck bat but by
the spark of movement that goes through the infielders in the first second that
the ball comes flying at them; and once it gets beyond them, "It's mine," you
call, "it's mine," and then after it you go. For in center field, if you can get to
it, it *is* yours. Oh, how unlike my home it is to be in center field, where no
one will appropriate unto himself anything that I say is *mine!*

Unfortunately, I was too anxious a hitter to make the high school team—I
swung and missed at bad pitches so often during the tryouts for the freshman
squad that eventually the ironical coach took me aside and said, "Sonny, are
you sure you don't wear glasses?" and then sent me on my way. But did I have
form! Did I have style! And in my playground softball league, where the ball
came in just a little slower and a little bigger, I am the star I dreamed I might
become for the whole school. Of course, still in my ardent desire to excel I
too frequently swing and miss, but when I connect, it goes great distances,

Doctor, it flies over fences and is called a home run. Oh, and there is really nothing in life, nothing at all, that quite compares with that pleasure of rounding second base at a nice slow clip, because there's just no hurry anymore, because that ball you've hit has just gone sailing out of sight. . . . And I could field, too, and the farther I had to run, the better. "I got it! I got it! I got it!" and tear in toward second, to trap in the webbing of my glove—and barely an inch off the ground—a ball driven hard and low and right down the middle, a base hit, someone thought. . . . Or back I go, "*I* got it, *I* got it—" back easily and gracefully toward that wire fence, moving practically in slow motion, and then that delicious DiMaggio sensation of grabbing it like something heaven-sent over one shoulder. . . . Or running! turning! leaping! like little Al Gionfriddo—a baseball player, Doctor, who once did a very great thing. . . . Or just standing nice and calm—nothing trembling, everything serene—standing there in the sunshine (as though in the middle of an empty field or passing the time on the street corner), standing without a care in the world in the sunshine, like my king of kings, the Lord my God, the Duke Himself (Snider, Doctor, the name may come up again), standing there as loose and as easy, as happy as I will ever be, just waiting by myself under a high fly ball (*a towering fly ball*, I hear Red Barber say as he watches from behind his microphone—hit out toward Portnoy; *Alex under it, under it*), just waiting there for the ball to fall into the glove I raise to it, and yup, there it is, *plock*, the third out of the inning (*and Alex gathers it in for out number three, and, folks, here's old C.D. for P. Lorillard and Company*), and then in one motion, while old Connie brings us a message from Old Golds, I start in toward the bench, holding the ball now with the five fingers of my bare left hand, and when I get to the infield—having come down hard with one foot on the bag at second base—I shoot it gently, with just a flick of the wrist, at the opposing team's shortstop as he comes trotting out onto the field, and still without breaking stride, go loping in all the way, shoulders shifting, head hanging, a touch pigeon-toed, my knees coming slowly up and down in an altogether brilliant imitation of the Duke. Oh, the unruffled nonchalance of that game! There's not a movement that I don't know still down in the tissue of my muscles and the joints between my bones. How to bend over to pick up my glove and how to toss it away, how to test the weight of the bat, how to hold it and carry it and swing it around in the on-deck circle, how to raise that bat above my head and flex and loosen my shoulders and my neck before stepping in and planting my two feet exactly where my two feet belong in the batter's box—and how, when I take a called strike (which I have a tendency to do, it balances off nicely swinging at bad pitches), to step out and express, if only through a slight poking with the bat at the ground, just the right amount of exasperation with the powers that be . . . yes, every little detail so thoroughly studied and mastered, that it is simply beyond the realm of possibility for any situation to arise in which I do not know how to move, or where to move, or what to say or leave unsaid. . . . And it's true, is it not?—incredible, but apparently true—there are people who feel in life the ease, the self-assurance, the simple and essential affiliation with what is going on, that I used to feel as the center fielder for the Seabees? Because it wasn't, you see, that one was the best center fielder imaginable, only that one knew exactly, and down to the smallest particular, how a center fielder should conduct himself. And there are people like that walking the streets of the U.S. of A.? I ask you, why can't I be one! Why can't I exist now as I existed for the Seabees out there in center field! Oh, to be a center fielder, a center fielder—and nothing more!

This backhand paean to the box score appeared in the New York *American* on September 17, 1920. How much of the doubleheader's detail can you fill in? And don't you wish that today's box score, though improved by adding the "pitching box," had retained the individual fielding totals and the pinch hitters' lines?

DAMON RUNYON

The Soul of Wit

The Sporting Ed. says, "Cut 'er short!
There's not much space to-day for sport.

"Between the ads,
Between the news.
All excess words I must refuse."

So short it is.
Quite short you see.
Two ball games at the old P. G.

The Pirates won.
The Giants won.
Scores: Three to one, and four to none.

The Sporting Ed. says:
"That'll do."
The box scores tell the rest to you.

FIRST GAME.

PITTSBURGH	ab	r	h	o	a	e	NEW YORK	ab	r	h	o	a	e
Bigbee, lf	4	1	1	2	0	0	Burns, lf	4	0	1	1	0	0
Cutshaw, 2b	2	0	0	2	1	0	Bancroft, ss	4	0	0	0	2	1
S'thworth, rf	4	2	3	3	0	0	Young, rf	3	0	0	4	1	0
Nicholson, cf	4	0	1	3	0	0	Frisch, 3b	3	1	1	1	3	0
Whitted, 3b	4	0	3	2	3	0	Kelly, 1b	3	0	1	15	3	0
Grimm, 1b	3	0	0	9	0	0	King, cf	3	0	0	3	0	0
McKechnie, ss	4	0	0	3	3	1	Grimes, 2b	3	0	1	1	4	0
Schmidt, c	2	0	0	3	1	0	Snyder, c	3	0	0	1	3	0
Hamilton, p	3	0	0	0	0	0	Barnes, p	2	0	0	1	2	0
							bGriffin	1	0	0	0	0	0
							Douglas, p	0	0	0	0	1	0
Totals	30	3	8a	26	8	1	Totals	29	1	4	27	19	1

a Kelly out: hit by batted ball.
b Batted for Barnes in eighth inning.

| Pittsburgh .... | 0 | 0 | 0 | 0 | 0 | 2 | 0 | 0 | 1—3 |
| New York .... | 0 | 0 | 0 | 0 | 0 | 0 | 1 | 0 | 0—1 |

Two-base hit—Whitted. Stolen bases—Frisch. Kelly. Sacrifices—Young. Grimm. Cutshaw. Left on bases—Pittsburgh, 4: New York, 4. Bases on balls—Off Barnes, 3: off Hamilton, 2. Hits—Off Barnes, 3 in 8 innings: off Douglas, 3 in running. Struck out—By Hamilton, 3. Losing pitcher—Barnes. Umpires—O'Day and Quigley. Time—One hour and forty-five minutes.

SECOND GAME.

PITTSBURGH	ab	r	h	o	a	e	NEW YORK	ab	r	h	o	a	e
Bigbee, lf	3	0	0	0	1	0	Burns, lf	3	1	0	3	0	0
Cutshaw, 2b	3	0	0	3	4	0	Bancroft, ss	4	0	0	2	2	0
S'thworth, rf	3	0	1	3	0	0	Young, rf	4	1	1	4	0	0
Nicholson, cf	3	0	0	4	0	0	Frisch, 3b	3	0	0	0	0	0
Whitted, 3b, 1b	3	0	0	2	2	0	Kelly, 1b	4	1	2	6	1	0
Grimm, 1b	2	0	0	8	1	0	King, cf	3	1	1	1	0	0
aCarey	1	0	0	0	0	0	Doyle, 2b	3	0	1	2	2	0
Trainor, ss	0	0	0	0	0	0	Smith, c	3	0	1	7	1	0
M'K'ie, ss, 3b	3	0	0	2	1	0	Nehf, p	3	0	1	2	0	0
Schmidt, c	3	0	0	1	1	0							
Ponder, p	2	0	0	1	2	0							
bBarbare	1	0	0	0	0	0							
Totals	27	0	1	24	12	0	Totals	30	4	7	27	6	0

a Batted for Grimm in eighth inning.
b Batted for Ponder in ninth inning.

Pittsburgh 0	0	0	0	0	0	0	0	0—0
New York 1	1	0	0	0	0	1	1	0—4

Two-base hit—Kelly. Home runs—King. Young. Stolen bases—Burns. Nehf. Left on bases—Pittsburgh, 1: New York, 4. Bases on balls—Off Nehf, 1: off Ponder, 3. Struck out—Ry Nehf, 7: by Ponder, 1. Umpires—Quigley and O'Day. Time of game—One hour and thirty minutes.

The play's the thing. Here are three contributions from the Bard, or in his manner, beginning with some gleanings from the plays by Henry Chadwick in 1868, then A. Donald Douglas's 1912 parody of Hamlet's soliloquy, and concluding with a witty, contemporary piece by Louis Phillips, published in a 1985 issue of the *Saturday Review*. Shakespeare's other recognized contributions to baseball's dramatic literature are *The Comedy of Errors*, *A Midsummer Night's Dream*, and, of course, *The Speed Merchant of Venice*.

WILLIAM SHAKESPEARE (& friends)

Bard at the Bat

Old Billy, ye play writer, must have been ball player once. Read what he says:

"You base (foot) ballplayers."—*Lear*.
"Why, these balls bound."—*Merry Wives*.
"Now, let's have a catch."—*Twelfth Night*.
"I will run no base."—*Merry Wives*.
"And so I shall catch the fly."—*Henry V*.
"Hector shall have a great catch."—*Troilus and Cressida*.
"More like to run the base."—*Cymbeline*.
"As swift in motion as a ball."—*Romeo and Juliet*.
"Ne'er leave striking in the field."—*Henry IV*.
"After he scores."—*All's Well*.
"Ajax goes up and down the field."—*Troilus and Cressida*.
"Have you scored me?"—*Othello*.
"He proved best man i' the field."—*Coriolanus*.
"The word is pitch and pay."—*Henry V*.
"However men do catch."—*King John*.
"What foul play had we?"—*Tempest*.
"Unprovided of a pair of bases."—*Titus Andronicus*.
"No other books but the score."—*Henry VI*.
"These nine men in buckram."—*Henry VI*.
"His confounded base."—*Henry VI*.

"I will fear to catch."—*Timon.*

"What works, my countrymen, in hand? Where go you with *bats* and clubs?"
—*Coriolanus.*

"Let us see you in the field."—*Troilus and Cressida.*

"The very way to catch them."—*Coriolanus.*

THE BATTER'S SOLILOQUY

By A. Donald Douglas

*(In the ninth inning, with a man on third, two gone,
and the score 2–2)*

To wait, or not to wait,—that is the question:
Whether 'tis nobler in this game to suffer
The taunts and yells of the outrageous fans,
Or to dodge the curves and drops of an erratic pitcher,
And, by my coolness 'scape them? To wait—to walk,—
No more; and by a walk to say we stroll
To first, and then be daring like Ty Cobb,
And work the Double Steal,—'tis a consummation
Devoutly to be wished. To walk—to steal,—
To steal. Perchance to score. Ay, there's the rub;—
For in that Double Steal what chance may come
When we have rattled the opposing pitcher,
Must give us runs: there's the respect
That makes a walk of so long life;
For who would bear the yells and taunts of fans,
The umpire's wrong, the bleachers' contumely,
The pangs of disprized hope, the game's delay,
The insolence of gamins, and the spurns
That one must take from the unknowing
When he himself his fame might make,
By a 2-bagger? Who would roastings bear,
To grunt and swear under a weary game,
But that the dread of something after it,
The Minor Leagues, from whose ranks
No old-time star returns, startles the mind;
And makes us rather bear those ills we have
Than fly to others whence we ne'er return?
These bleachers do make cowards of us all;
And thus the fumble of a hard-hit grounder,
Is yelled at by the bleacher mob,
And thus in places of great chance and moment,
We all make bonehead plays that lose the game.

SHAKESPEARE MAKES BASEBALL'S GREATEST PLAYS

By Louis Phillips

At one time, Shakespeare owned part interest in a ball club—the Stratford Variorums—and this team once played a series of exhibition games against a team consisting of America's all-time great players. The night of the season opener, Shakespeare and his sister invited me to attend the game with them. We were unfortunately late in arriving at the ballpark, so Shakespeare hurried me to my seat:

SHAKESPEARE: "But, sirrah, make haste, Percy is already in the field." (*Henry IV*, IV, ii, 74–75)

It took me a moment to realize that Shakespeare was referring to his center fielder—Joe Percy. Falstaff, the manager of the Variorums, came onto the field to change pitchers. Falstaff wanted a fresh hurler to face Ruth.

ME: Tell me, who's your catcher?
SHAKESPEARE: "Passion, I see, is catching." (*Julius Caesar*, III, i, 283)
ME: Number 38. Yogi Passion, catcher. This is a strange lineup.
SHAKESPEARE: "Now name the rest of the players." (*A Midsummer Night's Dream*, I, ii, 39)
ME: We have Hector Richmond in right field, Joe Percy in center, Jory Richmond in left, Al Richmond at third, Ajax Richmond at second, Laertes Richmond at first, Titus Richmond at short. . . .
SHAKESPEARE: "I think there be six Richmonds in the field." (*Richard III*, V, iv, 11)

Claudius let fly with a fast ball. Ruth hit a towering fly to right.

SHAKESPEARE: "Hector shall have a great catch." (*Troilus and Cressida*, II, i, 99–100)
HECTOR *(to himself, in right field)*: "I'll catch it ere it come to ground." (*Macbeth*, III, v, 25)

Alas, Hector did not catch it. He overran the ball, scoring Mantle from second.

SHAKESPEARE: "That's monstrous. O that that were out!" (*Two Gentlemen of Verona*, III, i, 365–66)

Claudius was replaced by a young pitcher named Aumerle (related to Rudy York). A great home-run hitter took his place in the batter's box.

SHAKESPEARE: "Here Aaron is; and what with Aaron now?" (*Titus Andronicus*, IV, ii, 54)
ME: A home run, I should guess.
SHAKESPEARE: "Strike him, Aumerle." (*Richard II*, V, ii, 85)

Hank pounded a hard grounder to the first baseman. Ruth broke for third.

SHAKESPEARE: "Come, for the third, Laertes, you do but dally." (*Hamlet*, V, ii, 297)

Laertes fired a perfect strike to the third baseman. Ruth hit the dirt.

SHAKESPEARE: "The fool slides. . . ." (*Troilus and Cressida*, III, iii, 215)
ME: That was a great throw from Laertes!

Ruth leaped to his feet and began to argue the call. Bill Martin, manager of the All-Stars, stormed out of the dugout.

SHAKESPEARE'S SISTER: Be calm, brother. Let the umpire decide the question.
SHAKESPEARE: "There is three umpires in the matter I understand." (*The Merry Wives of Windsor*, I, i, 137)
ME: The Babe was safe!
SHAKESPEARE:"Out, dog, out, cur!" (*A Midsummer Night's Dream*, III, ii, 65)
ME: Safe! Al missed the tag!
SHAKESPEARE: "Out, I say!" (*Macbeth*, V, i, 35)

Martin was finally ejected from the game. Al Simmons stepped to the plate.

ME: He's going to hit it.
SHAKESPEARE *(taunting the batter)*: "Thou canst not hit it, hit it, hit it. Thou canst not hit it, my good man." (*Love's Labor's Lost*, IV, i, 125–26)

The pitch was thrown. Simmons swung, missed, and missed again. Edwin Snider was annnounced as the next batter. He hit a pop fly to Percy.

ME: It's an easy out. . . . Percy's under it.
SHAKESPEARE: "No doubt but he hath got a quiet catch." (*Taming of the Shrew*, II, i, 331)

The lead of the American All-Stars held up. Nonetheless, Shakespeare had completely fallen under the spell of baseball. As he and I and his sister left the stadium he turned to me and said:

I'll make a journey twice as far t'enjoy a second night of such sweet shortness." (*Cymbeline*, II, iv, 43–44)

In addition to the standard scholarly histories of baseball by Harold Seymour and David Voigt, there are many anecdotal chronicles of the sport; of these, none is more entertaining and erudite than Robert Smith's *Baseball*, first issued in 1947 and then again in substantially different form in 1970. Fred Dunlap, The Only Nolan, Joe Start, Silver Flint, Deacon McGuire, Toad Ramsey—although these names may be unfamiliar to today's fans, they were heroes in their day.

ROBERT SMITH

Of Kings and Commoners

In the 1880s a man who was best at his trade would be called King, or sometimes he would be "The Only." Baseball's greatest King and the only one who wore the title to his grave was Mike Kelly. Everybody in the land has heard of Kelly, for he is as famous as Casey—the legendary figure who batted for Mudville in the poem by Ernest Thayer. Some used to say that Casey himself was modeled after Kelly, but this was not a fact. There was only one Kelly, and no figure in fact or fiction ever approached him. He was the Kelly who used to slide and whose name on that account has become a catchword in the tongue, still used by men and women who never knew the fellow who made it famous.

"Slide, Kelly, slide!" the fans in Boston used to sing.

"Slide, Kelly, on your belly!

"Slide, Kelly, slide!"

Although Mike Kelly was not the first to slide in order to avoid a tag, he was the most earnest practitioner of this dodge, and he invented ways of sliding to base that few of his contemporaries ever dared to try. He not only slid on his belly; he slid on his backside, and he slid on his thighs. He would fall away from a base in his slide and then reach out to grab it as he coasted by. Or he would ride in on the seat of his pants with his two feet flicking so that the man with the ball did not know where to put the tag. Or, in the days before they had remembered to make a rule about runners passing each other on the base paths, he might get the man running ahead of him to stop suddenly in front of home plate, legs aspraddle, to let Kelly slide in between the man's feet to tag the plate and score a run.

To get on base to do his sliding, Mike of course had to hit the ball. And for a time he was one of the games' mightiest hitters. But he learned his trade slowly and for a time did not seem at all sure to make it.

Michael J. Kelly was born in Troy, New York, then known as Lansingburgh, before the Civil War began. His father, still only a few years out of Ireland, enlisted in the Union Army when the war started, then reenlisted when the war was over and brought his family down to live in Washington, D.C., where he was stationed. Baseball was important in Washington in those days, for it was the era of the Nationals and of George Wright and the many others appointed to government jobs so they might play the "noble game" for the glory of the capital city. Young Mike, in school, where he was the fastest runner to be found, grew up on stories of the great games the mighty Nationals played all over the land. But in his school it was not the grown-up game that was played but "burn ball," one of the oldest versions of baseball, in which runners could be put out by "burning" their shrinking hides with a hard-thrown ball when they wandered off the base. To stay alive on the baselines in that game, a youngster had to be particularly agile, and none was more agile than Mike.

But the New York game, as played by the Nationals, still was real baseball to Mike and to those of his mates who were best at it. So Mike joined the Keystones, a club of juniors, to play New York ball. At that time Mike's private hero was Old Reliable Joe Start (he never dropped a throw), the husky first baseman of the New York Mutuals; when Mike grew old enough to raise a mustache of his own, he grew one just like Joe's. When ill health forced the elder Kelly out of the army, the family moved to Paterson, New Jersey, where Mike organized a baseball club of his own and insisted it be named the Keystones. In this collection of scrawny young Irishmen, not one of whom could brag of scratch enough to buy a whole uniform, Mike was the best—the hardest thrower, the fastest runner, the most reliable batsman. Among the dozen youngsters on the club, there was just one baseball cap—an authentic, multicolored, hard-billed cap almost exactly like the one Joe Start wore. It had cost fifteen cents. Mike had no fifteen cents to buy it with, but he insisted he would not play for the club in match games if he could not wear the cap. So when the Keystones took the field, there was no mistaking Kelly—the only one with a baseball hat on. And when the game began, there was no missing him, either— the boy who moved the fastest, hit the ball the farthest, and was having the most fun.

Mike Kelly liked to catch, because the catcher, facing the whole club, really ran the team, got into all the action, and took the most punishment. The club had a strong-arm pitcher named Nolan, who, by the time Mike had become King Kelly, was himself known the baseball world over as The Only Nolan. Eddie Nolan at that time was a railroad fireman, building his shoulder muscles by firing hungry freight engines along the Hudson River. Mike Kelly was working in a Paterson mill for three dollars a week.

The Nolan-Kelly battery made the Keystones invincible for three years; then Eddie began to play the game for money and moved away. Young Mike stayed on, still playing for fun and earning his income now by bringing the New York papers into Paterson at dawn. This job meant getting up at four in the morning, but it gave Mike every bright afternoon to play ball. By the time he was eighteen, Mike had become a semiprofessional ballplayer. In the wintertime, he undertook to learn to be a silk weaver, for it was a rare baseball job in that day (1876) that could offer a man enough to live on the year around. Mike quickly found he was no weaver, nor did he ever have any stomach for the twelve-hour day the mills offered—it being acknowledged even by the nation's advanced thinkers that a shorter workday would simply mean disaster for the laboring man. Mike decided he was never meant to be a laboring man, so he took a full-time job in the spring with the professional baseball club at Port Jervis, New York, but a buggy ride from home.

From Port Jervis, where he quickly proved himself the class of the lineup, young Mike advanced to the Cincinnati Buckeyes of the National League—a revival of the team that had died when the Red Stockings were born. Whether it was homesickness or curveball pitching, no one now can say, but Mike started off the 1879 season in Cincinnati in a sorry state indeed. In his first twenty-one times at bat he reached first but once, and that time through a fielding error. His baseball career might have ended right then, and history would have had to seek another slider, for the manager of the Buckeyes—Cal McVey, once the star of the Atlantics—had sent for a new ballplayer to haul his team out of the slump. To make room for him, Cal told himself, he would drop either Kelly or Dickerson, an outfielder who had been too ill to play regularly but who still was batting better than Kelly. When young Mike got wind of this, he took off like a man possessed. The very next day, in four times at bat, he hit two doubles, a triple, and a home run. In the next game against mighty Chicago, Kelly batted in every one of Cincinnati's runs and beat the White Stockings—and saved his place in the major leagues.

There was no World Series in the fall then, but ballplayers often stretched the season, and kept the paydays coming, by joining one of the many barnstorming teams to show big-time baseball to the Far West. Most famous of the great barnstorming clubs of that era was the Hop Bitters team of Rochester, New York, wearing the name of a patent medicine. The Bitters, a minor-league outfit, were the equal of many a big-league club and listed a number of famous players on their roster. But Kelly, in California, playing with a club made up chiefly of Cincinnati and Buffalo men, punched the Hop Bitters club full of holes. Adrian Anson, then the "captain"—that is, manager—of the Chicago club was so impressed with Kelly that he undertook at once to sign him for the White Stockings. It took the two of them—the dour Anson and the merry Mike—more than a week to settle a difference of $100 in the salary offer. But they decided on a figure finally, and Mike moved to Chicago, where he soon became the most famous baseball player in the world.

Mike was sometimes referred to as a "big fellow," and indeed, at the top of his fame, he did seem to stand out beyond all the players on his club. His uniform was always a bit more flamboyant than the other players', with letters on it that stood out almost an inch from the shirtfront. His shoulders were broad, his eyes agleam, his mustache flourishing, his hair neat and luxuriant. But at his best he weighed only 170 pounds, and he stood a scant 6 feet off the ground. Cap Anson himself was a bigger and broader man. But no one else cut quite the figure that Kelly did, in the press, on the field, or along the street.

A he-man in that day was a "hearty" man who could ingest abnormal quantities of food and drink. Mike Kelly loved whiskey and good roast beef with the ardor of a medieval friar, but Cap Anson, who believed in severe conditioning of his ballplayers, let no man on his squad load himself with lard. By the time he was ready to open the season with Kelly, Mike was greyhound lean, faster than ever in the field and on base, sharp-eyed at bat, and quick as a spider behind the plate. His great deeds on the ball field grew into legends, until some were exaggerated beyond belief. It was said he never tagged third base on his way home and sometimes went from first to third by way of the pitcher's box. No doubt he did frequently cut a base when the lone umpire was watching a play in the other direction. At least once he scored from second base without getting close enough to third to reach it with a pole. But much of his improvisation did not break the rules. It simply took advantage of loopholes the rule makers had left.

There was a rule that allowed a substitute to enter a game "on notice to the umpire." Kelly, learned in these careless phrasings, once leaped from the bench (where he might have been left to heal a hangover), shouted to the umpire, "Kelly now catching," and put away a foul ball the regular catcher could not have reached. The umpire would not allow the out, even after Kelly showed him the rule. After that they changed the rule.

Kelly performed most of his wildest feats in exhibition games, where he played for applause or strove to excite or anger the spectators. In one such game, when the ball he had hit became lost in the outfield brush, Kelly added suspense to the proceedings by leaving the baselines to run a solemn circle around each outfielder before he ran home. At a game in St. Louis, where the cheap seats were often crammed with denizens of the Kerry Patch—the Irish ghetto—Kelly, playing the outfield, invited the fans behind him to join in a chorus of "The Battle of Boyne Water"—an Orangeman's song calculated to curdle the whiskey of any true son of the sacred soil.

Still no one ever held a grudge against Kelly, who was the "King" to fans and "Kell" to his teammates. There was never an ounce of malice in the man, and there was a hogshead full of kindness and generosity in his heart. The opponents he beat, the umpires he taunted or hornswoggled, the fans he sometimes enraged, all finally adored him and begrudged him not a penny of the sudden wealth his fame brought him.

Eventually, Kelly was sold to Boston—sent away from Chicago "because of a woman," it was whispered. The price the Boston Beaneaters paid for him was $10,000—enough in those days to buy a ballpark. Promptly Kelly was named "The $10,000 Beauty," after a stage lady who used that title in her promotion. And the Boston Irish swarmed to make him welcome. His fans even chipped in one day to buy him a spanking pair of grays and a gig to go with them, so that the King of the Diamond could ride out on Washington Street in style, in gloves and gleaming top hat and needle-toed button shoes.

Like many a latter-day baseball king, Kelly thought money was made to spend, and he never laid by a nickel. Friends, acquaintances, even unhappy strangers who needed a fiver, could count on Kell to produce it. The little old lady who sold flowers in the street could unload her entire store of blossoms on old Mike. Although his salary ($2,000 dollars for playing ball and $3,000 for "use of his picture") was thought large enough to support a prince and was supplemented by money he took in for reciting "Casey at the Bat" on the vaudeville stage, Kelly was always a week or two ahead of the paymaster.

His play in Boston began to flag a little. On days when he had time to take aboard a proper helping of whiskey before the game began, he might circle unsteadily beneath an easy fly ball and then miss it altogether. Secure in the love the fans felt for him, Kelly never let such lapses fret him. "By God, I made it hit me glove," he would exult, and put it from his mind. It was not long, however, before even the most devoted fans grew tired of seeing precious ball games go home with the other side just because Mike Kelly had a drop taken. The Boston club shipped Mike to New York one day "on loan." Mike, in the big city, cut an even wider swath, and the loan was very quickly repaid, with hardly any thanks.

It was downhill after that for Kelly. He played awhile in Allentown and was dismayed when the fans not only failed to laugh at his antics but even hissed and booed at his failures in the field. *Ah, well,* he consoled himself, *they still love old Kell in the theater.* But now the audiences no longer laughed at the way he imitated De Wolf Hopper. Kelly tried running a saloon, too, along with Honest John Kelly, the umpire. But all this seemed to mean was that for a while he got his drink wholesale. When he was thirty-seven years old, he took a boat to Boston to fill a vaudeville engagement there, and on the boat he came down with pneumonia, as so many big, hearty men were prone to do. He was carried off on a stretcher and put to bed in his hotel, where he seemed to be getting better. Then suddenly his temperature shot up again, and he was rushed to the Boston Emergency Hospital, where he breathed his last under an oxygen tent.

Then finally the baseball world mourned him and remembered the way he had been at his best—so devil-may-care, so fast on his feet, so quick to slide, to slide, to slide.

Adrian Constantine Anson was very nearly the opposite of Mike Kelly in nature, yet nearly as widely known to fame in his day and every bit as fearsome a foe. Anson was dour and given to self-discipline, whereas Kelly was gay and a stranger to restraint. Anson was taller and heavier than Mike, a mightier man at bat but a leader rather than a member of a team, and a cross-grained, self-sufficient fellow as bitter in his prejudices as he was indomitable in his convictions. Anson played big-league baseball for more than twenty seasons, from 1871, when he was just turned twenty, to 1897, when he was past forty-six. He played every position on the diamond, including pitcher, but for the greater part of his career he was first baseman and captain of the Chicago White Stockings, who eventually became the Cubs. At the start of his career he was known as "Baby" Anson, or the "Marshalltown Infant." (He had been the first white child born in Marshalltown, Iowa.) Long before he was finished, he was known as "Pop," from being so much older than anybody else on the field. For a time after he left the Chicago club, they were known as the "Orphans," because they had lost their Pop.

Anson was known in his day as "an inveterate coacher," a coacher being one who was given, of course, to coaching. But coaching, in the seventies and eighties, as has been noted earlier, did not mean giving instructions or advice. It meant bellowing encouragement and derision at friend or foe. Some people came to the park as much to hear Anson yell as to watch him hit. He yelled at everyone. Standing near third base, towering over the enemy baseman, he would roar an invitation to the batter: "Knock the ball down here! This is the weak spot!"

Umpires, naturally, felt the rough side of Anson's tongue. He even scared one umpire—poor Dickey Pearce—into reversing a decision and ordering back to the plate a man who had just been awarded first base for being hit with the ball.

Teammates, too, could expect a public hazing by Anson if they booted a ground ball or let a fly elude them. But most treasured by true Anson fans were the orations that Cap would often deliver when he found umpires, foes, and fans all conspiring against him. Then he would turn to face the stands, and in a voice calculated to start rocks to rolling on a distant hill, he would berate the people who were hooting at him, belittle the city that housed them, and warn them of the humiliations his club would hang about their ignorant necks.

Anson was a homely man, not given to dandified dress. His nose was off center, and his ears were not mates. In his earlier days, according to the mode, he let his mustache grow and even waxed the ends a little. But his size and the obviously oak-hard condition of his body impressed all who faced him. And the voice that would have silenced the Bull of Bashan demanded attention and obedience. When he had delivered one of his orations to the enraptured stands, he would pound his great hands together like two wooden hammers and bellow:

"Come on, fellows! Play the game!"

And the game would be played.

Anson was one of the great batters of baseball. He swung a heavy stick and could hit the ball hard and far. But he always taught his players to choke up a little on the bat, the better to control it. This was known as "stopping it down" in that day and was a habit sometimes decried by those who thought a real man should try to break the ball in two whenever it came his way. Anson himself had no use for bunting, which he ridiculed as "the baby act." But he was one of the first to teach the advantage of keeping control of the bat in order to "hit the ball where it was pitched" instead of trying to lay into it with all one's power, to pull it into the batter's favorite field.

For himself, Anson always cradled the bat loosely in his arms at the plate, as if he were not certain how he might take hold of it. He did not cut the air with the bat or pound the plate, nor did he, as some of the ostentatious batters of that era did, stand with the bat "charged"—rifle style—toward the pitcher. Like Ty Cobb, a fiery batsman of a later day, Anson kept his hands well apart on the bat handle so he could choke up, or swing a long bat, depending on the pitch. The ball Cap Anson hit was the dead ball, not wound so tightly as the modern ball and without the cork center. Still, even with the pitcher only fifty feet away, big Cap set records that no modern hero would be ashamed of.

In 1884, Cap Anson hit five home runs in two days. When he completed his playing career, he was still batting better than .300. His fielding, however, was stodgy, and today he would be called dead on his feet around the base. He never felt that it was his part to scamper up the baseline to field a ground ball. Rather, he left that to his miraculous second baseman, the great Fred Pfeffer, who owned the biggest mustache in the game. Fred, having to cover all the ground between first and second base, often could stop a ground ball only by flinging himself full length on the turf, while Big Anse stood watching him from a few feet away. Then Fred, having stopped the ball, would have to flip it to Anson while lying facedown or on his side. But if he got it anywhere near the big man, that was enough, for Anson seemed able to stretch himself 5 yards in any direction, while still keeping a toe on the bag. Chicago fans used to scream with delight to see Anson reach high, high into the air and pluck a wild throw with his tiny glove.

Anson's real pride, however, was his ability to find good ballplayers almost everywhere he looked. While he led the Chicago forces, they owned many of baseball's greatest names—not only Kelly and Pfeffer but John Clarkson, Anson's best pitcher, and Silver Flint, the white-haired catcher who was sometimes known as The Only Flint. If Spalding, seeing a chance to trade off a star to advantage, approached Anson to test the captain's feeling about it, Anson never chewed the matter over for more than a minute. Even when Spalding, with some trepidation, brought the news to big Anse that Mike Kelly might be traded, Anson snapped his answer immediately:

"Sure! Trade anybody!"

There were always new ballplayers to be brought in and developed, and Anson was confident he could find them, as he had found Kelly out on the Coast with a bunch of barnstormers. Sometimes he could turn a fairly good ballplayer into a star just by seeing to it that the man kept his weight down and his reflexes sharp. He was one of the few managers in that far-off day who did not feel it was good for a player to fill himself chock full at the dining table. He gave his men gymnastics to do every day and laid down training rules designed to keep them out of the saloons and put them into their beds at a decent hour. Nor did he ever ease up on himself. He never drank strong liquor. He checked his weight as jealously as a jockey. His own pregame fare was a bowl of bread and milk. He sought his lone bed soon after the sun was gone. And he saved his money.

Like many another he-man of his day, Anson felt there was something two-fisted about exhibiting scorn for Negroes. He helped create the "unwritten rule" that barred black men from big-league baseball for sixty years and still keeps them from becoming managers. In Anson's days there were several ballplayers of African descent who performed in the major leagues without once threatening the ruin of the state. The first to enter the majors was Moses Fleetwood Walker, who, with his brother Welday, had starred in baseball at Oberlin College. Fleet Walker became a catcher with the Toledo Club of the American Association (a major league in the 1800s), where he teamed with ambidextrous Tony Mullane to help the likely lad from Cork win thirty-five games in a season. (Brother Welday played in the outfield at Toledo.) But here and there throughout the circuit, Walker met men who refused to share the diamond with any man so lost to good manners as to wear black skin. And crude Cap Anson, one day at Newark, where Fleet Walker and another black athlete, George Stovey, played minor-league ball, indignantly demanded that the Newark management "get those niggers off the field!" This request, hastily honored by the Newark bosses, set a style that was followed in organized baseball until 1945, when Branch Rickey hired Jack Roosevelt Robinson to play for Montreal.

There was another "King" in professional baseball besides King Kell, but the title never stuck to him as it did to big Mike, perhaps because it did not fit quite so alliteratively—or perhaps because Fred Dunlap, the King of Second Basemen, never cut quite the figure Mike did either off the field or on. Still there were numberless ball kranks in that day who would not have swapped you a Dunlap for three Mike Kellys.

The nickname that did stick to Dunlap was Sure-Shot, for Fred was noted for the sharpshooting accuracy with which he could fire the ball from any angle into the first baseman's glove. Fred, who played second base for Cleveland and St. Louis, was also the strongest man in professional baseball and the most fearless. More than one amateur bully who tried to misuse Fred Dunlap carried home a set of bruises that lasted him a month.

Fred was only 5 feet 8, small enough for a drunk to pick on. But he had been an athlete all his life and never let himself grow soft. He had spent his entire youth playing ball, from the time he was ten, when his parents had died. The elderly couple that took him in required only that little Fred fetch a growler of beer every morning in return for his board and keep. After that he was free to attend school or play baseball as he chose. Fred chose baseball and never learned to read or write until he was past eighteen, when someone helped him to spell out his name so he could sign papers.

Little Fred learned to run like a rabbit, not from fear but from eagerness to get from base to base or to run down a baseball and get into the game. His hands were really too small for a ballplayer, being dainty as a girl's. But endless practice made him adept as a monkey at grabbing a sizzling ground ball in either hand and firing it off from the very spot he seized it. His whistling throws, which seemed to clear the grass by no more than half a foot, never seemed to lose an inch of altitude in flight and almost never missed the mark by more than an inch or two. It was King Kell who, after watching Fred fire the ball to base, gave him the name of "Sure-Shot." Kell also agreed that Fred could outdress him, for Fred delighted to spend his money on clothing—as do so many poor boys who have known the humiliation of hand-me-downs. Fred was also, despite his short stature, an impressive and graceful figure off the diamond. He cultivated refined manners, wore spotless linen, and knew how to behave at a polite dinner table, even though he could never have read the menu.

What he did know most of was baseball. An alert, fast-thinking man who had studied the game since he began to play it as a tiny boy on a Philadelphia vacant lot, he seemed always able to stay a play or two ahead of the enemy. While team baseball in Fred's day was at its very beginning, with the great stars often scorning to move out of their positions and with basemen frequently anchored to the base, Fred moved about the diamond as George Wright had done and as Charlie Comiskey was beginning to do—backing up throws, trying for balls that technically "belonged" to another fielder, and diving for ground balls that no one seemed to have a prayer of reaching. Lying flat on the ground, Fred could still uncork a throw that would sting the palm of the first baseman and hit right in the center of the glove. If Fred found it difficult to get his right arm free for a throw, he could throw just as hard and just as accurately with his left, for he wore no glove on either.

Fred was also as fierce a slider as King Kell was. He handled himself on the baselines without fear or hesitation and would hurl his small, hard body into a base with such desperation that he would sometimes scare the baseman half out of his pants. He was sometimes called on to pitch and was ready to play any other position, too, as he had often had to do on the Philadelphia meadows to fit himself into a lineup.

In 1884, when players, outraged by the new "reserve rule," which bound them for life to the club that signed them, decided to join the new Union Association, Fred Dunlap became manager of the St. Louis club in that league. He was then twenty-five years old, lean, hard, and brown as an Indian from his constant being outdoors. He had the nose of an Indian, too, and deep brown eyes. But he weighed only 160 pounds, and despite his fierce and dignified demeanor, he did not scare Curt Welch of the rival St. Louis Browns. One day Welch, having talked himself into a froth of anger at the upstart "Onions," who were trying to take the bread out of his mouth, swaggered into the Union park and "called out" Fred Dunlap. Fred calmly went to meet the rugged Welch and within three minutes had beaten the big man so badly that Curt had to have help to get home.

Fred's inability to sign his first contract (with the Philadelphia Acmes), the humiliation of having to make an X where his signature should have gone, was what prompted him to learn to write his name. When it came time to sign the biggest contract of his life—the $6,000 contract with the St. Louis Maroons of the Union Association—Fred was able to write Fred Dunlap on the proper line even though he could not read a word of what preceded it.

After the Union Association folded up, Fred returned to the National League as manager of the St. Louis Browns, then was reduced to the ranks for his next few seasons with St. Louis and Detroit. In 1887 he starred in the great traveling World Series between Detroit and St. Louis, when the two teams played fifteen games in Pittsburgh, Brooklyn, New York, Philadelphia, Washington, Boston, Baltimore, and Chicago as well as in the two home cities. For his work in this series Fred pocketed a few hundred dollars extra. But Fred was never hard up while he was playing ball and never dropped money at the racetracks and saloons, as Mike Kelly did.

Fred's greatest playing days were spent in Cleveland, from 1880 to 1883. Here he belonged to the combination acknowledged the greatest of his era—Big Bill Phillips at first, Dunlap at second, Jack Glasscock, the King of Shortstops, next, and tough Mike Muldoon at third base. After his terms at St. Louis and Detroit, Fred went back to managing in Pittsburgh but lasted only one full season. He played a few games for Pittsburgh in 1890 and one for New York. He ended his career the next season, with Washington. He was said to have laid up $100,000 and had nothing to worry him for the rest of his life, having gone into the building business, where fortune seemed assured. But eleven years later a Philadelphia policeman, in the local morgue, saw a body that looked like Fred Dunlap's. He persuaded Lave Cross of the Philadelphia Athletics to come view the body, and Lave confirmed that this was the man he had often faced on the diamond, the King of All the Second Basemen, penniless, dead, alone, and destined now for Potter's Field.

If a man were not named King, he might instead be called The Only to indicate that there was none other like him on the globe. In the 1880s there were two "Onlys," but one was awarded the name when he played with the original—when Silver Flint was set to catching the fiery fastball of The Only Nolan, Flint became The Only Flint. But Nolan became Only because he was the only one of his kind—a pitcher who threw thirty games one season in which he did not allow the enemy a run. Indeed, his average "earned run" allowance in 1877 was half a run per game, in seventy-six complete games. He won sixty-four of these games, for an average of .941. When fans called him The Only then, no one in baseball disputed the title.

Eddie Nolan had played ball with Mike Kelly's Keystones in Paterson, New Jersey, where Nolan had a job firing freight engines for the Lackawanna Railroad. Eddie developed such strength in his shoulders on the job that he seemed able to throw fastballs forever. But he also had a startling curve, in that day when a curveball of any degree would cause men to marvel. Eddie's curve was labeled an "inshoot," for it broke sharply toward a right-handed batter. Actually it was probably the natural hop that an overhand fastball often shows when it is thrown with great strength. And there were no pitchers of that day any stronger than Eddie Nolan. Eddie pitched from the 50-foot distance, so many a batter caught no more than the briefest glimpse of Eddie's fastball.

Only or not, Nolan's big-league career was brief. He started with the minor-league club in Columbus, Ohio, when he was eighteen years old. When he defeated the mighty Indianapolis club, allowing only four hits and striking out twelve, the Indianapolis owner, W. B. Pettit, promptly hired Eddie away from Columbus by offering him one of the top salaries of the day—$2,500 a year, there being at that time no reserve rule to keep a club from luring a player away.

During Eddie's first year at Indianapolis, the club belonged to a loose sort of league called the "League Alliance," which had no set schedule and no real organization. Two big-league clubs did belong to the Alliance—the New York Mutuals and the Philadelphia Athletics, both expelled from the new National League for failing to complete their schedules. So Eddie Nolan faced opposition as strong as any other pitcher in the game. His record, however, not having been made in an organized league, has no official standing.

Next year, The Only Nolan pitched in the National League, but his record did not approach that of his first season. He began, apparently, to look upon the wine when it was red and in other ways do despite unto the lords of baseball; suddenly he found himself expelled from the league for failure to show up for a game—and presumably for giving his boss a short answer when he was questioned about it. Eddie was out of the game for a whole season until the Indianapolis fans raised such a howl that he was reinstated and assigned to the Cleveland club. But he never again showed the skill and strength that had made him the only one of his kind. To this day, however, no one has matched him. There has never been an earned run average posted that even approached Nolan's. Even in the old days, when pitchers might work several times a week, no other pitcher ever pitched seventy-six games and lost only four of them. Eddie Nolan, therefore, brief as was his fame and deep as it has been buried, still remains The Only.

Charles Radbourne might himself have been named The King or The Only because he was certainly *sui generis* and for a time topped all the pitchers in the game. But instead Radbourne was named for his willingness to show up for work when lesser men might have kept to their beds. He was known as the Old Hoss. And true to his name, he could be hitched to the wagon, any wagon, any day, and would plug along until he dropped. Nor did he, until he had been cruelly put upon, ever offer his employer any trouble over the wage he was awarded. Radbourne first earned his fame as a hitter, and he might have built himself a longer career and earned greater fame had he not been so given to homesickness. He would work all day and all night if need be, but he didn't want to be taken too far from the barn.

Radbourne, born in Rochester, New York, was moved to Bloomington, Illinois, while a baby. As a teenager he was living in Danville, Illinois, and became a brakemen on the Indiana, Bloomington and Western Railroad. In his off time he played baseball, like practically every healthy young man of his day, except that he was better at it than most. He played in exhibition games in the area, sometimes took a short trip with one of the traveling professional clubs, and once even pretended to be a college boy to pitch for Illinois Wesleyan against a team of pros. (That episode gave rise to a story that he was "a college graduate." Actually, he never went beyond the seventh grade.) Finally, at the age of twenty-four, he was talked into joining the Peoria Reds, as right fielder and a full-time pro. His salary was just about what he had been earning on the railroad—$55 a month. After one season, however, big Charlie decided that was all the professional baseball he wanted. It kept him away from home too blamed long.

That winter one of early baseball's ablest promoters, Ted Sullivan, at that time manager of the Dubuque Rabbits of the Northwestern League, woke Radbourne up late one chilly night to offer him a grand cure for homesickness—a salary of $75 a month plus room and board to come play for Dubuque.

Rad's career as pitcher began with Dubuque. The Rabbits being about the only team in the league strong enough to deal with a club mightier than the Bloomer Girls, the Northwestern League folded early, and Ted Sullivan took his Rabbits for a run around the small towns of the Midwest. In town after town, before crowds of farmers who might have traveled half a day to see him, big Rad showed off his pitching skills. It was soon offered as gospel among the kranks of that area that this big-shouldered sharpster from back in Illinois was throwing a "crooked baseball." How else could he make it hop this way and that on its flight to the plate? And how could it be that the strongest lads in the farm country could do no more than feebly trickle Rad's pitches along the ground?

But inasmuch as Rad seemed able to pull the same tricks even with the home club's baseball, a few of the shrewder observers in the grain belt concluded that Rad was perpetrating an optical illusion or using some form of hypnotic suggestion. And to assure themselves that such deeds were really being done, villagers and farmers by the hundreds hastened out to the local ball lot when the Rabbits came to town. And Ted Sullivan let Rad work every day.

While Rad was not really hypnotizing anyone, he was studying the art of pitching as few had done before him. He was forever trying out new deliveries. But his best, according to Sullivan, was his underhand fastball that hopped upward as it neared the batter. He could throw a reverse curve like the modern screwball, and he invented a pitch he called a "spitter," although he used no spit on it. Apparently it was some type of knuckle or fingertip ball—the "dry spitter" of the early twentieth century—for it had a way of dropping like a stoned duck just before it reached the batter. "It would," said contemporary batters, "come straight at you, then change its route all of a sudden." It was this "slow ball" that became Rad's most famous weapon and the one that made simple folk wonder if Rad were not in league with the devil.

Although Rad pitched into the era when overhand pitching was allowed, he always threw the ball underhand. This helped him get through his toughest season, when he won the pennant for the Providence Grays, for there was many a morning that year when Rad could not raise his poor arm high enough to brush his hair.

Providence had two pitchers that season (1884), and each was in his own way a difficult man. Rad was moody, perhaps still given to spells of longing for his own little home in Danville. The other pitcher, Charles Sweeney, supposed to be the speediest pitcher in baseball at that time, was nervous and quick to violent wrath. (He ended his days in San Quentin prison, convicted of homicide.) Rad and Sweeney, instead of pulling loyally together like one Old Hoss beside another, pulled in opposite directions. Sweeney liked to brag, and Rad liked to put Sweeney down. After Sweeney struck out nineteen batters in a game against Boston and commented on the record once or twice, Rad expressed irritation. Then, after Hugh Daily, Chicago's one-armed pitcher, also struck out nineteen Boston batters, Rad gave Sweeney a loud hoss laugh. Why, even a *cripple* could fan that bunch! Sweeney might have put a mark or two on Rad's shining countenance had not Manager Frank Bancroft halted the row while it was still nothing but bad words. Rad told the manager what he thought of his interference, and he was rewarded with a five-day suspension. (Nowadays, a pitcher with a five-day suspension might not miss a turn. Rad probably would have missed two or three.)

Providence had to get another "change" pitcher at once, to keep in right field in case Sweeney ever tired. They brought in Cyclone Joe Miller from the Chicago Unions. Sweeney, in his next game, built up a fat lead over Philadelphia so Bancroft decided to take a look at Cyclone Joe in action. He instructed Sweeney to change places with the right fielder. To Sweeney this was a public humiliation, and he damned the whole notion to hell, then walked off the diamond, never to come back. (He took a train to Boston to join the outlaw "Onions"—the St. Louis club in the Union Association.) Bancroft then had to lift Rad's suspension and had to beseech Rad to carry most of the burden for the remainder of the season.

Would he do it? *Could* he? Rad, no sorehead, promptly agreed. He thereupon won eighteen ball games in a row, lost one to Jimmy Galvin of Buffalo, then won eight more. Some days, to get his sore arm working, he would have to start warming up gently two or three hours before taking the mound. But the Old Hoss never halted and never complained. With Rad doing most of the work, Providence won the pennant. Rad promptly had offers from nearly every team in the "outlaw" league. But he accepted a small advance in salary to stay with Providence.

Eventually, however, Radbourne learned that loyalty worked only one way in Organized Baseball. He joined Boston in 1886, where he earned a salary (the league maximum) of $4,500 and was paid an under-the-table bonus. He won twenty-seven games for Boston the first year and twenty-four the second year. In 1888 he fell off to seven victories and in 1889 was handed a salary cut. He won nineteen games that year, but the next season, along with almost all the other stars of the game, he joined the Brotherhood Strike and played for the Boston Club in the Players' League, winning twenty-seven games.

Next year, back in the National League, the Old Hoss began to crack. It was said that the livelier ball used in the Players League had ruined his arm. But before many years were out symptoms of advanced syphilis showed up in the sturdy frame, so it seems fair to assume that physical deterioration had already set in as his baseball career ended. Rad retired to Bloomington, where he opened a combination poolroom and café, which drew patronage from many fans who came to goggle at the baseball greats who would appear from time to time to shake the hand of the mighty Old Hoss. In 1895, Rad lost part of his face and one eye in a hunting accident, and he never left home again. Two years later he died, at the age of forty-two.

Radbourne was not by any means the only professional ballplayer who ever drank strong waters and stayed out late at night. Drinking, cursing, and dalliance were just as popular among athletes of the 1880s as they are with the paid performers of today. But there were always some who eschewed such behavior or took such small helpings as to be practically doing without. Such straitlaced examples to the young were usually nicknamed "Deacon," although sometimes, if they were given to particularly gracious behavior, they might be dubbed "Lady"—a name that in that less sophisticated era suggested no perversion and was accepted as all in fun.

The most famous Deacon of all was Deacon McGuire, who stayed in professional baseball so long there were kranks grown to manhood who could not recall when the Deacon had not been playing for money. The Deacon's given name was James, and he started his working life as an iron molder in Michigan. Because he had hands about twice the size of a normal man's, he took easily to baseball and became a catcher in the barehand days when a man who took on that job knew full well he was inviting two hands full of broken fingers, an almost certain broken nose, a mouth half bereft of teeth, and possibly a vagrant eye, as well. But the Deacon was tougher than bull beef, and he never quailed before a pitcher in all his career, which lasted from 1884 until 1912.

When he started out, he was the battery mate of a fast and tricky pitcher named Charles Busted Baldwin, who was called "Lady" Baldwin because of his gentlemanly ways. Lady threw a "snake ball" that tantalized the batters of the day with its sudden deviations from the expected path. But it never fazed Deacon McGuire, who took every pitch in his oak-hard hands, snagged all the foul tips he could reach and refused to let finger fractures keep him from the game. The Deacon could get away from the iron foundry only on Saturday afternoons and Sundays, so Lady Baldwin became a weekend pitcher, there being no one else in that part of southern Michigan who could hold Lady's fastball.

It was said of Deacon McGuire, even before he had become a major-league catcher, that he "could catch a cannonball." No one ever tested the accuracy of that claim, but it seems certain that if any *had* sent a cannonball the

Deacon's way, he'd have stabbed for it with one hand or the other. Both hands were equally battered when Deacon was still a youth, and by the time he was permitted to wear protective equipment behind the bat, his hands looked like two ancient cypress roots torn out of a swamp.

After playing for Terre Haute and Toledo, Deacon McGuire entered big-league baseball with Detroit, where he teamed with Wild Bill Donovan, the original wild man, who could aim for the strike zone and put the ball over the grandstand. Once the Deacon signaled to Donovan for a pitchout, and Donovan, firing full strength, very nearly pitched the ball out of the park. McGuire leaped for the ball, just took a small piece of it with his longest finger, and had the finger bent straight back by the force of the throw. The flesh was stripped right off the bone, neat as a filet of flounder. Bald Bob Emslie, umpiring behind the plate, took one look at the finger and fell in a faint. But the Deacon remained erect, had the finger attended to, and was catching again before the end of the week. "We were short of catchers," he explained.

By that time, the Deacon was using a catcher's glove with a little padding in it, but his meat hand had been nearest the ball. In semipro ball in southern Michigan and while at Terre Haute, Deacon used only the thin fingerless gloves permitted. (Sometimes they were flesh colored to hide the catcher's shame.) At Toledo, Deacon caught the pitches of Hank O'Day, who earned his greatest fame as an umpire. O'Day was even faster than Lady Baldwin, so McGuire would usually tuck a piece of beefsteak under the skin of the tight glove on his left hand. After the game it was not always easy to see where steak stopped and McGuire began.

In 1895, Deacon McGuire, while playing with Washington, caught every inning of every game his club played—all 133 of them. And in that season, there being no foul-strike rule to shorten a batter's stay at the plate, an inning might last partway to forever.

Deacon went on to play on the clubs that won pennants for Charlie Ebbets of Brooklyn, a thrifty gentleman in the true clubowner tradition, who awarded his club a $4,000 bonus ($160 each) for taking the 1899 flag and then, when they won the championship again in 1900, blessed each man with a pair of cuff links. The Deacon after that played again for Detroit, then came to New York to catch for the American League club from 1904 to 1906. He was sitting on the bench in 1904 on the day Happy Jack Chesbro flung that famous wild pitch that lost the pennant to the Puritans (later the Red Sox) from Boston. Had the Deacon been on the job, he might just possibly have brought that ball down and have been with another pennant winner. But he had no fault to find with Red Kleinow, the catcher who could not reach the ball even though some of Happy Jack's partisans insisted afterward the pitch should have been called "passed ball by the catcher."

"There wasn't a chance of stopping that spitter," said McGuire. "It might as well have gone over the top of the grandstand."

(In the next inning, McGuire went to bat for Chesbro and received a base on balls, but he did not score.)

Three years later, McGuire himself was in Boston, managing the club now called the Red Sox. In 1909, 1910, and 1911 he managed the Cleveland club and in 1912 returned to Detroit as a coach. That year, while the club was playing in Philadelphia, all the regulars went on strike to protest the suspension and fine of Ty Cobb, who had climbed into the stands in New York one day to punch a fan who had been screaming insults at him. To protect the franchise, manager Hughey Jennings had to hire a bunch of new ballplayers from among the local semipros. Deacon McGuire went behind the plate to catch his last big league game. He made one hit, scored one run, and was charged with two errors. Detroit lost 24–2. Deacon Jim at that time was fifty years old.

Old Hoss Radbourne's slow pitch that dropped dead before it reached the batter was improved upon by many practitioners of that era and those who came after. None ever labored on this project more effectively than did an unreformed bricklayer named Thomas "Toad" Ramsey, who was "discovered" pitching (at the age of sixteen) in a vacant lot beside a firehouse in Indianapolis. His discoverer was a man named Jack Kerins, who ran a baseball team for one John T. Brush, president of the When Clothing Company. (Brush eventually became owner of the New York Giants.) Kerins saw young Toad striking out boys of all sizes, and he signed him on as a relief pitcher for the semipro club known as the "Whens." Despite his youth and despite the fact that he stood flatfooted in the pitching box and cranked his left arm twice around like a windmill before letting the ball go, Toad Ramsey soon became the best-known and the ablest left-handed pitcher in the land. Because his career was short, his name did not live long in baseball annals and his accomplishments will never be misremembered at Cooperstown. In his day, however, he was a greater marvel to most men than the electric trolley car.

Toad almost moved right into the major leagues at seventeen, because Indianapolis was awarded an American Association franchise the year after Toad joined the Whens and Kerins was made manager of the big-league club. But when Kerins asked if he could bring along his young pitcher, who had led the Municipal League the previous season, the owner said no. A major-league ball club, the owner decided, was no place for a teenaged boy. He was probably right, but it is doubtful if Toad's morals were nourished with quite the care they required, even with the club he did join—Chattanooga of the Southern League. Toad led that league in strikeouts and was sold next season to Louisville of the American Association, a big league at that time. In 1886, after one uncertain season with Louisville, Toad began to strike out everyone in sight. In an exhibition game against Detroit, a team that carried the heaviest hitters of the day—Dan Brouthers, Deacon White, Hardy Richardson, and Larry Twitchell—Toad Ramsey struck out thirteen, including all the four sluggers. When he faced Pittsburgh, he struck out twelve, and two days later he beat Cincinnati with fourteen strikeouts. He next took on the St. Louis Browns, the top club in the game. He struck out sixteen of them in ten innings. Altogether that season he had 499 strikeouts and twice fanned seventeen. His sixteen-strikeout game against St. Louis had spread his fame through the nation, and he continued to earn headlines all summer.

Toad Ramsey, just twenty-two years old that year, also pitched a no-hit no-run game against Baltimore in July, although the records do not give him credit for it. He struck out seventeen in that game and did not even grant the Baltimores a long fly. There were no hits listed in the Baltimore *Sun* boxscore next day, and the writer acknowledged that it was the "greatest game ever seen in Baltimore," with not a single hit by the home club. Since that day, however, someone has tucked a base hit in after Baltimore center fielder O'Connell's name.

Two days later, Toad faced Baltimore again and in twelve innings struck out seventeen. He granted one hit this time and had the home fans howling with laughter at the manner in which the locals flailed in vain at young Ramsey's "drop ball."

Next season, Toad might have really pitched himself into the Hall of Fame except that the professional thinkers of the game decided to see how baseball would work if the batter were allowed four strikes. This rule made the hill a whole lot steeper for Toad. But he won ball games and struck out batters all the same. On June 21, 1887, he struck out seventeen Cleveland batters, granting each one of them four strikes, just as the book said he should. A week later he struck out sixteen St. Louis batters. Altogether he pitched sixty-five games that season and won thirty-seven of them, with a total of 355 strikeouts.

How did he do it? It was all an accident. Or at least his trick pitch that caused men to disbelieve their eyes came about as a result of a stupid accident that befell him when he was a bricklayer's apprentice and should have been in school. Somebody dropped a hod of bricks or some such trifle on young Tom's left hand and cut the tendon in his middle finger so he could not flex it. As a result, he could merely perch this finger atop the ball and so threw a natural knuckleball. He practiced the pitch faithfully as a boy, and when he had become a professional, he could drop four out of five pitches right on the plate—and often did so to win side bets.

Some years later a young man christened Mordecai Peter Centennial Brown (he having been born in 1876) suffered a similar accident. He lost the better part of his right index finger in a corn chopper and so could not grip a baseball tight. As a result, he, too, threw a ball to which the thumb imparted most of the spin and which would drop, or seem to, with extreme suddenness as it reached the plate. But Brown did not become a pitcher right away, perhaps feeling that his handicap prevented him. In amateur ball he was always an infielder. When he joined the St. Louis club in the National League in 1903, he was throwing a wide curve that dropped very quickly away from the batter. But he did not use his pitch with full effect until he came to the Chicago Cubs in 1904. Then he ran off eight winning seasons in a row and pitched the club to a pennant in 1908. Whether his pitch was any more mystifying or any better controlled than Toad Ramsey's is a question. But he had far better control of his appetites.

Poor Toad Ramsey, sulking because the thrifty Louisville manager would not reward his winning thirty-seven games by offering him a small raise in salary, took to sharing his sorrow with whatever bartender would listen. In 1888, he was seldom in condition to play baseball, and he won only eight games out of forty-one that he tried. In 1889 Toad gave his full attention to drinking and for three solid weeks during the baseball season was not even able to find the ballpark. After this he was sold to the St. Louis Browns. There Toad took the pledge—even though the club owner, Chris Von der Ahe, self-styled "greatest feller in baseball," had taken up baseball as a means of promoting the sale of beer. In 1890, while most of baseball's big stars were playing in the Players League, Toad remained among the scabs and won twenty-six games. But Von der Ahe thought Toad should win every game—just he as decided, after seeing a right-field home run, that all balls should be hit to right field—and he scolded his loyal employee for losing occasionally. Toad lost his temper and promptly his job, as well. He completed his playing career by wandering from club to club in the South, and he resumed his drinking career at the same time. He wound up with the Admirals of Indianapolis, back home again, broke and without control of his magic pitch. In one game against Lebanon, Toad issued fourteen walks.

After that Toad did some umpiring, organized a minor league so he could find a pitching job (with Kokomo), learned he was unable to find the plate even in Kokomo, and so went back to bricklaying. Mordecai Brown, whom Toad might have matched, wound up in the Hall of Fame. Toad has been forgotten.

The composer of "The Washington Post March" was born in that city in 1854 and grew up among such future big-timers as Paul Hines, Charley Snyder, and Joe Gerhardt. John Philip Sousa was not only a baseball fan but also a baseball player, pitching for a team composed of members of his own traveling band. This bit is excerpted from an article the "March King" published in *Baseball Magazine* as "The Greatest Game in the World."

JOHN PHILIP SOUSA

Balls and Batons Forever

I played ball off and on from my sixth year until about my forty-fifth. The last game I played, probably the grand finale of my diamond career, was with a nine composed of members of my band. In the report of the game, my forty years of off-and-on service was dismissed by the following criticism of a reporter:

> It has long been apparent to those who have watched Sousa leading his band that if he ever got into a pitcher's box he would be too swift for the eye to follow. The only trouble was that the March King had no control over the ball when he started to wrap himself up and you could not tell whether the ball was coming out in the direction of the batsman or the center fielder.

And this scathing criticism simply because, in one inning, I gave four men bases on balls and forced in a run! Ye gods and little fishes, but I was sore on that reporter! Handing out such a line of talk to a man who had been in the game for almost forty years! But I knew that there must be something wrong, and I decided to quit the game.

In my band we have had a ball team for many years. Playing at the Exposition in Paris in 1900, on our natal day, the Fourth of July, our team played the nine of the American Guards on the Bagatelle Field in Paris. What could have been more appropriate for two American organizations in a foreign land to do on the glorious Fourth?

Last June, a year ago, at Willow Grove, Philadelphia, our band played the Marine Corps nine, my old colleagues, for I was for twelve years bandmaster of the U.S. Marine Corps. The following is the account of a baseball reporter of that, to us, great event:

If Connie Mack could have witnessed the game of baseball yesterday morning he would have been tempted to make John Philip Sousa an offer. The March King proved a wonder in the pitcher's box, and although he lasted but one inning, he retired Lieutenant O'Leary's colts in one, two, three order; then Mr. Sousa retired to the coaching line, where he gave an imitation of Arlie Latham that caused the spectators to howl with delight. When Umpire Schlotterbeck said "play ball," the versatile athlete musician, composer and author cast an eagle eye over the field, noted that his men were all in place and ready to come in on the first beat; then he spat on the new ball, threw his right leg around in front of the left, raised his arm above his head, lunged forward, and the umpire said "Strike one!" Suffice it to say Hopkins fanned. It was a surprise for the Marines. They had been looking for something easy, and no one imagined that any man could write a march to

King Edward VII and twirl the sphere for a strike out on big Hopkins, the slugger, all in the same season.

The following is from *Musical America*, 1907:

To the baseball player who must stand in the sizzling sun hurling a baseball as nearly as he may over a home base, the swinging of a baton by the conductor of an orchestra seems lazy work, and he might be surprised to learn that when John Philip Sousa wants to rest, it is in the pitcher's box that he seeks diversion. For it's true, no matter how astonishing it may seem, that the composer of the worldwide-known marches and exceedingly tuneful operas is really a pronounced baseball fan; not one whose fandom merely leads him to a seat in the bleachers or grand stand to yell at plays or misplays, but one who is a captain of a ball team of his own, who is a pitcher of no mean skill, who strikes 'em out with the best of them, and whose players in one campaign won eleven out of thirteen games played. . . .

Jules Tygiel is professor of history at San Francisco State University and commissioner of the Pacific Ghost League (a computerized "Rotisserie League" of considerable sophistication and bonhomie). There is ease in Tygiel's manner, whether in the groves of academe or the green fields of the mind. His 1983 book, *Baseball's Great Experiment: Jackie Robinson and His Legacy*, is a masterful blend of these twin devotions. Jackie Robinson's entrance into Organized Baseball has been documented often, though never better than in Tygiel's book; here are the less well known stories of Sam Jethroe, Luke Easter, Bob Thurman, Ray Dandridge, Chuck Harmon, and Piper Davis.

JULES TYGIEL

"The Only Thing I Wanted to Do Was Hit the Major Leagues"

I was explaining the "situation" to Luke shortly after he joined our team. I told him that a few fans might not like him because of his race, that he must overlook their boos. But Luke explained the whole thing to me when he said, "Mister Starr, everybody likes me when I hit that ball!"
San Diego Padres president William Starr, 1949

I

Luscious Easter was a figure of Bunyanesque proportions. His massive 6-foot 4-inch frame radiated awesome strength, yet he charmed people with his gentle manner and humor. Easter's tastes in fashion included "racy pinstripe suits" and a diamond ring that resembled "the headlight of the Santa Fe Chief." His age was indeterminate; his background shrouded in mystery. The records list his birth date as August 4, 1921, but Luke referred to that as his "baseball birthday" and hinted that he might be five, or perhaps ten, years older. Despite his advanced age, Easter had not appeared in the Negro Leagues until 1947, when he materialized on the Homestead Grays as the power-hitting replacement for the late Josh Gibson.

Upon arrival in the Pacific Coast League two years later, Easter remained a relative unknown. Bill Veeck made a special excursion to Puerto Rico to sign

the giant slugger during the winter and offered his services to the San Diego
Padres. Veeck advised Padres President William Starr that his latest discovery
"could hit the ball as hard and as far as Babe Ruth." "I thought he was kidding
me," admitted the incredulous Starr. In the Padres first six games Easter pounded
two prodigious home runs and two blistering line-drive triples. Starr and the
baseball fans of the western slope knew that Veeck had not exaggerated.

The arrival of Luke Easter in the Pacific Coast League in 1949 heralded the
advent of widespread minor-league integration. During the next few years
Easter and other black athletes introduced interracial baseball to cities and
towns throughout the nation, enduring regional variations of prejudice and
discrimination while struggling to advance to the major leagues. To younger
players the lower classifications represented the gateway to stardom. But for
many Negro League veterans, trapped by the persistent racism of the newly
integrated sport, the minor leagues at mid-century marked the final frustration
of a lifetime of exclusion.

Easter was not the first black player in the Pacific Coast League. In 1948
the Padres had fielded John Ritchey, a promising young catcher who batted
.300 as a part-time performer. Ritchey's debut had elicited minimal reaction
in the West. The following season, the Padres signed a working agreement
with the Cleveland Indians, who assigned Easter and shortstop Artie Wilson
to join Ritchey on the roster.

Easter quickly captured the imagination of Coast League personnel and fans.
In his first fifteen games the black first baseman batted .436 with 5 home runs
and 23 runs batted in. Observers hailed him as the "greatest natural hitter the
Coast League has seen since Ted Williams." "I've seen a lot of powerful hitters
in my time," reflected Sacramento Manager Del Baker, "but for sheer ability
to knock the ball great distances, I've never seen anybody better than Easter."
Manager Fred Haney of Hollywood agreed. "I wish they'd get him out of here
before he kills every infielder in the Coast League," exclaimed Haney.

The prowess of the massive black athlete became legend on the West Coast.
Scouts marveled at Easter's "amazing fielding" and his speed, labeling him
"the fastest big man in baesball." Writers compared his batting and drawing
power to Babe Ruth. As early as March 23, the *Sporting News* reported, "fans
are coming here from miles away to see him bust the apple." In a four-week
tour of Oakland, San Francisco, Los Angeles, and Hollywood, the Padres attracted 240,000 customers, setting new records in Los Angeles and San Francisco. In the latter city, an estimated 1,000 fans stood atop automobiles to gaze
over stadium walls at the conquering hero. When Easter came to bat, both
blacks and whites in the crowd rose to their feet, tossing hats and seat cushions
in the air when he hit safely. "When he takes his turn at batting practice,"
described sportswriter Frank Finch, noting the unusually early crowd arrival,
"the other players, the sportswriters, the goober salesmen and fans rivet their
eyes on the batting cage to watch Luke powder the ball."

Easter's tape-measure home runs combined with his status as one of the few
blacks in the Pacific Coast League to make him the frequent target of brushback

pitches. A month into the season, League President Clarence Rowland, in response to complaints about close pitches directed at Easter, issued a memorandum cautioning against the use of the beanball. Easter seemed unperturbed. Against Portland in April pitchers "low bridged" him twice. The first time up Easter hit the next pitch for a home run, and the second time he "lashed a savage drive" right back at the pitcher.

Remarkably, Easter performed his spectacular feats while playing with a painful injury. During spring training Easter had broken his kneecap in a collision. Although surgery was required to repair the damage, doctors advised Easter that he could continue to play without incurring irreparable harm. Easter was determined to complete the season, but by late June the pain had become unbearable. On July 1 Easter's career with the Padres came to an end. He had played in eighty games and batted .363 with 25 home runs and 92 runs-batted-in. To the chagrin of Coast League owners, attendance dropped to pre-Easter levels after his departure. Owners estimated that Easter's injury cost them $200,000 in gate receipts.

Luke Easter was the most spectacular of the wave of black athletes who entered Organized Baseball in 1949. With major-league teams signing non-whites in greater numbers, blacks appeared in every Class AAA and Class A minor league in 1949. (Both AA circuits, the Texas League and the Southern Association, were in the Jim Crow belt.) Major- and minor-league organizations, finally convinced that integration had become a reality, found the cream of the Negro Leagues at their disposal. They purchased many aging stars and young prospects from that dying institution. Generally underestimating the quality of play in the Negro Leagues, baseball officials placed most of the new recruits in classifications far beneath the players' talents. As a result, blacks compiled astounding statistics in the early years of integration.

In the Pacific Coast League, "prompted by the record-breaking box-office draw of Luke Easter," several clubs entered the hunt for black talent. In late May, Commissioner Chandler voided Artie Wilson's contract with the Cleveland Indians, who released him from their San Diego franchise. The Oakland Oaks quickly signed the shortstop, and the spindly, spray-hitting Wilson immediately established himself as the outstanding infielder in the Pacific Coast League. Wilson won the league batting championship with a .349 average, also pacing the league in hits and stolen bases. The Portland Beavers and Los Angeles also added blacks to their rosters during the 1949 campaign. Within two years every Pacific Coast League club fielded blacks.

Integration proceeded more slowly but no less successfully in the American Association. Roy Campanella had broken the league color line in 1948. At the start of the 1949 season, young Jim Pendleton, a fleet shortstop for the St. Paul Dodgers, was the sole black in the Association. His isolation ended on June 5 when the New York Giants assigned Negro League veterans Dave Barnhill, a pitcher, and Ray Dandridge, an infielder, to their Minneapolis Millers franchise. Barnhill met with indifferent success; Dandridge became the sensation of the American Association.

When he signed with the Giants, Dandridge stated that he was twenty-nine years old. He admits now that he actually was thirty-six. Many believe that even that figure stretches the truth. He had begun his playing career in 1933 with the Detroit Stars. One year later, he joined the Newark Eagles, where he played third base in the "black million-dollar infield" alongside shortstop Willie Wells, second baseman Dick Seay, and first baseman Mule Suttles. Roy Campanella called it the greatest infield alignment he ever saw. In 1940 millionaire Jorge Pasquel lured Dandridge to the Mexican League, lavishing favors and bonuses on his star infielder for the next eight years. Mexican fans, recalls Dandridge, treated him like a king. While Jackie Robinson broke the color line in 1947, Dandridge was serving as player-manager of the Alamendares club in the Mexican League.

Those who witnessed this short, stocky, strikingly bowlegged athlete in action agree that he may well have been the premier third baseman in baseball annals. Historian Richard Crepeau, who watched an almost-forty-year-old Dandridge in the twilight of his career, calls him the greatest performer at the hot corner that he ever observed. Sam Lacy asserts that Dandridge's "quick hands would give the efforts of Billy Cox and Brooks Robinson the aspect of a replay in slow motion." Plus, adds Lacy, "he could hit far better than either of them." Monte Irvin concurs. "There's never been a third baseman who could play better than Dandridge. I don't care who it was—Brooks Robinson, Graig Nettles, Pie Traynor—nobody." Yet in 1949 even the most knowledgeable of white baseball fans had never heard of Ray Dandridge.

Dandridge arrived in Minneapolis hoping that his play in the highest minor leagues would earn him an opportunity in the majors despite his advanced age. On June 5 he debuted against Warren McDermott, a young fastballing strikeout artist. "You know what he did to me," Dandridge states rather than asks. "I had to eat dirt. He throwed at my head." The veteran rookie was undaunted. "I didn't pay it no mind. So I get back up. Next one, he came down the groove with it, and I hit it right by his head, dead centerfield." Dandridge did not reach base on that play, robbed by an outstanding infield stop. The following night he began a twenty-eight-game hitting streak. He complemented his batting with the acrobatic fielding that had made him a legend among Negro and Mexican League patrons. Local reporters dubbed him "Old Bandy Legs the Dandy" and the "Black Honus Wagner." Minneapolis fans idolized him. Dandridge completed the season with a .364 batting average, just two points shy of the league lead. "Ol' Man Dandridge" finished second in the American Association balloting for Rookie of the Year.

The third Triple A minor league, the International League, had featured black players on the Montreal team since 1946. In 1949 league President Frank Shaughnessy boasted before the season, "We will have the most colorful league of all time." Both the Jersey City franchise, affiliated with the Giants, and the Yankee farm team at Newark added blacks to their rosters. On all three clubs blacks approached the high standards set by Easter, Wilson, and Dandridge.

At Montreal the Dodger farm club, which had already treated Canadian fans to Robinson, Campanella, and Newcombe, offered Dan Bankhead and Sam Jethroe. Reporters labeled Bankhead, working his way back to the major leagues, "the wild man of the International League." Nonetheless, he posted a 20–6 record while leading the circuit in strikeouts and walks. Jethroe, nicknamed "The Jet" and "Mercury Man," emerged as the foremost gate attraction in the league. He batted .326 and scored 151 runs. His 89 stolen bases established a new league record.

The Little Giants of Jersey City featured three black players: Monte Irvin, Hank Thompson, and pitcher Ford Smith. While Smith experienced a disappointing season, both Irvin and Thompson won promotion to the Giants in July. Irvin, the thirty-year-old former Newark Eagle, whom many had deemed the most likely prospect to break the color line before World War II, amply demonstrated his still-considerable talents. In 63 games with the Little Giants, he batted .373 and drove in 52 runs. (In 1950 the parent club again asked Irvin to start the season at Jersey City. In 18 games he batted .510 and drove in 33 runs, earning him the appellation of "Mr. Murder, Inc." and a hurried call to the Polo Grounds.)

The Yankees had less success with their initial signees. Angel Marquez and Frank Austin began the season with the Newark Bears, and both played well. In May, when Chandler awarded Marquez's contract to the Indians, however, the Yankees also sold Austin, leaving their top farm team with no black players. The Bears, struggling at the box office, remained all white until late July, when the Yankees purchased outfielder Bob Thurman and catcher Earl Taborn from the Kansas City Monarchs. Thurman was the more impressive prospect of the two. The *Courier* described him as a "home run hitter deluxe," who, despite his powerful six-foot one-inch, 210-pound frame, had "tootsies lined with mercury." The *Courier* added that Thurman, a former pitcher, "could throw with the best of them."

Thurman immediately lived up to his advance billing. In his first game he hit two singles and then powered "one of the longest homers ever seen at the [Newark] ballpark." Thurman hit two more home runs in his first week of play, including a grand slam. Like Easter, his former Negro League teammate, Thurman astounded spectators with the sheer distance of his drives. All of his home runs traveled over 400 feet, and at least one exceeded 500 feet. After a month with Newark, Thurman was batting .371, though a hand injury dropped his average to .317 at the season's end.

At times, the black players in Triple-A baseball in 1949 appeared so unstoppable that rival managers devised unique strategies to thwart them. In the Pacific Coast League, where Artie Wilson's opposite-field swinging produced 211 hits, San Francisco Manager Lefty O'Doul applied a "reverse shift," bringing his center fielder in to play shortstop and placing all of his fielders except the first baseman to the left of second base. The strategy failed to significantly deter Wilson. At Buffalo, Manager Paul Richards defied conventional baseball logic and intentionally walked the pitcher when there were two outs and nobody on base to pitch to leadoff hitter Sam Jethroe. "If we get the pitcher out," explained Richards, "we have Jethroe leading off. . . . [If] he gets on base, he's going to steal second and very possibly third." On the other hand, argued Richards, if he walked the pitcher, even if Jethroe reached base, "He can't hurt us with his speed because he's got the pitcher in front of him."

The black influx was not confined to the Triple A level. Throughout the minor leagues in the North and West blacks appeared for the first time with comparable results. At Wilkes-Barre, Harry "Suitcase" Simpson established himself as "one of the greatest sluggers" ever to perform in the Class A Eastern League, clouting "the longest drives hit in three of the loop's parks." His teammate Roy Welmaker, a veteran Negro League pitcher, registered twenty-two victories. Wilkes-Barre attendance increased dramatically. In the New England League, George Crowe batted .365 and drove in over 100 runs.

Needless to say, not all the black players active in 1949 attained these levels of performance. Many were given brief tryouts and then released; others displayed routine abilities. Nonetheless, given the relatively small numbers of black players in Organized Baseball, a high proportion produced not just good seasons but spectacular ones. At the same time, the black standard-bearers in the majors continued their outstanding examples. Robinson, Doby, Campanella, and New-combe all appeared in the All-Star Game. Robinson enjoyed his finest season as a professional. He batted .342 and won the National League Most Valuable Player Award, leading the Dodgers to the pennant. Newcombe became the Rookie of the Year. Paige, alone among the five black major leaguers who played an entire season, fared poorly, registering only four wins in eleven decisions.

In the age of Jim Crow common stereotypes had depicted black ballplayers as road-show clowns, far inferior to their white counterparts. The high standards established by baseball's racial pioneers created a new, no less stereotypical, image of the black athlete. "They have an inborn advantage in natural speed and strength," concluded Boston Brave scout Jack Zeller, "and when they also possess high intelligence, they are better athletes, as a class, than whites." The black ballplayer loomed as a "mercury-footed" daring base runner, like Robinson, Jethroe, and Wilson; the author of gargantuan home runs, like Doby, Easter, and Thurman; a pitcher of blazing speed, tinged with a touch of wildness, like Newcombe and Bankhead. Americans readily assimilated the new image of blacks. As "natural" athletes, blacks depended on brawn and reflex rather than brain or reason; as entertainers, they entered a domain in which they were already accepted. But these exacting standards raised the expectations for all blacks who entered baseball in the 1950s. Lesser performances provoked a chorus of boos and provided baseball executives with a rationale for keeping above-average, though not exceptional, black players in the minor leagues.

II

"I am a man of substance, of flesh and bone, fiber and liquids—and I might even be said to possess a mind," lamented the black protagonist in Ralph

Ellison's novel *Invisible Man*. "I am invisible, understand, simply because people refuse to see me." Ellison's portrayal of black America won the National Book Award in 1952. That same year, eighteen-year-old John Roseboro began his professional baseball career in the Dodger farm system. For the next several seasons Roseboro played in cities like Pueblo, Colorado, Sheboygan, Wisconsin, and Danville, Illinois—a pioneer on a frontier that few realized existed, an invisible man in baesball's vast minor-league domain.

Most Americans perceived racial prejudice as a southern problem, but hostility to blacks knew no regional boundaries. The introduction of black minor-league athletes was an unwelcomed occurrence in many communities, particularly those in which few blacks resided or in which *de facto* segregation prevailed. "There isn't a Nigger in Sheboygan," Roseboro wrote his parents during his first season. "Send your clippers to me. The peckers don't know how to cut a nigger's hair." In most towns, Roseboro and his black teammates lived in run-down boardinghouses separate from their white colleagues. Restaurants often refused them service. In Salt Lake City, aware that most eating places would not welcome them, the black players on the Pueblo Dodgers tried a small Chinese restaurant. The waiters ignored them until, following a long wait, the Chinese owner asked them to leave. At rustic minor-league ball parks, fans taunted Roseboro with cries of "Sambo," "Chocolate drop," and "Snowball."

The Dodgers, states Roseboro, "have always been a first-class organization." The team that had broken the color line, it remained throughout the 1950s more sensitive to the problems of black players than other clubs. Nonetheless, they offered little in the way of advice or assistance to the young black prospects in the farm system. "At the same time when they signed blacks and Latins," asserts Roseboro, "they should have made sure they would be welcome. If the black Dodgers weren't welcome in a motel, hotel, or theater, the white Dodgers should have fought for their rights and walked out." Instead, Roseboro discovered that "the Dodgers didn't care if I had race troubles to go with my growing-up troubles and playing troubles."

"You ache with the need to convince yourself that you do exist in the real world," asserted Ellison's invisible man. Recalling the indignities of his minor-league career, Roseboro relates, "I'm sorry I didn't have the guts to do anything about it. . . . But what could I have done? Gotten locked up for disturbing the peace? I didn't know what to do about bigotry."

Throughout the nation black athletes re-created Roseboro's experiences amidst the indifference of baseball officials. Minor-league intermediaries rarely, if ever, relayed reports of race relations, and afraid to jeopardize their careers, the players themselves rarely complained. Major-league executives remained blissfully unaware of conditions in their farm systems, an ignorance born of insensitivity and unfamiliarity rather than malice.

The reception accorded black athletes varied from region to region and city to city. Blacks who played in the Northern League in Wisconsin and Minnesota have fond memories of towns like Eau Claire and St. Cloud. Other areas were far less appealing. Piper Davis, the former player-manager of the Birmingham Black Barons, entered organized baseball in 1950. During the next eight years he appeared in four different minor leagues. As a barnstormer in the Negro Leagues and as a basketball player with the Harlem Globetrotters, Davis had traveled extensively throughout the United States. When young players would ask him about conditions in the South, Davis would reply, "They love me in the South. They tell me where I can go. They got signs up that say, 'Negroes here and whites here.'" In the North, on the other hand, Davis explained, "You don't know where you can eat. You go into a restaurant in the lower part of Illinois and Indiana, the waitress pass you up ninety miles an hour. And finally you come up and say, 'Can we get some service?' They say, 'We don't serve Negroes.'" Black players, alleged Davis, were refused service more in the West than in the South.

Other athletes agreed with Davis's tongue-in-cheek observations. Pitcher Dave Hoskins, who later became the first black in the Texas League, experienced the harshest treatment of his career with Grand Rapids of the Central League. Former major leaguer Leon Wagner contends that "conditions in southern Illinois were worse than I ran into in Tennessee." Syracuse, New York, ranked as one of the worst spots for blacks in the International League. Davis reports that in Pacific Coast League cities, where the large wartime and postwar migration of blacks had unleashed widespread racist sentiments, "I learned more names than I thought we had."

Fans routinely hurled racial insults at black athletes, with certain spectators reappearing regularly to taunt them. Bob Thurman recalls an old man in Baltimore who always called him an "African Bohemian." An Oakland fan would sit behind the dugout with a bottle of Jim Beam, and when an opposing black player would appear, he would howl at Davis, "Hey, Piper, here comes your cousin." Artie Wilson had a personal heckler in Sacramento who "called me all kinds of names." Most players rarely responded outwardly. "Every time I would hear a racial remark, I'd look straight ahead, and I'd just ignore it," says Davis. "I played mad a lot," laughs Thurman. "But I didn't let on. I was burning right in there, but I'd just take it out on the ball."

Local displeasure at the appearance of black players also manifested itself outside of the ballparks. Piper Davis attended spring training in Oakland in 1951 and stayed with the local Oaks at the California Hotel. When the season began, the team stopped paying for players' housing, and his welcome evaporated. Returning from his first road trip, Davis discovered that the hotel had not reserved a room for him. Teammate Hank Behrman arranged to have a rollaway bed placed in his room to temporarily accommodate Davis. "Checkout time was two o'clock Monday," recalls Davis. "I made it my business to be right over there at two o'clock for checkout. No room. Tuesday, no room." On Wednesday hotel officials assigned Davis a room on the mezzanine right next to the elevator. "Looked like the elevator was in the room, it was so close," says Davis. When the team left for its next road trip, Davis attempted to reserve lodgings for his return. The clerk informed him that the hotel would no longer accommodate him. In many cities black players regularly faced this type of treatment as they learned the limits of racial acceptance.

Minor-league teams exacerbated this situation with their own segregation policies. Ball clubs rarely assigned blacks and whites as roommates. Where a team fielded more than one black, they always lived together. Where a solitary black appeared, he would normally have his own quarters. Only on rare occasions did teams violate this rule. In 1947, when Don Newcombe returned for a second season at Nashua without Roy Campanella, he roomed with his new catcher, Gus Gallipeau. At Olean in the Pony League, Chuck Harmon shared his lodgings with white teammate Paul Owens, who later became the general manager of the Philadelphia Phillies. In 1949 when shortstop Artie Wilson reported to Oakland, he relates, "I was supposed to room by myself, but I had one who chose to room with me, so I had no trouble at all." The "one" was Wilson's double-play partner, Billy Martin.

These examples represent the exceptions. Throughout the 1950s and well into the next decade, most teams took precautions against interracial accommodations. "I played on four different Triple A teams by myself, and that was rough," recalls Bob Thurman. "I'd go to the movies by myself." Teammates rarely invited the genial Thurman to accompany them socially. An invitation by a new teammate on the San Francisco Seals to go to a movie so shocked Thurman, he "almost fainted." At the night's end, the two players returned to the hotel with "two blondes." Four days later the Seals traded away the white player. Thurman sorely felt the absence of social companionship. "If you had a bad day, you didn't have anybody to talk to. You'd talk to yourself," he remembers. "You had to be like a steel man to take being alone."

Despite the absence of social contact and friendships, Thurman and most blacks who played in the 1950s have few complaints about their teammates. "I never had any trouble with any players," says Thurman, "because I respected the players and they always respected me." Wilson describes his white colleagues as "super." Piper Davis recalls only one instance of conflict with his teammates. After he swung at a pitch and fell off balance, he heard a voice from the dugout call, "Get up, Uncle Remus." Davis sat down next to the culprit when he returned to the dugout and in his firm, quiet way let it be known that he would not tolerate future remarks. No further taunts reached Davis.

The racial tension inherent in the early years of integration notwithstanding, fights between black and white teammates proved rare. In 1949 in the Eastern League, pitcher Roy Welmaker and his white catcher squared off on the field following the catcher's refusal to support Welmaker's protests on close pitches. The pair exchanged several blows before teammates separated them. The following year, white pitcher Marino Pieretti and black shortstop Frank Austin of the Portland Beavers battled after a batting-practice dispute. "It wasn't a racial fight; it was just a baseball fight," concluded reporters, none of whom wrote of the incident until several decades later. Other minor flare-ups doubtless occurred, but contrary to the fears of integration opponents, little overt friction ever surfaced among blacks and whites involuntarily united on the same squad.

Nonetheless, every season after 1947 witnessed incidents of interracial conflict on the diamond. During the International League play-offs in 1948, "they came close to fighting the Civil War all over again," claimed Dink Carroll. Syracuse catcher Stan West attacked Montreal hurler Don Newcombe after the latter had brushed him back at the plate. Newcombe, not usually known for his even temper, ducked West's charge and refused to fight. "Had he tangled with West," reported Carroll, "there might have been a race riot in the stands that would have made a tornado look like a zephyr." The next season, Luis Angel Marquez engaged in two altercations with white players in the Pacific Coast League.

These episodes, and others like them, were typical of baseball battles; despite enraged tempers, minimal combat ensued. The first true racial donnybrook occurred in Oakland in 1952. San Francisco Seals pitcher Bill Boemler regularly aimed fastballs at Piper Davis and Ray Noble, the Oaks' two black stars. In mid-July he hit Davis on the elbow, sidelining him for a week. On July 27 Boemler twice forced Davis to sprawl in the dirt. Davis responded with a two-base hit. On the next play, he attempted to score with Boemler covering home plate. "I said, 'Here's my chance,'" recalls Davis, "and I bowled him over." According to accounts of the game, Boemler attempted to tag Davis with a "vicious blow in the face." Davis "tore into the pitcher with both fists." Teammates and black and white fans soon joined the pair. Noble, according to a sportswriter, "knocked down San Francisco players as though they were ten pins." And Davis states, "Noble was hitting everything white coming towards him." One reporter described the battle as "one of the most slambang baseball fights ever witnessed." Several days later, a San Francisco-based "Group of 19" threatened violent retaliation against Davis and Noble when the pair appeared at Seals Stadium. The Oaks turned the matter over to the local police and FBI, and both men played as scheduled. They encountered no difficulties.

The Coast League free-for-all constituted a rare event. It was triggered, however, by the most common weapon of antiblack hostility, the beanball. During the 1949 season when blacks first appeared in the minor leagues in significant numbers, a near epidemic of beanings resulted. Beanballs hospitalized one out of four black nonpitchers in Triple A baseball in 1949. In June, Hank Thompson had to be carried off the field and hospitalized after being hit in the head by a pitch. Two weeks later Jim Pendleton in the American Association was rushed to the hospital, the victim of a Lew Burdette fastball. On July 26 an "errant" pitch knocked infielder Parnell Woods, recently acquired by the Oakland Oaks, unconscious, and attendants removed him on a stretcher. "As soon as you walked up there, you'd get knocked down," recalls Thurman of his first year in Organized Baseball.

The inordinate number of black victims did not decline as integration progressed. The 1951 season began with the beaning of Portland shortstop Frank

Austin on March 31. Six weeks later Bob Boyd of Sacramento received X rays at the hospital, after a pitch struck him in the head. In the Western League "errant" pitches found Denver second baseman Curt Roberts four times in one day. Roberts established a Western League record when pitchers struck him for the fifteenth time that season. The following year a beaning hospitalized the unfortunate Roberts.

That so many black players required hospitalization indicates that these were not always routine "brushback" pitches calculated to intimidate the batters but included "beanballs" designed to injure them. Throughout the early years of baseball integration and even beyond, black players, particularly those pioneering in a new league, faced greater dangers than the average performer. Where a black pitcher also appeared, the potential of retaliation offered a modicum of protection. On occasion, blacks would protest and fight back. But most players accepted this harassment as part of the game. "I was knocked down in the Negro Leagues so much," asserts Thurman, "this didn't bother me." In one instance, Thurman shouted out to his opponent, "You got guts enough to knock me down, show the fans you got guts enough to throw some strikes now." Thurman hit the next pitch for a home run. "Boy, did I ever suck him in," he laughs. "Man, that thing is still going out!"

If a player hoped to ascend to the major leagues, he ignored the physical and verbal taunts tossed before him. "You just go out there and try to work harder and you end up having guys that are calling you names come up and shake your hand," says Chuck Harmon philosophically. "That meant more to me than wanting to punch them in the mouth."

Harmon's minor-league record reveals the success of his policy. During three seasons with Olean in the Pony League, Harmon batted .351, .374, and .375. Promoted to higher classifications, Harmon remained a .300 hitter. Nor was Harmon an exceptional case. Despite the adversity that confronted them and their relatively small numbers, blacks appeared regularly among the league leaders wherever they played. In 1952 and 1953 five blacks finished among the top-ten American Association hitters. In the Pacific Coast League, Bob Boyd, Piper Davis, and Artie Wilson finished in the top three spots in batting in 1952. The following season, black hitters won the batting championship in both the American Association and the Pacific Coast League, while for the second straight year, a black was named the Most Valuable Player in the International League. Blacks duplicated these performances at many lower levels, as well.

Jackie Robinson had endured his pioneering ordeal amidst considerable fanfare and publicity. In the aftermath of his accomplishment, scores of other blacks performed in the unexposed corners of the United States, re-creating his trials and triumphs. Their remarkable achievements and contributions to the cause of racial equality rarely received acknowledgment. But at a time when segregation remained an unyielding American reality, they, like Robinson, carved out and affirmed the black man's niche in the national pastime.

III

For Negro League veterans the minor leagues marked the final stepping-stone on a prolonged odyssey. Their careers had encompassed the Jim Crow circuits, the interracial barnstorming tours, and the international flavor of Caribbean baseball. Finally allowed into Organized Baseball, many hoped for one last opportunity to play in the major leagues. In most cases, however, baseball officials continued to deny them. Philadelphia Athletics General Manager Art Ehlers confessed in 1953 that many Negro League players should have advanced rapidly in previous years. "The majors were reluctant," stated Ehlers, "and the men who were ready became overage and lost their opportunity." While minor-league spectators thrilled to the exploits of Ray Dandridge, Piper Davis, Artie Wilson, and others, these great talents remained unknown to baseball's broader audience.

Among the greatest mysteries of the early 1950s were the ages of the Negro League players flooding into the higher minor leagues. To enhance their possibilities for advancement, blacks routinely lied about their age, shearing off anywhere from two to ten years. Sug Cornelius recalls truthfully telling scouts who approached him that he was thirty-nine years old. "Then I read in the paper . . . out in San Diego, about eight or nine guys I had played with were playing," says Cornelius. "They were all twenty-six, twenty-eight years old. I could have kicked myself. I should have told him I was younger." Many players did just that. Pitcher Roy Welmaker walked into the Cleveland training camp in 1949 claiming to be twenty-seven. He won twenty-two games for the Class A Wilkes-Barre team that season and the Indians promoted him to San Diego in 1950. Welmaker won eight of his first ten Pacific Coast League decisions and was hailed as "the best lefty to come down the pike in many moons." But Welmaker "admitted he would never again see his thirty-sixth birthday," and the Cleveland management proclaimed him too old for a trial in the majors.

The assumption that black players were older than the years they claimed sometimes worked to their detriment. "Why, my Pappy isn't that old," exclaimed Dan Bankhead in response to rumors that he was thirty-nine. When Buzz Clarkson reported for a brief stint with the Boston Braves in 1952, a reporter described him as "a comparatively ancient colored shortstop," whose "indeterminable" age "was the only thing against him." Sam Jethroe charges that suspicions that he was older than his thirty-one years in 1953 may have shortened his major-league career.

The major-league antipathy for aging players doomed most of the surviving stars of the Jim Crow era to the Triple A arena. Only a handful played in the majors for any prolonged period of time. Satchel Paige fared better than most. Cleveland released Paige after he won only four games in 1949. It was not coincidental that Bill Veeck, Paige's patron, had relinquished control of the club. In 1951 Veeck purchased the hapless St. Louis Browns, and he immediately returned Paige to the spotlight. At least forty-three years of age, Paige established himself as one of the outstanding relief pitchers in baseball during the next three seasons. In 1952, pitching for a team that won only sixty-four games, the great hurler won twelve games and saved ten more. Veeck sold the Browns after the 1953 season. The new owners proclaimed a youth movement and dropped Paige.

The indefatigable Paige spent two years on the barnstorming circuit before Veeck, operating the Triple A Miami Marlins, beckoned again. Paige literally descended from the heavens on opening day, deposited by a helicopter. Marlin Manager Don Osborne believed Paige's appearance was another Veeck publicity stunt, but the "old man" hurled a four-hit shutout in his first start. Used primarily as a relief pitcher, Paige posted an 11-4 record with 16 saves and a remarkable 1.86 earned run average. "He stood out on the mound, and you could hear his stomach growl," recalls John Roseboro. "With all his windups and deliveries and soft stuff, it was a thrill just to bat against him." Paige remained in the International League for three years. In his final season, he won 10, lost 10, and boasted a 2.96 earned run average.

Luke Easter's Organized Baseball career paralleled that of Paige. At the close of the 1949 season the Indians rushed Easter to Cleveland, amidst much fanfare, to help in their abortive pennant drive. Easter, overweight and still recuperating from his operation, batted only .222 with no home runs. The disappointed Indian fans made Easter "the most booed player in the history of Cleveland Stadium." The *Sporting News* quickly pointed out, "There was no racial connotation. He was expected to hit and he didn't." In the spring of 1950 Easter started the season slowly, evoking more jeers. In mid-May he finally uncoiled his power. At the season's end he had belted 28 home runs and driven in 107 runs. Over his first three seasons with the Indians, Easter averaged 29 home runs and 100 RBIs. Nearing the age of forty and continually plagued by knee and ankle injuries, he appeared in only sixty-eight games in 1953. The following year, Easter returned to the minors.

Easter's playing career had not ended. For the next decade he reigned as the toast of the International League, appearing first with the Buffalo Bisons and later for the Rochester Red Wings. As the years passed, Easter could barely run, and his defensive range grew more limited, but he remained a dangerous hitter, ever capable of launching one of his prodigious projectiles. As late as 1957, Easter hit forty home runs. At Rochester, fans greeted his appearances with cries of "Luuuuuke, Luuuuuke, Luuuuuke" and waited through one-sided defeats in hopes that he might pinch-hit. He became the most popular player in the league, particularly among the younger fans. "In the early 1960's," writes sports columnist Bob Matthews, who grew up in Rochester, "I was convinced Luke Easter was the greatest man alive." It was not until 1964, at the age of forty-three or perhaps forty-eight or maybe fifty-three, that Luke took his last swing as a Red Wing.

Several other Negro League stars also had relatively brief careers in the major leagues. Sam Jethroe won the Rookie of the Year Award in 1950 as a Boston Brave, but failing eyesight, poor defense, and an influx of younger black players on the Braves banished him to the International League in 1953. After wandering through the Triple A maze for five years, Bob Thurman finally won promotion to the Cincinnati Reds in 1954. Already thirty-three years old, Thurman seved primarily as a pinch hitter for five seasons, slugging 16 home runs in only 190 at bats in 1957. Pitcher Connie Johnson also amassed a five-year major-league career despite a belated start while in his mid-thirties.

Baseball players refer to a brief tenure in the major leagues as "a cup of coffee." Artie Wilson received his "cup" of big-league life with the New York Giants in 1951. The former Black Baron shortstop had batted .348 and .312 in his two seasons in the Pacific Coast League. In spring training he earned a place on the Giants with a .480 batting average. But Wilson engaged in little regular-season action, registering only twenty-two at bats. "I was a rookie," he explains, "and a rookie does not get to break in with a[n infield] combination like Eddie Stanky and Alvin Dark." In late May the Giants had to make room for another rookie—Wilson's former Black Baron teammmate, twenty-year-old Willie Mays. Wilson was dispatched to Minneapolis where he performed briefly before his former owners in Oakland requested his return to boost lagging ticket sales. He remained in the Pacific Coast League for the rest of his career. A consistent .300 hitter, Wilson never again received a major-league offer.

Quincy Trouppe also received a brief taste of life in the big leagues. A powerfully built catcher who prided himself on his defensive skills and general knowledge of baseball, Trouppe had been a player-manager on several Negro and Mexican League clubs. At the age of thirty-nine, he received an opportunity to play for the Cleveland Indians in 1952. "I guess no one who has ever broken into Organized Baseball could have felt any better than I did when I inked my name to that new Cleveland contract," writes Trouppe in his autobiography. But in two and a half months in the majors Trouppe batted only ten times. In June, Cleveland assigned him to Indianapolis. "The terrible disappointment nearly choked me," states Trouppe. He protested his demotion but was advised, "You don't have a record to go on." The veteran catcher "thought about all the highs and lows that went into putting together twenty-two years of playing ball on two different continents and on islands in between." Yet, according to Organized Baseball logic, he had no record. Trouppe reported to Indianapolis in the American Association, where he hit six home runs in his first two weeks, but the Indians never recalled him. At the season's end, Trouppe retired.

Although denied the full measure of fame and achievement that they deserved, players like Trouppe and Wilson at least had the satisfaction of playing in the major leagues. Other black stars, like Piper Davis and Ray Dandridge, were not as fortunate.

There is little doubt that Lorenzo "Piper" Davis possessed major-league abilities. "If he'd had a chance when he was young," asserts Clyde Sukeforth, who scouted Davis for the Dodgers, "he'd have been outstanding." The versatile line-drive-hitting Davis performed ably at all positions. In 1945 the Dodgers considered him in their initial search for black players. In 1947 the St. Louis Browns took out an option on his services. But when the Browns released Hank Thompson and Willard Brown, they also allowed the option on Davis to expire.

Three years later, the Boston Red Sox made their initial foray into the black player market when they purchased Davis from the Birmingham Black Barons. The Red Sox paid Barons' owner Tom Hayes $7,500, with the promise to double that figure if Davis remained in the Boston organization past May 15. Davis, the player-manager of the Barons, claimed to be twenty-nine years old, cutting two years off his real age. Red Sox General Manager Joe Cronin told reporters that he had obtained the "sleeper" of the season in the "twenty-six-year-old" Davis. "He's a fine kid," boasted Cronin. "I'm going to try him out with the Scranton, Pennsylvania, club. If he makes good, I'm going to waste no time in moving him on to Boston." Scranton, although only in the Class A Eastern League, was Boston's highest affiliate above the Jim Crow region.

Davis reported to the Red Sox training camp in Cocoa, Florida, in the spring of 1950. On the first day of practice, he recalls, "I took the routine exercises, got ready to throw. I patted that ball around for a minute or more, but it felt like fifteen. Nobody spoke to me." Another player finally offered to toss the ball with Davis. Local custom forbade Davis from dressing, living, or eating with his teammates. "I lived in the city with one of the waiters," remembers Davis. "I'd eat in the waiters' quarters. The team ate out in the dining room. I had to dress in the visitors' clubhouse." Davis did not start in the first exhibition game, but in the late innings he emerged from the dugout as a pinch hitter. "Well, I'll be damned," he heard a fan exclaim. "Boston done got a nigger." "That's one of the times I said my prayers in baseball," Davis relates. "I said, 'Lord let me hit this ball, please,' and I hit a screaming shot. If I'm not mistaken, I hit it over the boards."

The Scranton farm team played several exhibition games in southern towns, but Red Sox officials dispatched Davis directly to Pennsylvania rather than challenge the Jim Crow laws. The veteran Negro League performer rejoined the club at the start of the regular season and proceeded to batter Class A pitching. On May 13, two days before Boston was required to pay the second half of Davis's purchase price to the Black Barons, he led the team in batting, with a .333 average, home runs, runs batted in, and stolen bases. When the Scranton general manager summoned Davis to his office, the athlete antici- pated a promotion to the Red Sox Triple A farm club at Louisville. Instead, the general manager informed him that the Red Sox had released him for "economical reasons."

The action infuriated Scranton field manager Jack Burns. Burns assured Davis that he had played no role in the decision. The manager escorted Davis to the locker room and advised him, "You just take anything in here you want." Davis declined the offer. "I just took my cap, because I knew they wouldn't want my cap, anyway. They gave me my own brush and comb. They had all the combs up on the shelf. They gave me my own private brush and comb."

The Scranton club did not even offer Davis a train ticket to return to Birmingham. Ironically, at Union Station in Washington, D.C., where law required all blacks to detrain and relocate to the blacks-only cars, Davis suddenly found himself face-to-face with Joe Cronin. Cronin awkwardly repeated the tale of "economic woe" that led to Davis's dismissal before the two men went to their respective Jim Crow seats. Cronin later sent Davis first-class transportation and meal money to pay for his trip home.

Davis never accepted the Red Sox explanation of "economical conditions." "I knew that was a joke," he asserts, "because [Red Sox owner] Tom Yawkey's one of the richest men in the East." Indeed, the financial fortunes of the Red Sox had reached a new peak. The club had shown a profit in four of its previous five seasons, and the value of its assets had tripled during that period. In 1949 Boston attendance had surged to a record 1.6 million, a figure that would not be topped for eighteen years. Red Sox officials asserted that "at thirty-three, the Negro first baseman was not considered a major league prospect." In the eyes of the Boston management, Davis, really thirty-one, had aged seven years in a few months. Four seasons passed before Yawkey's Red Sox signed another black player; not until 1959 did a black man even don a Boston uniform in spring training.

In 1951 Davis joined the Oakland Oaks. For the next six years he delighted the Pacific Coast League fans as a utility infielder-outfielder, twice batting over .300. In 1956, ten years after the Dodgers had declined to sign him, Davis was traded to the Brooklyn farm team in Hollywood. The following season the Dodgers assigned him to their AA franchise at Fort Worth. "In the Texas League," recalls Davis, "I couldn't eat with [the team] anywhere and stay with them, either. I couldn't even play in Shreveport." When the team arrived at a restaurant to eat, Davis waited in the bus until they brought him food. On one occasion, when they forgot to bring him a meal, Davis advised his manager to ignore it. "I'm not worth waiting for, anyway," he exclaimed bitterly. The following season, the Dodgers sent him a new contract, but Davis returned it unsigned. A retired athlete at thirty-eight years of age, Davis had never played in a major-league game.

Like Piper Davis, Ray Dandridge deserved a chance to perform at baseball's highest levels. A perennial All-Star in the Negro and Mexican leagues, Dandridge compiled three consecutive outstanding seasons with the Giants' top farm club at Minneapolis. At third base, reported the *Sporting News*, "He astounded veteran observers with his plays. . . . The bowlegged Dandridge moves like a cat." After batting .364 in 1949, he won the Most Valuable Player Award in the American Association in 1950, hitting .311 and leading his team to the pennant. In 1951 he continued to harass Triple A pitchers with a .324 average, while pacing all third basemen in fielding. In May, Dandridge watched Willie Mays, his young black roommate, ascend to the Giants, but the great black veteran remained behind.

"My biggest point in life was that I wanted to put my foot in major-league ball," Dandridge asserts. Several stars on the Giants called for this elevation. Monte Irvin recalls that he and Hank Thompson urged Manager Leo Durocher to promote Dandridge. White pitcher Sal Maglie, who had befriended the third baseman while both played in Mexico, snarled, "Why the hell don't you bring that son of a bitch out of Minneapolis?" Durocher and the Giant front office steadfastly refused.

Ironically, the Giants were a pioneer club in baseball integration and seemed less conscious of a racial quota system than other teams of that era. Chub Feeney, then a Giant executive and now the president of the National League, explains, "Ray was considered several times, and the strange thing about it was that [owner] Horace [Stoneham] loved him. Called him 'Dandy Dandridge.' " Age, not race, blocked Dandridge's chances according to Feeney. "Ray was probably in his early forties, and by that time we had Henry Thompson and then Bobby Thomson at third base. There just never came a time when there was a real need." In retrospect, Feeney admits, "Probably we could have brought him up at the end of the season or something . . . if we'd recognized the fact that he had felt that need."

Dandridge believes that his immense popularity in Minneapolis provided another reason for the failure of the Giants to promote him. Stoneham, he says, told him that the organization wanted him there because of his drawing power. Dandridge charges that the Giants turned down offers from other teams in order to keep him in the Twin Cities. Years later he rebuffed Stoneham at an Old-Timers' Game. "I said, 'Horace, I don't even want to talk to you,' " he heatedly recalls. " 'You had the chance to sell my contract. You had the chance to bring me up, and you wouldn't do it. The only thing I wanted to do was hit the major leagues. . . . You could have called me up for even one week! I could have said I hit the major leagues.' "

"I loved baseball and everything in it. My life has been nothing but baseball," Dandridge told a reunion of Negro League players in 1980. His audience remembered him as perhaps the finest third baseman to ever play the game. Most other baseball fans do not know him at all. Long the victim of racism, in the end Dandridge fell victim to the universal experience of aging and the insensitivity characteristic of the newly integrated national pastime. For Ray Dandridge, Piper Davis, and countless others who ended their obscure, yet sparkling careers in the minor leagues, the demise of segregation occurred too late.

Bob Uecker's lifetime batting average through six major league seasons was .200; he never hit a triple or stole a base. When asked his secret for catching the knuckleball, he replied, "It's easy—I just wait for it to stop rolling, then I pick it up." Like Joe Garagiola before him, Uecker shrewdly transformed a mediocre career (yes, mediocre, not terrible) into a running joke and himself into a national celebrity. The Milwaukee-born catcher went into play-by-play broadcasting for the Brewers, funny beer commercials, stand-up comedy, and, inevitably, autobiography. Here is Uecker's last hurrah, with the 1966 Phillies.

BOB UECKER

Catcher in the Wry

The Phillies, like the Cardinals, were a team trying to regroup. No manager had survived more adversity than Gene Mauch. His first team had established a major-league record by losing twenty-three straight games in 1961. Near the end of the streak, they came off a road trip to find a large crowd waiting for them at the airport in Philadelphia. They figured, obviously, it was a lynch mob. A pitcher named Frank Sullivan called out, "Leave the plane in single file. That way they can't get us with one burst."

But the fans came to welcome them home again, to cheer, to give them support. There is no way to know what makes a Phillies fan tick. They rallied behind Gene Mauch, and in time he gave them a contender, only to see the Phillies blow a ten-game lead in the nightmare season of 1964. The next year they were never a factor, and now Mauch had decided to retool the club.

I felt at home with the Phillies when I reported to camp at Clearwater in March. The roster included such cashews as Richie Allen, who liked everything about a ballpark except getting there; Bo Belinsky, the flamboyant left-hander who thought he had been Rudolph Valentino in a prior life; and John Boozer, a pitcher whose idea of fun was to eat bugs and worms and watch people gag. He did a better job in the clubhouse than D-Con. He would be talking to a writer, and one of the players would hand him a live worm or a beetle. Some of the reactions were terrific.

Belinsky reported to camp two days late, explaining that he had been trapped by a snowstorm in Texas on the drive from California. Those Texas snowstorms can be murder.

In addition to the ex-Cardinal trio, Mauch had traded for Phil Linz, an infielder the Yankees had fired for playing the harmonica on the team bus after a loss, and Jackie Brandt, who once watched part of an All-Star Game while sitting in the dugout in the nude.

The Phillies had a terrific roster. I don't mean in talent but in names, the kind that headline writers loved, like Wine and Boozer, and the kind that just had a certain ring, like Ferguson Jenkins, Cookie Rojas, and Clay Dalrymple.

I had been brought in to back up Dalrymple, a seven-year vet and an underrated fellow, whose .213 average in 1965 was well below his form. Clay hit from the left side, which meant that once again I would have a chance to start against the left-handers. It was hard to tell if I had made any progress. I had been traded to my third team in three years. The Phillies issued me uniform No. 10. I had worn 9 in St. Louis and 8 in Milwaukee. Was this progress?

When the players talked about the best and the brightest managers, the name of Gene Mauch often came up. He was quick-tempered, but he did not give up on people easily. His career as a player had been similar to mine. He was a shortstop who always seemed to line up behind someone better, such as Phil Rizzuto, with the Yankees, or Pee Wee Reese, with the Dodgers.

Frustrated, still a kid, Mauch once confronted his manager, Casey Stengel, in the dining room of a hotel where the Yankees stayed. "Dammit, Casey," he blurted, "I've got to play."

Stengel looked up from his soup and nodded. "Go talk to Mr. Rizzuto," the old man said. "If it's okay with him, it's okay with me."

Mauch was the most intense manager I ever knew. He would sit on the bench with his arms folded, and his eyes never stopped moving. He didn't miss a thing. They used to tell a story about when Mauch was playing for the Red Sox and on the way to the airport the team bus got stuck under an overpass. The driver and the team got out to study the problem. Finally, Mauch said, "Let the air out of the tires and fill them up on the other side." And so they did.

I was in the lineup on Opening Day, 1966, caught Chris Short, and drove in a run with a single as we beat the Reds and Joe Nuxhall, 3–1. Then a really uncharacteristic thing happened. I hit home runs on consecutive days at the end of April. In my first six games I had produced four hits, half of them homers, and driven in six runs. A curious start, it was worth three stars and a full, hand-lettered page in the scrapbook:

TWO HOMERS
IN TWO
DAYS!

BIG UKE
IS STARTING TO
FIND THE RANGE

ONLY 505 CAREER
HOMERS BEHIND
MAYS & OTT!!

Ah, yes, the future stretched ahead as smooth and inviting as the Pennsylvania Turnpike. When I connected for my third homer on Memorial Day, against the Mets, Mark wrote a story for the school paper at Drury and mailed a copy to Bob Howsam. The Cardinals were in the process of sending Mahaffey and Johnson to the minors. The trade was looking rather one-sided for the Phillies.

The story went like this:

> Bob Howsam has finally, publicly, admitted in May that he was completely wrong in October. The story we got then was that we were trading White, Groat, and Uecker for Johnson, Corrales, and Mahaffey because we (the Cardinals) were fully committed to our youth movement.
>
> Well, it doesn't look too good for smiling Bob. How can you say you're in a youth movement and trade a thirty-one-year-old slugger like White and then keep a broken-down, thirty-seven-year-old pitcher named Curt Simmons, who only pitches against the Phillies and can't beat them?
>
> With his homer, double, and three runs batted in on Memorial Day, and his two singles two days later, Uecker raised his average to a lusty .266. With three homers . . . he seems likely to get a new career high in every hitting department, and last year had been his best. He's hitting better than either Bill White or Dick Groat, the men he was traded with, and that ought to make him the big man in the deal. The key man in the deal!
>
> Howsam, you're an idiot.

With aplomb, Howsam wrote back:

> Dear Mr. Stillwell,
>   Thank you for sending along the article which appeared at Drury.
>   It's nice to know, too, that you have remained Cardinal fans.
>   We hope you and your Fan Club will have the opportunity to visit the new Busch Memorial Stadium and see the Cardinals play. I think you'll enjoy it.
>   Kindest regards,
>   Bob Howsam
>   General Manager

The first time the teams met in 1966, the Phillies edged the Cards 5–3. Bill White singled home our first two runs. I singled to open the winning rally and scored the tie-breaking run on a bases-loaded walk to Groat, who had two hits. It's true, hitting well is the best revenge.

On June 3 I slugged my fourth homer of the year, equaling the total for my entire big-league career. The blow was off an ex-teammate, Ray Sadecki, then pitching for the Giants. By the All-Star break I had raised my total to six, the same number as John Callison, a guy who was usually good for twenty-five to thirty a season.

I would have felt great except that everybody around the Phillies kept wondering what was wrong with Callison. Four teams figured to stay in the pennant race most of the way, the Dodgers, Giants, Pirates, and the Phillies. We needed a big year from Callison. In fact, we needed a big year from everybody.

The point should be made right here that it can be harmful for a fellow who doesn't hit homers to suddenly start banging a few. It is like a guy who discovers girls late in life and thinks he can catch up all at once. And the next thing you know, you are in a jar at the Harvard Medical School.

But sooner or later you have to try. You see a Richie Allen twitch a muscle, and the ball flies off the bat and lands 500 feet away. And you think, *Is there any reason I can't do that?* The next thing you know, your hands are down at the end of the bat, and all your weight is on your heels.

In a way, those homers, hitting in the .270s, and getting four (4) votes for the All-Star Game may have been my undoing. Up to then my theories had stood the test of time, like milk of magnesia: (1) The more I played, the closer I was to getting shipped out, and (2) the better I performed, the more they expected.

If I had been content to just hit .200 every year, all singles, and throw out a runner now and then, I might have played as long as Gaylord Perry. Your body doesn't wear out very fast when you catch a game every four or five days.

On July 17 I tagged my seventh homer in what turned out to be a fifteen-inning win over the first-place Giants. On the Phillies, only Allen and Bill White had more, even though a total of twelve players had started more games.

I had no personal goals in mind, which was just as well, because I did not hit another homer during the rest of the season.

Harry Grabiner was the penurious Charles Comiskey's general manager with the White Sox, the bearer of ill tidings come contract time and thus the object of considerable ill will from players such as Joe Jackson and Eddie Cicotte. But Harry was a solid and competent company man, and when Bill Veeck bought the Cleveland Indians, he brought him over from Chicago to help keep the franchise solvent. In 1948 the long-dormant Indians were the surprise of baseball, giving Harry Grabiner his first winner since the Black Sox of 1919. From *Veeck—as in Wreck.*

BILL VEECK with ED LINN

An Epitaph for Harry Grabiner

One of the great joys of our quick success at Cleveland was watching the fun Harry Grabiner was having. After all the years of scrimping at Chicago, Harry was showing them all how he could operate when he had a chance to go first-class. As a man, he had always traveled first-class. Harry had a wonderful family. His daughter was June Travis, a Hollywood actress of some note before her marriage. His wife, Dottie, was a woman of such beauty that if you placed her and June side by side you could not tell which was the mother and which the daughter.

Reserved as Harry normally was, he was a wild and uninhibited rooter. During the course of a game he would keep jumping out of the office to run to the top of the stairs and cheer our boys through every rally. Harry was a hitter. Early in our association I learned to stay away from those stairs during my tours around the park, because Harry could pound you black and blue. In Cleveland, he was finally getting a chance to root home a winner.

He was a tremendous asset in running the business end of the club, because he was always practical. When it came to paying $100,000 for a Zoldak, he'd say, "Great." But he would suggest some alternative that would serve the same purpose at about half the price.

I have said before that Harry was an honorable man. Let me give another example. I had dealt with Harry quite a bit in Milwaukee, in both the buying and selling of players, and out of our old friendship in Chicago we always leveled with each other. I had a forty-year-old pitcher named Earl Caldwell whom I had bought from the Texas League, a sidearm, almost underhanded pitcher who had been up with the Athletics fourteen years earlier and had later put in time with the Browns. By the time he reached us, he was a fussy old guy who always wore rubbers and carried an umbrella. The rest of the players called him "Grandmother."

When I got Caldwell, I promised him I'd do my best to get him another shot at the majors, a promise I made to almost all my players. Although he had only a middling sort of year, I called Harry and told him I thought Caldwell might be able to help the White Sox in relief. Harry didn't want him. The next year, though, Caldwell had a pretty good season. I was operating the club out of the Corona hospital as the year ended, and this time I told Harry I was sure Caldwell would help him.

"But he's nine hundred years old," Harry said. "I wouldn't have any idea what to offer you for him and—I don't have to tell you—I don't have any money to fool around with."

I said, "Harry, pay me five thousand dollars, then pay me what he's worth to you after you have him. If you don't think he's worth anything, send him back on June 15 and I'll give back the five thousand dollars, and at least I've got him into the majors again like I promised."

Caldwell surprised even me. He pitched brilliantly for the White Sox from the start, far better than he had ever pitched before in his life. In the middle of May, Harry sent us $10,000. I immediately called to thank him and to let him know I was very well pleased with the price. Caldwell continued to pitch well, and in mid-August another $10,000 arrived.

That was the kind of fellow Harry was. He had agreed to pay me what the man was worth to him, and he was scrupulous about keeping his word. To my immense delight, Grandmother Caldwell was an even better pitcher for Harry the next year, far and away the best relief pitcher in the American League.

Now let's go back to Cleveland. Before the 1948 season we had set an attendance goal of 2 million people. As the season progressed, it became increasingly evident that we were going to roll right over our goal and go on to smash all records. Harry had a paper schedule of our home games on which he kept track of the attendance. He had three columns of figures. In the first column were the figures he had projected at the beginning of the year to show the attendance we would have to have, game by game, in order to reach our 2 million goal. In the second column, he would write down the actual attendance of each game as the season progressed. In the third column, he kept adjusting his original projection, game by game, to show what he now estimated our final figures would be, based upon our advance, our position in the race, and the constantly rising enthusiasm. It was all pretty complicated.

Harry and I shared the same office, and it became a sort of ritual for him to stop off at the desk every day to fill in the previous day's attendance and perhaps make a new projection. He kept the schedule in the inside pocket of his jacket, folded in three parts, and by the time we entered our last home stand of the season, it had been folded and unfolded so often that it had come completely apart. Harry would have to hold the frazzled, dirty pieces together on my desk while he ran down the attendance column, adding in his head, as always, because with his machinelike mind he never bothered to make a footing and write down a total.

We had been home on that last home stand for about a week when Harry stopped by at about five o'clock to go through the usual routine. He was in marvelous spirits. Our attendance was already half a million over his original estimate, and, more important, we had started the winning streak that was to carry us back into first place. I was sitting at the desk, as usual. Harry, as usual, seated himself on the very edge of the desk itself, leaning down over the tattered schedule. All things as usual. In a minute or two we would each get up and go our separate ways. I would step out into the stadium and begin to mix with the early customers. Harry would go up to the press room to sip his usual cup of tea and act as host to the writers.

And all of a sudden I heard him say, "I can't add. I can't add."

I looked up, startled. In his eyes, I could see . . . what? No, not fear, but a sort of dull shock. For Harry not to be able to add was like me not being able to talk.

"Harry," I said, "what's the matter?"

"I can't add." The same incomprehension. The same dull shock.

"You're just tired," I said automatically. I was frightened to death. "You're tired, Harry," I said. "Come on over to the couch and sit down."

But he reached out for my hand, and in that same quiet voice he said, "I can't think. Bill, hold my hand. I can't think."

I knew at that moment that it was something serious, something more than a stroke. Harry Grabiner was spilled there across my desk, grabbing on to my hand, the three sections of his schedule spread out around him, broken and awry. And Harry Grabiner was saying that he couldn't think. Harry Grabiner. I knew this was it, that it was over, that from one second to the next he had died there on my desk. No question about it. No question.

While we were waiting for the doctor, I brought Harry over to the couch and held him in my arms like a frightened child. The moment anyone came into the office, he would huddle closer to me in terror and whimper, "Don't let him get near me, Bill. Don't let him get near me." The only other person he wasn't afraid of was Ada Ireland, our telephone operator.

The doctor took one look at him and told me there was nothing he could do. "I could open his head, look in, and sew it back up," he told me. "All that would do would make him die a little sooner. I know what I'd see without cutting him open."

I left Harry huddled in Ada's arms and went out front to put in a rush call to a psychiatrist I knew quite well. A last, forlorn hope. I introduced him to Harry not as a psychiatrist but as a friend who had dropped in to say hello. He didn't have to ask Harry more than three or four questions before he knew it was out of his field. "Something inside his head has been eaten away," he told me. "His mind is about gone."

I had called June immediately, and she had quickly flown in from Chicago with her husband, Fred Friedlob. Harry was taken back to Allegan, where, through some hidden reservoir of strength and will, he held on until we won that play-off game in Boston. He wanted so badly to win that pennant, his first pennant after all those years. He walked around outside the house all during the game, listening to the radio broadcast, and the moment it was over and we had won, he walked back into the house and collapsed.

Harry had always wanted to show them that he was a good operator.

"East is East and West is West," wrote Kipling, "and never the twain shall meet"—not even in that shared obsession, baseball/*besuboru*. Baseball in Japan goes back to 1873, when a visiting American professor taught the rudiments of the game to his students at what is now the University of Tokyo. American major leaguers toured the land of the rising sun repeatedly, beginning in 1913, and by 1936 Japan had formed its own professional baseball league. American imports first appeared in 1951 and have been an important, yet controversial, part of the Japanese game for much of the postwar era. Whiting, who lives in Japan, is the author of *The Chrysanthemum and the Bat: Baseball Samurai Style*.

ROBERT WHITING

You've Gotta Have "Wa"

"I don't know what it is they play here," grumbled former California Angel Clyde Wright after his first season as a Tokyo Giant. "All I know is, it ain't baseball." Wright had learned what many expatriates in the Land of the Rising Sun had known for years: baseball, Japanese style, is not the same game that's played in the United States. Since adopting the sport, the Japanese have changed it around to incorporate the values of samurai discipline, respect for authority, and devotion to the group. The result is a uniquely Japanese game, one that offers perhaps the clearest expression among all sports of Japan's national character.

Like the American game, the Nippon version is played with a bat and ball. The same rule book is also used, but that's where resemblance between the two ends. Training, for example, is nearly a religion in Japan. Baseball players in the United States start spring training in March and take no more than five or six weeks to prepare for the season. They spend three to four hours on the field each day and then head for the nearest golf course or swimming pool.

Japanese teams begin training in the freezing cold of mid-January. Each day they're on the field for a numbing eight hours, and then it's off to the dormitory for an evening of strategy sessions and still more workouts indoors. Players run 10 miles every day, and one team, the Taiyo Whales, periodically performs the "Death Climb," twenty sprints up and down the 275 steps of a nearby Shinto shrine.

That's only the beginning. The average Japanese game is more like a board meeting at Mitsubishi than an athletic event. As each new situation arises, there is so much discussion on the field among the manager, coaches, and players that most games last three hours.

Unlike their counterparts in the States, losing managers in Japan are seldom fired outright. Instead, they go through an elaborate, time-consuming ritual designed to save face all around. It culminates with a public apology by the deposed skipper, his resignation, and, often, an all-expenses-paid trip to the United States for him to "study baseball."

Such phenomena are the tip of the iceberg. Below the waterline are the concept and practice of group harmony, or *wa*. It is this concept that most dramatically differentiates Japanese baseball from the American game.

The United States is a land where the stubborn individualist is honored and where "doing your own thing" is a motto of contemporary society. In Japan, *kojinshugi*, the term for individualism, is almost a dirty word. In place of "doing your own thing," the Japanese have a proverb: "The nail that sticks up shall be hammered down." It is practically a national design.

In Japan, holdouts are rare. A player takes what the club gives him, and that's that. Demanding more money is *kojinshugi* at its worst, because it shows the player has put his own interests before those of the team. Katsuya Nomura, the Nankai Hawk catcher who has hit 652 home runs in his career, said, upon quietly accepting a minuscule raise after winning yet another of his numerous home-run titles, "If I had asked for more money, the other players would have thought I was greedy."

The U.S. player lives by the rule: "*I* know what's best for me." In Japan, the only ones who know what's best are the manager and coaches. They have the virtues Orientals most respect going for them—age and experience, hence, knowledge. Their word is law. In the interest of team harmony they demand that everyone do everything the same way. Superstar Sadaharu Oh must endure the same pregame grind as the lowliest first-year player. At thirty-eight Shinichi Eto, a three-time batting champion and a ten-year All-Star, found that forty minutes of jogging and wind sprints before each game left him exhausted by game time. He asked to be allowed to train at his own pace. "You've been a great player, Eto-*san*," he was told, "but there are no exceptions on this club. You'll do things according to the rules." Eto lost weight, his batting average dropped, he spent the second half of the season on the bench and then reluctantly announced his retirement. Irrational? Perhaps, but any games lost because Eto was dog tired were not as important as the example he set.

In the pressure-cooker world of U.S. pro sports, temper outbursts are considered acceptable and at times even regarded as a salutary show of spirit. Unreleased frustrations, the reasoning goes, might negatively affect a player's concentration. Japanese players are expected to follow Sadaharu Oh's example. "When he strikes out," says an admirer, "he breaks into a smile and trots back to the bench." Oh has been known to be glum during a batting slump, but temper tantrums—along with practical joking, bickering, complaining, and other norms of American clubhouse life—are viewed in Japan as unwelcome incursions into the team's collective peace of mind. They offend the finer sensitivities of the Japanese, and as many American players have learned the hard way, Japanese sensitivities *are* finer.

Michio Arito was the captain of the Lotte Orions, a ten-year veteran and the team's longtime batting mainstay. Because of a badly bruised hand he had been able to play only by taking a lot of painkillers, and before a crucial game that would, as it turned out, mean the pennant for the Orions, the manager decided to replace him with a healthier player. When Arito heard he'd been benched, he yelled, threw his glove, and slammed his bat against the bench. Next day, at the Orions' victory party, Arito was summoned forth to atone for his sins. After bowing deeply to all, he said, "I am sorry for my childish actions yesterday. I have upset our team spirit, and I deeply apologize."

Jim Lefebvre, a former Los Angeles Dodger infielder who spent five years in Japan, can still not quite believe what he saw there. "It's incredible," he says. "These guys are together almost all the time from January to October. They live together, eat together, play baseball together. I've never seen one fight, one argument. In the States, there's always somebody who mouths off and starts trouble."

If you ask a Japanese manager what he considers the most important ingredient of a winning team, he would most likely answer, *"Wa."* If you ask him how to knock a team's *wa* awry, he'd probably say, "Hire an American."

Former American major leaguers have been an active part of Japanese baseball for eighteen years. The somewhat lower level of play in Japan has given these *gaijin* (outsiders) a temporary reprieve from the athletic scrap heap. And although the Japanese have paid the *gaijin* high salaries, they have not been elated with the overall experience of having them on their teams.

Money is a particular sore point. Foreigners make two to three times as much as Japanese players of similar ability. This, combined with the free Western-style house and the other perks that the *gaijin* seem to view as inalienable rights, sets them too far above their teammates. And more than one American player has brought in an agent to negotiate his contract. That is considered to be in very bad taste. A contract discussion is regarded as a "family affair," with the official team interpreter, despite his obvious bias, acting as a go-between.

Avarice is only part of it, however. Deportment is the rest. Although few Americans hold a Japanese batting or pitching record, many have established standards in the area of bad conduct. For example, the amiable former Dodger Norm Larker set the Japan single-season high for smashed batting helmets with eight. Joe Stanka, a six-foot five-inch 220-pound behemoth, was ejected from games a record four times in his seven-year stay in Japan. Ken Aspromonte, who later managed the Cleveland Indians, was the first man in the history of Japanese baseball to be fined by his manager for "conduct unbecoming a ballplayer."

Aspromonte pulled off this feat during a sojourn with the Chunichi Dragons of Nagoya back in 1965. Furious after being called out on strikes, Aspromonte stormed back to the bench, kicked over chairs and launched the inevitable attack on the water cooler. He was just doing what comes naturally to many American players, but Dragon Manager Michio Nishizawa did not enjoy the show. He yanked Aspromonte out of the game and suspended him. An incredulous Aspromonte was fined $200 and required to visit Nishizawa's home and issue a formal apology to get back in his manager's good graces.

Other Americans have followed in Aspromonte's footsteps. Ex-Giant Daryl Spencer was one of the more memorable. Like most former major leaguers, Spencer insisted on following his own training routine, and it was considerably easier than everyone else's. One night, as he was lackadaisically going through his pregame workout, his manager on the Hankyu Braves, Yukio Nishimoto, decided something had to be done.

"You don't look sharp, Spencer-*san*," he said. "You need a rest."

"What do you mean I need a rest?" Spencer growled. "Who's leading this team in home runs, anyway?"

"I don't think you can hit this pitcher," Nishimoto said.

"I can't hit him? I'm batting .340 against that guy!"

"Not tonight. That's my feeling. You're out."

That was too much for Spencer to take. He was in the dressing room changing into street clothes when he heard his name announced in the starting lineup. Nishimoto had put Spencer down as the third batter, but only because he was planning to "fool" the opposition by inserting a pinch hitter in the first inning.

Now Spencer was smoldering. When the game began and he heard the name of the second batter over the loudspeaker, he decided to get even. Clad in a pair of shorts and shower clogs, he headed for the dugout. Grabbing a bat and smirking in the direction of Nishimoto, he strode out to the on-deck circle to take a few practice swings.

Spencer's entrance delighted the fans and his picture was in all the papers the next day. Nishimoto was not amused. He ordered Spencer off the field and slapped him with a suspension and a $200 fine. Spencer paid up, later reporting with a wide grin, "It was worth every penny."

In 1972, John Miller became the first American to be released solely for his misconduct. Miller, who played briefly for the Yankees and Dodgers, arrived in Japan in 1970 and soon became the most dangerous batter on the Chunichi Dragons. He was a battler. A U.S. coach once said, "Miller is the kind of guy I'd want on my team. He'll fight you with everything he has. He doesn't know how to quit."

However, Miller wasn't the kind of guy the Japanese wanted. He was seldom on time for practice. If a workout was scheduled for 2:00 P.M., Miller would arrive at 2:10. This was more serious than it sounds, because his teammates would invariably be raring to go by 1:50.

"He always had some excuse," says a team official. "One day it would be because the traffic was heavy. Another day, he'd missed the train. He never once said he was sorry."

When reprimanded for being late, Miller responded in a most un-Oriental way. "Japanese customs are too military. I do good in the games, don't I? What else matters?"

Miller's hot temper sealed his fate as a Dragon. The coup de grace came in the twelfth inning of a big game. Miller had been slumping, and he had a bad game. He had been up four times without a hit. The fifth time, with the score tied, he was removed for a pinch hitter.

Miller blew his top. "You didn't have to take me out," he railed at his manager. "I've had it. I don't want to play for you anymore. I don't care if this team wins or not."

To Americans it would have been a fairly routine example of blowing off steam. To the Japanese, however, Miller might just as well have slit his throat. Although he later apologized and finished the year as the team leader in home runs, he was released at the end of the season. A second American on the team, Barton Shirley, who batted .190, was kept. He wasn't a battler.

Willie Kirkland, who had played for the Giants and Indians, was a happy-go-lucky sort who liked to tease his teammates. One day Kirkland was bemusedly watching an aging infielder who had recently been elevated to player-coach straining through a batting drill. "Hey, man, you're a coach now," Kirkland yelled playfully. "You don't have to practice anymore."

The player-coach took Kirland's jest as a comment on his declining usefulness, and he launched a roundhouse right that barely missed. It took half a dozen men to restrain him.

"I was just joking," Kirkland protested. "He was making fun of me," the unappeased coach retorted.

Kirkland left Japan with at least one enemy and considerable doubts about the Japanese sense of humor.

The Japanese didn't find Richie Scheinblum a barrel of laughs, either. A noted clubhouse wit in the United States, Scheinblum spent his two years as a Hiroshima Carp baiting the umpires. Shane, as he was known on the club's official roster, was frequently agitated by the plate umpire's idea of Scheinblum's strike zone. It was considerably larger than the one Shane had in mind.

Scheinblum searched for a Japanese phrase to convey his sentiments to the men in blue, something that would really get under their collective skins. A Japanese friend came to the rescue, and soon Scheinblum was saying, "You lousy Korean," to arbiters who crossed him.

There is as much love lost between Koreans and Japanese as, say, between William Buckley and Gore Vidal. To the umpires, Scheinblum's taunts were intolerable. To stop him, they imposed a stiff fine each time he uttered the dreaded epithet. When Scheinblum finally departed Japan for the last time, no cries of "Come back, Shane!" were heard—at least not from the umpires.

It wasn't until Clyde Wright came along that rules of behavior for foreigners were finally codified. Wright, a pitcher of some note with the California Angels, made his first Japanese appearance, with the Yomiuri Giants, in 1976. A self-described "farm boy" from eastern Tennessee, Wright was regarded by those who knew him in America as a tough-as-nails competitor who didn't believe in hiding his feelings.

The Giants are something of a national institution in Japan. They are the oldest team, the winningest (twelve pennants in the past fifteen years), and by a million miles the most popular. Their games, all of which are nationally televised, get high ratings, and one out of two Japanese will tell you he is a Giant fan.

Their manager, Shigeo Nagashima, is the most beloved sports figure in the land. As a player he won a Central League-record six batting titles and was personally responsible for the most exciting moment in Japanese baseball history, a game-winning (or *sayonara*) home run in the only professional game Emperor Hirohito has ever attended. Sadaharu Oh plays for the Giants.

The Giants are the self-appointed custodians of national virtue. Popular belief has it that their players are neater, better mannered, more disciplined, and more respectful than those of other clubs. Their *wa* is in better tune. In early 1977, when one writer, a former Giant player turned magazine reporter, suggested otherwise in print, he was forever banned from the team clubhouse. Among his blasphemous revelations were: (1) some Giant players did not like other players on the team; (2) a few players thought Nagashima could be a better manager; (3) some younger Giants did not especially care for the Saturday night 10:00 P.M. curfew at the team dormitory; (4) some Giant wives objected to the season-long "energy-conserving" rule forbidding them to have sexual relations with their husbands before "important" games. Tame material as far as exposés go, but to the *shoguns* of Yomiuri, the Giant name had been desecrated, and someone had to pay.

Wright also faced the difficulty of being a foreigner on a team that traditionally liked to consider itself pure-blooded—Oh's Chinese ancestry and the few closet Koreans on the Giants notwithstanding. Wright was only the second non-Oriental *gaijin* to play for the team, and the sight of a fair-skinned American in a Giant uniform was a bit unsettling to the multitudes. Wright soon gave them reason to be even more unnerved. In the sixth inning of an early-season game, with the score tied 1–1, Wright allowed the first two batters to get on base. Nagashima walked out on the field to take him out of the game. Few American managers would have removed him so abruptly. It was Nagashima's feeling, however, that Wright was getting weak, and that was that.

When Wright realized what was happening, he blew a gasket. To the horror of 50,000 fans at Tokyo's Korakuen Stadium and a Saturday night TV audience of millions, he brushed aside Nagashima's request for the ball and stalked off the mound, an angry scowl on his face. Halfway to the bench, he threw the ball against the dugout wall, cursed, and disappeared into the clubhouse.

Once inside, he kicked over a trash can, ripped off his uniform, shredded it, and flung it into the team bath. Amid a rapid-fire discharge of obscenities, he said something that the official team interpreter was able to understand: "Stupidest damn baseball I've ever seen. If this is the way the Giants treat their foreign ballplayers, I'm going. I've had it."

Nothing like this had ever happened on the Giants. Other teams had problems but not the proud *Kyojin*. No one had ever shown this much disrespect for Nagashima. Crazy Wright, as he was instantly renamed by the press, became headline news in the sports dailies the next day. Letters, telegrams, and phone calls poured into the Yomiuri offices. Outrageous! Inexcusable! Unforgivable! Wright should be sold. Released. Deported. Shot. Drawn and quartered. And not necessarily in that order.

Only Nagashima kept his cool. First, he patiently explained to his American pitcher that what he had done was not "stupid" baseball but simply the Japanese way of playing the game. It's a group effort. Then the manager faced the angry masses. There would be no disciplinary action. He was glad that Wright cared so much about winning. And he wished that some of his Japanese players would show as much fight.

Such benevolent words from the prince of Japanese baseball dissipated much of the public's antagonism toward Crazy Wright. It did not, however, pacify the front office. Management was not as eager as Nagashima-*san* to let Western ways penetrate their organization. They issued a set of ten rules of etiquette that Wright and every other American player the Giants might henceforth deem worthy of their uniform would be obliged to obey.

The Japanese press quickly gave it a name: The *Gaijin* Ten Commandments. This is how they went:

 1. Obey all orders issued by the manager.
 2. Do not criticize the strategy of the manager.
 3. Take good care of your uniform.
 4. Do not scream and yell in the dugout or destroy objects in the clubhouse.
 5. Do not reveal team secrets to other foreign players.
 6. Do not severely tease your teammates.
 7. In the event of injury, follow the treatment prescribed by the team.
 8. Be on time.
 9. Do not return home during the season.
10. Do not disturb the harmony of the team.

Willie Davis, then a practicing Buddhist, thought it would be different for him. Davis was perhaps the best all-round American player ever to come to Japan. He was a seventeen-year veteran of the major leagues and a former captain of the Los Angeles Dodgers. He had been an All-Star; he could run like a deer and hit and field with a grace and skill that few American big leaguers, let alone Japanese, possessed. Even at thirty-seven, Davis could have continued to play in the United States—in fact, he has been a pinch hitter for the Angels this season—but when the chance to go to Japan came in 1977, he took it. Not for the money ($100,000), he insisted, but "for the good of baseball."

Davis was a product of his times, of America's "quest for meaning." While others were exploring the wonders of Transactional Analysis, est, and the like, Davis was a devout member of the *Soka Gakkai,* the Nichiren Buddhist sect that had America chanting. Because Japan was the birthplace of the *Soka Gakkai,* Davis assumed he would be right at home. It was a misguided assumption.

The religion's sacred chant, *namu Myoho renge-kyo,* was an important part of Davis's daily life. He did it faithfully, because it brought him inner peace. When he joined the Dragons, he naturally continued this practice—in the morning, at night, in his room, in the team bath, and on the team bus. When not intoning the chant himself, he would play tapes of it on a portable cassette recorder.

Davis reasoned that the chanting would be music to his teammates' ears. Instead, it drove them nuts. They complained: there was no peace and quiet on the team; they couldn't sleep. The incantatory chant that supposedly would bring inner harmony to anyone who regularly intoned it was rapidly eroding the Dragons' collective *wa*

What particularly annoyed the Japanese players was Davis's locker-room chanting. Before each game, he would pull out his beads, and off he'd go. "*Namu Myoho renge-kyo, namu Myoho renge-kyo, namu Myoho renge-kyo.*"

"He'd pray that he'd do well, that the team would win, and that nobody would get hurt," his manager, a Japanese-Hawaiian named Wally Yonamine, says, "but it gave the others the feeling they were at a Buddhist funeral."

When the game began, Davis was a ball of fire—at least during the first half of the season. He was by far the most feared Dragon hitter, and on the base paths he displayed a flair the Japanese had never seen before. Nonetheless, the team was in last place. Key players were injured, and the pitching was subpar. Team *wa* was out of whack, and many Dragons blamed their American Buddhist for it.

It was more than the chanting, which Davis soon modified to please his teammates. There was, for example, the matter of his personal attire. Davis liked his Dragon training suit so much he had half a dozen made in different colors. He wore them in public, agitating club executives, who felt Davis was tarnishing the team's dignified image.

Davis would sometimes practice in stocking feet, and he once appeared for a workout with his comely wife, who was wearing hot pants and who jogged with him on the field. "It's so . . . so unprofessional," one sportswriter observed. "Davis is destroying our team's spirit in training," grumbled a player. "We can't concentrate on what we're doing."

Several players complained that Davis had special privileges. They referred to him as "Davis, the King," and as "Davis, our precious black *gaijin.*"

Yonamine was caught in the middle. "I'd try to tell them not to worry about it," he says. "Forget about how much money a man makes or how little he practices. What he does in the game is all that counts." Few Dragons were willing to accept that piece of American advice.

Davis's biggest liability was his gregariousness. "People didn't understand him," says a team official. "He was loud. He'd get excited. He'd yell a lot and wave his arms. It was all in English, and people didn't have the faintest idea what he was saying, but it looked as though he was arguing."

Once he reproached a teammate for not attempting to score on a play that Davis had initiated. "Why didn't you try for home?" Davis shouted. That was the wrong thing to do, because the player was not only the team captain but also a playing *coach*. In Japan, a player does not yell at a coach, much less question his judgment.

In August 1977, when Davis had 25 home runs and a .306 batting average, he broke a wrist in a collision with the outfield fence. It put him out for the year. The Dragons immediately went on a winning streak. During the last two months of the season they had the best record in the league and missed finishing second by a hair.

"It's our pitching," Yonamine insisted. But if you listened to Dragon supporters and students of Japanese baseball, it was all because the team *wa* had been restored.

"I knew Willie as well as anyone,," says Lefebvre, a teammate of Davis's on the Dodgers. "He had his quirks, but then we all do. He was named captain, and you're not chosen captain of a team like the Dodgers if you're a troublemaker. If you can't get along with Willie, you don't belong on a baseball team."

The Dragon front office apparently felt that it was Davis who didn't belong on a baseball team—at least not theirs. They traded him, and at the start of the following season the most exciting player ever to wear a Chunichi Dragon uniform was laboring in the backwaters of Fukuoka, contemplating the infinite and subtle mysteries of *wa* in between playing for the lowly Crown Lighter Lions.

Of course, not every American who comes to Japan wreaks havoc on his new team. There have been some, notably Felix Millan, Clete Boyer, and George Altman, who did their best to please their Japanese hosts. In turn, the Japanese liked them, describing their demeanor as being *majime*. It means serious, sober, earnest, steady, honest, faithful. They did everything that was asked of them. They kept their mouths shut, their feelings to themselves.

Some, like Boyer, paid a substantial price for the goodwill they engendered. The former Yankee fielding whiz had three reasonably good seasons for the Taiyo Whales, but in his fourth year, when he began to reach the end as a player, he ran smack up against the cultural wall.

Boyer decided that he needed to be used more sparingly, and he asked the club to rest him every third game. "I hit in the first two, but then I get tired," he explained. "I'd do a better job with an extra day off."

The team trainer argued that what Boyer needed was not more rest but more training. Because he was older, the trainer reasoned, Boyer would have to work harder to keep up with the others. The team owner, after considering the probable reaction of the fans to an $80,000-a-year *gaijin* sitting on the bench a third of the time, agreed with the trainer. Boyer reluctantly acquiesced. In an effort to keep his energy level up, he took massive vitamin injections and worked very hard. Still, he finished the season hitting .230 and then retired to coaching. His goodwill, of course, remained intact.

Lefebvre, too, obeyed all the rules, yet he ended up incurring the largest fine in Japanese baseball history. His manager on the Lotte Orions, Masaichi Kaneda, Japan's only 400-game winner and the "God of Pitching," had personally recruited and signed Lefebvre—to a multiyear contract worth $100,000 a year—and had predicted that Lefebvre would win the Triple Crown. Lefebvre hit only .265 with 29 home runs his first season. Hampered by a leg injury, he fared even worse in succeeding years.

Kaneda was so embarrassed that he resorted to open ridicule of his "star" in an effort to regain lost face. Once, after Lefebvre had committed a particularly damaging error, Kaneda apologized to the other players for the American's "poor play." Another time, after a similar misplay, Kaneda temporarily relegated his *gaijin* to a farm team.

Lefebvre tried logic in appealing to Kaneda. "Look, you won four hundred games, right?" he said. "That makes you the winningest pitcher in Japanese history, right?"

"Right," Kaneda proudly replied.

"You also lost 250 games, didn't you?"

"Yes."

"Then that also makes you the losingest pitcher in Japanese history."

"Yes, but . . ."

"But what? Don't you see? Even the greatest in the game have bad times. Give me a break, will you?"

But Kaneda kept up the pressure. And the unhappy Lefebvre endured it until his fifth season. After being summarily removed from the lineup in the middle of an important game, Lefebvre finally lost control. Walking back to the bench, he threw his glove at the dugout wall, producing a rather loud *whack*.

Kaneda, sitting nearby, assumed that Lefebvre had thrown the glove at him. He sprang to his feet and raised his fists. "You want to fight me?" he yelled. Lefebvre, who saw his playing career rapidly coming to an end, anyway, stepped forward to meet the challenge. Coaches intervened, but after the game Kaneda levied a $10,000 fine against his American "troublemaker" and suspended him.

"It was a big game, and I wanted to stay in it," says Lefebvre, "but what made me even madder was the way Kaneda took me out. He waited until I'd finished my infield warm-ups; then he came and waved me out. That's embarrassing. But I certainly wasn't trying to throw the glove at him. It missed him by *five* feet."

Kaneda wasn't interested in Lefebvre's version of the incident. If he had misunderstood his *gaijin*'s intentions, perhaps others on the team had, as well. What would they think if it appeared that the "God of Pitching" tolerated that sort of behavior?

Refused a private audience with Kaneda, Lefebvre took his case to the public. He called a press conference. Yes, he had lost his temper. That he regretted. But, no, he was not guilty as charged. A standard fine of 50,000 yen (about $250) he could understand. But there was no way he would pay the outrageous sum of $10,000. There was no way he *could* pay it. Kaneda was just getting back at him for his failure to win the Triple Crown. Or Kaneda was making him the scapegoat for everything else that was wrong on the team. Or perhaps Kaneda was simply taking this opportunity to demonstrate his skills as a "*gaijin* tamer." Whatever the reason, Lefebvre wasn't going to take it all lying down.

When Kaneda heard that he was being openly opposed, he called his own press conference and vowed that Lefebvre would "never, ever, again wear the uniform of the Lotte Orions."

Lefebvre was in limbo for weeks while the coaching staff and management covertly worked to find a solution. At one stage they suggested secretly dropping the fine but making an announcement that Lefebvre had paid it. As long as Kaneda, and his public, didn't know the truth, they concluded, Kaneda's ego and image would suffer no damage. Lefebvre refused. He had his own ego and his own image to worry about. He appealed to a highly placed baseball official in the United States, whom he refuses to identify. The official made a call to Kaneda, and the next day the fine was quietly dropped. Lefebvre was allowed to put his uniform back on.

In the eighteen years since Don Newcombe and Larry Doby became the first ex-major leaguers to play in Japan, not a season has passed without a controversial incident involving a *gaijin* player. Last year's "villain," for example, was a former San Diego reserve infielder named John Sipin, who twice during the season took exception to deliveries apparently aimed at his person and engaged the offending pitcher in hand-to-hand combat. After the second melee Sipin was hit with a three-day suspension, fined 100,000 yen ($500), and castigated by the press for his "barbaric" behavior. One sports-page editorial likened his conduct to that of a *yakuza* (Japanese gangster), while another called Sipin a throwback to the days of the U.S. military occupation when, to hear some Japanese tell it, American GIs regularly roamed the streets, beating up on the local citizenry.

"If Sipin doesn't want to get hit by the ball," said one commentator, "he should jump out of the way. There is no place for fighting on the field." In the face of such reasoning, Sipin had no recourse but to acknowledge his sins and promise to mend his ways.

Japanese team officials have understandably grown weary of the perennial conflicts wrought by their foreign imports and in recent years have tried to be more selective in signing Americans. Character investigations have become a standard part of the recruiting process, and more and more managers are going for those quiet, even-tempered types who keep their feelings to themselves and fit into the Japanese system. The 1979 crop of twenty-four *gaijin* (there is a limit of two per team) is the most agreeable, mildest-mannered group of foreign players ever to play in Japan. It includes Wayne Garrett, Felix Millan, Lee Stanton, and Carlos May, as well as a number of unknowns who never quite made it in the majors. There is even an American manager, Don Blasingame. Collectively they are so subdued that one American player's wife says, "This is the best-behaved bunch of ballplayers I've ever been around, either here or in the States. I just can't believe it."

Garrett, a former Met, is so obliging that he agreed to get up at 7:30 and join his teammates in their daily "morning walk." Stanton, late of the Angels and Mariners, amicably allowed the Hanshin Tiger batting coach to change his batting style. May, an ex-White Sox and Yankee, is so low-key that some fans can't believe he's American.

Millan, a former Brave and Met, has been the quintessence of propriety. When he arrived last spring for his second year as a Taiyo Whale, he politely refused an offer to let him train as he wished and instead endured all the rigors of a Japanese preseason camp with his teammates. When he was benched on Opening Day, he sat quietly in the dugout, a shy smile on his face, intently watching the action. When he got his chance to play a week later, he went 4-for-4, won his spot back, and of late has been leading the league with a .354 average.

Davey Hilton, a former Padre, is setting new highs in cross-cultural "understanding." Last year's Central League All-Star second baseman and a hero of the Japan Series, he undertook an off-season weight-training program and arrived in camp this season a proud 20 pounds heavier. He was immediately accused by his suspicious manager of loafing during the winter, reprimanded for being "overweight," and told to reduce. A few days later he developed a sore arm and asked permisison to ease up in fielding practice. He was coldly informed that no one got special treatment and was cautioned not to let his American head get too big for his Japanese cap. To top things off, after getting only two hits in his first three games of the season, he was benched and was ordered to take extra batting practice and to alter his batting stance. Through it all Hilton remained calm. "This is Japan," he told himself. "They do things differently here." Predictably, his average began to climb. By mid-season he was over .300, out of the doghouse, and on his way to becoming an All-Star again.

Japanese observers are somewhat baffled by this outbreak of civility. One reporter speculated, "It must be the sagging dollar, the recession in the U.S. Americans have it good here, and they're afraid of losing what they have." American players, who pay both Japanese and U.S. income taxes and who wince at such Japanese prices as $50 for a steak dinner, attribute their good manners to other factors: adaptability and a new awareness of cultural differences.

Whatever the reason, the new tranquillity is certainly producing results. Americans are having their best year. Twelve of them are batting better than .300, and the affable Chuck Manuel, an ex-Minnesota sub, is leading the Pacific League in home runs despite having been sidelined for fifty-eight days with a broken jaw.

Of course, a Reggie Jackson might look down his nose at the accomplishments of Manuel and his confreres—given the smaller parks and the slightly inferior level of play in Japan. But with his stormy background it is doubtful that Jackson-*san*, in spite of his considerable abilities, will ever be invited to come over and prove he can do better.

America's poet expounded on America's game in this little-known June 18, 1858, editorial from the Brooklyn *Daily Times*. (For calling it to my attention, thanks to Jim Carothers.) But these were not Whitman's only published words on the national pastime: in the 1855 edition of *Leaves of Grass* appears the line "Upon the race-course, or enjoying picnics or a good game of base-ball"; and in the Brooklyn *Eagle* of July 23, 1846 (only one month after the Knickerbockers' first match game!), he wrote: "In our sun-down perambulations, of late, through the outer parts of Brooklyn, we have observed several parties of youngsters playing 'base,' a certain game of ball." By the way, in the box score you'll note a heading "H.L."—this signifies "Hands Lost," or outs made at bat or on the base paths; you'll also note Pierce at shortstop for the Atlantics—this is Dickey Pearce, profiled earlier in this volume by Sam Crane.

WALT WHITMAN

On Baseball, 1858

Base Ball

The game played yesterday afternoon between the Atlantic and Putnam Clubs, on the grounds of the latter club, was one of the finest and most exciting games we ever witnessed. The Atlantics beat their opponents by four runs, but the general opinion was that the defeat was as much the result of accident as of superior playing.

On the fourth innings the Putnams made several very loose plays and allowed their opponents to score nine runs, and those careless plays were sufficient to lose them the game. On every other innings, they played carefully and well, as the score will show. They were also particularly unfortunate in having three of their men injured in the course of the game. Mr. Master, their catcher, being disabled from occupying his position on the fifth innings, was compelled to take the first base and his place taken by Mr. Burr, who in his turn was disabled on the seventh innings and his place supplied by Mr. McKinstry, the fielder, Mr. Burr taking the third base. Mr. Jackson was injured on the eighth innings so much as to be compelled to discontinue playing, and Mr. Ketcham was substituted in his stead, so that at one time no less than three men on the Putnam side were so seriously injured as to be unable to run their bases. Notwithstanding these accidents, however, the score is highly creditable to the Putnams (always excepting the fourth innings), and we doubt if any other club can show a better one in a contest with such opponents. The Atlantics, as usual, played splendidly and maintained their reputation as the *Champion Club*. Messrs. M. O'Brien, P. O'Brien, Boerum, Pierce, and Oliver of that club cannot easily be surpassed in their respective positions. Messrs. Master, Gesner, and McKinstry, of the Putnam Club, also deserve special commendation.

The score is as follows:

ATLANTIC	H.L.	Runs	PUTNAM	H.L.	Runs
Price, 1st base	3	3	Burr, field	2	2
M. O'Brien, ptchr.	4	2	Meserole, field	4	2
Boerum, catchr.	3	2	Dakin, ptchr.	5	0
Mann, 3d base	3	2	Kelly, 1st base	5	0
P. O'Brien, field	2	2	Gillespie, 3d base	2	2
Pierce, short	4	0	Gesner, 2d base	2	2
Oliver, 2d base	4	2	Master, catchr.	3	1
Hamilton, field	1	3	Jackson, field	2	2
Ireland, field	3	1	McKinstry, short	2	2
		17			13

RUNS EACH INNINGS

Atlantics:—1st, 1; 2d, 1; 3d, 1; 4th, 9; 5th, 2; 6th, 1; 7th, 1; 8th, 0; 9th, 1 = 17.
Putnam:—1st, 0; 2d, 0; 3d, 2; 4th, 0; 5th, 1; 6th, 2; 7th, 6; 8th, 2; 9th, 0 = 13.
[June 18, 1858]

This good-humored grab bag of baseball bits reflects the serious interest of a serious fan and the love of a conservative man for a conservative game. A football fan (Andy Rooney, say) might accuse baseball of being old-fashioned; a baseball fan would heartily concur, adding that archaism in the defense of virtue is no vice. Sidelight: I now know that I am not the only father to have rendered "Take Me Out to the Ball Game" *sotto voce* at my children's bedtime.

GEORGE F. WILL

Don't Beep in My Outfield

It has been said that baseball is to the United States what revolutions are to Latin America, a safety valve for letting off steam. I think baseball is more serious than any Latin American revolution. But, then, I am a serious fan.

How serious? I like *Sports Illustrated*'s baseball issue even more than its swimming-suit issue. I would sell my soul for the thrill of hearing a manager say of me what Joe DiMaggio's manager said when asked if DiMaggio could bunt. The manager said he didn't know and "I'll never find out, either." The last words my four-year-old daughter hears at night are ". . . at the old ball game." (On the "as the twig is bent" principle, my parenting involves the use of "take me out to the ball game" as a lullaby.) I have one son who even knows the names of the first-base coaches. That is like knowing the name of the secretary of commerce. I have told my other son that if he can hit a slider when he is sixteen he can quit school. I believe in incentives, and Rogers Hornsby, who said: "Don't read, it'll hurt your eyes." So much for my credentials, okay? Now, listen up. The Japanese have gone too far.

Gadget

I am not talking, as everyone else is, about how crummy the Japanese are being about American exports. I am talking about a Japanese export, another electronic gadget. It is a sonar system that beeps to warn an outfielder chasing a fly ball that he is approaching the fence. My objection is not that the technology is Japanese. My nationalism stops short of that of the Cub pitcher who, when asked if he threw spitballs or otherwise violated the rule against doctoring the ball with foreign substances, replied: "I don't put any foreign substance on the baseball. Everything I use on it is from the good ole U.S.A." My objection to talking fences is not patriotic but aesthetic.

The thought of beeping fences intrudes jarringly on April, a month of buds and box scores. The philosopher in us is consoled by the thought that, although ours is an age of dizzying flux, baseball retains a healthy Luddite hostility to modernity. But already some degenerate teams are using infernal machines, rather than honest manual labor with a fungo bat, to propel balls for fielding practice. And now beeping fences? If this insensate lust for high-tech baseball does not abate, baseball will become as bad as—this is harsh, but it must be said—football.

That football fans have coarse characters and frayed moral fibers cannot be a matter of mere chance. The explanation has something to do with a fact noted here before: football combines two grim features of American life, violence and committee meetings (huddles). It also has something to do with football's lunatic fascination with technology. The coaches stalk the sidelines wired up like astronauts so they can talk to the assistant coaches with whom they have spent the previous six days doing computer analysis of game films. The NFL is even considering "helmet radios" so that quarterbacks calling plays at the line of scrimmage can be heard clearly by receivers.

Baseball's emphasis in not on machinery, it is on mind, although some players modestly deny this. Bill Lee, Red Sox pitcher, said: "When cerebral processes enter into sports, you start screwing up. It's like the Constitution, which says separate church and state. You have to separate mind and body." Rot. Baseball's emphasis on mind accounts for its fine sense of moral nuance, as in the batter who, after being brushed back by a pitch, said: "They shouldn't throw at me. I'm the father of five or six kids." Mind, in the form of mastery of facts, is also required of baseball fans.

Martin Nolan, who edits the editorial page of the Boston *Globe* but is not otherwise dangerous, is a typical fan. The highlight of his life was when he walked into a saloon and answered that day's question: name the only player active when Ruth hit his last home run and Aaron hit his first (Phil Cavaretta). Heinie Groh boasted that he held the record among non-Yankee, non-switch-hitting third basemen for playing in the most World Series with the largest number of different teams. Ah, but somewhere out in this broad land there is a young right-handed non-switch-hitting third baseman with visions of the glory that will be his when he breaks Groh's record. As baseball folks say (stop me if you've heard this), records are made to be broken. Or, as Yogi Berra wired Johnny Bench when Bench broke Yogi's career record for home runs by a catcher, "I always thought the record would stand until it was broken."

Cash

One baseball scholar whose mind may have snapped assures me that Harry Chiti, who was a catcher, sort of, holds this record: he is the only player ever traded for himself. Detroit traded him to the Mets for cash and a player to be named later. The Mets looked him over and designated him the player to be named later. Chiti was, of course, an ex-Cub. Before the Cubs attained their current grandeur, Cubness was the subject of a quiz compiled by a sadist and sent to masochists like me: (1) What Cub slugger dislocated his shoulder carrying his suitcase down to the hotel lobby? (2) Why was it bad that Cub pitcher Bill Hands recorded fourteen straight strikeouts? (3) What Cub batter holds the major-league record for leaving the most runners stranded on base in a nine-inning game? (4) What Cub right fielder, trying to throw a runner out at the plate, beaned the bat boy? (5) Cub catcher Cuno Barragon hit a homer in his first major league at bat. How many did he hit in his career? (6) The Cubs once set a major-league record by scoring five times in the bottom of the eleventh inning. Who won? (7) The Cubs once blew a 13–2 lead and lost on a home run. Who hit it? (8) The Cubs scored twenty-two runs and lost on a home run. Who hit it? You could look it up. But you only need to look below.

Last week baseball posed, for this fan and other Tories, a metaphysical puzzle. It expanded the league championship series from best-of-five to best-of-seven games. This puts in conflict two principles that are moral absolutes. One is: the more baseball the better. The other is: everywhere, but especially in baseball, change is deplorable. Well, some absolutes are more absolute than others, and the former principle is absoluter.

Answers: 1. Dave Kingman. 2. He did it as a batter. 3. Glen Beckert. 12. 4. Mike Vail. 5. One. 6. The Mets, who scored six in the top of the inning. 7 and 8. Mike Schmidt.

Ted Williams's relations with the press—notably the hometown reporters, and most notable among these, Dave Egan—ranged from rancid to rabid. So when he made his farewell speech to Fenway fans on September 26, 1960 (prior to the game, which he capped with a home run in his final at bat), he couldn't resist one last jab: "Despite the fact of the disagreeable things that have been said of me—and I can't help thinking about it—by the knights of the keyboard out there [tilting his head up toward the press box], baseball has been the most wonderful thing in my life." And Williams was the most wonderful hitter anyone under the age of fifty ever saw. In this opening section of his autobiography, *My Turn at Bat*, he gets a lesson in press relations from the world's greatest athlete.

TED WILLIAMS

Jousting with the Knights of the Keyboard

I'm glad it's over. Before anything else, understand that I am glad it's over. I'm so grateful for baseball—and so grateful I'm the hell out of it as a player. This business of managing the Washington Senators might yet prove a terrible mistake, but it's a new course, and I'm excited about it. I certainly do not have a youth wish. I mean, I wouldn't go back to being eighteen or nineteen years old, knowing what was in store, the sourness and the bitterness, knowing how I thought the weight of the damn world was always on my neck, grinding on me. I wouldn't go back to that for anything. I wouldn't *want* to go back. I've got problems now. I've always been a problem guy. I'll always have problems. But I'm grateful that part of my life is over.

I wanted to be the greatest hitter who ever lived. A man has to have goals—for a day, for a lifetime—and that was mine, to have people say, "There goes Ted Williams, the greatest hitter who ever lived." Certainly nobody ever worked harder at it. It was the center of my heart, hitting a baseball. Eddie Collins used to say I lived for my next turn at bat, and that's the way it was. If there was ever a man born to be a hitter, it was me. As a kid, I wished it on every falling star: please, let me be the hitter I want to be.

I remember the first time I saw Carl Yastrzemski, a youngster in the Red Sox batting cage a few years ago, and how much he reminded me of myself at that age—I mean he positively *quivered* waiting for the next pitch. And I have to think there was nobody who had any more opportunity than I did, along with the God-given physical attributes and the intense desire. Almost always the first at the ballpark, almost always the last to leave. I'm talking about from a kid on. I have to laugh now at my last five or six years in Boston, how I just wanted to get in and get out, to beat the crowds, to get it over with.

I should have had more fun in baseball than any player who ever lived. I played in what I think was baseball's best-played era, the years just before World War II, and then the real booming years, 1946 through the early '50s. We were always fighting for a pennant; we played before the biggest crowds. I won batting championships and home-run championships and Most Valuable Player Awards, and when it was all over, I made the Hall of Fame. I had people around who encouraged me—a real hitter's manager like Joe Cronin, who would sit around the clubhouse for hours talking hitting, and I always loved that, and Joe McCarthy, who in my mind was the best of managers.

I played before the greatest fans in baseball, the Boston fans, and I know what you're going to say about *that:* Old Teddy Ball Game loved those fans, all right. He spat at them and made terrible gestures and threw a bat that conked a nice old lady on the head one day, and he never tipped his hat to their cheers. And you would be right. But there came a time when I knew, I *knew*, they were for me and how much it meant to me, and I will get into that later. As for tipping my hat, I did my first year but never afterward. I couldn't, not if I played another twenty years. I just couldn't. I was fed up for good with that part of the act.

Certainly baseball doesn't owe me anything, a not too well educated, not particularly smart guy who played probably the only game in which he could excel. And *to* excel, to participate, to see things, to have a few material things, I'm grateful for all that. I think at the same time I've taken a lot of undue abuse. My twenty-two years in baseball were enjoyable, but many times they were unhappy, too. They were unhappy because I was in a shell an awful lot. I felt a lot of people didn't like me. I did things I was ashamed of, and sorry for, and yet know in my heart I would do again under the circumstances, because that was me. I felt—I *know*—I was not treated fairly by the press, and I'm not going to go soft on that now. And I'm not going to say the Boston management did not deserve part of the blame for those bad relations, because it did, especially when I was a young player, when I needed and should have had some protection, some common meeting ground to head these things off before they got worse, which they always did.

Oh, I hated that Boston press. I've outlived the ones who were really vicious, who wrote some of the meanest, most slanderous things you can imagine. I can *still* remember the things they wrote, and they still make me mad: how I was always trying to get somebody's job—the manager's, the general manager's, the guy's in the radio booth—and I never coveted another man's job in my life. Or how I didn't hit in the clutch and yet drove in more runs per time at bat than anybody who ever played this game except Babe Ruth and got on base more times per at bat than anybody, *including* Babe Ruth. I was a draft dodger. I wasn't a "team" man. I was "jealous." I "alienated" the players from the press. I didn't hit to left field. I took too many bases on balls. I did this, I did that. And so on. And so unfair.

I remember the time I broke my elbow in 1950. I'd had one of my best years in 1949. I batted .343, I hit 43 home runs, I drove in 159 runs, I was voted Most Valuable Player in the league, and gee, we missed winning the pennant on the very last day. I had started 1950 like it was going to be an even better year for me. I felt great. Then in the All-Star Game, first inning, Ralph Kiner hit one deep into left center in Comiskey Park. I ran a long way and caught it and crashed the fence with my elbow. I didn't know then how serious it was. The elbow swelled up, and there was pain, but I played seven more innings and even got a single in the fifth inning to put the American League ahead, 4–3. Later they X rayed and found that I had broken thirteen little chips off the head of the radius, and they were talking about taking out the whole thing, which would have finished me for good, but they managed to make a repair.

This *has* to be the greatest disappointment of my career, because as time went on and my arm never completely came around, I knew I would never again be the hitter I was. It was two months before I played again. I could barely straighten the elbow. To this day I have trouble with it. But the Red Sox were anxious for me to get started because we were hot in the pennant race. I went back into the lineup. It was a mistake, because I wasn't ready. For two weeks I hit like an old woman. I was miserable. I wanted to play, but I wasn't doing the club any good. We lost in the last week to the Yankees, and do you know what they wrote in Boston? They wrote, "The Red Sox do better without Williams." That's the kind of writers they were.

There's no doubt, of course, that things got started and grew worse partly because of my temperament, because of my emotional, explosive nature. I have never been regarded especially as a man with great patience. Certainly as a young player I had none at all with myself. I was impetuous; I was tempestuous. I blew up. Not acting but *reacting*. I'd get so damned mad, throw bats, kick the columns in the dugout so that sparks flew, tear out the plumbing, knock out the lights, damn near kill myself. *Scream*. I'd scream out of my own frustration.

There was the time in Minneapolis. I've still got the scars on my wrist. It was 1938, the year before I went up to the Red Sox, and to appreciate how intense I was, you have to remember that it was a year any nineteen-year-old kid ballplayer would love to have had. I led the American Association in everything—runs, average, RBIs, homers, everything. I had a wonderful manager, Donie Bush, who put up with me. The town was mine, and I loved it.

Anyway, Lloyd Brown was pitching for St. Paul, a tough little pitcher with a good curve. I got him to 3 and 1 in the first inning, bases loaded, short right-field fence. Now he has to come in with the fastball. He does. Right there. Perfect. If I'd gotten that much more bat on the ball, it would have gone 440 feet, but I hit just under it and popped it up, and the St. Paul first baseman reached over the boxes and made a hell of a play. Boy, I'm mad now.

I go back to the bench, this little wooden bench, little cracker-box dugout in Minneapolis, and I'm so mad I don't know what to do. I sit down, and here's this big water cooler right there next to me. About half full of water. And I just can't contain myself. *Whoomph, kerr-rash.* I hit it with my fist. They must have thought a cannon had gone off in the dugout. It just exploded. Blood's flying, glass, everything. Well, I was lucky I didn't cut my hand off. There was one cut that went pretty deep and just missed a nerve. You don't have to cut very much there to do real damage. I could have ended my career before it started. As it was, it wasn't even bad enough to take me out of the game. But that shows you how intense I was.

I was never able to be dispassionate, to ignore the things people said or wrote or implied. It just wasn't in me. In my heart I don't believe I am any more sensitive to criticism than a lot of athletes, but I am certainly in the upper bracket of sensitivity, maybe the top 3 percent. In a crowd of cheers I could always pick out the solitary boo. I don't mean to say that criticism affected my hitting, because the boos always seemed to have the reverse effect. My last real outstanding season was in 1957, when, as an old man pushing forty, I hit .388. I spent the season being mad at the world for one reason or another. I don't think I said two words to the Boston writers all year. That hardly made life pleasant.

I read recently where Joe DiMaggio said that he felt the Yankees always tried to win without him. There had never been anything written like that; he just sensed it. So Joe's got to be a sensitive guy, too. And there he was in New York with the grandest press support in the world—because the Yankees won.

And there I was in Boston, where there must be more newspapers per capita than any place in the world, with writers vying for stories, all trying to outdo the others, all trying to get a headline, all digging into places where they had no business being. They—one of them—sent a private detective to San Diego in 1942 to find out if I really did support my mother. They went out into the street to take a "public opinion" poll on my parental qualifications in 1948 when I happened to be in Florida fishing when my daughter Bobby Jo was born—*prematurely.* That type of thing.

Well, I had been a fresh kid. I did a lot of yakking, partly to hide a rather large inferiority complex. When somebody asked a question, I answered it. Never very coy, never very diplomatic. As a result, I would get myself in a wringer. I'd say to myself, Damn, I wish I hadn't said that, or said it that *way,* and sure as hell when I pick up the paper it's even worse than I thought.

There were people, friends of mine, even writers in other cities who I liked, always telling me to try harder, and I'll tell you a story. I was demonstrating fly casting at the Sportsman's Show in New York one year, something I still do, because if I didn't make it as the greatest hitter, I'm not far from being the greatest fly caster. This was one year Jim Thorpe was on the program. Right off I was carried away with Thorpe. He looked the part of the big Indian—not the big, *big* Indian but a *big* Indian. Boy, just one look and you knew he had it. He was about sixty-five then, and I was so impressed with how quiet and attentive he was, how he would listen to people. Here's Jim Thorpe, all-time all-time, and he'd listen to anybody. He'd smile and he'd laugh and he'd listen.

Well, Thorpe had played some in the big leagues, and somebody told him, "Look, you can help Williams. He's getting into trouble with the press, charging around like he does, and you can give him some advice. He looks up to you." So about the sixth day of the show, Thorpe took me aside for a heart-to-heart on how I should try to get along with the press.

He said, "You know, they can make it awful miserable for you, but they can make it easier for you, too. It's better to get along with 'em." He kept going on in this real easy way, and then we started talking about hitting.

I said, "How long did you play in the big leagues, Jim?"

"Oh, five-six years."

"How good a hitter were you?"

"I was a pretty good hitter. Everybody said I couldn't hit the curveball, but I hit .327 one year."

I can see I'm getting him stirred up a little bit now.

He says, "The writers were always saying I couldn't hit the curve, and not only that, one of them wrote one day, 'And Thorpe isn't very good for the team, either.'" I could see this bothered Thorpe an awful lot.

"You know," he says, "I thought about this a long time, that I wasn't a team player. And one day this writer comes into the clubhouse. I went right over to him and told him, 'I don't think that was a very fair article. I'm hitting .323. I must be hitting *something*, if I can't hit a curveball. But the thing that really hurts me is you say I'm not a team man. I'm a little upset with that.'"

Well, if you ever met Jim Thorpe, you would realize that if he was upset a little bit, he was *upset*. So he says to this writer, "What do you think you would do if somebody wrote something like that about you?"

And Thorpe said the writer answered, "Well, I guess I'd punch him in the nose."

Thorpe smiled that big Indian smile and says, "So I punched him in the nose, and down he went." We both laughed like hell.

This beautiful passage is from a letter the novelist sent to baseball writer Arthur Mann on February 16, 1938, only seven months before his death and two weeks after Mann had taken him to the annual New York dinner of the Baseball Writers Association of America. There Wolfe—who at that time was developing the character of ballplayer Nebraska Crane for his novels *The Web and the Rock* and *You Can't Go Home Again*—sat star-struck, gazing at the likes of Ruth, Wagner, Foxx, and Gehrig. Baseball and the weather of our lives—a fitting conclusion to this *Armchair Book of Baseball*.

THOMAS WOLFE

The Sound of the Ball, the Smell of Old Dry Wood

I cannot tell you how much I enjoyed the Baseball Writers' dinner and how much I think I got out of it. Not that I learned so much, but I think there was a big value in verification—in seeing the animal at first hand and in communication with his fellows. The point is, one of the characters in this immense long book that I am writing is a baseball player,* and I realize from past observation how easy it is for a writer to go wrong when writing about a professional athlete: the sporting writer, or the writer of baseball fiction, does it best of all, I think, because they put him in a certain limited setting—on the field or on the bench or at the training camp. My problem is a different one: I think I may have told you that one reason I have always loved baseball so much is that it has been not merely "the great national game" but really a part of the whole weather of our lives, of the thing that is our own, of the whole fabric, the million memories of America. For example, in the memory of almost every one of us, is there anything that can evoke spring—the first fine days of April—better than the sound of the ball smacking into the pocket of the big mitt, the sound of the bat as it hits the horsehide: for me, at any rate, and I am being literal and not rhetorical—almost everything I know about

* Nebraska Crane.

428

spring is in it—the first leaf, the jonquil, the maple tree, the smell of grass upon your hands and knees, the coming into flower of April. And is there anything that can tell more about an American summer than, say, the smell of the wooden bleachers in a small-town baseball park, that resinous, sultry, and exciting smell of old dry wood.

431